"This is a novel reflection on informal settlements and their conditions linking a robust range of contexts at multiple levels of urbanization with crucial issues of environmental regeneration, economic as well as social equality and racial justice. Inevitably, the discourse on sustainable and responsible practices encompasses the urgency to prioritize a human centered design approach in order to observe and register those patterns. It is in this pursuit of interdisciplinary contributions through the lens of sustainability, where the book might well make compelling revelations."

Maria Perbellini, Dean and Professor, School of Architecture and Design, New York Institute of Technology, USA

"Antonino Di Raimo, Steffen Lehmann and Alessandro Melis explore new directions into understanding the phenomenon of Informality. Presented as a three-part unified framework, Informality opens new research directions and is a must-read for future multidisciplinary thinking and creation of sustainable urbanized worlds."

Tom Kovac, Professor, RMIT University, Australia

"A breakthrough book outside of stereotypes! The authors demonstrate with clarity and methodological rigor that cities are never the product of a single deterministic will, but they are the result of the rise of sudden innovations, of independent – often informal – dynamics which are consolidated by the creativity of the inhabitants, by actions produced by individual and collective actors, whose outcome often exceeds the intentions and control of the most powerful actors. The book explores different resilient communities that, through fertile bricolage, produce powerful alliances between intentionality, spontaneity, causality and design."

Maurizio Carta, Full Professor of Urban Design, University of Palermo, Italy

Informality through Sustainability

Informality through Sustainability explores the phenomenon of informality within urban settlements and aims to unravel the subtle links between informal settlements and sustainability.

Penetrating its global profile and considering urban informality through an understanding of local implications, the authors collectively reveal specific correlations between sites and their local inhabitants. The book opposes simplistic calls to legalise informal settlements or to view them as 'problems' to be solved. It comes at a time when common notions of 'informality' are being increasingly challenged.

In 25 chapters, the book presents contributions from well-known scholars and practitioners whose theoretical or practical work addresses informality and sustainability at various levels, from city planning and urban design to public space and architectural education. Whilst previous studies on informal settlements have mainly focused on cases in developing countries, approaching the topic through social, cultural and material dimensions, the book explores the concept across a range of contexts, including former Communist countries and those in the so-called Global North. Contributions also explore understandings of informality at various scalar levels – region, precinct, neighbourhood and individual building. Thus, this work helps reposition informality as a relational concept at various scales of urbanisation.

This book will be of great benefit to planners, architects, researchers and policymakers interested in the interplay between informality and sustainability.

Antonino Di Raimo, *FEA*, is a Reader in Architecture at the University of Portsmouth's School of Architecture (UK), where he is also a Co-Lead in research. He joined the University of Portsmouth in 2017. Prior to this, he had been teaching in Italy (University of La Sapienza) and Albania (Polis University, Tirana).

Steffen Lehmann, *Assoc. AIA, RIBA, AoU*, is Director of the School of Architecture at the University of Nevada Las Vegas (USA), and a full Professor of Architecture. He is also Founding Director of the interdisciplinary Urban Futures Lab and Director of the Future Cities Leadership Institute.

Alessandro Melis, *RIBA, ARB, AoU*, is a full Professor of Architecture Innovation at the University of Portsmouth (UK) and the co-director of the Cluster for Sustainable Cities. He is the curator of the Italian Pavilion at the 17th International Biennale of Architecture in Venice 2020–21.

Earthscan Series on Sustainable Design

Series Editor: Professor Steffen Lehmann (Steffen.Lehmann.Cities@gmail.com)

All books in this series are authored and/or edited by leading academics and practitioners in the field of sustainable design.

While there has been an immense amount of theory and technology focused writing published on the topic of sustainable design, many of these books have failed to introduce readers to the wider challenge of what the re-thinking of design, production, operation and recycling of all products, buildings and cities really means.

Sustainability is not a passing fashion and people are constantly searching for more information, ideas and products in this area. This new book series will aim to develop a more coherent theoretical framework for how different theories of sustainable design might engage with the practice of architects, designers, urban planners and related professions. The knowledge gained from this book series will equip the readers with the tools for realising the full potential of the good intentions of sustainable design.

The aim is that these books will provide a novel alignment of interdisciplinary perspectives on the problems of global consumerism, sustainable design and strategies to avoid resource waste, on the scales of products, buildings, districts and cities.

The books will become essential reading for architects, industrial designers, urban designers and researchers/students in these disciplines. Potential readers for the books will also include industry and government agencies. Global relevance and the potential for use as textbooks will be essential.

The book series will become a highly useful addition to the literature on sustainable design, urban development and city culture, focusing on the key topics encountered by students and scholars of urban studies, pointing towards related bibliographic material.

If you have an idea for the series then please contact the series editor.

Designing for Zero Waste: Consumption, Technologies and the Built Environment
Edited by Steffen Lehmann and Robert Crocker
December 2011 | Paperback: 978-1-84971-435-8 | Hardback: 978-1-84971-434-1

Motivating Change: Sustainable Design and Behaviour in the Built Environment
Edited by Robert Crocker and Steffen Lehmann
July 2013 | Paperback: 978-0-415-82978-6 | Hardback: 978-0-415-82977-9

Low Carbon Cities: Transforming Urban Systems
Edited by Steffen Lehmann
October 2014 | Paperback: 978-0-415-72983-3 | Hardback: 978-0-415-72982-6

Growing Compact: Urban Form, Density and Sustainability
Edited by Joo Hwa Philip Bay and Steffen Lehmann
May 2017 | Paperback: 978-1-138-68040-1 | Hardback: 978-1-138-68039-5

Informality through Sustainability: Urban Informality Now
Edited by Antonino Di Raimo, Steffen Lehmann and Alessandro Melis
December 2020 | Hardback: 978-0-367-35477-0

For more information about the series, please visit: https://www.routledge.com/Earthscan-Series-on-Sustainable-Design/book-series/EARTHSD

Informality through Sustainability

Urban Informality Now

Edited by Antonino Di Raimo, Steffen Lehmann and Alessandro Melis

Routledge
Taylor & Francis Group
LONDON AND NEW YORK

earthscan
from Routledge

First published 2021
by Routledge
2 Park Square, Milton Park, Abingdon, Oxon OX14 4RN

and by Routledge
52 Vanderbilt Avenue, New York, NY 10017

Routledge is an imprint of the Taylor & Francis Group, an informa business

British Library Cataloguing-in-Publication Data
A catalogue record for this book is available from the British Library

Library of Congress Cataloging-in-Publication Data
Names: Di Raimo, Antonino, 1973- editor. | Lehmann, Steffen, 1963- editor. | Melis, Alessandro, editor.
Title: Informality through sustainability : urban informality now / [edited by] Antonino Di Raimo, Steffen Lehmann and Alessandro Melis.
Description: New York : Routledge, 2021. | Series: Earthscan series on sustainable design | Includes bibliographical references and index.
Identifiers: LCCN 2020035062 (print) | LCCN 2020035063 (ebook) | ISBN 9780367354770 (hardback) | ISBN 9780429331701 (ebook)
Subjects: LCSH: Squatter settlements. | City planning–Environmental aspects. | Urban policy. | Urban ecology (Sociology)
Classification: LCC HD7287.95 .I544 2021 (print) | LCC HD7287.95 (ebook) | DDC 307.1/216–dc23
LC record available at https://lccn.loc.gov/2020035062
LC ebook record available at https://lccn.loc.gov/2020035063

ISBN: 978-0-367-35477-0 (hbk)
ISBN: 978-0-429-33170-1 (ebk)

Typeset in Gill Sans and Times NR MT Pro
by KnowledgeWorks Global Ltd.

Contents

Figures

PART I

CHAPTER I

CHAPTER 2

CHAPTER 3

CHAPTER 4

CHAPTER 5

CHAPTER 6

CHAPTER 7

CHAPTER 8

PART 2

CHAPTER 9

CHAPTER 12

CHAPTER 13

CHAPTER 14

CHAPTER 15

CHAPTER 16

CHAPTER 17

CHAPTER 18

CHAPTER 19

CHAPTER 20

CHAPTER 21

CHAPTER 22

CHAPTER 23

CHAPTER 24

CHAPTER 25

Cover Image: © Urban forms, courtesy Endrit Marku

Tables

CHAPTER 12

CHAPTER 13

CHAPTER 18

CHAPTER 19

CHAPTER 22

Editors and contributors

Co-editors

Dr. Antonino Di Raimo, *FEA,* is a Reader in Architecture at the Portsmouth School of Architecture (PSA), where he is also a Co-Lead in research. He joined the University of Portsmouth in 2017. Prior to moving to Portsmouth, he had been teaching in Italy (University of La Sapienza) and Albania (Polis University, Tirana).

In Albania, Antonino served as the Dean of the Faculty of Architecture Design and Engineering (2012–2017) where he contributed to the innovation of the school's curriculum, to the interdisciplinarity between the courses and to the school's research. At Polis University, Antonino has also been the Head of the Innovation Factory Research Unit, a pioneering institute aimed at unravelling the role of innovation within the unique Albanian reality.

In 2016, Antonino was appointed the curator of the Albanian Pavilion at the XXI Triennale in Milano, *Design after Design.* In the same year he curated the first Albanian Architecture Biennale, TAW–Tirana Architecture Weeks.

His specialist teaching, supervisory, and research interests lie in the fields of computation and ecology, focusing on the relation between the human body and the architecture space both in design and in the field of architecture and criticism.

Antonino holds a Ph.D. in Architecture Composition and Theory (University of Rome, La Sapienza). He has been part of various international architecture competitions and projects. In addition, he has been writing for various trade magazines, and contributing with various articles to several books. He is the author of the books 'François Roche Heretical Machinism and Living Architecture of New Territories.com' published within the IT Revolution book series (Edilstampa, 2014, Italian and English edition) and 'Mente, corpo, informazione. Per un'agenda dell 'Embodiment in architettura' (Mind, Body, Information. For an Embodiment architectural agenda, Quodlibet, 2016).

Dr. Steffen Lehmann, *AIA RIBA AoU,* is Director of the School of Architecture at the University of Nevada Las Vegas (UNLV), and a full Professor of Architecture. He is also Director of the interdisciplinary Urban Futures Lab and Director of the Future Cities Leadership Institute.

Over the last 18 years, he has been a tenured full professor on three continents, in the US, in the UK, and in Australia. Steffen has published 20 books with prestigious publishers, and countless articles on architecture and sustainable urban development. In the 1990s, he coined the pioneering concept of *Green Urbanism*. In recognition of the international significance of his work, he held from 2008 to 2010 the UNESCO Chair for Sustainable Urban Development in the Asia-Pacific. He has held senior positions at several universities across Europe, Asia and America; including as tenured full Professor of Research and Innovation at the University of Portsmouth (UK); and at the University of South Australia, where he led the university-wide theme 'Sustainable Cities'; and as Founding Director of the *Cluster for Sustainable Cities* in the UK.

For over 13 years he was a full professor and Chair at leading universities in Australia, where he served in a range of senior leadership roles, including Director of Research; and Head of School in Perth, where he was responsible for over 3,000 students and 150 academic, professional and casual staff, with offshore programs in Malaysia and Hong Kong. He was invited as Visiting Professor at the University of California Berkeley, TU Munich (DAAD Professor), TU Berlin, NUS Singapore, Tongji University Shanghai; and in 2018–20 he is a Distinguished Visiting Professor at Xi'an Jiaotong University in China; and a Visiting Professor at the University of Portsmouth.

In 1991, Steffen graduated with the AA Diploma from the Architectural Association School in London, and in 2003 completed a Ph.D. in Architecture and Urbanism at the Technical University in Berlin. Before establishing his own practice *Steffen Lehmann Architekten GmbH* in 1993 in Berlin, he worked with Pritzker-Prize winners James Stirling in London and Arata Isozaki in Tokyo.

Dr. Alessandro Melis, *RIBA ARB AoU*, is a professor of architecture innovation at the University of Portsmouth (UK) and the co-director of the Cluster for Sustainable Cities in the UK. In 2019, he was appointed by the Italian Minister of Cultural Heritage (MIBAC) as the curator of the Italian Pavilion at the 17th International Biennale of Architecture in Venice 2020. In 2020, he was appointed by the Italian Ministry of Foreign Affairs as Ambassador of Italian Design.

He joined the University of Portsmouth in 2016. His specialist teaching, supervisory, and research interests lie in the fields of community resilience, environmental policies, radical theories, and criticism. Previously, at the University of Auckland, he was the head of the technology area and director of postgraduate engagement at the School of Architecture and Planning. He has been a guest professor in Austria (Die Angewandte, Vienna) and in Germany (Anhalt University, Dessau).

He holds a Ph.D. in Architecture design from the University of Florence. He has been a member of the academic body of the Foster Foundation and an honorary fellow at the Edinburgh School of Architecture. He has also been invited as a keynote speaker at the China Academy of Art, the MoMA New York, the University of Cambridge, TED, the Italian Institute of Culture in London, and the UNESCO Headquarters in Paris.

In 1996, he founded Heliopolis 21, a multi-awarded architecture practice based in Italy, Germany, and the UK. The SR1939 Institute of the University of Pisa, the Stella Maris Hospital, and the Auditorium of Sant'Anna, inaugurated by the president of the Italian Republic, Sergio Mattarella, are acknowledged both in scholar publications and in popular magazines as examples of excellence in sustainable design.

The recognition of Alessandro's research is corroborated by a record of over 130 peer review journal publications and by as many citations, including in popular periodicals such as *Wired*, the *New York Times*, the *Independent*, *Reuters*, and the *Conversation*. His work was the object of several exhibitions and of a recent monograph (Rome, 2020) edited by Francesco Fallacara Chirico, titled "Alessandro Melis, Utopic Real World."

Contributors

Teddy Cruz is an American architect, urbanist and Professor in Public Culture and Urbanism at the University of California, San Diego. Together, they are the principals of Estudio Teddy Cruz + Forman, a research-based political and architectural practice in San Diego, and co-directors of the UCSD X-Border Initiative.

Fonna Forman is a professor of political theory and the founding director of the Center on Global Justice at the University of California, San Diego. Together with Teddy Cruz she codirects the UCSD Cross-Border Initiative and the Estudio Teddy Cruz + Fonna Forman.

Kathy Waghorn is associate professor in Huri te Ao/The School of Future Environments at AUT, the Auckland University of Technology. Her research and practice sits at the intersection of art, architecture and urbanism. As co-founder of the collective Hoop-la.nz she collaborates with others to develop civic engagement initiatives in Tāmaki Makaurau Auckland.

Pablo Martínez Capdevila, PhD, is a Senior Lecturer at the University of Portsmouth, School of Architecture.

François Roche is a French architect, co-founder of the architecture studio and research platforms, New-Territories including LabM4, R&Sie(n), [eIf/bʌt/c], Mindmachinemakingmyths, among other names.

David Franco Santa Cruz, PhD, is an Assistant Professor of Architecture at Clemson University, School of Architecture.

Sotir Dhamo, PhD, is a Professor of Urban Design at Polis University, Tirana.

William Carpenter, PhD, is a Professor at Kennesaw State University, Department of Architecture.

Mitchell Joachim, PhD, is Co-Founder of Terreform ONE and an Associate Professor of Practice at NYU.

Nicholas Gervasi is an Architect/Head Researcher at Terreform ONE.

Simone Sfriso is an Italian Architect, Co-Founder of TAMassociati, an international practice active in Social Design.

Massimo Lepore is an Italian Architect, Co-Founder of TAMassociati, an international practice active in Social Design.

Raul Pantaleo is an Italian Architect, Co-Founder of TAMassociati, an international practice active in Social Design.

Barbora Melis is an Urban Planner and PhD student at the University of Portsmouth, School of Architecture.

Charlotte Malterre-Barthes, PhD, is an architect, scholar, urban designer and assistant professor of urban design at Harvard Graduate School of Design, US.

Dario Pedrabissi is a Senior Lecturer at the University of Portsmouth, School of Architecture.

Paul Jones, PhD, is Associate Professor and Director of the Master of Urban and Regional Planning at The University of Sydney, School of Architecture, Design and Planning.

Mohammad Swapan, PhD, is a Senior Lecturer in Urban and Regional Planning at the School of Design and the Built Environment, Curtin University, AU.

Atiq Zaman, PhD, is a Lecturer at Curtin University, School of Design and the Built Environment.

Daniela Perrotti, PhD, is Professor of Landscape Architecture at University Louvain, Faculty of Architecture, Architectural Engineering and Urban Planning.

Danny H. Ortega is Professor of Landscape Architecture and Associate Director of the School of Architecture, University of Nevada, Las Vegas.

Janice Perlman is a Professor and Senior Research Scholar at Columbia University. She is also the Founder and President of The Mega-Cities Project, Inc.

Ata Chokhachian is an architect and university lecturer at Technical University of Munich, holding Research Associate position at the chair for Architecture Informatics and Architecture Research Incubator.

Daniele Santucci is a practicing architect, building scientist, and research associate at the Chair of Building Technology and Climate Responsive Design at the Technical University of Munich.

Thomas Auer, PhD, is Professor and Chair in the Building Technology and Climate Responsive Design at the Technical University of Munich, Department of Architecture. He is also managing director of Transsolar.

Dorina Pojani, PhD, is Senior Lecturer in Urban Planning at the University of Queensland, School of Earth and Environmental Sciences.

J. Antonio Lara- Hernandez, PhD, is an Architect and Researcher in Urban Studies.

M. Yazid Khemri is a PhD student at the University of Portsmouth, School of Architecture.

Besnik Aliaj, PhD, is a Professor of Urban Design and Planning and Rector of Polis University, Tirana.

Alessandra Lai, PhD, is an urban planner and independent researcher holding collaborations with several universities.

Francesco Carcri, PhD, is an architect and Associate Professor at the University of Roma Tre, Department of Architecture. He is also a founding member of the Stalker/Osservatorio Nomade urban art workshop.

Olufunto Ijatuyi, PhD, is a lecturer in the Department of Architecture at the Federal University of Technology, Akure Nigeria.

Ayoola, Hezekiah Adedayo, PhD, is a Senior Lecturer in the Department of Architecture, Federal University of Technology, Akure, Nigeria.

Cristina Dreifuss, PhD, is an architect and Research Coordinator at the Universidad de Lima, School of Architecture.

Aseem Inam, Ph.D. is Professor and Chair in Urban Design at Cardiff University in the UK and Director of TRULAB: Laboratory for Designing Urban Transformation. He is the author of numerous award-winning journal articles, book chapters and books, including *Planning for the Unplanned: Recovering from Crises in Megacities,* and *Designing Urban Transformation.* He has practiced as an activist, designer and urbanist in Brazil, Canada, France, Greece, Haiti, India, Morocco, United Kingdom, and the United States.

Acknowledgements

This book is the outcome of many months of work and commitment of numerous people. We would like to express our thank you for the generosity of everyone involved, especially all authors who made this comprehensive study possible.

The book emerged as result of many conversations held on the topic of urban informality and shared by the three Editors at the Portsmouth School of Architecture, since 2018.

The first and the third editors would like to thank Professor Steffen Lehmann at the University of Nevada Las Vegas for his prompt interest and enthusiasm to collaborate on the book as part of the Earthscan Book Series on Sustainable Design (Routledge), based on the main idea: our belief that architecture and sustainability should encompass informality as a matter of great relevance and concern.

In the editors' view, this book is a cross-cultural project, aiming at exploring the fundamental relevance and benefits of informality as a global phenomenon. However, its relevance to sustainability and architecture is still often neglected.

The editors want to thank and acknowledge all the book's contributors for their interest in this book project, and for their patience and commitment to the book's completion even through the Covid-19 outbreak.

As in our view, cultural statements should firstly involve early career researches, and we would like to acknowledge the support by some of our PhD students at the University of Portsmouth: Claire Coulter, Ph.D. student in the Strategy, Enterprise and Innovation group; and Barbora Melis, Ph.D. student at the School of Architecture, in the Faculty of Creative and Cultural Industries.

Our warmest thanks go to Professor David Turnbull for the Preface.

We would finally like to thank Francesca Ford and Trudy Varcianna at Routledge for their trust, help and prodigious assistance during the production of the book, especially in light of the present difficult times.

We would also like to thank all photographers, authors, architects and archives for making information and images available. Every effort has been made to trace the copyright holders, and we apologise in advance for any unintentional omission.

—Antonino Di Raimo, Steffen Lehmann
and Alessandro Melis (Co-Editors), August 2020

Preface

David Turnbull

Innocence

It has been a long time, too long perhaps, since I started thinking about 'informality' in architecture and urbanism. When I was younger it was possible to enjoy processes of contamination, indeed it was obligatory. The spectral adversary was formal. The charge—'formalism'. The remedy ... a realism, of some kind. The real destabilised the ideal—perfection was rendered imperfect, and by implication, authentic. Any alibi could be used—in a poetics of contagion, infection and death ... finality, finitude ... living in end-times, searching for the end that was always the beginning of something new, something fresh, found in the garbage dump of history. It was fun. It seemed relevant, even revelatory. Like the fragments of papyri discovered at Oxyrhynchus, confirming Sappho's brilliance, the incomplete, the unfinished communicated love, a loving relationship with others ... with other people, other things, and other places—love in pieces, peaceful love, declared with a whisper, a murmur rather than a manifesto. For a while there were no grand narratives. Total War eliminated the hubris of pre, post or inter, flattening the curve of creative potential measured against time, dispensing with ages, golden, gilded, tarnished ... even schools of thought ... in favour of ubiquity, hidden behind a mask of multiplicity. The technologies of production and dissemination fabricated many masks, protecting the subject—a cover-up, perhaps, but not a cover-all. The virus became a model. Ideas went viral. New narratives proliferated ... dreams became nightmares, that became dreams, recursively.

Informality transformed the practice of architecture, as far as I am concerned, in 1953. I am sure that this is a ridiculous assertion, but I will make it anyway. I remain convinced that the deliberate, careful documentation of informal settlements, mapped and drawn, exhibited as a weapon to be used in a battle of wits with an older generation of architects, was instrumental in the destabilisation of CIAM, and the emergence of Team X. I do not need to provide evidence, there is plenty, but I may need to qualify this statement, by invoking the privilege of age. My generation of architects was taught by the surviving members of the battle of Aix-en-Provence, CIAM IX, and their followers. As parochial as this sounds, which it does, I can say, I think reasonably, that in the echo-chamber of Europe, the ideas of Team X remain in the substrate of architectural discourse, sometimes unwittingly, and that, mobilised as rumours, they have become increasingly active in the imagination of younger architects who have no connection to the ancestral voices. Also, without wishing to overburden the genealogy, I believe that these rumours have produced their own echoes around the world.

I could claim that the British or Dutch influence in the formation of Team X may have been overstated. The French would agree that drawings by Roland Simounet prepared for Team Alger, and photographs presented by Team Maroc had a decisive impact, when 'ATBAT—Afrique' colleagues, Vladimir Bodiansky, Georges Candilis, Michel Écochard, Henri Piot and Shadrach Woods confronted the Charter of Athens' working assumptions concerning health, hygiene, sanitation and sociability—the bidonvilles of the French colonial cities in North Africa, where the desert meets the sea, provided proof that the resilient complexity of the 'shanty-town', where progress meets its alter-ego in 'the violence of poverty and mud', could not be ignored. Candilis, from Casablanca, persisted—the 'habitat' for 'the greater number', should learn from the conditions in which the greater number already lived. Simounet, a brilliant draughtsman, in Algiers, made extraordinary drawings of rooms in the 'informal settlements' of the city—drawings populated with figures, sleeping, standing, sitting, and artefacts, pots and cooking utensils, bedding, clothing, toys, books, food—dimensioned, and carefully annotated. One drawing, made in 1952, assembled domestic artefacts, found objects, on a loosely defined grid, with compartments that were scaled appropriately, a place for everything—a gas-burner, pots and pans, a bottle or flask, oil, water, maybe some spices … everything that was needed to make and share a meal. Compartments intersected, some overlapped, objects in front of a sub-division, others behind—everything precisely delineated and carefully arranged. His composite figures were a celebration of necessity.

I remember Camus, writing about the 'Summer in Algiers' (1938):

'Does the Algiers in me need any special signs or sounds to embrace these short instants where the day tips into night? When I've been away from this land for a while, I imagine its twilight as a promise of happiness. On the little hills that dominate the city, roads wind through the mastics and the olive trees, and it's to them that my heart returns. I see gatherings of black birds rise above the green horizon. In the sky, suddenly emptied of its sun, something unwinds: masses of red clouds spread out until they are reabsorbed into the air. Just a moment later, you see the first star begin to form and harden in the thickness of the sky. And then, all of a sudden, the night, all-consuming.

These fleeting evenings in Algiers, what unique power do they have to unravel so much within me? This sweetness that the evenings leave on my lips, I don't have time to tire of it before it has already disappeared into the nighttime. Is this the secret of its persistence?'

His devotion, like Simounet's, unconditional … accepting—his vision synoptic.

In 'L'Étranger' (1942), Camus, in prison, learns 'the trick of remembering things'—'Sometimes I would exercise my memory on my bedroom and, starting from a corner, make the round, noting every object I saw on the way. At first it was over in a minute or two. But each time I repeated the experience, it took a little longer. I made a point of visualising every piece of furniture, and each article upon or in it, and then every detail of each article, and finally the details of the details, so to speak: a tiny dent or incrustation, or a chipped edge, and the exact grain and colour of the woodwork. At the same time I forced myself to keep my inventory in mind from start to finish, in the right order and omitting no item. With the result that, after a few weeks, I could spend hours merely in listing the objects in my bedroom. I found that the more I thought, the more details, half-forgotten or malobserved, floated up from my memory. There seemed no end to them.'

Ten years apart, Camus' 'L'Étranger', and Simounet's drawings for CIAM—Alger's 'grille', employ an encyclopaedic exhaustion of detail, a surplus of description that demands attention while insisting on detachment … detail that attracts, and repels—details that bind and details that fail. Failure, proximate, inevitable and necessary adheres to informality, like dust. Like decay. Like mould. Like George Candilis in 1953, in Aix-en-Provence, I will persist—like Simounet I will draw a line. My line, as drawn in purple crayon, why not, will reveal a continuity of thought, with an origin in the past that is sufficiently remote that it remains invisible … and another in the future that appears on the horizon as a point of light, radiating in all directions. In between, embedded in an almost incoherent scribble, distinct figures appear as vivid demonstrations of potential. Looking back, not so far, but far enough—the romantic poets, symbolists and melancholics … Baudelaire's 'Les Fleurs du mal' (1857), the anarchists, Pierre-Joseph Proudhon, Mikhail Bakunin … Peter Kropotkin's 'The Conquest of Bread' (1892). Looking forward, from 1953, not yet the present—specific moments, singular artefacts, and declarations of purpose … Guy Debord and Asger Jorn's 'Naked City' (1957), Friedensreich Hundertwasser's 'Mould Manifesto' (1958), Colin Ward's 'Anarchy in Action' (1973), Hakim Bey's 'Temporary Autonomous Zone' (1991), and various attempts at negotiating the regulated and unregulated, authorised and unauthorised, toward an aesthetics of freedom, and an alternative society of small self-governing communities based on voluntary cooperation, that are functionally egalitarian and sufficiently productive … 'without greedy elites maintaining their privilege with propaganda and force'.

In my mnemonic tangle I am certain that I will also find the seminal work of John F.C. Turner (1927–), and Paul Oliver's extraordinary 'Shelter in Society' (1969), and Martin Pawley's 'Garbage Housing' (1975). I am certain, because then—at Aix-en-Provence in 1953, in Paris in 1957, Vienna in 1958, London in 1969 or '73 … in the Antilles in 1990, or New York in 1991—whenever then is determined … or now, there was, and remains a widespread realisation that informality must be understood, the self-organising formalisms of informality should be explored, and the ecosystemic behaviour of informal settlements examined.

My generation came of age with, and in spite of informality. I joined the New Architecture Movement, read the proceedings of the meetings of the Architects Revolutionary Council, refused to be registered as an Architect, declined the offer of membership of the profession, and yet, ultimately, in love with Architecture, fascinated by the challenges of urban design, I went over to the other side. I was not alone. Desperation drove a desire for a rapprochement—formality and informality reconciled, in arbitrarily ad hoc accumulations of archetypes, simulated variety, collision composition, and more recent algorithmic simulation … complicated surrogates standing in for the real complexity of the city. The example of Algiers or Casablanca, the bidonvilles, recast—as dirty realism is declared too real to be realised, but real enough to be adopted as a dream, 'as the day tips into night', with tenderness … with love. I lie awake at night, remembering the smell of Kibera, in Nairobi, the squatter settlements in Abuja, and Accra, the city of the dead in Cairo … the density, the tragic absence of clean water and sanitation, the stench of human waste … and the hubris—cell phones and satellite dishes, photovoltaics and pilot projects, water filters, toilets, temporary or permanent—the debris of good intentions.

I find Édouard Glissant's 'Poetics of Relation' (1990), useful … because he knew 'the violence of poverty and mud' and will not allow it to be forgotten, but also because his catalogue of 'relationships', good and bad, is too pertinent to be ignored—of domination, fascination, multiplicity and contagion, of polite subservience or mockery, of tangency, subversion or intolerance ... and, for me, the critical confrontation between the written and the spoken, in which the informal invariably finds in favour of orality, the vernacular, against the official, the academic, the dominant discourse, without being submissive. Indeed, it is mockery—oral insubordination—that persists as the master signifier in the discourse of informality ... the rebellious voice of the multitude that commands respect—the relational aesthetics that defeats the phantasm of disciplinary autonomy. Herein lies hope, resisting authority, rising above the green horizon, in the pursuit of happiness—'for the greater number'.

So, how can informality, as a construct, be embraced as a disciplinary obligation, now, without compromise ... recognising the risks associated with any attempt to codify the patterns and procedures that determine the indeterminate? How can the unconditional acceptance found in Camus' twilight in Algiers, in the innocence of Roland Simounet's drawings of the 'bidonvilles', a love affair with the ungovernable—how can hope become programmatic again, as it was for the architects assembled in Aix-en-Provence in 1953. I doubt that the editors and authors who have worked tirelessly in unprecedented circumstances to complete this book would be naive enough to express their shared goals in these terms, but I will. Recalling an inventory of influences, from the despair of Baudelaire's 'Tableaux parisiens' (1861), to Peter Sloterdijk's 'Terror from the Air' (2002), writing under 'lockdown' I feel compelled to restate that the future they wanted, and we want ... that has been declared so many times, that underpins the UN Sustainable Development Goals ... was not a promise. It was a challenge. This collection of essays confronts the complexity of the challenge posed by the desire for change with the potential of the informal, real and imagined. The editors, Antonino Di Raimo, Steffen Lehmann and Alessandro Melis revive the informal as fact and motivation, within the domain of architecture, in the city, and in behaviour. Their examination of informality is presented as a provocation, recuperating the past, projecting the future. The diversity of contributions echoes the complexity of the informal settlement, and may appear unsettling. I believe that this is appropriate, even necessary.

I have been writing this preface intermittently for six months marked by the paradox of solidarity in isolation. I worried that the pandemic may render the argument of this book unarguable. I vacillated, perplexed by internal conflict, hubris and despair. In favour of acceptance, I imagined the challenges faced by the early Christian Desert Fathers ... finding in their solitude the possibility of redemption. In my dreams, remembering Camus, I saw gatherings of black birds rising. An omen. The graphs could not lie. The news was bleak. The virus changed everything. Informality retreated from the public sphere to the private bubble. The grand narratives returned, good and bad—among them, resistant, resilient, informality. In the morning, on the streets, the multitude marched in time with death. In the evening, on the screen ... in the chipped edges of reality, in the details of the details, in private lives made public ... informality became the medium and the message. In the twilight ... hope echoed, around the world.

Introduction

Antonino Di Raimo, Steffen Lehmann and Alessandro Melis

According to the most recent estimates, about 25 percent of the world's population currently lives in informal settlements (Un-Habitat, 2013). The term *Informal Settlement*, a label, which in the last decades became very popular as much in urban policies as in academia, identifies those communities, *which are not in compliance with building norms and property and urban planning regulations* and this is *the main reason for qualifying them as "informal"* (Zárate, 2016). Indeed, different studies conducted on informality as well as many good practices and pilot projects, show that as a subject, rather than a simple label, Informality may greatly benefit from being investigated through different research perspectives, and not only from the usual approaches which often rely on the negative mark associated with the dimension of illegality, which Informality implies.

However, as Zárate has rightly reiterated, the mark of illegality doesn't concern so much the built environment, or the legislative framework which informal settlements do not comply with; rather, it subtly marks those who live in the informal neighborhoods, those individuals who keep constructing the settlements and who transform them into a complex network inundated with activities, negotiations and even creativity. The stigma of Informality undeniably often prevents even consideration of real life within an informal urban area. Therefore, the association between the illegality of a settlement and the criminal status of those who live in, can become too obvious and contribute to acknowledge the status of the Informal more as an urban bias rather than a subject. The informal label, as we use it, ends up producing a prejudice rather than an opportunity for knowledge. The editors would like to argue in this book along with all the contributors, that informality as an array of proto-urban conditions, is not only extremely vital, and even capable to trigger novel forms of societies, but it could even be recognised within the umbrella of Sustainability.

Therefore, in this book, we would like to claim that Informality can now be a laboratory of urban production, resourcefulness and creative knowledge, rather than a mere label of a very complex and diversified phenomenon. Furthermore, we believe that informality might need to be investigated and considered as the counterpart of any conversation or study that focusses on urban and architectural design. Rather than dealing with an allurement of informality, we are more interested in unraveling the subtle links between informal settlements and the broader discourse of sustainable urbanization, which currently characterizes architecture and urban design. Indeed, informality seems to encompass different topics ranging from the dichotomy determined-undetermined in the urban and architectural morphology, to the question of the residents as the vital vectors who organize, implement, protect and maintain these urban transformations. It is therefore also a discourse about the shift in the way we look at informality today, and how we acknowledge its profound correlation with the human element, the people behind the production and movement of the city. This shift has been emphasized by the *movement, described as Social Production of Habitat,* which *intends to highlight the positive and transformative characteristics of so-called "informal settlements", which involve people-driven and people-centered processes to produce and manage housing, services, and community infrastructure*, as Zárate pointed out in a simple way (Zárate, 2016).

If on one hand, producing buildings certainly is not automatically making architecture, on the other hand, it results in making cities, or in other words: producing complexities. Additionally, informal settlements reveal their nature which greatly depends on both, the geographical context and the urban scale. Although we can find common features, Informal Settlements still cover an extreme and diverse range of organizations depending on the local socio-economic situation and the ability of people in self-organizing structures. The property of self-organization, as one of the most emerging properties within informal settlements (Eizenberg, 2019; Nations & Commission, 2013), perhaps the result of the *processes of practical problem solving for achieving human dignity and a better quality of life* (Zárate, 2016), should therefore be regarded as the link towards a renewed approach to the described phenomenon.

In 1987, the United Nation defined *Sustainability* as *meeting the needs of the present without compromising the ability of future generations to meet their own needs* (Visser & Brundtland, 2013). Although Sustainability is a fragile concept and very susceptible of different definitions and articulations, there is no doubt that its major conceptual strength is the coexistence between humans and nature co-existing in a reciprocal balance and keeping development in balance with its proper conditions.

Therefore, in the perspective of systemic thinking, Informal Settlements can be considered a rich source of knowledge and a diverse catalogue of different approaches to the human setting, which along of the problematic dimension it can offers, it can also be considered a resource of human creativity in the transformation of the built environment.

Because of the different declinations that Informality offers, including different spatial and morphological urban qualities along with a plethora of behavioural patterns, the generalization of the word *informal* appears very limiting. This book presents the thinking of over 30 recognized scholars on the topic: it offers an overview of different versions of Informality aimed at illustrating how this diverse and multi-faceted phenomenon occurs in different contexts. For obvious reasons, we couldn't cover all the different locations we would have liked to cover, however, we would like to highlight how many of the cases presented in this book share common roots, and at the same time are extremely diverse. Informality is certainly not a problem limited to low income groups, cities or countries, among which it further differs, rather it even concerns developed countries and emerging economies. Perhaps, given the evidence about the many ways Informality articulates itself, we should use the word *Informalities*.

Informalities, rather than describing a coherent and unique phenomenon, is in the urgent need to be reformulated, articulated and pluralised. We need Informal voices to talk about it.

Within this perspective, Informalities seem to challenge, unconsciously or not, contemporary urban as well as architectural culture. Indeed, if the only common denominator among Informalities is the absence of authority, Informal Settlements are left in a *gray space* where the authorities, in the guise of political power, can benefit (Yiftachel, 2009b, 2009a) while architects with some exceptions often leave this topic to the urban planners.

Informality then is also about policy, namely a matter of coexistence within individuals belonging to a certain society, although this is not a book written by political scientists. As architects and urban designers, we acknowledge how the wishes of individuals, their memories, and their ideas about architecture and cities undoubtedly play a crucial role in the way Informality happens. Undoubtedly it regards disadvantaged people and may be paradoxical emerges in those contexts where a relative economic availability allows the need and the relative freedom of something emerging as urban and architectural transformation.

The latest incarnation of Informality then, can be considered ground zero for a whole series of global battles: from climate change and social justice movements to economic regeneration and city design and planning.

The book's editors ask the following question: how could informality be considered through the lens of sustainability? Or rather, how the concept of sustainability could help in unfolding the hidden layers of informality in all of its declinations?

If the concept of sustainability, as it merged over the last decades, is fundamentally an attempt to work with the whole ecology of the Planet, how can this idea reveal the hidden dimensions of the informal, which goes far beyond the simple fact of illegality?

What does the informal tell us about the multitude of individuals who transform despite their socio-economic conditions?

To answer these questions, we have conceptually divided the book into three parts, which reflect three different dimensions of the way we could look at the informal.

The three parts of the book

The first part, entitled *What does Informality have to say to Architecture? Decolonising the enquiry and the enquirer,* works in a more speculative way and opens up the definition of informal to the specific field of architecture rather than the city. It is aimed at unraveling how the concept of Informality could be regarded as a subtle link between contemporary architecture discussions and the city.

It is a part that tries to argue around the thread which links the informal with architecture, the former regarded as a transformative practice of individuals beyond the control of the discipline of architecture itself. We argue that the Informality can reflect different articulations of contemporary architecture research, which embrace both the speculative and technological sides. Furthermore, Informality in its different incarnations seems to involve the question of the bottom-up design processing, the idea of the design emerging from a set of negotiations, rather than from an authorial gesture. Yet, it could be argued that Informality concerns architecture in relation to the problem of the form, perhaps in its being determined or undetermined, completed or unfinished, an ever-going transformation or a finished object.

The second part, entitled *Informality as a Mode of Sustainability,* presents a series of chapters that were developed by different scholars and practitioners with an interest in the potential link to Sustainability. This is a central core of the book in which, rather than giving definite answers, allows for further questions to arise. It is argued that Informality can even be a mode of Sustainability, namely that the latter has the potential to turn the analysing of Informality into a more comprehensive spectrum, providing new keys to understanding the different social, economic, environmental and geographical implications that informality currently presents in the contemporary world. If the first part deals with what the informal has to say about architecture; this part unravels what informality has to say to sustainability.

Indeed, a close enough look at any urban settlement will reveal informal patterns of growth and inhabitation, which as we argue, presents aspects like self-organization, continuous negotiations among the habitants, and perhaps a broader sequence of sustainable latencies. Lehmann's chapter deals with the spatial character of public space and its modus operandi. Malterre-Barthes discusses the contradiction between housing sprawl and the loss of agricultural land in Egypt. Pedrabissi examines the informality within a large housing block in Seoul, while Perrotti describes the informal found in the metabolism of the 21st century landscape. Swapan, Zaman and Lehmann describe the informal patterns of use found in the public space of megacity Dhaka, while Jones explores informal settlements in Bandung, Indonesia. Ortega is fascinated by everyday practices in the urban landscape of Southern Los Angeles, and Perlman tracks the failures of public sector interventions in the favela in Brazil. Finally, Williams et al. examine how the digital technology of the smart phone can be used to visualise the operation of Matatus, the informal bus systems in Nairobi.

The third part is titled *Informal Behaviour as a Form of Community Resilience*. It explores the informal hypothesis as an opportunity aimed at resilience to redefine the paradigms of human coexistence and the urban fabric in times of global crises.

This position is considered here as a consequence of the failure of the deterministic approach to town planning as the default mode of colonisation of the planet and leads to the study of informal behavioural patterns as a contribution to resilience through an understanding of low consumption practice and coexistence with non-human species.

The three parts therefore come together into a unitary and possibly integrated framework, without which, the authors think informality couldn't be fully addressed. The authors do not pretend to give an exhaustive picture of the phenomenon, rather they think this book constitutes a first attempt to open new directions in the research around Informality, including the creative and problematic contradictions which profoundly relate it to sustainability.

References

Eizenberg, E. (2019). Patterns of self-organization in the context of urban planning: Reconsidering venues of participation. *Planning Theory*, *18*(1), 40–57. https://doi.org/10.1177/1473095218764225

Nations, U., & Commission, E. (2013). Self-made cities. In *Self-Made Cities*. https://doi.org/10.18356/b38f6f47-en

Un-Habitat. (2013). *Streets as Public Spaces and Drivers of Urban Prosperity*.

Visser, W., & Brundtland, G. H. (2013). Our common future ('The Brundtland Report'): world commission on environment and development. *The Top 50 Sustainability Books*, 52–55. https://doi.org/10.9774/gleaf.978-1-907643-44-6_12

Yiftachel, O. (2009a). Critical theory and "gray space": Mobilization of the colonized. *City*, *13*(2–3), 246–263. https://doi.org/10.1080/13604810902982227

Yiftachel, O. (2009b). Theoretical notes on "gray cities": The coming of urban apartheid? *Planning Theory*, *8*(1), 88–100. https://doi.org/10.1177/1473095208099300

Zárate, L. (2016). *They are Not "Informal Settlements"—They are Habitats Made by People–The Nature of Cities*. https://www.thenatureofcities.com/2016/04/26/they-are-not-informal-settlements-they-are-habitats-made-by-people/

Part I

What does informality have to say to architecture?

Decolonising the enquiry and the enquirer

Antonino Di Raimo

The informal city, like informal architecture, as well as being a topic that has been well-investigated and debated, is above all an increasingly emerging reality implied by the development of the contemporary city. Taking a closer view, informality not only concerns the urban realm, but rather, we would like to argue, it also matters to architecture.

As has been already introduced in this book, one of the main aims of the first part is to disclose and emphasise how informality can imply architectural discourse. Perhaps at the architectural level, as has been said before, we should use the plural version of the word, namely referring to the informalities which we can observe, rather than informality as a unique and coherent phenomenon. Therefore, in this introduction to the first part of the book, I would like to argue for the need to consider informality in its multiscalar sense, implying different manifestations from the point of view of architecture, and not just from the points of view attached to such disciplines as urban studies or planning, as has traditionally happened. Although these have provided valuable research on the topic, the privileged level of observation rarely intercepts the architectural realm, while informality naturally also acts at the architectural level despite the potential difficulties in fully addressing this.

Within an empirical observation it is very common to choose a point of view which can rely on the account of emergent qualities rather than on singularities. Hence, I would like to argue that the phenomenon of informality is perhaps a significant and missing link between the problems presented by the growth of contemporary cities as complex places embodying social transactions and contracts, and architecture design, which still holds to the scale of the individual or groups of individuals. The architectural dimension of informality, I would like to claim, should be regarded as an imperative dimension to be observed and investigated, rather than being – *sic et simpliciter* – subsumed by the urban and planning dimensions. Informality starts with an architectural action that doesn't derive from any acknowledgment of the urban and the planning. Perhaps informality could specify the urban articulations of a city or even implement planning expectations, but it could also contradict them. I would like also to argue that informality represents what we need to look at from an architectural point of view, just as our concerns with sustainability and ecology are authentic actions aimed at embracing our planet's priorities within the discipline, rather than being merely marketing labels that may be useful at this stage, while being scrapped as soon as other priorities arise. Roy says that, "*In many parts of the world, the site of new informality is the rural/urban interface. Indeed, it can be argued that metropolitan expansion is being driven by informal urbanization*" (Roy, 2005). Yet, informality, according to this emblematic sentence, might have the status of an interface, namely, "*the place at which independent and often unrelated systems meet and act on or communicate with each other*" (Interface, n.d.). Roy, as has been highlighted, moved the label of informality to an epistemological level, aiming at extending the word as a tool for knowledge. I would like to assume and to extend this definition by claiming that informality, through being an *interface* between the rural and the urban as Roy significantly pointed out, can also be regarded as an interface between many other dichotomies such as the urban and the architectural, the legal and the illegal, the peripheral and the central, the individual and society, and so on. Informality as an interface, which in our view is a phenomenon fully belonging to what we call the built environment, should be primarily regarded as a physical, tangible, material interface with a proper morphology that is anything but *unformal*. As architects, we are interested in the way that informality as a material interface can work in architectural terms. Like a strange corollary of the city as a theoretical notion, informality takes its physical reality in the form of turbulent borders combining different areas of our contemporary cities. It emerges as an anarchic appropriation of the city's interstitial spaces. We might recognise informality even in those areas in which, depending on different socioeconomic factors, a proto-urbanisation is occurring. Informality has taken hold according to different modalities up to the point that it can even be acknowledged as a palpably emerging different genre of landscape.

In our experience, informality is already part of our everyday life. It occurs when we enter a city, going across the areas which mark its borders. Whether we are arriving in the city by train or exploring its immediate suburbs, the feeling of informality is palpable. In some cases, informality as a physical phenomenon has ceased to be hidden and has turned out to be a quality to be exhibited. Paradoxically, travel agencies offer tours in the favelas of Rio De Janeiro in Brazil or in the slums of Klong Toei in Bangkok.

So why is it still so difficult for informality to be fully acknowledged as a part of architectural discourse?

From an urban point of view, informality is grounded in a solid research tradition dating back to the seventies. Over the following decades, scholars, researchers and stakeholders, each from different backgrounds, developed an extensive range of studies, resulting in a broader understanding of the phenomenon aimed initially at decreasing the dichotomy between the formal and the informal, and the stigma applied to informal settlers.

Informality now embodies inclusive meanings, allowing us not only to overcome prejudices surrounding informal settlements and their inhabitants, but also showing that there is a wide range of social and economic conditions that do not always fall into the simple category of poverty. Yet, informality is a very nuanced phenomenon, and even if it has often been associated with categories such as *marginality*, informal settlements can display creative meanings, though this may seem contradictory, and a richness of distinct values. The pioneering work developed by Janice Perlman since the seventies has shown the importance of the demystification of categories often associated with informal settlements, like marginality, poverty and segregation (Perlman, 2002). An extensive overview that summarises this long path for the recognition of informality as a complex phenomenon not falling within a dualistic vision, along with several other contributions, can be found in UN-Habitat's New Urban Agenda (Alfaro d'Alençon et al., 2018).

From these highly relevant studies it is worth noting that the physical and morphological aspects implied by informal settlements, especially at the level of architectural scale, remain fields that are relatively unexplored, or at least they have only been explored sporadically and never systematically. This is a sign of the stigma and prejudice attached to informality, which prevents it from being part of the architecture agenda. Significant exceptions exist in some architecture practices, while others belong in the didactic and research activities developed in architecture studios at the university level, which take the informal as a possible field for the application of architectural ideas; the more analytical of these, focusing on the study of urban morphology, are the most common. Yet, in an era of the proliferation and pervasiveness of architectural images, even a certain figurativeness which might be considered an implicit feature of informality through its recurring motifs reaches the architect's imagination, such as the reproduction of small derelict housing units and their 'in progress' appearance. To a certain extent informality seems to influence architecture, at least in some proposals which emphasise features like self-sufficiency, flexibility, open-ended process and sustainability, though perhaps this needs to be firmly be established by targeted research.

Even if the architect's imagination and the presumption of aestheticisation implicit in their work is inevitable, romanticising informality and not distinguishing between basic conditions related to poverty and inequality, including a lack of sanitised water and toilets, and the informalities which act as a set of practices at the socioeconomic and urban levels carried out beyond any legal framework, may further imply a fundamental disengagement between architecture and urban speculations, and their capability to address real problems.

Monika Grubbauer argues about the importance of what she calls the "*modes of (dis)engagement between urban theory and professional practices*" (including architecture) within the context of post colonialism urbanism. A paradoxically interdisciplinary debate which relies on an "*eclectic mix of statements*", and often the "*dominance of the global architect*" – a figure who works as a vehicle for polarising the debate and creating "*architecture as urban theory's 'other'*", reinforcing the reciprocal "*epistemological difference*" between architects and social scientists instead of opening up a space for a mutual exchange of ideas and knowledge (Grubbauer, 2019). Despite the production of knowledge produced by architects who have been involved with informality, "*exhibitions are often not shown and publications are not available in the cities of the Global South which serve as sites of these projects*" (Grubbauer, 2019). In the meantime, she points out that "*Leading Western architects and designers active in cities of the Global South, for instance, are frequently criticised for their actions by urban scholars. At the same time, ongoing changes in the intellectual foundations of the field of architecture and urban design have not received much recognition in urban scholarship*" (Grubbauer, 2019).

Other authors have made significant comments on the involvement of global architects such as Rem Koolhaas with the Global South's megacities, as in Lagos, "*where he turned the dysfunctionality of the African city into a sort of virtue in so far as it can be understood theoretically to incubate the future. In an attempt to overturn the prevalent apocalyptic view of a doomed urbanisation strategy, Koolhaas sees a continued functionality in the slumscape of Lagos and other megacities of the South, making a case to revise our existing theories, tracing instead a new kind of urbanism in this anomaly*" (Arabindoo, 2011). And, as Gandy critically points out, "*Koolhaas urges us not to 'anguish over its shortcomings' but instead to celebrate the 'continued, exuberant existence of Lagos and other cities like it', and the 'ingenious, alternative systems' which they generate*" (Gandy, 2005). There is, of course, a significant disengagement between actors who are dealing with informality on different levels, and from different disciplines and social backgrounds.

In an alternative and tangible way, many architects, among them Teddy Cruz, stand out for their capability to assume that informality is a complex physical and social field in which architecture is not a tool aimed at producing disengagement, nor at simply formalising the informal. Cruz's work for instance contemplates architecture as a set of disciplinary tools capable of extrapolating informality's socio-physical properties, along with the conflicts that they embody, as the basis from which a project can be developed. The architecture proposals here are clearly based on the informal features of the context, and rather than being purified they become a set of design actions encompassing language properties and compositional aspects emerging in the architecture proposal. Cruz, who is perhaps a representative of architecture's capability 'to listen' to a context, has been interviewed in the first part of this book by Kathy Waghorn.

On a more experimental and certainly disruptive degree is the work of François Roche, who with his historical and elusive architecture platform *New-Territories* has confidently and consistently contemplated the dynamics and perhaps the bottom-up implications of what we know as the decisive properties of informal settlements. Although he never uses the word informality, we should recognise his non-neutral concerns about architecture as a problem of transactions between people, and conditions both geographical and historical, as well as environmental. If there is a way to rethink architecture in the light of informal processes, this should contemplate the process, which is a *protocol* rather than a methodology. The protocols in the belief of *New-Territories* encompass *the multitude* at their core, rather than the users – the environment as ecology, counting both the natural and artificial, and including the fundamental presence of robotic apparatuses. The *social body* which generates, *protects* and maintains a settlement, namely the individuals, also generates a complexity of biological, social, and emotional transactions which are mediated by robotic agents, which may even be perturbed by the contradictory signal disclosed by these humans (Di Raimo, 2014). The settlement emerges from this set of negotiations between individuals, and the individuals and the context, as an open-ended process, a morphological multitude of clusters, as happened in the *I Have Heard About* project and later in *An Architecture 'des humeurs'* (Le Laboratoire, 2010).

In a way, and from different perspectives, these pieces of architecture research seem to highlight that understanding informality cannot transcend the dimension of the individual, their molecular articulation and therefore their desires, which represent them and define them psychologically. In other words, informality also seems to reclaim the individual dimension, which is perhaps often missing from systematic attempts aimed at framing it as a phenomenon acting only on a geographical/territorial and/or urban scale.

The individual behind environmental transformation

When I suggest that the first part of the book is also aimed at discovering the individual dimension behind informality, I am not alluding to Hernando De Soto's work, which enhances the individual heroism of informal settlers as being equally capable of creativity and entrepreneurism as individuals in the West (De Soto, 2000), I am referring instead to individuals as embodied agents, whose embodied condition constitutes the link between the lived experience of the settler and the built environment. Considering the *individual sensorimotor capacities* as being *embedded in a more encompassing biological, psychological, and cultural context* (Varela et al., 1992) is highly significant for unravelling the complexity emerging from the embodied action of the settlers, the material production of architecture and the urban environment.

As an example, Desai et al. (2015) develop a *focused analysis of the relationships of the body to the diverse materialities of sanitation infrastructure* in order to *understand open defecation in the unequal city.* Within an informal context, they seek to understand the *everyday geographies of disgust, contamination and the unsanitary city,* highlighting that the *practices of improvisation* implemented by settlers to face a lack of local toilets are *too often neglected in accounts of urban infrastructure and political ecologies.* They also highlight the importance of analysing *the lived worlds of urban infrastructure* (Desai et al., 2015).

While open defecation, accompanied by disgust and a loss of dignity, may be very common in informal settlements, especially those which are also characterised by poverty, there *has been scant research on open defecation despite its widespread prevalence in many cities in the global South. Perhaps one reason for this is that open defecation is perceived to be at complete odds with the modern city* (Desai et al., 2015).

The incongruity between open defecation and the modern city exposes the crucial relationship between the physiological needs of the human body and the hygienic protocols established by the Modern Movement. Claiming the existence of the toilet, and even better the *plumber,* to use the title of one of the most iconic famous essays about Modernism (Loos, 1987), could perhaps be regarded as the juncture where the ideology of modernism, and therefore the idea of a Modern Architecture, took shape and became inextricably linked to the idea of civilisation. Rightly or wrongly a lack of toilet facilities started to become almost equivalent to a lack of architecture, employing architecture itself, and even possibly the architect, to be the medium in charge of allowing the 'civilisation' advocated by Loos and many others within the Modern Movement.

It is not the case, as argued by some scholars, that "*there was no Postmodern toilet, no desire to return to Greek plumbing while celebrating Classical pediments. Nor is there a Critical Regionalist or Parametric toilet. Robert Venturi and Denise Scott-Brown didn't offer a complex and contradictory toilet experience. Even the High-tech architects who see all architecture as a form of glorified plumbing largely stay away from the toilet.* Furthermore, *we live in an age in which some of the biggest battles in the media and in the courts are about the toilet – and what it means to share a toilet with someone whose secrets you may or may not want to know, whether in terms of transgender rights or the vast community for whom the toilet as a little space cut off from daily life is simply unthinkable: the diapers of the super young and super old; the assorted bags of the seriously ill, invalids, incontinent, and paralyzed; the prisoners sleeping with their toilet; communal toilets in villages; or the vast group of the world's poor who live in the world before the toilet that modern architects tried to so urgently address*" (Colomina & Wigley, 2018).

Informality seems to be at odds with the modern idea of the city, even before considering architecture.

Indeed, informality is directly correlated with the existence of the city as a product of modernisation and globalisation; it is worth emphasising that the Modern Movement in architecture has always been marked by dichotomies which have shaped the debate, its evolution, and its respective crises. It could be argued that it is not informality as we know it today, but rather its range of different incarnations (the vernacular, the organic, etc.), which are the basis of these dichotomies.

In a way, although this is never fully acknowledged, it could be argued that informality as a subtle tension within modernisation has played a significant role in architecture. Marion Von Osten explains from different points of view how the works of Bernard Rudofsky and Colin Ward, as two "*perspectives identifying a condition that emerged during decolonization, in which a massive crack appeared in the modernist movement and its vision of top-down planning,*" constituted examples of how the lexicon, perhaps more focused on aesthetics in the case of Rudofsky and more on politics in the case of Ward, already reflected the physical characters or the modalities belonging to informality (Von Osten, 2009).

Decolonising research and the researcher (Datta, 2018)

In my years teaching and researching at Polis University in Tirana, Albania, I worked with several colleagues on the topic of informality. Despite the fact that informality, often under the euphemistic label 'spontaneous,' is widespread in the Mediterranean and in the Italian territory, where it often assumes the form of abusive and landscape-devastating building-speculation, in the strength and the visual impact of informal Albanian settlements and those in the European Western Balkans, an exceptional energy is unravelled, and although these are comparable to other experiences described in the literature, in their local variety they showed inventiveness and even a certain anarchic character. When using the word anarchic in terms of Albanian informality, I am trying to subtly imply a certain desire of architecture, recognisable in the many artsy and ungrammatical architectural elements embedded in that built environment.

Certainly in Tirana the energy exuding from some informal urban aggregates, or from growths close to and in-between buildings belonging to the Communist era, was as much the result of long repression, and therefore liberation following the collapse of the dictatorial regime, as of the introduction of neoliberal economic policies. It became clear to me and my colleagues that they were both simultaneously a sign of desperation and of a euphoria, which dramatically demanded to be listened to and understood. Tirana's informality should have been considered by looking at what could have been the desire for physical transformation, and perhaps for architectural development expressed by individuals in the historical context of the roughly 20 years following 1991. An empathetic attitude to reading the urban and architectural settlement, and above all to understanding it, was not just a concern, rather it became a need.

At Polis University, the two faculties of architecture and urban planning, although providing two different degree courses, often contemplated joint architecture and urban design studios, where with our students, we worked on informality through an interdisciplinary approach aimed at providing a common envisioning between planners and architects. This was a hallmark of the school, derived from the experience in daily hands-on practice in participatory planning that the founders of the university introduced into the Albanian reality through the NGO CoPlan following the collapse of communism, dealing with settlers who quite obviously detested planning.

While I was teaching architecture design, with a focus on computational procedures and taking to an ecological approach, I learnt about informality by experiencing it first-hand with my Albanian colleagues, therefore appreciating it not only on the urban scale but also the architectural one. Diverse conversations, observations and experiences based on analysis of the existing, and envisioning a possible design, were shared and generated with our students.

Commonly arising questions were related to informality as a real and omnipresent medium in the Albanian built environment, perhaps even more real than the

Figure 1 View of Tirana city from its surrounding hills (2014). Informality often manifests itself as an interface between different parts of the planned city.

Source: Author.

scenographic transformations that the new powers were eventually preparing to put on stage in the city. Despite all of the architectural exercises based in informal areas, which consisted of the regeneration of the informal areas their 'distillation,' it became increasingly clear to us that informality showed us something that we could identify as its proper voice. Informality could even have a proper terminology, and perhaps language, ranging from stammering through to rude screaming, passing through a series of disciplinary accidents, grammatical distortions and unimaginable words.

The process of listening to the informal and understanding it not only within a socioeconomic and political perspective, but also in architecture terms couldn't be possible if approached according to my Italian background in architecture education. In Tirana, it was difficult to identify something by relying on intellectual categories belonging to a taxonomy which could work well for an Italian city, but not for Tirana.

Our understanding of informality was then triggering a parallel critical appraisal of the academic model that "*continues to deny the colonised and historically marginalised other space to communicate from their own frames of reference*" (Chilisa, 2012). We also realised that this process of recognition, as opposed to simple neglect, also implied "*a process of change that does not necessary involve destroying Western knowledge but*

Figure 2 Tirana city, Don Bosko Area (2014). There is no informal, rather there are different informalities, which appear as inconsistent, disconnected, yet capable of emerging in a certain urban atmosphere.

Source: Author.

rather decentring it or perhaps deterritorialising it (making it something other than what it is)" (Le Grange, 2016).

The informal, therefore, far from having any architectural citizenship, and more than constituting a simple spontaneous building contingency – certainly a reassuring category – was not so much about *an architecture without architects* in the manner expressed by Rudofsky, nor did it articulate any political position. Rather, informality expressed a condition of desire, whose architectural features were expressed without any intellectual mediation, such as one which might have been offered by an architect. Apparently, informal settlers in Albania, and I suspect everywhere, were not only doing without architects, but it is likely they replaced that professional figure with themselves.

While this could leave us architects dismayed, as it dramatically shows architecture's inability to even take informality into consideration, with the exception of those architects who made this their professional foundation, at the same time it shows a need to look at and even to learn from informality, beyond setting it in reassuring categories such as the vernacular and the picturesque.

This biographical interlude, which is aimed at sharing the experience which I have gained about one of the possible incarnations of informality, tries also to emphasise some important points which are the basis of not only the first part of the book, but also of its overall structure. Recalling the words of a scholar coming from indigenous education, we understand that we need to decolonise the process of observation and inquiry, and construct the possibility for conducting research within informality by placing it as an indigenous voice with its own proper epistemology, in the centre of the research process (Smith, 1999).

In the case of architecture, a discipline that in its historical, philosophical and political tradition takes the form and the transformation of the built environment and its formalisation as its epistemological core, putting an epistemology of the informal at the centre of its theoretical discourse would not only imply contemplating a diversity of manifestations of the form in which we live, but more importantly would imply enclosing phenomena that affect architecture even though they are considered merely the emergence of a pathological condition. Despite the common belief that architecture is a resolver-healer discipline, perhaps stemming from its the complex intertwining with the ambiguous concept of civilisation (Burkitt, 1996), architecture is certainly not a problem solving discipline, and "*terms such as civilization and* its counterpart *barbarism have a social and normative origin, their function being to define the behaviours of one set of people as morally good and superior, and the behaviour of others (the lower classes and those of other cultures) as debased and inferior*" (Burkitt, 1996).

By placing it at the centre of architecture, informality would not mean the absence of the architect, rather it would exploit the lack of the conventional discourse around *formality*. It is emblematic that while informality has been investigated, studied and deconstructed according to its economic, political and social meanings, the formality, namely that which should constitute its counterpart in architecture and urban design, has never been mentioned nor named as a such. Paradoxically, while it is quite clear what the informal might constitute in the built environment, and how many phenomena could fall under this label, it would be really difficult to understand what we would classify as the formal, if this category were to exist. Should we say that several

Figure 3 Tirana city, Don Bosko area (2014). Informality seems to always implies basic residential units. A unit which can be micro or macro in terms of size would eventually emerge, through subsequent aggregations, in larger configuration.

Source: Author.

centuries of experience in architecture, urban planning and design have to be classified as the formal? Should we accept that, because of the negative value placed on the informal, we hold an idea of architecture, an urban transformation, that should therefore fall under the formal simply because, in the face of informal, it should be called formal? The informal then seems to hold a subtly reassuring role in establishing what architecture is and what it is not. And I hope this will be the matter of further study.

Therefore, recognising the dimensions of architecture which informality implies, be they manifest or latent, or even irrational, should be an imperative for all those concerned with urban settlements, architecture and sustainability. Informality doesn't simply seek a diversity of formal architecture manifestations; informality seeks inclusivity.

Inclusivity

So, what does informality have to say to architecture? And what is there in informal settlements that should be discovered, analysed, and studied through the official lenses of architecture discourse? And how do these points connect with the other two parts of this book?

Without any doubt, the first argument that informality puts into play is the need for an inclusive (and not exclusive) attitude by architects. Informality, if truly considered from the point of view of the individuals or small communities who generate it, has a lot to do with the relationships between these actors, the spaces that they create, and the official city. Informal settlers belong to the city as much as the inhabitants of formalised settlements. The concerns about their reasons, their desires, their memories and even their imagination should be studied from a closer point of view. Any study should look at the individuals who constitute the real agency behind this phenomenon. Informality can unfold into diverse architectural categories, which are often already part of many contemporary architecture experiments and speculations. Informal settlements in their diverse range are complex areas, resulting in laboratories of coexistence, creative communities and even architectural debate.

Complexity and levels of observation

In considering an approach to informality and to urban space in general, it is worth mentioning that there is no linear way to deal with this. Portugali (2006), who sees in complexity the potential to bridge the culture of space and place, aiming at reconciling the hard and soft sciences in the understanding of human geographies, advocates for a contemporary approach to the observation and description of the urban phenomenon. Complexity as a contemporary scientific paradigm could undoubtedly be the ideal milieu for tackling a renewed tradition of urban and architectural observation, in which the formal and the informal, rather than being dichotomic categories, would intertwine with the agents of transformation within a given environment. It would be a systemic and inclusive approach.

The complexity approach to the field of urban phenomena is a very broad research front, and, has been recently explored by several scholars as a potential for studying informality. The need to move this approach from a metaphorical dimension to one that is methodologically rigorous and quantifiable has been highlighted by many researchers (Boeing, 2018). Some have applied it to urban sprawl, which is often a form of informality, with some scholars highlighting the relevance of computational models such as cellular automata and fractal forms of organisation in order to obtain an understanding of its genesis (Bosch et al., 2019). Other recent studies have focused on the well-known concept of agents, emergence and self-organisation (Alberti et al., 2018). Complexity consequently shows the potential for the use of computational techniques and algorithmic paradigms, with Agent Based Modelling and the Cellular Automata being the most used.

It seems promising that in the modelling and simulation of complex urban phenomena some features characterising informal areas, such as self-organisation and multiscalar features, can be recreated through abstract computer simulations, with their role as stabilising factors able to be observed and documented (Barros, 2008). However, while the results of these simulations allow us to quantify data, extrapolate relationships, and therefore construct models aimed at a better articulation of the phenomenon, the need to incorporate uncertainty is still relevant. Although the outcomes are interesting, the computational models remain fundamentally deterministic, and like all models recreated as computer processes they can fail to account for the noise, redundancy, and essential non-deterministic character of informal settlements.

Morphology, architectural dirtiness and ecology

There is still a fundamental need to obtain a full observation and understanding of informality at the architectural level, possibly using the traditional tools of the discipline. Dovey & King (2011) articulate a taxonomy of the modalities through which the informal takes place and emerges into urban and architectural features (Dovey & King, 2011). The proposed methods are of interest not so much for their absolute value, as each category can coexist with one or all of the others, but for their capability to disclose architectural actions within the built environment. The articulation proposed by Dovey & King (2011) consists of three types – *settling, inserting, attaching* – which on looking closer highlight the way that agents root in an environment in order to inhabit it: "*the first is simply settling, as on unclaimed and often unbounded land as indigenous villages and towns have come about over millennia. Second is inserting, into the uninhabited, abandoned or leftover fragments of urban space. Third is attaching, as informal accretions or excrescences grow out of, or attach onto, the structures of the formal city. These processes of settling, inserting and attaching occur in a diversity of urban situations, unused land, urban infrastructure, edges to formal settlement, rustbelt districts*" (Dovey & King, 2011).

These three categories emerge in morphological types, entangling both the geological support conditions and the existing urban fabric, giving rise to informal types such as *the district, the waterfront, the backstage and others* (Dovey & King, 2011). From this exemplary morphological and definitely non-functional classification, the places generated by informality resemble the idea of the ecological niche, precarious balanced, with redundancy and flexible features based on local contingencies. It is about an open-ended process alongside the writing of the settlement, which almost always take place either incrementally room by room (Kamalipour & Dovey, 2020), or by erasing i.e. a detrimental rewriting. "*Although informal morphologies may appear as random and chaotic, there is often an underlying logic to the emergence and growth of various forms of informality*" (Kamalipour, 2016).

I would like to propose that, despite the lack of observations on the architectural level, the urban fabric still emerges from a set of rules carried out and generated by an individual's actions in something that should be acknowledged as an unconscious interpretation of architecture. "*The logic of informality is the complex commingling of spatial geometry, context-specific conditions, social transactions, historical events, and ethical norms that produce hybrid urban fabrics that show both regularity and irregularity*" (Lejano & Del Bianco, 2018).

Perhaps extending architectural discourse to include informality would mean considering architecture as a hybrid phenomenon encompassing not only what architects do, but also what all of the agents responsible for a physical transformation do. On the other hand, in order to extend informality to the architectural realm, along with considering theory we should also consider practice-based research (Candy, 2006).

This first part then, which aims at interrogating architecture in the light of informality, comprises not only theory-based chapters, but also practice-based and practice-led experiences where informality emerges more closely as a fundamental category, embodying physical or cultural dimensions, in a context in which architecture occurs to the procedures and even the architectural outcomes.

In the first part of the book, Waghorn, in conversation with Teddy Cruz and Fonna Forman, highlights the political milieu employed by informality in re-establishing the conflicts, transactions and the role of architects working as medium within the lived experience of informal areas.

Martínez Capdevila explores how, even within the experience of the radical architecture avant garde, the dimension of informality conveyed by the dissolution of the city could be identified as a subtle and latent tension.

Roche, embracing architecture in its innovative, ecological, and political meanings since 1993, shows three case studies developed by his platform *New-Territories* aimed at unravelling and demystifying technology, which he sees as a vector for 'informal' transformations of a context. If there is a need today for *informalising* architecture, as claimed by Dovey (2013), we should take the work developed by Roche as a paradigm.

Santa Cruz aims at extending informality to the domestic realm of American rural poor communities, unveiling their dissenting self-sufficiency as the opposite of urban and suburban overconsumption.

Dhamo unfolds the case of the city of Tirana, focusing on the agents responsible for the transformation, unveiling the dimension of individual arrangements as a significant case for the urban and architectural dimension of an emblematic contemporary case of informality.

Carpenter sets his practice-based research, often involving informal and temporary appropriation of the space, within the broader concept of resilience.

Joachim and Gervasi's work extends informality to a greater ecological realm, focusing on informal migrations of humans and insects across an administrative border.

Sfriso, Lepore, Pantaleo and Foerster highlight how the use of informal tools in their practice, and more generally the notion of informality, could be an alternative tool with respect to the deterministic and paternalistic planning approach of the Western world.

Conclusions

In conclusion, this first part of the book aims at emphasising how the presence of informality in the built environment, according to its various incarnations within a complex perspective, should be listened to and understood at the architectural level in the light of an approach based on relationships rather than on separations. This means encompassing all of the dimensions that informality implies, namely the historical, the cultural, the psychological and the biological. At the architectural level, informality seems to show both the house and the waste, the faeces and the urine which flows down in the street, because although the sewer is missing, you still have a toilet. Informality, even when you are not in a condition of poverty, can still materialise on the architectural level as a space where all of the dirtiness, which is normally removed through modern hygienic practices, is quietly displayed rather than being "*brought together at both a functional and symbolic level*" (Campkin & Dobraszczyk, 2007). Informality calls for us to revise our idea of sustainability and ecology in architecture.

As some authors have claimed, embracing the notion of resilience defines informal settlements and their inhabitants as entities in search of "meaningful identities, lives and livelihoods in the interstices of fast changing and intersecting urban worlds" (Alfaro d'Alençon et al., 2018; Beall et al., 2010), Informality needs to be observed at the architectural scale. What does informality really represent in architectural terms? Can we merely leave this question to those who observe the world only on the urban and territorial scales? As claimed by Grubbauer, "*design practitioners are clearly expanding their tools and methods of operation through their renewed activist and participatory engagement.* Furthermore, she argues for *learning from in-depth narratives about alternative and bottom-up projects needs both first-hand encounters and observations on site, or thorough reports and analyses from people who are involved and have the skills and the capacity to produce such accounts*" (Grubbauer, 2019).

Informality indicates that there is more than a realm made by urban and/or architectural objects. The built environment works more as an *ambience* where the presence of "*agents structurally coupled with their environment*" transforms it into a continuous process of adaptations, and mutual developments within a history of perturbations occurring in a specific setting (Maturana & Varela, 1991). The nature of informality has a lot to do with a profound ecological dimension, and it manifests itself on a horizontal plane of direct and transparent actions, a well-regarded fact due to the lack of any external authority, including that of the architect who translates and negotiates, or even censures individual actions. Informality can still be a formidable interface between architecture as a discipline and the complexity of our built and unbuilt environment.

Although recently the argument for "*the possibility of an absolute architecture*" (Aureli, 2011), has been regarded by several architects as a new perspective for the reintroduction of an open political position "*within and against advanced capitalism*", informality, belonging neither to the architectural domain nor to rampant and boundless urbanisation but being instead a fragile phenomenon in the middle, might have a lot to say to architecture. If there is an absoluteness of architecture as "*the specific condition of the architectural form* (...) *to separate and be separated*" (Aureli, 2011), the informal underlines instead the urgency for architecture to abandon any kind of absoluteness and to profess itself as a discipline capable of establishing relationships rather than separations.

References

Alberti, M., McPhearson, T., & Gonzalez, A. (2018). Embracing urban Complexity. *Urban Planet, May*, 45–67. https://doi.org/10.1017/9781316647554.004

Alfaro d'Alençon, P., Smith, H., Álvarez de Andrés, E., Cabrera, C., Fokdal, J., Lombard, M,...& Spire, A. (2018). Interrogating informality: Conceptualisations, practices and policies in the light of the new urban agenda. *Habitat International, 75*(April), 59–66. https://doi.org/10.1016/j.habitatint.2018.04.007

Arabindoo, P. (2011). *Rhetoric of the 'slum.' 4813*. https://doi.org/10.1080/13604813.2011.609002

Aureli, P. V. (2011). *The Possibility of an Absolute Architecture*. MIT Press.

Barros, J. (2008). Unifying Themes in Complex Systems IV. *Unifying Themes in Complex Systems IV, January 2008*. https://doi.org/10.1007/978-3-540-73849-7

Beall, J., Guha-Khasnobis, B., & Kanbur, R. (2010). Introduction: African development in an urban world: Beyond the tipping point. *Urban Forum, 21*(3), 187–204. https://doi.org/10.1007/s12132-010-9086-5

Boeing, G. (2018). Measuring the complexity of urban form and design. *Urban Design International, 23*(4), 281–292. https://doi.org/10.1057/s41289-018-0072-1
Bosch, M., Chenal, J., & Joost, S. (2019). Addressing urban sprawl from the complexity sciences. *Urban Science, 3*(2), 60. https://doi.org/10.3390/urbansci3020060
Burkitt, I. (1996). Civilization and Ambivalence. *The British Journal of Sociology, 47*(1), 135–150.
Campkin, B., & Dobraszczyk, P. (2007). Architecture and dirt: Introduction. *Journal of Architecture, 12*(4), 347–351. https://doi.org/10.1080/13602360701614623
Candy, L. (2006). Practice Based Research: A Guide. *CCS Report, 1*(November 2006), 19. Retrieved from http://www.creativityandcognition.com/resources/PBR Guide-1.1-2006.pdf
Chilisa, B. (2012). *Chilisa, B. (2012). Indigenous Research Methods*. Los Angeles: Sage Publication.
Colomina, B., & Wigley, M. (2018). *Toilet Architecture: An Essay About The Most Pyschosexually Charged Room In A Building*. Retrieved from https://pinupmagazine.org/articles/toilet-modern-architecture#11
Datta, R. (2018). Decolonizing both researcher and research and its effectiveness in Indigenous research. *Research Ethics, 14*(2), 1–24. https://doi.org/10.1177/1747016117733296
DeSoto, H. (2000). *The Mystery of Capital: Why Capitalism Triumphs in the West and Fails Everywhere Else*. Basic Books.
Desai, R., Mcfarlane, C., & Graham, S. (2015). The politics of open defecation: Informality, body, and infrastructure in Mumbai. *Antipode, 47*(1), 98–120. https://doi.org/10.1111/anti.12117
Di Raimo, A. (2014). *François Roche. Heretical Machinism and Living Architecture of New-Territories.com*. Roma: EdilStampa
Dovey, K. (2013). Informalising architecture: The challenge of informal settlements. *Architectural Design, 83*(6), 82–89. https://doi.org/10.1002/ad.1679
Dovey, K., & King, R. (2011). Forms of informality: Morphology and visibility of informal settlements. *Built Environment, 37*(1), 11–29. https://doi.org/10.2148/benv.37.1.11
Gandy, M. (2005). *Learning From Lagos*.
Grubbauer, M. (2019). *Postcolonial urbanism across disciplinary boundaries: modes of (dis) engagement between urban theory and professional practice. 2365*. https://doi.org/10.1080/13602365.2019.1643390
Interface. (n.d.). The Merriam-Webster.Com Dictionary. Retrieved August 14, 2020, from https://www.merriam-webster.com/dictionary/interface
Kamalipour, H. (2016). Urban morphologies in informal settlements. *Contour, 3: Agency/Agents of Urbanity*, 1–10.
Kamalipour, H., & Dovey, K. (2020). Incremental production of urban space: A typology of informal design. *Habitat International, 98*(January), 102133. https://doi.org/10.1016/j.habitatint.2020.102133
Le Grange, L. (2016). Decolonising the university curriculum: leading article. *South African Journal of Higher Education, 30*(2), 1–12.
Le Laboratoire. (2010 January 22- 2010 May 16). *An architecture "des humeurs"*. Paris.
Lejano, R. P., & Del Bianco, C. (2018). The logic of informality: Pattern and process in a São Paulo favela. *Geoforum, 91*(June 2017), 195–205. https://doi.org/10.1016/j.geoforum.2018.03.005
Loos, A. (1987). *Spoken Into the Void: Collected Essays, 1897–1900*. Graham Foundation for Advanced Studies in the Fine Arts, Chicago, Ill., and the Institute for Architecture and Urban Studies, New York, N.Y.
Maturana, H. R., & Varela, F. J. (1991). *Autopoiesis and Cognition: The Realization of the Living*. Springer Netherlands.
Perlman, J. E. (2002). *Marginality: From Myth to Reality in the Favelas of Rio de Janeiro. 1969–2002*. Department for International Development.
Portugali, J. (2006). Complexity theory as a link between space and place. *Environment and Planning A, 38*(4), 647–664. https://doi.org/10.1068/a37260

Roy, A. (2005). Urban informality: Toward an epistemology of planning. *Journal of the American Planning Association*, *71*(2), 147–158. https://doi.org/10.1080/01944360508976689

Smith, L. T. (1999). *Decolonizing Methodologies: Research and Indigenous Peoples*. Zed Books.

Varela, F. J., Rosch, E., & Thompson, E. (1992). *The Embodied Mind: Cognitive Science and Human Experience*. MIT Press.

Von Osten, M. (2009, May). *Architecture Without Architects—Another Anarchist Approach*. Retrieved from https://www.e-flux.com/journal/06/61401/architecture-without-architects-another-anarchist-approach/

Chapter 1

Visualizing the political

Teddy Cruz and Fonna Forman, in conversation with Kathy Waghorn

Teddy Cruz, Fonna Forman and Kathy Waghorn

This chapter records a conversation that took place in 2019 by email with architect Teddy Cruz and political scientist Fonna Forman. Since 2012, Cruz and Forman have worked together to address the central challenges of urbanization, especially those occurring at the Mexico/US border at Tijuana/San Diego. This contested metropolitan zone, where they live and work, is the largest bi-national urban region in the world. Blurring conventional boundaries between theory and practice, and situated at the intersection of architecture, art and civic engagement, their practice is committed to exploring the invisible trans-border flows that define this territory and that shape the identities of everyday life in this part of the world.

Pixilation: visualizing the border

Kathy Waghorn: The editors of this book describe informality as the "tangible reflection of the incredible strain between processes of urbanization and urban inhabitants", or in short, that "social, economic, and political factors have real spatial and human consequences" (Di Raimo, Lehmann, & Melis, 2019). *In my proposal to the editors I suggested we focus on your use of visualization to distil and propagate your research. I am going to begin with your work re-imaging, and re-imagining, the border at Tijuana/San Diego. You have consistently drawn attention to this boundary zone, denying its border properties, saying instead that "it is actually the flow and circulation across the wall that has historically shaped the transgressive hybrid identities of everyday life in this part of the world" and that what is needed is "a more encompassing lens focused on shared practices, norms, interests, and aspirations – all of which typically flow unimpeded across border walls".* (Cruz & Forman, 2017, *p. 105*).

The first work of yours that I became aware of, and that has stuck with me, is your mapping of the 'pixilation' that intervenes in the large-scale mono-density of the San Diego region as migrants bring with them the mixed-use density that characterizes their neighbourhoods back home (see Figure 1.1). *In your work at this time, your exposition of the border as a zone of exchange and possibility shuttled between different types of visualization – from photomontage (for example the Levittown houses crossing the border, an image almost in the vein of John Heartfield) to diagrams of social relations, to this more cartographic mapping, and is both richly visual and textual; here I'm drawing attention to your use of language that also makes images – 'pixilation', 'living rooms at the border, 'micro-policy', 'neighbourhood as developer' etc.*

Figure 1.1 Mapping of land use in the Tijuana/San Diego region. The finely pixelated Mexican city presses up against the border wall. Further north, as migrants bring with them the mixed-use density that characterizes their neighbourhoods back home, the large-scale mono-density land use of San Diego also begins to 'pixelate'.

Source: Cruz and Forman.

How did your use of these forms of visualization arise? As an implicit part of your research, who is this graphical articulation aimed at? What agency does the capacity to make such imagery give you, and is this part of the expanded role of the architect/advocate/activist – to make complex situations and ideas visible (and compelling)?

Teddy Cruz and Fonna Forman: In our practice, architecture is not only, or primarily, about spatial-material intervention, but about constructing methods for visualizing political and civic processes. We have been interested in visualizing the urban conflicts and controversies that result from the collision between top-down policies of exclusionary urbanization and bottom-up social and ecological networks. We have often asked ourselves: How can one tackle the urban crisis without visualizing the often invisible institutional mechanisms that have produced it? In other words, for us, the visualization of the contested power relations inscribed in the territory – what we call 'conflict urbanization', is the essential creative tool to reimagine the city today.

Conflict urbanization comprises precise global, regional and urban borders, where discriminatory and alienating policies – by design – exert pressure on the spatial, territorial and environmental conditions, making these critical thresholds hot spots of social and economic inequality, and injustice. It's been essential for us to shift our gaze, from the privileged sites of development, to these peripheral zones of crisis. Along the way we have realized that this shift requires challenging our own methods of representation, a new praxis of intervention, beginning with engaging the 'conditions' themselves that have produced such collisions as the material for design.

Urban conflict is a point of departure in our design and thinking process, and it requires expanded modes of practice, through which architects act as interlocutors of institutional memory, and imagine counter spatial procedures, political and economic structures that can produce social and spatial justice. We maintain that exposing and altering the exclusionary politics and economics of urban development is the radical context from which to produce new programmatic, formal and aesthetic categories for design, and that this process of engagement begins with using images as political tools.

In our work, the *visualization of the political* then entails the exposure of the contested political, social and economic processes that have produced urban border zones, as catalysts to retool our own practice, and the prerequisite for a more effective and inclusive urban and architectural vision and intervention. This is a double project of research and action, that begins with positioning ourselves dialectically within the specificity of these urban conflicts, exposing hidden institutional histories, in order to piece together a more accurate, anticipatory urban research and design intervention. For us, then, the visualization of the political does not stop with naming, or 'measuring' the problem, but involves producing research and design strategies to transcend it, including the pedagogic systems that enable communities affected by the problem cognitive access to the complexity of the urban forces that have caused the problem, to begin with.

Our projects always begin with a *Conflict Diagram*, as a way to name a particular urban conflict. This includes visualizing a relational cartography of the multiple conditions inscribed in a contested site, exposing critical top-down and bottom-up, political, social and economic power relations, as well as the myriad stakeholders involved in the conflict, the ones who produced the crisis, those affected by it, and those activist practices that are positioned and inspired to tackle it. The Conflict Diagram's script is organized around direct questions and provocations, consolidated by, what we call, the "5 W's": The Why, Who, Where, What and When of the problem, and its opportunities.

The Conflict Diagram is really a generative tool for proposition, rooted in the controversies, contingencies and opportunities of a given site, exposing the complex power vectors embedded in any crisis, and assembling the edifice upon on within which 'things can happen'. For us, this opens the most important aspect of images as political tools: the agency that visualizations can have to increase community capacity for political action. In other words, for us, images are not an end in themselves but are tools for political mobilisation and representation, to give voice to the marginalised, serving as evidentiary material, to translate the emancipatory potential of bottom-up stealth urban dynamics, in order to demand changes in top-down policy.

Where is our public imagination?

In your work you return time and again to the crisis of the public. In this, you usefully warn against the risk of abstracting or romanticizing this idea, explaining that "rethinking the public cannot begin without exposing the controversies and conflicts that define the unprecedented social and economic inequality in cities across the globe today" (Cruz & Forman, 2016, *p. 73*). *From what I know of your work, concerned as it is with the local, I don't see this as a monolithic public (as in the concept of 'the public good') but a more multiple and specific public – perhaps akin to the publics that arise around 'matters of concern' to use Latour's phrase* (Latour, 2004). *You see "the widening gap between institutions of knowledge and the public" as a key site of intervention, which requires new practices, research methods and protocols, that is "learning to speak in languages that communicate beyond our own professional knowledge"* (Cruz & Forman, 2016, *p. 76*).

Can you expand on what the public is in your terms, and specifically how the knowledge of multiple publics is made visible and mobilised in your work?

Yes, one major question we ask ourselves and others, as we continue to experience the violent blow that neoliberal political and economic policies have exerted on our shared economic and environmental resources is precisely: Where is our collective imagination today? And in the context of the death of the social welfare state, the erosion of public thinking, and austerity everywhere, we also ask: what do we do in the meantime?

In the absence of a top-down public that can mobilise investments in public infrastructure, housing and services, one that prioritizes re-distribution of wealth and justice, can we imagine a bottom-up public? This pertains to the informal urban practices, distributed across sites of urgency where bottom-up social and economic dynamics have been stitching together, through collective action, a praxis of survival, constructing an informal shared urbanity of resilience and solidarity.

Our practice is an unconventional partnership between a political theorist and an architect, converging around our interest in 'informal' urban dynamics and emergent collective practices – social, moral, economic, political, spatial. We are particularly interested in how people in conditions of scarcity, on the margins of formal institutions, build informal settlements, markets of exchange, governance practices and general strategies of collective survival. Our research has always been motivated by the positive impact of immigrants on the city. Their ingenious strategies of adaptation and survival in conditions of scarcity have inspired our urban vision. For us, border neighbourhoods are sites of urban and political creativity that can generate more inclusive imaginaries of urban development. As such, then, we maintain that peripheral communities are not passive victims of poverty. They are intensely active urban agents who are capable of challenging the dominant models of growth that have excluded them, and denied their rights to the city. This creative knowledge needs to trickle up, to inspire policy-makers and planners to rethink their approaches to the city. We believe that the monolithic public, one that has been decimated in the last years by the hegemony of the private, has been forced to morph into more localized distributed social practices that are found in such informal, marginalized communities. It is here, within geographies of conflict like our own border zone, where the agency of the public is exercised in small acts of collective will, beyond walls, as an anticipatory 'activist public', committed to the incremental re-stitching of a more socially inclusive collective imaginary.

In this context we see the notion of the 'public', less as an abstract adjective, which is always susceptible to being encroached into and hijacked by the private, and instead as an operative set of practices that enable specific points of access to urban rights. In fact, we have come to see urban rights less as a set of mandates designed from above (the conventional way of thinking about rights), and more as a set of performative urban actions from below. This bottom-up action can take the shape of emergent, everyday lived practices among marginalized communities, or more deliberate strategies of urban intervention designed to counter exclusionary political and economic power. We have argued that these bottom-up social and economic exchanges, spatial flows and actions are the building blocks for a more just and equitable city, a more accountable public institution. Urban rights should be understood as a bottom-up public, a collective practice of resistance to unjust power structures in the city – the urban norms, policies, procedures and spaces that perpetuate uneven patterns of urban development.

This is the reason we believe that urban activism needs to focus on increasing public knowledge; how to intervene into the mythologies that have manipulated entire segments of society to mistrust the 'public', (at least in the US *public* seems a forbidden word in our political language); how to reject the hierarchical social norms that have validated neglect, exploitation, dispossession and disinvestment the city? A bottom-up public, then, involves a new urban pedagogy, capable of reigniting civic dignity; repairing collective trust; and restoring a belief in community agency at the local scale, to demand institutional accountability.

Tactics of translation

In the dialogue between the formal and the informal you are not only concerned with these dimensions as they relate to urban form, but in how they also generate and allow different forms of knowledge. You are interested in the complexity of urban knowledge and the ways this knowledge might be transferred across these poles, from the bottom up to the top down.

Over the last few years you have been looking closely at the radical social transformation of Bogotá and Medellín in Colombia, and other Latin American cities that have over decades developed more democratic forms of urbanization. You have said that "the stories of Bogotá and Medellín helped us to clarify something essential in our own urban and political research: that an informal act in the city, whether through stealth spatial alterations, jurisdictional encroachment, or social behavior, does not have to stop at the small and symbolic gestural scale, but it can trickle upwards with enough self-assurance to construct a political process that can ultimately transform top-down policy" (Cruz & Forman, 2016, *p. 88*). *While notably wary of short lived 'pop-ups', a more fulsome mobilisation of the 'bottom up' is imperative to the generation of what you call 'citizenship culture', and in your practice you have developed operational and creative tools to facilitate this transferal – or 'tactics of translation' that can be employed to expose and visualize urban conflict. In many cases these tools begin from (but are not limited to) your capacity to make images that can communicate phenomena that are palpably present but that need distillation and explanation to be grasped in a productive fashion.*

Can you give an example of a new practice, tool or method that you've employed from this exchange with Latin America? How have these ideas translated into the 'bi-national region' that you work in? How is the 'UCSD Cross-Border Initiative' influenced in functional or practical, as well as political and philosophical ways, by your Latin American colleagues and collaborators?

Yes, it is from Latin America that we have learned most about designing political (municipal) and civic processes that yield more equitable forms of urbanization in a neoliberal world of uneven growth. In the last years, we have been interested in translating these Latin American lessons and carrying them back to the Tijuana–San Diego border region, precisely because we believe that some of these lessons can be operationalized across our border region, where we have been committed to facilitating new alliances between municipal and grassroots agendas on both sides of the wall, as well as choreographing the interface between top-down resources and bottom-up creativity, across immigrant neighbourhoods flanking the wall. Ultimately, two main concepts from our research of Medellín and Bogotá have stayed with us, inspiring a set of conceptual tools and initiatives. One is the idea that before transforming the city physically we must first transform social norms, restore public trust and mutual accountability – in essence, construct a new 'citizenship culture'. And the other is that this citizenship culture can be spatialized when it is articulated as a space of knowledge-exchange and education, where citizenship and collective imagination can be mobilised through cultural action.

We recently developed a series of projects from this research. One is the *Medellín Diagram* (see Figure 1.2), which consists of a visualization of the political and civic processes that made the mythical transformation of Medellín possible. Many architects and urbanists across the world have celebrated the physical transformation of Medellín, from being the most violent city in the world in the mid-'90s to becoming an example of an urbanization of social justice just a few years later. While everyone was admiring the architecture, few were asking how this transformation happened, and so rapidly? The focus had been on the physical interventions in the city, not taking into account that the transformation of Medellín was primarily a political project, one that involved a robust institutional reformation. As we deepened our research, it became clear that this was an institutional project, resulting in the reinvention of governance, from opaque, corrupt and inefficient bureaucracy into an agile and creative form of public management that was inclusive of community-based needs and imaginaries. In close partnership with Sergio Fajardo who led this new political vision during his four years as mayor of Medellín, and architect Alejandro Echeverri who directed its urban strategies, we developed the *Medellín Diagram* from a series of interviews and conversations among dozens of civic actors who participated in the transformation of this city. Graphic Designer Mattias Görlich collaborated on the visual system. Ultimately, the *Medellín Diagram* became our compass, to retool our practice, and to orient an aspect of our work dedicated to the visualization of institutional memory.

The project that more fully elaborates an answer to your question is the tool-method we call the *Cross-Border Citizenship Culture Survey*. This is an initiative that we led in collaboration with Bogotá mayor, Antanas Mockus, who led important interventions in that city in the 1990s, during its most intense period of violence and breakdown. We had been inspired by several foundational commitments in Mockus's approach to governance: 1) that 'law and order' does not produce new public values; and 2) that art and culture are powerful engines of civic engagement. Mockus fought violence in Bogotá not with guns but with community processes, to reignite a bottom-up sense of civic commitment, that had been crushed beneath decades of violence and inequality, and to inspire a model of shared responsibility across sectors. We wanted to bring these lessons back with us to the Mexico–US border: to claim that citizenship can

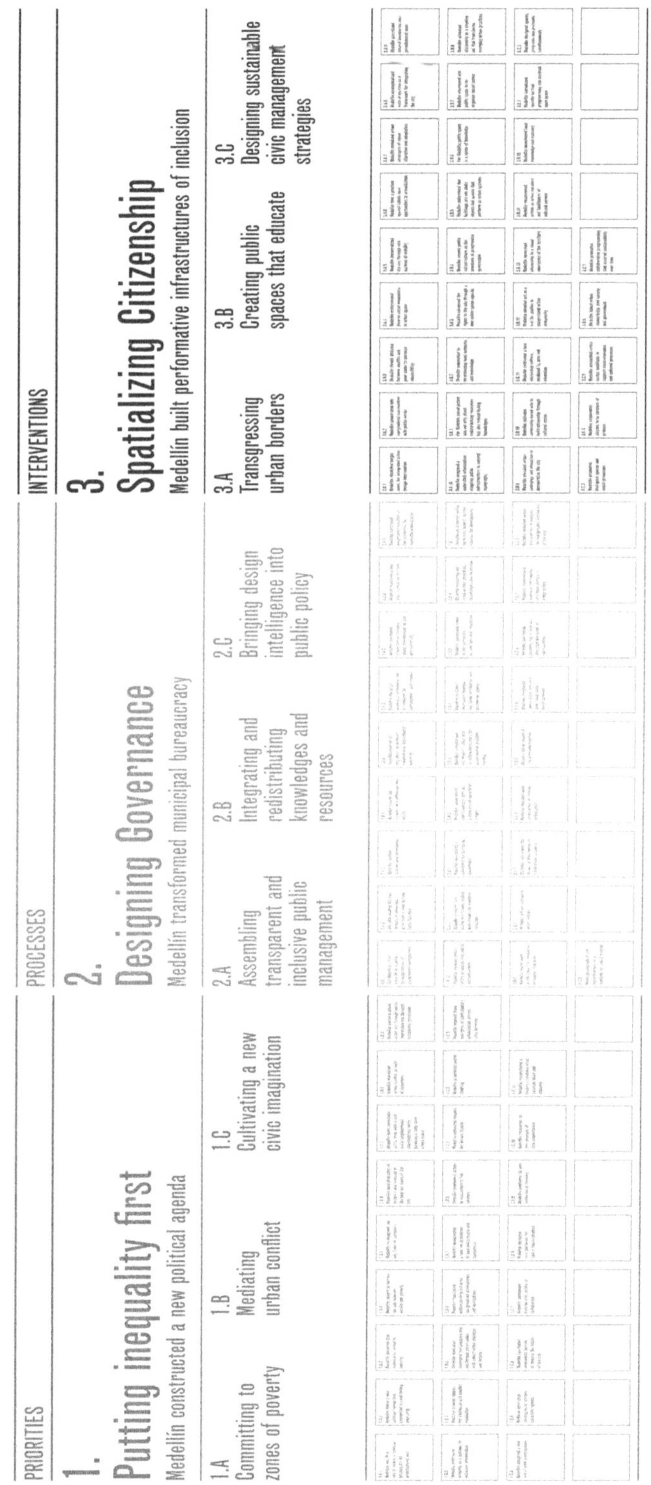

Figure 1.2 Medellín Diagram. A visualization of the political and civic processes that made the mythical transformation of Medellín possible.

Source: Cruz and Forman.

become more than 'us versus them', but instead a unifying cultural force, a tool for collective awareness and interdependence, particularly inside divided communities, and across sites of unimaginable polarization.

We shared with Mockus our belief that the border wall ultimately cannot disrupt the informal normative, social, economic and environmental flows that define our bi-national region, and that therefore this site of imposed division and fragmentation could be an ideal backdrop to test a new version of his *Citizenship Culture Survey*, a tool he had designed and implemented across 50+ cities in Latin America to measure public trust, vertical relations between institutions and publics, and horizontal capacities for social coordination and solidarity. His experiments had always focused on one city at a time, not on two cities, simultaneously, two adjacent communities divided by a wall, so he was excited about the idea of investigating citizenship culture that crossed an international threshold.

Mockus understood that a re-tooled survey could help us advance our documentation of the informal flows that transgress the border wall, to compel a new era of public self-knowledge, as well cross-border municipal and cross-sector collaboration – in essence, to develop the idea of a 'cross-border citizen', whose conception of citizenship is organized around the shared values and social norms, common interests and sense of mutual responsibility around which a new bi-national citizenship culture could emerge. We wanted to move a sense of solidarity beyond the formal jurisdictional boundaries that too rigidly define both cityhood and citizenship in the United States.

So in 2015, we brought Mockus to the San Diego/Tijuana border region to help us rethink citizenship in this contested territory. We worked with the mayors' offices on both sides of the border and a cross-sector team of stakeholders to design the *Cross-Border Citizenship Culture Survey*, a tool to help us identify a latent regional 'citizenship culture' that transgressed the line. The results confirmed many of our intuitions: publics on both sides were open to collaborating on issues of mutual concern, ranging from border wait times and immigration to public health and environment – even though they did not think their governments were ready. By documenting invisible connections and flows across the wall, the *Cross-Border Citizenship Culture Survey* became a mirror for our region, helping people on both sides appreciate what they share and recognize that their destinies are intertwined. Insights like this – while intuitive for the activist – become powerful and more generative when they are cast as manifestations of collective sentiment and will.

For us, the *Cross-Border Citizenship Culture Survey* became a script to instigate grassroots action and intervention. It established new criteria from which to articulate projects and initiatives to straddle the border. At a moment when we were growing increasingly dissatisfied with the many temporary gestures of resistance deployed at the border by artists and architects (as important as these ephemeral gestures can be, no one seems to wonder about the day after), the survey helped us orient our commitment to a more embedded and long-term set of cross-institutional collaborations on both sides of the border wall.

As a result of the survey, we founded the UCSD *Community Stations*, a network of field-hubs in under-represented immigrant neighbourhoods on both sides of the border, where education and research is curated *collaboratively* between university researchers and community-based non-profits, advancing a new model of long-term community-university partnership and cross-border cultural action. This distributed platform of shared spaces straddling the wall, designed for urban pedagogy, dialogue and performance achieves its goals by enacting 'unwalling' experiments that are co-curated by grassroots organizations, university researchers and cultural producers.

Too often, universities perceive marginalized communities as recipients of charity or subjects of research, rather than as participants with knowledge and agency. Instead, the *Community Stations* are committed to a long-term 'partnership model' with communities. This means adopting a stance of ethical engagement, through trust and honouring mutual commitments. Central to the *Community Stations* concept is that university-community engagement is a *reciprocal* activity. While the university enters into the field (sharing its specialized knowledge and resources), the field also enters into the campus (sharing community-based knowledge and changing the culture of pedagogy and research inside the university).

This effort demanded the design of a curatorial apparatus to choreograph how participants would perform the many cultural strategies we employ to circulate knowledges across the border. For example, this included: Bridge Curators, who manifest shared management between community and university, coproducing the protocols, the tools for engagement, and the management of circulations and interfaces between the institution and the community. They also translate the narratives, research, and capabilities developed through the many reciprocal activities and programs into urban policy and development support systems; Public Mentors are university students and neighbourhood youth who follow each other over the course of an academic year, and participate in curated activities, physical and virtual, which cultivate recognition and tolerance as well as awareness of regional interdependencies. University students serve as mentors; youth serve as ambassadors and guides to the issues of everyday life in their neighbourhoods; and the bridge curators trigger dialogue; Public Scholars are community activists who enter the institution to co-teach with researchers and faculty, and bring with them the social, economic, and environmental urgencies of their communities. While they are not 'qualified' by university standards, they bring essential knowledge into shared programming, and must be validated as a matter of equity, we argue, by stipends that compensate them for their time, the use of their spaces, and their social capital.

The co-production of research includes cultural strategies and activities such as Cross-Border Tele-Learning, a telecommunications platform that enables virtual transgression of the wall with technology, to facilitate virtual cross-border dialogues, workshops, and performances with people who cannot or do not want to cross the border physically; The Co-production of Evidence enables community activists, residents, and researchers to assemble bottom-up data and visualizations that are impossible to access through conventional top-down institutional research methods; Nomadic Planning/Itinerant Workshops involves the construction of urban pedagogical tools that mediate urban conversations and debates, to redraw the territory through narrative, anecdote, and everyday practices, including Radical Cartographies: Geographies of Coexistence as a series of experiments elevating the visual cognition of the territory as a requisite for the urban curator.

Nature's nation – communicating a bio-region

The editors suggested that this book would explore "the phenomenon of informality within urban settlements (…) to unravel the subtle link between informal settlements and sustainability" (Di Raimo, Lehmann, & Melis, 2019). *In your earlier work, the informality of Tijuana was documented as 'flowing' into San Diego, re-shaping the formal 'zoned' city through the more localized and everyday pragmatics of less formal urbanization and settlement. However your more recent work through the UCSD Cross-Border Initiative, and especially through the project MEXUS, has sought to reimagine the border zone as a 'transnational environmental commons', an 'eco-region'. A key dimension of this is to "rethink citizenship itself – opposing conventional jurisdictional or identitarian ideas that divide communities and nation-states with a more practical idea focused on the shared social norms, everyday practices, interests, and aspirations that typically flow across boundaries."* (Cruz & Forman, 2018, *p. 416*). *The informal in urban terms has long been studied as a social paradigm, as localized groupings of people, culture, goods and knowledge that emerge organically (practically) from given situations. What is now coming to the fore is the correlation between this and the 'informality' of the environment – an understanding that the 'smooth control' that formal borders seek to uphold is continually disrupted by the movement of water, air, insect and animal life (viruses and bacteria) and climate systems. Your research on and understanding of the informal seems to have primed or prepared you in to engage with these environmental issues in certain ways. Can you talk about this?*

Yes, MEXUS, in fact, emerges from the many bottom-up nomadic planning activities and the community-engaged research developed through our Divina Community Station in Laureles Canyon, an informal settlement of 85,000 people, adjacent to the US border wall. As we discussed earlier, we investigate 'informal' urban dynamics and emergent collective practices – social, moral, economic, political, spatial, as the constituent elements of a more practical idea of citizenship.

By 'informal urbanization' we mean the micro social, economic and spatial conditions that evolve endogenously, organically from the bottom-up. Informal, everyday urban dynamics can be understood as 'extra-official' since they are often off-the-radar of the formal institutions of planning. These stealth urbanizations sometimes evolve as strategies of survival in the absence of government support, to address the urgent needs of immigrant, displaced or local marginalized populations. Survival urbanization has intensified in recent years with the explosive growth of cities across the planet and the rapid peri-urbanization of world populations produced by political instability, climate change, food scarcity and the neoliberalization of the world's economy. Informal urbanization also sometimes manifests as deliberate bottom-up resistance, and defiance, to the privatization and gentrification of our cities.

While we have always found the ingenious bricolage of informal urbanization aesthetically compelling, we are advancing informality not as an aesthetic category or style, but as a praxis, a set of emergent counter-procedures responsive to social emergency, a set of urban practices that transgress imposed political boundaries and top-down economic models, where individuals construct their own spaces, their own norms, economic relations and governance structures. We engage these environments not primarily as sites of institutional alienation, poverty and exploitation, though of course they are, but as laboratories for reimagining the city. In our own region, we have witnessed how small border neighbourhoods have constructed practices of retrofit, adaptation and resiliency that transgress imposed political and economic forces, pointing to other ways of constructing city. In essence for us the informal is the spatialization of citizenship, the performance of social justice.

Recently, we have been interested in linking social and environmental justice, unrecognized bottom-up agency and ecological networks. This relationship between the social and the ecological is perhaps most dramatic as the border wall moves across the Tijuana landscape, reaches its western-most limit, and sinks into the Pacific Ocean. As this militarized artefact descends into the depths of the water, the site is simultaneously strangely poetic and hugely tragic, manifesting physically the contradictions that characterize the border landscape, where two disparate urban horizons meet, where the top-down and the bottom-up collide, where the conflict between the political and the natural yields dramatic social alienation.

This is how *MEXUS* became a visual exercise in unwalling the thickened system of social and ecological interdependencies between the US and Mexico. In this project, (see Figure 1.3), which was recently exhibited at the Venice Architecture Biennale (2018), we wanted to provoke thought about the border beyond the jurisdictional line of the nation state. As you accurately pointed out in your reflections regarding this question, *MEXUS* is a visualization of the continental border region without the jurisdictional line, presented instead as a transnational bio-region composed of eight

Figure 1.3 MEXUS, exhibited at the Venice Architecture Biennale (2018). A visual exercise in unwalling the thickened system of social and ecological interdependencies between the US and Mexico, provoking thought about the border beyond the jurisdictional line of the nation state.

Source: Cruz and Forman.

watershed systems shared by Mexico and the United States, and as such provokes a more inclusive idea of citizenship based on co-existence, shared environmental assets, and co-operative opportunities between divided communities.

Through *MEXUS* we maintain that the recognition of informal social-ecologies is paramount to the reconstruction of a new cross-border imaginary that advances empathy and cooperation as new political tools. The need to reimagine the border through the logic of informal natural and social systems is the foremost challenge for the future of this bi-national region and of many other border regions across the globe.

The political equator

I have been thinking about scale in your work. The project that most helps me feel about for this question is the "The Political Equator" (see Figure 1.4). *This project is one of ongoing research that leverages a diagram as a platform to express conflict along borders. In the diagram the conflicts of US/Mexico, the strait of Gibraltar and the Mediterranean, India/Pakistan, Israel/Palestine and North Korea/South Korea are arranged as a series of red dots along a line overlaid across the world map, with each dot emanating a series of red circles arrayed outwards, filling the map. This visually positions these crises as ones of global proportions; although concentrated at certain geographical points, the conflicts are indicated as spreading well beyond those regions. In contrast to this, much of your work is*

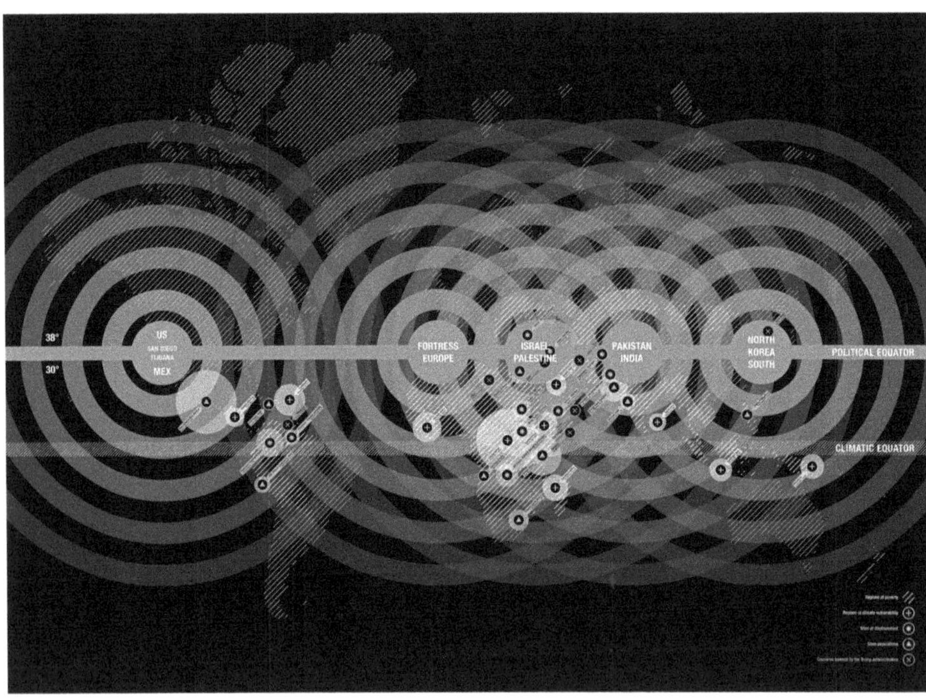

Figure 1.4 The Political Equator. This map links the most contested geographies of conflict across the world between the 30–38 degrees north parallel.

Source: Cruz and Forman.

concerned with micro-sites of exchange, where you are committed to elevating the creative intelligence, resiliency and empathy prevalent in specific migrant communities and situations. For example, the work and projects that take place at the Cross-Border Community Stations really zeros in on these sites of local exchange. My point is that as a practice you are able to move across and between these scalar poles, seeing an issue (and making an issue visible) at these different scales, in the same way that you move across and between political theory and activism/practice. This is very unusual ... could you comment on this?

Our research-based practice has forwarded the Tijuana/San Diego border region as a global laboratory for engaging the central challenges of urbanization today: deepening social and economic inequality, dramatic migratory shifts, urban informality, climate change, the thickening of border walls and the decline of public thinking. And now that Tijuana/San Diego has become the main site of arrival for people seeking asylum from Central American violence and poverty, and a lightning rod for American nativism and hatred, geopolitics has once more turned intensely local. Our practice is committed to localizing the global, moving from a *critical distance*, the abstraction of globalization (the 'out there,' somewhere in the world), into the specificity of the political inscribed in the physical territory, a *critical proximity* (the 'here and now,' of our immediate social-political context).

"The Political Equator" links the most contested geographies of conflict across the world between the 30–38 degrees north parallel. When this political equator is visualized alongside the climatic equator, the convergence of environmental and social injustice across the world becomes evident, as communities most affected by political marginalization likewise often bear the brunt of the accelerating impact of climate change. The collision of geo-political borders, environmental crisis, political marginalization and human displacement is the great crisis of our age, demanding collective action.

As one descends in scale from this global threshold to the continental site between the United States and Mexico, then, our *MEXUS* project investigates the ruptures and collisions between natural and political systems along the entire trajectory of the US–Mexico continental border, and imagines a new cross-border zone of interdependence – a thick, bio-regional set of social-ecologies framed by the existing structure of shared bi-national watersheds systems.

And then in our work, our interventions take place in the San Diego/Tijuana border, which becomes a microcosm of all the conflicts and depravations that globalization has inflicted on the most vulnerable populations everywhere. It is our protagonistic conflict zone, where our practice has deepened its strategies of research and intervention, by visualizing hidden correspondences between global, regional and metropolitan crises, and critically observing and tracing the specificity of cross-border conflicts. Obviously this means moving simultaneously across scales, from the global border, to the border region, to the border neighbourhood and back; to understand the implications of global conflict in shaping the contested power relations inscribed in the everyday lives of people impacted by those conflicts on the political ground itself.

This confluence of the local and the global, the broad and the specific, is fundamental for our work, because geographies of conflict such as the San Diego/Tijuana border are proving to be the anticipatory scenario of the 21st century global metropolis, where the city will increasingly become a battleground in which strategies of control and tactics of transgression, formal and informal economies, legal and illegal occupations will meet/clash (see Figure 1.5 "Practice Diagram"). Cities are contested

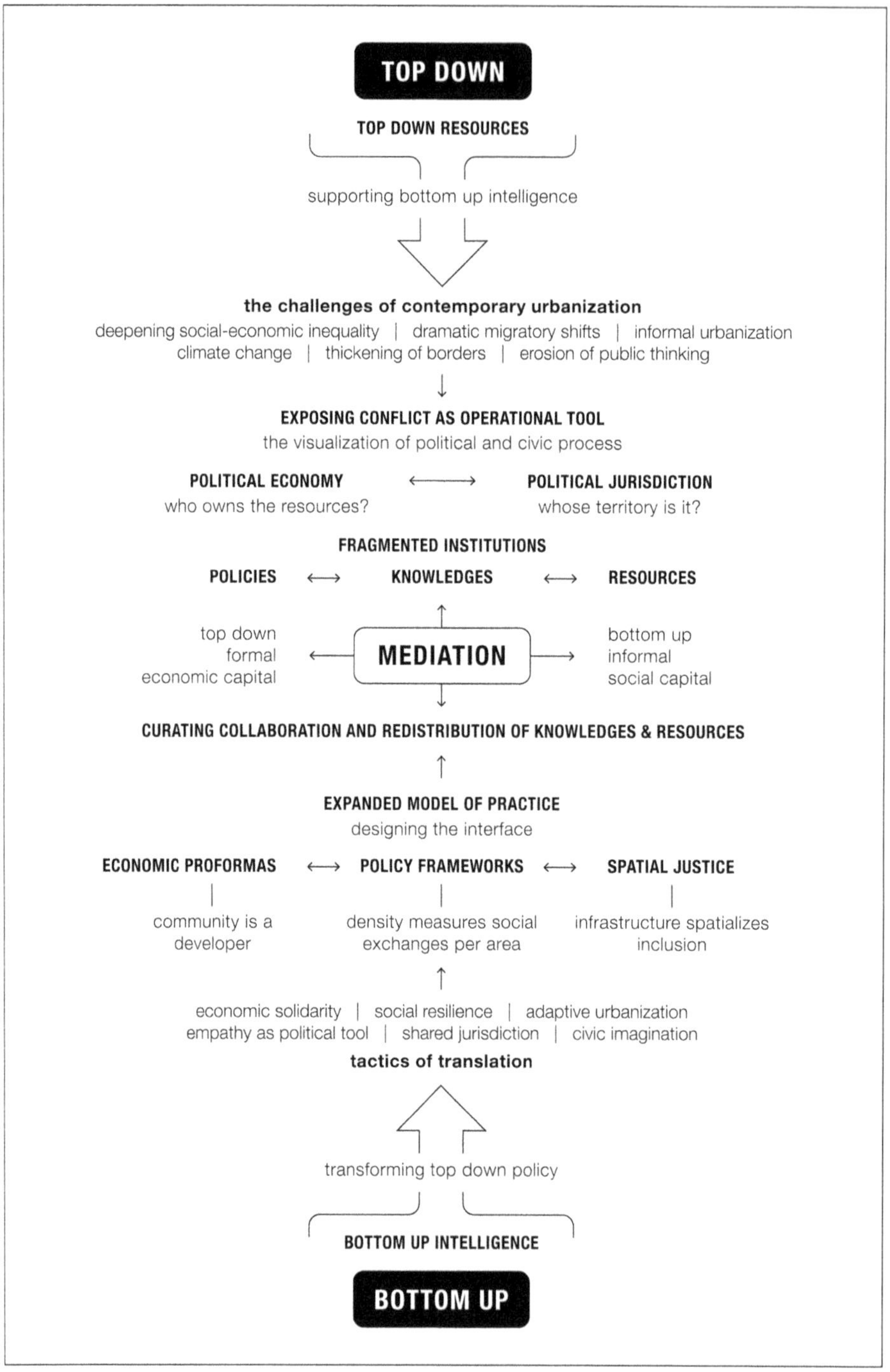

Figure 1.5 A practice diagram that details the mediation of local and the global, the broad and the specific, and the universal and fundamental in their work.

Source: Cruz and Forman.

geographies from which we can challenge today's and tomorrow's protectionist walled-worlds, whose political economies are organized around the criminalization of immigration and the ubiquity of urban surveillance, the polarization of top-down and bottom-up systems of urbanization, and the expanded gap between wealth and poverty everywhere.

Additionally, from the perspective of global justice and the need for urgent interventions to remediate injustice, it is essential that we forge new bi-directional flows between global and local knowledges, imperatives, resources, capacities and actions. Institutions need to learn to incorporate practical knowledge on the ground, and this extends to global institutions and actors as well. Exploring these correspondences is a large and important project – how the top-down and the bottom-up need to converge in their knowledges and strategies to confront poverty and injustice across the globe.

References

Cruz, T., and Forman, F. (2016). The Destruction of Destruction. In J. Burton, S. Jackson & D. Willsdon (Eds.), *Public Servants: Art and the Crisis of the Common Good* (pp. 71–90). Cambridge, Massachusetts: MIT Press.

Cruz, T., and Forman, F. (2017). Unwalling Citizenship. In J. Graham, A. Anderson, C. Blanchfield, J. Carver, J. Moore & I. Kirkham-Lewitt (Eds.), *And Now: Architecture against a Developer Presidency* (pp. 97–109). New York: Columbia University Press.

Cruz, T., and Forman, F. (2018). Citizenship Culture and the Transnational Environmental Commons. In K. Kusserow & A. Braddock (Eds.), *Nature's Nation: American Art and Environment* (pp. 416–427). New Haven: Yale University Press.

Latour, B. (2004). Why Has Critique Run out of Steam? From Matters of Fact to Matters of Concern. *Critical Enquiry*, 30(2), 225–48.

Di Raimo, A., Lehmann, S., and Melis, A. (2019) Informality Now: Urban Informality through Sustainability, Book Synopsis, un-published.

Chapter 2

From a Marxist arcadia to high-tech favelas

The latency of informality in Archizoom and Andrea Branzi

Pablo Martínez Capdevila

The *No-Stop City*

I will not attempt to provide a detailed account here of Archizoom's *No-Stop City* (1969–1971), without doubt one of the best-known and most discussed projects of the *architettura radicale* of the 1960s and 1970s, nor to thoroughly explain its political dimension and the influence of Italian Marxism and *Operaismo*, since they have already been analysed and discussed multiple times (Varnelis, 2006; Gargiani, 2007; Scott, 2007; Aureli, 2008, 2014). However, I will touch briefly on said political dimension since it is not only essential to fully understand the proposal, but also its main *raison d'être*. When it was first published in the July–August 1970 issue of *Casabella*, the lengthy text by Archizoom presented it as a sort of architectural rendering of Manfredo Tafuri's 1969 article *Toward a Critique of Architectural Ideology* (Tafuri, 1998/1969). The group tried to dispel any suspicion of reformism or utopianism, which had been forcefully disapproved of by Tafuri and others (Gargiani, 2007), by stating that their proposal was not a project but "a theory," and hence it was not meant to be an alternative or future city, but rather a "critical Hypothesis related to the system itself" (Archizoom Associati, 2006a/1970, p. 157).

Notwithstanding its many paradoxes (Martínez Capdevila, in press), what Archizoom aimed to produce was a sort of demystified allegory of a state of total capitalist integration wherein the entirety of society had been organised according to the model of the factory. Its texts and images were intended to reveal a "city of capital" and a state of total proletarianisation that somehow had already been achieved, but that remained hidden by the discontinuous formal structures of the bourgeois city. Paradoxically, said structures, which acted as an ideological superstructure meant to legitimise the capital, also prevented its full development by slowing down the economic cycle. Archizoom wanted to erase that ideological and formal layer and replace it with a continuous and homogeneous urban model that, by being fully coherent with the quantitative and efficiency logics of the system, would accelerate the economic cycle, eventually making the "Brain of the System mad." The No-Stop City was therefore a sublimated representation of a perfect capitalist city that would maximise the contradictions of capital, ultimately causing its takeover by the working class.

Hypertrophy, dissolution and insignificance

Beyond its political agenda, the project was triggered by the awareness that framed structures, elevators, air conditioning and artificial lighting had allowed some building types, such as car parks, factories or supermarkets, to grow beyond the dimensional limits imposed by natural lighting and ventilation.

Archizoom's most crucial decision was to extend said technification of the environment to all functions, and ultimately to the whole city. The outcome was the No-Stop City: a homogenous, generic, neutral and potentially endless container that thoroughly undermined the canonical (western) architectural object.

Arguably, the clearest and most influential definition of said object was put forward by Leon Battista Alberti in his *De re aedificatoria* (1485), through the description of the ideal centrally planned temple. According to Alberti, such a perfect building would have a specific function, would be free standing, composed of different parts articulated following strict hierarchical, geometric and compositional rules, would have a distinct centre and periphery and its exterior and interior envelopes would be essential by conveying symbolical meaning. Furthermore, the building was understood as a finished, perfect and stable object to which nothing should be added or taken away. Although, obviously, architecture has changed dramatically since the Renaissance, this paradigmatic description has been deeply rooted in the discipline and is still relevant today. In fact, most buildings still comply, especially in terms of the fundamental role of architectural form and the overall permanence and stability of buildings. Given that Alberti's canon still embodies the dominant understanding of architectural form, it could also be useful to put forward, *via negativa*, a possible definition of informal architecture. We could then argue that it would be generic and functionally indeterminate, it would lack complex compositional principles and hierarchy, its shape and image would be irrelevant and meaningless and it would be transient. Ultimately, instead of a stable, closed and defined object, informal architecture would be an adaptable, open and amorphous system (see Figure 2.1).

As I have argued elsewhere, this dissolution of architecture in the No-Stop City was paradoxical because it did not arise from a 'lack' of architecture but, rather, from an 'excess' of it (Martínez Capdevila, in press). The boundless and homogenous growth of the building necessarily implied the dissolution of an architectural object that has been traditionally defined by its finitude and its heterogeneity. The members of Archizoom were fully aware that their endless and shapeless urban model would eliminate architecture as they knew it, in fact in its first publication they stated: "The ultimate goal of modern Architecture is the 'elimination' of architecture itself." (Archizoom Associati, 2006a/1970, p. 170). In their texts they presented the No-Stop City as the outcome of the unlimited application, *ad absurdum*, of modern technology and rationality. By doing so, they suggested an analogy between the end of capitalism and that of architecture, since for both cases their disappearance was presented as the inevitable consequence of the full unfolding of their internal (whether technical or economical) logics: of a state of plenitude and apogee that would cause their eventual demise (Martínez Capdevila, in press).

The most obvious consequence of this 'dissolution by hypertrophy' was turning the overall shape and outer envelope into traits that were completely inconsequential and trivial. By doing so Archizoom fully developed a condition that they had previously explored in their entry for the *Mostra dell'Artigianato* competition in Florence's *Fortezza da Basso* (1967), a neutral and isotropic building whose shape had been generated 'automatically' by trimming it following an offset of the existing walls. In the case of the No-Stop City, the actual irrelevance of architectural form is clearly

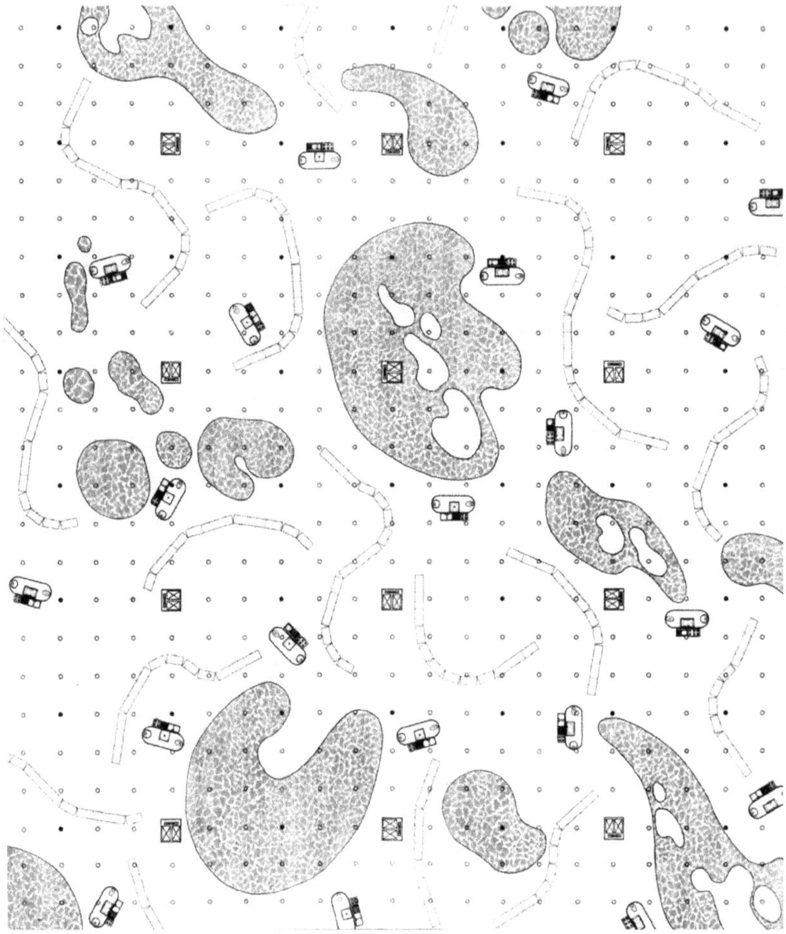

Figure 2.1 Archizoom Associati: *No-Stop City: Residential Park* (1970).

Source: Studio Branzi.

conveyed through the many different and contradictory illustrations of it that were produced by the group between 1969 and 1971: sometimes it was depicted as a solidified magma whose shape was dictated by the coastline or the topography, other times it was presented as a huge rectangular volume, or as an endless repetition of identical volumes, or as an upward extrusion of *Central Park* in New York or as a linear stripe along a river. This variety clearly conveyed that the shape and outer envelope had become negligible. In fact, the facade – understood as a specialised surface mediating between the inside and the outside that conveys meaning and defines architectural identity – has disappeared altogether. “The perimeters of these continuous horizontal structures fall on a basis of ‘chance’ or a ‘criterion’: in any event, they only represent a vertical section of the phenomenon” (Archizoom Associati, 2006a/1970, p. 174). In fact, and not surprisingly, among the many drawings of the No-Stop City produced by Archizoom, there is not any elevation.

The crisis of architectural shape and the ensuing disappearance of the facade were again not at all accidental. When describing their entry for the *Università degli Studi* competition, which was a version of the No-Stop City, Archizoom said:

> The only architectural form that we would have liked to propose was a drifting fog bank over the plain between Florence and Pistoia ... in the sense that we refuse to design an object and prefer, instead, to design its use ... The outer perimeter of the whole is not identified or represented: we do not care about its shape.
> (Archizoom Associati, 1972, pp. 11–12)

But Archizoom went beyond a mere physical shapelessness and pointed towards a further dissolution of both architecture and the city by envisioning a sort of immaterial urban condition: "The metropolis ceases to be a 'place' to become a 'condition': in fact, it is just this condition which is made to circulate uniformly, through Consumer Products, in the social phenomenon. The future dimension of the metropolis coincides with that of the Market itself" (Archizoom Associati, 2006b/1971, p. 177). The No-Stop City, therefore, announced a radical change in the comprehension of the urban fact, that was understood as a virtually ubiquitous condition detached from its physical medium; an idea that radically opposed Aldo Rossi who, in *The Architecture of the City* (1966), had put forward a comprehensive urban theory based on the concepts of *locus*, monument and type, all of which stressed the irreducible identity, memory and specificity of cities, interpreted as big architectural artefacts.

The group was fully aware of the new role of media and electronics in shaping a new sphere for the human experience: "... now the use of electronic media takes the place of the direct urban praxis" (Archizoom Associati, 2006b/1971, p. 177). This prophetic intuition derived from a very popular figure at the time, Marshall McLuhan, whose "global village" was mentioned twice in the first publication of the project in Casabella (Archizoom Associati, 2006a/1970, p. 157, p. 169). The belief that mass media, the emergence of telecommunications and the virtual elimination of physical distances had inaugurated a radically new era is central in the work of McLuhan, who formulated the idea of a "global village" for the first time in his 1962 book *The Gutenberg Galaxy*:

> ... certainly the electro-magnetic discoveries have recreated the simultaneous 'field' in all human affairs so that the human family now exists under conditions of a "global village." We live in a single constricted space resonant with tribal drums.
> (McLuhan, 1962, p. 31)

Later on, in *Understanding Media* (1964), he further developed these insights towards themes that are particularly relevant for our subject by describing a sort of neo-nomadism and the dissolution of cities:

> [the nomad state] is global, and it ignores and replaces the form of the city which has, therefore, tended to become obsolete. With instant electric technology, the globe itself can never again be more than a village, and the very nature of city as a form of major dimensions must inevitably dissolve like a fading shot in a movie.
> (McLuhan, 1994/1964, p. 343)

Similarly, the new urban "condition" depicted by Archizoom implied an increasingly irrelevant and secondary role for the traditional built environment and, crucially, stressed the fact that our everyday experience had become more and more shaped by phenomena that are, to a great extent, omnipresent and ungraspable: information and a virtually limitless market.

Soon after the last publications of their project, and apparently in line with their refusal to design tangible formal structures, the group produced what could be considered the clearest and most poetic rendering of that immaterial condition foreseen in the No-Stop City's texts: two collages called *Gazebo a scala territoriale* (see Figure 2.2) that were published in the magazine *IN. Argomenti e immagini di design* in 1972. Each image showed a huge dematerialised volume, which was only outlined by dashed lines on its edges and letters on its vertices, encompassing a seemingly arbitrary territorial area without any visible relation with it, like a drifting fog bank.

Figure 2.2 Archizoom Associati: *Gazebo a scala territoriale* (1972).

Source: Studio Branzi.

Pop art and the (eco)system of objects

The city's homogenous hypertrophy not only turned its form into something inconsequential, but also allowed informality to arise in its interiors, where architecture escaped its traditional primary role in the formal, functional and iconographic qualification of space. As happens in the *Bürolandschaft*, said role was taken over by a constellation of furniture and objects that programmed the space. The stark contrast between the homogenous, neutral and stable building and these diverse, specialised and transient objects asserted a radical autonomy between built form and function: architecture became a mere container, a pure and continuous background for a life that, somehow, had become independent from it.

> ... we have finally freed ourselves from architecture, we have reduced it to a technical envelope. [...] dwelling is carried out through the products; we are also interested in designing the products, up to the design of the clothes. The form of architecture is an absolutely secondary problem: it is an endlessly transformable and endlessly adaptable event.
>
> (Deganello, n.d.)

As Paolo Deganello states, in those years Archizoom designed several pieces of furniture such as the *armadio abitabile* (habitable closet, 1970), a transformable equipment that would allow dwelling anywhere in their interior city, as well as clothes such as their *Dressing Design: Nearest Habitat System* (1970). Along the same lines, most images of the No-Stop City show habitats shaped by all sorts of furniture and objects. A drawing called *Schema di Montaggio di Abitazioni Temporanee* (assembly diagram for temporary dwellings, published in *Domus* 496, 1971) highlighted their mobility and flexibility by showing a forklift moving a container from which a bathroom, a kitchen and a bed were deployed to set up a full, albeit transient, domestic environment.

Consequently, the small scale of objects absorbed many of the roles traditionally attributed to the discipline and shaped an informal habitat freed from architectural logics and values. In fact, although objects have obviously a form, their nature is very different from that of architecture, since they are mass-produced, lightweight, movable and replaceable elements, a perpetual renewal that is required by the market. Moreover, their combination creates dispersed ephemeral and adaptable habitats, an informality that turns the interior of the city into something analogous to a natural ecosystem.

The analogy between artificial and natural is especially noticeable in some plans where furniture is combined with natural elements (rocks, bushes, rivers, lawn spots) to form naturalistic and 'picturesque' compositions, hence suggesting shared underlying principles. In addition to that, many of the images bore captions clearly inspired in nature ("residential park," "residential wood," "interior landscape," etc.) while the texts described a city transformed into a "habitat of services" and a capitalism turned into a "deep nature." By doing so, Archizoom suggested that the market, a market that they perceived as an all-pervading reality, had become not only a sort of second nature but also our primary habitat.

The functional, sociological and iconographic centrality of objects reflected the influence of Pop Art, which had been key in the previous trajectory of the group (Gargiani, 2007). Pop Art detected and, at the same time, encouraged the commodification of all spheres of life, including leisure and intimacy, and portrayed a new situation where people's desires and subjectivities had to be as 'manufactured' as any other product. In this respect, it is very telling that Andrea Branzi has illustrated, over the years, several of his texts with Richard Hamilton's 1952 work *Just what is it that makes today's homes so different, so appealing?* (Branzi, 1984, 2006a, 2006b & 2014). This collage, widely considered the foundational artwork of *Pop Art*, can be considered a premonition of the No-Stop City, not only because the scene is located in a completely blank and superfluous interior but, more importantly, because it shows a domestic environment fully shaped by objects and consumer products ready to meet any need, any desire. What made that home 'so different and appealing' was not architecture but the market. A market that we inhabit and that inhabits us.

As noted by Rodríguez Pedret (1991, p. 103), in Hamilton's collage the limits between public and private are blurred, generating a domestic internalisation of the urban space and a simultaneous urban externalisation of the domestic space. The scene recalls the No-Stop City interior dioramas (see Figure 2.3) although, while in Hamilton's work the home has started to dissolve in the market but still exists as separated space, in Archizoom's city said dissolution has gone one step further: the

Figure 2.3 Archizoom Associati: *No-Stop City, paesaggi interni* (interior landscapes, 1971).

Source: Studio Branzi.

enclosed domestic space has disappeared altogether. It seems as if the overall internalisation of all urban activities and spaces that took place in the project implied the parallel disappearance of the traditional interior space: that of domestic privacy.

Nomadism and deterritorialisation

The demise of stable and enclosed housing, together with the presence of sleeping bags, tents and other movable equipment, suggested a nomadic existence that was coherent with the retribalisation process announced by McLuhan:

> Before the huddle of the city, there was the food-gathering phase of man the hunter, even as men have now in the electric age returned psychically and socially to the nomad state. Now, however, it is called information-gathering and data-processing. But it is global, and it ignores and replaces the form of the city which has, therefore, tended to become obsolete.
>
> (McLuhan, 1994/1964, p. 283)

McLuhan's nomadism did not actually imply an effective physical mobility but, rather, a new stage of human experience wherein consciousness would be free to wander through unprecedented landscapes: the open and vast horizons of delocalised information. However, while his "information-gatherers" were nomads in a psychical and metaphorical sense, in the case of No-Stop City we witness a literal nomadism that implied physical mobility. Hence, the potential dissolution of the city foreseen by McLuhan became effective in the interior and informal landscapes of the No-Stop City, since sedentary life and permanent dwelling have been the primordial conditions for the existence of cities. At the same time however, housing did not disappear completely but was dissolved into the public space. It could then be argued that the entire city became a sort of expanded and diffuse home. After all, nomads carry their dwellings with them, transforming the territory with their passing and turning it into their home. A transience that epitomises informality and where, as McLuhan explains, the distinctions between skin, clothing, housing and city blur.

> If clothing is an extension of our private skins to store and channel our own heat and energy, housing is a collective means of achieving the same end for the family or the group. Housing as shelter is an extension of our bodily heat-control mechanisms—a collective skin or garment. Cities are an even further extension of bodily organs [...] Literate man, civilized man, tends to restrict and enclose space and to separate functions, whereas tribal man had freely extended the form of his body to include the universe
>
> (McLuhan, 1994/1964, p. 123–124)

Archizoom's agenda to eliminate architecture as an ideological superstructure did not only dissolve it into the city, but triggered a broader and generalised dissolution of the primary categories through which the built environment has been thought and organised (public, private, house, building, city, territory). The resulting scenario is an informal and fluid habitat shaped by the 'micro' sphere of objects and the 'macro' and immaterial sphere of information: an environment that is radically different from any previous city or settlement and recalls, instead, an ever-changing natural landscape. The market and information are thus presented as the nemesis of architectural and urban form and as the ultimate agents of dissolution and deterritorialisation.

Eros and liberation

This latent nomadism went hand in hand with a certain 'neo-primitive' condition that puts the No-Stop City in line with the categories of the "pastoral" and the "primitive" that Catherine Rossi has detected in other exponents of the Italian *Radical* movement such as Superstudio, Ricardo Dalisi or the 9999 group (Rossi, 2014). The clearest indication of this condition, which was not mentioned in the project texts and seems to contradict its character of technological utopia, was its peculiar inhabitants. They were depicted for the first time in a collage published in *Design Quarterly* in 1970 (see Figure 2.4) that showed four naked women in a surreal interior landscape including hills, trees and a deer.

Naked figures of men and women appeared again in one of the four interior dioramas published in *Domus* in 1971, in this case accompanied by geese and other domestic animals. Simultaneously, the group published a series of drawings of interior rooms, called *allestimenti di stanze* in the magazine *IN* which have been subsequently published as part of the No-Stop City (Branzi, 2006b). In sharp contrast with the "micro-climatised" container, two of these illustrations showed rudimentary structures of branches and animal pelts and a group of children and bearded men that looked like savage hunter-gatherers. Even if Archizoom did not describe or prescribe any specific lifestyle for their interior city, the shared trait of these individuals allow

Figure 2.4 Archizoom Associati: *No-Stop City* (1970).

Source: Studio Branzi.

to read them not so much as eccentric or marginal groups but, rather, as members of a wider society of Rousseauian "noble savages" or, using Branzi's later jargon, "neo-primitives."

More precisely, both their nudity and the latent anti-authoritarian dimension place the No-Stop City in line with Wilhelm Reich's original Freudo-Marxism, as evidenced by the expression "character armour," which is mentioned in the texts of the project as something to be transcended. According to Reich, while these psychic structures protect the individual from frustration or anguish, they also inhibit pleasure and the satisfaction of drives, blocking a full personal fulfilment based on *Eros*, the "life instinct" that opposes the aggressive and destructive "death instinct" (*Thanatos*). Archizoom extended this concept, which in Reich referred to the psychic realm although it had psychosomatic implications, to the whole society and human habitat. The No-Stop City's life scenes seem to adhere to the propositions of other Freudo-Marxist thinkers such as Herbert Marcuse who, in books like *Eros and Civilization* (1955) and *One-Dimensional Man* (1964), had argued that the political potential of *Eros* could lead to a new cooperative and solidary social form where imagination, creativity and sublimated needs could be fully developed, destroying all repressive domination.

This communitarian and anti-authoritarian vision not only opposed capitalism and bourgeois values but also the cultural conservatism and puritan morality of the old Italian Communist Party. The PCI *ethos* was equally challenged by the cornucopia of consumer goods shown in many of the images that was nevertheless consistent with the political strategy of *operaismo*. In Archizoom's texts, consumerism was not understood as something intrinsically negative or alienating but as something liberating that should be extended, in line with Mario Tronti's motto "more money and less work" (*Più soldi e meno lavoro*). The *en masse* incorporation of workers to consumption would force capital to recognise the mystifying and artificial nature of its mechanisms of exploitation and power. Being influenced by McLuhan, Freudo-Marxism and *operaismo*, Archizoom depicted a society that opposed the most canonical depictions of the proletariat produced from orthodox Marxist positions, which have tended to represent it as a compact and austere class, toughened by hard work. The No-Stop City neo-primitives, instead, seemed to shape a nomadic society relishing the market and enjoying an uninhibited, playful and hedonistic existence. A lifestyle, in short, much closer to that of hippie communes or to the *Homo Ludens* that inspired Constant's *New Babylon*, than to that of alienated industrial workers or Stakhanovist heroes.

Hence, the will to overcome architectural ideology triggered a process of dissolution that spread from architecture to the whole human habitat and to society at large. The No-Stop City acted as a sort of liberating machine where its most obvious informal traits reflected the demise of any sort of alienating constraint, whether material or moral, physical or psychical, individual or collective.

The neo-primitive style: fragmentation and animism

After the dissolution of Archizoom in 1974, Andrea Branzi moved to Milan and was among the promoters of design groups such as CDM, Alchimia or Memphis, becoming one of main protagonists and ideologues of the so-called "Nuovo Design." Although he progressively moved away from the Marxist ideology and political antagonism that had marked Archizoom's work, he continued to develop many of their themes. In his article "We are the Primitives" (Branzi, 1986) he described a new neo-primitive condition underpinned by the "Integral Naturalism" of art critic Pierre Restany and the new postmodern condition depicted by the philosopher Jean-François Lyotard, that is to say, as the decay of metanarratives and the subsequent proliferation of small narratives. Branzi portrayed a society made up of small groups and marked by the proliferation of identities and the recovery of ancestral cultural forms. A situation where design had become a means for the construction of identities, which implied the prevalence of expression over functionality. This would have brought about a "rediscovered centrality of the body" that became a carrier of signs and meaning. "The body thus becomes the central point of expression of that emerging phenomenon defined as neoprimitivism, and that, in reality, represents one of the extreme poles of the postmodern condition." (Branzi, 1986, p. 27)

These ideas were applied in the furniture series *animali domestici* (1985–86) that combined artificial and natural materials (tree trunks, branches, furs) into hybrid pieces, hence suggesting that the division between natural and artificial could be overcome in order to achieve a mutual enrichment. The series' name posed a diffuse animism by inviting to see this furniture (and, by extension, all domestic object) as a sort of pets or animated entities with which we maintain relationships that are much richer than those traditionally acknowledged and expressed by modern industrial design. Due to their totemic character and their ability to appeal to our unconscious, they would exemplify a "neo-primitive style" that would refer to a world of greater integration and harmony between artefacts, man and nature: "So the moral of the fable of these domestic beasts is that a hybrid love between different creatures is possible." (Branzi & Branzi, 1987, p. 15).

In the Western world, new consumption patterns and an increasingly fragmented market would have led mass culture to a radical refoundation:

> The Bauhaus concept of design research sought to custom definitive objects able to provide once and for all the basic necessities for a society of equals. Since the 1970s, however, design has been required to provide objects aimed not at nonexistent and gray majorities, but products able to select their own users, aimed at partial markets...
>
> (Branzi & Branzi, 1987, p. 6)

While the No-Stop City was marked by a bold political antagonism aimed towards a collective emancipation, the neo-primitive condition outlined by Branzi in the mid-80s seems to have abandoned any revolutionary agenda. In fact, its aim was to endow industrial design with a theoretical support that would enable it to meet the needs of an increasingly diversified market. The neo-primitive style did not only respond to the parallel fragmentation of identities and subcultures, it actually encouraged them by promoting the construction of subjectivities demanded by a saturated market that needed to expand itself internally and accelerate its renovation cycles. A situation in which, as happens in natural ecosystems, the constant renewal of the "micro" ensures the survival and overall stability of the "macro", which appears as a natural and, therefore, inevitable reality (Martínez Capdevila, 2017).

Weak urban models

In 1988, Branzi put forward the concept of an "ecology of the artificial" which had a remarkable impact in the field of Design Theory (Branzi, 1988). This theoretical proposal did not intend to incorporate environmental sustainability into the design practice; instead, it was meant to reconsider the relations between humans and the artificial sphere by pursuing unstable balances analogous to those found in nature. Ecology was hence used as a conceptual tool to manage the increasing complexity of the contemporary world, somehow developing an insight that was already present in the No-Stop City, where the city was conceived as a sort of functional ecosystem in a state of continuous evolution and renewal.

Agronica (Branzi et al., 1995) was the first of Branzi's "models of weak urbanisation," which were explicitly inspired by the *pensiero debole* (weak thought) of Italian philosopher Gianni Vattimo (Waldheim, 2010; Martínez Capdevila, 2016). Branzi noted that the electronic revolution and the complexity of the contemporary metropolis had deepened the split between form and function. Places had lost their functional, typological and stylistic identity while buildings would become part of a "metabolic" territorial system where programs dissolve and recombine in novel ways:

> The physical form of a new construction, one starting from scratch and lacking any earlier historical manifestation to refer to, would not have any structures corresponding to the functional density of the present metropolis. Its ground plan would instead resemble that of the shapeless metropolis of the third world.
>
> (Branzi et al., 1995, p. 104)

Agronica posed a hybridisation between rural and urban that was far removed from Arcadian or picturesque idealisations. In fact, agriculture was not seen as a reservoir of moral or aesthetic values but, rather, was understood as an advanced and flexible technological universe compatible with an urban existence and fully integrated into a unitary and unopposed economic system. If agriculture is able to adapt and take full advantage of the cycles and inherent mutability of the natural environment, Agronica used it as a conceptual model to respond to economic conditions that Branzi presented as analogous (Martínez Capdevila, 2019).

Its territory was dotted by poles and a variety of items such as diaphragms, canopies, sunshades or suspended platforms hovering over the ground. A number of lightweight constructions, resembling industrial storage systems, acted as generic functional containers devoid of any architectural, typological or symbolic connotations. A drawing entitled "Abacus of part of the elements of the hybrid dwelling system" showed these containers in twenty-one different functional configurations, somehow stressing the divorce between form and function and reflecting a state of total functional liquefaction. Overall, Agronica deployed a lightweight and modular constructive apparatus that minimised the contact with the ground and conveyed a sense of full adaptability and reversibility (see Figure 2.5).

Significantly, Agronica's text starts by describing it as a "partial or incomplete" utopia, setting it apart from previous "positive utopias (such as La Ville Radieuse) and critical utopias (such as No-Stop City)" (Branzi et al., 1995, p. 103). While the No-Stop City, despite its ambiguous character, can still be read as a classical utopia, that is, as a unique and totalising scenario that excludes any other possibility, Branzi's models of

Figure 2.5 Andrea Branzi, Donegani, Petrillo, Raimondo: *Symbiotic Metropolis Agronica,* 1955.

Source: Studio Branzi.

weak urbanisation explicitly deny any unique or final state of perfection. If the former (or, at least, its built container) still mirrored the unique, homogeneous and orderly scenario of modernity, the latter seem a direct translation of the fragmented scenario of postmodernity marked by the proliferation of partial narratives and Vattimo's weakening of Being (Martínez Capdevila, 2016). A new situation devoid of the horizon of completion (*telos*) and the historical purpose that characterised the modern project.

While the dissolution of architecture in the No-Stop City was the paradoxical outcome of an "excess" of architecture that turned it into an omnipresent and trivial background for a city that was shaped functionally and symbolically by furniture and objects, the dissolution of architecture in Agronica was the outcome of an "absence" of architecture caused by its transformation into something analogous to furniture, that is, into objects that are smaller, lighter and more transformable and ephemeral than traditional buildings. In fact, while the constructions of Agronica could be read as the logical evolution of the furniture that programmed the No-Stop City, they did not show any similarity whatsoever with its endless built container that, significantly enough, has disappeared altogether.

A new urbanity for the 21st century

Andrea Branzi has continued to explore the implications of a dissolution of architecture that electronic technology has deepened. While, in 1972, he claimed "Cities instead, all cities, are one toilet every 100 m^3, and that's it" (Branzi, 1972, p. 33), more recently he has said that "the city has become a computer every 20 square meters" (Branzi, 2010a/2007), p. 179). The book *Weak and Diffuse Modernity* (Branzi, 2006a) and his manifesto for a *New Athens Charter* (Branzi, 2010b) synthesised his urban discourse after the turn of the century. Branzi sees the city as a dense and immersive environment made up of services, products, information, networks, microclimates, sensorial structures "... that are contained within architecture, but cannot be represented by architecture's figurative codes" (Branzi, 2006a, p. 9). One of the themes developed in these texts is the intuition, already hinted in Agronica, that the shapeless metropolises of the third world, beyond their many socio-economic issues, could in fact be better adapted to a society in permanent renewal. In fact, one of the points of the *New Athens Charter* is "To consider the city as a high-tech favela. Avoid rigid and definitive solutions and foster reversible, incomplete and imperfect devices that allow the urban space to adapt continuously to new unplanned and un-programmed activities." (Branzi, 2010b, pp. 180–181)

Furthermore, the animistic dimension of his *domestic animals* opened the door to a surprising pantheistic conception of the artificial sphere. A good example is his proposal *Città Reale. Modello teorico della civiltà merceologica* (2010) displayed at the 12th Venice Biennale. The piece is an allegory of the anthropological importance of the perishable and apparently superfluous sphere of objects in the form of an urban centre made up of consumer products, touristic souvenirs and figurines of fictional characters or oriental deities.

Over the years, Branzi has developed a consistent and methodical agenda for the dissolution of architecture that thoroughly undermines its Vitruvian foundations and challenges the established conception of the architectural object based on its physical, functional and temporal stability. A programme that goes beyond architecture itself to posit a radical rethinking of the whole human habitat and that has the value of having enlarged the fields of architecture and design by recovering a series of anthropological dimensions that had been forgotten or ignored for too long. A journey which started almost fifty years ago that may help us to rethink and challenge the dominant understanding of what architectural and urban informality could be.

References

Archizoom Associati (1970). "No-Stop City. Residential Park, Climatic Universal System." *Design Quarterly* 78–79, n.d.

Archizoom Associati (1972). "Progetto di Concorso per l'Università di Firenze." *Domus* 509, April.

Archizoom Associati (2006a). "City, Assembly Line of Social Issues: Ideology and Theory of the Metropolis." In Branzi A (ed.) *No-Stop City: Archizoom Associati*. Orleans, France: Editions HYX (Originally published in *Casabella* 350/51, July/Aug. 1970).

Archizoom Associati (2006b). "No-Stop City: Residential Parkings, Climatic Universal System." In Branzi A (ed.) *No-Stop City: Archizoom Associati*. Orleans, France: Editions HYX (Originally published in *Domus* 496, Mar. 1971).

Aureli PV (2008). *The Project of Autonomy: Politics and Architecture within and Against Capitalism*. New York: Princeton Architectural Press.

Aureli P V (2014). "Manfredo Tafuri, Archizoom, Superstudio and the Critique of Architectural ideology." In Deamer P (ed.) *Architecture and Capitalism: 1845 to the Present*. London: Routledge.

Branzi A (1972). "La Gioconda sbarbata. Il ruolo dell'avanguardia." *Casabella* 363.

Branzi A (1984). *La Casa Calda. Esperienze del nuovo design italiano*. Milan: Idea Books.

Branzi A (1986). "We are the Primitives." *Design Issues*, 3 (1), 23–27 (Original published as: "I primitivi siamo noi," *Modo* 80, June 1985).
Branzi A (1988). "An Ecology of the Artificial." In *Learning from Milan: Design and the Second Modernity*. Cambridge, Mass.: The MIT Press.
Branzi A (2006a). *Modernità debole e diffusa. Il mondo del progetto all'inizio del XXI secolo*. Milan: Skira.
Branzi A (2006b). *No-Stop City: Archizoom Associati*. Orleans: Editions HYX.
Branzi A (2010a). "La città è un computer ogni 20 mq." In F La Rocca (ed.). *Scritti presocratici. Andrea Branzi: Visioni del progetto di design 1972/2009*. Milan: Franco Angeli Edizioni (Originally published as "La scrittura d'architettura" in *Interni* 571, May 2007).
Branzi A (2010b). "Per una Nuova Carta di Atene." In F La Rocca (ed.). *Scritti presocratici. Andrea Branzi: Visioni del progetto di design 1972/2009*. Milan: Franco Angeli Edizioni.
Branzi A (2014). *Una generazione esagerata. Dai radical italiani alla crisi della globalizzazione*. Milan: Baldini & Castoldi.
Branzi A & Branzi N (1987). *Domestic Animals: The Neoprimitive Style*. Cambridge, Mass.: The MIT Press.
Branzi A, et al. (1995). "Symbiotic Metropolis Agronica." In E Manzini, M Susani (Eds.), *The Solid Side: The Search for Consistency in a Changing World*. The Netherlands: V+K Publishing, Netherlands, pp. 100–120.
Deganello P (n.d.). *Narrate, uomini, la vostra storia. (transcription of his conference in the Facoltà di Architettura Civile*, Milan, 2006, January 18). Retrieved from: https://sites.google.com/site/paolodeganello/articoli/narrate-uomini-la-vostra-storia (accessed January 2018).
Gargiani R (2007). *Archizoom Associati 1966–1974: Dall'onda pop alla superficie neutra*. Milan: Electa.
Martínez Capdevila P (2016). "Towards a weak architecture: Andrea Branzi and Gianni Vattimo." *Cuadernos de Proyectos Arquitectónicos* 6.
Martínez Capdevila P (2017). "An Italian Querelle: Radical vs. Tendenza." *Log: Observations on Architecture and the Contemporary City* 40.
Martínez Capdevila P (2019). "Demystified Territories: City vs. Countryside in Andrea Branzi's Urban Models." In F Lemes, I Mell (eds.). *Planning Cities with Nature: Theories, Strategies and Methods*. Switzerland: Springer.
Martínez Capdevila P (in press). "A Paradoxical Imago Mundi. The No-Stop City by Archizoom Associati." In G Marinic (ed.). *The Interior Urbanism Theory Reader*, London: Routledge.
McLuhan M (1962). *The Gutenberg Galaxy: The Making of Typographic Man*. Toronto: University of Toronto Press.
McLuhan M (1994). *Understanding Media: The Extensions of Man*. Cambridge, Mass.: The MIT Press (Originally published 1964).
Rodríguez Pedret C (1991). "Miradas 'pop' en la ciudad contemporánea." *Annals d'arquitectura* 5.
Rossi C (2014). "Crafting a Design Counterculture: the Pastoral and the Primitive in Italian Radical Design, 1972–1976." In G Lees-Maffei, K Kjetil Fallan (eds.). *Made in Italy: Rethinking a Century of Italian Design*. London: Bloomsbury Academic.
Scott FD (2007). *Architecture or techno-utopia: Politics after modernism*. Cambridge, Mass.: The MIT Press.
Tafuri M (1998). "Toward a Critique of Architectural Ideology." In K M Hays (ed.). *Architecture Theory since 1968*. Cambridge, Mass: The MIT Press. pp. 6–35 (Originally published in *Contropiano* 1, Jan./Apr. 1969).
Varnelis K (2006). "Programming After Program: Archizoom's No-Stop City". *Praxis: Journal of Writing and Building* 8.
Waldheim C (2010). "Weak Work: Andrea Branzi's 'Weak Metropolis' and the Projective Potential of an 'Ecological Urbanism'." In M Mostafavi, G Doherty (eds.). *Ecological Urbanism*. Baden, Switzerland: Lars Müller Publishers.

Chapter 3

"I'm an imposter"

[a Gödel-Cassandra incompleteness]

François Roche

The '*management des humains*,' from their self organisation to their disciplinary control, could be seen as the Ariadne's thread of each of the societies whose primary function is aimed at integrating and regulating the '*doxa*' of its proper morality; that so-called modus operandi of '*vivre ensemble*,' from its glorious expansion up to its fall. The hegemonic limits that this thread imposes upon the subjects, or rather citizens, who make it up, result in territories that are alienated from it ... It emerges in a political and territorial overlap determined by a State and/or a Nation which have the right to apply the authority of institutional structures permissive and/or repressive on human organisations.

The management of humans implies methods of control and supervision/surveillance, as widely analysed by post-structuralist philosophers, first by Michel Foucault. We acknowledge that Foucault was the first to highlight the distinction between two medical treatment systems and their implications. The first is related to the hare, and the second to the plague. The latter, which aims at excluding, under the pretext of divine punishment, the whole infected community at the gates of their city, and which develops the segregation and isolation of this pariah society on the principles of contemporary apartheid, namely to each his/her own territory ... the former, that of the hare, which applies a quarantine to the whole infected city, emerging in a network aimed at controlling, which is performed by neighbourhoods. It is enacted house by house, floor by floor, with the aim of removing sick members and placing them in a lazaret, prior to their cremation and thus preserving the health, vitality and hygiene of everyone and everybody. The power and management of the epidemic has gone from a territorial cartographic mapping based on the principles of separation and autonomy (the hare), to that of a corporeal and nominal cartography of individuals, namely the inhabitants (the plague).

The evolution of human management then seems to find its apogee at the beginning of the twentieth century, with the establishment of places for imprisonment, the *Panoptic Institution*, and repressive medicine based on an organisation which associates knowledge and power with disciplinary scope. From the man under control through to that so-called Ideal Man, it was apparently enough to make a semantic shift. And the Modern Movement according to the significance of what we usually call the "modern period" has not ceased to make this concentrationary enterprise flourish e.g. from the Voisin project (1925) financed by the eponymous car company, to Futuramal supported by GM Motors (1939), to the Vertical City (1925) by Hilberseimer, up to the ennobling autopia highway (1971) in Los Angeles imagined by Reyner Banham, just to recall the most famous and emblematic examples. All of these examples – and I apologise in advance for what will be written here – are not extraordinary. It is not the case that these same principles of control and planning were implemented by a Bauhaus architect, Fritz Ertl, who designed the buildings in the concentration camp for extermination at Auschwitz-Birkenau. How ironic that these ways of organising and monitoring human bodies are adorned with utopia, even with radical architecture, and maybe with new propaganda and control systems (see Pinterest).

I want to claim that not only is the coercive and concentrationary city of Hilberseimer (from the Bauhaus) not remotely utopian or radical, but that the result of the violence of the state, implemented by its architects, will emerge in the legitimisation of any subsequent production, like top-down master planning, large sets of envisioning and ultimately a glorification of the elites ... This can be seen as "for the good of all"... Namely the same ideological offspring that we can say today, suddenly open to those countries where human rights have been banned (countries in the Gulf, Azerbaijan, China). The ghosts of Pinochet or Ceausescu could commission from the same architects a work that they would accept... Emerging from a "shake" in the architecture, shapes as puppets of "progress", ultimately designed to mask the social ones that are still, yes indeed, living in feudal structures.

On the other hand, see the historical antidote to Fritz Ertl ... Let's remember that David Georges Emmerich (partner in GEAM) was an Auschwitz survivor. His early association with Yona Friedman led to a requisitioning of the legitimacy of the architect, the bottom-up self organisation of the "creative unemployed," to quote Constant, the dismissal of the architect's posture 'deus ex-machina', and as collateral effect, unbolting our own falsification of "professional de-expertise."

We have always the choice between both sides...the Mephistopheles Survey, where architects play for their 'übermensch' success, Doctor Faustus or... the de-organisational artifacts of the Survivor, who doesn't pretend to abolish the desire and the risk of being a human on the planet, with our own vulnerability and procrastination, without the need for a "discourse of the master" to guide and rule the appetite for life... in fact...another agenda for architecture.

Another crack appears, which we have already evoked, in the late 1950s, following the trauma of the Second World War, with GIAP and GEAM (amongst others), both heroic and radical (oh, pardon, this word has become a trap). We will deal later in this text with what this desirable machine factory implies (Friedman's "Spatial City", Constant's "New Babylon", Chaneac's "Interdite Architecture", amongst others ...) as a way of aesthetic and political resistance: not yet the "machine for living," but the factory of machines to be made and unmade, to be lived together, weakening, if not just demystifying the protective and deadly image of omnipotent architecture. Numerous collections and series like the Frac Orleans, or the book like Radicals by Gianni Pettena in 1996 draw its vertiginous paths ... and their demotion.

Concerning more ourselves, another period, which is still too close to be fully understood and analysed, emerged from the digital (r)evolution of the mid 1990s, a period of some 10 years lasting until its first class burial, in 2004, on the occasion of the "Non-Standard" exhibition at the Centre Pompidou.... As the opposite of the diagram that identified and associated the representation of society with a flying vision, the 'modus operandi' of this proto-digital period was initially intending to conquer, appropriate, caress and corrupt new tooling methods, situations and processes made possible by the democratisation of computers. Very close to the 'concept of modulation' from Deleuzc and Simondon, (re)opening the Pandora's box of relations between matter and form, shape/shapelessness and computer intrinsic logic-illogic, which renegotiate the ontological division and opposition between human life and machines, articulating their co-dependencies, where machines are constituted by human realities, dreams, nightmares, illusions, fiction, in the sense of Foucault to knot and unknot realities and illusion... de-alienating the managerial-official storytelling by insiders, workerism and operaist strategies... recomposing the full chain of production and the division of labour, with a permanent shift or drift in design and fabrication processes, renegotiating the posture-position of the architect, and mainly developing a format of "resistance-resilience," if I may quote Log 25, which was published later, in 2012. This proto-digitalism was perverting the ancient order, postmodern Rotary Club, design merchandising, over designed technology from the nineteenth century in the pursuit of the Crystal Palace, etc.

This movement, which is not unique, which through the synchronicity of its authors' pretentions, has been voluntarily and strategically turned into the Blob Architecture caricature.... that the Bézier curve is replaced by the line, that the topology, previously called "analysis situ" by Euler, that is to say the analysis of the situation, has replaced the determinisms and the little story of the professional builder, hostage to political systems, brutalised by his professional status, patronising and reactionary ... whereas the corporate ways of alienation and reproductions, which are considered as Tractatus ... But this could not be ... And the caricature (blob) allowed to confine and metabolise their potential dangers.

In these times of disciplinary "grand narrative", classic, modern, postmodern (obviously in architecture, light years after Jean François Lyotard's postmodernism), and now post-digital, architecture is written in capitals letters... Nothing emerges which is not an image of the mechanisms of power, like its intrinsic representation, its DNA, a sort of echo, or a performative and cynical reflex that finally ends in the petrification of matter, in the act of doing, to mark its pompous and pretentious ideological aesthetic perenniality.

But there are also "in between" periods, which work like historical cracks, such as the Baroque so well described in the fold of Deleuze. He associates the torments and the fold of the soul, of the "I is another," with descriptive geometry's topologies, with the discovery of heliocentrism, the infinite repetition of the *mise en abîme* of the line, up to Bernini's Ecstasy of Saint Teresa, to the voids of the conflicts of the Christian world, where politics and the relationship with the divine stammer between Luther's Reformation and the orgies of the Borgia family. This crack in time and in the mechanisms of knowledge will produce the Copernican revolution and the asymptotic curve of Leibnitz, as a critique of the world and its own representation ... It is about a symbolic temporal zone that disposes of Alberti's Greco-Roman precepts aimed at generating its own "Perversions": Kepler and Francesco Borromini.

In this process we can identify the attributes of what Freud calls "*Spekulation,*" in the sense of the Siamese and antinomical drive, death drive and pleasure, *eros* and *thanatos*. At the same time, it is about a "death drive" that denies itself to any organisation, namely the result of castration mechanisms (political and professional ideological structures) in order to free the forces of anti-production from a posture and a production suitable to corrupt the dominant discourses of doing, saying and knowing-doing... But also, and in fact, it is the result of their schizophrenia, in the sense of Guattari's schizoanalytic cartographies, changing one power for another. These cracks are also generative of the "desiring machines," the antidote to the death or masochism that drives them. In a contradictory way they inscribe their own fragility in the institutional flaws – the Don Quixote of their authors – or sometimes the lack of opportunity invites them to close up shop, to disappear; without grasping the statute which they themselves contributed to displace.

These "desiring machines" inoculate the germs of the desire production or the production in desire as the place of the possible, that of the real – even if at the end of his life Borromini does not want to see this real anymore and both at night and during the day he closes its doors so as not to notice it anymore. Their fictions are mostly made of words and processes (from the discovery of Baroque optics to Bits and Pixels), but paradoxically increasingly these fictions produce a narration from which the dream is banned, plus their reality potential is exercised as a plausible counterpower.

According to Deleuze, these desiring machines are neither the result of 'the imaginary' nor of 'the symbolic,' rather they are a modulation of real production in the actual (i.e., in contingency, within digital/computer and manufacturing the methods are similar to mould and clay modulation). These desiring machines are by nature within the machines of the visible (the social, the political, the aesthetic, the institutional, the technical), but they themselves are not subdued; they recondition from inside the territories of libido and production, through relational diagrams. These diagrams have nothing to do with the control diagrams of Eisenman or Superstudio, already prefiguring their commercialisation. The diagrams I refer to here make up assemblies of singularities, the emergencies of flow that at the same time pass through them and constitute them. They work in such a way that forces capable of creating devices of knowledge, both artificial and natural, analogue and digital, human matter and electronic circuits, converge. These hybrid data streams combine vitalism and machinism, a beautiful gateway along with resistance, lightning exultation and masochism, ambivalence of the death drive and desiring machines, which renegotiate the act of producing, in the sense of Marx. At the same time, the express place of the technique, of the machine and its appropriation, but also of the human structures (not) subdued, engaged in their result.

Let me express a criticism here. I claim that downgrading digital culture in architecture to the "Infinite Monkey theorem" as successfully orchestrated in the Centre Pompidou in 2005 is a fact: 90% of the architects participating as authors came to an end of their production. This castration enterprise from the French house of culture is not so anodyne. But on the other hand, aren't institutions made for this? ... to normalise? (See the following expo that stretches the carpet to lobotomised technicalities, 3D printing or codes on the subtle condition of being innocent and harmless, while the reality of the world isn't ...) Calling it a fun culture for petty bourgeois and Parisians is a pleonasm, so much that the city has been emptied of its 'popular neighbourhoods'. The latter reason, amongst others, for New-Territories' departure for the Andaman Sea, with cat, computer and robot following along. All of this marked the end of this decade of the 1990s of "desiring digital machines" (1994–2004) and fulfilled the prophecy of the death drive, a masochistic instinct that underlies them, and which naturally crosses every movement which was born from these cracks in time...

Where are we now? As Burroughs or Bowles said about the Interzone of Tangiers, "there is nothing left to spoil anymore".... The digital has come back as a system of control, simultaneously developing a superficial, naïve jiggling methodology to mask its content (in a neolibertarian parametricism for an illiberal regime). Computation and robots are used for decorative "Christmas" exhibitions... academia are engaged in the use-abuse of tooling in a purely formalist way, detoxified, sterilised and lobotomised as in some Anglo-American spots for wealthy time-rich Asians which profits of the globalization, de-territorialisation of economy, impoverishment of the western middle class, intellectual normalisation of campuses, de-politized and business oriented, for cash-flow purposes. It's time to announce the defeat of the digital in terms of a re-questioning of thinking and making within the post-capitalist age... Architecture plunges again into a system of Tractatus, where repetition, plagiarism and 'déjà vu' is 'la raison d'être' for its existence ...Waiting in sleeping mode for the next trans-door... The next singular synchronicity...The next crack in time to accomplish again its own schizophrenia.

Should we suspect that digital "arch" is meant now to be used as a glamorous lure, a blue sleeping pill, to entertain those who produce it, just as turpentine intoxicates the painter, and for its consumers, to help maintain their belief in the illusion of positivism, progress, emancipation through science and novelty gadgets? Yes, I would say this is a fact. At the end of this proto-digital, in 2004, Zaha Hadid and her multiple epigones started to use computers... And her legatee now pretends to legitimate and legislate the right way to manage computing...What an irony. We could say that le phantom of le Corbusier and his five points are back. it's a real advantage to work with these blinkers, no need to check the political regime or the concentration of power to over design a totemic twisted geometry! So, the post-digital drove us into the backlash world of the "Ancient Regime," in the sense of the division of labour, delegation of power and concentration of databases, which mask their powerlessness, their impotency.

Principally, I would argue, because we are in the midst of a paradigm shift, to quote Thomas Kuhn, between two inherently incommensurable systems. The old system that uses technology to reproduce and perpetuate top-down "creative" authority, in fact very romantic and a new system that needs to discover its potential, its limits, constraints in order to renegotiate the scenario of means and meaning "but" architecture... for protocols more disruptive than linear, more heuristic than deterministic, more anthropo-technological (Sloterdijk would say) than purely dedicated to accuracy, performativity, expertise, now analysed as one symptom of what I define as the copy-based syndrome...

But.... what could the next synchronicity be that is able to scratch our comfort... in the collapsing age of the planet or eschatologist "zeitgeist"... we are becoming the particles of a systemic accelerationist agenda...

Antonio Negri already suggests it in his work 'Empire' "we slipped from a disciplinary society that authorises and punishes the one which it has decreed to be sick, to a more insidious and flexible system, an individualised control system, a definition inherited by William Burroughs, which deals not only with bodies, but with "data and Psyche", "cookies" that navigate like the Trojan horse. We ourselves have become the vectors of its efficiency, of its diffusion, in a voluntary enslavement of belonging. A society called 'postmoderne, et dans laquelle les mécanismes de maîtrise se font toujours plus "démocratiques", toujours plus immanents au champ social, diffusés dans le cerveau et le corps de citoyens.'

How to act when we are tossed right and left, to unmask the real from its deception, the elements of language and fake news, the small scams and the washing machines, a financial and ideological recycling system, when we need to separate the wheat from the chaff on several levels? As Deleuze would say:

- Facing the lure of romantic ecology, which was the best companion to the twentieth century's most barbaric regimes. Lenin and Goering were highly concerned with animal rights and nature… as expressed by a multitude of laws.
- Facing the hoax of industrial ecology, where greenwashing (from the Tesla battery to any photovoltaic device/Cobalt and silicon are not harvested; they are produced through the fossil-fuel energy chain) appears the ultimate performative and cynical discourse for post-capitalism to sell illusive moralism and "save Willy" gadgets (what beautiful incestuous lovers).
- Facing a political and intellectual high drama in which sceptical environmentalist lobbyists, obscene liars, opportunistic evangelists and many others… spread their influence through the complicity of newspapers, journalists and other media in the hands of the billionaires.
- Facing the scientists of the IPCC (Intergovernmental Panel on Climate Change) who were misjudged or ridiculed as Cassandras 20 years ago, with the aim of metabolising or ignoring their warnings… to the situation here and now where they appear to be logically tumbling into catastrophism… into a "too late – run for your life" resignation/Any deep, extreme, virtuous transformation (degrowth) in our consumerist symptoms will de-impact the decay of Gaia for the kids of Greta Thunberg for at least the next two generations! Tell the dinosaurs, before their global extinction, that they need to sacrifice to save a hypothetical future…
- Facing the revenge of nature (Katrina, El Niño, the cyclones Jeanne, Tomas and Nargis, the Xynthia storm, the Ewiniar typhoon, the Indonesian and Japanese earthquakes, collateral tsunamis all the way to Fukushima…) in a mutiny against the organisation of man-power, in a faltering of the original chaos…
- Facing the newspeak propaganda about deep learning and the post-human, which fantasises and entertains global lobotomisation to hide and mask the major program of alienation, domination and the concentration of profit, resources, data, material and immaterial… underway since the nineteenth century…

The word still exists, we're going to have to wheel it out again, facing those multiple hypo-crisis and trap, push it into the very heart of whatever situation, like a hesitation of time's arrow, here and now, here and elsewhere, elsewhere but not just anywhere, avoiding the futurist past as much as the positivist future… Quite the opposite… And anyway, why would "It" be more moral, why would it have some right over the whole collection of good wishes and good consciences? There are so many people who are happy to carry morality's flag, they're legion, as numerous and powerless as criminals…without being digital-romantic, computation addicted, eco-masturbator, socio-moralist, … but just architects, snaking in the crack of abuse, idolatry, idiocracy, propaganda, self-complaisance, bio-hoax, social network lure, etc…

The crack of time closed in 2005, it is up to us to reopen it ... the wound will bleed profusely, ultimately oozing black bile ... our melancholy.

Three case studies

1996: In Orlando-Soweto, South Africa, the first of Johannesburg's townships, in fact our first digital scenario, on the grave of Hector Pieterson, one of the kids shot during the uprising of teenagers in 1976 against Afrikaner Apartheid.

2018: In Okayama, Japan, our last scenario, in a city which was erased by the first Napalm Carpet Bombing in 1945, using the paper-wood traditional jap. housing as a factor in its erasing, by fire. Okoyama received a comparable blowing up to Hiroshima.

2019: In Brastislava, a typical teaching studio where we applied our system of synesthesia between tooling, process, means and meaning, mainly about post-ecology in the collapsing age, through a display, a movie, a public output, launched in May 2019.

This scenario is located in Japan, at Okayama, near Hiroshima. On 28 June 1945, four hundred and eighty-seven B-29's flew four missions against secondary cities. Only one B-29 was lost, according to US Air Force Reports. Mission 234 included one hundred thirty-eight 58th BW B-29s, which attacked Okayama destroying 2.13 square miles or 63% of the city. Precision/The B-29 used Napalm Bombing (to optimise destruction of the wood and paper environment).

Process: Disruptive logic and design...from scanning a Okayama Parcel, to extract digitally through ground-penetrating radar (12 m deep) the obstacles from the past and the residue of the Allied bombing night/an architecture emerges from the underground DATA onto the surface through robotic heuristical trajectories, directly impacted by the feedback of the underground strata, in real time... a computing scenario against amnesia...

Simple room hotel, in the middle of Okayama, on a global program of ten rooms disseminated in the urban tissue, using the existing city as corridors, hotel facilities and services.

This project was commissioned by Foundation Ishikawa/Architect/New-Territories/2019.

Process:

1. Scanning of the underground with ground-penetrating radar over 500 m^2.
2. Developing a rubber fibber concrete, in Thailand, to assume a soft geometry and elastic behaviour.
3. Analysing in real time the underground signals to disrupt the nozzle seven axes robot trajectories, extruding a continuous line of rubber concrete, just as Ariadne's thread in the Minotaur Maze.
4. Mirroring the substructure landscape through this seismographic condition to develop, in the middle of the vibrations... a glass slump house, in direct echo of the echo (of the underground), as a "mise en abime" of the time reverb.
5. Revealing a glitch/uncertain past-future, which is able to trigger an architecture, shapeless emergence.

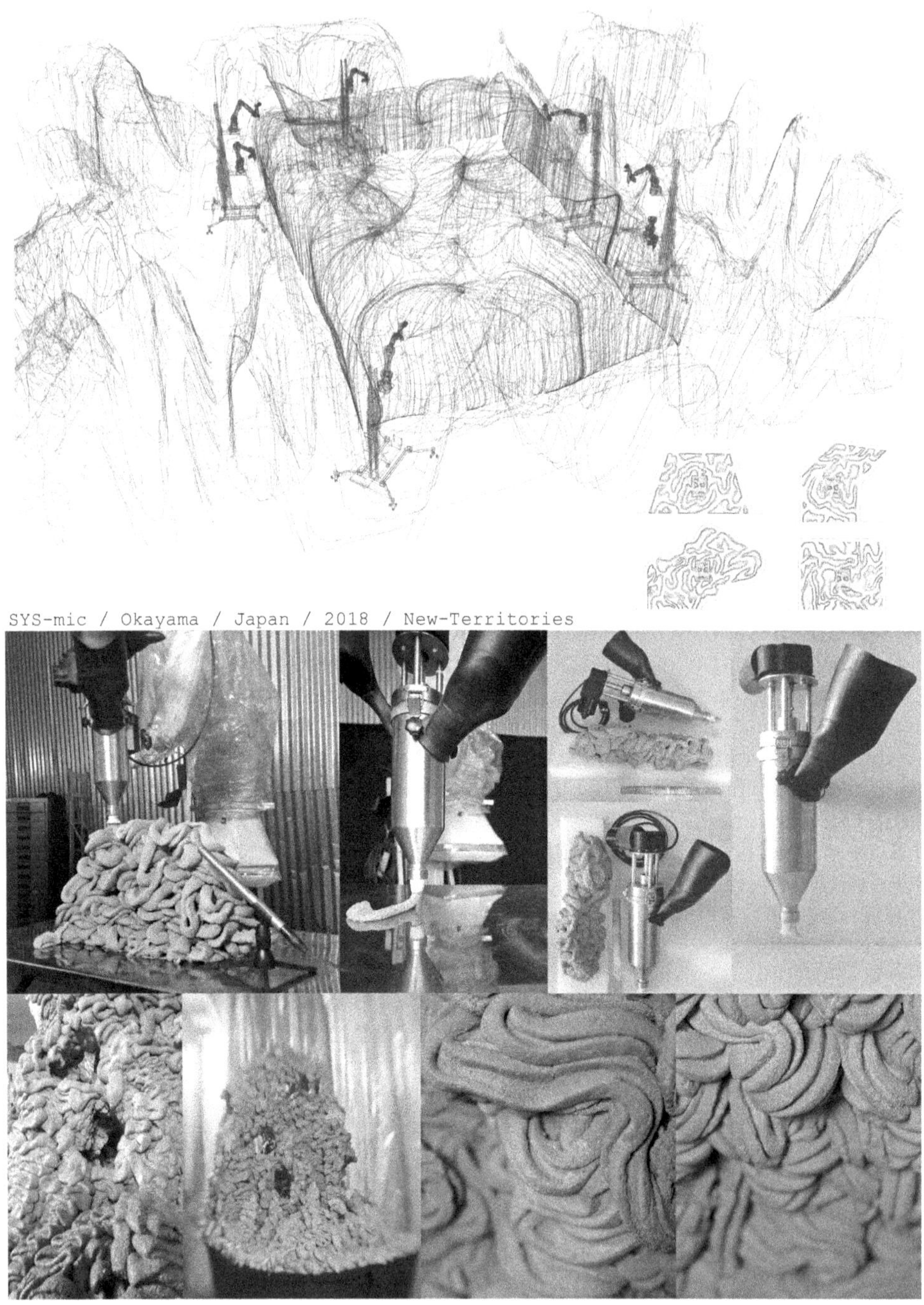

Figure 3.1 New-Territories: SYS-mic, Okayama, Japan (2018).

Source: François Roche.

Processes

Scenario of NewT, including Sys-Mic proceeded by robotic from catatonic feedback of human-history-situation pathologies to environmental strategy to reveal those "amnesia" and failures. Those signals, whether analogue or digital, in real time, are the subtracts, the intrinsic logic of fabrication. As in many scenarios in Bangkok, the making of the "prop" is developed from this non-linear and conditional robotic processes, from AI task algorithms to absorb the misapprehension of human and environmental pre-conditions.

Those 'modulations' (in the sense of Simondon-Deleuze) reveal the relationship between the mould/robot and the clay/matter/extrusion...in interdependences and co-relation with real sensor interface (RSI), signals, inputs, analogue-digital, collected through UPD signal and the chain of Processing, Firefly, Grasshopper, Rhinoceros, and re-injected (every 2m/s) in the 'parcours' of the machine, creating a permanent conditional position, between 'the point where the machine was' to 'the point where the machine should be', as a vector of translation in an iterative redefinition ... without ever reaching any vanishing intention as a goal of achievement, producing perturbations and stochastic positioning, in real time, where the trajectory of the nozzle and its secretion are reacting to the robot's very noise, to the humans' very vibes (mental or physical), to the environmental suppression and amnesia ... Those agents corrupted the programmed predictable work and modified in real time the path of the fabrication, as a stuttering feedback coming from the intrinsic protocol of doing, increasing the intricate meanders of the tool in an ever permanent inaccuracy of positioning, introducing non-linear processes ... as a way of territorialising technologies, but under the condition to never ignore the diagram of their relationships... where data, algorithm are neither inoffensive nor innocent, and participate to the diagram of control, of servitude, repression, merchandising...

This is a memento in our work. The question was about the participation in '94 in the political, or better symbolic, transformation of Southern Africa, initiated and carried out by Nelson Mandela. At the time we were located between the Reunion islands and Mauritius, as on a sort of escape with our first two kilo-euro PC, a 3D Studio max and Windows NT. 3.51. So we were almost within a regional context of proximity. Perhaps it was a matter of luck or just the case that we were working on the design of the memorial dedicated to Hector Pieterson, killed during the 1976 uprising, following the new law which obliged children of the South Africa townships to use Afrikaans rather than English.

It was very easy to justify that a petrified memorial would not have been enough in this specific case. The archives of the ANC (African National Congress), derived from SANNC, were spread widely across foreign universities or hidden from the South African settler's view. It was an opportunity to make them visible and accessible. And through offering a working tool and a research economy on all of those places of discrimination and racial struggles. The project rather than emerging as a grave, something that already was, resulted in a transformation of its activities program, therefore it was a storage and a demonstration space, as well as the whole of the reception, restaurant services ... etc. changing the activities program as the first political-aesthetic action was not anodyne.

Therefore, we elaborated an architectural remodelling, a fold, with the tomb of the young Ettore in the middle. In order to avoid justifying the presence of an architectural

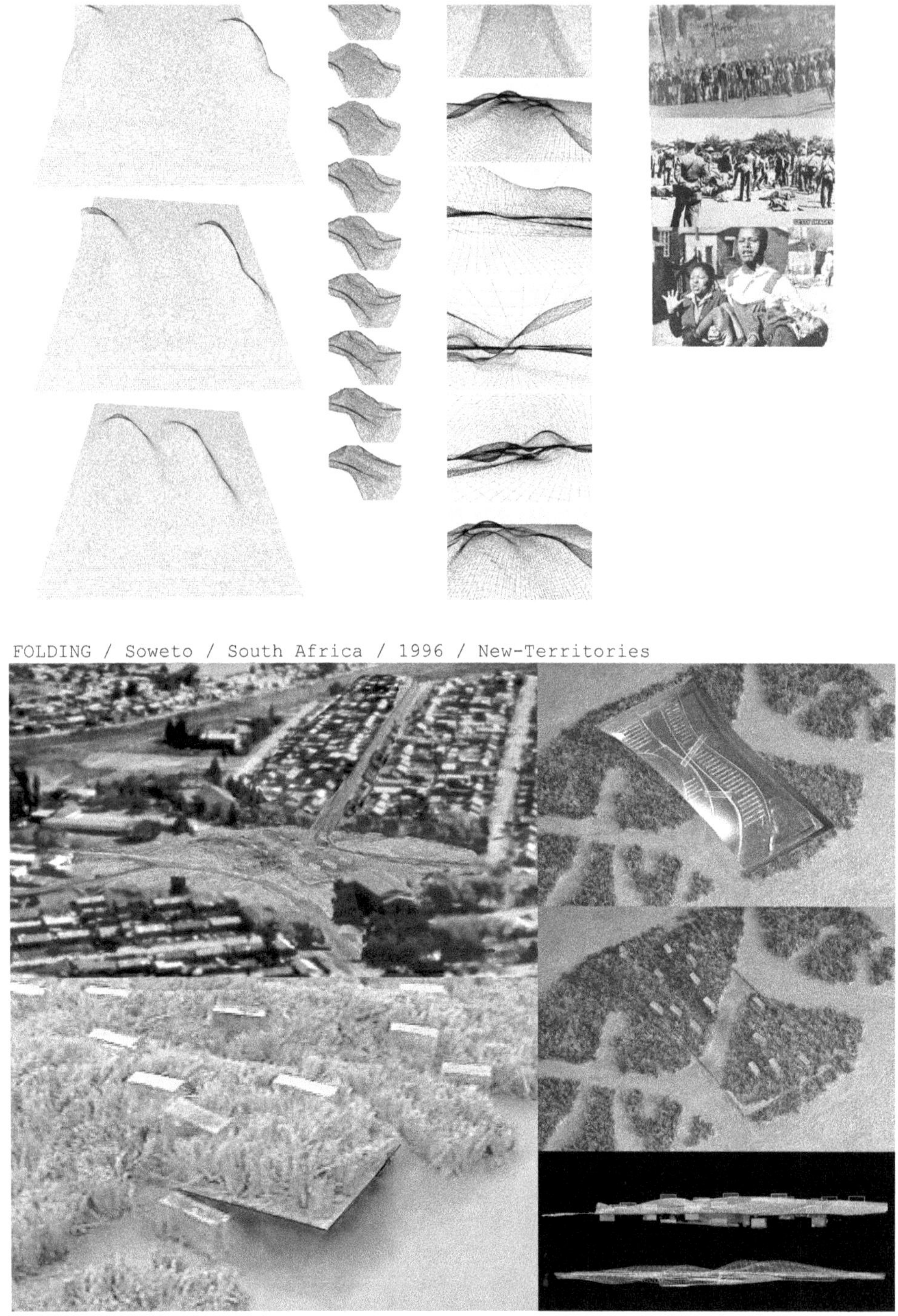

Figure 3.2 New-Territories: *Folding*, Soweto, South Africa (1996).

Source: François Roche.

totem, nothing was shown. Only some glass containers abandoned in a bush (grasses burned by the sun) perforated the wave morphology. In the centre, the grave, full layers of soil ... The soil of Soweto, offered and thickened by the most powerful of the gold extractors, Mr. Oppenheimer, whose confessed objective was to "stalaguer" his future low-wage labour.

The fact that a simple kinetic and kinematic "display" with intensity variation could bring out a new geography in 3DSMAX, did not cease to amaze us. We were in the game or in a mastery with the parameters under the cursors and its variables editable in real time ... Indeed the two aspects together.

Because of our naivety we informed the French representation's services in South Africa, who hurried to ask us to inform the competent ministry and its architectural direction ... we were urgently summoned to Paris in a meeting "under the gilding of the Republic" to justify and criticise us for an initiative that politically had not been validated upstream ... by the state services on a subject said to be sensitive ... as they say in post-colonial diplomatic circles ... Africa and France, what hypocrisy ... since those times ... where I saw our republican monarchy ... François Barré was the ass-hole on duty ... but in fact despite him ... he still occupied the function ....

Design of a museum-memorial on the tomb of Hector Pieterson, integrating the archives of the township (exhibition hall, archives, conference room, restaurant) and a landscaped area of 3 hectares in 1996.

Process:

1. Undulation of the skin of the bush (high vegetation burned by the sun) to preserve the tombstone and its destitution.
2. Deformation of the programming layers according to this movement (basement).
3. Random positioning of the glass containers emerging from the bush tablecloth.
4. (Referring to the usual township installations done by ship containers).
5. Moving of all archives of the Apartheid Soweto history and facts, disseminated in many Johannesburg institutions, to trigger possible economy of researchers within the township.
6. Ownership of the new "groundunderground" for people who were "used and abused" in the gold mines, under the apartheid regime of South Africa.

This scenario is included in the mythomaniaS series, which has been developed since 2012 mainly in Bangkok where we test-taste environments and architecture in paranoid symptoms, with psychotic machines (robot in real time feedback), psychotic apparatuses and fragments with... human and Bodies in verse... meeting the stories and the fabrication of the shelter of their symptoms... The 'forbidden' is reintroduced as a possibility, and, what was rejected or considered as an improper ingredient within our computer graphic idealisation of the world is coming back like one of George Bataille's substances... in a repulsive 'curiouser and curiouser' affinity.

A part of the work is an apparatus and display on the Public Art gallery of the AFAD School, where newt was doing a three-month master class, including movies on robot done in BKK, a large scale computation fragment, developed by double signal in Grasshoper-Rhino to discover output as intricated artifact... with some prototypes, a movie with actor, scenario, story board, cinematography and 4k camera... as a fiction on architecture and digestive animal matter: 5 km of pork intestine/from

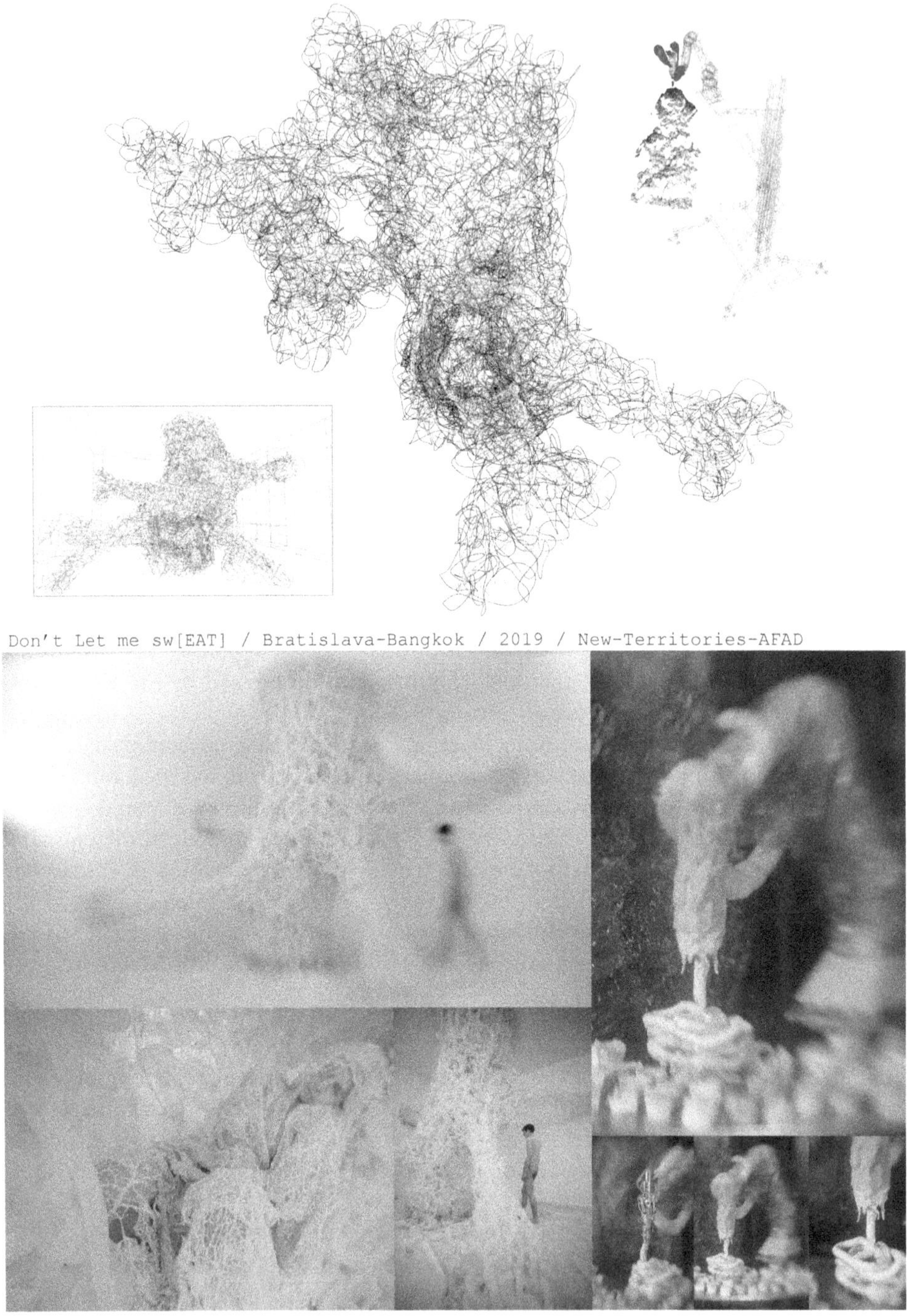

Figure 3.3 New-Territories-AFAD: *Don't Let me sw[EAT]*, Bratislava, Bangkok (2019).

Source: François Roche.

Slaughter houses and 250 animals/30kg of Stomach/The price of barbarian practice to exorcise guiltiness/as an ecology of human symptoms.

Scenario

Based on the Decameron of Boccaccio, few people decided to renegotiate the ritual, the ceremony, the vitalism of life, facing the collapsing Anthropocene age, trespassing the evidence of global failure... to reformulate an ethico-aesthetic paradigm, where philosophy, physiology, sexuality and technologies are intertwined, intricate. This specific 'ZeitGeist' definitively altered the rules of human behaviour, using emerging logic as apparatuses of knowledge and simultaneously processes of fabrication, assuming (n)certainties, (n)determinism, disruptive logic, heuristic feedback as agents of attitudes and form, where lines of subjectivities are the triggering principle of realities and strategies for escape. Where biology, technology, robotics, anthropology are in symbiosis & synesthesia; from Carnivore to Vegetarian, to Vegan, to Liquidarian, to ...Breatharian, in a long agony of their digestive machine, from the hunter condition to a "Monism" co-relation, humans are reaching the limbo of dead-alive physiology in organic psyche matter, where obsession with food, bulimia, overeating, anorexia, overcalculations, overthinking, an omnipresent imagery of food, consumerism, overconsumption, a substitute for happiness, pleasure food, comfort food, food as an excuse, excess, food as an accessory, food as a fashion, as a statement, kitchen studios, house centralised around kitchen and toilet, society determined around table and drink, lifestyles consolidated around digestive matter, mind suppression projected in food, eating guilt away, guilty food, the murder of the beast for our pleasure, the fart of the sheep-cow, environmental disaster, attempts to run away from this loop, from the predator, and vegetarian and vegan practices, and what else...questioning, exploring 'clichés', stereotypes of the insider. Loosening individualism, who is master who is slave, emancipation of or from technologies, empowering, reliance, dependency, humans are becoming part of the whole, not the top of the chain, on the breast of machines, humans are becoming flesh, irrigated by pulsion of death and life, in degradation to data, as a material for consumption, consumed, barely an input for an independent process of a machine, emergent, self-generative, self-sufficient, post-human era. The opposition is losing control over human evolution, leaving it to nature, losing the artificiality, the tools, the hands leaving the grid, leaving the network by being the network in co-relation, with desires of instincts, crossing hedonism, epicureanism, Dionysian point of view versus Apollonian, taming desires with rationalism, stoicism, monism... Trying out all the roles in society, a struggle to find a way. Bored to stay in one, numb to all stimuli and excitement. In need of something less. Draining the earth. Abstinence.

Translated by Claire Coulter
Credits/
Concept by New-Territories, M4 with AFAD school/Brastislava 2019
AFAD Partners/Štěpán Krahulec, Michaela Krpalová, Jakub Samuel, Sára Krčmáriková, Natália Štundová, Patrícia Chamraz, Chloé Tissier, Elisa Coquel, and Júlia Kolláthová, assistant production.
Actor/Lukáš Mráz.
A part of New-Territories 'mythomaniaS' case studies.

References

Bataille, G., Hamilton, A., & Hamilton, C. L. T. S. P. H. I. A. (1973). *Literature and Evil.* Calder and Boyars.
Cioran, E. M., Howard, R., & Thacker, E. (2012). *A Short History of Decay*. Arcade Publishing.
De Honnecourt, V., & Bowie, T. (2012). *The Medieval Sketchbook of Villard de Honnecourt*. Dover Publications.
Deleuze, G., & von Sacher-Masoch, L. R. (1989). *Masochism: Coldness and Cruelty*. Zone Books.
Egan, G. (1997). *Distress: A Novel.* HarperPrism.
Foucault, M. (1971). Orders of discourse. *Social Science Information*, 10(2), 7–30.
Guattari, F. (1995). *Chaosmosis: an ethico-aesthetic paradigm*. Indiana University Press.
Kaufmann, E. (1952). *Three Revolutionary Architects: Boullée, Ledoux, and Lequeu*. American Philosophical Society.
Lacan, J. (1990). *Television: A Challenge to the Psychoanalytic Establishment*. W.W. Norton.
Lautréamont, comte de, Dalí, S., & Dent, R. J. (2011). *The Songs of Maldoror*. Solar Books.
Leibniz, G. W. G. W. (2018). *The Monadology.* CreateSpace Independent Publishing Platform.
Lyotard, J.-F., & Benjamin, A. E. (1989). *The Lyotard reader*. Oxford, UK: Blackwell.
Milton, J., Fenton, E., & Johnson, S. (1821). *Paradise Lost*. John Bumpus.
Price, C. (2003). *The square book*. Chichester, West Sussex [etc.]: Wiley-Academy.
Ragon, M. (1978). *Prospective et futurologie: histoire mondiale de l'architecture et de l'urbanisme modernes*.
Rudofsky, B. (1964). *Architecture without Architects: An Introduction to Nonpedigreed Architecture*. Museum of Modern Art; distributed by Doubleday, Garden City, N.Y.
Venturi, R., Drexler, A., Stierli, M., of Modern Art (New York, N. Y.., Scully, V., Scully, V., Art, M. M., for Advanced Studies in the Fine Arts, G. F., & Brownlee, D. B. (1977). *Complexity and Contradiction in Architecture*. Museum of Modern Art.
Vincent, J.-D. (1990). *The Biology of Emotions*. Oxford, UK: B. Blackwell.
Wittgenstein, L., & Ogden, C. K. (1998). *Tractatus Logico-Philosophicus*. Dover Publications.

Chapter 4

Informality and dissent

The culture of self-sufficiency of the American rural poor

David Franco

Introduction

Architects and planners have been fascinated by the free aesthetics and social complications of informal housing practices since at least the late 1960s. However, most of that interest has focused on settlements in metropolises in developing countries, such as Rio de Janeiro, Lagos or Lima, which sustained fast population growth from rural migration flows. In contrast, there has been surprisingly little attention given to informal housing practices within rich countries such as the United States. Few have acknowledged that a tradition of informal housing does exist in the US (Durst & Wegmann, 2017; Mukhija & Monkkonen, 2007; Ward, 1999, 2014), although it is unevenly distributed across the country's geography and – unlike Latin American countries – closely intertwined with formal housing. In this chapter, I will consider the importance of informal practices exerted by the American rural poor, both as part of a long history of scarcity and resourcefulness, as well as a tactical response to the current housing affordability crisis, affecting rural communities across the United States (White, 2015).

I would like to look at this phenomenon over the background of neoliberal culture, in which the colonization of the domestic sphere by consumerism is certain (Cohen, 2004) and housing, instead of being defined by the traditional organization of work or by everyday life, has fully turned into a commodity (Forrest & Williams, 1984; Pattillo, 2013; Marcuse & Achtenberg, 1986). If we consider informal practices such as junk accumulation, domestic farming or unregulated self-construction – also seen as markers of poverty and failure – against a context in which 'the pursuit of profit in housing is coming into conflict with its use for living' (Madden & Marcuse, 2016), they turn into actions of dissent. Actions that not only question the architectures produced by the market and accepted by society but that, in the context of the ongoing debate about sustainability and the built environment, demonstrate the ability of lifestyles defined by scarcity to produce alternatives.

While urban poverty epitomizes the prevailing debate on housing informality, this chapter looks at the less-noticed practices of the rural poor in the US, as part of a long-standing tradition of self-sufficiency, but also in the context of the current housing crisis. The growing difficulty to find affordable homes in urban centres like New York City, Seattle or San Francisco is already part of the national political conversation (Richardson, 2019). However, a similar process is silently taking place in rural America, as much as it may seem difficult to understand how affordable housing can be scarce when the cost of life is much lower (White, 2015). Not only are poverty rates higher and average income lower when we compare them to their closest urban neighbours (United States Department of Agriculture, 2017), many rural areas in America are also undergoing an unexpected growth in population – often urban retirees looking for lower living costs – that affect the real estate market in a sort of rural gentrification (Nelson & Nelson, 2010). Unlike what happens in cities, rural renters have virtually no options – a longer commute or a smaller apartment – when rental prices get higher. Therefore, many of them end up living in unhealthy manufactured homes, houses in disrepair, or even in campgrounds or cars, without minimum living conditions (Patrick, 2017).

Non-urban environments like these were always the stage of the self-sufficiency dreams that emboldened the 1960s do-it-yourself ethos, which surged with hippie culture. A typical protagonist in those dreams was the 'countercultural bricoleur' (Kirk, 2015), whose legendary manual, the *Whole Earth Catalog,* provided a roadmap for DIY building practices, as well as a guide to adapt our everyday life to the environment as a whole (Sadler, 2008). We might need to look back at this foundational link between self-construction's modern culture and the global environmental discourse in a time like ours, when self-sufficiency might not just be a way of putting sustainable ideals into action, but also to purely dodge homelessness. In this context, the rural poor – a figure with a powerful presence in the American collective imagination (Cunningham, 1999) – takes the role of protagonist.

According to sociologists Manuel Castells and Alejandro Portes (1989, p. 12), informal activities are those that are 'unregulated by the institutions of society, in a legal and social environment in which similar activities are regulated'. The rural poor have been performing material practices outside of the limits of what is socially acceptable in the USA for centuries. And while there are plenty of nuanced differences between, for instance, rural black poverty in the deep South and white trash poverty in the rural Appalachians, they do coincide in several important aspects. Sociologist Cynthia Duncan (2014) has presented a cross-section of persistent poverty in rural America by exploring several communities in very different areas of the country. Social classes are similarly stratified in the dominantly white Appalachian coal fields and the black Mississippi Delta: 'upper-class families that control the resources and participate in mainstream economic and political life, and lower-class families that are powerless, dependent, and do not participate. The poverty of the have-nots is inseparable from the privilege of the haves' (Duncan, 2014, p. 237). Unlike cities and suburbs, where different social classes are distinctively segregated, the life of poor families in rural communities is spatially intertwined with that of the wealthier ones. Power dynamics are not hidden, and the size, quality and upholding of someone's house constitutes a visible marker of their standing in the community. In this context, as Duncan points out, the middle classes 'consciously put themselves in a group with the very wealthy, whom they emulate and often envy, and distance themselves from the poor, whom they deride as lazy and deviant' (2014, p. 239). The informal houses, sheds and yards built by the rural poor are an important – and very visible – part of the cultural deviance that the middle and upper classes perceive when they look at them. This chapter approaches the question of housing informality looking at this context, and recognizing informality as the materializations of class conflict within rural America, rather than as the expression of global inequality, as it has usually been understood.

Figure 4.1 Alfred Lee Johnson's Backyard, Eutaw, Alabama. Photographer: Vaughn Sills.

Source: Vaughn Sills.

Such an approach comprises two parallel perspectives with regard to architecture. First, a sociohistorical reinterpretation of the American rural vernacular, which finds its expression in very distinct ways, from the informal gardens that African Americans have traditionally built by recycling all kinds of used objects (see Figure 4.1) to the resourceful – and messy – material culture of the rural white trash. Second, a renewed look at domesticity as the main stage for sustainable practices within the built environment. As opposed to corporate-based consumerism, this approach reclaims the home as a sustainable unit of production towards a life-serving, rather than extractive, economy. Both perspectives constitute expressions of dissent against the established order, which manifest through informal practices. Ultimately, this chapter is an exploration of the ways in which these expressions can broaden, and maybe complicate, our current understanding about informality in architecture, hopefully overcoming the limitations of recent debates about this issue.

The politics of informal housing and sustainability

If we had to look for an origin story for the theorization of informality in architecture, that would lie in the publications by British architect John Turner in *Architectural Design* in 1963. Turner worked on the ground from 1957 until 1965, studying informal settlements in Latin America – mostly focused in Lima's urban slums – in a period when the continent's metropolises received millions of rural migrants who ended up living in slums on the edge of cities. By defining the self-help practices that he had observed not only as valid tactics to build homes and neighbourhoods but furthermore as a way of empowerment for the urban poor, Turner established one of the dominant discourses on informal housing amongst architects and academics. He was one of the first scholars 'to portray the urban poor not as victims but as heroic pioneers at the edges of Latin American cities' (Van Ballegooijen & Rocco, 2013), and with that, he opened a new front in the critique against large-scale modern housing projects as undemocratic and alienating. To defend the possibilities and freedoms enjoyed by low-income squatters in Lima's *barriadas*, Turner (1968, 1972) compared them to the alienated urban poor in wealthier countries, like the USA, who couldn't achieve such a level of autonomy due to the pressure of the authorities to organize and control. His skepticism against centralized power delves into the notion of autonomy, which like much of his thinking was strongly influenced by anarchist theorists like Peter Kropotkin. Ironically, Turner's work on informal housing in Latin America became highly influential in establishing the housing agenda of international institutions like the World Bank (Harris, 2003), whose power was essential in the foundation of the neoliberal world order.

However, his vision of informal settlements as real alternatives to the inaction and incompetence of the state to provide housing has provoked a steady series of responses from the Marxist left. Among others, Rod Burgess makes a particularly virulent critique of what he calls the 'Turner school of development' (1982, p. 59) arguing that advocating for an expansion of self-help projects to cover the section of low-income population that the regular market won't reach gives a clear political message of distrust public housing systems. Which entails giving up any radical change of the status quo and, ultimately, accepting the reality of 'the government abandoning people to survive (or not) on their own devices' (Bower, 2016, p. 90).

During the last decade we have witnessed a resurgence in the interest for informal and DIY practices among architects, which has reignited the old discussion about the politics of informality within an updated context. Echoing Burgess' account, several critics have questioned the mystification of informality by Rem Koolhaas (2001) or Alfredo Brillembourg (Brillembourg & Klumpner, 2005), who present it as a challenge against the rigidity of urban planning and a defense of spontaneity in architecture (Van Ballegooijen & Rocco, 2013). While some critics have also signaled the problematic interpretation of unknown sociocultural elements by first world architects (Roy, 2004), most concentrate on how the new defense of informal housing as an alternative to formal planning might entail a renewed critique against the state, in the context of neoliberal economy. Van Ballegooijen and Rocco (2013, p. 1808) have argued that the discourse supporting self-help housing practices often detaches them from their actual political context, by misleadingly suggesting 'that the enormous urban problems of tomorrow's metropolises could simply be solved in the private realm'. To recover that context, we should remember that the notion that the state is unable to efficiently organize the built environment – or any other economic sector – and that instead we should just rely on private citizens' entrepreneurship is paradoxically shared by anti-establishment activists like John Turner, and supporters of hard neoliberalism like the economist Hernando De Soto (1989).

Urban thinker Neil Brenner points at the recent enthusiasm for incremental and informal urban actions as being openly infused of a 'stridently anti-planning rhetoric' that, despite its combative appearance, hardly 'engenders any serious friction against the neoliberal order, much less subverts it'. On the contrary, informal housing might even strengthen the neoliberal status quo by 'temporarily alleviating' some of its worst 'disruptive social and spatial effects, but without interrupting the basic rule regimes associated with market-oriented, growth-first urban development' (Brenner, 2015).

Environmentalism and dissent

However difficult it is to disagree with Brenner and other critics about Turner's mystification of self-sufficiency and the subsequent depoliticization of informality, the great distance between both positions – one defending informality as a real alternative to formal planning and the other acknowledging it not as a solution but as the symptom of larger socio-economic problems – reduces the discussion to a deadlock. Is there a different way to look at informal housing – the way in which a third of the world's population inhabits the built environment (World Bank, 2014) – from an architectural perspective without crashing against its problematic politics?

Two basic shifts – the first in the geography under consideration and the second regarding our thematic approach – might help to open a more productive conversation. I already hinted at this geographical shift when I raised the need to look at informal practices in the context of developed countries, like the United States, instead of studying them only in poorer countries whose social and political nuances are hardly translatable to our own circumstances. The second shift would incorporate informal spatial practices into the larger thematic arch on architecture and the environment. The growing perception of climate change as a highly incendiary political issue (Klein, 2014, p. 31) turns questions usually associated with economic inequality, such as housing affordability, into questions of environmental justice. In that regard, journalist and activist Naomi Klein, as many others, has argued that the only realistic way of undertaking climate change is by tackling capitalism as a whole. That approach would require understanding environmentalism as a political force that should not be limited to dealing with the effects but also with the general causes of the problem. In the architecture profession, in particular, the search for higher energy efficiency regarding envelope design or the defense of denser neighbourhoods versus suburban ones, have progressively become mainstream assumptions. However, there is little questioning – or little discussion for that matter – around the environmental effects of the commodification of the built environment within capitalist societies. The common environmental critique about oversized McMansions focuses on their disproportionate carbon footprint, but not on the way in which they embody the values of a society obsessed with consumption and structurally defined by economic inequality.

From that perspective, the acknowledgement of informality as an array of practices with the potential for meaningfully transforming the built environment, cannot be limited to the effective use of material and energy resources. It also has to recognize how they circumvent the cultural logics of consumerism and challenge the laws of free market, turning material and spatial practices into forms of productive dissent within contemporary capitalism. A new discussion about informal housing might open if we stop seeing it just as an interesting fringe activity taking place in distant countries, like arguably Koolhaas, Brillembourg and others do. But rather as an overlooked part of both the urban and rural economies of developed countries. To that end, we might have to overcome Turner's ideals of self-help and autonomy – upheld as the opposites to formal planning – and instead consider the notions of self-sufficiency and self-expression as the opposites to passive overconsumption. In societies built around material abundance, the very idea of resisting the commodification of domestic life that consumption carries with it entails an intrinsic attitude of opposition. When Margaret Crawford and others (2008, p. 10) introduced the concept of 'Everyday

Urbanism', they asked us to rethink the contemporary city by looking at how small everyday practices overcome formal design. In that way, they recognized the dissentive power of spatial informality. According to Crawford, if the desires behind all the small everyday gestures that give form to informal spaces could acquire a political language, 'they would make a new set of personal and collective demands on the social order'. Therefore, everyday practices – like self-construction or transformation of domestic environments outside normalized models of consumption – can lead the way towards social and environmental change, 'not via abstract political ideologies imposed from outside, but instead through specific concerns that arise from the lived experience of different individuals and groups' (Crawford, 2008, p. 10).

From the countercultural DIY to the vernacular of the rural poor

The question of self-construction obviously has very different implications in Latin America than it does when we look at it in the context of the United States. However, it would be a mistake to interpret the latter as a simpler or less ideologically charged framework. Cathy Smith has studied how American countercultural DIY manuals, such as the *Whole Earth Catalog*, not only worked as educational platforms to disseminate construction technology's practical knowledge, but also provided 'the philosophical and cultural ethos of the movement – a direct challenge to mainstream American values and lifestyles' (Smith, 2014, p. 1). Countercultural manuals shared an essential ideological component with commercial DIY catalogues from the 1940s and 1950s, because both types of publications connected self-construction practices with the idea of social transformation. Far beyond merely providing the way to obtain the building materials and the technical instructions to assemble them, these manuals supported the idea that DIY building practices had intrinsic social benefits, both individually and collectively (see Figure 4.2).

The decorating manual *Better Homes and Gardens* describes specific spatial techniques for 'the creation of an ideal home supporting and indeed producing the family unit and its attendant lifestyle (Smith, 2014, p. 5). The ability to self-organize a family's home appears here as an important ideological component for the fulfilment of the traditional suburban American dream. Despite the practicality of the techniques illustrated in the book, its suggestions are indeed, 'positioned within the context of comprehensive social aspirations'. However, a tension arises between the embracing of individual self-expression, which is an essential part of DIY culture, and the sense of social compliance that the suburban ethos arguably favours (Goldstein, 1998; Starr, 1941). The autonomy to self-construct distinct spaces through individual choices is weakened by the conflicting aspiration of conformity within mainstream lifestyles. DIY was part of the new mid-century suburban identity, but it was also essential in the 1960s countercultural reaction against that very identity. Although these two DIY sensibilities are fueled by two different notions of social transformation, both share a role in the expansion of consumerism throughout American society. While 1950s suburbia marked the acceleration of modern mass-consumerism, the counterculture movement of the late 1960s and early 1970s was ultimately co-opted by businesses that saw an opportunity to redefine – and expand – the possibilities of consumption in the creation of new lifestyles (Frank, 1997).

Figure 4.2 John and Marie's House with Buffalo Bill's loft, 1977. Image by John Wehrheim, as part of the photograph series compiled in the book 'Taylor Camp', http://findingutopia.org/taylor-camp-products.html, and appearing in the film 'THE EDGE OF PARADISE: Taylor Camp, Kauai 1969–1977'. www.theedgeofparadisefilm.com.

Source: John Wehrheim.

A more class-based analysis could conclude that both suburban and countercultural DIYs, however different they seem, were in reality part of the same cultural baggage of the well-off mid-century middle class. During those same decades, the material culture of the working rural class was slowly accruing a set of practices that we may call a deviant vernacular, defined by their lack of ideological connotations and their survivalist ethos. Although it might seem the contrary, this is not necessarily an antimodern or even an antiurban vernacular. To build a shack, customize their trailers or to beautify their front yards, the rural poor were repurposing the debris left by the material abundance of twentieth century America.

Simon Sadler (2012) argues that 1960s countercultural architecture contains a dialectical tension between Buckminster Fuller's ideal dome and the imperfection of the unfinished shacks that proliferated in hippy communities like the Morning Star Commune in California, or Taylor Camp in Kauai. While the technical perfection of the dome offered a glimpse of the alternative world that hippie culture craved for, the shacks were a direct reflection of the pragmatism of countercultural DIY. In a sense, the vernacular of the rural poor is also built around a similarly pragmatic attitude, but fully devoid of any utopian tension. Their only aspiration resided within the very process of material transformation and the elemental urges – shelter, beauty, leisure, reconnection with nature – it satisfies.

The environmental implications of the counterculture's DIY and its explicit rejection of consumerism belong to a well-rooted ideology that connects social change with environmentalism (Castillo, 2015). As Sandler explains, one of the ultimate goals of such ideology was the 'ethical cleansing of its adherents' relationship to consumption', which clearly evokes the project of the late nineteenth century Arts and Crafts movement that 'hoped that commodity production and exchange could be reformed into a social bond' (Sadler, 2012, p. 78). But nothing further from these notions of wholeness and cleansing than the impure and messy ways in which the rural poor transform the environment around them. In its lack of an ideological ambition, their spatial informality seeks neither a wholesome alternative to consumerism, nor being intentionally friendly or respectful to the environment. Unlike countercultural attempts of self-construction, rural DIY does not try to replace a failed architectural model, like the ever-present suburban nightmare that hippies detested in its uniformity and lack of imagination. Instead, the informality of the rural poor constitutes an active deviance from mainstream spatial practices or, to put it in other words, a pragmatic expression of spontaneous dissent. Anthropologist Mary Douglas (1966) has explained the importance of the ideas of purity and pollution in the definition of cultural orders. In that sense, the image of the chaotic and dirty shacks, worn-out trailers or impoverished farmsteads documented by Dorothea Lange (Meister, 2020) as the home of the rural poor, constitute an aggressive response to the pastoral aura of the wealthy plantation, the respectability of the mill worker house or the feeling of upper mobility of the suburban home (see Figure 4.3).

Figure 4.3 Arkansas squatters. Three years in California. Near Bakersfield, California. Photographer: Dorothea Lange, 1935.

Source: Library of Congress.

The deviant self-sufficiency of the white rural poor

This is not a new phenomenon. Historian Nancy Isenberg (2016) maintains that the figure of the rural vagrant – a jobless and landless poor person living on the fringe of rural communities – was characteristic of the American colonies where, coherently with Douglas' notion of pollution, they were literally called 'waste people'. Their lack of stability and their constant change of location became their own form of spatial culture, a way of occupying and transforming space through informal material tactics and illegal squatting. We can see them in action in Harper Lee's classic novel *To Kill a Mockingbird* (1960), where the Ewell family represents the opposite of the main character, Atticus Finch, a dignified and deeply moral Southern gentleman. The divergence between these two moral poles, which is essential to the racial discourse of the novel, is not only confirmed by the Ewells' behaviour – their cowardice, immorality and idleness – but also by the architecture of the disheveled cabin where they live. Lee describes the house with precision and disgust, as a shack resourcefully built with the remainder of other construction projects: 'the plank walls were supplemented with sheets of corrugated iron, its roof shingled with tin cans hammered flat, so only its general shape suggested its original design.' Architectural elements like the windows, are cunningly reduced to almost nothing, 'merely open spaces in the walls, which in the summertime were covered with greasy strips of cheesecloth to keep out the varmints.' The improvised construction of the backyard enclosure is described sarcastically: 'what passed for a fence was bits of tree-limbs, broomsticks and tool shafts, all tipped with rusty hammer-heads, snaggle-toothed rake heads, shovels, axes and grubbing hoes, held on with pieces of barbed wire.' The dirty yard contains the 'fruits of their industry' in their harvesting of the city dump, a collection of assorted abandoned objects: 'a discarded dentist's chair, an ancient icebox, plus lesser items: old shoes, worn-out table radios, picture frames, and fruit jars, under which scrawny orange chickens pecked hopefully.' (Lee, 1960)

In these brief passages Harper Lee outlines two of the typical aspects of the informal spatial techniques employed by the American rural poor. In the first place, she clarifies that the tactics used by the Ewells to build their house, collect materials and gather them in their yard mark them as social pariahs. It is their specific form of architectural informality that signals the ethos of those who live in dissent, beyond the law, as excluded elements of society. In the second place, the very nature of these tactics – collecting and reusing existing objects, finding imaginative ways of living with the bare minimum – gives the Ewells' action a minimum impact, it makes them environmentally friendly without a conscience beyond their pragmatism. Lee's emphasis underscores the neglect of the Ewells' house, which she portrays as 'the playhouse of an insane child', but the building itself is far from abandoned. In reality, both the house and the yard are unfinished assemblages in a state of continuous reorganization by their users. One of the main objectives towards sustainable development according to the UN Guidelines for Sustainable Consumption and Production (United Nations Development Programme, 2010), is 'doing more with less' and, 'reducing the use of resources.' The improvised ugliness of self-built shacks or trailers, which the Ewells' house exemplifies so well, is the result of building practices that do a lot with very little, and that the American rural poor put into practice – unlike those studied, for instance, by John Turner in Lima – in the midst of a wealthy, consumption-based society.

It is important to acknowledge – especially for those less familiar with the intricacies of racial politics in the USA – that Lee's fictional portrayal as well as Isenberg's historical account refer specifically to the white rural poor; the American white trash who historically have been perceived – and probably still are – as 'squatters, vagrants, and informal occupants of the land' (Isenberg, 2016). A social group characterized not only by the hardship in which they live, their dangerous behaviour or their frontal rejection of respected cultural practices, but also, and importantly, by their unstable and chaotic ways of inhabiting and transforming the built environment.

African American vernacular as informal architecture

However different and conflicting their common history, another group that exercises informal practices similarly to the white rural poor are African Americans. There is a very detailed historical account of informal construction and gardening by black communities in rural areas across the Southern region of the USA. Richard Wesmacott, (1992) has analyzed how domestic gardens became not only an essential source of food production for black families during the first decades following emancipation after the Civil War, but also places of social interaction and ornamental display. Yards were more than the outdoor extension of the bare interiors of self-built shacks and cabins where cooking, washing and other everyday activities took place. They also functioned as the open frame for informal aesthetic settings (Bakare, 2020; Sills, 2010), in which found objects – much like in Harper Lee's description of the Ewells cabin – combined with sticks, tree branches or leaves, took unexpected functions like edging elements or even as part of a larger masonry wall. Used items like car tires, pots, bricks, glasses, bottles, plastic buckets, egg cases and other things, which in most households are discarded, became valuable building materials. Historian and curator Paul Arnett (2000) claims that the best way of understanding the nature of these compositions of used objects in gardens and backyards is to consider them as a form of African American vernacular. Although these works have been studied and labeled by Arnett and others as artistic practices, they doubtlessly can also be seen as informal domestic architecture (see Figure 4.4).

Dinah Young (Arnett & Arnett, 2000, 2001), an elderly African American woman living in a small town in Hale County, Alabama, is known for transforming the yard around her small house through spatial actions like marking the ground, completing existing structures or building new structures around trees, using recovered material like tarp, plastic bottles, tree branches or stones. Although these are small, simple actions, the sheer accumulation of them completely transforms her backyard and porch, so 'every tree, bin, shed and post had things leaning against it' (Arnett & Arnett, 2001). When interviewed, Young always gives pragmatic reasons to do it – arranging piles of wood, trash or junk so they are available to burn them later, putting up a tarp so she is protected from the sun, covering the windows and doors with wooden sticks 'to keep the cold wind out' (Arnett & Arnett, 2001, pp. 347–350) – while firmly denying any artistic intent behind her work.

The yard work that Southern black Americans like Dinah Young have been practicing for more than a century expands and complicates our understanding of what informal architecture can be. The undifferentiated mixture of natural elements and reclaimed industrial objects that she uses, and the natural merging of centuries-long

Figure 4.4 David Washington's Yard, New Orleans, Louisiana, 1995. Photographer: Vaughn Sills.

Source: Vaughn Sills.

aesthetic traditions with present-day recycling, demonstrates that the relationship between contemporary environmentalism and vernacular culture should be part of the debate on informality and architecture (see Figure 4.5).

Conclusions – informality, sustainability and dissent

The intimate interaction between vernacular depth, contemporary materiality and natural landscapes that we see in the small domestic arrangements in rural black America, resonates with recent and highly influential calls for a new culture of sustainability in architecture. In his proposal for a new ecological urbanism, Mohsen Mostafavi (2010), echoes Felix Guattari's *Three Ecologies* (2000) – mental, social and environmental – to define a new ethico-aesthetic dimension for the design of the built environment. Mostafavi (2010, p. 48) recognizes that 'Guattari's conception of an ethics of the ecological is an inherently political project with a commitment to countering the global dominance of capitalism.' As with many contemporary thinkers, he seems merely to contemplate how such a new ethical projection of architecture and the environment materializes in cities and on a global scale. However, other models of ethical counteraction to capitalism that intentionally separate themselves from the urban have recently emerged. Shannon Hayes' defense of the figure of the *radical homemaker*

Figure 4.5 Structure beside Dinah Young's house. Photographer: William Arnett.

Source: Souls Grown Deep.

(2010), who reclaims domesticity from consumer culture, is one of them. According to Hayes, radical homemakers – very much like Dinah Young or even the Ewells – leverage the potential of rural environments to facilitate new forms of self-sufficient domesticity. To do so, similarly to how the American rural poor have done for generations, they use specific skills like food gardening, canning or self-construction, to be less dependent on a dominant system fueled by the exorbitant use of resources and household overconsumption. From this point of view, rural America's informality is not only a mere set of survival tactics within a context defined by scarcity. It is the pioneering expression of a new culture of socio-environmental dissent that – following Hayes' radical homemaking (2010, p. 9) – rejects the dominant logic of global extractive economies, turning families and individuals into units of production instead of units of consumption. It is precisely from this perspective – in which rural informal architecture responds to questions of both environmental and class politics – that I would like to formulate the final thoughts or conclusions to this chapter.

Since John Turner pioneered its study, the dilemma that has constantly framed the contested territory of informality in architecture is the one outlined by the opposition between formal planning and informal housing. As I have argued, this opposition ends up in a deadlock, since seeing informality as a real alternative to planning, as Turner does, usually entails the romanticization of its social context. The first conclusion of this chapter's argument is that a more constructive framework could be, instead, defined by the opposition between rural informality and urban (and suburban) overconsumption. In that way, informality and, more broadly, self-sufficiency emerge as qualities that can transform mainstream non-sustainable lifestyles, while helping us retrieve at least some parts of the domestic sphere from commodification, and back into the circuit of everyday life (Lefebvre, 2003; Madden & Marcuse, 2016). While the politics of sustainability applied to architecture tend understandably to focus on global scale problems like energy consumption, efficiency or CO_2 emissions, the contribution of architectural informality to this debate can however operate on the much smaller scale of the domestic.

Certain practices of rural self-sufficiency, like the ones I have explored during this chapter, challenge the ways in which contemporary culture has shaped mainstream domesticity, opening a path for its re-politicization and subsequent transformation. These practices are not just a straightforward approach to do-more-with-less. They also constitute a way to indirectly express dissent against dominant trends in the domestic sphere, such as household overconsumption or the digitalization of relationships and culture. As I have illustrated throughout the chapter, such dissent appears in distinct ways. On one hand by providing what we may call patterns of spatial behaviour – as we saw in the domestic architecture created by the Ewells – specific ways of using and transforming space through self-sufficiency that are common for the rural poor, and that are being reproduced by new radical homemakers. On the other hand, and I know this might be a riskier conclusion, through a specific material and formal language that seems to naturally emerge when these patterns of spatial behaviour are put into practice. A language based on the radical acceptance of impurity and improper mixtures: the trashy combination of recycled materials and the chaotic blending of improvised forms, as we saw in Dinah Young's vernacular yard work. Ultimately, this might be the main conclusion to this chapter. The notion that, instead of being founded on a renovated technical paradigm built around energy, a radical approach to sustainable architecture could instead be grounded on improvised forms, recycled materials, and self-sufficiency. To develop the ethics of such an approach we may need to question consumerism as a whole, and look at the typology of the rural, informal, pragmatic shed, defined by scarcity and resourcefulness, as a real alternative.

References

Arnett, W., & Arnett, P. (2000). *Souls Grown Deep, Vol. 1: African American Vernacular Art of the South: The Tree Gave the Dove a Leaf.* Atlanta: Tinwood Books.

Arnett, W., & Arnett, P. (2001). *Souls Grown Deep, Vol. 2: African American Vernacular Art of the South: Once that River Starts to Flow.* Atlanta: Tinwood Books.

Bakare, L. (February 2020). Hanging trees and hollering ghosts: the unsettling art of the American deep south. *The Guardian.* Retrieved from www.theguardian.com

Better Homes and Gardens (1961). *Better Homes and Gardens Decorating Book.* Des Moines, Iowa: Meredith Publishing Company.

Bower, R. (2016). Who Decides and Who Provides? The Anarchistic Housing Practices of John Turner as Realizations of Henri Lefebvre's Autogestive Space. *Alternatives: Global, Local, Political 2016, Vol.* 41 (2), 83–97. https://doi.org/10.1177/0304375416684856

Brillembourg, A., & Klumpner, H. (2005). Towards an Informal City. In A. Brillembourg, K. Feireiss, & H. Klumpner (Eds.), *Informal City: The Caracas Case.* Munich: Prestel.

Brenner, N. (2015). Is Tactical Urbanism an Alternative to Neoliberal Urbanism?. In N. Brenner (Ed.), *Critique of Urbanization.* Basel: Bauwelt Fundamente Series.

Burgess, R. (1982). Self-Help Housing Advocacy: A Curious Form of Radicalism: A Critique of the Work of John F.C. Turner. In P. W. Ward (Ed.), *Self Help Housing: A Critique.* Oxford: Alexandrine Press.

Crawford, M. (2008). Introduction. In J. L. Chase, M. Crawford & J. Kalinski (Eds.), *Everyday Urbanism. Second Edition*. New York: The Monacelli Press.
Castells, M., & Portes, A. (1989). World Underneath: The Origins, Dynamics and Effects of the Informal Economy. In M. Castells, A. Portes & L. Benton (Eds.), *The Informal Economy: Studies in Advanced and Less Developed Countries*. Baltimore: John Hopkins University Press.
Castillo, G. (2015). Hippie Modernism: How Bay Area design radicals tried to save the planet. *Places Journal, October 2015*. https://doi.org/10.22269/151026
Cohen, L. (2004). A Consumers' Republic: The Politics of Mass Consumption in Postwar America. *Journal of Consumer Research* 31 (1), 236–239. doi:10.1086/383439
Cunningham, C. (1999). To Watch the Faces of the Poor: "Life" Magazine and the Mythology of Rural Poverty in the Great Depression. *Journal of Narrative Theory*, 29 (3), 278–302. Retrieved from www.jstor.org/stable/30225735
De Soto, H. (1989). *The Other Path: The Invisible Revolution in the Third World*. New York: Harper and Row.
Douglas, M. (1966). *Purity and Danger. An Analysis of the Concepts of Pollution and Taboo*. New York: Routledge.
Duncan, C. M. (2014). *Worlds apart: Poverty and politics in rural America*. New Haven: Yale University Press.
Durst, N., & Wegmann, J. (2017). Informal Housing in the United States. *International Journal of Urban and Regional Research Volume* 41 (2), 282–297. https://doi.org/10.1111/1468-2427.12444.
Forrest, R., & Williams, P. (1984). Commodification and Housing: Emerging Issues and Contradictions. *Environment and Planning A: Economy and Space*, 16 (9), 1163–80. https://doi.org/10.1068/a161163.
Frank, T. (1997). *The Conquest of Cool: Business Culture, Counterculture, and the Rise of Hip Consumerism*. Chicago: The University of Chicago Press.
Goldstein, C. (1998). *Do It Yourself: Home Improvement in 20th Century America*. Washington and New York: National Building Museum, Washington and Princeton Architectural Press.
Guattari, F. (2000). *The Three Ecologies*. New York: Continuum.
Harris, Richard. (2003). A Double Irony: The Originality and Influence of JOHN F.C. Turner. *Habitat International*, 27. 245–269. https://doi.org/10.1016/S0197-3975(02)00048-6.
Hayes, S. (2010). *Radical Homemakers: Reclaiming Domesticity from a Consumer Culture*. Richmondville, NY: Left to Write Press.
Isenberg, N. (2016). *White Trash. The 400-year untold history of class in America*. New York: Penguin.
Klein, N. (2014). *This Changes Everything: Capitalism vs. the Climate*. New York: Simon & Schuster.
Kirk, A. (2016). Alloyed: Countercultural Bricoleurs and the Design Science Revival. In D. Kaiser & W. P. McCray (Eds.), *Groovy Science: The Countercultural Embrace of Science and Technology over the Long 1970s* (pp. 305–336). Chicago: University of Chicago Press.
Koolhaas, R. et al. (2001). Lagos: Harvard Project on the City. In Koolhaas R. et al (Eds.), *Mutations* (pp. 651–720). Barcelona: ACTAR.
Lange, D. & Rochkind, M. (2015). *Dorothea Lange: 500 FSA Photographs*. CreateSpace.
Lee, H. (1960). *To Kill a Mockingbird*. New York: Hachette.
Lefebvre, H. (2003). The Urban Revolution. Minneapolis: University of Minnesota Press.
Madden, D. J., & Marcuse, P. (2016). *In defense of housing: The politics of crisis*. London: Verso.
Marcuse, P., & Achtenberg, E. (1986). Toward the Decommodification of Housing. In R. Bratt, C. Hartman, & A. Meyerson (Eds.), *Critical Perspectives on Housing* (pp. 474–83). Philadelphia: Temple University Press.
Meister, S. (2020). *Dorothea Lange: Words & Pictures*. New York: MOMA.
Mukhija, V. & Monkkonen, P. (2007). What's in a name? A critique of 'colonias' in the United States. International Journal of Urban and Regional Research 31.2, 475–88.

Mostafavi, M. (2016). Why Ecological Urbanism? Why Now?. In M. Mostafavi & G. Doherty (Eds.) *Ecological Urbanism. Revised Edition*. Zurich: Lars Muller.

Nelson, L., & Nelson, P. (2010). The Global Rural: Gentrification and Linked Migration in the Rural USA. *Progress in Human Geography* 35 (4), 441–459. https://doi.org/10.1177/0309132510380487

Patrick, E. (May 2017). Appalachia at Risk: Housing Crisis threatens Mountain Life. *Citizen Times*. Retrieved from www.citizen-times.com.

Pattillo, M. (2013). Housing: Commodity Versus Right. *Annual Review of Sociology. Vol.* 39, 509–531. https://doi.org/10.1146/annurev-soc-071312-145611

Richardson B. (January 31, 2019). America's Housing Affordability Crisis Only Getting Worse. *Forbes*. Retrieved from www.forbes.com.

Roy, A. (2004) Transnational Trespassings: The Geopolitics of Urban Informality. In A. Roy & N. AlSayyad (Eds.), *Urban Informality: Transnational Perspectives from the Middle East, Latin America and South Asia*. New York: Lexington.

Sadler S. (2008). An Architecture of the Whole. *Journal of Architectural Education*, 61 (4), 108–129. https://doi.org/10.1111/j.1531-314X.2008.00194.x

Sadler, S. (2012). The Dome and the Shack: The Dialectics of Hippie Enlightenment. In I. Boal, J. Stone, M. Watts, & C. Winslow (Eds.), *West of Eden: Communes and Utopia in Northern California*. Oakland: PM Press.

Sills, V. (2010). *Places for the Spirit. Traditional African American Gardens*. San Antonio, Texas: Trinity University Press.

Smith, C. (2014). Handymen, Hippies and Healing: Social Transformation through the DIY Movement (1940s to 1970s) in North America. *Architectural Histories*, 2 (1). http://doi.org/10.5334/ah.bd

Starr, J. (1941). *Fifty Things to Make for the Home*. New York: McGraw-Hill Book Company.

Turner, JFC. (August 1968). The Squatter Settlement: An Architecture that Works Architecture of Democracy, *Architectural Design*. Retrieved from: http://www.communityplanning.net

Turner, JFC. (1972). The Re-Education of a Professional. In JFC Turner & R. Fichter (Eds.), *Freedom to Build* (p. 123). New York: Macmillan Education.

United States Department of Agriculture. (2017). *American Community Survey*. Retrieved from https://www.ers.usda.gov/topics/rural-economy-population/rural-poverty-well-being

United Nations Development Programme. (2010). *United Nations Guidelines on Sustainable Consumption and Production*. Retrieved from www.un.org.

Van Ballegooijen, J, & Rocco, R. (2013). The Ideologies of Informality: Informal Urbanisation in the Architectural and Planning Discourses. *Third World Quarterly*, 34 (10), 1794–1810. doi: 10.1080/01436597.2013.851890

Ward, P. (1999). *Colonias and public policy in Texas and Mexico: Urbanization by stealth*. Austin, Texas: University of Texas Press.

Wesmacott, R. (1992). *African-American Gardens: Yards In Rural South*. Knoxville: University of Tennessee Press.

White, G. (January 20, 2015). Rural America's Silent Housing Crisis. *The Atlantic*. Retrieved from: www.theatlantic.com

World Bank. (2014). *Population living in slums (% of urban population)*. Retrieved from: https://data.worldbank.org/indicator/EN.POP.SLUM.UR.ZS

Chapter 5

The urbanism of individual arrangements

Understanding specific realities – the case of Tirana

Sotir Dhamo

Tracing the main characteristics of Tirana's ID: Blurring authority through cyclic waves of spontaneity

Tirana began at the beginning of the 17th century as an organic settlement (Frashëri, 2004, p. 17), at the intersection between the regional commerce routes, when this territory was under the domination of the Ottoman Empire. The genesis and the evolution of the first nuclei was nourished by a combination of factors, including topographic constraints, land divisions and other "*physical determinants*" such as preconditions of irregular city form (Kostov, 2003, pp. 53–59, 62); social practices rooted in the model of a patriarchal enlarged family; and a premeditated strategy based on the system of "*kulliye*" (Ingersoll & Kostov, 2013, p. 439) as a city foundational device and charitable institution embraced by Ottomans in the 14th century to promote "*Islam and the Ottoman way of life*". The next step in Tirana's process of urban generation relates to the process of "*synoecism*" (Kostov, 2003, pp. 59–62) as several of the urban nuclei merged into a bigger and more consolidated urban core around the central mosque and the Old Bazaar. The fluxes, generated in and around the regional intersection of the Old Bazaar, controlled the entire form of the settlement. Based on previous studies, I classify the generations and traces created under these conditions under Historic Organic Pattern #1 (see Figure 5.1).

At this point, some important persistent aspects that have influenced both the genesis and future growth became clear. These aspects include the main natural values and historic conditions that forged a local culture and anthropological substratum, which still prominently underlie the city shaping process; and most importantly, the modality of growth that combined spontaneous processes with a premeditated strategy through city foundational devices, acting as agents.

Tirana stayed as a small organic town until it was declared the capital of Albania in 1920. The first attempts to move from spontaneous to organised urban planning started at the beginning of the 1920s with the first ideas to map and regulate the city. Interventions became especially intense during the period of the monarchy, starting in 1925, with ideas for the Europeanisation of Tirana, which signaled the beginning of a new era that lasted up until the end of the Second World War. This includes King's Zog "*Grand Travaux*" for opening and broadening some of the main generative paths from organic Tirana, or for establishing the first designed ceremonial urban square, etc. From 1939 onwards, under the fascist occupation of Albania, this strategy continued with the monumental interventions of Italian Fascism and the import

Figure 5.1 Traces of Historic Organic Pattern: a visceral labyrinth.

Source: Sotir Dhamo.

of "*Stile Littorio*" as a monumentality separated from the social reality (Frampton, 2007, p. 215). These are the first layers of "disturbance" to the continuity of organic structures. The main representative element is the Grand Boulevard as a generator for a new restart of Tirana, imposing a new geometric order over the organic layers. This axial scheme can be seen as deriving from the topographic features, but is also a reflection of the political power that is manifest in this case through absolute celebrative characteristics triumphing over the organic city. At the end of this period, two Tirana(s) with legible architectonic and morphological features were created: one rooted in the organic paths of the city's origin, and the other one, recently started, rooted in the geometric axis of its re-foundation. A new urban scale, and most importantly a new typology of public space appeared in Tirana. The enmeshed islands routed in Ottoman culture and the dead end labyrinths with closed perspectives existed in contrast to the open and continuous perspectives of the avenues of the orthogonal grid. This can be seen also as a clash between Ottoman and Western civilisation, represented in the diametrically different ways of living and in the respective principles of generating space. However, despite serious attempts to dilute the Ottoman influence, this lay dormant in niches in the visceral parts of the city, persisting over five centuries. The ambition for the Europeanisation of Tirana in such a relatively short period remained incomplete. The real historic substrata of Tirana still remained in the original organic town, which was intimately embodied in its old neighbourhoods. Structures and traces formed under this attempt at geometrising constitute the base for Recording Over Pattern (#2).

A new era started when the communist government was installed after the end of the Second World War, lasting until the collapse of the dictatorship at the beginning of the 1990s. Architecture and urban planning embraced ideological principles to support the so-called revolution and social progress. During this phase Albania oscillated between two extremes: from being an integral part of the Eastern Bloc during the two first decades, to totally self-isolating at the end of this period (see Figure 5.2).

Figure 5.2 Authoritarian space: the main ceremonial urban square in Tirana.

Source: Sotir Dhamo.

Under the centralised economy significant changes happened to the city structure. What transformed Tirana for the most part were the so-called low-cost, 4 to 5 story, standardised, collective housing blocks, built in the centre and next to industrial zones on the periphery. In fact, the urban space created by such a-stylistic collective blocks, designed according to very strict and basic norms, induced desolation and the perception of being in a condition of emptiness. The asceticism and the isotropy of the urban environment, reflected the ideological aim to kill differences in a space where everybody was supposed to be equal, but in fact were equally poor. These blocks were supposed to birth a new model of life that was never born. On the contrary, the social experiment resulted in the creation of a ghost city, deprived of any personal identity. Consequently, everybody wanted to leave the condition of emptiness created by the so-called new city. The frames of the housing blocks were another important base for Recording Over Pattern (#2) that emerged or re-emerged especially after the 1990s.

Tirana was designed by demolition, and transformed internally by the forced insertion of standardised freestanding housing blocks, totally different typologies detached from any historic organic traces. Tirana was also transformed externally, because of new extensions to the periphery, mostly for industrial purposes, based on the political directives enacted by the Congresses of the Party.

A new era started after the collapse of the communist dictatorship, which is still underway. The vacuum that was left behind, both physically and psychologically, was the origin of the dramatic and uncontrolled political–economic–social collision that happened afterwards. In this new situation, the state was removed from the role of absolute control, including over territory. In less than three decades, Tirana has changed more than ever: the city changed in its internal structure, in its size and in its behaviour; in its typological structure and in its binary relationship with city shaping.

In this context the first informal suburbs emerged. The uncontrolled urbanisation in Tirana, as reactive revenge to something that was denied in the past, had two chief tendencies: infill densification in the centre, or infiltration of massive volumes (6 to 12 floors). This progressive process contributed to the loss of most of the open vacant spaces, or vacuums. Instead, in periphery a shapeless "vaporised city" emerged, that at first approach demonstrates characteristics of chaos and a lack of structure. It consolidated on former agricultural land, swallowing pre-existing villages, former state *kooperativas*, resulting in a bigger, unstable organism. The self-organised city found its own way without any disturbance or assistance from the government. This was a kind of return to the organic processes and spontaneous waves of the city's origin. The city was reborn again. Evidently, the "proletarian city", or the "city of social progress," did not fully succeed in sterilising the human and the physical energy. Life invaded the city again.

Analysis of satellite imagery conducted during 2001 by the team of Strategic Planning for Greater Tirana showed a massive population expansion in the Greater Tirana area: from an area of 12 km^2 prior to 1991, to 32 km^2 in 1994 and 56 km^2 in 2001, or almost a five-fold increase. Tirana, the biggest city in the country, experienced an annual population increase of almost 7% during the first ten years after the political changes. The first tentative plan to create a vision beyond the traditional borders, on the Greater Tirana scale, dates back to the early 2000s; however, a new plan for Tirana could only be officially approved in 2012, and was soon substituted with a new one in 2017. Neither plan represented a real qualitative shift in methodology or in what it proposed. On the contrary, while too much effort was spent on the redesign of the central areas and on city beautification, the periphery and the newly created suburbs were totally neglected.

Different labels are used to characterise the informal neighbourhoods around Tirana, such as "informal," "illegal," "without permission," "sprawl," "newcomers' city" etc. While sprawl is a term borrowed from other social contexts, the other terms, such as illegal or informal, carry a prejudicial connotation and are mostly related to legal status. This semantic misconception has hindered a deep understanding of the phenomena and the related urban impacts. For this reason, I use the term New Organic, in direct reference to the historic organic city. In the following paragraphs I try to give theoretical interpretations of the organic city, and explore how it can be understood under the complexity approach. Therefore, generations and traces formed under this condition are mainly analysed under the New Organic Pattern (#3) (see Figure 5.3).

At the conclusion of this section, it becomes clear that Tirana started as an organic city, and waves of spontaneity returned several times in the course of its history, including over the last twenty-five years. Meanwhile, there is a wide range of oscillations across which Tirana fluctuates: from the organic urban nucleus that emerged in the middle of agricultural lands to the urban abstract axis of the boulevard; from the system of *kulliye* disseminated through the Ottoman culture to the straight line open perspectives that pierced the city in the name of Europeanisation; from a solely

Figure 5.3 Waves of spontaneity: the city of small-scale individual arrangements.

Source: Sotir Dhamo.

spontaneous entity to a city that was also designed; from dictatorial interventions/foundations to spontaneously self-made incremental housing and neighbourhoods; from concentric rigid rings to the dissolved vaporised archipelago city; from big scale interventions to small scale pixelated infill(s); from single reality to multiple realities; from linear to complex; from foundation to re-foundation; from an extremely strict application of the rules to the total abolishment of the rules; from clear to both unclear and clear; from "Tirana" to spontaneous "Greater Tirana" and "Durana"; from small to big.

This spontaneity that inherently characterises Tirana, which among other things reflects concerns at the individual level, is related to the interpretations of the *organic city* explained in the following section.

Reframing the taboo of informality – organic, fractal and complex as alternative ways to understand informality – the order beneath

Following the brief description of the main historic events and their reflection in the fluctuation of the urban fabric, it becomes clear that the specific relationship that Tirana has had with spontaneous actions has emerged from the bottom up, at the individual or group level. At this point it is important to give some theoretical background to the concept of organic. First, it is important to better understand the human processes that drive the organic. Second, I will present a more scientific explanation of the organic as a complex of self-organised individual relationships arranged on the smaller scale, and emerging from the bottom up. I will argue also that concepts like planned–unplanned or regular–irregular are reductive, and belong to the old mechanical paradigm. This path of reasoning highlights the fact that we cannot fully understand these processes unless we change the theoretical lenses related to the way in which we observe and analyse the phenomena.

Organic characteristics

First, I present some characteristics of the organic cities. As Kostov argues, the simple formulas about "*planned*" and "*unplanned*" cannot satisfy a complexity of factors concerning the fluctuation of the urban form (2003, p. 51). While the first is mostly characterised by a centrally planned geometrically ordered scheme, "*set down at one moment*" and decided by a controlling authority; the second, often called spontaneous, is "*chance-grown,*" "*generated*" or "*geomorphic.*" Its form is *irregular* and "*organic*" with a random distribution of open spaces and path intersections. This form results from activities in the daily life of citizens, acting within the framework of pre-existing physical determinants, or other prior geometries and social arrangements. It is the passage of time that gives way to an "*unplanned evolution*" or "*instinctive growth*" (2003, pp. 43–44).

It is important to also say that in the "*continuous effort for adjustment*" there is no permanent dichotomy between regular and irregular. They often exist side by side. Because of that, "*the reworking of prior geometries over time leaves urban palimpsests ...*" (Kostov, 2003, p. 47).

From this point of view, there is a continuously mutable/flexible interactive process between regular and irregular, or planned and organic in Tirana. This is typical in most of the residential blocks built during the dictatorship, especially in cases where a geometric grid was imposed over the organic one. For example, the organic labyrinth of cul-de-sacs and narrow winding streets, although damaged, persisted after the imposition of the regular frameworks for the standard residential blocks. After almost three decades, the hidden layers that were considered eradicated spontaneously re-emerged. Currently these blocks are internally and externally worn and corroded (see Figure 5.4), particularly along the main formative lines. However, similar processes also happened in Tirana in the cases where the housing blocks were built ex-novo as a geometrically regulated form. This kind of reemergence that is happening in many neighbourhoods of Tirana as a recording-over or fill-in geometry (described in the previous chapter) has a lot to do with what Kostov calls "*steps in the process of deregulation*" (2003, p. 48).

At this point it is important to highlight that there are two main organic patterns in Tirana: organic as a foundation device, represented in the Historic Organic Pattern (#1), and organic as a Recording Over or Fill-In device (#2). Despite the fact that the essential qualities of spaces in both cases are different, the formative logic is similar: in both cases, it is a self-organised spontaneous action, based on individual arrangements and social consent, without any help from a central controller, and informal from the legal point of view.

Figure 5.4 Organic as a Recording Over process of the 4–5 story, standardised collective housing blocks.

Source: Sotir Dhamo.

Organic as fractal

Batty and Longley in Fractal City (1994) speak about the "*organic city*" (1994, p. 31) and *"the city of pure geometry*". As these authors state, they follow the spirit of Kostov by putting more emphasis on the way that cities grow and coordinate on the smaller scale. Right from the beginning, they clarify that with the irregular form of the city, they *"... do not mean that it is disordered or chaotic, but that it is not smooth ..."* in the Euclidian sense (1994, p. 3). Most importantly, these authors try to *'avoid any association between "organic" cities and the notions of uncoordinated ... growth'*. On the contrary, they are the "*product of many detailed and individual decisions which have been coordinated in the small*" (1994, p. 28), adapting to individual or social preferences, economic, technological and natural constraints.

In fact, fractal cities try to overcome the concept of disordered cities: this type of form reveals a degree of order which is deeper than the order associated with the city of pure geometry. Planned and unplanned are just superficial perceptions of the urban form, and are more of a hindering factor. Related to this, as Batty and Longley argue, the main idea of fractal cities is to identify "*systems in which elements are repeated in a similar fashion from scale to scale. If this similarity is strong in a geometric sense, then it is referred to as self-similarity or in its weaker form as self-affinity*" (Batty & Longley, 1994, p. 47). Therefore, "*the visual quality of such organic development ... is in terms of its informality, its idiosyncrasies and its picturesque properties and occasionally in its exploitation of the dramatic natural features, but never in terms of the power of its geometry*" (1994, p. 35). According to these authors, cities in general display a mixture of both organic and pure geometry.

Another aspect presented by Batty and Longley is that the concept of organic is dependent upon history and culture. According to them, countries where "*social and economic norms are closer to those of the past ... still generate cities which are organic ...*" (Batty & Longley, 1994, p. 32). Albania has its own characteristics related to this. Because Albania did not go through the industrialisation process at the same pace as most the European countries, cities were characterised by very slow organic growth and an extensive structure up until the end of the Second World War, which is reflected in these cities even now.

Organic as complex

What has been described so far about the organic as coordinated or self-organised from the bottom up, leads us to see this phenomenon also through the logic of complexity theory. As Mitchell says, self-organised behaviour, called emergent, is produced by simple rules that generate a "collective whole." This behaviour has its base in the individual behaviour (rooted in social and cultural principles), and networks of individuals interacting based on "*signaling and information processing*" (2009, pp. 4, 12–13). Portugali argues that cities are self-organised systems and that self-organisation is the principal property of complex systems (2000, p. 2). In the "paradigm of pattern formation" and "paradigm of pattern recognition," Portugali, (2000, pp. 57–58) explains the common path in self-organisation, describing how the smaller parts of the system interact and produce structure and pattern at macroscopic level through "control parameters", "order parameters", that "enslaving" the behaviour, strengthens and reproduces the "order parameters", entering thus into a "circularly casual fashion". This has also been explained by Kelso, Stolk & Portugali (2016, pp. 44–46) in "Synergetics" and "Inter-representation Networks". This theory, diametrically different from the theory and practice of rationale planning (Portugali, 2000, p. 230), provides a strong interpretative and methodological framework that raises doubts about urban and regional planning.

Based on the concepts above, to better understand how dynamics are set in motion in bottom-up self-organised neighbourhoods (individuals/groups), and how new structure and pattern owning site-specific essential qualities emerges from interaction, I introduced the notions of human motive and behaviour. Therefore, the challenge is to identify how in a site-specific place the arousal effect that originated from a human motive, triggers a specific individual behaviour, translates this into collective intelligence (social normative), interacts and creates the essential quality of patterns. The new emergent reality results from the arousal effect created by internal/external relationships, within a large number of individuals aiming to solve housing problems outside of central control.

How reality works? The city of individual arrangements – conceptual gaps

From the historic overview of Tirana and from the theoretical concepts above, it becomes clear that the organic phenomena in Tirana played the role of an opposing force to the city that was largely planned. Not only were organic processes important initially as foundation devices, but they also played a primary role in the extension of informal peripheries, and/or as a device that blurred or carved the rigid blocks built during the dictatorship. However, there is a continuous and arrogant persistence on the part of the authorities to further reinforce the centralisation of the planning system. There is enough evidence in Tirana showing that any period characterised by an attempt to exert extreme central control over the territory is followed by another period characterised by a larger wave of spontaneity at all levels of the city hierarchy. The top-down order imposed over the organic city (often only as formal geometry) is not only incapable of solving its problems, but is shown to be a temporary form of sterilisation that cannot erase the myriad activities of everyday life and interrelationships, because it represents a superficial reaction to the urban form. In fact, life grows and invades again with similar energy, because the organic/spontaneous remains responsive and flexible to adapt. The so-called irregularity, understood in Euclidean terms, is a rejection of thinking in a complex way.

As such, Tirana "restarted" several times, by the authorities pretending to re-initiate the city, and by ordinary people that *de facto* set their own rules. Tirana lives in a specific urban condition where there are no clear limits between that which is planned and unplanned, designed or un-designed, and where the geometrically designed city is "by default" organically deregulated by continuous erosion through filling-in or parasiting of the urban spaces. The ideas coming from architects and planners are reworked by the spontaneous "imagination" of ordinary citizens who played a role in shaping Tirana as a physical and ideal structure. Elements such as commercial activities, housing, etc., interlock in an intricate and complex space where "friendly" occupiers of public spaces (starting as temporary structures) create a succession of spontaneously transformable and planned spaces. This lends Tirana the aspect of being unfinished, being ready for a new equilibrium and the next signal of change. However, the reworking of city morphology on different scales went through tensions and incurred social costs, making Tirana a city "moving" between dreams and a reality that is difficult to manage.

Because of this, in Albania, and in Tirana especially, there is no trust in the centrally formulated regulatory instruments that they will solve the real problems. The abolishing of plans after the change in political mandates clearly demonstrated a non-functional planning system and discredited this instrument. The two last regulatory plans for Tirana, approved in 2012 and in 2017, both formulated with international assistance and the participation of star architects through a typical top-down process, are only the latest evidence of this ill-planning system and the use of this instrument for manipulation. A blurred condition created by the interaction between spontaneous developments and planning decisions is typical on different scales, from a single building to the entire city.

This is reflected also in the difficulty in classifying some fundamental categories, such as public–private, designed–non designed (even in the legal sense) or different functional use relationships, etc. These categories simultaneously contain different in-between states that, depending on the specific circumstances, may leap to another intermediate state in-between these categories. For example, two neighbours initially test through perception whether it is permissible to approach (step by step) one or another intermediate states between two extreme categories (example: control over semi-private states between public–private). This indeterminacy is related to a mentality that consciously generates unclearness and blurred situations in order to give parties the full potential to explore the intermediate statuses in-between public-private categories, through actions that vary between invasion-mediation, interference-combination, interlocking-adhesion, etc. These characteristics make the legibility of Tirana's urban condition a very challenging exercise. In fact, as Arida argues, speaking about exclusivist and inclusive approaches, in open systems the extreme categories, more than opposing notions ("*either/or*") constitute complementarities ("*both/and*") or transitional (*indeterminate*) conditions of elements ("*propensity*") (2002, pp. 142–145, 150).

Conceptual gaps – interrelationships as the basis for a more holistic understanding of new emergent realities

In a city like Tirana, where the organic origin of the city is still legible, where planning instruments were used or misused mainly for political capital or as ideological instruments (by the monarchy, fascism, communism and post-communism); where planning was almost totally abolished after the collapse of the dictatorship and the city went spontaneously through a rapid process of urbanisation, where people implicitly know that planning serves only as an alibi to support land speculation, alternative methods that are sensitive to place, people and processes need to be explored.

The spontaneous "instinct" of city making should be turned into a conscious process. To reach this objective we need to bridge the discrepancy between the so-called atypical urbanism of Tirana and the order understood in a simplistic, mechanical logic. For this we need additional theoretical lenses that help to obtain a more holistic view of reality. We need to understand the conceptual leap from the mechanical view of reality as a perfect machine where the whole is the sum of its parts, to the inter-relational holistic quantum view of reality, and its other components such as fractal, chaos and complexity theories. According to the "quantum worldview" (Arida, 2002, p. 68), reality is a container of interactions where "things" enter into correlations in a larger whole; it is an infinity of potentialities full with tendencies to exist, or tendencies to occur, and it becomes meaningful only if we observe it. For this reason, in the following paragraphs I give three interpretations of wholeness and the way in which I use this in the urban realm, as emerging from relationships, under the quantum, fractal and complexity approaches.

Wholeness as unbroken web of relationships

As Zohar and Marshal say, wholeness is an "unbroken web of overlapping … internal relationships" (1994, p. 62) created by the wave aspects which give rise to new systems with a "new corporate identity." This is because the "particle aspects tend to stay … separate"; instead their associated "… wave aspects merge" and overlap giving rise to a new "emergent reality", which is not the sum of parts (Zohar & Marshall, 1994, p. 54). This web or relationship created by the overlapping wave effect is what Arida calls "society-space-time (SST) continuum … as an energy field of potential events" (Arida, 2002, p. 157).

Wholeness as a system-structure

According to the "fractal city" approach, wholeness is seen as relationships or dynamics in the system-structure made of interacting forces that give rise to self-similar/affine recursive behaviour by elements assembled in hierarchies that create the invisible structure of form that underlies the external form. At the base of this behaviour remains the repetitive nature of irregularities across scales. However irregular a form may seem, if we look at its internal as something resulting from a relationship, a common pattern of irregularity may be discovered (Batty & Longley, 1994, pp. 43–44, 47, 58–59).

Wholeness as a self-organised macroscopic behaviour

According to the complexity approach, wholeness is seen as relationships within a bottom-up self-organised "collective whole," or macroscopic behaviour, which arouses through the interaction between large numbers of entities that tend to self-regulate, interacting through signaling, information processing (Mitchell, 2009, pp. 4, 12–13). How the smaller parts of the system or individuals interact and produce structure and pattern at macroscopic level is already explained.

Historic organic pattern in Tirana as a wholeness

In the following paragraphs, I apply these concepts for a more holistic understanding of one of Tirana's patterns by bringing some subtle interactions into the sphere of the conscious. Community ties and behavioural principles remain the basis of interrelationships that create the unbroken web of the energy field (the overlapping of the wave factor) that connects the past, the present and the future. These ties and principles motivate the interaction of specific human behaviours through which a common sense emerges at the group or social level, which in itself is "imposed" as a collective intelligence from the top of the system downwards, or "order parameter" (Portugali, 2000, pp. 57–58). This energy field processes the information that moves single entities toward self-organisation, giving birth to emerging new realities within the macro-system.

For example, in the case of Historic Organic Pattern (#1) in Tirana, analyses show how the Visceral Quality of space is created. With the word 'visceral' I intend an interiorised neighbourhood (cluster or house) through an inward aggregation process aiming to hide in itself through refraction that isolates and wraps inwardly and outwardly. This is preconditioned by a motive forged in history, such as the right to visual privacy, acting as the associated wave factor triggered by the original event: a tradition based on religious practices. This motive acts as a "control parameter" at the bottom of the system enacting an introvert behaviour and interaction between individual parts. The introvert behaviour is an individual interfering pattern, aroused and detectable in the local–temporal reality at the level of individual arrangements, acting as the dynamics of the system-form. Because of information exchange at the individual/group level, this behavioural pattern concretises in recursive refraction of the straight line during the settling process. This is a social pattern (collective intelligence), imposing a common sense from the top of the system downwards, and translating the aimed for essential quality of space in a social normative fashion. The modality of refraction (to guarantee the right to visual privacy) is a recursive action that applies on the straight line to replace it and scale it down. This is also considered an "order parameter" created at the macroscopic level of the system that "enslaves the behaviour" of individual parts. In doing so, they reinforce and reproduce the order parameter by entering in a "circulary casual" process (Kelso, Stolk, Portugali, 2016, pp. 44–46). These constitute the internal system of interrelationships that define the specific quality of space. Human interactions play an important role in shaping/arousing the new emergent realities, which are more than spatial systems. This logic helps to go beyond the concept of territoriality understood only in physical terms.

Conclusions

Is planning a human trap? Rejection of plans

The situation in Tirana is evidence that we cannot correct the naturalness of the city through restrictive legislation. This approach is a reminder of old paradigms and authoritarian systems. It tends to be a temporary precarious equilibrium, which inevitably drives the system from extreme rigidity to total freedom, or a near entropic situation. The waves of spontaneity that cyclically returned in Tirana, demonstrate also the failure of conventional planning to create correspondence with the patterning model of society.

This supports the idea that specific realities cannot be corrected by closing systems and cutting the energy exchange with the environment through planning instruments. On the contrary, first we need to understand those realities through observation and analytical methodologies in order to allow the communication channels within the socio-cultural environment, or as we called it, within the "unbroken web" (Zohar & Marshall, 1994, p. 62), or within "society-space-time (SST) continuum" (Arida, 2002, p. 157). Then we can include these inputs in the way that we design and transform the city.

The real city challenges traditional planning practice because it does not fit within the idea of a strictly controllable model. At this point, we may question the predictability of the city through plans. In this regard, the condition created by the continuous interaction between spontaneous developments and planning decisions may be considered the basis for a new methodology where prediction in the "classic" sense is neither the only, nor the most important element. As (Batty, 2018) says in "Inventing Future Cities", predictability is something related to the closure of the system. As I explained throughout this paper, cities are complex organisms and as such, it is impossible to conform to any grand plan that is considered to be the closure of the system. We cannot reverse the tendency of cities to develop in a certain way, just for the sake of our outdated mindsets. In this regard, the paradigms under which the city is observed, and our ability to include without prejudices the entire urban phenomena, becomes important. People can be part of the design not only through direct participation, typical for the 1970s and 1980s (which arrived in Albania after the 1990s), but also through "catching" the intrinsic logic in the patterning process and embodying it in a potential emerging reality. This can be achieved through modelling processes where the computational nature of urban phenomena go along with the historic anthropological background.

The paper tries to illustrate with a concrete case this conceptual shift, which requires the enlargement of the observable base, and more sensitivity to interpret the latencies of a multiple reality. It brings visible occurrences into a conscious sphere, whether they are excluded or not, and most importantly, it helps to overcome mechanical concepts related to territoriality as something strictly physical and predictable. At the same time, enlarging the base of conscious information inspires us to go through courageous experimentations towards the emergence of urban realities/forms that fit within the anthropological model of society. We can try to express those qualities in a model that reflects the understanding of the specific urban phenomena.

References

Arida, A. (2002) *Quantum City*, Publisher: Routledge, Architectural Press.

Batty, M., & Longley, P. (1994) *Fractal City, a geometry of form and function*, Academic Press, San Diego, CA and London.

Batty, M. (2018) *Inventing Future Cities*, The MIT Press.

Frampton, K. (2007) *Modern Architecture, a Critical History*, fourth edition, Thames & Hudson world of art.

Frashëri, K. (2004) *Historia e Tiranës, Historia e Tiranës si qytet deri më 1920*, vëll.1, Botimet Toena.

Ingersoll, R., & Kostov, S. (2013) *World Architecture: A Cross-Cultural History*, Oxford University Press, New York, Oxford.

Kelso, J.A.S., Stolk, E., & Portugali, J. (2016) Self-organization and Design as a Complementary Pair, Chapter 3, In book: *Complexity, Cognition, Urban Planning and Design*, Springer Proceedings in Complexity.

Kostov, S. (2003) The City Shaped – Urban Patterns and Meanings Through History (Fourth edition), Bulfinch Press AOL Time Warner Book Group, Boston, New York, London.

Mitchell, M. (2009) *Complexity a Guided Tour*, Oxford University Press.

Portugali, J. (2000) *Self-Organization and the City*, Springer.

Zohar, D., & Marshall, I. (1994) *Quantum Society, Mind, Physics, and a New Social Vision*, Quill William Morrow, New York.

Chapter 6

Informality and temporary appropriation in Atlanta as a prototype for resilient communities

William Carpenter

The Peccioli Charter proposes a bold global vision for the country of Italy as a "Nation of Resilient Communities" and it also creates a global network of practitioners and scholars of design centered in Peccioli on urban innovation. The new technical tools, such as digital fabrication and visualisation, allows us to examine the environmental crisis in new ways. The charter for the new Italian Resilient Communities movement states: "we believe that sustainable development is not an obsolete option or concept, but a collective commitment that must be based on solid pillars of a new development paradigm that defines a new alliance between space and society, between individuals and community."

To highlight four of the main points of the Peccioli Charter, we can further understand how temporary appropriation and design-build practices align and exponentially expand how to examine and implement these principles.

Promote innovation
Innovation becomes an important catalyst in this thinking: Resilient Communities want to promote innovation, always and everywhere, sharing their experiences, their actions of resistance, their resilience practices, learning from each other and presenting themselves as new knowledge platforms.

Reimagine cities and life spaces
In the Resilient Communities each actor must promote a radical rethinking of the urban fabric, starting from the suburbs, and its environment to transform cities into virtuous non-erosive and dissipative systems that react actively to climate, economic, social and cultural changes, generating mitigations.

Be sensitive and effective
The capacity for reaction and transformation of the urban fabric must characterize the Resilient Communities of the future, through timely actions that pass from the late reaction to effective prevention.

Be polycentric
The Resilient Communities will facilitate relations between settlement systems based on territorial identity, specialization and the distribution of urban-rural functions in a polycentric and reticular perspective.

Temporary appropriation and informality: A prototype

Introduction

The organic growth of informal systems in cities creates a densification of interstitial suburban spaces. This is an in-between condition of natural boundaries and urban density. It is this gray space between figure and ground, and this allows for areas of the city worthy of temporary appropriations. This gray zone is a healing condition of resiliency. For the Peccioli Charter we emphasize innovation, sensitivity and a polycentric approach. The following prototypes show partnerships the author has been involved in leading which form a prototype that is transferable to other sites; each example helps to solve a specific urban issue or set of issues.

With the advent of Covid-19 and the worldwide protests regarding racism, we see a watershed change regarding temporary appropriation of urban space. For example, social distancing alone redefines and reframes our experience of each other and of the city.

Selected prototypes

As an architecture professor in Atlanta for the past 28 years, I have witnessed profound change in the city. After the 1996 Olympics, the city nearly doubled in size to over 6 million people. The need for urban housing became foregrounded and over 100,000 units have been built in the past 10 years. The following projects are a glimpse into some of the prototypes regarding temporary appropriation and design build approaches in the city. If we examine the urban plan of Atlanta, you will see three main grids which collide along a topographical ridge (Peachtree Street) which is a strong organizing device and a historical Indian trail.

Cutting through the historic urban grids is the interstate connector which plows through the historic districts like a gouge and cuts off the Auburn Avenue district from the downtown, effectively damaging it for the past 50 years. The decision was intentional by the former state governor and certainly racially motivated.

Rem Koolhaas writes about Atlanta and informality:

> "Less a city and more a landscape, Atlanta is a delicate and sparse carpeting of dwellings and supreme composition of small fields. In this photo essay, this non-city is examined through an incisive and questioning lens that focuses on the city's most important contextual references; vegetation and infrastructure. A new aesthetic operates in Atlanta: the random juxtaposition of entities that have nothing in common except their coexistence? **Atlanta** is a creative experiment, but it is not intellectual or critical: it has taken place without argument. It represents current conditions—without any imposition of program, manifesto, ideology."
>
> (Koolhaas and Mau, 1997)

He goes on to describe Atlanta as a "convulsive architecture that will eventually acquire beauty, instead of a navigable street grid, a sensible zoning code or a dominant housing type, it is green space, both public and private, that weave together our disparate neighborhoods and commercial monuments into something approaching a cohesive whole" (Koolhaas and Prat, 1999).

The following projects are interventions into the urban context which help reveal cultural and societal needs and allow for students and faculty to investigate learning objectives and outcomes which are complex, multilayered and constantly evolving. The faculty member faced many obstacles in helping get these projects realized. The influence of several visits by Rem Koolhaas and Samuel Mockbee became formative in the direction and pedagogy for these projects.

Mad housers

The first example in Atlanta is a collaboration project between the homeless advocacy group "The Mad Housers" and my students at Kennesaw State University. This group is mainly composed of military veterans who build their own shelters from recycled materials and create encampments on illegally used land. Even though the land is considered there are certain political structures that allow the city to "look the other way." For example, one resident has attached his dwelling to a railroad bridge which is evocative of the Lebbeus Woods high houses in London. This leads to a stealth-like existence creating a guerilla camouflage that allows for a symbiotic relationship use of shelter and infrastructure. It is an understanding of sympathy and a verve for survival (Carpenter, 1997) (Carpenter, 2009) (Madhousers.org).

Normally these units are 4 feet wide by 8 feet deep and about 10 feet high. The materials palette is usually recycled wood from demolished buildings or donated sources. They are usually timber frame and they contain a heat source wood stove which is also a cooking device devised by the group. This device has kept many of these homeless

Figure 6.1 Mad Housers Prototype: Temporary Appropriation of Urban spaces. The prototype can be assembled in 8 hours and includes a stove for heating, cooking and rainwater collection. Size: 50 s.f. Budget $348.00

Source: William Carpenter.

Figure 6.2 Mad Housers Prototype – image with doors open. Size: 50 s.f. Budget $348.00

Source: William Carpenter.

residents from freezing to death and has been emulated by many other homeless advocacy groups.

This project emphasizes the gray laminal spaces between urban infrastructure and the urban core. Many of these projects were prefabricated in the shop and then delivered to the sites at night.

Miss Mattie's garden

The second example is that of a project in downtown Atlanta called "Miss Mattie's Garden." This project is a former garbage dump and drug sales house that was reappropriated into a community garden by my Design for Humanity studio. The project was temporarily occupied while construction took place without permits through a creative interpretation of the term "garden structure" in the building code. Because of this loophole, we are able to build the project without a building permit. The project transformed this dump into a meaningful urban park that continues to patina and grow over time with meaning and sensitivity.

Juxtapositions of the temporal qualities of the site and materials of this project allow for a kind of freezing in time when one visits the site. The stone walls frame the site and topography and the light wooden structures are organic and temporal. The project creates a meditative space through its winding paths and gathering spaces and allows for contemplative reflection of lost loved ones in this neighbourhood.

Figure 6.3 Miss Mattie's Garden, Entry view from the street. Size: .25 acres Budget: $6,000.00

Source: William Carpenter.

This project still offers many transferable lessons. It has become an important gathering place for the community and has taken a dangerous site on this street and turned it into a desirable contemplative garden.

Reynoldstown Gateway Park

This site turned one of the most dangerous areas of the city into a flourishing landmark and urban park as a design-build studio involving simultaneity. The project uses the temporary appropriation of this part of the city and involves local graffiti artists in its creation. Local children worked to create the detailed mosaics and the steel was fabricated in a nearby steel plant where the students worked alongside local residents and steel workers. The project now marks an important threshold of the city and announces this important neighbourhood of former African-American slaves who moved to Atlanta after the United States Civil War. Many of these residents are talented and internationally known quilters, jazz musicians, hip hop artists and visual artists.

Odd lots (for future consideration)

The odd lots purchased by artist Gordon Matta Clark in New York, mainly at local tax auctions, reveal temporary appropriation in an interesting way. He was essentially buying small vestiges of land, some only centimeters wide, but they reveal temporary

Figure 6.4 Miss Mattie's Garden, Reflection pavilion. Size: .25 acres Budget: $6,000.00

Source: William Carpenter.

appropriation through the potential uses and reconciling of ownership of private and public entities. Matta Clark bought a total of fifteen sites in the New York City area and before his death he intended these for future use. The odd lots of Matta Clark are a form of informality and temporary appropriation; we can examine these examples in any city as they form a negotiation between urban overlays of public, private and semi-private ownership. What are the leftover parcels/spaces and how can they be energized and appropriated? This example offers us a transferable method to understand the dynamic morphology of the city and the notion of ownership.

Figure 6.5 Reynoldstown Gateway Park. Team Leaders: Students B.J. Goodman and Michael Rickman. Collaborators: James Fausett FAIA, Young Hughley Jr. (executive Director of the Reynoldstown Revitalization Corporation and Shannon Sanders Mcdonald AIA). Size: .85 acres Budget $740,000.00

Source: William Carpenter.

Figure 6.6 Reynoldstown Gateway Park; Steel entry pavilion. Size: .85 acres Budget $740,000.00

Source: William Carpenter.

Conclusions

These examples offer the Peccioli Charter as set of prototypes of how academic partnerships with local industries and practices can create projects that involve and expand the interstitial spaces of the cities and to solve complex urban problems in the design build studio.

Resilience and the self-healing city are compelling definitions of informality and its manifestation of temporary appropriation in urban morphologies and dynamic spatial systems. These Atlanta projects are examples of temporary appropriation and design build studios which allow for liminality and simultaneity to occur while also giving back to communities.

As we examine the ideas of Informality and Temporary Appropriation, we should ask how the projects contribute to student learning, faculty exploration and how the projects contribute to community. Each of these projects navigated or carefully avoided complex codes and the teams worked closely with community members to achieve these goals.

Working Definitions

Informality – Organic natural and manmade growth patterns in urban morphology which reconcile, or attempt to reconcile, the collision between certain natural systems such as topography, forests, rivers, infrastructure and urban densities.

Temporary Appropriation – The making of a thing, (such as) urban spaces, building, shelter, public space into your own which sometimes implies illegal or temporary use.

Framing – Our view of the world is defined by frames: door frames, window frames and surrounding paintings, screens and cellular and television signals. Frames contain, order and systematize their contexts (Porter, 2015).

Design-Build – When designing and building occurs in relation to making. In architectural practice, it usually relates to cost saving and speed of construction in building; in academia, it normally relates to service-learning based projects or component-based material and systems-based artifact studies which can be used in research or practice (Carpenter, 1997).

Simultaneity – When designing and building occurs at the same time or in overlapping sequences. Normally simultaneity is studied in relation to haptic cognition and materials-based learning and the neurosciences.

References

Carpenter, W. *Learning by Building*. New York: Van Nostrand Reinhold, 1997.
Carpenter, W. *Design Build Studio*. New York: Lightroom Press, 2009.
Koolhaas, R and Mau, B. *SMLXL*, New York: Monacelli Press, 1997.
Koolhaas, R. and Prat, R. *ATLANTA*. New York: Actar, 1999.
Rowe, C. and Koetter, F. *Collage City*. Boston: The MIT Press, 1978.

Chapter 7

Effected butterflies

Informal urban migration of Monarchs and humans across the US–Mexico border

Mitchell Joachim and Nicholas Gervasi

Global urbanization trends have led to denser and more populous cities but unfortunately concurrent increases in poverty and inequality. While GDPs are soaring, gaps have been created that further isolate marginalized groups. The monetary pie is larger, but its divisions have shifted unequally in favour of those already in formidable financial positions. These undesired consequences have manifested in the proliferation of informal settlements. When affordable housing fails, cities have failed. Informal settlements represent the strive and ambition that those who want a better life are willing to sacrifice to be a part of cities. The safety and health concerns associated with these living conditions are cast aside in order to find a way forward. Clustered in peripheries or along borders, informal settlements have a dense ecological footprint, which has an innate level of sustainability. Bastions of interdependent communities, these settlements exemplify tempered resource management.

Furthermore, with each successive wave of human migration, local biota and biodiversity have seceded territory and number. (Kolbert 2015) Whether it be intentional or accidental, the proliferation of humans in an area strains the plants of that ecosystem to produce glucose as an energy source for the dependent organisms. Our settlement practices typically do not consider our impact on local ecosystems. (Sachs 2015) Conventional development projects inextricably lead to habitat destruction. Especially when cities are located on or adjacent to natural resources, the built environment replaces habitats. The tabula rasa approach ever-present through humans' inhabitation of the planet, eliminates naturally occurring processes and species. We simply do not recognize the significance of indigenous species and ignore their geographic ties. Rarely studies or environmental impact assessments are conducted to the resolution to determine the true cost of an office park or luxury housing development on a local population of herbivore. For example, with Monarch butterflies, these developments tear down crucial links in the flyway that provide reproduction points, wayfinding and key generational transitions. This systematic conversion of green fields to the built environment leads to missing links and breeding grounds for Monarchs.

Obliterating crucial niches and the redundant ecosystem services critical to resiliency, the built environment grows weaker in its defense against the effects of climate change. Resilience and regeneration are derived from a high level of ecosystem elasticity in that entities can step in, override or supplant others in order to maintain the balance between living things and their resources. Ecosystems possess a certain degree of abundance in order to compensate for feast or famine type spikes. This abundance allows for the entire system to remain healthy. Losing different types of ecosystem drivers downgrades the system's ability to continue to function. Just as a tree is only as strong as the forest around it, losses in resiliency lead to a positive feedback loop of increased losses.

Communities within the geopolitical boundaries that define the USA and Mexico endure many persistent conflicts. Tensions stem from turmoil in Central America, as migrants attempt to escape poverty and violence, seeking asylum in the United States. (Taylor 2013) Bottlenecks occur at the border from the rejection of their request. (Barbassa et al. 2019) These are the effects of conflicts and coup d'états 50 and even 75 years old. (Srikrishnan & Heldiz 2018) As many as 60 million people cross the San Diego–Tijuana checkpoint every year, which makes it the most trafficked border point in the world. (Cruz 2014) With close to five million people in the conurbation, about 1.6 million of those people live in border communities called "colonias" settlements along the US side of the US–Mexico border, often living separated from family members. (Cruz & Forman 2017) A similar number of people live on the Tijuana side divided by an eighteen-foot steel wall completed in August 2019 as part of a 147-million-dollar border wall replacement project. The project originated in 2009 under the Obama Administration and was granted funding in 2017 by the Trump Administration.

Architects and urban designers have observed that construction debris and reclaimed materials travel in the opposite direction from San Diego to Tijuana. These materials, garage doors, aluminum siding and plywood from formwork often become walls, roofs and decks of informal settlements. (Cruz 2014) This reclamation of discarded materials into amalgamated structures speaks to the ingenuity of the settlements. (Misra 2017) Modesty in architecture as those who are less privileged hold themselves to a higher standard of sustainability than their wealthier counterparts.

In February 2019, President Trump declared a national emergency in his effort to expedite receiving funds for the wall. Desperately trying to act on a campaign promise that had rallied his supporters, President Trump exercised his executive power to invoke the declaration. By May 2019, the Pentagon had redirected the funds necessary to build 256 miles of barriers along the border, which included 63 miles within the first six months. These initiatives are attempting to disguise the conflicts at the border by hiding them from view.

Ecosystems don't stop at borders. Neither do their services. A chief component of sustainability is recognizing local action; however, this is not at odds with understanding the larger regional goals of a location. (Sachs 2015) Regions have shared resource pools and inputs, such as ground water or arable land. Border divisions, if they are arbitrary, ignore these features and their importance to sustaining life.

Turbulent political disputes around immigration and ethnic diversity have reached a hyperbolic frenzy. The failure to understand our differences has allowed fear to drive policy concerning passage across the border. Moreover, neglecting the motivations and intentions of migrants has led to false assumptions and biases about their goals. (Botti 2019) Concentrating around anthropocentric interests of unlawful migration, the fierce transnational clash excludes other forms of organic life. This dispute breeds resentment and ultimate disregard of the value of entities different from each other. Extending to biodiversity, if our values on diversity are flawed; we execute poor treatment of the surrounding environment. This parallel is exacerbated by architecture that burdens its site with buildings agnostic to living systems.

There are philosophical connections between biodiversity and human diversity. Complex biodiverse systems in nature can prove to be exemplars for promoting human diversity. For example, witnessing the interworkings of the cloud forests of Ecuador, emphasizes how a huge variety of bird species can co-exist within the slopes of the Andean mountains. Metaphors can be drawn from this large species variety living in close proximity to city dwellers living in dense clusters. Diversity does not imply competition.

Often the drastic concerns of social injustice overshadow the unplanned discriminatory behaviour against flora and fauna. Critically endangered and threatened populations of various animals, birds and insects are almost never as important as societal struggles. Expansion of what defines social justice to living creatures beyond humans will bolster our values and provide more platforms to illustrate the positive effects of it. Inclusivity must embrace the natural world, not just the trials of human society. Our treatment of plants and animals reflect our values on society.

As clusters of human activity and environmental impact, cities need to recognize their role in promoting biodiversity within their ecological footprints. Often settled around or atop relics of natural habitats, such as forests or rivers, cities inherited biodiversity due to these resources. Humans specifically chose regions to settle with gargantuan amounts of resources to convert and exploit into economic gains. As centres of importation, cities spread and naturalize invasive species. These actions have negatively shifted growth patterns and distribution. As we traverse and infiltrate areas previously undisturbed, we bring with us our methods of extraction and waste production, ultimately leading to the decline of the non-human sector.

Case study

Our case study highlights the positive socio-ecological principles that a building can promulgate and serve as an example of what should be expected of sustainable architecture. This case study illustrates the ecosystem integration capabilities of architecture. For a building to be a generator, contributor and habitat within its regional context versus a reducer. Operating at the macro and micro scales, we examine overall conservation strategies and high resolution interventions to foster these overarching values.

Monarch sanctuary: Integrated biodiversity in double-skin façade

The Monarch Sanctuary (Lepidoptera terrarium) will be eight stories of new commercial construction in Nolita, New York. Programmatically, the building space will mostly contain retail and office life. Yet central to its purpose is a semi-porous breeding ground, waystation and sanctuary (Figure 7.1) for the Monarch butterfly (Danaus plexippus). It is a pioneering building – one that aims to be ecologically generous, weaving butterfly conservation strategies into its design through the integration of open Monarch habitat in its facades, roof and atrium. Not just a building envelope, the edifice is a new biome of coexistence for people, plants and butterflies (Figure 7.2).

Figure 7.1 An architecture that aims to be ecologically generous, weaving butterfly conservation strategies into its design through the integration of Monarch habitat in its façades, roof and atrium. Not just a building envelope, the edifice is a new biome of coexistence for people, plants and butterflies.

Source: Joachim and Gervasi.

The Monarch butterfly of North America is an at-risk species. The US Fish and Wildlife Service is currently assessing whether the Monarch needs to be granted "endangered species" status, while the Monarch population erodes due to the combined forces of agricultural pesticides and habitat loss. This process was initiated in 2014 by a petition to the USFWS to add the Monarch butterfly to the list of species protected under the Endangered Species Act. The petitioners included the Center for Biological Diversity, the Center for Food Safety, the Xerces Society and Dr. Lincoln Bower. (U.S. Fish and Wildlife Service 2020) The USFWS agreed to conduct a Species Status Assessment to determine whether the Monarch warrants the protection. This SSA framework assess the species' needs in terms of current availability or condition of those needs as well as the species' condition, factoring in future availability of its

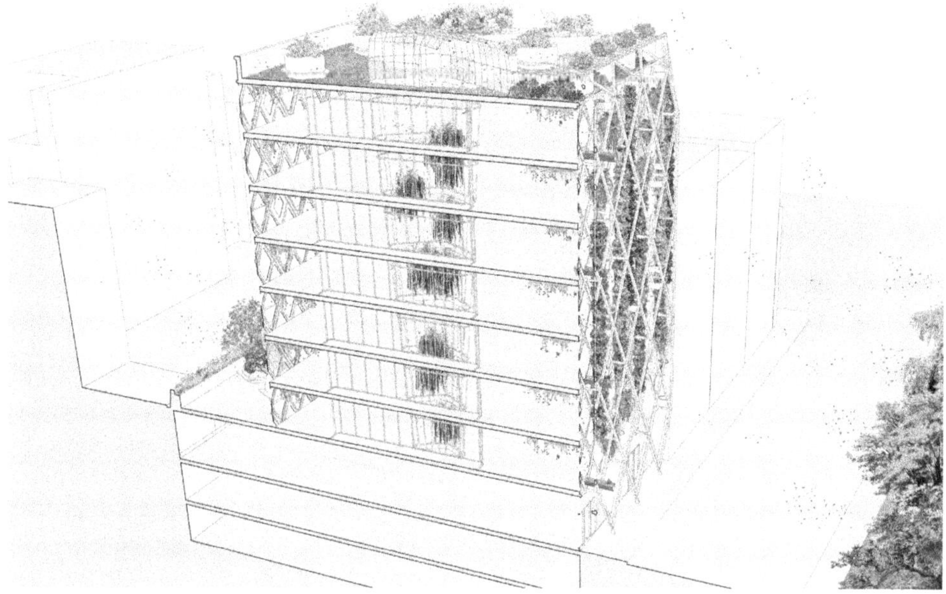

Figure 7.2 Building section perspective mapping the trajectory of butterflies from across the street Petrosino Park through the double-skin facade vertical meadow finally up to the pollinator rooftop garden.

Source: Joachim and Gervasi.

needs. Compiling and analysing the best available information on the species, which includes taxonomy, life history and habitat, the agency also examines the ecological needs at the individual, population and species level to understand how environmental factors will act upon the species. The goal is to determine the species ability to sustain populations in the wild over time based on the current and future abundance and distribution with its ecological settings. The USFWS had until June 2019 to develop the status review. In May 2019, the deadline was extended by the courts and approved by the petitioners to December 2020. (U.S. Fish and Wildlife Service 2020)

However, awaiting the decision should not be used as a reason to stall efforts to promote Monarch population resurgence. Monarchs are a delicate presence in New York City, migrating each year to Mexico and Florida from the city's precious green spaces to lay their eggs on the milkweed plant. Milkweed is essential for Monarchs as it is the only plant their caterpillars will eat. (Agrawal 2017) Monoculture farming practices have culled out naturally growing milkweed embedded in fields. For example, in Iowa it is estimated that cropland lost 98% of its milkweed from 1999 to 2012. (Agrawal 2017) The cropland in the overall Midwest region has lost 64 percent of its milkweed; this is the primary zone of the flyway for adult butterflies.

Scientists have determined Monarch's population has dropped 90% from the 20-year average population that overwinters in the mountain hillsides in oyamel fir forests in Mexico. (Agrawal 2017) The Xerces Society's annual survey of California western Monarch populations revealed a loss of 86 percent decline in 2018 as compared to the previous year. In total, California has lost 97 percent of its Monarch population since the 1980s.

The region one hundred kilometres northwest of Mexico City has now become the Monarch Butterfly Biosphere Reserve and it is climatically suited for Monarchs. By holding a temperature between 0 to 15 degrees Celsius, these forests provide an ideal microclimate for butterflies as the butterflies do not have to use their stored fat reserves. (Agrawal 2017) Their energy conservation is further bolstered by the humidity in the forest, which keeps the Monarch's wings from drying out.

After overwintering in Mexico, Eastern North American Monarchs travel north into spring breeding grounds correlated with month/temperature warmings. In March, they fly north into Texas and other southern states to begin feeding and breeding. Next, in April and May, the first generation of offspring fly further north, spreading even as high as Canada. Finally, the second and third generations breed throughout the summer until mid-August, when the sojourn to Mexico begins. (Oberhauser et al. 2015) (Figure 7.3)

This project will vitally serve as a large-scale Lepidoptera terrarium. A permeable vertical meadow, the Monarch Sanctuary is a double-skin facade integrated with an open garden that serves as a crucial waystation and habitat for the at-risk butterfly. It will bolster the Monarch's presence in the city through two strategies: open plantings of milkweed and nectar flowers on the roof, rear facade and terrace will provide breeding ground and stopover habitat for wild Monarchs, while semi-enclosed colonies in the atrium and street side double-skin facade will foster Monarch population growth. The insects will have fluid open access to join the wild population, enhancing overall species population numbers.

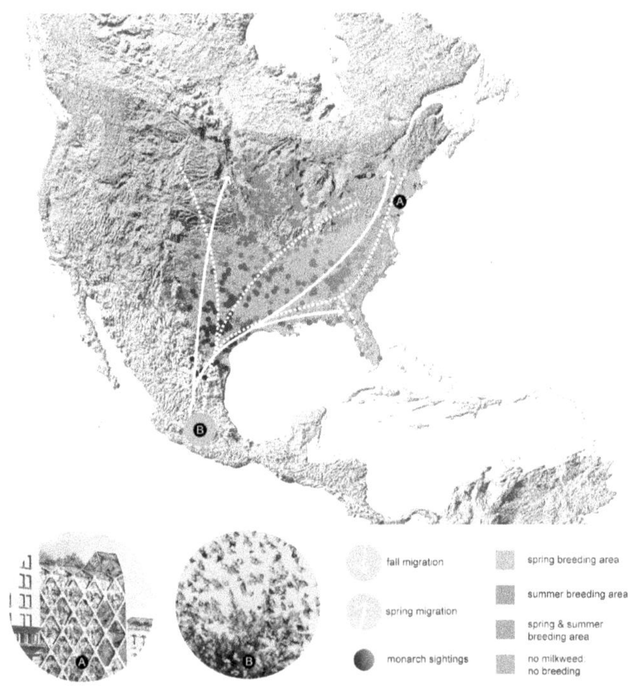

Figure 7.3 Annual migration pattern of Monarch butterflies from the United States to Mexico.

Source: Joachim and Gervasi.

This building functions as a waystation to minimize the spread of disease and allow for release. Release is crucial to the process. Captivity based systems promote disease, loss of genetic diversity and risk of parasite spread over time. Due to the exponential potential of Monarch breeding, as one female can lay two hundred eggs, disease and poor behaviours can become alarmingly present in a population. Thus, the waystation model prevents these issues that are prevalent in captive breeding. The building is conceptually a tilted field of milkweed and flowers meant to substitute for the fields of milkweed that have been obliterated in rural areas.

Our connection to the community of NYC is essential. The prime location will attract attention and educate the public on Monarch extinction. It has a total area of 30,000 square feet and is to be located in the heart of Nolita, between Soho and the burgeoning art district along the Bowery, and a few blocks west of the New Museum. The site is just around the corner from the Storefront for Art and Architecture and currently exists as two plots occupied by small residential buildings, which will be combined into a single property. Although it is a relatively small commercial building by New York standards, the building will present a striking public face and a powerful argument in favor of a diversity of life forms in the city. It will face Petrosino Square, a small triangular paved public park, named after a fallen NYPD lieutenant. The façade of the Monarch Sanctuary building will add a lush vertical surface to the edge of the square. Taking of advantage of this heavily trafficked area, the building will broadcast images and live streams of its habitat monitoring systems to the public via oversized screens on the exterior.

The double-skin street façade, with a diagrid structure infilled glass at the outer layer and with "pillows" of ETFE foil at the inner layer, encloses a careful climate-controlled space, three feet deep and seven stories tall. This "vertical meadow," the terrarium proper, serves as an incubator and safe haven for Monarchs in all seasons (Figure 7.4). It contains suspended milkweed vines and flowering plants to nourish the butterflies

Figure 7.4 Simulated rendering depicting concrete panel system of habitats for butterflies.

Source: Joachim and Gervasi.

Figure 7.5 Photograph of 3D printed sponge nectar feeder.

Source: Joachim and Gervasi.

at each stage of their life cycle. Hydrogel bubbles on the ETFE help maintain optimal humidity levels, and sacs of algae help purify the air and the building wastewater. Solar panels on the roof provide renewable energy to assist in the powering the facilities. Butterflies can come and go as they need from inside the building skin system and roof.

Other features of the project are equally in service of the insects. LED screens at the street level provide magnified live views of the caterpillars and (Figure 7.5) butterflies in the vertical meadow, which also connects to a multi-story atrium adjacent to the circulation core. Interior partitions are constructed from mycelium, and additional planting at the ceiling enhances the interior atmosphere and building biome. Hovering around the building, a few butterfly-shaped drones take readings and maps of the immediate microclimate. They return every few minutes to recharge, and their combined real-time data works to maintain the butterfly health.

The building is intended to serve as an object lesson in enhancing the urban environment with green technologies, including plant life and other creatures, in designing for other species, and in conveying images of new possibilities for the urban environment. This project alone will not save the Monarch but it will crucially raise awareness about our much-loved insect residents.

Part of this building as object lesson objective was to identify novel research trajectories especially the overlap between technology and ecology. We sought to develop the form of the building based upon butterfly affinities for sunbathing, feeding, frolicking, perching and mud puddling. Designing a building around species conservation requires knowledge beyond the scope of architecture. Delving into ecology, entomology and biology, we synthesized information from university, non-profit and governmental experts to infuse our design with sound principles. Throughout the design and research process of this project, we engaged these experts on various components of the design to understand what has been previously tested with butterflies and what unstudied territory remains.

Artificial and natural sources of nectar are featured within the façade system in order to regulate the quantity and quality of sucrose available to butterflies. A typical flower's nectar levels fluctuate based upon seasonal conditions and number of visitations by a butterfly. (Oberhauser et al. 2015) So, in effect, a butterfly could expend energy to travel to a flower that has diminished nectar reserves, thus this butterfly would have to continue on to more flowers. By supplementing natural sources with artificial ones, we can monitor the sucrose levels within the system to ensure its plentiful. The University of Minnesota Monarch Lab emphasized that Monarchs taste with their feet, but they find based on flower shape and color. Since Monarchs see different wavelengths, they can spot patterns invisible to the human eye. (Oberhauser et al. 2015) We tested various colours and surface treatments and deduced from live observation that red or orange on a perforated shell performed the best. The shell enclosed a sponge soaked with sucrose and the perforations allowed butterflies to sink their feet into the sponge to detect the food source. Natural systems must be calibrated to allow for blooming during late August to mid-September for butterflies to build mass for their migration. Any system, natural or artificial, cannot be treated with neonicotinoid insecticides, which make the flowers toxic.

With the Trump Administration dismantling key conservation measures in the seminal Endangered Species Act, the architecture of environmental stewardship could not be more pertinent. Regulations stymie climate change based arguments on intervention due to an overarching goal of minimizing climate action. Overhaul of substantive environmental laws creates a cognitive dissonance between our actions and their consequences. The Administration is steadfastly attempting to counter the decades long efforts of species protection by utilizing of unreliable economic assessments to determine the whether or not a species is worth it. These financial models are dubiously filled with erroneous assumptions and typically lack foresight into future innovations that are lost due to a potentially medicinal plant going extinct.

References

Agrawal, A. A. (2017). *Monarchs and milkweed: a migrating butterfly, a poisonous plant, and their remarkable story of coevolution*. Princeton, NJ: Princeton University Press.

Assessing the status of the monarch butterfly. (2020). *U.S. Fish and Wildlife Service.* Retrieved from https://www.fws.gov/savethemonarch/SSA.html

Barbassa, J., Peterson, M., & Rossback, A. (2019). Along the U.S.-Mexico border. Retrieved from https://www.nytimes.com/interactive/2019/01/10/world/americas/crossing-us-mexico-border.html

Botti, D. (2019). Long before border walls, entering the U.S. from Mexico was as easy as crossing a street. Retrieved from https://www.nytimes.com/video/us/100000006456208/mexico-border-wall-immigration.html

Cruz, T. (2014). The informal as inspiration for rethinking urban spaces: architect Teddy Cruz shares 5 projects. Retrieved from https://blog.ted.com/architect-teddy-cruz-shares-5-projects/
Cruz, T., & Forman, F. (2017). "Enough preaching to the choir," say Teddy Cruz and Fonna Forman in new manifesto. Retrieved from https://www.metropolismag.com/cities/teddy-cruz-fonna-forman-manifesto/
Kolbert, E. (2015). *The sixth extinction: an unnatural history*. London: Bloomsbury.
Misra, T. (2017). Architect Teddy Cruz and political scientist Fonna Forman want to turn the line between the U.S. and Mexico into a site for creative problem solving. Retrieved from https://www.citylab.com/equity/2017/01/the-urban-laboratory-on-the-san-diego-tijuana-border-teddy-cruz-fonna-forman/512222/
Oberhauser, K. S., Nail, K. R., Altizer, S. M., & Oberhauser, K. S. (2015). *Monarchs in a changing world: biology and conservation of an iconic butterfly*. Ithaca: Comstock Publishing Associates, a division of Cornell University Press.
Sachs, J. (2015). *The age of sustainable development*. New York: Columbia University Press.
Srikrishnan, M., & Heldiz, A. (2018). Border report: the long-simmering tensions that led to the border shutdown. Retrieved from https://www.voiceofsandiego.org/topics/news/border-report-tensions-border-shutdown/
Taylor, A. (2013). On the border. Retrieved from https://www.theatlantic.com/photo/2013/05/on-the-border/100510/

Chapter 8

Informality and commons

*Simone Sfriso, Massimo Lepore,
Raul Pantaleo and Barbora Melis*

Premises

The contemporary debate on the direction to be given to architecture in recent years has been characterised increasingly by a strong reference to the social impact of the discipline (Fathy, 1973; Friedman, 2006).

The physical and conceptual sphere of speculation is represented by the great changes that, in a different way and in the presence or otherwise of conflicts, cross the planet and represent the challenge for its future (Bauman, 2016).

Strategic issues such as environmental protection, climate change, growing urbanisation, migratory phenomena and the rational use of resources raise the question of whether architecture, with its own disciplinary tools, can be somehow part of a process aimed at guaranteeing access to greater social justice (Correa, 2000).

In this context, each responsible designer is called to reflect on the social, economic and environmental outcomes that each architectural work can induce, thus expanding the typical skills of the discipline: from composition, technique, expressive use of materials, towards local and global effects that the different choices inherent in an architecture path can activate (or not activate) in terms of sustainability, inclusion, access to norms, frameworks and protections, with particular attention to projects in marginal places (Aquilino, 2011; Mehrotra & Vera, 2013; Mostafavi, 2013; Mazzanti & Schenk 2014).

This chapter therefore explores the possibilities of practice-based research in marginal and extreme environmental conditions in the Global South.

Background of the research

Reflection on the issues mentioned in the premises has generated a discussion between two different polarised positions. One, attentive to the great challenges that contemporaneity brings to the agenda, is decidedly in favour of a "new" architecture aimed at considering the value of the social impact of the discipline (and its access by the weaker sections of the population), with a particular sense of responsibility towards the environment and the management of human and material resources; the other, more focused on the specificity of the so-called "disciplinary autonomy" of architecture, is linked to a careful control of technique, shape and materials, more oriented to the value of expressive research, and to offering the individual ability of the architects to the client (Aravena, 2016; Schumacher, 2016).

From our point of view, the aforementioned debate appears to be conditioned by a vision too concentrated on the role and prerogatives of the discipline, within a hierarchical vision of knowledge, while it should be moved more towards the use and potential of architecture as a practice capable of building circular knowledge; but above all, the discussion should be conducted by carefully evaluating the disruptive social and productive changes that are characterising our time (TAMassociati, 2016).

Design cultures increasingly tend to meet in open platforms, all the more effective and more capable of cancelling the traditional hierarchical scales of knowledge to activate generative processes thanks to the continuous comparison and exchange of information. This holistic vision of the project leads to a different conception (and representation) of the figure of the designer, which must become part of a complex and participatory process, in which creativity takes place in the concurrence of individual contributions, and is also self-generative in marginal places and borders (Aquilino, 2011; Mostafavi, 2013).

In this process, therefore, the new qualities required of projects are measured: the flexibility in proactively involving a multiplicity of subjects, primarily the users/clients; the ability to metabolise available resources, to generate sustainability and self-sufficiency; the ability to transfer information in the form of replicable knowledge, the attention to generate processes in which the growth of local human capital constitutes the most important added value (Mazzanti & Schenk, 2014).

In this process, the design culture will have to be increasingly intertwined with new "support" disciplines, to interface the project with the objectives contained in the various agendas dictated by the many agencies that operate interactively for the fair and sustainable development of the planet. These practices involve, just to cite a few examples: the management of open and non-hierarchical decision-making models; the systematisation of self-generative and informal processes of necessity; the interpretation of complex variables connected to increasingly structured databases; the assimilation of knowledge aimed at sharing information on common platforms; the assessment of the production/reuse life cycles and environmental compatibility.

In short, this is an inevitable "revolution," precisely because it is dictated by a change that involves the structure of knowledge itself in its relationship with needs and which seeks to pilot the effects that will ensure a better management of available resources; we believe that, in particular, in these areas and not in others, we should direct the debate on the contribution that architecture can give to those governing this disruptive change. The issues at stake also concern above all the emerging countries of the southern hemisphere where needs, scarcity of resources and informal creativity overlap.

Accordingly, our design practice, TAMassociati, has started a design-led exploration in these regional contexts, of which the current chapter can be an initial reflection in textual form.

Comparative practice-based research

As previously stated, this chapter aims to explore the impact of TAMassociati practice-based research in marginal and extreme environmental conditions in the Global South.

By extreme conditions here we mean both climatic and war conditions and their social and health consequences.

The environmental crisis is largely due to the emissions of the formal settlements of the Western world, whose economic and political interests often contribute to fomenting the wars cited.

World Health Organization (WHO) and United Nations reports have warned us of the impact that these conditions will have on the regions with the least infrastructure.

In these contexts, the need to embrace the notion of informality as an alternative tool with respect to the deterministic and paternalistic planning of the Western world emerges ever more strongly. If, in fact, the causes lie elsewhere, why is it believed that the criticality in city planning is at its most vulnerable ends, such as in slums?

In this part of the text, through case studies, we try to outline a series of possibilities for a more sustainable design, economically, socially and environmentally, making use of more informal tools, such as co-design, open source design, vernacular and regional technologies, to support local communities.

The three case studies taken into account regard the design of TAMassociati, which, thanks to decades of experience in the field, has been able to experiment and respond effectively to the research question through professional practice.

The case studies are H_2OS Eco-Village in Senegal, an Emergency NGO Paediatric Centre in Sudan and two health centres in a refugee camp in Iraq.

The study cases have been selected on the basis of their emblematic nature with respect to the aforementioned social and environmental issues, including desertification in the sub-Saharan area, the lack of infrastructure dedicated to health in the war areas, and the extreme conditions of the refugee camps.

Case study 1: H_2OS, anti-desertification eco-village in Senegal, 2017

H_2OS is an eco-village located in an area without electricity, water or school and health facilities, in Keur Bakar, 200 km away from Dakar, in Senegal.

TAMssociati aims, here, at an open source, autonomous and sustainable design as a model for the whole region to respond to desertification, school dropouts, and emigration (see Figure 8.1).

The initiative has been promoted by the Circolo Sunugal (Senegalese Migrant Association) in Venice, and Onlus Musoco (Venice) in collaboration with the NGO Union pour Solidarité et l'Entraide (USE) in Dakar. The project has been funded by the Italian trade unions (CGIL CAAF Nord-Est), the Walsensian Church, Livenza Tagliamento Acque (LTA), and is supported by the AUTODESK FOUNDATION (USA) and Idee per Risorse Collettive (IdRiCo), by the Friuli Venezia Giulia Region and by the provincial association Arci Trieste.

The eco-village is intended as a symbol of eco-modernity, consistent with the technical, managerial and agricultural self-sufficiency of local communities, which are also involved in the design process.

Economic and social sustainability are also embodied in the cost of the work: less than 200 Euros per metre. On-site maintenance is part of the broader self-sufficiency scenario.

The community 'eco-maison' is the first phase of the eco-village, and it is the heart of the new village, and is used as a research, training and information centre and includes arts and crafts workshops.

Figure 8.1 TAMassociati: *H_2OS, anti-desertification Eco-Village in Senegal* (2017).

Source: TAMassociati.

The structural construction material is rammed earth. Utilities and mechanical systems are developed by specialised technicians who, at the same time, train the local workforce.

The sustainable approach includes rainwater collection, the filtration systems and natural ventilation, passive strategies, clean energy generation, phytodepuration and photovoltaic energy.

Next to the community building are the well, washhouse and farming lots, cultivated mostly by women and irrigated thanks to the collected rainwater (see Figure 8.2).

Figure 8.2 TAMassociati: *H_2OS, anti-desertification Eco-Village in Senegal* (2017).

Source: TAMassociati.

Working at this model project led designers and stakeholders to consider that the participatory approach, and aspects such as self-sufficiency and the use of local technologies have greatly contributed to ensuring the ecology of the design.

Although the aforementioned convergence may seem obvious, we must consider that, as evidenced by our professional experience and that of many colleagues, in the conventional world of Western construction, the economic, social and environmental aspects of sustainability are often considered to be conflicting and uncooperative aspects.

Case study 2: Emergency NGO paediatric centre in Port Sudan, 2012

The project was the result of the first prize assigned to the artist Massimo Grimaldi, for an art competition for the MAXXI Museum in Rome.

Grimaldi donated 92% of his fees (€643,800) for the construction of the hospital. His art work proposed for the competition was in fact a photo-shoot of the new hospital construction progress, then shown in a video format on the entrance wall of the MAXXI.

Port Sudan offers the only sea access in Sudan. The expansion of the harbour, the abandonment of the countryside due to increasing droughts and refugees from various conflicts led to a dramatic population growth from 30,000, in 2000, to 500,000 inhabitants.

The clinic, born thanks to an artist philanthropic intuition, is located in a desert area in the north-west suburb of the city, with a high concentration of refugees, and is one of the few child healthcare institutions within the whole region.

The one-floor building covers 780 square metres and includes 14 in-patient beds, 4 intensive care beds, 3 outpatient clinics, a pharmacy and diagnostic services.

On the east side of the hospital, a park, irrigated by a wastewater treatment system and used for leisure and sport activities, is an effective regeneration and social catalyst for the whole area.

In Port Sudan, the temperatures often exceed 50°C with humidity between 5 and 10%.

These weather conditions, together with the problem of dust generated by the strong desert winds, have required a detailed study on passive technology able to minimise costs, while balancing comfort and construction simplicity (see Figure 8.3).

The plan organisation is reminiscent of the principles of Arab houses.

It is distributed around a series of courtyards with a limited number of external openings.

The entrance is dominated by a tree in the middle of the waiting area, a fragment of life and continuity with the outdoor garden. The direct solar radiation is controlled through limited exposed openings and through shielding with natural fibre panels.

Limiting the number and the size of openings has significantly reduced the direct solar intake during the day. In this context, the use of solar protective systems on the facades has become an integral part of the building's environmental strategy. Braided bamboo shields have been placed to protect the walkways and waiting areas – a technique inspired by traditional fences and especially used in refugee camps. This has been important both from a cultural perspective as well as a functional point of view.

Figure 8.3 TAMassociati: *Emergency NGO Paediatric Centre in Port Sudan* (2012).

Source: Massimo Grimaldi.

So, the spaces are physically and ideally isolated from the outside heat with a succession of cool and protected rooms lit by overhead light sources that serve as vents for latent heat deriving from the common areas, in a way which rethinks and revives the atmosphere and the types of traditional living.

Another factor distinguishing the main façade was the use of wooden sun shades inspired by Ottoman buildings: the typical wooden shutters were such that women could observe activity on the streets without being seen. This is a distinctive element that can be found throughout what used to be the Ottoman world from the Balkans to Africa.

It was not easy to propose these wooden sunshades and relaunch them in a place where the memory of past knowledge had been lost.

The use of thick walls with an interposed ventilated air chamber allowed the heat accumulated during the day to be dissipated and the flow of heat through the wall during the hottest hours of the day to be reduced.

In the main façade, we wanted to diversify the construction materials by inserting fragments of "traditional" building systems, in coral stone, retrieved from the demolition of old buildings. The whole city was built with this material (no longer available from quarries). The same construction technology was used in the Ottoman Suakin (the Coral City) at the beginning of the 16th century up to the mid-1800s. Suakin, a few kilometres from Port Sudan, is now an important archaeological site.

The roof structure is made of brick vaults called jagharsch (from harsch, which, in Arabic, means arc) protected from direct solar radiation with a secondary metal roof which thermally isolates the jagharsch coverage and creates a ventilated air space between the two structures.

The use of the thermal mass of the walls was not sufficient so it was also necessary to ensure an adequate natural and forced (when needed) ventilation.

In this context, air circulation was designed for using a system of natural treatment called badgir (inspired by Iranian traditional systems of natural ventilation) integrated into a mechanical cooling system with an industrial type "water cooler".

The eight-metre outdoor chimneys catch the prevailing winds from north to south; the air is then directed into the basement of the building through a labyrinth of walls; the shock caused by the impact against the walls of the labyrinth, in addition to the slowdown of the speed of the air, allows most of the sand and dust contained in it to be deposited. The simple system has proved to be very efficient and cost effective and requires almost no maintenance, except occasionally cleaning of the basement (see Figure 8.4).

For the treatment of the air, we adopted an adiabatic absorption system with two industrial "water coolers", with an electric absorption of the entire system of 6KW for cooling and the exchange of air. This system allowed a reduction in electricity consumption for air conditioning estimated at about 70%.

To obtain a minimum value and acceptable cooling power for the system, it was necessary to properly size the air flow in the two air treatment units (UTA). The adiabatic systems are necessarily "all outside air" (given the need to ensure a continuous intake of water in the air treatment), which is a particularly favourable condition in hospital environments.

After several tests, we achieved a 10°C reduction even in the harshest conditions. For example, with an incoming temperature of 38.7°C and humidity at 21%, in the hospital we recorded a comfortable temperature of 28.4°C and 44% relative humidity.

Figure 8.4 TAMassociati: *Emergency NGO Paediatric Centre in Port Sudan* (2012).

Source: Massimo Grimaldi.

Adiabatic systems are a novelty for Sudan as well as for all sub-Saharan areas, despite their low cost and simplicity.

Hence, the building site has become a regeneration laboratory able to reactivate a sense of belonging, also thanks to the implementation of traditional passive strategies which have allowed the reduction of mechanical cooling systems for the benefit of the construction costs and future maintenance of the clinic.

This project has taught us that in crisis areas, due to civil war and exacerbated by the poverty of refugees and external environmental conditions, architecture can become an opportunity to combine health and environmental needs.

Paradoxically, using that wealth of knowledge of local traditions, on which informal architecture often relies, results can be achieved with very low construction and maintenance costs. At the same time, precisely the use of those passive devices, coming from local and regional culture, contribute to the regeneration, both social and psychological, of a sense of belonging to a place.

Case Study 3: Refugee camp in Sulaimaniya, Iraq, 2015

The survivors of the Syrian butchery and that of the self-styled Islamic State moved to an area between Sulaimaniya and Khanaqin, away from the war.

A situation characterised by "all against all" has made Syria and Iraq places where the only possible choice is escape. Thus, thousands have sought refuge in an increasingly less hospitable Europe, while the most desperate and poor have found a way out in neighbouring areas, such as this corner of Iraq.

The NGO Emergency has been called on to intervene in the refugee camps in the province of Sulaimaniya, in Iraqi Kurdistan, to bring health and "human reconstruction" facilities including the Arbat camps.

Refugee camps are like small cities, with schools, places of worship, police, houses, fire-fighters and hospitals. A refugee camp is microcosm of life, with the same spaces, rhythms and times of an inhabited centre. Why not think, therefore, of going beyond basic needs, imagining spaces for sociality and living?

Thus, one aim of the transformation of two clinics, already operating in Arbat, is to make them more functional and welcoming, transforming anonymous containers into buildings, abandoned spaces into places, the rocks that surround them into gardens. In this desert of stones and humanity, trees are the first sign of rebirth.

In the two clinics that we are building in the Khanqin camps, a few kilometres from Baghdad, and very close to the front, we want to demonstrate how it is possible to face the emergency by focusing not only on functionality, but also on the rights of people to be treated in worthy places. It is a difficult challenge in a context where the emergency prevails, as if the refugees were numbers and not people. However, the use of our clinic as a standard model proposed by the Kurdish-Iraqi Ministry of Health is early evidence that the challenge is possible (see Figure 8.5).

In our projects, we use the same standard prefabricated modules present in all fields and used for clinics: the same number, with the same finishes and the same cost. As designers, we are embedded in the processes through which refugee camps are created, trying to demonstrate that with those budgets, those space-time limitations, those materials and elements, human places can be generated, simply using colour,

Figure 8.5 TAMassociati: *Refugee camp in Sulaimaniya, Iraq* (2015).

Source: Alessandro Rota.

creating welcoming spaces, giving an identity to buildings, making architecture become a recognisable landmark.

The use of the emergency entrance to the Qoratu clinic as the main entrance is a further acknowledgement of the quality of the work.

This impact of this relatively limited project has convinced us that architecture can still be an integral part of the psychological healing process. Thus, the real challenge is to design, even in these contexts, for people as they were before the emergency.

Conclusions

In an overall picture as outlined in the background of the research, the need to reconsider architecture as a collective work capable of "common good" in the service of the community emerges strongly.

The process of generating and implementing an architectural project must therefore be structured in such a way as to involve designers, institutions and users in the construction of a "common good" capable of transcending the mere utility or aesthetics of the architectural object.

The examined case studies corroborate the idea that architecture, by its definition, can be an agent in the processes of positive manipulation and transformation of goods (whether private or public), while it can also contribute to the consolidation of common values such as identity, awareness and appropriation (Nicolin, 2014; TAMassociati, 2016).

Thus, placing architecture in to the context of the common good, or outcomes that are of interest to the community, means recognising the value of the production and the management of the process of the goods themselves. In this regard, Davide Tommaso Ferrando writes: "The Commons are not defined in objectual but relational terms – the "commoning" process, which concern indifferently material or immaterial goods, is their distinctive aspect – as well as architecture, once it is introduced into the sphere of common goods, will be characterized more by the ability to activate collective processes of re-appropriation and transformation of the urban environment, than by taking on a specific physical form" (TAMassociati, 2016).

In the places of informality and in the peripheries of the world, such as those taken into consideration in the case studies here, local communities face difficulties, in spite of expressing a vitality which follows necessity, in response to individual primary needs. These are often precarious, transitory, rough answers to primary questions. Here architecture must challenge marginality and resignation through quality, culture, protection of rights, and support for the incentive of collective services.

The search for "empathy" with the physical and social context constitutes the true foundation of each building, which balances the environmental impact, resources, ambitions and respect for local cultures.

In conclusion, the case studies confirm that, in the analysed context, an inclusive architecture implies beauty and appropriateness, precisely because it is anchored to a commons paradigm which is shared by both designers and users.

References

Aravena, A. (26.05.2016). Interview with the curator of the International Architecture Exhibition Biennale di Venezia 2016: https://www.youtube.com/watch?v=aHpS8uFT1eE

Aquilino, M.J. (Ed.). (2011). *Beyond shelter. Architecture and human dignity*. New York: Metropolis Books.

Bauman, Z. (2016). *Scrivere il futuro*. Roma: Lit Edizioni.

Correa, C. (2000). *Housing and Urbanization: Building Solutions for People and Cities*. London: Thames & Hudson.

Fathy, H. (1973). *Architecture for the poor*. Chicago: The University of Chicago Press.

Friedman, Y. (2006). *L'architecture de survie. Une philosophie de la pauvreté*. Paris: Editions de l'éclat.

Mehrotra, R. & Vera, F. (Eds.). (2013). *Kumbh Mela. Mapping the Ephemeral Mega City*. Berlin: Hatje Cantz.

Mostafavi, M. (Ed.). (2013). *Architecture for Life*. Zurich: Lars Muller Publishers.

Mazzanti, G. & Schenk, M. (2014). *Architecture as mechanism for building community*. Delft: TU Delft.

Nicolin, P. (Ed.) (2014). *Commons*. Lotus International *(153)*. Milan.

Nicolin, P. (Ed.) (2015). *People in motion*, Lotus International *(158)*. Milan.

Schumacher, P. (2016). Interview about Impressions of the International Architecture Exhibition Biennale di Venezia 2016: https://vimeo.com/169518191

TAMassociati (Ed.). (2016). *Taking Care – Designing for the common good*. Catalog of the Italian Pavilion, Venice Biennale 2016, Padova: Becco Giallo.

Ward, C. (2016). *Architettura del dissenso*. Milan: Eleuthera.

Part II

Informality as a mode of sustainability

Steffen Lehmann

Informality and sustainability

The term *informality* means 'the absence of formality'. It describes an unregulated non-formality that relates to the 'unplanned', the part of a city which evolved and has grown organically outside of a regulatory framework or system – without any formal arrangement or management. Informality is therefore frequently characterised by its relaxedness, organically shaped structure and easy accessibility as 'the unofficial version' of the city. However, these definitions imply that informality is widely unrestrained by regulations such as building codes and is likely to include the characteristics of spontaneity, efficiency and flexibility (as pointed out by AlSayyad, Roy, Holston, Hasan, Pieterse, Dovey, Perlman and other scholars who have been working on a better understanding of urban informality for decades).

This second part of the book will look at how informal urbanisation can be interpreted in different contexts and how it frequently embeds principles of sustainability. Therefore, this part explores the different types of informality in the context of sustainable urban development and its relationship to environmental concerns. It links informal activities and patterns of informal development to ecological behaviour and to the unplanned growth patterns of cities as informal urbanisation can often be observed in emerging or rapidly expanding cities. The chapters in this part explore the deep underlying principles behind the dynamics and seemingly chaotic ordering systems of cities as they *grow* (expand) or *decline* (shrink). For instance, which urban characteristics support the communities in the slums of India and in the favelas of Brazil, making them so resourceful and resilient?

Urban informality in particular relates to the unplannable, but it is far more than poor squatter settlements or slums in the Global South. Much relevant research over the last two decades has examined the organisational structures of slums and squatter settlements (see Figure 1). As a consequence, the editors feel that the term requires a wider definition. Urban informality is a phenomenon clearly not limited to the Global South (despite the fact that in Africa, six out of ten urban dwellers live in slums today). It can be found in many forms as a mode of metropolitan urbanisation, such as in homelessness in developed cities, displacement, micro-entrepreneurship along streets, or city-ward migration (Harvey 2009).

In *Architecture without Architects*, Bernard Rudofsky (1964) asked for a new aesthetic, and even a science of cities, to better understand the interconnectedness of all

Figure 1 Aerial photo of Mumbai, India.

Source: Johnny Miller, Millefoto, Cape Town, 2018.

kinds of actions and user patterns that occur within cities. The lifelong question that kept driving him could be summarised in one simple sentence: What makes a good city? In his seminal book, Rudofsky states that 'Architectural history, as written and taught in the Western World, has never been concerned with more than a few select cultures' (36). He attempted to break down the limited idea of this architectural history by contrasting it to the vast theory and wise world of 'non-pedigreed architecture' (an adjective he used to describe informal, vernacular, ephemeral, indigenous and often anonymous contributions to the built environment).

The makeshift balconies of the prefab-Soviet housing in Kiev (Ukraine) are a good example for architecture without architects: the residents of the housing slab live in very small apartments and have turned their balconies into additional living space, and due to the self-built DIY-extension, each balcony addition is different in material, shape and size. This freedom of expressing of ownership and private space adds a uniqueness to the otherwise anonymous, standardised and uniform Soviet architecture, turning it into an example of informal architecture (see Figure 2). German architect Otto Königsberger taught that urban planners in the developing world/Global South should be prepared to dynamically adapt their plans, and involve local communities and techniques, as opposed to imposing a static master plan based on Western ideas – an approach he called *Action Planning* (1975).

The concept of informality emerged in the early 1970s, at this time defined as the informal sector of the urban poor and limited in its focus to people living in slums and squatter settlements (Moser 1978). Today, we have gained a clearer and wider view of urban informality and its modus operandi. However, infrastructure, high unemployment and a lack of affordable housing in all kinds of cities and geographies have made a clear differentiation between formality and informality even vaguer (Bardhan, Jana

Figure 2 The individual balcony extensions at this housing slab in Kiev (Ukraine) are informal architectural elements.

Source: Roman Blazhan, Kyiv, Ukraine, 2019.

and Sarkar 2019). Particularly among younger urban residents it has often become impossible to afford the high cost of housing, which has made their life both precarious and transient.

It is estimated that informality is the daily condition of at least one-sixth of our world's population. It seems that the real life of cities takes place in the corners where no one is watching, where communities coalesce and develop organically, where the thousands of people who might call the place 'home' interact on the human scale, in everyday ways. Researchers have frequently noted that one can find two opposing perspectives on the meaning of urban informality: the first perspective is the 'emancipatory perspective', which frames urban informality as a practice that can foster autonomy, entrepreneurship and social mobility; the other perspective sees informality more critically, through the lenses of political exclusion, inequality and urban poverty.

Architectural design and urban planning decide where social interactions take place in urban areas. This part of the book aims to shed light on the dynamics generating the urban areas and conditions of urban informality, including 'shadow citizenship', and to contribute towards a better understanding of the drivers of urban inequalities that pose such significant challenges to the existence of our urban societies. Just think of the interstitial urbanisation that is happening in major metropolises, leading to informal spaces and spontaneous occupation (examples could range from the anti-gentrification movement in Berlin to the democratic uprising in Hong Kong). In this regard, urban economist Joseph Stiglitz noted, "The more unequal a society is, the more the likelihood of its social polarisation to intensify; and, the wider the spatial and social inequality, the lower the economic growth of a country or city, and consequently the higher the threat to the sustainability of its welfare state" (Stiglitz 2013).

One could say that urban informality is the result of ineffective bureaucracies or even the lack of top-down democratic processes. Is it then justifiable to see urban informality as a fertile breeding ground for bottom-up democracy and political participation? In addition, how is it expressed spatially?

Urban informality is not automatically a fertile breeding ground for bottom-up democracy or political participation. Urban informality happens rather 'outside' the order of formal urbanisation, planned and built by non-professionals (AlSayyad & Roy 2004; Lehmann 2009) and it can be a 'rich source of learning'. However, the urban character and concept of informality have often been misunderstood (as argued by Perlman 1976; Harris 2018). Favelas and slums were too often the study of aesthetic interests and romanticisation. Informal urbanism can appear "picturesque, but one should never aestheticise or romanticise poverty" (Yiftachel 2009; Dovey 2013). On the other hand, every favela or slum is an active recycling centre, an extremely resourceful and dynamic form of complex settlement (although this resourcefulness of informal communities comes at a social cost, as the residents are not setting out to be resourceful by their own choice).

Learning from informality should therefore become a key aspect of our planning approaches. While cities are great social laboratories, there is still not enough learning going on between cities and decision makers on issues of urban informality and the unplanned. Increasingly, researchers are engaged in revealing the underlying urban patterns and hidden data of informality, e.g., data on movement, trading of goods or the intrinsic behaviour of people in public space (Huchzermeyer & Karam 2006).

Urban informality and the temporary appropriation of public space are therefore two closely related phenomena. Temporary appropriation is usually read as a form of informal practice, e.g. in the form of micro-entrepreneurship in the streets and plazas. Some concepts of informal behaviour in urban settings could be better understood when viewed as a form of temporary appropriation, as there is clearly a need for a deeper understanding of the relationship between informality and spatial appropriation. This is still an under-researched field (Lehmann and Zaman 2017). There is also the challenge that – while we have plenty of useful data – architects and urban designers rarely perform a deep data analysis, and data sets are too fragmented or disconnected to be analysed (e.g. in numerous cities, reliable data on household consumption or health data is still lacking).

It is obvious that a whole range of questions arise out of the lenses of discussion presented in the second part of the book. For instance, in the future, how precisely will experts be able to predict and forecast the behaviour of humans in cities? Can we anticipate new social conditions ten to twenty years in advance? Moreover, what kind of public spaces will society need to empower its citizens to lead fulfilled lives? Could there be a way to learn from urban informality to enhance design decisions in developed cities (for instance, to improve liveability and citizen participation and ensure better health outcomes)? How best can society meet the needs of the ageing population, in which health issues such as depression, isolation, dementia and obesity are rapidly on the rise?

Cities are the key to social integration, and they are essential for localising the UN's Sustainable Development Goals (United Nations 2015). However, city layouts have been surprisingly stable over a long period and resistant to change, making it almost impossible to quickly transform developments or reverse urban sprawl. Obviously, it is much more difficult (and expensive) to provide infrastructure retroactively or to retrofit a neighbourhood, compared to using infrastructure newly planned from scratch. Here, informality provides constant services at a very low cost and keeps cities inclusive and running (for example, in many of the world's growing cities in Africa and Asia, semi-formal buses form the basis of public transit systems). However, in the process of rolling out the North American model of suburban car-dependent sprawl, the chances for any informality to occur remain minimal.

In defense of cities: The chapters in Part II

There is a diversity of voices and view angles in the chapters of the second Part. The eight various chapters address questions of urban informality related to ecology, economy, digitalization, mobility, demography, work, entrepreneurship and housing. Some chapters explore novel methods and strategies, as well as technologies and digital tools to tackle the challenges posed by urbanisation and climate change and aim to link design in situated environmental conditions with territorial scale regional development.

In chapter 9, entitled "*The Self-Organising City and Its Modus Operandi: Informal Urbanism and Public Space*," Steffen Lehmann explores various cases from Chile, the US and China that illustrate the dilemma of the relationship between informality and public/private space today. One of the chapter's conclusions is that informality is a deregulated self-help system that redefines relationships with the formal. It discusses tactical urban interventions, surveillance, facial recognition, public health crisis and de-densification.

Chapter 10 is entitled "Housing the majority, destroying agrarian land: the irreconcilable dilemma of Cairo's informal areas." Charlotte Malterre-Barthes looks at the case of the city of Cairo in Egypt and its informal housing and waste collection systems, and discusses the contradiction between new sprawl and food security. Topics are Cairo's informal growth and housing crisis, and the speed of illegal construction of informal settlements in an ever-growing metropolis, losing agricultural land to grow food. Urbanisation has manifold increased to footprint of Cairo over the last years, but this economic liberalization comes at a cost.

Chapter 11 by Dario Pedrabissi discusses "Informality and Mass Housing in Seoul: The Role of the Informal Settlements in the Formation of Megaprojects." In Seoul, 1970s mega-housing projects were inserted into the high-density low-rise fabric of the city. Pedrabissi's chapter retraces the history of housing evolution during the twentieth century, with a focus on informal settlements and their role on the establishment of an urban model that is representative of the South Korean cities.

Paul Jones writes in chapter 12 on the "Role of Adaptation in Changing the Micro-Morphology of Informal Settlements." He argues that the main form of change in informal settlements is through incremental adaptations to housing, such as dividing and extending existing rooms, adding a floor and balcony or converting roof space. He discusses the case study of an informal settlement (*kampung*) in Bandung, Indonesia, to argue that understanding micro-morphological changes are critical.

In chapter 13, Mohammad Swapan, Atiq Zaman and Steffen Lehmann discuss research on Dhaka mega-city in Bangladesh. First they examine the transformation of the term "urban informality" to move into a discussion about the effects of "elite informality" on sustainable urbanisation in the city of Dhaka. The chapter continues to explore the contested spaces along the urban periphery in order to better understand the increasing involvement of power and politics in shaping the entire planning regime in Bangladesh. The role of the state's re-adjustment of the structure plan in favour of powerful stakeholders is more like an "act of retrospective rationalization" of the informal (i.e. illegal) activities as defined by Bent Flyvbjerg (1998). More informed citizenship and responsive planning negotiation is needed.

Daniela Perrotti discusses in chapter 14, entitled "Landscape–Infrastructure: Formal–Informal Entanglements Across Political Ecologies of Resource Use," a new model of thinking about landscape, leading to the metabolism of the 21st century landscape. To shed new light on informality today (or our "informality age") and resulting speculations in design, Perrotti propose to turn towards the emergence of landscape urbanism and its recent evolutions. She uses Taichung Gateway Park in Taiwan as case study and argues that landscape infrastructure can be understood as a concrete constellation, which can act as an infrastructural catalyst (in the landscape urbanism's language). This, she notes, can demonstrate a capacity to engage with the complexity of contemporary urban living while favouring a new understanding of the interlinkages between institutionalised urban regimes and informal practices.

Daniel H. Ortega argues in chapter 15, entitled "Contested Ground, Sustainable Informal Settlement and Human Consequence in the Urban Landscape of South Los Angeles", that everyday practices performed in the urban landscape can act as critically determinant factors in the shaping of our contemporary understanding of a sustainable, informal, urban settlement. The case study of an urban farm in South Los Angeles does not present a case for informal housing, but a responsive case of urban agro-ecology (Peña, 2006) as an additional offering to consider within the lexicon of informal settlement typologies. Ortega is fascinated by everyday practices in the urban landscape of Southern Los Angeles.

Janice E. Perlman asks in chapter 16 if informality is a model for sustainable cities or a result of scarcity. Using the Brazilian favela Rocinha in Rio de Janeiro as case study, she examines choice or consequence of living in a favela. While the favela is a dangerous and challenging place to live, she recognizes the resourcefulness, affordability, central location, self-reliant qualities of the favela as a reason for the development of a close-knit community. These obviously positive characteristics are relevant for any sustainable urban development of the future. However, since living in conditions of insecure occupancy and instability, the vulnerability of favela residents is a chronic condition leading to constant stress associated with informality, marginality and precarious neighborhoods. Perlman argues that a more integrated approach would help to understand the way cities work in real space and time.

Living in informal settlements is informal settlements are the daily condition of at least one-sixth of our world's population (see Figure 3).

Figure 3 Informal settlements are the daily condition of at least one-sixth of our world's population.

Source: Steffen Lehmann, 2019.

Understanding informality through the lenses of sustainability

Today, in terms of understanding urban informality, we have probably reached a turning point. New readings of urban informality are emerging. Therefore, chapters in this part of the book explore the link between informality and sustainability in greater detail, including the differences on how to transform a typical North American or European city into a sustainable city. Some of the chapters demystify the notion of sustainability concerning informality and an architecture of transgression. The chapters include aspects of growth management, considering tensions between population growth, suburbanisation, mobility, temporary appropriation, surveillance and resource protection (such as green space, water resources, food supply, social media and public space).

Clearly, it is significant what can be learnt from the incremental, ephemeral modes of informal urbanism that are opposed to the ideological, formal urban planning theory of the twentieth century. This is the reason the editors have chosen to explore this fascinating topic and to compile a book: to gain an alternative and better understanding of urban life in our contemporary cities, learn from informal processes and refresh formal city planning.

References

Roy, Ananya, and Nezar AlSayyad, eds. *Urban Informality*. New York: Lexington, 2004.

Bardhan, R, A Jana, and S Sarkar. 'Informality'. In *The Wiley Blackwell Encyclopaedia of Urban and Regional Studies*, edited by Anthony M. Orum, p. 360, New York: J. Wiley & Sons, 2019.

Dovey, Kim. 'Informalising Architecture: The Challenge of Informal Settlements'. *Architectural Design* 83, no. 6 (November 2013): 82–89, https://doi.org/10.1002/ad.1679.

Flyvbjerg, Bent. *Rationality and Power: Democracy in Practice*, Chicago: University of Chicago Press, 1998.

Harris, Richard. 'Modes of Informal Urban Development'. *Journal of Planning Literature* 33, no. 3 (November 2018): 267–286, https://doi.org/10.1177/0885412217737340.
Harvey, David. *Social Justice and the City*. Athens, GA: University of Georgia Press, 2009.
Huchzermeyer, Marie, and Aly Karam, eds. *Informal Settlements: A Perpetual Challenge?* Cape Town, South Africa: University of Cape Town Press, 2006.
Jones, Paul Roger. *Unpacking Informal Urbanism: Urban Planning and Design Education in Practice*. Bandung, Indonesia: ITB Penerbit Press, 2016.
Königsberger, Otto. *The Absorption of Newcomers in the Cities of Developing Countries*. Report to the United Nations, New York, 1975.
Lehmann, Steffen. *Back to the City: Strategies for Informal Urban Interventions*. Stuttgart, Germany: Hatje Cantz, 2009.
Lehmann, Steffen and Zaman, Atiq. 'Changing the masterplanning paradigm for China's urban future', in: *Rethinking Masterplanning: Creating Quality Places*, AlWaer, H. & Illsley, B. (eds), 2017, ICE Publishing and Th. Telford Ltd, London; p 135–148.
Moser, Caroline O.N. 'Informal Sector or Petty Commodity Production: Dualism or Dependence in Urban Development?' *World Development* 6, no. 9–10 (September–October 1978): 1041–1064.
Peña, D.G. (2006, 4, March). Farmers Feeding Families: Agroecology in South Central Los Angeles. *Lecture Notes, Keynote Address presented to the National Association for Chicana and Chicano Studies*, Washington State University, Pullman, WA. https:www.ucdenver.instructure.com.
Perlman, Janice. *The Myth of Marginality: Urban Poverty and Politics in Rio de Janeiro*. Los Angeles: University of California Press, 1976.
Rudofsky, Bernard. *Architecture without Architects: A Short Introduction to Non-pedigreed Architecture*. The Museum of Modern Art. Garden City, NY: Doubleday, 1964.
Stiglitz, Joseph E. 'The Measurement of Wealth: Recessions, Sustainability and Inequality'. In *Contemporary Issues in Macroeconomics*, edited by Joseph E. Stiglitz and Martin Guzman, 63–76. International Economic Association Book Series. London: Palgrave Macmillan UK, 2013.
United Nations. Sustainable Development Goals 2015. Online: https://sustainabledevelopment.un.org/?menu=1300.
Yiftachel, Oren. 'Theoretical Notes on "Gray Cities"'. *Planning Theory* 8, no. 1 (February 2009): 88–100.

Chapter 9

The self-organising city and its modus operandi

Informal urbanism and public space

Steffen Lehmann

Introduction

Cities are many different things to many people. At their best, they offer essential breathing spaces that facilitate social inclusion and encounters, allowing for the unplanned and enabling a diverse range of informal activities to occur. They support autonomy, empower people to 'do their thing' (for instance, as micro-entrepreneurs) and give them the freedom to thrive and lead a happy life. The city is never an easy cocktail to get right. It needs the optimal mix and balance between efficient public transport systems, a walkable public space network, integrated green space, fair and decent quality housing, good workplaces, cultural vitality and great health care and education. Social inclusion is of particular relevance, as it is the process by which efforts are made to ensure equal opportunities – that everyone, regardless of their background or social status, can thrive and achieve their full potential in life (Alexander 1979; Whyte 1980). Gentrification, excessive control of space and the increasing privatisation of public space are constant threats to this potential.

Over the last fifty years, urbanisation has become an inevitable, fast-moving global phenomenon, and informality has emerged as an inseparable feature of this process in numerous cities, not limited to developing cities in the Global South. However, the process of urbanisation can be ruthless and is frequently driven by greed and one-sided monetary motives. Therefore, in most large-scale urban developments, residents, planners, and government and decision makers make efforts to ensure social inclusion can occur once the project is completed. These efforts include policies and actions that promote equal access to public services, space and amenities; reduce the threat of gentrification; and enable citizens' participation in the decision-making processes on developments that frequently affect their lives in cities.

The concept of informality emerged in the early 1970s, at this time simply defined as 'the informal sector of the urban poor' and limited in its focus to people living in slums and squatter settlements (Moser 1978; Koolhaas 1998). Informality was closely associated with urban poverty and deprivation; and indeed, it often involves the lower-income group that falls into the informal sphere. However, with globalisation's enabling of social mobility and the levelling of economies, we have gained a much wider view of urban informality and its modus operandi. This led to a more differentiated and multifaceted view of informality. More recently, the lack of affordable housing, functional infrastructure and high unemployment are present in all kinds of cities and geographies, not limited to cities in the Global South, and have made a clear differentiation between formality and informality more difficult and vaguer (Bardhan, Jana and Sarkar 2019).

Redefining urban informality

It is estimated that *informal* is the daily condition of at least one-sixth of our world's population. This chapter explores some examples of informal urbanism and its relationship to public and private space. The author believes that the informal sector offers important lessons on the adaptive capacity and use of space in general, and on its social role. For instance, it is fascinating to examine the ways in which 'marginal groups' appropriate informal urban spaces in Mexico City and how this adds to a city's character, entrepreneurship and success (Lara-Hernandez, Melis and Lehmann 2019).

The characteristics of informal, interstitial spaces within the contemporary city, and the numerous creative ways in which these spaces are appropriated, challenge the prevalent critical discourse about our common understanding of 'public space', place-making and the character of social order in the city. One could say that informality redefines our relationship with the formal. Unplanned informal spaces punctuate the homogenous, controlled, 'official' pattern of the public space network and the everyday ubiquitous spaces of the contemporary city. However, they are often overlooked or relegated simply as messy 'left-over space' or 'urban voids'. Informal spaces are excluded from what is commonly defined as the *ideal* concept of the controlled city because they run contrary to the dominant image of an ordered city, such as that promoted in conventional masterplans and the clean marketing of the official urban scenarios (Sennett 2018).

How urban informality, public space, growth and inequality are interconnected has long been a field of scholarly reflection and research. It has been argued that cities exist because people tend to agglomerate around space for social, economic or political reasons. Increased job access, trade, housing and amenities, combined with safety and fewer restrictions on personal choices, indicate some critical advantages of urban informality. However, depending on its context, the definition of informality varies greatly. In constantly evolving cities, there exist very different types of informality, for instance, in the context of sustainable urban development and in its relationship to environmental sustainability. It's worthwhile to explore how informal urbanisation can be interpreted within such different contexts and how it frequently embeds principles of sustainability, such as reuse, recycling, resourcefulness and resilience.

Frequently, the informal is defined as 'casual', with a lack of legal status. However, 'informal' should not be equated with 'illegal', as a legal option may not exist. Urban informality conceptualises and illustrates temporary appropriation of space as a phenomenon that contributes to the conformation of relevant themes within the urban agenda, including topics such as citizenship, inequality, social inclusion, migration, urban social sustainability, health care, employment, growth, informal entrepreneurialism and resilience. The informal temporary appropriation of urban space has behavioural, economic and cultural dimensions, and forms of appropriation are not always immediately obvious: they are not mentioned in building codes and can often be subversive or unexpected, emerging in the grey area between formal and informal activities in the city.

As life must adapt to site-specific solutions, the real life of cities often takes place in the corners where no one is watching, where communities coalesce and develop organically, and where the thousands of people who might call the place home interact on a human scale. Offering a better understanding of the space appropriation phenomenon, this chapter poses the following questions: How could our streetscapes and plazas better cope with the new and complex forms of informal appropriation, increasing pressures from homelessness and urban nomadism? How can we design our public spaces to better facilitate the informal components of economic life and social inclusion in cities?

As discussed, informality is likely to contribute huge potential to solve all kinds of urban challenges, such as the housing crisis or the threat of gentrification, which often accompanies urban regeneration activities. A good example of this is the housing project by Elemental in Constitution, Chile. The project allows for infill and self-built completion (as a tactical intervention) by the inhabitants over time, at a later stage. Architect Alejandro Aravena argues that 'half a house can build a whole community' (McKnight 2016), as a low-income family cannot afford a large house immediately. The idea is to build a 'half house' that residents can finish by themselves incrementally and informally over time, allowing people to build whatever they like for themselves within a given frame. This informal, incremental, self-built completion leads to an unplanned and unexpected variety that makes each house unique. Residents provide their own time, labour and any extra materials to complete the second half of the house later, which delivers affordability and allows for more funding to uplift and improve the surrounding public space. In addition, the architects provide the complete residential designs as an open-source resource on their website for free download to help tackle the affordable housing crisis (see Figure 9.1).

Cities built for cars?

Cities form when people try to take advantage of shared infrastructure (e.g. by creating marketplaces for trade and information) and cultural amenities. In cities, companies and workers benefit from knowledge creation, job opportunities and matching, as well as information sharing.

For most of urban history, city streets and public spaces were for everyone. There was the shared road that led to public space such as a market, plaza or playground. Nevertheless, streets that serve the needs of motorists first create an automobile lifestyle that favours private vehicles passing through over the people who live there. Over the last seventy years, as our cities have continued to sprawl and as more and more people are forced to live in car-dependent suburbs, we have been making it harder for social interactions and human connections to occur. The urban planning school of thought that promoted zoning and separation led to strict segregation of the various functions of a city (as embedded in simplistic zoning regulations) and made walkable, mixed-use and compact neighbourhoods almost impossible. The twentieth-century zoning laws simplified the idea of a city with strictly separated places for living, working, shopping and recreation. While such a planning system might have the advantage that it is easier for planners to understand and control, it bans complexity and restricts freedom (Sennett 1974; Brahmblatt 2015; Lehmann 2019).

Figure 9.1 Housing by Elemental in Constitution, Chile: individual two-storey half houses for informal, incremental self-building by the residents (2010). Aravena has championed an approach he describes as 'incremental', in which governments fund construction of 'half a good house', with residents completing the other self-built portion informally as resources allow.

Source: Elemental.

In the mid-twentieth century, with the emergence of the car-dominated city, the new notions of freeway, shopping mall, suburbs and parking lots became dominating forces of our urban lives. This new conception of a city based on movement through private vehicles and a network of freeways has reduced the level of social interaction and walkability and increased anonymity. It has also increased the need for informal solutions on the pedestrian scale. Recognizing that cities are places where both problems emerge and solutions are found at the citizen level, urban activism has been increasingly considered an important part of the governance processes, as local actors desire to participate in politics, influencing decision-making through legal tools and participatory practices.

According to Lewis Mumford, social and spatial inequalities are an intertwined phenomenon, and to understand them, we must address them simultaneously. In developing cities, for example, factories are often located far from the barrios and informal settlements where workers live, forcing them to endure long daily commutes back and forth from home to work. Chouinard refers to migration when he describes urban informality as 'places of shadow citizenship and entitlements' (1997) in which inequality and injustice proliferate. His research sheds light on the dynamics generating the urban areas and conditions of urban informality, including the condition of 'shadow citizenship', and aims to contribute to a better understanding of the drivers of urban inequalities that pose significant challenges to the existence of urban societies. Stiglitz notes that the more unequal a society is, the greater the likelihood that its social polarisation will intensify; and the wider the spatial and social inequality, the lower the economic growth of a country or city, and consequently the higher the threat to the sustainability of its welfare state (Stiglitz 2013, 36).

Charles Montgomery notes that 'cities have always been a happiness project' (Montgomery 2013). His research shows that *happiness* in urban living depends on criteria such as commute times, air quality, housing affordability, crime rates and access to local green spaces. Urban residents tend to be happier if a great public space or garden is just around the corner. Public plazas, parks and other meeting places, for example, can encourage new social connections and interactions while giving residents a sense of common ownership over the space, where everyone has a stake in the city's success. Access to multiple modes of mobility – from trains and buses to bike shares and e-scooters – can help remove one's sense of isolation amidst the crowds. Pedestrian-friendly streets boost the city's overall well-being by encouraging active lifestyles and even more face-to-face interactions. However, nothing could be more important to the health of urban dwellers than diversity in its population, its housing opportunities, its variety of public space and its employment opportunities (Montgomery 2013).

Placeless, auto-dependent and socially-isolating sprawl has always created more problems than it solved. Density, on the other hand, can resolve many of our current challenges: it makes mass transit possible and allows for a better public space network, with active streetscapes and more affordable housing. It creates environments where people can walk, supports public hospitals, vibrant cultural institutions and allows us to curb climate emissions. The era of the car-centric suburb is over. However, gentrification, growing privatisation of public space and lack of affordable housing, as well as lack of accessibility to high-quality public spaces and parks, have exacerbated the urban conditions of inequality. More compact urban form and infill supports all forms of active mobility, such as walking and cycling; facilitates public transport; and reduces the capital costs for infrastructure. It is the walkable city that facilitates all forms of urban informality. Making cities more compact and walkable has always been a key to social integration, and essential for localising the UN's Sustainable Development Goals (UN 2015). Thus, engendering the dynamics of the United Nations' 2030 Agenda for Sustainable Development (with Goal 11 specifically calling for cities and human settlements to be 'inclusive, safe, resilient and sustainable'), spatial inequality and particularly inequalities exacerbated by the economic crisis and austerity measures have been addressed by activists through the means of political protest and social innovation (Rivera 2013).

Charles Montgomery (2013, 36) notes that "The city is not merely a repository of pleasures. It is the stage on which we fight our battles, where we act out the drama of our own lives. It can enhance or corrode our ability to cope with everyday challenges. It can steal our autonomy or give us the freedom to thrive. The good city should be measured not only by its distractions and amenities, but also by how it affects this everyday drama of survival, work and meaning.... The city is ultimately a shared project, like Aristotle's polis, a place where we can fashion a common good that we simply cannot build alone."

Urban informality and socio-economic inequality

The concept of *informality* has its origin in the emergence of the 'informal sector', which was coined as a concept in the early 1970s. Caroline Moser (1978, 1051) described the informal sector as simply 'the urban poor', or as the people living in slums or squatter settlements. Today, most scholars agree that this definition fell short of the many facets that informality can display. In the 1980s, the definition became more refined, and informality was understood not solely as poverty, inequality, illegality or marginality per se; to paraphrase Castells (1983), it was seen not as a product but as a process, constantly in the making, shifting and redefining relationships (in many cases dependent and essential) with the formal. Rakowski emphasised the link to the economy when she argued that informality in peripheral societies is the expression of the uneven nature of capitalist development (Harvey 1989; Rakowski 1994).

Informality plays a different role in different cities. In cities in India, for example, slums are an essential part of the cityscape and all major cities have massive areas devoted to informal settlement growth (see Figure 9.2). Roy (2009, 2012) describes the complicated relationship between what is legal and illegal in the Indian city, or authorised and unauthorised, arguing that informality is a deregulated system not

Figure 9.2 The edge where the formal city meets the informal city in an aerial photo of Mumbai. Informal settlements have developed on public land along the river, and the inequality and spatial separation are visible from above.

Source: Johnny Miller, 2018.

synonymous with poverty. Scholars, including Porter (2011), as well as Bardhan, Jana and Sarkar (2019), point out that informality is not outside formal systems, but is instead produced by formal structures and always intimately related to them. They have equated informality with a kind of self-help arising from the inability of the government and market forces to provide essential services like affordable housing and employment, as is the case in the Indian example.

Urban informality in particular relates to the unplannable, but it is far more than poor squatter settlements or slums in the Global South. AlSayyad and Roy emphasise the importance of income-generating, entrepreneurial efforts and expenditure saving, such as resource-efficiency or recycling activities (2004). Today, a new reading of these forms of informality is emerging. New forms of informality are constantly emerging, while old forms re-establish themselves in a manner which makes it difficult to distinguish between globally driven and locally based informality (Kundu 2019). Agglomeration forces strengthen centralisation trends, resulting in urbanisation and spatial distribution of location choices and investments, in terms of infrastructure and innovation activities, within cities (e.g. the decision about the route of a light rail system, or the choice of where a recycling centre is built).

The importance of public space is in the manifestation of social relations and is a social relation itself (Florida and Mellander 2018). Although accelerating urbanisation can have a significant impact on the spatial outcomes of economic activity and inequalities, it affects social inclusion in urban areas in contradictory ways (Lefebvre 1974). Cities in the developed world experience a paradox wherein rising levels of human capital, economic activity and employment are accompanied by a trend of increasing levels of socio-economic inequality, gentrification and spatial segregation. While agglomeration effects in cities can act as engines of urban growth, they can also be drivers of gentrification and inequality, not only in economic terms but also in a wide range of quality-of-life aspects (Lehmann 2019). Such increasing inequalities have become a multi-scale issue. It is evident that the urban environments of developed cities face a situation in which, despite their continuously rising shares of economic activity, employment and wealth, levels of socio-economic inequality are increasing and express a spatial footprint in cities as well as between neighbourhoods.

Tactical urbanism as a form of informality

The use of public space changes over time, and urban informality is closely linked to the unplanned, dynamic use of public urban space. Consequently, numerous public spaces are linked to temporal informal activities such as pop-up markets and demonstrations, or as spaces for particular celebrations. For example, just think of the carnival celebrations every February in South America that temporarily change public spaces. Informal spaces are often perceived as 'unplannable', as informality tends to occur in a deregulated rather than an unregulated realm.

Public spaces offer endless opportunities for *tactical urbanism* as a form of informality. In contrast to institutionalised urbanism, tactical urbanism is defined as temporary (short-term), low-cost projects that aim to make a part of a city more lively or enjoyable. It is frequently referred to as guerrilla urbanism, pop-up urbanism or DIY

Figure 9.3 Tactical urbanism includes ephemeral appropriation and temporary interventions in public space. An example is the transformation of Times Square in Manhattan simply by adding lawn chairs to create a traffic-free area.

Source: New York City Department of Transportation, 2009.

urbanism. It includes quick, low-risk, temporary changes ('interventions') to the built environment, intended to improve local neighbourhoods and city gathering places. Figure 9.3 shows an example of tactical urbanism in the public space of Times Square, Manhattan.

The outcomes of large-scale institutionalised urban developments have frequently been disappointing in their results (Oswalt et al. 2007; AlWaer & Illsley 2017). Conventional hierarchical master plans are struggling to deliver on their many promises because society has much more complex requirements today. Therefore, the question arises: can a city still be planned or predicted? In *Back to the City: Strategies for Informal Urban Interventions* (Lehmann 2009), I described the power that tactical and improvised interventions in underused public spaces can have and their ability to become catalysts for long-lasting urban change. Use of vacant and derelict sites for new programmes, activities and citizens' participation has allowed for the reshaping of disregarded urban spaces. It represents a 'messy and imperfect grassroots design activism and spontaneous Guerrilla urbanism' (Lehmann 2009), in which community-driven small-scale projects often become the embodiment of unexpected outcomes that a formal planning process would have rarely achieved. These dynamic 'everyday' urban design processes and interventions can operate in contrast to the institutionalised over-regulated planning process.

Dynamic micro-entrepreneurship needs walkable streets

There is growing recognition that informal jobs and informal housing constitute significant proportions of urban economies (Castells 1983; Haas and Olsson 2014; Bardhan, Jana and Sarkar 2019), and this form of self-employed micro-entrepreneurship is thought of as economic empowerment. Urban informality has taken on new forms under the forces of globalisation that cannot be disentangled from public space. In addition, informality today is not limited solely to a geography of periphery or urban core, nor to poverty, inequality, illegality or marginality per se.

Like Disneyland, the Las Vegas Strip is a carefully choreographed urban machine that provides rare high-quality walkable space not often found in US cities: it presents a walkable, mixed-use city centre densified with sensory pleasures of consumable goods and decorated with vernacular or historical facades. Both places, the Strip and Disneyland, are privatised 'quasi-public spaces'. They require a vast urban system behind the scenes to support the experience machine. It is no accident that every visit to the Strip (just like to Disneyland) "begins and ends with a walk along Main Street USA: a parade of cartoon-cute shops and unhurried bustle that simulates the perfect small town cliché" (Montgomery 2013, 31). Visitors delight in Main Street USA and the experience of walkable public space, which is very different from the car-dependent suburban sprawl they are used to in their home cities of Phoenix, Houston or Los Angeles.

Informality, once associated with squatters and slums in the Global South, has now become a generalised urban form in most cities of the developing and developed worlds (AlWaer and Illsley 2017). Many of the informal activities that occur within the formal city are driven by the micro-entrepreneurship of immigrants trying to make a living. These micro-business operations of marginalised immigrants are usually happening in unregulated space, at street level, uncovering ephemeral opportunities and temporal potential. Ortega describes the impact of the informal mobile car wash vendors' business on the formal street life in Las Vegas (Ortega 2015, 115). He found that the group of mobile car wash vendors in Las Vegas occupy the edges of parking lots and strip mall developments, forming part of a resistant cultural infrastructure' (see Figure 9.4). The car wash vendors are an informal entrepreneurial group appropriating the streetscape to sell their services in a non-regulated grey zone, side-by-side with the formalised and regulated tourist activities concentrated along the boulevard. This includes the mobile activities of self-employed male or female street hawkers, shoeshine boys and other marginalised groups. Their activities occur along the busy streets of cities, where globalisation and economic liberalisation have given rise to new dynamic geographies. There is demand: the informal sector steps in to provide products and services that are in demand but not offered affordably by the formal sector. This is the reason Hernando de Soto described informality as 'heroic entrepreneurship' (2000). Low-paid and self-employed residents have no financial buffer to fall back on, but we all rely upon their work to keep the city moving. In numerous big cities, informal workers are the backbone of the urban systems, keeping these cities functioning.

Figure 9.4 A temporary, informal pop-up car wash station along Tropicana Avenue in Las Vegas. Micro-entrepreneurship creates new opportunities for 'shadow citizens' and indicates a more spontaneous use of public space.

Source: S. Lehmann, 2020.

Burning man: Informal versus formal arrangement

This book chapter examines cases ranging from self-built housing in Chile to car wash vendors in Las Vegas to tactical urbanism in New York's Times Square. There are two more case studies:

- the Burning Man City, a temporary festival town in the desert of Northern Nevada, a once small-scale spontaneous construction that has evolved into a gigantic event.
- the negative impact that new digital technologies for control, surveillance and facial recognition have on public spaces in China.

The Burning Man spectacle is an interesting case of informal tactical urbanism. Every year, volunteers erect a temporary 'desert city' over the short period of two weeks in remote Northern Nevada, outside Reno. In two weeks, an entire, dense city is built, lived in for nine days, and disappears without leaving a trace. What started in 1991 as an annual festival of self-expression and spontaneous gathering in a deregulated space has now grown into a massive urban development that exists for only a short time every year. However, since it has grown to over one hundred thousand people, the festival city has become one of the most regulated initiatives, planned over months down to the smallest detail. The explosive growth of the countercultural event, due to its utopian vision of peace and love, meant that it needed a more structured organisational system with a full city infrastructure and medical stations.

Urban planner Rod Garrett is credited with developing the master plan for Burning Man City, also called Black Rock City (see Figures 9.5 and 9.6). Its simplistic but

Figure 9.5 Aerial photo of the temporary, semi-circular city of the annual ephemeral Burning Man festival, Nevada.

Source: Photo courtesy of Jason Bean, 2019.

Figure 9.6 The temporary Burning Man City grew over the last decade, and in 2018 and 2019 it housed 100,000 people. Ironically, the informal event is organised within a highly formal, radial figure-ground plan that forms a ring.

Source: Photo courtesy of Jason Bean, 2019.

practical figure-ground plan of a concentric semicircle has a gigantic sculpture in its centre. Its formal layout is flexible enough to allow for all kinds of informal activities within its rigid structure to flourish. People stay in thousands of tents, trucks, cars, recreational vehicles and camp sites that together form the gigantic C-shaped circular 'city'. Movement along the circular and radial roads of this self-referential shape happens by walking or biking, not by driving. This temporary city plan is built around the spectacle of art, music and human interaction. While the earlier festival occupied random sites that brought feelings of dislocation, the circular design was naively intended to express a sense of communal belonging. The city plan needed to be easy for all those arriving to grasp because it would be built within two weeks. Everyone who attends needs to know their place within the bigger picture. The area closest to the centre is reserved for art installations, creating a park-like zone that complements the 'residential neighbourhoods'. The early dynamic, informal and messy guerrilla grassroots beginnings of Burning Man, with its unpredictable nature, are long gone, and the institutionalised mass event it has become has a significantly negative environmental impact. Here, ironically, the informal complex event is organised within a highly formal, radial figure-ground plan of the ring.

Reno Mayor Hillary Schieve believes that there are lessons in urban planning to be learnt from this temporary city for permanent cities: "*Burning Man* stretches your definition of art, and of what is possible in city-building with cooperation and shared values. There's an impression that it's a lawless, anything-goes atmosphere, but that couldn't be further from reality. You can see arts and culture as vital to the soul of a city, and public spaces that bring people together. Every year, when the city is rebuilt, it is with accumulated lessons from over the years. Even the city plan – the crescent that circles the 'Man' that is burnt on the final night – isn't a fully closed circle because it's responsive to the wind conditions on the Playa. It's designed with nature in mind." (Hillary Schieve, mayor of Reno, Nevada, where Burning Man is happening, in an interview on May 16, 2020 on *ArchDaily*)

Government regulations, surveillance and new technologies in Chinese public spaces

For centuries, architects and urbanists have observed people's movement and behaviour in public space, and these observations have often informed their design decisions. For instance, the discreet distinction between private and public space, or the sense of belonging that we can experience in good public space, have been guiding themes for new urban plans. However, in the twenty-first century, urban space is challenged and changing under the pressure of technological advancement and a new relationship between the city and digital technologies. This process is closely connected to how new technologies – artificial intelligence, big data and autonomous technologies in particular – have commenced to impact public space and urban life (Ratti 2019). Facial recognition technology has turned Chinese cities into the largest areas of constant mass surveillance (see Figure 9.7). Data models are constantly feeding and optimising our urban experience, and the urban landscape of tomorrow will depend not only on human-to-human relationships, but more and more on machine-to-human relationships that drive and optimise the invisible systems and connections that keep the city moving. This evolving relationship between urban space and technological

Figure 9.7 Facial recognition technology allows for the complete surveillance of Chinese citizens, diminishing the quality of public space. Will this total control mean the end of informal activities in the public spaces of Chinese cities?

Source: Gilles Sabri 2019.

innovation, the cultural integration of fast-evolving digital technologies and their environmental contradictions, is still little understood and under-researched.

Facial recognition technology has been around for a while, but in 2019 it became a facet of life in China. Facial recognition systems are being rolled out in public spaces such as railway stations, schools and shopping centres across the country. Enabled by a vast network of cameras, the government is using the technology for total surveillance, turning its cities into a police state. China has installed some 200 million cameras by its own estimate (2019), feeding into a surveillance-based biometric dataset of millions of people. Part of an effort to monitor ethnic minorities in the name of national security, it has now become mainstream in Beijing, Shanghai and numerous smaller cities. Citizens are indexed by information such as their criminal history, and facial recognition data records whether they were bearded or wearing a mask and what ethnicity they were.

China's facial recognition technology is now so advanced that it can positively identify 98.1 percent of human faces within 0.8 seconds, according to the *China Daily* (2019). So far, there has been little pushback in China against facial recognition technology and data harvesting. While this is not entirely surprising (after all, the Chinese Communist Party is well known as an oppressive authority), these surveillance systems are being deployed extensively and invasively to achieve total control of its people and their behaviour in urban areas. What we need instead is the use of technology that helps and supports the daily lives of people. Following the 2020 Coronavirus pandemic, which started in the city of Wuhan (China), the Chinese Government justifies the excessive surveillance of its citizens as a necessary public health measure.

Considering the impact of the pandemic on city life, Richard Sennett raises caution about the authoritarian control and social isolation 'that might outlast it' and warns of the danger of social surveillance (Sennett 2020). He warns that power structures exploit crises and use them to legitimate expanded authoritarian rules and total control even when the crisis has passed. In particular, rules regulating public space and dictating social distance are likely to persist even after we have the medical means to suppress the virus. To prove this case, Sennett reminds of regulations following the 9/11 disaster where this was the case: "regulations restricting public gatherings, controlling access to buildings, and the specification of how bombproof buildings should be constructed, stayed on the statute books" (Sennett 2020).

The quality of public space in authoritarian countries is being diminished by exorbitant control and surveillance (Hamm & Feireiss 2015). Spaces for spontaneous informal interaction without regulation, control and commitment to consumption are a good thing for society. Flourishing cities have always relied on such informal spaces and activities to function, enabling a mix of possibilities that allow for surprises and the unplanned to occur. This is why the extensive surveillance of Chinese public space and its excessive control is an invasion of people's privacy and detrimental to the vitality and quality of these cities and their public spaces.

Re-examining the architecture of density. How the 2020 public health crisis will leave its mark on cities and erase informal activities

The 2020 pandemic, like all other extreme and painful experiences, offers some important lessons and architects and urban planners have much to learn from the situation. Like the Great Depression and World War II, the Covid-19 pandemic (along with the climate change crisis) has altered how we think about the economy, globalisation, travel, tourism, the workplace and public space in the everyday situation. The significant impact a pandemic can have on urban development, economic productivity and urban informality is nothing new. Since the global cholera and tuberculosis outbreaks in the nineteenth century, pandemics have reshaped cities, and some of these consequences can include increased surveillance, de-densification of neighbourhoods, remote working from home (made possible by the intensification of digital infrastructure) and even the introduction of new urban systems (e.g., around 1850, European cities introduced modern drinking supply and sewerage systems as a direct result from the devastating cholera pandemic).

For centuries, urban planning decisions have been shaped by public health agendas. Pandemics can radically alter the way we think about and move around cities: during the 2020 Covid-19 health crisis, people have self-isolated, stayed at home and avoided contact with others. At time of writing, it is still unclear how this pandemic will alter our urban life and what exactly will be the impact from this crisis on cities and their informal sector.

Cities are made of collective sites, shared green spaces and public spaces. The author still believes in human contact as a necessity of urban survival. For centuries, the promise of social interaction has always shaped public space. In the same way, our cities, public spaces and buildings have also been shaped by public health concerns. So what can we expect the lasting impact from the Covid-19 pandemic on our public spaces to be? Some of the usual priorities of design are likely to give way to more epidemiological considerations: how does this space perform in a pandemic? Can it be cleaned? Can it perform, technically, spatially and aesthetically under new rules of interaction and social distance?

In future, with the risk of infection, there will be much less person-to-person connection. So, how can we socialize in an age of social distancing? What will be the impact on the informal sector? The pandemic challenges urbanists to rethink cities and public space. What has become clear is that a major challenge in our cities is the loneliness of people: for instance, how to deal with the large number of elderly people living alone (e.g. in Paris, 68 percent of the elderly are one-person households). Are there any new concepts of community for the elderly (such as mutual care networks) that would contribute to avoid isolation?

In 2020, for an extended period, more than one-third of the world's population was forced to spend most of their time inside their homes. This global lockdown caused by the coronavirus has brought the shortcomings and social inequality inherent in modern housing to the forefront. Housing is limited in its capacity to be multipurpose and its shortcomings reflect inequalities. In future, our homes will need to deal with working remotely, online shopping and online learning; in this new world, there will be much less opportunity for urban informality.

Our living spaces have become the places where we work, shop, socialise, exercise, study and so on. The windows, balconies and roof gardens have become interfaces with other people and a vehicle of collective expression and social interaction. As a consequence of the pandemic, residents lose access to outside amenities such as parks, cafés and cultural and sporting facilities. The restricted movement has shown that most housing is not designed for multiple uses and has no suitable spaces for home offices, to productively work from home. It is particularly difficult for people who live in confinement in small spaces or apartments with limited views. All this will need to be better considered in future housing design.

Some architects have developed post-coronavirus design principles, envisaging how the design of workplaces, mobility and public spaces with social distancing will change. Post-pandemic, it is likely that future houses will accommodate more home offices and specific working-from-home areas, while the open-plan office layout seems to be passé.

Obvious questions also exist in regard to density and mobility

How might our built environment – our cities, streets, squares and landscapes – need to transform to accommodate this conflicting desires for connection and social-distance during a pandemic? Cities have been hit hard by Covid-19, leading to new concepts of urban space and the potential revival of the more spacious suburbs. Jack Shenker (2020) suggests that in future, "urban planners will face the apparent tension between densification – the push towards cities becoming more concentrated, which is seen as essential to improving environmental sustainability – and disaggregation, the separating out of populations, which is one of the key tools being used to hold back infection transmission". This indicates also an emerging conflict between the competing demands of public health and the need to stop climate change: denser cities of short distances are necessary to reduce the need to commute and CO_2 emissions. In an almost predictable urban future, in times of a pandemic, informal activities will increasingly be push out or made impossible. Oppressive regimes could soon employ total surveillance and security robots to control and patrol all public spaces, and check the identity and medical condition of people, leading to a fundamental shift in social relationships and loss of freedom.

All this doesn't mean that higher-density cities are necessarily more vulnerable, or lower-density cities more resilient to the pandemic (Hong Kong and Seoul, for instance, performed reasonably well through the health crisis). External city density matters less than internal density of occupancy, inside buildings. The density that matters most is internal population density (e.g. when working in a crowded open-plan call centre), as there is much less transmission through casual contacts in outdoor spaces such as streets or parks (Pafka 2020).

De-densification will not resolve the public health challenges. Density and diversity have always been the rationale for cities and their public space. The concentration of activities in a city stimulates economic and social activity. The concentration of people on less land is also a good ecological principle in dealing with climate change, by saving on infrastructure resources. The pandemic requires us to do a radical rethink of density. Sennett suggests that "to prevent or inhibit future pandemics, we may need to find different physical forms for density, permitting people to communicate, to see neighbours, to participate in street life even as they temporarily separate" (2020). New types of courtyard buildings could help creating this.

In general, density is not bad for our health, as it enables walkable cities, an active public space network and bustling commercial corridors, which in turn fosters health, makes communities more resilient and allows us to curb climate emissions – a public health problem of an entirely different kind. In all the discussion about the health risks of density and concentration of uses, it is important to remember that urban density can provide for health, resiliency and space for informal activities that are integral to our society. We will need to rebuild trust in public space and rethink the types of public space and their role as spaces of shared values (see Figure 9.8).

Public transport is probably the most challenging issue, as the benefits of public transport consist of efficiently massing numbers of riders together, but that isn't a healthy form of densification. The walkable, compact and mixed-use "city of short distances" (Lehmann 2010) would offer a solution to reduce the need to commute. Cycling has again become very popular during the crisis. Flying is becoming again a much more exclusive activity, and if we cannot travel, it will narrow our horizons.

The economy, sustainability and informal opportunities

Global cities act as both locus and regulator of the 'uneven processes of capitalism' (Harvey 1989), and places where increasing investment in the financial sector rather than in other productive activities has shaped the geography of unequal development. However, the growth of spatial inequality is not limited to global cities. Geographical inequalities are frequently a reflection of an out-of-equilibrium economy characterised by the dynamic coexistence of regionalised growth and localised decline, unequal interactions and asymmetrical power relations between the urban core and peripheries.

Figure 9.8 Temporary marking grid on an Italian public plaza to guide people in their social distancing, city of Vicchio near Florence.

Source: Caret Studio

Since the sidewalk and market vendors of the Greek agora, the public realm has always been a place to sell goods and services. The impact of the 2008 economic crisis and subsequent austerity measures, accompanied by the persistent stagnation of some economies (along with rapid technological changes in the world of communication and work), have caused conditions of inequality to further proliferate. Alongside regions and cities that have functioned as poles of attraction for private capital investment and innovation, boosted by ad hoc public and private interventions, are areas in which economic hardship has been coupled with not only private-sector but also public-sector retrenchment. Therefore, opportunities for social and economic development generated by global economic, financial and political trends have not benefited all countries, cities and populations equally, nor have these opportunities been distributed evenly across regions, cities and neighbourhoods or among people (Sassen 1991; Lefebvre 1996; Marcuse et al. 2009).

The 2008 economic crisis and the ways governments have sought to address it, either with austerity measures or with strategic growth packages, have contributed to strengthening long-established patterns of unequal territorial and spatial development. Places better equipped with human, infrastructural and social resources have greatly benefited and have had further opportunities to overcome the crisis, while areas with a weaker combination of such factors keep lagging behind. In this scenario, old divisions, such as *centrality* versus *periphery* in terms of regional or urban economic and political centres, have exacerbated pre-existing territorial inequality patterns. In Europe, for instance, these inequality patterns can be found between Southern and Northern Italy, or West and East Germany, or Northern and Southern England, where a two-speed development has created gated communities and immigrant ghettos.

Numerous scholars have elaborated on the learning that can be gained from the richness of informal settlements, their non-hierarchical systems and their resourcefulness such as described by Dovey (2013), AlSayyad and Roy (2004), Jones, and others). This is why, increasingly, research has focused on the localised clustering of economic activity and the importance of informal entrepreneurialism, for instance, the conditions which enable the intense informal activities that can occur along busy city streets and on plazas. Massey's (1984) work on labour policies and the consequential spatial division of labour indicates that each stage of economic growth creates new spatial divisions of labour; each period reflects different socio-spatial configurations, introducing new dimensions of inequalities and relations of dominance and dependence among activities in different places and involving different people. Uncovering the relationship between informal spaces and the economy is crucial to understanding the benefits informal urbanism can provide.

The opportunity to reclaim the 'democratic' public space that privatisation and gentrification have conquered lies in the sphere of civil society, where the urban problems are being defined, articulated and addressed. However, the juxtaposition between spatial inequality and social stratification has dramatically constrained opportunities for specific categories of individuals. Those experiencing a combination of spatial and social disadvantages (e.g. the elderly, urban poor or disabled people in need of health care services) find themselves entrapped in a cycle of deprivation. This spiral of deprivation reveals the interlocking systems of power that have an impact on the most marginalised in society and resonates with Crenshaw's (1989) 'intersectionality of structural identities' based on categories such as gender, race, sexuality and class, which interact with each other in various ways and further create inequalities and discrimination. In this context, the significance of opportunities for informal activities and appropriation of public or private space for micro-entrepreneurship becomes obvious, and the need to facilitate informality gains an entirely new dimension (Florida 2003).

Conclusion – enabling urban informality is relevant

The Greek agora was a truly public place where commercial goods, information and ideas were traded freely. Cities are full of contradictions, particularly when one considers the complexity inherent in places that mix living, working, shopping, recreation and other functions. Cramped market streets and urban informality lead to serendipitous encounters with other people and places, distractions, conversations and outdoor life that enable the benefits of messy public space. Planners frequently display a tendency towards simplification of inherently complex systems to avoid unplanned urban informality; with a new understanding, accepting and enabling informality will become part of the planner's future toolbox.

Addressing urban informality is a pressing issue and important in guiding the expansion and transformation of cities. Informality is a phenomenon that cannot be disentangled from space and urban planning. We can now think of new people-oriented organisational urban models of 'flexible density' that facilitate informal activities.

Many of the urban theories remain rooted in the developed world and urban studies are still dominated by the idea that the First World/Global North provides 'models' for Third World 'problems'. It is time for urban studies to move beyond this simplistic dichotomy and value learning and solutions from Third World cities' implementation of and policy responses to informality (Roy 2005 and 2012, see page. 13). In these settings, the 'unplannable' is a welcomed exception to the formal order of urban planning (Hall and Pfeiffer 2000).

The traditional concept of a rigid master plan as a set of rules and set-backs has become outdated, since the narrow perspective of master planning as a design-led activity frequently neglects the human dimension and is not sufficiently flexible and resilient to successfully deliver sustainable outcomes. This has resulted in the creation of places unable to deal with informal activities and change. There is, therefore, a need for an improved way of thinking: a new, integrated approach to master planning aimed at addressing the unpredictable nature of community development and accommodating elements of change (climate change as well as shifts in employment).

This chapter examined a range of different cases. It found that informal spaces emerge because these are beyond the realm of planning controls. In the case of the informal settlements that have developed on public land along rivers in Mumbai (see Figure 9.2), the urban poor have built their own city without any reference whatsoever to the overarching bureaucratic apparatus of planning and control in the formal city next door (Hall and Pfeiffer 2000).

At Burning Man City in the desert of Northern Nevada, city dwellers from all over the US created their idea of an ideal city based on a simplistic approach and radial model. Just because a structure is temporary or ephemeral like this one does not necessarily make it informal. In the case of China, the increasing control of public space, such as through facial recognition technology, is detrimental to the quality and diminishes the enjoyment of public space.

The 2008 economic crisis and subsequent austerity measures – along with rapid technological changes in the world of communication and work – have caused conditions of urban inequality to further proliferate. This process increased the need for more informal opportunities: with a large number of people depending on informal means and activities to sustain their livelihood, informality is a vital aspect of cities and needs to be facilitated. The question for decision makers should therefore be less about how to manage informality and should instead ask whether informality needs management at all. Informality will continue to be part of cities' socio-economic systems, and too much control (such as in the Chinese case) will only reduce the quality and enjoyment of public space.

This chapter explored some examples of informal urbanism and its ambiguous relationship to public and private space, where the informal sector can offer important lessons about the adaptive capacity of these spaces, its unexpected use and its social role. It examined various ways in which specific groups appropriate informal spaces and how these can add to a city's character, entrepreneurship and success. The characteristics of informal, interstitial spaces within the contemporary city and the numerous creative ways in which these temporary or permanently used spaces are appropriated (which are not always immediately obvious) continue to challenge the prevalent critical discourse about our understanding of 'authorized planning', formal place-making and the character of social order within the city in relation to these informal spaces. The necessary step is to integrate the concepts of the 'healthy city' with the related concepts of the green city and the city of short distances. In conclusion, one could say that informality is a deregulated self-help system that redefines relationships with the formal. The presented cases from Chile, the US and China illustrate the dilemma of the relationship between informality and public/private space today. How do we undo the rigidities of the "master plan" that disable informality?

References

Alexander, Christopher. *The Timeless Way of Building*, New York: Oxford University Press, 1979.

AlSayyad, Nezar, and Ananya Roy. 'Urban Informality: Crossing Borders'. In *Urban Informality: Transnational Perspectives from the Middle East, Latin America, and South Asia*, edited by Ananya Roy and Nezar AlSayyad, 1–6. Lanham, MD: Lexington Books, 2004.

AlWaer, Husam, and Barbara Illsley, eds. *Rethinking Masterplanning: Creating Quality Places*. London: ICE Publishing/Thomas Telford, 2017.

Bardhan, R, A Jana, and S Sarkar. 'Informality'. In *The Wiley Blackwell Encyclopaedia of Urban and Regional Studies*, edited by Anthony M. Orum, p 360. New York: J. Wiley & Sons, 2019.

Brahmblatt, V. 'Messy Urbanism'. In *Now Urbanism: The Future City Is Here*, edited by Jeffrey Hou, Benjamin Spencer, Thaisa Way, and Ken Yocom, 13–25. London/New York: Routledge, 2015.

Castells, Manuel. *The City and the Grassroots: A Cross-Cultural Theory of Urban Social Movements*. California Series in Urban Development, Book 2. Berkeley, CA: University of California Press, 1983.

China Daily 'Facial Recognition Aids Police Efforts' (11 Sep. 2019), He Wei, Beijing, 2019.

Chouinard, Vera. 'Structure and Agency: Contested Concepts in Human Geography'. *Canadian Geographer* 41, no. 4 (December 1997): 363–77.

Crenshaw, Kimberle. Demarginalizing the Intersection of Space and Sex: A Black Feminist Critique of Antidiscrimination Doctrine, *Feminist Theory and Antiracist Politics*. The University of Chicago Legal Forum 1989, no. 1, art. 8 (1989): 139–67.

De Soto Polar, Hernando. *The Mystery of Capital*. New York: Basic Books, 2000.

Dovey, Kim. 'Informalising Architecture: The Challenge of Informal Settlements'. *Architectural Design* 83, no. 6 (November 2013): 82–89, https://doi.org/10.1002/ad.1679.

Hamm, Oliver G., and Kristin Feireiss, eds. *Transforming Cities: Urban Interventions in Public Space*. Berlin: Jovis Verlag, 2015.

Florida, Richard. *The Rise of the Creative Class: And How It's Transforming Work, Leisure, and Everyday Life*. New York: Basic Books, 2003.

Florida, Richard, and Charlotta Mellander. 'The Geography of Economic Segregation'. *Social Sciences* 7, no. 8 (July 2018): 123.

Haas, Tigran, and Krister Olsson. *Emergent Urbanism: Urban Planning and Design in Times of Structural and Systemic Change*. Stockholm, Sweden: Routledge, 2014.

Hall, Peter, and Ulrich Pfeiffer. *Urban Future 21: A Global Agenda for Twenty-First Century Cities*. London: Spon, 2000.

Harvey, David. 'From Managerialism to Entrepreneurialism: The Transformation in Urban Governance in Late Capitalism'. *Geografiska Annaler: Series B, Human Geography* 71, no. 1 (1989): 3–17.

Koolhaas, Rem. 'Whatever happened to urbanism?' In *S, M, L, XL*, edited by Rem Koolhaas, Bruce Mau, and Hans Werlemann, 567. New York: Monacelli Press, 1998.

Kundu, Debolina. 'Urban Informality'. In *The Wiley-Blackwell Encyclopaedia of Urban and Regional Studies*, edited by Anthony M. Orum, p 412. London: J. Wiley & Sons, 2019.
Lefebvre, Henri. *Writings on Cities*, Oxford, UK: Blackwell, 1996.
Lefebvre, Henri. *The Production of Space*. Paris, France: Anthropos, 1974.
Lehmann, Steffen. *Back to the City: Strategies for Informal Urban Interventions*. Stuttgart, Germany: Hatje Cantz, 2009.
———. (2010). The Principles of Green Urbanism. *Transforming the City for Sustainability*. London: Earthscan.
———. (2019). Urban Regeneration. *A Manifesto for transforming UK Cities in the Age of Climate Change*. London: Palgrave Macmillan.
Massey, Doreen. *Spatial Divisions of Labour*. London: Macmillan, 1984.
Marcuse, Peter, James Connolly, Johann Novy, Ingrid Olivo, Cuz Potter, and Justin Steil, eds. *Searching for the Just City: Debates in Urban Theory and Practice*. New York/London: Routledge, 2009.
McKnight, Jenna. 'Alejandro Aravena makes housing designs available to the public for free'. Dezeen (6 April 2016), https://www.dezeen.com/2016/04/06/alejandro-aravena-elemental-social-housing-designs-architecture-open-source-pritzker/.
Montgomery, Charles. *Happy City. Transforming Our Lives through Urban Design*, London: Penguin, 2013.
Moser, Caroline O.N. (1978). 'Informal Sector or Petty Commodity Production: Dualism or Dependence in Urban Development?' *World Development Report* 6, no. 9–10 (September–October 1978): 1041–64.
Ortega, Daniel H. 'NOSOTROS (We): 'Two Cultures of Sustainability and the "Present City' of Las Vegas"'. In *Now Urbanism: The Future City is Here*, edited by Jeffrey Hou, Benjamin Spencer, Thaisa Way, and Ken Yocom, 109–21. London/New York: Routledge, 2015.
Oswalt, Philipp, Klaus Overmeyer, and Philipp Misselwitz. 'Patterns of the Unplanned'. In *Loose Space: Possibility and Diversity in Urban Life*, edited by Quentin Stevens and Karen Franck, 281–87. London: Routledge, 2007.
Pafka, Elek (2020). "As coronavirus forces us to keep our distance, city density matters less than internal density", *The Conversation* (online May 12, 2020), Melbourne.
Porter, Libby. 'Informality, the Commons and the Paradoxes for Planning: Concepts and Debates for Informality and Self-Made Cities'. *Planning Theory and Practice* 12, no. 1 (March 2011): 115–153.
Rakowski, Cathy A. 'Convergence and Divergence in the Informal Sector Debate: A Focus on Latin America, 1984–92'. *World Development Report* 22, no. 4 (April 1994): 501–516.
Ratti, Carlo. (2019). '2019 UABB Shenzen Bi-City Biennale of Architecture/Urbanism'. Carlo Ratti Associati, https://carloratti.com/project/2019-shenzhen-bi-city-biennale-of-urbanismarchitecture/
Rivera, Manuel. 'Political Criteria for Sustainable Development Goal (SDG) Selection and the Role of the Urban Dimension'. *Sustainability* 5, no. 12 (November 2013): 5034–51.
Roy, Ananya. (2005). 'Urban Informality: Toward an Epistemology of Planning'. *Journal of the American Planning Association* 71, no. 2 (June): 147–58.
———. (2009). 'Why India Cannot Plan Its Cities: Informality, Insurgence and the Idiom of Urbanization'. *Planning Theory* 8, no. 1 (February 2009): 76–87.
———. (2012). 'Urban Informality: The Production of Space and Practice of Planning'. In *The Oxford Handbook of Urban Planning*, edited by Randall Crane and Rachel Weber. Oxford, UK: Oxford University Press.
Sassen Saskia. *The Global City: New York, London, Tokyo*. Princeton, NJ: Princeton University Press, 1991.
Sennett, Richard. *The Fall of Public Man*. New York: Faber, 1974.
Sennett, Richard. *Building and Dwelling: Ethics for the City*. New York: Allen Lane, 2018.

Sennett, Richard. 'How should we live? Density in post-pandemic cities', *Domus* 1046 (May 2020), Milano, 2020.
Shenker, Jack. *Cities after Coronavirus*. Newspaper article in: *The Guardian*, London, 26 March 2020.
Stiglitz, Joseph E. 'The Measurement of Wealth: Recessions, Sustainability and Inequality'. In *Contemporary Issues in Macroeconomics*, edited by Joseph E. Stiglitz and Martin Guzman, 63–76. International Economic Association Book Series. London: Palgrave Macmillan UK, 2013.
Whyte, William H. *The Social Life of Small Spaces*. Washington, DC: Conservation Foundation, 1980.

Chapter 10

Housing the majority, destroying agrarian land

The irreconcilable dilemma of Cairo's informal areas

Charlotte Malterre-Barthes

At the LafargeHolcim conference in April 2019 at Dusit Lake View, New Cairo

On stage, the keynote speaker, Laila Iskander, former Minister of Urban Renewal and Informal Settlements in the first President Abdel Fatha al-Sisi cabinet (2012–2015), delivers a convincing lecture on the informal waste collection system of the Egyptian capital—in front of five hundred architects and planners from around the globe. She speaks vibrantly of the *zabbaleen*, the well-known Coptic community leading the efficient mechanism that processes Cairo's waste—and in particular from construction activities. Iskander highlights how construction firms rumble from desert real estate development amounts for some 50 percent of the waste managed by the *zabbaleen*. To building industry professionals, she paints an image of low-tech intelligence and sustainability, surprisingly leaving out of the conversation the housing conditions of this community, and what was at the heart of her former position: informal areas. Of the 17 million inhabitants comprising the Greater Cairo Region, 65 percent of them live in informal housing. Most of the stock is built on former agrarian land, constructed without permits and seldom, if ever, conforming to building codes.[1,2] This is perhaps the most paradoxical question raised by informal development: On the one hand, this now prevalent mode of urbanisation literally devours thousands of hectares of arable fields on the periphery of Cairo.[3] On the other hand, informal areas are considered sustainable according to a number of criteria: affordable, compact, walkable, connected and dense.[4]

This chapter attempts to unpack this paradox by investigating the spatial characteristics of informal growth on agrarian land, and the mode of spatial production at work in the transformation of fertile 'Old Lands' of Egypt into informal urbanised areas. The research underlines land competition for two of the most basic human needs: food and shelter, examining this precarious imbalance between urban growth and agricultural land. The aim is to provide overdue insight onto the tensions amid urban dynamics, environmental concerns—with regard to local food supply and sustainable urbanism.

Housing the majority

High-rise concrete and brick infill construction sitting in fields are a common sight as one cruises along Cairo's peripheral Ring Road. Considered informal because they are built on former agrarian land, these housing settlements are spontaneous, having been erected without planning or permit. The pace of illegal construction on fertile areas on the capital's fringes has accelerated since the 2011 revolution, and, to reiterate, over 60 percent of Cairo's inhabitants live in informal housing.[5] In the Greater Cairo Region, with its population of approximately 20 million, rapid and uncontrolled urban sprawl has taken a dramatic turn as it continues to expand on agrarian land.

The chronology of Cairo's informal growth has been well studied up until 2011. In *Understanding Cairo*, David Sims claims that "in 1950 there were virtually no informal settlements around Cairo."[6] The first development on agricultural land appeared in the early 1960s following President Gamal Nasser's national industrialisation policies. An influx of rural migrants sought work in Cairo and built houses adjacent to public work opportunities. Ananya Roy and Nezar AlSayyad indicate in *Urban Informality* that large tracks of agrarian land were bought and illegally subdivided for housing in the late 1960s to accommodate those workers involved in the construction of Nasr City.[7] Public housing schemes only offered a fraction of what was needed, and even these inadequate schemes were discontinued after the 1967 war.[8] Fuelled both by rural migration and the influx of refugees from the Suez Canal Zone, housing demand grew steadily and the shortage of affordable housing became a chronic affliction of the Egyptian capital.

In 1970, encroachments on privately owned farmland were identified near villages north of Cairo. At the time, new construction was mainly expanding existing rural settlements on fertile land on the city's periphery (i.e., Boulaq al-Dakrour, Munira, Shubra al-Kheima, Matariya). In her chronological account of informal settlements, Sarah Sabry notes that "80 percent of the housing built in Cairo in the 1970s was informal in some aspect."[9] This informal urbanisation picked up pace following Anouar Sadat's *Al-Infitah*. Millions of Egyptian males relocated to the Gulf, sending remittances back to their families at home. These savings were invested in the so-called *ashwa'iyyat* because property in the formal market remained financially and technically out of reach. Despite Sadat's famous pledge to provide every citizen with a home, both public and private formal investment shifted to cater to the upper and middle-income classes.[10] Unable to afford and gain access to public or private housing, lower-income populations' demands for a place to live were routinely left unattended, inevitably leading to an increase in illicit forms of housing construction that contributed to the commodification of agrarian land as well as the consolidation of an informal real estate market.

Under Hosni Mubarak's government, no significant housing solutions for the majority were successfully implemented. As less foreign remittances came back into the country and as demographic growth and rural migration flows decreased in the 1980s, the construction of illegal settlements decelerated, only to pick up pace again in the following decade. Despite strict measures against spontaneous urbanisation, Cairo's informal districts grew steadily—reaching a rate of 3.5 percent a year during the late 1990s.[11] The 2000s saw increased densification as well as vertical and horizontal expansion of existing areas rather than the build-up of new areas.[12]

The speed of illegal constructions built on fertile land at the fringes of cities quickened after the 2011 revolution.[13] Illicit, post-revolution development took place even faster than previously, most likely due to the power vacuum left by the fall of the Mubarak government. Contractors grew confident during the short period of the

Supreme Council of the Armed Forces (SCAF) transitional government because the administration essentially remained oblivious to the issue. Undoubtedly, contractors were also emboldened during the brief term of Muhammad Morsi, who actually supported informal areas from where it had drawn political support, setting off a speculative building boom along the Cairo Ring Road.[14] Notwithstanding the fact that the right to adequate housing had been added to the 2012 Egyptian Constitution and that the amended 2014 Constitution addressed for the first time informal housing, little was done officially to alleviate unbridled urban growth and consequently, construction continued unabated.[15]

This was all supposed to change in 2016, when President el-Sisi pledged to "end the problem of informal housing within two years," although this appeared to be no more than mere conjecture.[16] For illegal urbanisation on agrarian land has, in truth, continued unhindered as the flagrant reality of urbanisation in Egypt. Symptomatic of the government's dismissive and superficial attitude toward informal housing, Prime Minister Mostafa Madbouly announced in January 2019 that "Egypt's ubiquitous red brick buildings convey an 'uncivilised' image [of the country]," following a Presidential order for these buildings to be painted in a "unified colour scheme of 'dusty' shade."[17,18]

There is—as of 2020—no post-2011 assessment of informal growth for the Greater Cairo Region. Based on fieldwork data and by compiling several GIS images of an area to measure ongoing development chronologically, the extent of encroachment on agrarian land has continued since 2011 (see Figure 10.1).[19,20]

Modus operandi

Agrarian land is subdivided, sold and built upon. The distinctive architectural typologies that emerge follow property lines and financial logic. The often untidy array of actors and protocols produces physical structures with homogenous standards and uniform aesthetics. Specific subdivisions and plot sizes, identical building structures, similar interior layout and circulation, comparable volumes and an unvarying materiality define the architecture of informality in Egypt.

Egypt's renowned irrigation system establishes the morphological configuration of the terrain. A continuous hierarchised grid of water channels stretches throughout the fertile Nile Valley and Nile Delta. Although the flooding irrigation method that dictated the construction of these canals is ancient and was rendered obsolete by the Aswan Dam, the system is still largely in place. Built or upgraded at the end of the nineteenth century in accordance with national development policies and directives for economic growth, the sizeable feeder canals (*rayahs*) remain operative. Branching from the barrages on the Nile, these canals in turn are subdivided into thousands of smaller secondary waterways, totalling some 32,000 kilometres in length.[21] Paths follow canal banks and dikes, allowing access to the farmland. This is the common setting within which the property lines of the Egyptian agricultural unit, the *feddan,* determine urban expansion on agrarian land. The *feddan* is a narrow strip of farmland, 100–300 metres long and 6–17 metres wide. Their geometrical shape (rectangular mostly) makes land subdivision easy. A *feddan* is divisible in 18, 20, 22, 24 or 30 *qirats*—the typical size of a *quirat* is 10–12 by 12–14 metres, that is, an average of 120–140 square metres, and rarely reaches 180 square metres. A consensual agreement

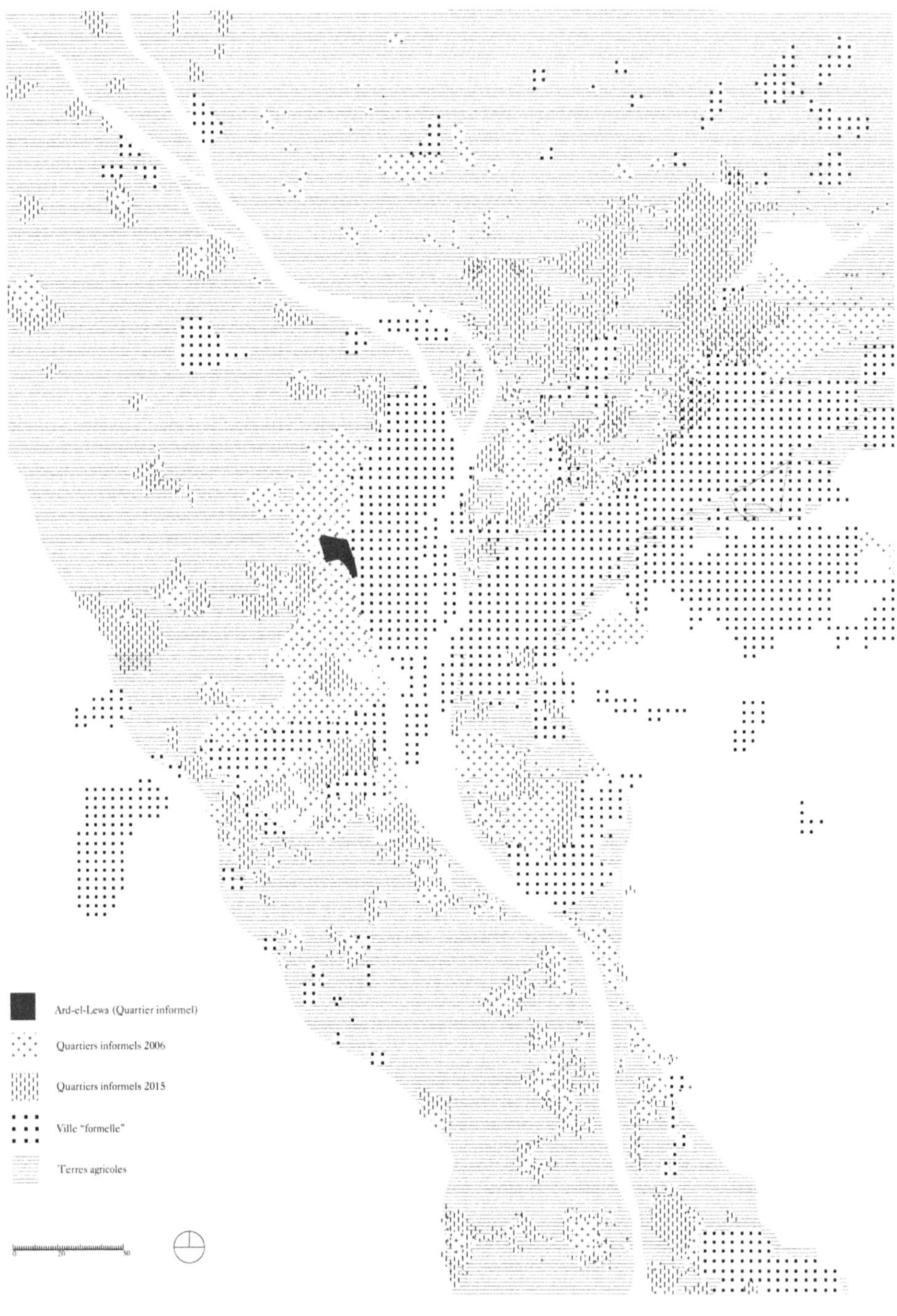

Figure 10.1 Aerial photo showing the location of the New Cairo and, even farther out in the desert, the location of the planned capital city and administrative centre. Ard-el-Lewa (Informal neighbourhood), Informal neighbourhoods 2006, Informal neighbourhoods 2015, "Formal" city, Agricultural Land.

Source: Malterre-Barthes/MAS Urban Design ETHZ.

between buyers is made regarding a setback of 1.5 to 2.5 metres that is left to create an access road. A circulation strip of 4 to 6 metres runs all along the *feddan* from one end to the other, creating what will later be the only public space in the unlikely form of an 'urban canyon', so to speak. In this regard, agricultural space can be said to prefigure its own forms of urbanisation, for this subdivided rural layout gives rise to the telltale architecture of informality in this context, determining its orientation, proportions, and circulation patterns as well.

Building typologies

The construction system of most buildings is based on a skeleton frame (columns, beam and slabs) made from reinforced concrete and filled in with mostly unplastered red brick.

In the 1970s, while single-story houses were the norm, with footprints from 75 to 125 square metres, and one or two small apartments per floor, scholar Davis Sims identified this typology as the "classical informal," characterised by simple brick and concrete buildings of one to 7 floors—the maximum acceptable height that can be accessed without an elevator.[22] Also recognised by Hisham Bahgat in "Housing Generation in the Informal Sector in Egypt" as a standard (*bayt*), this typology is still prevalent in most areas.[23] Buildings, comprising units of 60–75 square metres each, are often commissioned for an extended family—for example, an elderly couple and their son's family living in two apartments on one floor. The structure is left open on the roof for future expansion. There are countless variations of this type (i.e., *aimara,* a multi-family residential type of 3 to 6 stories and *rab'a*, a collective form of housing units for low-income families built around a common passageway).[24]

This said, the 'traditional' typology has evolved into speculative one-off towers constructed by developers or groups of small investors (see Figures 10.2, 10.3, 10.4, 10.5). The tower typology appeared in the mid-1990s, mainly on the fringes of Cairo. The building has a much larger footprint, averaging from 250 up to 1,500 square metres (six *qirats*), with larger apartments and several units per floor. Unlike the plain appearance of the brick and concrete construction of the simple types, towers are plastered and painted in bright colours to facilitate the sale and rental of units.[25] Buildings have up to 15 floors, and when inhabited, are equipped with elevators. After the January 2011 events and the collapse of the then-ruling government, contractors became more emboldened to pursue speculative illegal construction. High towers with balconies and ornamental facades appeared along Cairo's Ring Road.[26] This new typology exemplifies how the techniques of the formal sector market have been appropriated locally, with contractors and investors increasingly engaging in the production of a real estate stock to be sold 'informally' and in plain sight, thereby manifesting an advanced form of speculative informality, if there ever was one. In sum, it becomes clear that the architecture of informality is anything but chaotic (*ashwa'iyyat* in Arabic). Mirroring agricultural subdivision and irrigation patterns, buildings are standardised in terms of their dimensions, materiality, structure, internal organisation and alignment. Yet the flexible and adaptive mode of construction allows for a large range of different housing layouts. The noticeable variations (e.g., in height, corner arrangements and the surfaces of facades) appear to be a response to an increasingly formalised market demand. Insofar as middle-class populations turn to informal housing and ever more

Figure 10.2 New high-density housing blocks up to 14 stories are built on agricultural land.

Source: Bürgi and Malterre-Barthes.

Figure 10.3 New high-density housing blocks up to 14 stories are built on agricultural land.

Source: Bürgi and Malterre-Barthes.

capital is being invested in construction one can only assume that informal urbanisation will undoubtedly persist, destroying more and more agricultural land.

Following the given grid of *feddans,* this regular and efficient form of incremental urban growth adheres to the logic of a time-honoured water distribution infrastructure that had its origins in cultivating the land. Urban form, in other words, follows irrigation infrastructure—as default grid, structure, or system—upon which other networks are superimposed (i.e., streets, water utilities and sewer lines). Within such a framework, building after building continue to be constructed, incrementally and according to a set of precisely defined rules, while forming, overall, a kind of machine for urbanisation that operates at an unprecedented scale. Today, informal Cairo represents 40 to 60 percent of the total surface of the metropolitan area.[27]

Destroying arable land

Why precisely is agrarian land around Cairo consumed for informal construction? The answer to this question resides in the correlating factors that support informal housing demand: push-and-pull dynamics of migration, political geography and demography, social motives, economic incentives, administrative and economic policies, and governmental shortcomings, in particular in regard to rural population.

Figure 10.4 New high-density housing blocks up to 14 stories are built on agricultural land.

Source: Bürgi and Malterre-Barthes.

Figure 10.5 New high-density housing blocks up to 14 stories are built on agricultural land.

Source: Bürgi and Malterre-Barthes.

To comprehend the correlations between global and local food production, land-use, and urbanisation processes, and trace a narrative pertaining to how urban expansion operates against productive landscapes, it is useful to approach the subject from a rural perspective, rather than as seeing the countryside as the backdrop to the growth of cities.[28]

Agriculture versus urbanisation in Greater Cairo

The historical account of land tenure and agrarian policies reveals that food production systems and rural populations are subjected to various political programs and economic ideologies. Changes during the past four decades in particular have led to the current conditions challenging the nation. Despite its key role for food security and national agendas alike, agrarian land is continuously laid open to the oft-destructive forces of urbanisation.

Even with a regulated amount of fertile land of 3 million hectares, agriculture on 'Old Lands' is nevertheless extremely productive, with significant grain harvests yielded two or three times a year. This said, Egypt loses as much as 10,000 hectares of arable land every year.[29] While there are various causes cited for this annual loss, including high salinity and desertification, illegal urbanisation still accounts for the most conspicuous consumption of arable land. Desert land is also being promptly urbanised, but the direct consequences on the overall food system and on agricultural practices in Egypt are comparatively less acute. Since 1995, agricultural land has been lost to informal urban expansion at an ever-accelerating rate within the Nile Delta, the Nile Valley, and the Greater Cairo Region (GCR).

Meanwhile, thousands of tenants are solely dependent on the good will of landowners to keep farming and maintain a modest livelihood. Illustrating how the growth of cities is intertwined with long-term economic pathways and ideologies, this situation might at first appear to be a direct consequence of the spatial extension of the city. In reality, this situation arose from the revocation of the Nasser laws protecting the rents of farming tenants. This neoliberal move dating back to the Mubarak era has, in truth, facilitated the acceleration of urbanisation. By lifting the protection of tenants and allowing owners to fully control agrarian land tenure, Law 96/1992 essentially removed all impediments to the transformation of arable land into construction zones.[30]

The law was approved after intense lobbying from landowners serving in Mubarak's administration, overturned rent control guarantees installed in the 1950s. The law stipulated that rents should be freely negotiated between landlords and tenants "according to the principle of the law of the contractors, with the consequent result of freedom of the two parties to formulate the provisions of the contract."[31] At the time, those one million tenants of the country who were directly affected had no political representatives in the Parliament of Egypt. In the coverage of the events then, the media depicted farmers as "lazy peasants (...) abandoning the land."[32] This biased misrepresentation was ultimately used to justify the 'rightful' return of land to 'destitute' owners. Defined as a "balanced law that would achieve justice for both parties (owners and tenants), and (...) should also serve the aims of economic reform," the legislation was fully implemented in October 1997 after a five-year transition period.[33] Law 96/1992 resulted in inflated land rents that increased by as much as twenty times the original amount, leading to the mass eviction of tenants unable to pay the exorbitant sums ranging from LE200 to LE2500 per *feddan*.[34] With tenancy contracts renewed annually at the discretion of landowners, tenants who had been farming the same plot for some 40 years could suddenly be evicted overnight. As of 1997, an estimated one million farmers had lost their land, the majority being small landholders.[35] Combined with Law 96/1992, the modernisation strategies of the Mubarak era (1984–2011) brought about damaging transformations of the rural world that would have far-reaching ramifications. In the long term, years of government neglect for the lives of small-scale farmers led to an increase in the flow of rural migration to cities (sometimes temporarily) and consequently raised the demand for affordable urban housing, yet another phenomenon to which the state has failed to respond.

As the pace of urbanisation picks up speed, and as a result of the harmful conditions brought about by the density of neighbouring buildings, agrarian land is becoming less profitable for agriculture and more lucrative as a commodity for sale. The systemic mechanisms driving this tendency are implacable and tenants have no say in this process. The effects of this vicious cycle percolate ever further into socio-economic realms. In that sense, one might argue that the architecture of informality constitutes a direct material manifestation of the lost battle for land: built versus unbuilt, urban versus rural, real estate commodity versus land for sustenance. The architecture of informality also manifests the "death of peasantry" as a productive labour force and as a class altogether, as stated by Erich Hobsbawm in *The Age of Extremes*.[36] The Food and Agriculture Organization and other international agencies claim that "the future of agriculture [is] based on large-scale land ownership," that "farms are likely to decrease in number," and that the current balance between the rural and urban populations will shift in favour of the urban population by 2040 globally.[37,38,39]

Yet, there is an ambiguity in the transformation of arable lands into housing, and the very character of this informal urbanisation. On the one hand, a majority of small farmers experiencing the city's inexorable advances onto their fields belong to a part of the population that has been subjected to the inherent violence of economic liberalisation. Following the rollback of Nasser's redistribution land policies (1954–1970), they lost their plots and source of livelihood to market logics as casualties of a deteriorating local food system under Sadat (1970–1984) and Mubarak's economic reforms (1984–2011). On the other hand, the small developers responsible for this urban production have only responded to the needs of those poor populations abandoned by the state since the 1980s. Both groups have suffered from the state's failures in accommodating the most basic needs of its people, simultaneously victims of and directly accountable for the destruction of agrarian land and the construction of affordable housing. It is true that between the farmers engaged in agrarian production vital for national food security and those urban dwellers involved in "post-planning" production of the built environment, a contentious "silent violence of accumulation" has taken place, which has significantly transformed space.[40] Beneath the surface of this urbanisation, one side of the story that unfolds is that of rural dispossession and of environmental destruction of productive hinterlands. Yet it is in these very neighbourhoods abandoned by the state and devoid of public services that the first riots that brought down the Mubarak regime in 2011 originated. After decades of institutional neglect and public contempt, resistance emerged within these contested neighbourhoods. Young crowds walked from the informal district of Bulaq al-Dakrour down

Nahia Street, the first of many such demonstrations that would continue to Tahrir Square.[41] The youth of the informal areas built over agrarian land emerged from these repressed territories to criticise unjust urban practices and socio-economic dispossession, their slogans effectively linked sustenance to democracy and social justice (bread, freedom, social justice: *aīsh, hurriyya, 'adāla igtimā'iyya*).[42]

By standing up to routine injustices and demonstrating ability to rouse collective action, the precarious spatial order of the *ashwa'iyyat* offered a platform for contestation and the formation of political agency.

When Head of the Ministry of Urban Development and Informal Areas during short-lived el-Sisi's first presidential term, Iskander declared at the time citizen participation as being essential to its plans and set out to tackle the economic and social inequities that drive informal urban growth.[43] But as promising as such an agenda might have been and before any work to this end could commence, the ISDF was promptly dissolved as a distinct governmental entity in 2015 and subsequently integrated into the Ministry of Housing that had just introduced the more enticing prospect of a "New Capital" project—a massive desert development along the Suez Canal entailing the relocation of all administrative entities.[44] But there remains a modicum of hope, insofar as some local and international experts have called for a more considered and balanced approach to managing social and spatial imbalances. On the one hand, they have proposed the introduction of planning and legalisation measures in informal areas as a means to control rampant urban growth. On the other hand, they appeal for more support of conventional agrarian practices, which might not only increase crop yields and thus bolster more self-sufficient modes of farming, but might also preserve agrarian land that, in the long term, could lead to a more manageable and sustainable equilibrium between rural and urban areas, a way to alleviate some of the struggles brought about by Cairo's informal urbanisation.[45]

Notes

1 David Sims, *Understanding Cairo: The Logic of a City Out of Control* (Cairo: The American University in Cairo Press, 2010).
2 Stephen K. Mayo, *Informal Housing in Egypt: Draft* (Cambridge: Abt Associates, 1981).
3 Charlotte Malterre-Barthes, "The Limits of Control. Informal City Versus Agricultural Land at Cairo's Fringes," *TRANS* 23, 2013.
4 Heba Khalil, "New Urbanism, Smart Growth and Informal Areas: A Quest for Sustainability," in *Sustainable Architecture & Urban Development*, ed. Husam AlWaer and Jamal Al-Qawasmi Steffen Lehmann(Amman: CSAAR, 2010).
5 Amira Howeidy et al., *Cairo's Informal Areas between Urban Challenges and Hidden Potentials: Facts.Voices.Visions*, eds. Regina Kipper and Marion Fischer (Cairo: Egyptian-German Participatory Development Programme in Urban Areas (GTZ), 2009).
6 Sims, *Understanding Cairo: The Logic of a City Out of Control*, 96.
7 Ananya Roy and Nezar AlSayyad, *Urban Informality: Transnational Perspectives from the Middle East, Latin America, and South Asia* (Lanham, Md.: Lexington Books, 2004), 180.
8 Mahmoud Abdel-Fadil, *The Political Economy of Nasserism* (Cambridge: Cambridge University Press, 1980), 131.
9 Sarah Sabry, "An Introduction to Informal Housing in Cairo," in *Housing Cairo: The Informal Response*, eds. Marc Angélil and Charlotte Malterre-Barthes (Berlin: Ruby Press, 2016), 253.

10 "Food for every mouth, a house for every individual, and prosperity for all," in Sean F. McMahon, *Crisis and Class War in Egypt: Social Reproduction, Factional Realignments and the Global Political Economy* (London, Zed Books Ltd, 2017).
11 Howeidy et al., Cairo's Informal Areas between Urban Challenges and Hidden Potentials: Facts.Voices.Visions, 19.
12 Eric Denis and Marion Sejourne, "Isis: Information System for Informal Settlements," ed. Ministry of Planning (Cairo: GTZ, CEDEJ, 2002).
13 Charlotte Malterre-Barthes, "Housing Cairo. From Small-Scale Informal Housing Construction to Semi-Professional Speculative Urban Schemes," in *NO/LOW COST HOUSING* (ETHZ, Zürich: Architecture Department, 2016).
14 See Bernard Rougier et al., *Egypt's Revolutions: Politics, Religion, and Social Movements* (New York: Palgrave Macmillan, 2016).
15 "The Right to Adequate Housing in the Egyptian Constitution," *Tadamun*, accessed May 8, 2018, http://www.tadamun.co/2013/10/07/the-right-to-adequate-housing-in-the-egyptian-constitution/?lang=en#.Wgm2wEdryAx.
16 "Egypt's President Vows to End Problem of Informal Housing Within Two Years," *Egyptian Streets,* May 30, 2016, https://egyptianstreets.com/2016/05/30/egypts-president-vows-to-end-problem-of-informal-housing-within-two-years/.
17 "Egypt's President El-Sisi Issues an Order to Paint All Red Brick Buildings," *Egyptian Streets,* (2019). https://egyptianstreets.com/2019/01/18/egypts-president-el-sisi-issues-an-order-to-paint-all-its-red-brick-buildings/ (accessed 11 December 2019).
18 Ruth Michaelson, "Egyptian President Calls for Unified Colour Scheme for Buildings" *The Guardian* (2019). https://www.theguardian.com/world/2019/jan/21/egypt-presidential-decree-buildings-unified-colour-scheme (accessed 11 December 2019).
19 Google Earth imagery, 2011-2016, Ard-el-Lewa. See Appendix C.
20 Chris Webster, "Urban Morphological Fingerprints," *Environment and Planning* B, no. 22 (1995).
21 Godfrey Sykes, "Agriculture in the Nile Valley," *The Plant World* 17, no. 3 (1914).
22 Sims, *Understanding Cairo: The Logic of a City Out of Control*, 105.
23 Bahgat, "Housing Generation in the Informal Sector in Egypt."
24 Ibid., 214.
25 Maria Kouvari and Heechul Jung, "A New Vernacular. Typology, Construction, and Aesthetics" in *Housing Cairo: The Informal Response*, eds. Marc Angélil and Charlotte Malterre-Barthes (Berlin: Ruby Press, 2016).
26 Fieldwork by Charlotte Malterre-Barthes, 2014, Ard-el-Lewa, Greater Cairo.
27 Shaimaa Al-Aee, "40% of Egypt's Housing Is Informal: Deputy Housing Minister," *Daily News Egypt*, April 10, 2017, https://dailynewsegypt.com/2017/04/10/621607/.
28 Neil Brenner, *Critique of Urbanization: Selected Essays*, Bauwelt Fundamente (Basel: Birkhäuser Gütersloh, 2017), 217.
29 Humanitarian News and Analysis IRIN, "Egypt: Desertification Threat to Local Food Production," *Humanitarian News and Analysis*, July 11, 2011, http://www.irinnews.org/report.aspx?reportid=93193.
30 "Often, [landowners] would like to sell more land but cannot because they are unable to remove the tenants who have been farming the land for many years." in The Joint Land Policy Team, "Urban Land Use in Egypt," (Cairo: Ministry of Housing and Reconstruction (Arab Republic of Egypt) with Office of Housing Agency for International Development (USA), 1977), 95.
31 Nathalie Bernard-Maugiron et al., *Egypt and Its Laws* (Amsterdam: Springer Netherlands, 2002), 132.
32 Saad, "Egyptian Politics and the Tenancy Law," 391.

33 Bush, "More Losers Than Winners in Egypt's Countryside."
34 Saad, "Egyptian Politics and the Tenancy Law."
35 Fouad N. Ibrahim and Barbara Ibrahim, *Egypt. An Economic Geography* (London; New York: I.B. Tauris, 2003), 120.
36 See Hobsbawm, *The Age of Extremes: The Short Twentieth Century, 1914–1991.*
37 Mark Lindeman, "Russia Trip Report: Grain Outlook Favorable Despite Volga Valley Dryness," June 20, 2002, http://www.fas.usda.gov/pecad2/highlights/2002/07/russia_trip_report/.
38 "World Urbanization Prospects—the 2014 Revision," ed. United Nations Department of Economic and Social Affairs (New York: Population Division, 2014).
39 See Agricultural and Food Marketing Management, (Rome: FAO, 1997), accessed May 4, 2018 http://www.fao.org/DOCREP/004/W3240E/W3240E00.HTM.
40 Neil Brenner, *Critique of Urbanization: Selected Essays*, Bauwelt Fundamente (Basel: Birkhäuser Gütersloh, 2017), 220.
41 Khaled Adham, "Maqamat'imraniya: Navigating the Virtual and Real Urban Cartographies of the Egyptian," in *Beyond the Square: Urbanism and the Arab Uprisings*, eds. Deen Sharp and Claire Panetta (New York City: U505 Terreform, 2016).
42 Amira Mittermaier, "Bread, Freedom, Social Justice: The Egyptian Uprising and a Sufi Khidma," *Cultural Anthropology* 1, no. 29 (2014).
43 Kareem Ibrahim, "Urbanization, Informal Areas and the New Cabinet," *Mada Masr*, September 20, 2015, https://www.madamasr.com/en/2015/09/20/opinion/u/urbanization-informal-areas-and-the-new-cabinet/.
44 Shawkat, "Government Failure to Upgrade Informal Settlements in Egypt: A Brief History."
45 El-Hefnawi, "'Protecting' Agricultural Land from Urbanization or 'Managing' the Conflict between Informal Urban Growth While Meeting the Demands of the Communities (Lessons Learnt from the Egyptian Policy Reforms)."

References

Abdel-Fadil, Mahmoud, *The Political Economy of Nasserism* (Cambridge: Cambridge University Press, 1980).

Brenner, Neil. *Critique of Urbanization: Selected Essays* Bauwelt Fundamente. Basel: Birkhäuser Gütersloh, 2017.

"Egypt's President El-Sisi Issues an Order to Paint All Red Brick Buildings." *Egyptian Streets*, (2019). https://egyptianstreets.com/2019/01/18/egypts-president-el-sisi-issues-an-order-to-paint-all-its-red-brick-buildings/ [accessed 11 December 2019].

"Egypt's President Vows to End Problem of Informal Housing Within Two Years," *Egyptian Streets*, May 30, 2016, https://egyptianstreets.com/2016/05/30/egypts-president-vows-to-end-problem-of-informal-housing-within-two-years/. [accessed 11 December 2019].

Khalil, Heba. "New Urbanism, Smart Growth and Informal Areas: A Quest for Sustainability." In *Sustainable Architecture & Urban Development*, edited by Husam AlWaer and Jamal Al-Qawasmi Steffen Lehmann, 137–156. Amman: CSAAR, 2010.

Malterre-Barthes, Charlotte, "Housing Cairo. From Small-Scale Informal Housing Construction to Semi-Professional Speculative Urban Schemes," in *NO/LOW COST HOUSING* (ETHZ, Zürich: Architecture Department, 2016).*Housing Cairo: The Informal Response*, eds. Marc Angélil and Charlotte Malterre-Barthes (Berlin: Ruby Press, 2016).

Mayo, Stephen K., *Informal Housing in Egypt: Draft* (Cambridge: Abt Associates, 1981).

Michaelson, Ruth. "Egyptian President Calls for Unified Colour Scheme for Buildings" *The Guardian* (2019). https://www.theguardian.com/world/2019/jan/21/egypt-presidential-decree-buildings-unified-colour-scheme [accessed 11 December 2019].
Rougier, Bernard et al., *Egypt's Revolutions: Politics, Religion, and Social Movements* (New York: Palgrave Macmillan, 2016).
Roy, Ananya and Nezar AlSayyad, *Urban Informality: Transnational Perspectives from the Middle East, Latin America, and South Asia* (Lanham, Md.: Lexington Books, 2004).
Sims, David, *Understanding Cairo: The Logic of a City Out of Control* (Cairo: The American University in Cairo Press, 2010).

Chapter 11

Informality and mass housing in Seoul

The role of informal settlements in the formation of megaprojects

Dario Pedrabissi

Introduction

South Korea has developed due to incredible wealth and technological advancements over the last 60 years. It has progressed from being one of the poorest countries in the world in the aftermath of the Korean War (1950–53) into a robust leading economy, transforming its capital city into a world mega-city that combines both hyper-technological urban systems with a strong traditional character. Nowadays, Seoul accommodates 9.8 million people, whereas the Seoul Capital Area is an urban agglomeration that is comprised of 25.6 million people. This is almost 50% of the total 49.5 million people that live in the country, whereas 42.2 million people are urbanized (Economist, 2016, p. 20). In terms of economic output, South Korea is the thirteenth largest economy in the world and the thirteenth biggest economy according to purchasing power (Economist, 2016, p. 26). These crude figures help to understand the contemporary condition of South Korea and its capital city, although this fast progress has also implied dramatic events.

Informal constructions are always the product of specific political and economic condition. During the twentieth century, South Korea experienced critical historical events – Japanese colonization, the Korean War and military dictatorship. These have profoundly influenced Seoul's urban development. During the 1950s informal settlements proliferated in Seoul. Then, during the 1970s and 80s, they have been subjected to a series of redevelopment processes. Different policies have been implemented simultaneously, producing two different approaches: the complete destruction of the shanty towns with the consequently forced relocation of their inhabitants, alternated with the improvement of the area through key infrastructural works. The latter cases have then allowed the transformation of the temporary buildings into a series of different housing types throughout the 1970s and 80s.

In the first part of this article, the aim is to provide a clear definition of the historical and political factors that have transformed the urban structure of Seoul. This section starts with a brief explanation of the ancient urban composition of the capital city to define the nature of the urban fabric that is still significant nowadays. This is instrumental in introducing the first idea of coexistence between a formal gridiron organization of streets and an informal development of minor alleys. The section continues with the definition of the key infrastructural works that were carried out during the Japanese colonial period. This new form of organization is the first modern development of the city, and it is the basis on which further developments occurred, especially from the 1960s onward.

Section two focuses on the evolution of urban housing from the beginning of the twentieth century, mainly concentrating on the traditional urban *hanok* and its subsequent transformation. The study of the evolution of urban housing is essential in order to understand the multi-household dwellings that have come to substitute the urban *hanok*. This building typology has also been adopted in the initially informal settlements, creating new neighbourhoods that are based on the intricate street pattern that characterized the previous setting.

The final section presents the development of large housing complexes, introduced in the 1960s, that fully advanced during the 1970s and 1980s. This typology had a significant impact on the existing urban fabric present at that time. This prevailing urban environment was mainly informal, and it rose as an essential ecosystem to provide the necessary programmatic diversification missing in the new mono-functional large housing complexes. The resulting composition was the coexistence of formal and informal constructions. This became an urban model that also affected the contemporary planning strategy where the high-rise housing buildings are planned in relationship with new low-rise buildings that provide the necessary programmatic diversification. This system is now a Korean planning model that has been adopted throughout the country, and it is also implemented abroad, especially in South East Asia. In Europe, we strongly consider the compact city to be the best urban model that can convey the right balance of density, sustainable development and congenial space. However, is the Asian model a plausible alternative that can deliver a high-density condition while providing a high-quality urban environment?

Urban morphology in Seoul

Seoul's urban structure has been strongly modified during the twentieth century, and all of the different phases are a tangible legacy of the contemporary city. Three main stages have been analysed: the period before 1910, the Japanese colonization, and the urban transformation after the Korean War.

The urban fabric in Seoul before 1910

Seoul did not register any substantial spatial transformation from its foundation year (1394) to the colonization period. Starting from 1910, the "ordering of streets" urban policy altered the original street network, widening the existing thoroughfares and building new roads. The primary purpose was to introduce economic and military ideologies in the organization of the urban space, completely altering the traditional principles of the original city. Urban design before this time was based on a conventional oriental geomantic idea called Pungsu – Feng Shui in Chinese – which is a set of theoretical philosophies based on the study of the wind and water.

Seoul was built on the model of the first capital city in East Asia, Ch'ang-an, known first as Tahsing. This Chinese city was planned before the end of the sixth century, and it became, during the T'ang dynasty (618–907), 'the largest, richest and grandest city in the world of that time' (Boyd, 1964). Nowadays the city is the contemporary Xi'an, but in its original ancient composition, it has set new standards both in its size and its rigidity. It had 11 north-south streets, 14 east-west streets and the Royal Palace was placed at the northern end of the central axis, traditionally facing south. The administrative city adjoined it to the south, and there were two marketplaces (east and west). Within the rigid gridiron structure, the *bo* grid blocks were mainly rectangular with the long axis pointing east-west (Morris, 1972). This urban structure was also used in Japan for the construction of Naniwa, the first Japanese capital city built in 645 and based on the plan of Ch'angan. The next capital city, Heijokyo built in 710 by Emperor Genmei, was laid out using a similar gridiron structure. The city lasted for a period of some seventy years before, in turn, being superseded by Heiankyo (modern Tokyo) (Morris, 1972).

Seoul was built much later than the previously mentioned East Asian examples as it became the capital city of a new Korean dynasty, specifically the Joseon Dynasty founded by Yi Sŏng-gye in 1392. The city was built starting from 1394 and it followed the typical layout derived from Ch'angan imperial city. While the main urban fabric was based on a gridiron layout, there was a maze of secondary arteries. Gelézeau described the space between the axis as follows: 'Roads providing access to the houses branch chaotically, forming a convoluted maze of frequent dead-ends, all highlighting the essentially pedestrian nature of this network' (Gelézeau, 2015). Therefore, there existed a quite remarkable contrast between the formal gridiron structure of the main arteries and the informal nature of the inner streets of each block where the houses of the commoners were built on a more organic layout, embodying the coexistence of two different principles in a unique system: the grid and the maze. This traditional layout underwent a significant transformation when Korea started to be colonized by the Japanese in 1910.

Urban transformations during the colonial period

The first great modernization impact on the Korean peninsula occurred during the Japanese colonization period (1910–45). Japan exerted massive pressure on Korea even before its annexation as the first urbanization wave dates back to 1876. This was when Korea was forced to drop its long-held policy of isolation. Ten port cities and five inland cities were opened up to trade, generating new needs in terms of modern urban planning (Jung, 2013, p. 4). Starting from the 1930s, Japan designated the Korean colony to be an engine of the Japanese military complex for its imperialistic expansion plan. Consequently, a great deal of new infrastructure was developed around the country.

The city of Seoul was then remodelled according to the new modern urban standards that were first tested in Tokyo and later adapted to other cities such as Osaka, Kyoto, Taipei and Pyongyang (Jung, 2013, p. 9). Broad new boulevards were introduced, and existing roads were widened according to the City Ward Improvement Plans of 1912 and 1919 (Jung, 2013, p. 11). Further urban development occurred during the 1920s, but it is in the 1930s that the first modern planning acts appear, namely the 1934 Joseon City Planning Act and the 1936 Gyungsung City Plan. This also resulted in a significant expansion of the boundaries of Seoul (Lee, 2012).

In terms of architectural developments, new colonial Western Style buildings were introduced in the cities – mainly public buildings and transportation facilities – intended to be used as tools to consolidate colonial rule. The buildings adopted neo-classical eclectic styles mainly deriving their influence from Britain due to the well-established relationship between Japan and the U.K. The Japanese used the Western-style colonial architecture as a political tool to contrast with the Korean symbolic buildings in order to impose their culture. However, the most crucial role was played by the infrastructural works that advanced during the colonial period. After Japan was defeated in 1945 and after the Korean War ended in 1953, the time for reconstruction began. The Japanese street networks and plot subdivisions were kept, and new buildings were rebuilt using this existing urban structure.

Modern development after 1953

Seoul experienced one of the largest single country-to-city migrations ever recorded. Korea's economic 'miracle of the Hangang river' exploded and, starting from the early 1960s, this area experienced exponential demographic growth (Kim, 1999). Urban development in Seoul was impossible to control; thus, the urban method of organization introduced by the Japanese was kept. New large-scale public works projects were planned, and spontaneous developments were expropriated and destroyed (Gelézeau, 2015, p. 168).

The Republic of Korea (South Korea) was founded in 1948 as a constitutional democracy, although South Korea has gone through a 'succession of what are known as six different "Republics" since 1948' (Holcombe, 2017, p. 304). After a succession of authoritarian presidents, in 1987, South Korea held the first democratic election in years. A military dictatorship ruled South Korea from 1961–87, and during the leadership of President Park Chung-Hee (1961–79), the modernization process was especially key to the political agenda. This period was characterized by massive economic growth coupled with severe repression. President Park had the clear intention to use urban transformation as a tool for social reform, thus introducing large scale population control in Seoul. The construction of vast mass housing projects (called *ap'at'û tanji*) was seen as 'a very powerful tool for guiding and managing the social groups that have been at the core of South Korea's economic development' (Gelézeau, 2007, p. 186).

Modernity was thus seen as a political instrument to transform society. Seoul has developed by strictly applying the programmatic subdivision that was prescribed in the Athens Charter. The omnipresent large mono-functional housing complexes have proliferated, expanding the border of the city but also replacing the existing informal settlements that have been created after the war, forcing the poor to move far from the centre of the city. It is worth noting that in contrast to what has happened in the West, these standardized high-rise housing blocks were conceived for the middle and the upper-middle class.

In terms of urban planning, Seoul adopted an urban growth management strategy based on ring-radial roadway circulation, multiple centres and green belts. The proposed urban model was inspired by the Western New–Town Planning and Garden City ideas. The resulting 1966 Comprehensive Development Plan was put into place to facilitate the expansion of the city, proposing four ring roads at varying distances from the city centre and thirteen radial arterials (Rowe, 2005, p. 81). The junctions of these roads were to become subcentres.

This plan was followed by the 1972 National Development Plan which introduced a new greenbelt system, easily struck by unplanned development. The plan also pushed new development toward the south side of the Han River. By the mid-1980s, the expanse of urbanization on both the north and south banks of the river was equal (Rowe, 2005, p. 82). A further decentralization process occurred in 1989 with the construction of five new large towns – Ilsan, Jungdong, Sanbon, Pyeongchon and Bundang – with a planned variety in population density. Recent ambitious new town projects include Sejong Metropolitan Autonomous City and Songdo Smart City.

The modern development has profoundly modified the urban morphology of the traditional city. The old buildings that inherited their dimensions from the historic urban form are considered to be low value, and the small plots have often been merged to allow for large-scale urban interventions. The morphological and typological references with the historic city are thus disintegrated. Furthermore, the original inhabitants have pushed away from the centre, and the existing urban program is compromised due to the mono-functional character of the new intervention. Nevertheless, the new big urban plans have naturally created a juxtaposition with the multi-functional low-rise neighbourhood in their proximity to enhance the diversification of the urban program. This combination of different architectural types has been an accidental clash in the beginning of the process. However, it has turned out that this coexistence is capable of delivering high-density neighbourhoods with two very distinct urban programs that work in symbiosis.

Urban housing evolution in Seoul

In order to comprehend the contemporary low-rise urban area that played a crucial role in supporting the proliferation of large housing complexes, it is essential to analyse the evolution of urban housing. During the twentieth century, urban housing in Seoul has evolved several times. In the early modern development period, the traditional urban *hanok* was the most important housing typology, although other foreign types of houses have been developed in the city. After the Korean War, informal settlements grew indiscriminately in both the centre and at the fringes of the city. Different policies have been adopted, and some of the neighbourhoods have been kept and improved through essential infrastructural works. This process instigated the transformation of the temporary building into a sequence of different housing types that have evolved throughout the 1970s and 80s. This renovation process has been registered in both the initially informal urban area as well as in the former urban *hanok* districts. It is in these environments that the multi-functional urban condition that is intrinsically part of the Korean urban milieu can flourish and sustain the services for the large apartment complexes.

Early modern transformations

During the early modern development period, three distinct types of housing evolved in Korea: Western-style houses, Japanese-style houses and the urban *hanok*. While the Western-style houses maintained their original composition derived from other colonial modifications, the Japanese-style house was eventually adapted to the extremely

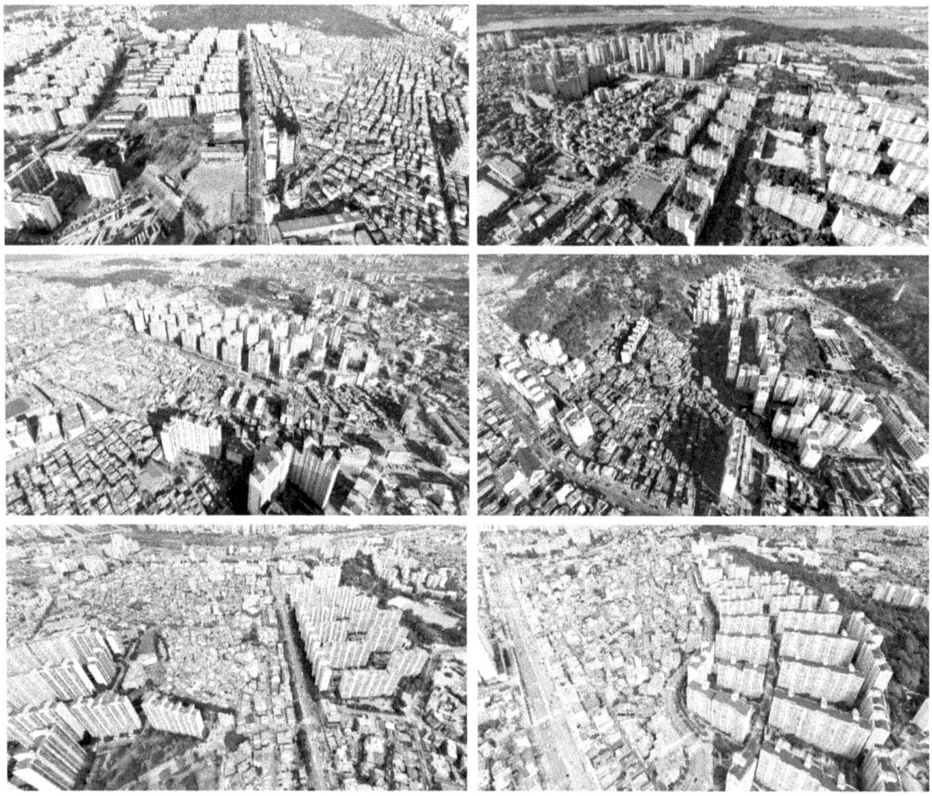

Figure 11.1 Aerial view of different housing complexes in the proximity of low-rise neighbourhoods in Seoul. From top left in a clockwise direction: Nowon-gu, Kangdong-gu, Enpyeong-gu, Dongjak-gu, Yeong Deungpo-gu, Seongbuk-gu.

Source: naver.co.kr. Image edited by the author.

harsh Korean winters. These houses were the middle-corridor type and the *machiya* passageway type, which eventually employed the traditional Korean heating system (*ondol*). This originated the first hybrid integration of a Japanese house with a Korean traditional technological feature (Jung, 2013, p. 28). The urban *hanok* was derived from the traditional Korean house – it first appeared in the 1920s and was the dominant type of urban housing built in Korea until the late 1960s.

The urban *hanok* saw great success as a house of the commoners due to its affordability and the preservation of the traditional housing layout. Its plan varied regionally, but in Seoul, the U-shaped plan was the most common. The L-shaped set of rooms was combined with an I-shaped annexe used for the entrance gate and services. The rooms were set around the *madang*, a central open courtyard that functioned as a distribution space but also as storage and as a common area. The rooms usually included a kitchen, a master bedroom, a second bedroom and a *maru (daecheong)*. This was a wooden-floored semi-open space placed between the two bedrooms to provide a ventilated area during the Korean summer (Lee, 1991). The traditional *ondol* heating system was fuelled by the kitchen, and for this reason, this room was connected to the master bedroom. This type of house then became a point of departure for the development of new types of urban housing to respond to new market demands and urban settings.

Before exploring the evolution of the urban *hanok* into a modern typology, it is crucial to understand the informal settlement phenomenon that took place in Seoul after the Korean War. The informal settlements flourished on the urban fringes of the city as well as in the central areas affected by the destruction of the war. Various terms are used to describe informal settlements in South Korea. 'The most common term is *panjachon*, meaning a settlement formed of houses made of timber-framed structures, panels and flimsy materials. They are also called *daldongne*, meaning a settlement of rental houses where many urban poor reside. When the focus is on legality, the same settlement can be named *mooheogachon*, of which the literal meaning is an unapproved settlement' (Kim, Park & Park, 2019, p. 272).

The Seoul Metropolitan Government (SMG) has implemented different strategies to cope with the proliferation of informal settlements in the city. In some instances, it has also adopted on-site upgrading plans, although large-scale forced eviction was the dominant implemented policy alongside an imposing building practice based on extensive and repetitive housing complexes. The resulting dichotomy between informal settlements that have eventually evolved into established urban areas during the subsequent decades and the modern planned neighbourhood is a constant reality in Seoul's urban environment nowadays. This is as the high-density condition of this mega-city generates situations that simultaneously juxtapose both the traditional milieu and a modern aesthetic.

The process that initiated the prevalent use of modern apartment buildings was developed through a series of typological transformations that originated when the traditional urban *hanok* became inappropriate to respond to the increasing urban population pressure. Two main housing types evolved from the urban hanok: the spec house and the multi-household dwelling. Moreover, the informal settlements that have been kept and improved from their initial illegal state experienced a similar transformation, replacing their temporary buildings with multi-family housing.

New housing transformations vs old urban fabric

The first evolution of the urban *hanok* was the spec house. This refers to a 'ready-built' single-family detached house known as *jipjangsajip,* which entered the scene in the 1960s (Jung, 2013, pp. 71–72). Small-scale developers built the spec house type by adopting new modern materials and techniques such as the brick façade with a reinforced concrete structure and gable roof. The house was either one or two stories, and the main innovative aspect was the introduction of the boiler heating system. This allowed for the transformation of the traditional floorplan arrangement, which had been defined by the strict relationship between the kitchen and the master bedroom due to the *ondol* heating system. This is where the cooking and heating occurred in the same place.

Another significant development is the internalization of the *madang*, the exterior court that once served as the circulation and relational space, even though the internal *madang* was initially used more like a hall instead of a proper living room. These two new arrangements introduced a novelty to the floorplan layout based on a living-dining (LD) and living-dining-kitchen (LDK) axis. These arrangements became very influential in the later apartment building floorplans (Lee, 1991, p. 70).

In 1985, the revision of the Building Act allowed the owners of single-family homes to convert their property and to build collective housings on the same site (Jung, 2013, p. 71). Consequently, two new urban housing types, the multi-household dwelling (*dasedaejutaek*) and the multi-family dwelling (*dagagujutaek*), began replacing the spec house. The law was intended to boost the ongoing urban densification process by allowing the transformation of the single-family home into collective dwellings. Thus, the neighbourhoods where the urban *hanok* and later the spec houses were first built witnessed another radical transformation with the advent of multi-household dwelling. This had a negative effect on the quality and quantity of open space, and for this reason, multi-household dwellings became the accommodation standard for low-income families.

The process in which the old urban fabric is maintained, and the building is subjected to further transformation is typical also in the districts that were initially formed as informal settlements. In this case, the street network is much more irregular than in the previous case, where the urban *hanok* were planned according to a quite rigid grid. The irregular pattern was derived from the original informal setting combined with the small scale of the new buildings that usually span between two to four floors. This composition has favoured the formation of small businesses, restaurants and even light industry interspersed between the housing buildings. As a result, the urban program of these areas is composed of a good variety of services that enrich the quality of the neighbourhood. This condition served as a support for the large apartment complexes that surround these districts (see Figure 11.2).

Figure 11.2 Clash between multi-functional areas and apartment buildings in Sanggye-dong, Seoul.

Source: Author.

Mass-housing and informality

Serial apartment complexes are the most common housing typology in South Korea. Their presence dominates the landscape everywhere in the country. As previously noted, their success was boosted by the developmental state strategy during the military dictatorship that targeted the large apartment complexes for the upper-middle-class. The modern aesthetic was seen as the advocate of a new urban and social order; thus, it was promoted by the regime for political purposes.

This section aims to introduce the history and features of the large apartment complexes in South Korea, retracing the evolution of their formation. The goal is to contextualize the big plans in the urban space, focusing on their coexistence with the organic neighbourhoods – originating in their initially informal condition.

Large apartment complexes

Modern apartment blocks have become the prevailing housing typology and, consequently, the dominant image of the South Korean landscape, spreading throughout both the city and countryside. As Florian Urban pointed out, 'serial construction methods became the prevalent technology of mass housing around the world, and simultaneously a stylistic principle of modern city design' (2013, p. 16). In the 1970s, the prefab high-rises comprised less than 4 per cent of the housing stock in South Korea, while this number rose to 50 per cent in 2000. Accordingly, in the same period, the percentage of individual houses decreased from 90 per cent to approximately 25 per cent (Hall, 2014, p. 356).

Korea's first apartment building, Mikuni Apartments in Hoehyun-dong, was constructed in 1930 by a Japanese company to provide accommodation for its employees. This was followed by a second apartment built in 1935 in Naeja-dong. In the same year, records show the construction of the Yurim apartment, which was the first to be built for rental purposes (Lee, 2010). None of these buildings survives today. We have to wait until 1958 to see the first apartment buildings built after Korea's liberation from Japan. The two examples worth mentioning are Jongam apartments comprised of three buildings that are four to five stories high, the first to be equipped with flush toilets. There are also Mapo Apartments – ten six-floor apartment buildings – which were constructed between 1962 and 1964 by the Korean National Housing Corporation (KNHC). They are equipped with individual hot-water heating systems. Although the formal policies that applied to the apartment buildings were defined later on, Mapo apartments established a set of planning principles for the layout of the *tanji*: collective housing consisting of at least 300 units with both autonomy and shared facilities (Gelézeau, 2007, p. 171).

The *tanji* realized exponential growth when the government launched the Housing Construction Promotion Act in 1972. Amended and strengthened in the early 1980s, the law promoted the construction of high-density residential areas within the city boundaries and other newly designated areas (Gelézeau, 2007, p. 176). The *tanji* was then defined as a grouping of large urban blocks containing mono-functional residential slabs interspersed with small commercial buildings and service facilities.

The construction model employed the Fordist production system. This is where residential slabs are built in a reinforced concrete structure with prefab elements. The main building types are slab buildings with a single-loaded corridor system and open corridors (gallery access), in addition to multiple vertical access. These slabs usually have the ridgeline of the building oriented east-west to maximize sun exposure, leaving the north façade as a functional element that is aesthetically forgotten. These features allow for maximum land use and minimal construction cost, but at the same time, it creates an entirely new environment that disintegrates the traditional landscape and social relationships. Nevertheless, the apartments became a symbol of a higher social status, and they are a highly desired product that is still very popular nowadays (see Figure 11.3).

In terms of interior design, the typical apartment floorplan is a combination of different influences. As analysed earlier, the traditional floorplan developed from the transformation of the urban *hanok* into the spec house, where the *madang* became an interior space and started to function as a living room. The Western influences travelled through Japan, adopting new building technologies and new spatial configurations. The typical LDK floorplan system (Living, Dining and Kitchen) was already developing in Japan starting in the 1940s before being employed in Korea, becoming the standard layout in modern Korean apartments. Nevertheless, these influences were combined with the traditional floorplan, creating a hybrid arrangement together with the foreign systems. This blended the continuity and consistency of the traditional plan into contemporary design (Lee, 1991).

Figure 11.3 View of boram apartments, Sanggye-dong, Seoul.

Source: Author.

The role of the low-rise buildings

As evident in Figure 11.1, contemporary Seoul's urban fabric is a collage of two distinct types of districts: the *tanji*, which is the formally planned mega-block composed of a repetition of identical large housing buildings, and the informally generated neighbourhood that is mainly colonized by multi-family houses. The coexistence between these two districts seems strident, although, in reality, the *tanji* is not entirely self-sufficient in terms of its public program. The *tanji* usually contains some interspersed service facilities, but the informal district in its proximity is essential in terms of providing the necessary functions that the *tanji* needs. This apparent clash is then a necessary condition for the balanced programmatic organization of the urban area. Consequently, this situation has now produced a symbiosis between the two urban apparatuses and paradoxically they have formed a precise urban model that is now used by the large real estate companies to plan new interventions.

South Korea has advanced its unique corporation system, defined by the country's large construction conglomerates (*chaebol*). These large companies have played, and still play, a key role in the urban and regional transformation where large housing projects are the instrument used to dominate the real estate market. Regarding contemporary South Korean urban planning, the clash between formal and informal urban conditions coexist in a clear planned intention. This has now become the Korean urban model. In fact, for the first large housing complexes, it was almost inevitable for them to be implemented in a site surrounded by traditional or informal architecture. Instead, the later urban transformations have carefully planned and adopted this hybrid combination of high-rise mono-functional housing blocks and low-rise multi-functional buildings as it provides the services that are needed for the neighbourhood.

As a result, we can assume that the real estate companies have learned from an initially accidental clash between the two distinct urban types. They have created a planning system that is unique to South Korean urban planning. This system is now adopted for large projects implemented outside of Seoul (see Figure 11.4), in particular in the construction of new towns or in the expansion of existing cities that play the role of satellite cities around Seoul. The intention is to alleviate the pressure on the capital city as well as to increase the housing supply. Furthermore, the large construction and real estate conglomerates are investing in foreign countries as the Korean market has started to become saturated. In particular, Southeast Asian countries are the main destinations of new speculative planning where the Korean culture is particularly cherished, mainly through their movies, TV drama, K-Pop singers, technology and food. Henceforth the Korean way of living is going to be exploited and exported via its distinctive urban model that is derived from decades of transformation.

Conclusions

South Korea has experienced dramatic changes in the last century. Major historical events have drastically transformed the urban environment in Seoul. The traces of these transformations are clearly visible in the contemporary city, and they have generated the construction of the modern city. Alongside the large housing complexes that have been built starting from the 1960s, the city has expanded through the construction of several informal settlements. These neighbourhoods have been improved

Figure 11.4 View of a new area in Cheonan. The high-rise residential towers are coupled with mixed-used neighbourhoods in a planned intention, which is reminiscent of the initial accidental clash between the two types.

Source: Author.

and transformed in recent decades, replacing the original construction with the typical Korean multi-household dwellings.

The key factor in this study is that the informal settlements have proven to be essential for the construction of large housing complexes that are a typical product of Korean real estate development. The combination of low-rise, spontaneous settlements, together with the high-rise housing complexes, is essential to provide a diversified urban program. The coexistence of a multi-functional area in support of the mono-functional housing complexes has proven to be a model that is now being developed further in the new plans. In this case, the clash between the low-rise buildings and the high-rise towers is now carefully planned, where the low-rise buildings are clearly designed to balance the urban program.

Thus, it seems that the Korean urban planners have learned from informality, and they have adopted a model that can reproduce the variety of functions that are generally found in these areas.

References

Boyd, A. (1964). Chinese architecture and town planning 1500 BC-AD 1911.

Economist, The (2016). *Pocket World in Figures 2017*. Profile Books.

Gelézeau, V. (2007). Korean Modernism, Modern Korean Cityscapes, and Mass Housing Development: Charting the Rise of Ap'at'ŭ Tanji since the 1969s. In Rüdiger Frank et al. (Ed.), *Korea Yearbook 2007, Politics, Economy, and Society*. Leiden & Boston: Brill.

Gelézeau, V. (2015). Streets and open Spaces in Seoul (1995–2010). A Cultural and Geographical View of Local Neighborhood. Retrieved from https://halshs.archives-ouvertes.fr/halshs-01174275/document

Hall, P. (2014). *Cities of tomorrow: an intellectual history of urban planning and design since 1880*. John Wiley & Sons.

Holcombe, C. (2017). *A History of East Asia*. Cambridge University Press.
Jung, I. (2013). *Architecture and urbanism in modern Korea*. University of Hawai'i Press.
Kim, B., Park, H., & Park, J. (2019). Seoul. The Evolution of Informal Settlers' Political Gains in Changing State Regimes in Seoul. In R. Rocco &J. van Ballegooijen (Eds.), *The Routledge Handbook on Informal Urbanization* (pp. 270–280). New York: Routledge.
Kim, Y.-W. (1999). Industrialization and urbanization in Korea. *Korea Journal*, *39*(3), 35–62.
Lee, C. K. (2010). Apartment City, Seoul. Replacing by Apartment. In K. H. Kwon (Ed.), *RE. PLACE.ING: Documentary of Changing Metropolis. Seoul* (Korean Pav, pp. 70–75). Arts Council Korea.
Lee, J.-J. (2012). *Spatial Development of Seou. Urban Development History & Prospect*. Seoul. Retrieved from http://english.seoul.go.kr/wp-content/uploads/2014/02/03_Spatial_Structure_of_Seoul.pdf
Lee, S. (1991). Continuity and Consistency of the Traditional Courtyard House Plan in Modern Korean Dwellings. *Tdsr: Traditional Dwellings and Settlements Review*, *3*(1), 65–76.
Morris, A. E. J. (1972). *History of urban form: prehistory to the Renaissance*. George Godwin Limited.
Rowe, P. G. (2005). *East Asia modern: shaping the contemporary city*. London: Reaktion books.
Urban, F. (2013). *Tower and slab: histories of global mass housing*. Routledge.

Chapter 12

The role of adaptation in changing the micro-morphology of informal settlements

Paul Jones

Introduction and context

Informality is most visible in the Global South and is increasingly being experienced in cities of the Global North (Harris, 2017). In countries of the Global South, informality and – more importantly – informal settlements are a normal 'everyday urbanism', as reflected in the upward trajectory of informal settlements and slums as a major source of housing supply. The latter are an entrenched mode of urbanization reflecting some of society's most visible indicators of social, economic and physical disadvantage (UN-Habitat & ESCAP, 2015). In 2015, approximately 25% of the world's population was estimated to be residing in informal settlements, including slums; globally, this is the equivalent of approximately one billion dwellers. This proportion of the world's population living in informal settlements is expected to double by 2030 (UN-Habitat, 2016). Despite the negative stereotypes that continue to pervade informal settlements, they perform valuable functions in city development by meeting a demand for affordable housing whilst providing the formal city with labour for construction and public services, as well as being a source of inexpensive services and goods (UN-Habitat, 2008). The literature increasingly indicates that informal settlements are highly organized and innovative: the processes of housing construction and settlement expansion are being undertaken and endorsed by residents in settings where official top-down rules and regulations may play little part in their development (Silva & Farrall, 2016). While issues of illegality, insecure tenure, overcrowding, social disorder, poor housing conditions, and inadequate or insufficient public services characterise the mainstream discourse surrounding informal settlements, such settlements and their communities remain integral to processes making and shaping the city (Das, 2017; Jones, 2019a). At a wider level, the concept of informal urbanism remains central to understanding patterns of exclusion and issues of social justice in the city (Jones, 2019b).

The emphasis on city-making is via formal codes, masterplans and regulations, but cities evolve through a mixture of both formal and informal practices and processes (Dovey, Pafka, & Ristic, 2017). A key stimulus for transformative physical change in cities has historically been planned new cities and city renewal, including infill, land readjustment and acquisition programs, provision of major transportation infrastructure, planning for public open space and peri-urban expansion (UN-Habitat, 2016). In Asia, city development driven by market forces and large government infrastructure projects, particularly in public transport, has led to accelerated city transformation.

This has increased the demand for affordable housing and land close to strategically located centers, whilst providing and stimulating the informal urban economy (Hou & Chalana, 2016; UN-Habitat, 2008).

The city transforms in a hierarchy of multiple scales, being multi-layered, contested, non-inclusive, emergent and can be spatial, temporal or functional. Such urbanism patterns and processes challenge policymakers, planners and architects to better understand the complexity of city urbanism which is 'bottom up', unfinished and continues to unfold (Jones, 2019b). This includes dense informal settlements which are generally characterized by fine-grain and irregular morphology, with most local human-scale transformations by residents occurring via small-scale socio-physical alterations and adaptations (Kamalipour & Dovey, 2019). This process of transformation in housing is typically incremental; change occurs by dividing existing rooms for privacy or accommodation, adding a floor, inserting a balcony, reducing setbacks to extend or add a new room, or to insert external stairs to access upper levels. These changes happen within a set of specific protocols where the same or similar socio-material, physical, and spatial identity is replicated. These horizontal and vertical 'bottom-up' transformations often result in transgressing the 'quasi-legal' or 'legal' front plot boundaries and introduce new built forms to the façade and building footprint. Importantly, the local changes collectively impact on wider neighborhood sustainability as they modify the way residents and traders undertake their livelihoods, as well as general practices of sociability in the public spaces framed by housing (Jones, 2016, 2019a).

Researchers have observed that informal settlements grow through generative processes of incremental adaptation and self-organization that meet residents' immediate priorities in contrast to longer term outcomes (Dovey, 2014; Jones, 2019a; Kamalipour, 2016a, 2016b; Kamalipour & Dovey, 2019; Rapoport, 1988). In an Indonesian Papua provincial context, for example, informal settlements result from unplanned adaptations. Self-help housing change is expressed through their different non-linear geometric forms, range of materiality and construction methods, and through the development of hybrid governance arrangements (Suhartini & Jones, 2019). In these contexts, adaptability and incremental steps in meeting housing needs emerge as both key processes and actions in the transformation process. Often these changes occur within a framework of groups and individuals who are capable of self-organization and co-evolution across space, time and society (Suhartini & Jones, 2019). At a national level, such changes are significant but underrecognized with official estimates in Indonesia, for example, estimating that 80% of housing development in 2013 was contributed through informal self-help systems (United National General Assembly, 2013).

Despite the above trends, comparatively little attention is given to planning and design practices that seek to better explore the impact of housing adaptation practices on the micro-morphological and wider spatial patterns in informal settlements. The emphasis in researching informal settlements has been on larger scale assessments of policy, governance and existing features of the 'informal city' (Davis, 2006; Neuwirth, 2004; Roy & Alsayyad, 2004) rather than their micro-scale practices (Dovey, 2012; Dovey & King, 2011; Jones, 2019a; Kamalipour, 2016a, 2016b, 2017; Kellett & Napier, 1995; McCartney & Krishnamurthy, 2018). The physical nuances of informal settlements are generally not well documented, often due to their classification as illegal.

Many settlements and their resident characteristics remain excluded from official local government plans and information systems (Patel & Baptist, 2012; Suhartini & Jones, 2019). The result is that there are limited analyses of the 'messier' morphological features in informal settlements, such as amorphous and fluctuating boundary lines, continual adjustments to building typologies, varied interpretations of shared space and ownership, and rights of way and access (McCartney & Krishnamurthy, 2018).

As the study of the urban fabric and structure, urban morphology has tended to emphasise examination of the attributes of function, form and changes in formally developed suburbs and cities based on registered cadastral boundaries, repetitive plot sizes and clarity of land-use rights (Conzen, 1960). The established mainstream methods and tools of morphological analysis do not address fluid property and building lines, irregular alleyway alignments, rights of use, incremental housing adaptation practices, and access to services and infrastructure resulting from private and public circulation space being negotiated, transgressed, and 'new' territorial boundaries and form changes being determined (Jones, 2019a). In this setting, cities are planned and regulated through a range of adaptive bottom-up mechanisms as seen in informal settlements plus through a combination of formal codes and plans. Housing and space forms are many and varied in informal settlements and one needs to be wary of generalizing and being too reductionist so as to miss generic and specific characteristics. Having stability in city planning yet recognizing the role and limitations of adaptive mechanisms is a key part of complexity-based approaches to managing and planning the evolution of increasingly diverse cities with multiple stakeholders and different development agendas (Rosner-Manor, Borghini, Boonstra & Silva, 2019). If a key objective of urban morphology is concerned with identifying processes and outputs of built form and space transformation, then understanding informal settlements as produced and shaped through fine-grain built and unbuilt forms of adaptation is a valid research aim (McCartney & Krishnamurthy, 2018).

Within this context, the aim of this chapter is to identify key processes and types of micro-adaptation by which housing, plots, and blocks transform and make distinctive and unique patterns of micro-morphology. In many informal settlements, transformation of plot sizes, housing form and alleyway spaces is locally self-organized and incremental through small-scale changes which are not readily discernible or acknowledged as important since they are perceived as chaotic and lacking formal order. Residents often undertake little or minimal consultation with neighbors or wider local government authorities when making changes, thus effectively taking on the role in part or full as planners, designers, architects and builders. With questionable land tenure, changes occur within a setting where built (housing and plots) and unbuilt spaces (alleyways) emerge as fluid because the processes of housing densification continually create new building lines, larger plots and irregular blocks, new interface types and alleyway alignments. The proper layout of services and infrastructure, for example, is not an immediate or longer-term concern for residents. Thus, the micro-morphology, namely, the study of the structure and form of small-scale urban fabric including the logic and processes of adaptation in informal settlements, takes on major significance in understanding the nature of both the "formal and informal" city.

The case study

Setting

Bandung is the third largest city in Indonesia and the capital of West Java, located 150 kilometers south east of Jakarta. Bandung has an estimated metropolitan population of approximately 10.5 million persons (2014) and has been subject to rapid urbanization. This includes containing around 38,450 hectares of 'slums', comprised mainly of *kampungs* that accommodate the urban disadvantaged and poorer households (Jones, 2017a). Located in the center of Bandung and divided by the Cikapundung River is the Tamansari valley and adjoining localities. The once-fertile agricultural area wedged between the Dutch planned areas of the city to the east and west was settled by people from West Java following civil unrest and political struggles over Islam gaining ascendancy in the 1960s. An influx of migrants saw the agricultural-based uses of Tamansari intensified with growing *kampungs* and population, with many original refugees and their descendants becoming long-term landowners (Reerink, 2011).

On the perimeter of Tamansari and eastern slopes of the Cikapundung River abutting Bandung Zoo is the *kampung* of Lebak Siliwangi. In 2015, the population was estimated at 4,240 persons, comprising approximately 1,080 families consisting of 2,098 males and 2,142 females. Current building works suggests a major population increase driven primarily by the demand for student accommodation. While resident livelihoods are diverse, including many home-based businesses, mini-stores and an array of street vendors, the *kampung* is increasingly home to many university students, especially those from the neighboring Institute of Technology Bandung University. This heterogeneity of population reinforces the nature of affordable housing that Lebak Siliwangi offers to "newcomers" such as university students, as well as longer-term low-income residents.

The existing structure of Lebak Siliwangi has evolved from the interplay of several factors, namely: (i) natural features, such as the major north-south Cikapundung River, (ii) topography, including the gradient fall from east to west to the Cikapundung River, (iii) past major development decisions driven by in-migration and settlement growth, such as a north-south irrigation channel (for rice paddies), a major eastern perimeter road, and two pedestrian river crossings, (iv) gradual land-use change from infilling rice paddies and fish ponds commencing in the 1950s to housing and associated small-scale commercial and more recently rental housing, and (v) the progressive introduction of 'urban' morphological units, such as irregularly sized plots, blocks, mosques (with their east-west orientation) and alleyways as the area has intensified and transformed to a dense inner-city informal settlement (see Figure 12.1).

Since the influx of migrants in the 1950s, the morphology of Lebak Siliwangi has seen rice paddies replaced by plots and buildings, open pathways reduced to alleyways, and services, infrastructure, and clarity of land tenure often following building occupation. With its inner-city location, space in Lebak Siliwangi is highly utilized. Housing construction is a mix of vertical and horizontal expansion as residents and landowners respond to spatial demands by family members within the context of available social and financial capital, plus the area of their plot. The varied alleyways that frame dwellings and the block patterns – many still in family or individual ownership – are the residual unused spaces from family plots, many of which are the original

Figure 12.1 The eastern boundary of *kampung* Lebak Siliwangi is the Cikapundung River, which acts as collector of refuse including untreated effluent and raw sewage.

Source: Author.

pathways that surrounded and linked the network of rice paddies that dotted Lebak Siliwangi in the mid-1900s. Formal government institutions exist in Lebak Siliwangi – for example, there are eight designated neighborhood units based around the government administrative units called *rukun warga (RWs)* and *rukun tetangga (RTs)* – but government influence and control via formal planning and design standards and approval does not exist (Jones, 2019a). As such, there is total freedom from 'top-down' regulatory planning, design, and building laws, which is reflected in the multiplicity of form adaptations, building styles and materiality that respond to the changing social and economic needs of individual households. The result is an irregular morphology of plot, block and alleyway patterns (see Figure 12.2).

Phases of transformation

A key element by which housing extends and modifies its form and function is by intruding into the width of the adjoining non-linear alleyways. Using variables of width, location, and functionality, alleyways can be classed as either major, minor, or one-way (that is, "live ends" leading to houses). Alleyways that connect major desire lines and have greatest motorbike and pedestrian 'traffic' – such as the north-south Gang Stone Alley adjoining the Cikapundung River – tend to have a greater

Figure 12.2 Block patterns in Lebak Siliwangi have evolved from the original layout of the rice fields with many terraced walls forming the network of major and minor alleyways remaining.

Source: Author.

proportion of economic and socio-cultural land uses as they cater for both *kampung* and wider city users. Major and minor alleyways provide pedestrian and transport permeability and connectivity, in which the consequences of changing interface form types between the built form of the house, plot and alleyway are enacted. While the overall connectivity of alleyways is determined by (i) their function and permeability, (ii) the distance to the desired destination, (iii) underlying physical structure such as the Cikapundung River, and (iv) grade changes including existing terraced walls, the alignment of alleyways remains flexible. This is primarily driven by the myriad housing types continue to redefine the interface of the housing frontage and alleyway. Hence, the alignment and form of key structural elements, such as alleyways, are in constant flux driven by private and communal interests. In this context, the major influence on current structure and the arrangement of morphological elements is the cumulative impact of multiple individual micro-adaptation decisions and changes occurring in housing types, plots and alleyways (see Figure 12.3).

Three main phases of transformation can be identified within which incremental micro-scale changes occur. These phases can be summarized as:

- Phase One represents the low-density plots changing from agriculture to housing in the 1950s as the population increased, primarily through in-migration. Rice paddies are slowly filled, and former rice paddy terraced walls are stabilised, and pathways begin to shape the physical form of the block boundaries. The typical dominant housing type in this period was single storey detached housing and featured a front setback, minor side setbacks and a rear boundary often containing a pond that was partitioned off from the former rice paddy.

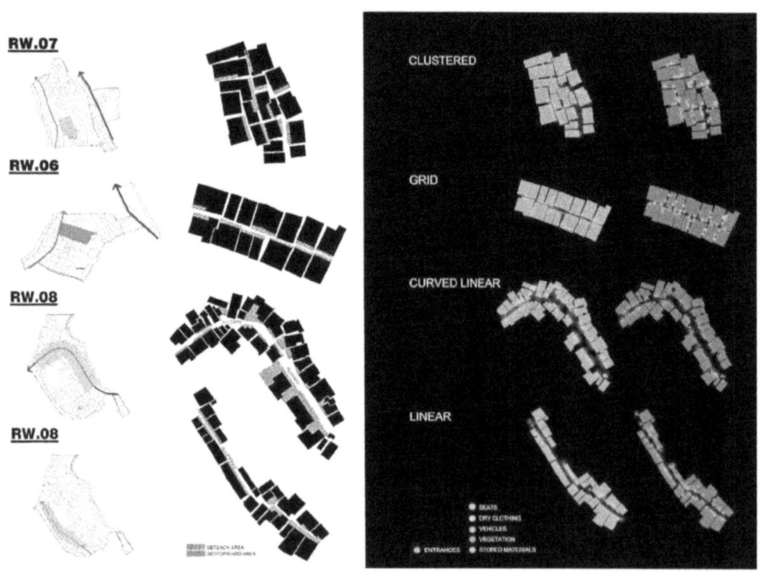

Figure 12.3 Examples of differing alleyway alignments in selected RWs that are driven primarily by housing encroaching and claiming the adjoining alleyway space.

Source: Author.

- Phase Two occurs in an increased period of intensification from the 1980s to 2000s, in which housing is expanded, primarily horizontally, and pathways are further encroached and formalized. Single storey housing reflects a shift in form to two storeys, land is subdivided by family members or sold, and housing expands by a combination of infill and moving forward on their plots, thus narrowing the alignment of the alleyway.
- Phase Three reflects further intensification via horizontal and increasingly vertical adaptations. Additional floorspace and new uses lead to unbuilt plot space being infilled and buildings are aligned, set-forward, or upwards, thus setting new building lines and notional boundaries. The transition in the current Phase Three is increasingly defined by fine-scale changes, typically half to one to two-meter maximum additions, reflecting an adherence to locally accepted rules by which housing adapts and adds to the overall transformation processes (see Figure 12.4).

Understanding how plots have been subdivided and housing is intensified through built form, plot, and land use change in Lebak Siliwangi is fundamental to understanding the current state and fluidity of micro-morphological patterns and *kampung* evolution. New subdivisions and house additions emerge from the demand for housing space generated at the household level. Former pathways are now alleyways adjoining houses and comprise the irregular edges of blocks of varying sizes. When land ownership is transferred (both registered and non-registered) and, in the absence of enforcement, many buyers continue to encroach further into the alleyway space. This occurs because the lands in effect remain under a family name despite the space being

Figure 12.4 During the current Phase Three adaptations, the main alleyway in *kampung* Lebak Siliwangi (named Gang Stone Alley) has become narrower, with form changes increasingly ad-hoc due to being both "set-forward and set-above", and functionality has become restricted.

Source: Author.

historically used as a public area. The gradual impact of encroachment over time is that as plots are sold and subdivided, new alleyway widths and configurations emerge, thus contributing to a non-linear alleyway alignment and "cookie cutter" morphological block patterns. The result is alleyways have become a labyrinth of de-facto public spaces framing irregular plot, block, and building patterns (Jones, 2019a).

Interface form types and "interface creep"

The transition zone that defines the connection of the private domain, such as a house to the adjoining public space and vice versa, is termed the 'interface' (Kamalipour, 2017). In mainstream planning narratives, the space defined by the wall of the building and horizontal juxtaposition of the street and public space has been used to interpret socio-spatial transgression and human-scale connectivity by examining the degree of connectivity, functionality, porosity and permeability from the dwelling to the public space (Dovey & Wood, 2015; Gehl, 2011). In high density informal settlements, the dwelling is inextricably linked to the alignment of the alleyway due to the small scale, multi-functionality and porosity of the alignment space. As such, the interface takes on multiple permanent and temporary forms and functions, being hyperactive at varying times of the day. The alleyways provide a shared space that is both dynamic and flexible, often functioning as the 'front yard' of a house as well as a domain for economic transactions. Housing and their varying built forms and front boundaries – legal, illegal or otherwise based on varying stakeholder understandings of social and spatial boundaries and territory control – adjoin each other in a variety of physical configurations to frame the non-linear alleyway. This unregulated variable width and alignment of the alleyway has been created by what has been termed "interface creep" (Jones, 2019a) and determines the subsequent functions and form responses of the alleyway. This constriction and reduction of space impacts on the movement of people, trading of goods, socialization, and wider *kampung* sustainability.

Within this dynamic interface, it is possible to identify the main interface form types through which the "interface creep" occurs; namely, the progressive encroachment onto private and public residual spaces. Set against contested interpretations of what residents and governance perceive as private, public, communal, semi-public, and shared space, four types of housing forms dominate the spatial pattern framing alleyways in Lebak Siliwangi: setback, aligned, set forward, and set above (Jones, 2019a). The progression through these interface forms from one type to another (and many in combination) align with the three phases of *kampung* intensification as previously outlined. Residents shift their physical and cadastral boundaries via adaptations to their built form while concurrently shaping and reconfiguring the nature of the alleyway edge and wider plot and block morphology. The notion of incrementalism and adding onto and extending housing at micro-scale levels is central to understanding how these form types "creep" and morph from one type to another in multiple iterations. The main form types defining "interface creep" in Lebak Siliwangi are summarized in Table 12.1.

Other interface form types adapt from a combination of these primary types; for example, edges can be defined by both setback and aligned, or both aligned and set forward. Within each interface form type, elements such as doors, windows, partial or full walls, and fences couple in different combinations to provide varying degrees of human

Table 12.1 The main interface form types defining "interface creep" in Lebak Siliwangi.

Type and description	*Elevation*	*Example*
1. Setback: A semi-private transition space between the front boundary and dwelling entry. The transition space may include a green area, pavement or a covered porch enclosed by a full, part, or no wall at the alleyway edge.	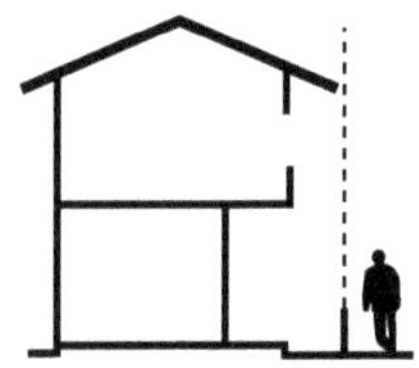	
2. Aligned (no setback): The front face and entry to the main dwelling is aligned to the front boundary. There is no transition space between the front boundary and the main dwelling entrance. Can combine with Setback, Set Forward or Set Above types.	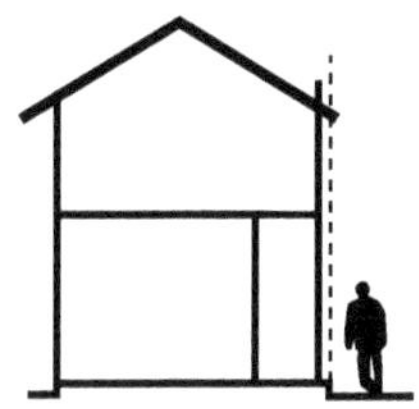	
3. Set Forward (no aligned): A dwelling which transgresses the property boundary or dwelling edge into the alleyway. The form of the Set Forward could be a (part) room, porch, seating, ramp or the like. Can combine with part Aligned and Setback.		
4. Set Above: A dwelling whose second and additional storey extensions incudes a verandah which extends over the front ground level boundary of the alleyway.	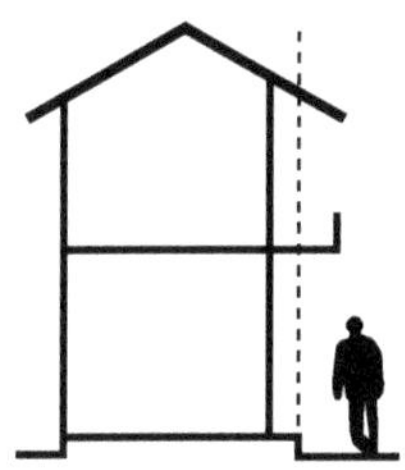	

Source: Adapted from Jones, 2019a.

scale accessibility, visibility, and socialization between the house and alleyway and vice versa. They also provide the opportunity for economic activities within the interface form types. For example, a window could be turned into a shopfront for part of the day, a setback or part setback could be used to park a mobile food stand or motorbikes, or stairs introduced as access for upstairs room rental within the setback or set forward (Jones, Maryati & Suhartini, 2018). Thus, the micro-morphology can be fluid or fixed depending on the social and economic drivers, as well as the type and function of the alleyway.

Micro adaptations: The physical increments of change

Through the progression from one interface form type to another, housing in Lebak Siliwangi expands horizontally and vertically within or over fluid plot and physical boundaries to maximize living area (Jones, 2017). Housing and their physical elements, such as walls, floors, roofing, balconies and doors are added in response to changing social, economic, and cultural drivers. Small-scale actions of adaptation and renewal in housing are progressively implemented and contribute to a high degree of diverse visual coherence and a multiplicity of functions and morphological form. Spatial and physical forms are made diverse through individual actions such as agreeing and affirming development changes and acquiring temporary or permanent building materials. Through the collation of human-scale actions at the level of individual houses, the urban fabric comprising plots, blocks, alleyways, and fixed and unfixed elements is in a continual state of change (Jones, 2019a).

If the processes and types of horizontal and vertical change are deconstructed by their form and function, the main physical increments of change and functional drivers can be identified. Table 12.2 summarizes the physical increments of change that reflect the ongoing processes of housing adaptation in Lebak Siliwangi and which

Table 12.2 Micro-Adaptation: The main physical increments of change and function, Lebak Siliwangi.

Main type of physical increment	*Main function of adaptation*	*Example*
1. Plot Subdivision and Amalgamation	• Increased capacity for floorspace/intensification and additional dwelling yields • Greater financial returns	
2. Vertical Extension by Adding Floor/s	• Additional living area and possible rental accommodation • Extra lighting and ventilation • Clothes drying areas	
3. Insertion of External Access Stairs	• Additional access for renting of rooms or meet existing household and lifecycle needs	
4. Insertion of External Services	• Improve basic services, e.g. water supply, drainage	

(*Continued*)

Table 12.2 (Continued)

Main type of physical increment	*Main function of adaptation*	*Example*
5. Material Replacement	• Increase lighting e.g. installing clear tiles • Ventilation e.g. installing louvred windows • Reduce gaze e.g. installing opaque fencing	
6. Verandah Add-Ons	• Additional living space, drying area, storage	
7. Temporary/Mobile Form Elements	• Economic driver to sustain livelihoods (e.g. window converted into mini store, part aligned and setback to accommodate cooking trolley) • Urban greenery	

Source: Author.

collectively impacts on wider micro-morphological patterns including unbuilt alleyway space. These are: (i) plot subdivisions and or amalgamations, (ii) vertical extension by adding floor/s, (iii) insertion of external access stairs, (iv) insertion of new external services (such as a rooftop water tank), (v) material replacement to allow lighting, ventilation, or reduce connectivity and visibility, for example, (vi) veranda add-ons and extensions, and (vii) temporary and mobile form elements, such as food trolleys placed at the front of housing. The progressive changes to housing collectively result in settlement densification through additional floorspace and rising population, and the reduction of public space such as through altering alleyway widths and functions. Through these adaptation processes, housing is being modified and transformed while also recalibrating the underlying micro-morphology of the plot, block, alleyway and wider settlement.

An observation from the fieldwork in Lebak Siliwangi is that there appears to be a connection between the legal status of the dwelling and the materiality of the physical increment of change. Where there is resident uncertainty of land and building tenure, there is a reluctance to invest in costly adaptations. In these circumstances, adaptations tend to be improvised with second-hand materials, while construction can also be more basic, with little concern for durability and aesthetics. Glass bricks are used for light and vertical vegetation used for screening. Tarpaulins, for example, are placed over permanent fencing to make them non-porous and provide screening to reduce visibility and gaze. Those residents who have secure tenure and can access financial resources appear more receptive to using permanent and new materials, often with an increased emphasis on aesthetics, such as painting and use of geometric 'modern' shapes.

Conclusions

Change in housing form in Lebak Siliwangi is progressive and incremental through small scale adaptation and renewal. There is a strong interplay between micro-morphological changes and the resulting patterns of physical form and structure, the physical, economic and social needs of the household, and settlement sustainability. Notions of form and function remain fluid; recognizing the nexus between alleyways and housing as innovation in space utilization demonstrates their extreme versatility. The freedom of households to make small-scale changes with modules of similar size without external regulation means boundary and or building lines continue to be challenged, new building and boundary lines are set, housing typologies are in constant evolution, and plot and block footprints form myriad patterns. Diverse block sizes and shapes are all interconnected being linked through a system of permeable alleyways. Thus, *kampung* form and structure is an assemblage of outcomes produced via a continuum of informal and formal practices, with bottom-up actions and processes at the household level being the major driver of incrementality in manipulating micro-morphology.

Residents territorialize space by small-scale adaptations as part of their process of housing production (Habraken, 1998) and publicly state their mode of occupation in physical terms. These processes may be spontaneous or well planned, with outcomes temporary or permanent. Most importantly, the shape of the micro morphology is a culmination of these incremental processes and multiple iterations (i.e., types) coalescing over time. Residents observe and replicate small-scale form changes, using a diverse and creative mix of materiality. This bottom-up driven environment of residents acting independently, albeit within an overarching spatial framework of 2–3 storey housing defined by small plot size, comes at a cost. Although small-scale changes facilitate household adaptability, multi-functionality and new interface permutations, they adversely impact on access, sociability, multifunctionality and economic modes of production through the process of "alleyway creep."

In this context, continued unregulated household actions strongly influences *kampung* sustainability in terms of eroding levels of sunlight, ventilation, access to services including drainage and emergency services, and reducing the diversity of functionality in public spaces. The desire to achieve private household outcomes supersedes and overrides consideration of wider public interest concerns. The continued pursuit of private actions is unsustainable, with adverse social, physical and economic implications for the *kampung's* physical and community fabric. This has been acutely highlighted by the current global COVID-19 pandemic where it is impossible due to the high-density settings and lack of public services in informal settlements for households and communities to apply the preventative measures as recommended by the World Health Organization. This includes limited resident access to clean water as well as the inability to maintain at least a one metre distance from others, one result being that social distancing is a "luxury" (Jones, 2020).

Aside from this chapter reinforcing the need for increased visibility of morphological approaches to understand the messy but rich patterns of urbanism in informal settlements, the narrative highlights the overdue recognition for self-help and self-organized housing initiatives in terms of technical and material credit assistance for residents. As is well noted by practitioners (for example, Turner, 1968) and researchers (for example, Dovey, 2014; Jones, 2019a; Kamalipour, 2016b), residents in informal settlements create their houses and homes through vastly different processes than currently extolled in city and neighborhood master plans, rules, and regulations. Considering the scale at which micro-adaptation is now occurring globally, self-help housing as an incremental form of upgrading needs revisiting in line with other larger-scale housing upgrading schemes currently being implemented. A greater focus needs to be placed on understanding and supporting the processes of adaptation, highlighting positive examples of governance that embody self-organization and co-evolution between formal and informal settlements, and their rules, regulations and protocols.

References

Conzen, M. (1960). *Alnwick, Northumberland: A study in town-plan analysis* (27ed). London, England: Institute of British Geographers.

Das, A. (2017). A City of Two Tales:Shelter and Migrants in Surabaya. *Environment and Urbanization ASIA*, *8*(1), 1–21. doi:10.1177/0975425316686501

Davis, M. (2006). *Planet of Slums*. London and New York: Verso.

Dovey, K. (2012). Informal urbanism and complex adaptive assemblage. *International Development Planning Review*, *34*(4), 349–368. doi:10.3828/idpr.2012.23

Dovey, K. (2014). Incremental Urbanism: The Emergence of Informal Settlements. In T. Haas & K. Olsson (Eds.), *Emergent Urbanism: Urban Planning & Design in Times of Structural and Systemic Change*. London and New York: Routledge.

Dovey, K., & King, R. (2011). Forms of Informality: Morphology and Visibility of Informal Settlements. *Built Environment*, *37*(1), 11–29. Retrieved from https://www.researchgate.net/publication/263381444_Forms_of_Informality_Morphology_and_Visibility_of_Informal_Settlements

Dovey, K., Pafka, E., & Ristic, M. (Eds.). (2017). *Mapping Urbanities: Morphologies, Flows, Possibilities*. New York: Routledge.

Dovey, K., & Wood, S. (2015). Public/private urban interfaces: type, adaptation, assemblage. *Journal of Urbanism: International Research on Placemaking and Urban Sustainability*, *8*(1), 1–16. doi:10.1080/17549175.2014.891151

Gehl, J. (2011). *Life between buildings using public space* Washington, D.C: Island Press.

Habraken, N. J. (1998). *The structure of the ordinary: form and control in the built environment* Cambridge, Mass: MIT Press.

Harris, R. (2017). Modes of Informal Urban Development: A Global Phenomenon. *Journal of Planning Literature*, *33*(3), 267–286. doi:10.1177/0885412217737340

Hou, J., & Chalana, M. (2016). Untangling the "Messy" Asian City *Messy Urbanism: Understanding the "Other" Cities of Asia*. Hong Kong: Hong Kong Scholarship.

Jones, P. (2016). *Unpacking Informal Urbanism: Urban Planning and Design Education in Practice* Bandung, Indonesia: Institute of Technology Bandung (ITB) University Press (Penerbit).

Jones, P. (2017). Formalizing the Informal: Understanding the Position of Informal Settlements and Slums in Sustainable Urbanization Policies and Strategies in Bandung. *Indonesia. Sustainability*, *9*(8), 1436. doi:10.3390/su9081436

Jones, P. (2019a). The Shaping of Form and Structure in Informal Settlements: A Case Study of Order and Rules in Lebak Siliwangi, Bandung, Indonesia. *Journal of Regional and City Planning*, *30*(1), 43–61. doi:10.5614/jpwk.2019.30.1.4

Jones, P. (2019b). Informal Settlements and The Concept of Informal Urbanism. In S. Maryati (Ed), *Understanding the Informal City*. Institute of Technology Bandung (ITB) University Press (Penerbit).

Jones, P. (2020). Too many left behind: the failing of COVID-19 prevention measures in informal settlements and slums. *The Conversation*. Retrieved from https://theconversation.com/too-many-left-behind-the-failing-of-covid-19-prevention-measures-in-informal-settlements-and-slums-137288

Jones, P., Maryati, S., & Suhartini, N. (2018). *The Form of the Informal – Understanding Lebak Siliwangi, Bandung, Indonesia*. Bandung, Indonesia: Institute of Technology Bandung (ITB) University Press (Penerbit).

Kamalipour, H. (2016a). Forms of Informality and Adaptations in Informal Settlements. *ArchNet International Journal of Architectural Research*, *10*(3), 60–75. doi:10.26687/archnet-ijar.v10i3.1094

Kamalipour, H. (2016b). Urban Morphologies in Informal Settlements: a case study. *Contour Journal*, *1*(2), 61. doi:10.6666/contour.v1i2.61

Kamalipour, H. (2017). Mapping Urban Interfaces: A Typology of Public/Private Interfaces in Informal Settlements. *Spaces and Flows: An International Journal of Urban and ExtraUrban Studies*, *8*(2), 1–12. doi:10.18848/2154-8676/CGP/v08i02/1-12

Kamalipour, H., & Dovey, K. (2019). Mapping the visibility of informal settlements. *Habitat International*, *85*, 63–75. doi:10.1016/j.habitatint.2019.01.002

Kellett, P., & Napier, M. (1995). Squatter Architecture? A Critical Examination of Vernacular Theory and Spontaneous Settlement with Reference to South America and South Africa. *Traditional Dwellings and Settlements Review*, *6*(2), 7–24. Retrieved from https://www.academia.edu/2044991/Squatter_architecture_A_critical_examination_of_vernacular_theory_and_spontaneous_settlement_with_reference_to_South_America_and_South_Africa

McCartney, S., & Krishnamurthy, S. (2018). Neglected? Strengthening the Morphological Study of Informal Settlements. *SAGE Open*, *8*(1), 1–11. doi:10.1177/2158244018760375

Neuwirth, R. (2004). *Shadow Cities: A Billion Squatters, a New Urban World*. London and New York: Routledge.

Patel, S., & Baptist, C. (2012). Editorial: Documenting by the undocumented. *Environment & Urbanization*, *24*(1), 3–12. doi:10.1177/0956247812438364

Rapoport, A. (1988). Spontaneous Settlements as Vernacular Design. In C. V. Patton (Ed.), *Spontaneous Shelter: International Perspectives and Prospects*. Philadelphia: Temple University Press.

Reerink, G. (2011). *Tenure Security for Indonesia's Urban Poor: A Socio-Legal Study on Land, Decentralisation and the Rule of Law in Bandung*. The Netherlands: Leiden University Press.

Rosner-Manor, Y., Borghini, S. G., Boonstra, B., and Silva, P. (2019). Adaptation of the urban codes – A story of placemaking in Jerusalem. *Environment and Planning B: Urban Analytics and City Science*. 0(0), 1–17. ttps://doi.org/10.1177/2399808319867712

Roy, A., & Alsayyad, N. (Eds.). (2004). *Urban informality: Transnational perspectives from the Middle East, Latin America, and South Asia*. Lanham: Lexington Books.

Silva, P., & Farrall, H. (2016). Lessons from informal settlements: a 'peripheral' problem with self-organising solutions. *Town Planning Review*, *87*(3), 297–319. doi:10.3828/tpr.2016.21

Suhartini, N., & Jones, P. (2019). *Urban Governance and Informal Settlements: Lessons from the City of Jayapura, Indonesia*. Switzerland: Springer.

Turner, J. C. (1968). Housing Priorities, Settlement Patterns, and Urban Development in Modernizing Countries. *Journal of the American Institute of Planners*, *34*(6), 354–363. doi:10.1080/01944366808977562

United National General Assembly. (2013). *Report of the Special Rapporteur on adequate housing as a component of the right to an adequate standard of living, and on the right to non-discrimination in this context on her mission to Indonesia.* Annex. Human Rights Council, New York.
UN-Habitat. (2008). *Quick Guides for Policy Makers 4 EVICTION: Alternatives to the whole-scale destruction of urban poor communities.* Retrieved from https://unhabitat.org/books/quick-guides-for-policy-makers-4-eviction-alternatives-to-the-whole-scale-destruction-of-urban-poor-communities/
UN-Habitat. (2016). *World Cities Report 2016 – Urbanization and Development Emerging Futures.* Kenya: UN-Habitat. Retrieved from https://unhabitat.org/books/world-cities-report/
UN-Habitat & ESCAP. (2015). *The State of Asian and Pacific Cities 2015: Urban Transformations Shifting from Quantity to Quality.* Retrieved from https://www.unescap.org/sites/default/files/The%20State%20of%20Asian%20and%20Pacific%20Cities%202015.pdf

Chapter 13

Urban (in)formality and the new unsustainable landscape of the Global South

Case study of megacity Dhaka

Mohammad S.H. Swapan, Atiq Zaman and Steffen Lehmann

Introduction

The term 'informality' has been a much abused, blurred and misunderstood concept in urban studies literature. It is often defined narrowly or loosely to characterise the urbanisation process, practice and outcome in the Global South. The concept has been preluded with neoliberal economics and governance thinking put forward by Castells and Portes (1989), Pierre (1999) and DiGaetano and Strom (2003). Informality has prevailed as a dominant characteristic of urbanisation of poverty as "either as an economic sector [e.g., street hawking] or as a form of shelter [e.g. slums and squatters] and service provision" (Kudva, 2009, p. 1614). The subaltern urbanism, which is defined by the informal process adopted by the urban poor occupies a vast landscape of the cities (Roy, 2011; Varley, 2013). In many cities, informality is so blended within society that the line between formal and informal practice is often hard to distinguish (Roy, 2009; Schindler, 2014). Several studies have affirmed that various forms of informality exist in the developing world that slip through the laws of urban space or fail to adhere institutional regulations (Adams et al., 2014; R. Harris, 2018).

The discourse of urban informality which is traditionally referred to as the Global South has "undergone critical transformation in recent scholarships" (Moatasim, 2018, p. 1010). Such transformation has challenged the dominant concept of informality (Song, 2016), often defines the poverty-led informality as partial view of the literature [such as De Soto (2000) and Davis (2006)]. In this regard, Roy cautions that informality is no longer synonymous to poverty but rather the term is also associated with various forms of wealth and power (Roy, 2005, 2009). A number of urbanists acknowledge that planning is not solely performed by planners but also other critical stakeholders including developers, builders, civil societies and residents, who often render and obscure what is considered as formal or legal. In extreme cases, a wider practice of informality "defines the entire planning regime" as seen in many countries in the Global South (R. Harris, 2018, p. 267; Roy, 2009). The premise of Roy's progressive view of 'informal urbanisation', is to treat it "as much the purview of wealthy urbanites as it is of slum dwellers" (Roy, 2009; 2011, p. 233). The literature suggests decreasing the role of the state and advocating to uphold the dynamic relationships and interactions among state and non-state actors. Different governance scales and frameworks offer different actors different patterns of relationships and influence, which reflect economic, political and ideological frameworks embedded in the planning process (Hackenbroch, Hossain, Altrock, Schoon, & Sterly, 2016). Therefore, capitalist development and the informal role of the state need to be unpacked to understand the new dimensions of informality in the Global South (McFarlane, 2012; Roy, 2005).

Roy's seminal work suggests informality as the mode of urban development which is politically constructed and increasingly manipulated by the urban elites to satisfy their own needs (Roy, 2009). Such elite driven urbanism has been widely featured in recent planning literature based on South Asian and African cities. For example, frequent bypassing of planning regulations to serve elite interests is increasingly evident in post-colonial cities in these regions (Moatasim, 2019; Morshed, 2014). The resurgence of elite informality is further reported in major cities in South Africa, Angola and Mozambique in terms of informal coalition between capitalists, state power and the foreign corporate wealth for reconstruction of modern/western-style development. This was mainly done by evicting and displacing urban poor from fringe areas (Arfvidsson, Simon, Oloko, & Moodley, 2017; Simon, 2015). Informal urbanisation is often produced due to a lack of capacity of the formal system and to justify politically constructed decisions. Elite informality has featured mostly within urban land and housing development contexts, which have remained as an uncontested landscape of cities in South Asian countries particularly in India, Pakistan and Bangladesh (Hossain & Hackenbroch, 2019; Moatasim, 2019; Morshed, 2014). It relies on the nexus between state (e.g., bureaucrats and political representatives) and non-state actors (e.g., private developers and investors) by creating extra-legal development mechanisms for the cities. The increasing desire of urban elites to live in the urban periphery separating themselves from urban poor often leads to serious environmental destruction. However, such environmental implications of elite informality are comparatively less featured in the urban studies literature (Baviskar, 2011; Follmann, 2015; Rumbach, 2017).

In this chapter, we aim to trace the characteristics of the recent trend of elite influence on the urbanisation (also termed as entitled urbanism) of the Global South. In this regard, we first discuss the materials and methods adopted to organise the chapter followed by a systematic literature review presented in the third section. Section four reports on the case study of megacity Dhaka (Bangladesh) and the perpetuating trend of elite informality at the periphery. The discussion section scrutinises entitled urbanism to demonstrate how political power and wealth intermingle to produce unsustainable landscape through a biased metropolitan planning and policy instrument. Finally, we conclude with commenting on implications of new trend of informality on sustainable urban growth in the Global South.

Materials and methods

A systematic literature review and scan of media reports and government documents were predominantly adopted to prepare this chapter. The systematic literature review provides a useful approach to unpack the body of knowledge as well as rigour and transparency in identifying conceptual evolution (Sengers, Wieczorek, & Raven, 2016). A media scan provides a comprehensive and popular overview of the case study, which engages critically in translating the concept in a contextual discourse.

Although the term 'elite informality' has been widely cited in recent years, the approach was evident since the early history of urbanisation. The key characteristics and recent trends of elite informality were analysed through a systematic literature review. Both Scopus and Science Direct database were used to identify the most relevant studies on urban informality. Since the main focus of this chapter is to understand the elite influence on urbanisation process, thus we used 'urban informality' AND 'elite'/'entitled' as the database search criteria. Our initial search identified 750 articles and 1950 articles in Scopus and Science Direct database respectively. Based on the relevance and number of citations, around 33 articles were selected finally and analysed to understand the elite informality in the Global South.

To report on such manipulation in major strategic plan and urban development projects in Dhaka, we have reviewed metropolitan policies and strategies, government reports, Detailed Area Plan (DAP) planning proposals and land use maps. To obtain critical insight to the resulted governance mechanism and outcomes along the formal process due to informality, we conducted an intensive media scan of the leading daily newspapers, online portals and blogs, between 2008 and 2018.

From subaltern urbanism to entitled urbanism: A systematic literature review

Elite informality in the Global South

The informality in the Global South is the outcome of exploitation of political, economic and social power, violation of planning norms under the name of greater goods or social benefits and finally the legitimisation of the all these practices though regulation and policy stemming from prejudice. Table 13.1 shows the key characteristics and drivers of elite informality around the world. By reporting on the systematic literature review, we have explored the conceptual development and forms of non-traditional informality in the Global South.

Based on the findings of the systematic literature review of the relevant articles presented in Table 13.1, it is evident that urban informality is not only limited to a lack of formal planning system in place but also by various other factors including corruption, exercising social connections and networks for economic and political gains, influencing and violating planning norms and codes. Although urban informality was initially driven by rapid urbanisation and to accommodate urban poor – street vendors, migrated labour and illegal workers, the review of previous studies indicates that the trend and dynamics of urban informality has changed over time. In the 1990s, urban elite formally appeared in influencing the city planning in the name of privatisation to promote self-help housing and poverty alleviation (Roy, 2005). The elite groups are not only violating the planning norms through their political power and networks, but also legitimise their corruptions by changing the planning regulations and court decision. The recent trends indicate that even the state has been influencing and contributing to the urban informality. The following section explores the characteristics of the urban informality in Dhaka city and how urban informality has changed over time due to various ramifications.

Table 13.1 The key characteristics and drivers of elite informality in the Global South

Country/Region	*Study areas*	*Central vs peri-urban*	*Key characteristics, drivers and development process*	*Authors*
Pakistan	Bani Gala	Central area and peri-urban	The key drivers of the elite informality in Bani Gala, Pakistan were mainly the use of political connection, corruption, influence the zoning regulation and finally legitimisation through court decision.	Moatasim (2019)
Jakarta	Greater Jakarta	Central and peri-urban	The informal development in the greater Jakarta is driven by both grassroots and elite people, mainly through the role of elite informal networks connecting the development industry with state actors.	Herlambang, Leitner, Tjung, Sheppard, and Anguelov (2019); Sheppard (2019)
India	Mumbai, Mangaluru, Bangalore, Delhi, Gurgaon	Central and peri-urban	Elite-biased both formal and informal development in urban areas is influence through informal tenure, land grabs – corruption and the hypocritical policing and violating planning norms. The absence of significant public or private investment, micro-political practices employed by non-state and state actors in bureaucratic, judicial, and political and market system.	Doshi and Ranganathan (2017); Doshi (2019); Follmann (2015); A. Harris (2018); Kadfak and Oskarsson (2017); Pethe, Nallathiga, Gandhi, and Tandel (2014); Roy (2009); Schindler and Kishore (2015); Srivastava (2014); Sundaresan (2017)
Bangladesh	Dhaka	Central and peri-urban	Although initially started by informal system, the informal development has transformed to a 'systemic invasion' of land around rivers, lakes and other water-bodies and wetlands by the 'elites'. The political influence and violation of planning code, lack of transdisciplinary planning and agencies collaboration bureaucratic acts, the existing power relations, and group interests considerably influence planning practice in Bangladesh.	S. Ahmed, Nahiduzzaman, and Hasan (2018); Hackenbroch et al. (2016); Alam (2014); Hossain and Hackenbroch (2019)
Philippines	Manila	Central	Manila's urban informality is influenced by the state actors, landlords, community residents and elite families through on-going gentrification and neoliberal urbanism.	Ortega (2016)
China	Chengdu, Beijing	Peri-urban	The state-controlled land ownership, high-level political and financial influence a "semi-formal" regulated system influence both informal and formal development.	Zeuthen (2018); Zhang and Zhao (2018)

(*Continued*)

Table 13.1 (Continued)

Country/Region	*Study areas*	*Central vs peri-urban*	*Key characteristics, drivers and development process*	*Authors*
Brazil	El Condado, Puerto Rico, Rio de Janeiro,	Central and peri-urban	A higher level of social inequality particularly a majority of lands controlled by very few elites, racial and privileged-class who influence state-level and local level public policy to drive the informal development in Brazil.	Ramos-Zayas (2019); Prouse (2019); Fahlberg and Vicino (2016)
Paraguay	Ciudad del Este	Peri-urban	Mainly two factors (i) "regulation by ambiguity"- legal opacity (the proliferation of contradictory regulations; sporadic, politicized enforcement of law; substantial de facto bureaucratic discretion) and (ii) spatial illegibility (a mismatch between official maps, land titles, and so on and the physical geographies they purport to represent) drive the informality.	Tucker (2017)
Africa	N/A	N/A	The grassroots informality is mainly driven by the economic and political context of associations, the nature of their relations with political elites, the governing powers of associations, the nature of their leadership.	Lindell (2018)
Eastern D.R. Congo	Goma	Central	Mainly hybrid modes of governance and fragmented paths of urbanisation, regulatory networks and new alliances among urban elites influence the informal development.	Büscher (2012)
Mexico	Mexico City	central	The real estate developers, politicians, and residents, informality motivates homeowners' associations to take on a neighbourhood-defending and state-monitoring role, influences planning decisions and access to land in urban Latin America.	Müller and Segura (2017)
Global South (in general)	N/A	N/A	Hyper-urbanisation in the Global South, 'insurgent' citizenship that destabilises 'entrenched' forms of citizenship. Privatisation, land right and a lack of participation in the market influence informality and create elite to exploit the system.	Banks, Lombard, and Mitlin (2019); (Roy, 2005); (Wagenaar, 2014)

Case study: Metropolitan planning in Dhaka

Dhaka is ranked 9th in the world's megacity list and is projected to take over the 4th position by 2030. The megacity covers an area of 1528 km^2 inhabited by 19.5 million people (UN, 2018). A recent report by the World Bank notes: "in Bangladesh, rapid and unplanned urbanisation has affected the liveability in the cities. Today, about 54 million Bangladeshis live in cities and the number will be more than double in the next 35 years. Yet, one-fifth of urban dwellers currently live in poverty" (WB, 2017). The city is bordered by several rivers and is susceptible to seasonal flooding (M. Swapan, Zaman, Ahsan, & Ahmed, 2017). In recent years, due to unplanned and informal development, Dhaka is highly vulnerable to flooding. Dhaka experiences an unprecedented frequent flooding challenge due to monsoon rains. In previous years, citizens faced devastating floods while around 50% of the city was completely inundated.

Paradise lost: Failure of strategic planning

The city experienced few organised metropolitan plans in the past though it faced significant influx of population. Being the centre of all economic and administrative activities of the nation, Dhaka is passing through a significant urbanisation process. The formal town planning for the capital city started in 1953 with the release of the first Master Plan. The plan was mostly shelved due to its non-sensitivity to local context and the city but there was no attempt to guide the urbanisation process until the 1990s. The Dhaka Metropolitan Development Plan (DMDP) released in 1995 by the RAJUK (Capital Development Authority), is a three-tier development control and growth management strategic plan for the core area and the hinterlands. RAJUK runs under the Town Improvement Act 1953 and controlled by a semi-autonomous management board. After the completion of the Dhaka Structural Plan (1st tier) and Urban Area Plan (2nd tier), the development of the Detailed Area Plan (DAP) was delayed due to a paucity of funds. In the meantime, the city experienced unprecedented and uncontrolled spatial development mainly inspired by private developers (Bari & Efroymson, 2009). After a long pause due to political developments and bureaucratic complexities, DAP was officially launched with government approval in 2004 with specific planning proposals for planning sub-regions within the DMDP areas.

The DAP was initially drafted by the planners from RAJUK and nominated consulting firms. The draft plan was then displayed only to a selected group of people for feedback. This step of the process carries a substantial risk of allowing in bias to suit vested interests of the select group members. To give top priority to environmental considerations and to ensure civil society participation in plan-making process, RAJUK organised a 13-member Technical Working Group (TWG) representing professional groups and environmental activists (Sheltech, 2010). The committee indicated several issues in the draft plan, especially with population projection, discrepancy in data, nonconformity of proposed land use and confusing planning norms (Ali & Alam, 2009; M. S. H. Swapan, 2014). In the meantime, the revised, and possibly biased, plan was put up for public hearing though RAJUK's field offices. According to section 73(4) of Town Improvement (TI) Act 1953, RAJUK carried out a two month long public hearing on the Detailed Area Plan around the end of 2008 (M. S. H. Swapan, 2014).

It is reported that the initiative only addressed planning errors occurred in the original plans but did not listen to the other complaints lodged by the affected citizens. Finally, DAP was gazetted in June, 2010.

The DAP defined two-thirds of the greater Dhaka as flood flow zones including low-lying wetlands (see Figure 13.1a), water retention ponds, ditches and canals which act as natural receptor of water during the monsoon. Main flood flow zone is susceptible to annual flooding due to overflowing of adjacent water bodies while sub-flood flow zone only inundates during high tides and storms. According to the land use plan of DAP (1995–2015), new development was almost impossible in the fringes as 73% of land was delineated as non-residential (e.g. agricultural, rural or wetlands) (Morshed, 2014) (see Figure 13.1b). However, the restricted areas soon became very attractive to powerful private developers, politicians and even to public agencies to capitalise the sky-rocketing increment of land values. Real estate data shows that land price of the fringes areas of Dhaka has increased enormously, with an average more than 70% annually during 2000–2010 (Alam, 2018). Another report shows that the agricultural land and waterbodies in DAP areas reduced by around 22% while residential areas increased by 33% during 2006–2013 (A. H. Mahmud, 2014) (see Figure 13.1c). As a result, the risk of flooding has escalated in recent years as the wetlands have been continuously filled up for housing development projects. Moreover, due to the illegal encroachment and landfilling, Dhaka lost around 19 km^2 of rivers and canals and 77 km^2 of wetlands during 1978–2009 (Asad & Ahsan, 2012). This causes a serious threat to the environmentally sustainability and liveability of the mega city. A continuous encroachment of lands important for water retention and drainage led to unprecedented urban flooding in 2005 and subsequent years (Roy, Sowgat, & Mondal, 2019).

Elite informality and unsustainable landscape

The DAP received significant obstacles in implementing specific planning proposals especially in the areas identified as a fragile environment in the fringe areas (e.g., flood flow zones, rivers and canals). Private developers have appeared as the dominant actor in land conversion around the fringes of DMDP areas. This is a common trend in most developing countries as subdivision at fringes is most profitable form of land conversion (Morshed, 2013). It is reported that proposed reserved areas for water retention and agri-based activities primarily belonged to private owners, who sold the lands to private developers to gain higher economic benefits (Alam, 2014). Recent data shows that around 181 housing projects have been developed by several powerful real estate developers converting the low-lying areas at the periphery of Dhaka of which 33% is located in the main flood flow zone and 14% is developed in sub-flood flow zone encroaching an area of 10,128.34 hectare (Alam, 2014; Bird et al., 2018; Jahangir Alam & Akter Mullick, 2014). Another report shows that 80% of ecologically critical areas is destroyed by the real estate companies (Ali, 2014) (see Figure 13.2). Such major land sub-division and land filling (up to 4–7 meter) contribute to significant impacts on the natural drainage system and ecologically critical areas of the city. Lack of legal enforcement, lingering bureaucratic process of DAP implementation and endemic corruption allowed these projects to grow and expand (Alam & Ahmad, 2013). Although RAJUK took legal actions against a number of housing project for violating related policies and conservation rules (e.g., Natural Water Body Protection Law, 2000), the

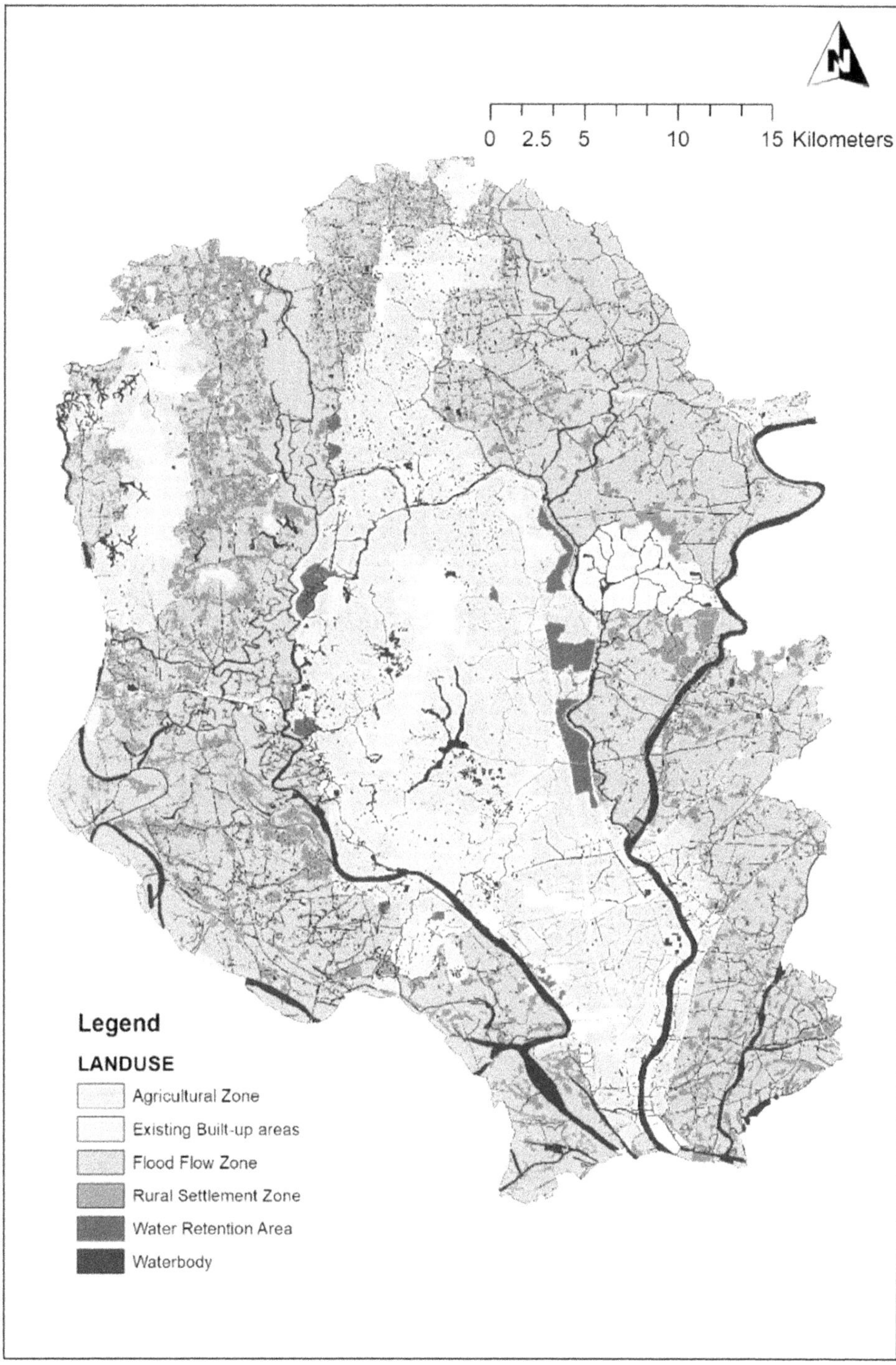

Figure 13.1 Detail of land use plan proposed by DAP (1995–2015).

Source: Bird, Li, Rahman, Rama, & Venables, 2018; Morshed, 2013; RAJUK, 2006.

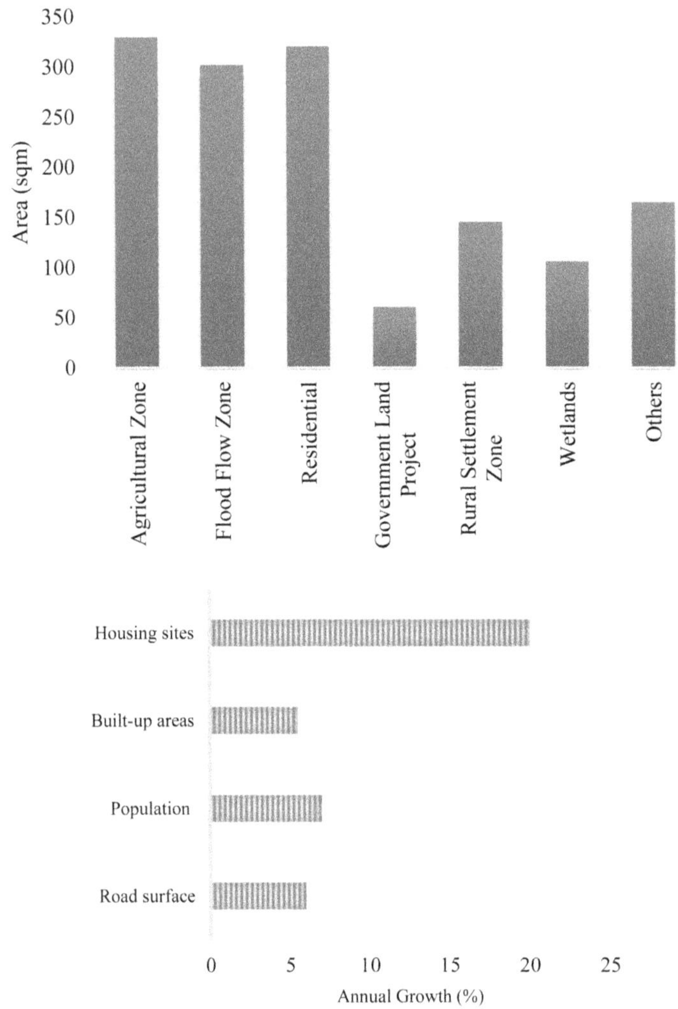

Figure 13.1 (Continued)

developers had already subdivided the land without any approvals from the development authority and sought political channels to avoid any uncertainties.

Dumni canal located in the north-eastern part of Dhaka (Purbachal 300-feet Road) (Hashim, 2017)	Private developers occupied the marshy land for land filling and residential subdivision (Husain & Sohag, 2017)

Ironically, (Alam, 2014) also reported five public housing projects which have even violated the DAP land use restrictions. These projects included 24,300 residential lots and 3,360 apartments, which were completed either at the cost of agricultural land or filling up large lakes at the periphery (Alam, 2018). Most of the projects were originally funded by the Ministry of Housing and Public Works to contribute to more affordable housing for middle and lower income groups. Alam and Ahmad (2013, p. 195) found

Figure 13.2 a and b Illegal encroachment of waterbodies and wetlands in DAP areas.

that these projects are in fact "developed because of the demand from different elites, national policy makers and upper class to avail the plots with a lower price under a quota system". In reality, only 5% of the subdivided plots were distributed to the affected owners, while 18% were reserved for the state's top officials and ministers and the rest of the plots were allocated to powerful groups of the society including business persons, high officials, political leaders etc. (Hossain & Hackenbroch, 2019). Although DMDP as well as National Housing Policy define the role of the government as only an enabler in the land market but state's direct involvement appears as a stark contradiction to it with direct violation of land use policy (RAJUK, 2006). Eventually, it further "encouraged more private developers to convert lands in the fringe areas of the city" (p. 55).

Later, power and politics interplayed significantly to change the direction of DAP. To avoid the legal barriers, project owners tried to manipulate planning decisions using informal network and political influence. RAJUK was also found to be supportive to these powerful stakeholders. A spokesman from RAJUK even mentioned that there was discrepancy in proposed land use by DAP as many built-up areas were identified as low-lying land and areas having existing residential buildings and industries were declared as restricted zone (BP, 2018). The recent adjustments, therefore, were deemed justified to the planning authority. Eventually, the Ministry of Housing and Public Works recommended relevant authorities legalise and approve a number of housing projects located inside the restricted land use of DAP. To deal with mounting appeals, application and mass unrest against illegal housing projects, another ministerial technical committee was engaged in 2015 to review the DAP proposals. It is interesting to note that RAJUK was not represented in the committee despite of being the main stakeholder of DAP. It is evident that several housing projects which were declared illegal by the High Court, gained favour from the newly formed committee as H. U. Ahmed (2018) noted in a news article:

> It approved as many as 158 changes during the past 8 years, through which the influential quarters got approval for filling up a large chunk of designated water-bodies and flood-flow areas.... Till now, 135 gazette notifications containing approvals made by the cabinet committee.... permissions were given for filling up water bodies through 34 amendments and flood-flow areas through 14 amendments. Agricultural and rural settlements have been cancelled through 20 amendments. ... [changes made] in the land use categories in overlay zones through 13 amendments.

Such deviation occurs in both micro and macro level planning in Dhaka city. A study conducted in 13 areas of the metropolitan area by Transparency International Bangladesh (2007) reveals that deviation in Building Construction Rules (1996) occurs between 80–100% of approved residential buildings. In most of the cases buildings encroaches the adjacent roads by violating setback rules. On the other hand, on an average 86% of approved commercial buildings are built without any parking facilities (M. A. Mahmud, 2007). Apart from this, wide-spread corruption of RAJUK is reported in media and study reports which leads to "poor enforcement of the Rules and the Code", political interference and favouritism and "the use of land as political patronage" (Sabet & Tazreen, 2015).

Discussion

The illegal encroachment of peri-urban areas in Dhaka by private developers as well as the state to deal with public housing issue has significant impacts including social, economic and environmental. It is reported that several land owners in the fringe

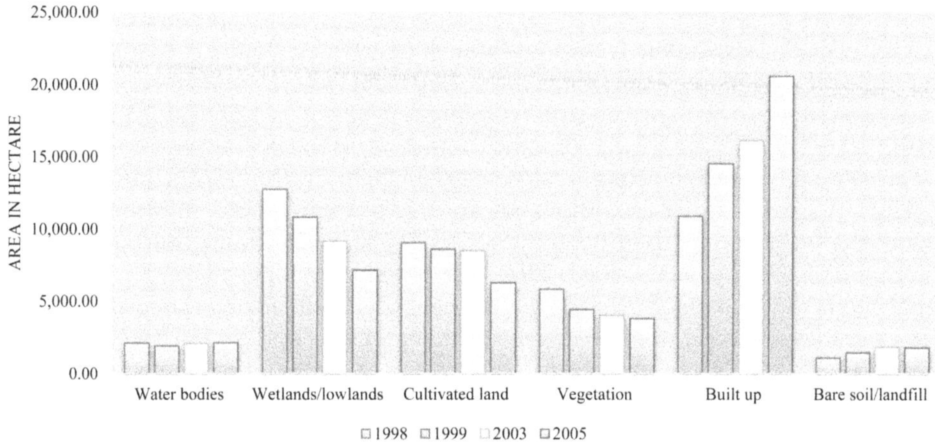

Figure 13.3 Land use change and loss of natural resources in Dhaka (1998–2005).

Source: Jahangir Alam & Akter Mullick, 2014.

areas faced eviction due to selling their land unwillingly to the real estate companies. (Akther & Hossain, 2011) found that 90% of the owner was either forced or trapped by pocket land as the developers secured all the lots around them and eventually compelled them to sell their land. A sudden increase in land conversion for housing also contributed to escalated land price in the fringe areas which attracted traditional farmers to sell their cultivable fields. As a result, around 1200 acres of agricultural fields were converted and significantly reduced crop yields (Jahangir Alam & Akter Mullick, 2014). Deviation from planning measures and lack of enforcement of planning regulation have led to continual encroachment of risk areas and ended up with significant loss of natural resources (see Figure 13.3). Filling up flood flow zones has also serious detrimental impacts on city's entire drainage system resulting in persistent flooding, decreasing ground water level and destruction of biodiversity.

The case study clearly demonstrates how urban elites based on financial resources and political patronage routinely participate in the production of informal and unsustainable space. As Moatasim pointed out, "elite informality as a relatively uncontested terrain where private developers, public agencies and in some cases coalition of these powerful networks can work to produce high-end spaces of informality for other elite citizens to enjoy" (Moatasim, 2019, p. 1010). In extreme cases as evident in DAP implementation, informality defines the entire planning regime where the state patronages powerful stakeholders and creates extra-legal arrangements to justify their acts even at costing city's lifelines. Roy (2009) further defines peri-urbanisation and such unsustainable conversion of environmental sensitive areas as 'privatisation of informality' which is as informal as squatter settlements (Morshed, 2014, p. 387).

The political context of Bangladesh yields various types of clientele and networks that eventually lead to illegal flow of resources and informal production of space. These networks, relying on networks built around patron-client relationships, have largely contributed to corrupting urban governance systems, rendering them inefficient (Sarker, 2008; Uberti, 2016). Various actors including politicians, bureaucrats, private developers form this complex patron-client relation for mutual benefits (Khan, 1998; Sarker, 2008). Traditionally such relation existed between urban poor and political leaders/powerful elites for voting rights and to seek access to formal urban services by the deprived groups living in squatter settlements (Przeworski, 2010).

The new landscape of informality in peri-urban Dhaka introduces "a non-monetary explanation, building on coalitions of power, flexibility, and informality" and negotiated space rationalised by extra-legal arrangements (Alam, 2014; Hossain & Hackenbroch, 2019, p. 3; Morshed, 2014). The private developers have the awareness, connections and capability to access and engage with the formal planning system. However, they are likely to disregard the formal planning system as it may be seen as irrelevant. They are more likely to use their political clout and social and businesses networks to bypass the normal or prescribed interface with the formal planning system while they seek to influence the formal planning system's decision-making in their favour. While the informality becomes the formal planning practice to serve the elites as the case study demonstrates, "statutory planning does not necessarily act for societal benefit and not even for environmental sustainability" of the city (Hossain & Hackenbroch, 2019, p. 2).

Conclusions

It is evident from the case study that the new dimension informality shaped by elite urbanism can be much more detrimental than the traditional subaltern urbanism in cities of developing countries. The coalition between the state and the powerful elites to politicise the entire planning regime could be more devastating in terms of long-term sustainability of the city. The study reveals some root causes of unsustainable landscape perpetuated through the elite informality in Dhaka. While urban poverty often contributed in informal production of space and economy resulted from subsistence concerns and to access urban services they are not entitled, the elites have more individualistic agenda and focused on economic benefits. In neoliberal context, the increasing investment of private developers is not always rationale in case of peri-urban Dhaka. A recent report has shown that only 35% of existing built-up area in the city is utilised for housing, therefore occupying wetlands is not a valid excuse (Ali, 2019). Furthermore, the role of the state in readjusting the structure plan in favour of the powerful stakeholders is more like an act of retrospective 'rationalisation' of informal (i.e., illegal) activities as defined by Flyvbjerg (1998). It urgently demands a more informed citizenship and responsive planning negotiation by the state. Otherwise the upcoming Dhaka Structure Plan (2016–2035) will deviate from normative planning principles like its predecessors and will obviously fail to achieve the targets of sustainable city as a whole.

References

Adams, M. A., Frank, L. D., Schipperijn, J., Smith, G., Chapman, J., Christiansen, L. B., … Sallis, J. F. (2014). International variation in neighborhood walkability, transit, and recreation environments using geographic information systems: the IPEN adult study. *International Journal of Health Geographics*, *13*. doi:10.1186/1476-072x-13-43

Ahmed, H. U. (2018). Flouting Detailed Area Plan and Dhaka's perilous future. *The Financial Express*. Retrieved from https://thefinancialexpress.com.bd/views/views/flouting-detailed-area-plan-and-dhakas-perilous-future-1524672521
Ahmed, S., Nahiduzzaman, K. M., & Hasan, M. M. U. (2018). Dhaka, Bangladesh: unpacking challenges and reflecting on unjust transitions. *Cities*, *77*, 142–157.
Akther, F., & Hossain, S. M. N. (2011). Impacts of Private Residential Land Development Projects in the Flood Flow Zones of DMDP Area: Case Study of Tetuljhora Union. *Journal of Bangladesh Institute of Planners*, *4*, 57–70.
Alam, M. J. (2014). "The organized encroachment of land developers"—Effects on urban flood management in Greater Dhaka, *Bangladesh. Sustainable Cities and Society*, *10*, 49–58.
Alam, M. J. (2018). Rapid urbanization and changing land values in mega cities: implications for housing development projects in Dhaka, Bangladesh. *Bandung: Journal of the Global South*, *5*(1), 1–19.
Alam, M. J., & Ahmad, M. M. (2013). Public Facilities in Public and Private Housing Projects in Dhaka, *Bangladesh. Urban Policy and Research*, *31*(2), 190–207.
Ali, T. (2014). 80pc flood flow zones filled up. *The Daily Star*. Retrieved from https://www.thedailystar.net/80pc-flood-flow-zones-filled-up-15165
Ali, T. (2019). Planned urbanisation and environment. *The Daily Star*. Retrieved from https://www.thedailystar.net/supplements/25th-anniversary-special-part-2/planned-urbanisation-and-environment-210874
Ali, T., & Alam, H. (2009). Dhaka's detailed area plan grossly flawed. *The Daily Star*. Retrieved from https://www.thedailystar.net/news-detail-84769
Arfvidsson, H., Simon, D., Oloko, M., & Moodley, N. (2017). Engaging with and measuring informality in the proposed Urban Sustainable Development Goal. *African Geographical Review*, *36*(1), 100–114.
Asad, R., & Ahsan, R. (2012). Structuring urban sustainability with water: a case of Kamrangir Chor, Dhaka, Bangladesh. *Journal of Social and Development Sciences*, *3*(8), 293–303.
Banks, N., Lombard, M., & Mitlin, D. (2019). Urban informality as a site of critical analysis. *The Journal of Development Studies*, 1–16.
Bari, M., & Efroymson, D. (2009). Detailed area plan (DAP) for Dhaka metropolitan development plan (DMDP): A critical review. Dhaka: WBB Trust.
Baviskar, A. (2011). What the eye does not see: The Yamuna in the imagination of Delhi. *Economic and Political Weekly*, 45–53.
Bird, J., Li, Y., Rahman, H. Z., Rama, M., & Venables, A. J. (2018). *Toward Great Dhaka: A New Urban Development Paradigm Eastward (Directions in Development)*. Washington, DC: The World Bank.
BP. (2018). Conspiracy around DAP (in Bengali). *Bangladesh Protidin*. Retrieved from https://www.bd-pratidin.com/home/printnews/328718/2018-05-09
Büscher, K. (2012). *Urban governance beyond the state: practices of informal urban regulation in the city of Goma, Eastern DR Congo*. Paper presented at the Urban forum.
Castells, M., & Portes, A. (1989). World underneath: The origins, dynamics, and effects of the informal economy. In A. Portes, M. Castells, & L. Benton (Eds.), *The informal economy: Studies in advanced and less developed countries* (pp. 11–40). Baltimore: Johns Hopkins Press.
Davis, M. (2006). *Planet of slums*. New York: New York.
De Soto, H. (2000). *The mystery of capital: Why capitalism triumphs in the West and fails everywhere else*. New York: Basic books.
DiGaetano, A., & Strom, E. (2003). Comparative urban governance: An integrated approach. *Urban Affairs Review*, *38*(3), 356–395.
Doshi, S. (2019). Greening Displacements, Displacing Green: Environmental Subjectivity, Slum Clearance, and the Embodied Political Ecologies of Dispossession in Mumbai. *International Journal of Urban and Regional Research*, *43*(1), 112–132.

Doshi, S., & Ranganathan, M. (2017). Contesting the unethical city: Land dispossession and corruption narratives in urban India. *Annals of the American Association of Geographers*, *107*(1), 183–199.

Fahlberg, A., & Vicino, T. J. (2016). Breaking the city: Militarization and segregation in Rio de Janeiro. *Habitat International*, *54*, 10–17.

Flyvbjerg, B. (1998). *Rationality and power: Democracy in practice*. Chicago and London: University of Chicago Press.

Follmann, A. (2015). Urban mega-projects for a 'world-class' riverfront–The interplay of informality, flexibility and exceptionality along the Yamuna in Delhi, India. *Habitat International*, *45*, 213–222.

Hackenbroch, K., Hossain, S., Altrock, U., Schoon, S., & Sterly, H. (2016). Informality, urban governance and the state: negotiations of space in Dhaka and the Pearl River Delta. *International Development Planning Review*, *38*(3), 229–253.

Harris, A. (2018). Engineering formality: flyover and skywalk construction in Mumbai. *International Journal of Urban and Regional Research*, *42*(2), 295–314.

Harris, R. (2018). Modes of Informal Urban Development: A Global Phenomenon. *Journal of Planning Literature*, *33*(3), 267–286.

Hashim, S. M. (2017). No need for water bodies! *The Daily Star*. Retrieved from https://www.thedailystar.net/opinion/no-frills/no-need-water-bodies-1510261

Herlambang, S., Leitner, H., Tjung, L. J., Sheppard, E., & Anguelov, D. (2019). Jakarta's great land transformation: Hybrid neoliberalisation and informality. *Urban Studies*, *56*(4), 627–648.

Hossain, S., & Hackenbroch, K. (2019). Whose interest finally counts? The statutory production of urban space at the fringes of Dhaka, *Bangladesh. Planning theory*, *18*(2), 167–190.

Husain, S. N., & Sohag, K. H. (2017). *Sustainable policy for the flood flow zone and effective Development Control Mechanisms: Dhaka City*. Paper presented at the Conference for Research on Climate Change in Bangladesh, Dhaka. http://gobeshona.net/wp-content/uploads/2016/08/template-PPT-Nazmul-Husain.pdf

Jahangir Alam, M., & Akter Mullick, R. (2014). Climate change effects upon massive land and housing development: Case of Dhaka, Bangladesh. *International Journal of Climate Change Strategies and Management*, *6*(3), 315–331.

Kadfak, A., & Oskarsson, P. (2017). The shifting sands of land governance in peri-urban Mangaluru, India: fluctuating land as an 'informality machine'reinforcing rapid coastal transformations. *Contemporary South Asia*, *25*(4), 399–414.

Khan, M. H. (1998). Patron-client networks and the economic effects of corruption in Asia. *The European Journal of Development Research*, *10*(1), 15–39.

Kudva, N. (2009). The everyday and the episodic: the spatial and political impacts of urban informality. *Environment and Planning A*, *41*(7), 1614–1628.

Lindell, I. (2018). Street Work: Dynamics and Trajectories of Collective Organizing. *Articulo-Journal of Urban Research*(17-18).

Mahmud, A. H. (2014). Dhaka land use pattern changes rapidly. *Dhaka Tribune*. Retrieved from https://www.dhakatribune.com/uncategorized/2014/04/08/dhaka-land-use-pattern-changes-rapidly

Mahmud, M. A. (2007). *Corruption in Plan Permission Process in RAJUK: A Study of Violations and Proposals*. Dhaka: Transparency International Bangladesh

McFarlane, C. (2012). Rethinking informality: Politics, crisis, and the city. *Planning Theory & Practice*, *13*(1), 89–108.

Moatasim, F. (2018). Entitled urbanism: Elite informality and the reimagining of a planned modern city. *Urban Studies*, 1–17.

Moatasim, F. (2019). Entitled urbanism: Elite informality and the reimagining of a planned modern city. *Urban Studies*, *56*(5), 1009–1025.

Morshed, M. M. (2013). Detailed Area Plan (DAP): Why It Does Not Work? In G. Rahman (Ed.), *Planned Decentralization: Aspired Development* Dhaka: Bangladesh Institute of Planners (BIP).
Morshed, M. M. (2014). Illegality of private subdivision and access to land for housing by the urban poor in Dhaka. *Habitat International*, *44*, 386–393.
Müller, F., & Segura, R. (2017). The uses of informality: Urban development and social distinction in Mexico City. *Latin American Perspectives*, *44*(3), 158–175.
Ortega, A. A. C. (2016). Manila's metropolitan landscape of gentrification: Global urban development, accumulation by dispossession & neoliberal warfare against informality. *Geoforum*, *70*, 35–50.
Pethe, A., Nallathiga, R., Gandhi, S., & Tandel, V. (2014). Re-thinking urban planning in India: Learning from the wedge between the de jure and de facto development in Mumbai. *Cities*, *39*, 120–132.
Pierre, J. (1999). Models of urban governance: The institutional dimension of urban politics. *Urban Affairs Review*, *34*(3), 372–396.
Prouse, C. (2019). Subversive formalization: efforts to (re) form land, labor, and behavior in a carioca favela. *Urban Geography*, 1–20.
Przeworski, A. (2010). *Democracy and the limits of self-government* (Vol. 9): Cambridge University Press.
RAJUK. (2006). *Dhaka Metropolitan Development Plan (DMDP), 1995–2015 [Structure Plan, Volume 1]*. Dhaka: Rajdhani Unnyan Katripakha (RAJUK).
Ramos-Zayas, A. Y. (2019). 'Sovereign Parenting'in Affluent Latin American Neighbourhoods: Race and the Politics of Childcare in Ipanema (Brazil) and El Condado (Puerto Rico). *Journal of Latin American Studies*, *51*(3), 639–663.
Roy, A. (2005). Urban informality: toward an epistemology of planning. *Journal of the American Planning Association*, *71*(2), 147–158.
Roy, A. (2009). Why India cannot plan its cities: Informality, insurgence and the idiom of urbanization. *Planning theory*, *8*(1), 76–87.
Roy, A. (2011). Slumdog cities: Rethinking subaltern urbanism. *International Journal of Urban and Regional Research*, *35*(2), 223–238.
Roy, S., Sowgat, T., & Mondal, J. (2019). City Profile: Dhaka, Bangladesh. *Environment and Urbanization ASIA*, *10*(2), 216–232.
Rumbach, A. (2017). At the roots of urban disasters: Planning and uneven geographies of risk in Kolkata, *India. Journal of Urban Affairs*, *39*(6), 783–799.
Sabet, D. M., & Tazreen, A. (2015). Governing growth: Understanding problems in real estate development in Dhaka, *Bangladesh. Journal of South Asian Development*, *10*(1), 1–21.
Sarker, A. E. (2008). Patron-client politics and its implications for good governance in Bangladesh. *Intl Journal of Public Administration*, *31*(12), 1416–1440.
Schindler, S. (2014). Producing and contesting the formal/informal divide: Regulating street hawking in Delhi, *India. Urban Studies*, *51*(12), 2596–2612.
Schindler, S., & Kishore, B. (2015). Why Delhi cannot plan its 'new towns': The case of solid waste management in Noida. *Geoforum*, *60*, 33–42.
Sengers, F., Wieczorek, A. J., & Raven, R. (2016). Experimenting for sustainability transitions: A systematic literature review. *Technological Forecasting and Social Change*.
Sheltech. (2010). *Preparation of Detailed Area Plan (Final Plan Report)*. Dhaka: Sheltech Pvt. Ltd.
Sheppard, E. (2019). Globalizing capitalism's raggedy fringes: thinking through Jakarta. *Area Development and Policy*, *4*(1), 1–27.
Simon, D. (2015). Uncertain times, contested resources: Discursive practices and lived realities in African urban environments. *City*, *19*(2-3), 216–238.

Song, L. K. (2016). Planning with urban informality: A case for inclusion, co-production and reiteration. *International Development Planning Review, 38*(4), 359–381.

Srivastava, S. (2014). Entangled urbanism: Slum, gated community and shopping mall in Delhi and Gurgaon. *OUP Catalogue*.

Sundaresan, J. (2017). Urban planning in vernacular governance: Land use planning and violations in Bangalore, India. *Progress in Planning*.

Swapan, M., Zaman, A., Ahsan, T., & Ahmed, F. (2017). Transforming urban dichotomies and challenges of South Asian megacities: Rethinking sustainable growth of Dhaka, Bangladesh. *Urban Science, 1*(4), 31.

Swapan, M. S. H. (2014). Realities of community participation in metropolitan planning in Bangladesh: A comparative study of citizens and planning practitioners' perceptions. *Habitat International, 43*, 191–197.

Tucker, J. (2017). City-stories: Narrative as diagnostic and strategic resource in Ciudad del Este, Paraguay. *Planning theory, 16*(1), 74–98.

Uberti, L. J. (2016). Can institutional reforms reduce corruption? Economic theory and patron–client politics in developing countries. *Development and Change, 47*(2), 317–345.

UN. (2018). *The World's Cities in 2018*. New York: United Nations Retrieved from https://www.un.org/en/events/citiesday/assets/pdf/the_worlds_cities_in_2018_data_booklet.pdf

Varley, A. (2013). Postcolonialising informality? *Environment and Planning D: Society and Space, 31*(1), 4–22.

Wagenaar, H. (2014). The agonistic experience: Informality, hegemony and the prospects for democratic governance. *Practices of freedom*, 217–248.

WB. (2017). *Bangladesh City Planning Must Be More Sustainable For Livability*. New York: The World Bank Retrieved from https://www.worldbank.org/en/news/press-release/2017/10/28/bangladesh-city-planning-must-be-more-sustainable-for-livability

Zahid, S. H. (2018). Disappearing urban water bodies *The Financial Express*. Retrieved from https://thefinancialexpress.com.bd/public/index.php/views/disappearing-urban-water-bodies-1524413790

Zeuthen, J. W. (2018). Whose urban development? Changing credibilities, forms and functions of urbanization in Chengdu, China. *Land use policy, 79*, 942–951.

Zhang, M., & Zhao, P. (2018). The determinants of informal housing price in Beijing: Village power, informal institutions, and property security. *Cities, 77*, 117–129.

Chapter 14

Landscape–Infrastructure

Formal–Informal entanglements across political ecologies of resource use

Daniela Perrotti

Introduction: A landscape constellation

In her 1990 essay *Landschaften,* German philosopher Ute (Guzzoni, 1990) unfolds the lexicon of a new *landschaftliches denken* (from the German *landschaft*, 'landscape', and *denken*, 'to think' or 'the act of thinking'). Here the landscape is described as a 'manifold contemporaneity of spatial and temporal relations between things', a 'mutable multiplicity of relations', through which the entity that we name 'landscape' becomes one, sole, precise, and complete in all its elements. Approaching the landscape as a network of material and immaterial relations among a heterogeneous range of elements suggests a sensorial experience rather than a univocal definition of the notion of 'landscape'. The philosopher subsequently introduces the metaphor of 'concrete constellation' (building on the Hegelian notion of the 'concrete universal') as a means to address the question of the relation between the individual and the universal in the landscape, between the entirety of the constellation and every single element that composes it. As a result of the combined action of all the individuals that form the universal, the concrete constellation is the image of the landscape universality: an entity that only comes into existence by virtue of the relations among its elements and that, at the same time, entails and encompasses a dialogue between them. Indeed, it is these very relations that determine the uniqueness of the combined action – the *jeu d'ensemble* – of the diverse elements in a constellation. Because of the mutability of the relations between the individuals in the universal, Guzzoni's concrete constellation is neither stable for eternity nor sharply delimited in space. Further, the relational character Guzzoni attributes to the landscape brings into focus mutual dependencies rather than simple cohabitation of elements.

To what extent is Guzzoni's *landschaftliches denken* reflected into contemporary landscape practice and its theory? Can it prompt an actualised landscape narrative and, through this, shed new light on formal-informal entanglements in urban living, resource management practices and their discourse in urban studies? To address these questions, first, I will use Guzzoni's work to navigate landscape and infrastructure epistemologies that led to emergence of the landscape–infrastructure nexus within the landscape urbanism approach and its recent evolutions. To this end, I will discuss the landscape–infrastructure nexus through examples in which infrastructures are conceptualised and orchestrated as landscapes (section 2) and urban landscapes as infrastructures for the provision of essential resources to both human and ecosystems' life (section 3). Second, I will explore opportunities for circumventing dualistic ontologies across institutionalised regimes and informal practices through assemblage thinking, using urban political ecologies of water as a paradigmatic case (section 4). Finally, I will conclude by pointing at perspectives and ways forward for the landscape–infrastructure nexus to inform a novel understanding of the divide between informal practices and institutionalised regimes in urban studies (section 5).

Landscape–Infrastructure 1.0: Infrastructure as landscape

Critical reviews of the landscape urbanism approach have suggested that its original definition of 'infrastructure' can echo Guzzoni's understanding of the multiple entanglements in the landscape constellation and its relational connotation (Waldheim, 2016; Perrotti, 2014). In the first landscape urbanism written manifesto (Waldheim, 2006), 'infrastructure' is defined as a 'preparatory substrate' and a 'networked system that supports and instigates' the environmental processes, social dynamics, and economic growth and degrowth of the urbanity. Infrastructure is subsequently described as both a physical vehicle supporting humans' relational existence and a conceptual instrument to temporarily disentangle philosophy and design (Allen, 2009; Bélanger, 2017a). The landscape urbanism definition of infrastructure reflects landscape architect James Corner's take on post-industrial metropolitan regions in North America (Corner, 2006). Metropolitan regions are conceptualised as an open-ended matrix of horizontal surfaces which organizes, collects, distributes and condenses the forces operating upon the city. The urban matrix functions as a 'living ecology' consisting of a thick living mat of accumulated patches and layered systems, with no singular authority or control. Infrastructural systems are an essential component of the urban matrix, since they support and instigate its development over time. In this sense, infrastructural systems are catalysts that landscape and urban designers can orchestrate to implant new potentials in the urban horizontal surfaces. As an instigator of such 'surface strategies', infrastructure can be considered as a model for the whole urban landscape (Waldheim, 2016).

Practical applications of this approach in the design and orchestration of infrastructural catalysts can be found in the work of architect and urban designer Stan Allen. As (Allen, 1999) points out, in landscape urbanism, infrastructures act as a scaffold for the complex series of events and mechanisms that leverage the growth and functioning of the urban matrix and cannot be anticipated by the architect. On these bases, and echoing James Corner's view of post-industrial metropolitan regions, he lays down a series of propositions for designers to identify the potential of infrastructural systems to prepare the ground and create the conditions for the urban matrix to be. Infrastructure systems should be designed as 'artificial ecologies' of a flexible (in both space and time) and anticipatory nature. On the one hand, infrastructural systems delineate distinct architectural elements within specific limits. On the other hand, they organize the flows of energy and resources on a site by creating the conditions necessary to respond to incremental adjustments in resource demand and supply, due to change in inhabitation or environmental conditions. Like Corner's, Allen's view on infrastructural systems focuses on the dynamic effects they can engender rather than on the forms they can take. He distinguishes between two kinds of effects produced by infrastructural systems that influence the 'field conditions[1]'in which the urban matrix unfolds: the 'capillary effects of scales', generated by a great number of small elements that compose infrastructural networks, and the 'effect of synergy' that originates where there is convergence and interchange between different systems in a network. Finally, infrastructural systems should be able to enhance the collective nature of the city and its 'shared narratives' instead of conveying self-referentiality or representing expressions of individual stakeholder groups. The conversion of the site of a former airport to the Taichung Gateway Park in Taiwan is one of Allen's project-manifesto to put theoretical speculations to work (Allen, 2008). The development of the 240-hectare multifunctional urban district and its central parkway over time is supported by a dynamic structure of new environmental and social ecologies (ecological reserves, park amenities and local waterways, alongside new event spaces connected by pedestrian paths and roads). This embodiment of Allen's *landschaftliches* thinking of infrastructure into an urban design exemplifies the way in which infrastructural systems can functions as landscapes in the post-industrial urban matrix.

Landscape–Infrastructure 2.0: Landscape as infrastructure

The cross-fertilization of Guzzoni's concrete constellation with the landscape urbanism definition of infrastructure offers the opportunity to look critically into the hybridisation between horizontal surfaces and infrastructural catalysts in the urban matrix. The first can acquire the same dynamic connotation of the second (Perrotti, 2014), while the second allows for the maintenance and growth of the urban matrix as a living ecology (Allen, 1999). Similar positions can be found in the work of previous generation's landscape scholars studying the interplay between the making of the landscape and the consolidation of communities. For example, (John Brinckerhoff Jackson, 1984) describes the landscape as 'a composition of man-made or man-modified spaces to serve as infrastructure or background for our collective existence'. Jackson's use of 'background' refers to the modern meaning of the word: 'that which underscores not only our identity and presence, but also our history.' Jackson's landscape background is a vertical and horizontal palimpsest that enables and sustains the coexistence of historical and present living while instigating future developments through their network of relations.

In recent years, the 'landscape as infrastructure' idea has gained significant popularity in the wake of the widespread of landscape-urbanism design speculations in the late 2000s, inspiring regional planning in post-industrial contexts (Bélanger, 2009, 2017b; Perrotti, 2014). 'Across a range of disciplines, landscape has become a lens through which the contemporary city is represented and a medium trough which it is constructed. These sentiments are evident in the emergent notion of "landscape urbanism"' (Waldheim, 2006, p. 15). More than a field, the landscape becomes the 'locus of intellectual, ecological and economic change of significance' (Bélanger, 2017a). Examples include making sense of social, economic and ecological mutations in the Great Lakes Region in North America in the wake of the significant logistical, economic and ecological transformations occurred since the second half of the 20th century, while calling into question methods and models for large-scale and long-range design as a response to such radical changes. This region was by many understood as a playground to test hypotheses and design responses challenging the *laissez-faire* dogma of neo-liberalist economics, Fordism-inspired civil engineering, and Euclidean planning policies as a legacy of the 20th century (Berger and Waldheim, 2008).

As argued by Canadian landscape architect and urban planner Pierre Bélanger, the legacy of industrial production, infrastructural decay, and pollutants fluxes on North American metropolitan landscapes (Kirkwood, 2001) has called for a radical re-evaluation of the role of infrastructure within the disciplinary debate about urban management, regional planning and design since the 1990s (Bélanger, 2009). For Bélanger this legacy has provided an unparalleled opportunity to liberate knowledge and practice from specialized disciplinary precincts and technocratic silos (Bélanger, 2017b). His analysis draws on the example of two paradigmatic urban environments in the geo-political region of the Rust Belt, Flint (Michigan) and Youngstown (Ohio), which have both been affected by an extensive deindustrialisation program originating in the post-industrial fallout of the early 1980s. Industrial de-corporation, land un-development, population unemployment and deurbanization have been consequences of a period of global outsourcing and industry relocations outside North America (Friedman, 2005). Flint and Youngstown exemplify two distinct politics of urban management in post-industrial shrinking cities. Flint's administration engaged in a high-cost regeneration program, converting the post-industrial landscape of the General Motors infrastructure into tourism facilities. By contrast, the former steel town of Youngstown worked towards a protracted shrinkage of the city rather than an increase in its former prosperity (Bélanger, 2009). The local administration pursued an urban management and financial investment strategy moved by both socio-economic and ecological motives and prompted the deurbanization process in order to capitalize on high vacancy rates and under-used public spaces. Their goal was to downsize the city by razing derelict buildings, cutting off oversized or unnecessary infrastructure, banking vacant land, and re-zoning heavy industrial districts. In this controlled de-urbanization process, the local landscape infrastructure was used as the basis for the programmed urban regeneration.

Pursuing the dual objectives of economic performance and ecological durability, Youngstown's urban management response to the local shrinkage dynamics provides an example of what a *landscape-as-infrastructure* strategy can offer. The decentralization of the urban structure together with the de-engineering of infrastructural systems through landscaping offered the opportunity to work across urban ecology and 'land-waste' economies (Berger, 2006). As seen in similar contexts in Europe (Perrotti, 2015; Galan and Perrotti, 2019), such global economic and financial reorganisations have triggered the transition from metropolitan regions heavily subsided from remote supply areas towards an alternative model of growth centred on de-urbanized landscapes as regional, decentralised infrastructural systems for the provision of water, food, energy, land and other essential resources. The closing of material loops and resource cycles requires the establishment of new politics of the urban space and alternative governance models in which landscape operations can underpin a more integrated model of urban economic regeneration and site redevelopment while achieving greater economies and ecologies of scale (Perrotti and Iuorio, 2019). 'These regional landscape operations can be considered self-generated and self-maintaining. At this precise moment – when these landscape operations are essential – they became infrastructural' (Bélanger, 2009, p. 89).

Informality as quasi-object in landscape–infrastructure assemblages

Thinking of infrastructure as landscape and landscape as infrastructure (and operating across both epistemologies as planning 'instigators') can generate a universe of reference in which the distinction between formality and informality becomes a wicked problem. Despite the ever-increasing popularity of 'informality'-labelled phenomena in post-colonial studies of fast-growing cities in the Global South, post-humanist and new materialist ontologies have revealed the inextricability of institutionalised urban regimes and formal mechanisms (structures of power, norms, reference standards, and cultural codes) from informal practices of inhabiting, working, leisure, and being (Lieto and Beauregard, 2016). For example, assemblage thinking (Farías, 2010; Brenner et al., 2011) and Actor-Network-Theory (ANT) (Latour, 1999) have worked towards their understanding as co-functioning bodies in the urban arena and encouraged their incorporation under the same knowledge framework to avoid oppositions (McFarlane, 2011). Both approaches can help recompose formal-informal dualisms in urban studies through the unfolding of flatter ontologies and by making sense of the urban micro-politics (Guattari, 2000 [1989]) that already exist in a site or can come into existence in a close or far future. ANT perspectives are even more compelling when landscape is infrastructure and infrastructure is landscape, since the landscape–infrastructure nexus does not seek for a relation between 'the material' and 'the social' world but acknowledges that this very division is an artefact (Latour, 2005). Following ANT, formal mechanisms and informal practices in landscape-infrastructure assemblages can be understood as entangled hetero-referential objects that establish relations of different types and nature. This idea builds on Latour's (1993) work on said '*objets chevelus*' (literally 'ruffled objects') and its genealogy in Michel Serres's (1982) definition of 'quasi-object' – an object which 'marks the boundary between the subjective and the objective', an intermediate object that both determines and is determined by the relations with other objects surrounding it. Because of their relational configuration in the landscape–infrastructure (one can only exist and be defined relative to the other), formal mechanisms and informal practices can be seen as *objets chevelus* when studied through ANT. They are objects that look like 'ruffled beings' with neither sharp boundaries nor separation between a hard-core and their environment but with a large number of connections, 'tentacles' or 'pseudopods' (Latour, 1993). Therefore, they are, by their own nature, inextricably interconnected with each other and with the environment that surrounds them, and can, through these very relations, be perceived as a wholeness with the 'universe' to which they belong (or as 'actants' in an assemblage). In this sense, formal/informal quasi-objects can be studied as entities that acquire their form, efficacy and meaning by virtue of their relational configuration sometimes independently from the human will (Anderson et al., 2012).

Urban political ecologies of water provide a paradigmatic case for illustrating the entanglement of formal and informal governance regimes and their understanding as 'quasi-objects' in the urban arena (Perrotti et al., 2020). When envisioned through the landscape–infrastructure lens, water systems show an 'intangible and imponderable recalcitrance' to be dissected; by their very nature, they resist the divide between formality and informality for classification purposes (Bennett, 2010). Since its inception, the landscape urbanism agenda has pushed for an understanding of watersheds as constructed ecologies resulting from the interplay between socioeconomic and bio-physical systems (hydrology, geology, climate) while preconditioning modes of urban production. Watersheds are an irreducible structural element of urban systems. In other words, they act as a basic infrastructure supporting the unfolding of the manifold economic, ecological, and cultural dimensions of urbanization including "informal" ways of living. For landscape urbanists, watersheds have been the repository of new strategies for economic and ecological regeneration at the level of neighbourhoods or entire cities (Bélanger, 2009). They are the locus of the co-dependency of the environment and the economy, of the landscape (the expression of our material existence) and the infrastructure (our mode of socioeconomic production).

The unfolding of grassroots initiatives in Mexico City illustrates that a strong intertwinement exist between informal practices of water management at the neighbourhood or household level and the economy and ecology of the city in its watershed. Here, over a population of nearly 9 million (2015 census data), approximately 250,000 people live without connection to the water network and many more are estimated to have an intermittent service or receive contaminated water (Isla Urbana, 2019). This condition is at odds with the history of the site since Mexico City lies on a highlands plateau (one of the four basins of the Valley of Mexico, at over 2,000 meters above sea level) that was originally occupied by the Texcoco lake. The lake was gradually drained with the Spanish colonizers seeking to expand the settlement area of the original Aztecan city (Aguilar et al., 1995). With the fast expansion of the urbanised area and the rapid population growth, the aquifer that used to be the main source of water has been pumped nearly dry and consequently the city has started to increasingly source its water from other basins outside the Valley of Mexico (Bojorquez-Tapia et al., 2000). To reduce the overexploitation of the aquifer, 30% of the water is supplied from the Lerma-Balsas and the Cutzamala river basins situated in other regions and pumped from 60 to 150 kilometres away and, vertically, over 1 kilometre (Tortajada and Castelán, 2003). The energy required to pump all the water is approximately equivalent to the total electricity consumption of a city of 1.5 million inhabitants (Isla Urbana, 2019). Even with such high environmental and economic costs, it is estimated that the supply is enough for only one third of the population (around 40% of the water is lost due to leakage in the system). Tank trucks are being used to respond to the Mexico City's water crisis, but the water they deliver is also of poor quality. Bottled drinking water has therefore become part of everyday life. Some families use up to 20% of their income just to buy water (Isla Urbana, 2019). Paradoxically, Mexico City is also struggling with too much water in the form of heavy rains. The Valley of Mexico is one of the few endorheic basins in the world. This means that all storm water is retained on site and converges into lakes or swamps, with no outflow to other external bodies of water (rivers or oceans) (Ezcurra et al. 1999). The problem is exacerbated by the high saturation of the soil and the clogging of the sewer system in many nodes. The progressive sinking of the city causes additional damages to the sewer system (Chelleri et al. 2015). The paradox of the "too little or too much" water is particularly acute in Iztapalapa, the most populous of Mexico City's 16 municipalities whose name (literally 'slates over waters') refers to its location at the lowest point of the Valley of Mexico (corresponding to the former south bank of Lake Texcoco). Here, not only the quality of water is poor and water supply is limited

(20% of Iztapalapa's population does not have access to water in their houses), but also, due to its localisation downstream, the frequency and intensity of flood events are particularly high and the borough's streets and buildings receive significant amounts of storm water that naturally flows in from the higher elevations (de Alba, 2017). Inhabitants of Iztapalapa and four other neighbourhoods in the south-east part of Mexico City (the most vulnerable to flooding) have coordinated a collaborative response to jointly address the problem of water scarcity and flood risk. A local NGO, Isla Urbana, has been working alongside them to promote the self-construction of low-tech rainwater harvesting systems at the household and community level (see Figures 14.1–14.3). The NGO estimates that these systems can supply a family with water for 5 to 12 months per year while potentially reducing the amount of flooded areas (Isla Urbana, 2019). The joint work of local residents and NGOs such as Isla Urbana in Mexico City shows the wicked problem arising from dissecting the role of informal practices in cities from the ecology and economy of water in which they operate. When operating across the landscape–infrastructure nexus, what logic should be applied as to make sense of the contribution of 'residual' practices falling outside 'formal' or statutory water management regimes?

Figure 14.1 Community rainwater treatment plant co-built in 2015 on a public building by the NGO Isla Urbana and the local residents in the community of Yuguelito, municipality of Iztapalapa, Mexico City. The plant can capture and purify up to 180,000 litres of water per year.

Source: 2015 Isla Urbana with permission.

Figure 14.2 View of the filtering tanks of the Yuguelito community rainwater treatment plant.

Source: 2015 Isla Urbana with permission.

Conclusions

Through this essay, I have invited the reader to look at the landscape as a concrete constellation that shares the same characteristics as the infrastructural catalysts in the landscape urbanism matrix. This originates in a reading of Guzzoni's *landschaftliches denken,* which, back in the 1990s, prompted an understanding of the landscape as a network of (neither isomorphic nor isotropic) relationships through which a landscape becomes a landscape. Therefore, Guzzoni's work has highlighted the need to think transversally across the universal and the individual in order to grasp the concrete constellation in its wholeness (rather than as the sum of individuals). Today, the cross-fertilization between Guzzoni's *landschaftliches denken* and the landscape-infrastructure approach in landscape urbanism theory and practice can bring greater focus on the landscape as a connective structure that supports and, at the same time,

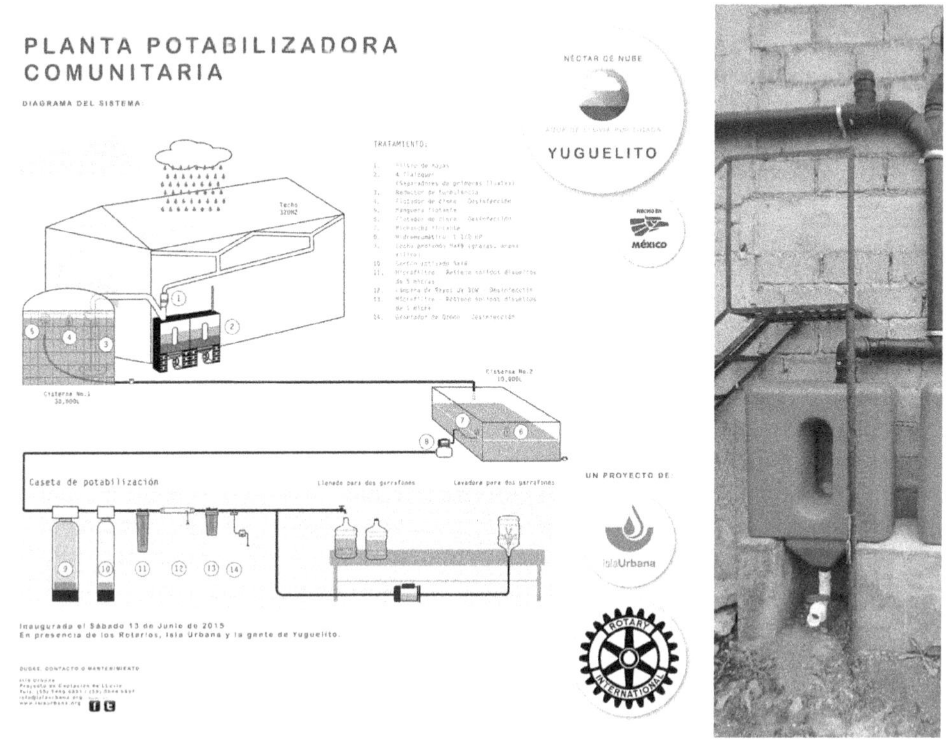

Figure 14.3 Flyer advertising the opening of the Yuguelito community rainwater treatment plant on 13 June 2015 with diagram illustrating the functioning of the rain collection and purification system.

Source: 2015 Isla Urbana with permission.

instigates change in the urban matrix. In this context, new landscape–infrastructure epistemologies can have the dual purpose of re-framing the conventional role of infrastructural systems in the 21st century urban regions and repositioning the landscape as a system of essential services, resources and processes that underpins socio-economic and ecological regeneration. Through the unfolding of these epistemologies, the landscape–infrastructure nexus can promote a novel understanding of the interlinkages between institutionalised urban regimes and informal practices while helping scholars and designers to engage with the complexity of contemporary urban living. This understanding of the landscape–infrastructure nexus acquires particular relevance in the wake of the landscape urbanism legacy today. Landscape urbanism strategies have paved the way to a new approach to spatial planning and design (Waldheim, 2016), where landscape is proposed as a medium for urban order in contemporary design practice. Through the landscape–infrastructure nexus, social and ecological questions can be synergistically addressed and responses provided that can nurture the micro-politics of desire (Guattari, 2000 [1989]) populating the urban concrete constellation. This involves maintaining the landscape–infrastructure as a functional 'conveyance or distribution network' (Aquino, 2011) assembling a variety of living systems for both human or non-human life while making room for future uses, collective and individual imaginaries, and unforeseen windows of opportunities.

Thirty years after Guzzoni's *landschaftliches denken* and the landscape urbanism inception, reconceptualising the landscape–infrastructure nexus can suggest that its ecology and economy need to be constantly regenerated by heterogenous 'anomalous/out-of-the-system/more-than-formal' practices for our concrete constellation to make sense and hold meaning for the urbanity to be. When considered from urban-assemblage or ANT perspectives, informal practices are essential to maintain heterogeneity as a condition for constant dynamic renewal in the landscape–infrastructure (Perrotti, 2012). Actualising Guzzoni's thinking through ANT can help make meaning of the role of informal practices as quasi-objects in an assemblage, instead of crystallising boundaries between 'informality' and its 'formal' alterity. In this sense, ANT can bring a clearer focus on the added value of thinking more fluidly through flatter ontologies and across relationships of scales and agencies in the urban realm; such approaches should acquire a more prominent position in urban studies as an alternative to, first, identify and, then, solve 'problems' arising from the role of informal ways of living and dwelling through definitive formulations. Hence, an ANT reading of the landscape–infrastructure nowadays can help to look critically not only at the divide between informal practices and institutionalised resource management regimes but also at the way we conduct urban studies. This can point to the limits of dualistic thinking and call into question the definition of boundaries between the 'formal' and the 'informal' in the political space that makes up the backbone of our cities.

Note

1 'Field conditions move from the one toward the many, from individuals to collectives, from objects to fields. The term itself plays on a double meaning. Architects work not only in the office or studio but in the field: on site, in contact with the fabric of architecture. "Field conditions" here implies the acceptance of the real in all its messiness and unpredictability. It implicates architects in a material improvisation conducted on site in real time. Field conditions treat constraints as opportunity. Working with and not against the site, something new is produced by registering the complexity of the given.' (Allen, 2009, p. 119).

References

Aguilar, A.G., Ezcurra, E., Garcia, T., Mazari-Hiriart, M., and Pisanty, I. 1995. The Basin of Mexico. In Kasperson, J.X., Kasperson, R.E. and Turner II, B.L. (Eds). *Regions at Risk: Comparison of Threatened Environments*, Tokyo: The United Nations University Press. pp. 304–366.

Allen, S. (1999). Infrastructural Urbanism. In *Points + Lines: Diagrams and Projects For The City* (pp. 48–57). New York: Princeton Architectural Press.

Allen, S. (2008). Taichung Gateway Project: A New Synthesis of Park and City. In *New Geographies* 0: 16–30.

Allen, S. (2009). From Object to Field: Field Conditions in Architecture and Urbanism. In Allen S., Agrest D. (Eds.) *Practice: Architecture, Technique and Representation*. London: Routledge, p. 119–143.

Anderson B., Kearnes M., McFarlane C. and Swanton D. (2012). On assemblages and geography. *Dialogues in Human Geography* 2(2), 171–189. https://doi.org/10.1177/2043820612449261

Aquino, G. (2011). Preface. In The Infrastructure Research Initiative at SWA (Ed.) *Landscape Infrastructure. Case Studies by SWA*. Basel: Birkhäuser GmbH, p. 7.

Bélanger, P. (2009). Landscape as Infrastructure, *The Landscape Journal* 28 (1), 79–95. http://doi.org/10.3368/lj.28.1.79

Bélanger, P. (2017a). Redefining Infrastructure. In *Landscape as Infrastructure. A Base Primer*. Bélanger, P. Oxon: Routledge, pp. 116–154.

Bélanger, P. (2017b). Infrastructural Ecologies. In *Landscape as Infrastructure. A Base Primer*. Bélanger, P. Oxon: Routledge, pp. 426–748.

Bennett, J. (2010). *Vibrant Matter: A Political Ecology of Things*. Durham, NC: Duke University Press.

Berger, A. and Waldheim, C. (2008). Logistic Landscapes, *The Landscape Journal*, 27 (2), 219–246. http://doi.org/10.3368/lj.27.2.219

Berger, A., (2006). *Drosscape. Wasting Land in Urban America*. New York: Princeton Architectural Press

Bojorquez-Tapia, L.A., Ezcurra, E., Mazari-Hiriart, M., Díaz, S., Gómez, P., Alcantar, G., Megarejo, D. (2000). The Basin of Mexico: A History of Watershed Mismanagement. In Ffolliott, P.F. et al. (Eds.) *Land Stewardship in the 21st Century: The Contributions of Watershed Management* (pp. 129–137). Department of Agriculture, Forest Service Forest Service Proceedings RMRS-P-13. Retrieved from: https://www.fs.usda.gov/treesearch/pubs/41990 (accessed 15/05/2020)

Brenner, N. Madden, D.J., and Wachsmuth, D. (2011). Assemblage urbanism and the challenges of critical urban theory. *City* 15 (2), 225–240. https://doi.org/10.1080/13604813.2011.568717

Chelleri, L., Schuetze, T. and Salvati, L. (2015) Integrating Resilience with Urban Sustainability in Neglected Neighbourhoods: Challenges and Opportunities of Transitioning to Decentralized Water Management in Mexico City. *Habitat International* 48, 122–130. https://doi.org/10.1016/j.habitatint.2015.03.016

Corner, J. (2006). Terra Fluxus. In Waldheim, C. (Eds.) *The Landscape Urbanism Reader* (pp. 21–34). New York: Princeton Architectural Press.

de Alba, F. (2017) Challenging State Modernity: Governmental Adaptation and Informal Water Politics in Mexico City. *Current Sociology Monograph* 65 (2): 182–194. https://doi.org/10.1177/0011392116657288

Ezcurra, E., Mazari-Hiriart, M., Pisanty, I., and Aguilar, A.G. (1999). *The Basin of Mexico. Critical Environmental Issues and Sustainability*. Tokyo: The United Nations University Press. Retrieved from: https://digitalrepository.unm.edu/cgi/viewcontent.cgi?article=1530&context=nrj (accessed 15/05/2020)

Farías, I. (2010). Introduction: decentring the object of urban studies. In Farías, I. and Bender. T. (eds). *Urban assemblages: how actor-network theory changes urban studies* (pp. 1–24). Oxon and New York: Routledge.

Friedman, T. L. (2005). *The World is Flat: A Brief History of the Twenty-First Century*, New York: Farrar, Strauss and Giroux.

Galan, J. and Perrotti, D. (2019) Incorporating metabolic thinking into regional planning: the case of the Sierra Calderona Strategic Plan. *Urban Planning* 4(1), 152–171 http://dx.doi.org/10.17645/up.v4i1.1549

Guattari, F. (2000 [1989]) *The three ecologies*. Trans. I. Pindar and P. Sutton. London and New Brunswick, NJ: The Athlone Press.

Guzzoni, U. (1990). Landschaften. In *Wege im Denken. Versuche mit und ohne Heidegger* (pp. 25–59). Freiburg/München: Karl Alber Verlag.

Jackson, J.B. (1984). The World Itself. In *Discovering the Vernacular Landscape* (pp. 1–8). New Haven: Yale University Press

Kirkwood, N. (2001). *Manufactured Sites: Rethinking the Post-Industrial Landscape*. London: SPON Press.

Isla Urbana (2019) Rain for All. Water sustainability for Mexico. Retrieved from: http://islaurbana.org/english/wp-content/uploads/2019/10/PRESS-IU_compressed.pdf (accessed 15/05/2020)

Lieto, L. and Beauregard, R.A. (2016) Introduction. In Lieto L. and Beauregard R.A. (eds) *Planning for a Material World* (pp. 1–9). London and New York: Routledge.

Latour, B. (1993). What Is a Quasi-Object? In *We have never been modern* (pp. 51–54). Trans. C. Porter. Harvard Cambridge, Massachusetts: University Press.

Latour, B. (1999) On Recalling ANT. In Law, J. and Hassard, J. (eds) *Actor Network Theory and After* (pp. 15–25). Oxford: Blackwell.

Latour, B. (2005) *Reassembling the Social: An Introduction to Actor-Network-Theory*, Oxford: Oxford University Press.

McFarlane, C. (2011) On context. *City*, 15(3-4), 375–388. https://doi.org/10.1080/13604813.2011.595111

Perrotti, D. (2012) La ruralité urbaine: de plateforme d'expérimentation à lieu de la mise en scène d'un nouveau modèle de durabilité: les territoires périurbains du Parc Agricole Sud de Milan à l'épreuve de l'Expo Milan 2015. *Environnement urbain / Urban Environment* 6(1): 100–117. https://doi.org/10.7202/1013715ar

Perrotti, D. (2014) Landscape as Energy Infrastructure: Ecologic Approaches and Aesthetic Implications of Design. In Czechowski, D., Hauck, T. and Hausladen G. (Eds.), *Revising Green Infrastructure: Concepts Between Nature and Design* (pp.71–90). CRC Press: Boca Raton.

Perrotti, D. (2015) Of other (energy) spaces. In Frolova, M., Prados, MJ. and Nadaï, A. (Eds.), *Renewable Energies and European Landscapes: Lessons from Southern European Cases* (pp. 193–215). Dordrecht: Springer. https://doi.org/10.1007/978-94-017-9843-3_11

Perrotti, D. and Iuorio, O. (2019) Green Infrastructure in the Space of Flows: An Urban Metabolism Approach to Bridge Environmental Performance and User's Wellbeing. In Lemes de Oliveira, F. and Mell, I. (Eds.), *Planning Cities with Nature: Theories, Strategies and Methods* (pp. 265–277). Dordrecht: Springer. https://doi.org/10.1007/978-3-030-01866-5_18

Perrotti, D., Hyde, K. and Otero Peña, D. (2020) Can water systems foster commoning practices? Analysing leverages for self-organization in urban water commons as social–ecological systems. *Sustainability Science* 15(3): 781–795. https://doi.org/10.1007/s11625-020-00782-1

Serres, M. (1982 [1981]). *The Parasite.* Trans. L.R. Schehr. Baltimore and London: Johns Hopkins University Press.

Tortajada, C, and Castelán, E. (2003) Water Management for a Megacity: Mexico City Metropolitan. *Ambio* 32(2): 124–129. https://doi.org/10.1080/07900620600671367

Waldheim, C. (2006). A Reference Manifesto. In Waldheim, C. (Ed.), *The Landscape Urbanism Reader* (pp. 13–19). New York: Princeton Architectural Press.

Waldheim, C. (2016). From Figure to Field. In Waldheim, C. (Ed.), *Landscape as Urbanism. A general theory* (pp. 2–11). Princeton and Oxford: Princeton University Press.

Chapter 15

'AQUI ESTAMOS Y NO NOS VAMOS'

Contested ground, sustainable informal settlement and human consequence in the urban landscape of South Los Angeles

Daniel H. Ortega

Introduction

The theme of this text, *Informality through Sustainability: Urban Informality Now*, welcomes an investigation into how everyday practices performed within the urban landscape can serve as critically determinant factors in the shaping of our contemporary understanding of a sustainable, informal, urban settlement. In attempting to determine whether or not this premise can be achieved, I will visit the everyday actions performed within the urban landscape by a group of community-based farmers known as the South-Central Farmers Feeding Families.

While the terms urban and landscape offer well-understood and often dichotomous definitions, the combined phrase urban landscape is somewhat less distinctive. For the purposes of this work, the term, urban landscape, can be defined as the same ambiguous ground that Margaret Crawford refers to as having "many overlapping and contradictory meanings – aesthetic, intellectual, physical, social, political, economic, and experiential." (1999, p. 8) It is my assertion that the specific acknowledgement of Crawford's definition of urban landscape is important in that it serves as foregrounding for positions that I will take later on in this writing. In addition, I will call upon specific definitions of settlement modelling, informality and sustainability, to support this work.

A history of conflict, rooted within a unique portion of the urban landscape of South Los Angeles, California, USA, will provide the substantive framework needed to ascertain how human need, cultural agency, and the everyday practices of low-income urban farmers can serve to inspire a much-needed change in those urban landscapes that are characteristically connected to people who live in poverty.

According to data gathered in the last U.S. census, which took place in 2010, the city of Los Angeles hosted a population of almost 3.8 million people, of which 725,000 of those residents can be federally defined as living in poverty. Additionally, using the same census data, 48.6%, or, 1.8 million of the city's total population were documented as being of Hispanic descent. While I am not claiming to make a direct correlation between the 2010 Hispanic population of Los Angeles and L.A.'s residents who live in poverty, this work is centred on an informal agricultural settlement executed by predominantly low-income Hispanic residents of the city. The settlement was formerly situated in South Los Angeles and took the form of an unsanctioned urban farm. The farm was initiated by 360 families and was organized by the South-Central Farmers Feeding Families.

The South Los Angeles urban farm in context

'Aqui estamos y no nos vamos' which translates as 'We're here and we're not leaving' was a slogan used by the South-Central Farmers Feeding Families in reference to their stance within the legal battle that took place between themselves, the city of Los Angeles, and a private real estate developer (see Figure 15.1). For more than two decades, the South-Central Farmers Feeding Families were engaged in litigation with said group over the contested ground that was formerly home to their fourteen-acre urban farm.

While the part of the city where the farm was located was formerly referred to as South Central Los Angeles, it is now simply referred to as South Los Angeles. The South Los Angeles Urban Farm occupied a parcel of land, which has been a location of controversy for over three decades. The farm was formerly located at the intersection of 41st Street and Alameda Avenue, south of downtown Los Angeles. This site is located in an industrial area adjacent to the Los Angeles Regional Food Bank and the Alameda Corridor, a multi-billion-dollar railroad project that links the port of Los Angeles with the city's downtown (see Figure 15.2).

In 1986, the City of Los Angles took possession of the property from its owner, real estate developer Ralph Horowitz, by implementing eminent domain. As mandated by law, the city paid the developer nearly $4.7 million in compensation for his property. After purchasing the land from Mr. Horowitz, city decision makers announced plans to construct a garbage incineration facility on the plot of land. However, public outcry, and organized political protest, against the incineration facility resulted in the legal defeat of the city's intended use for the land.

In 1992, through the suggestion of the then Los Angeles Food Bank's executive director, Doris Bloch, the city donated a small portion of the fourteen-acre site to be used as a community garden where low-income families could grow their own food. The city's decision to donate a community garden site to the food bank was twofold. The decision was made partly as a response to the ill feelings left behind by the garbage incinerator proposal, and in part to address social tensions and food shortages related to the city's 1992 'Rodney King Riots.'[1]

During the 1992 riots, many of the neighbourhood's grocery stores were looted and burned down, thus placing the area's predominantly low-income resident's food security in jeopardy. The small scaled community garden eventually gained popularity, and over a span of almost fifteen years, grew to become an informally aggregated farm of sub-divided plots that worked to feed 360 families. As such, the farm came to eventually occupy the entire fourteen-acre parcel. By doing so, the collected settlement shaped what was, at that time, the largest urban farm in the country.

In 1994, official legal ownership of the land was transferred to the Los Angeles Harbour Department, as a part of the Alameda Corridor project.[2] Mr. Horowitz' land holding company (LHIC) viewed the transfer as the legal equivalent of a re-sale of the land, which would have given them the right of first refusal to re-purchase the land. As such, between 1995 and 2002 LHIC entered into negotiations with the city to regain ownership of the property. When negotiations failed, LHIC filed a lawsuit against the city claiming that their right to first refusal to the property had been violated. In 2003, in an undisclosed closed door meeting, the city sold Mr. Horowitz the property for slightly more than their original purchase price.

Figure 15.1 Site plan and entry point of the South-Central Farm, an urban farm in South Los Angeles.

Source: Jonathan McIntosh – Own work, CC BY 2.5, https://commons.wikimedia.org/w/index.php?curid=775099. This image has altered in that it was converted to greyscale.

Figure 15.2 Site plan and entry point of the South-Central Farm, an urban farm in South Los Angeles.

Source: Google Maps.

As a result, the L.A. Regional Food Bank issued thirty-day eviction notices to the families farming the site in October of that same year. In response to the eviction notices, the farmers organized themselves into an advocacy group known as the South-Central Farmers Feeding Families. Among the group's first actions was to file for a temporary restraining order, and a temporary injunction against the city of Los Angeles and LHIC. The injunction claimed that the city's sale of the property back to Mr. Horowitz violated requirements set forth in the city of Los Angeles' Administrative Code and the Los Angeles City Charter as well as violating California Code of Civil Procedure, section 526 a, which regulates the expenditure of public funds.

The farmers also filed a lawsuit claiming that their constitutional and statutory rights to due process had been violated and that they were entitled to a prescriptive easement and, therefore, the right to continue to farm the land. The South-Central Farmers Feeding Families' bids for both the temporary restraining order and the temporary injunction were, for some time, successful on the grounds that city officials had indeed violated both the City Charter and the L.A. Administrative Code. These decisions temporarily prevented the city and LHIC from evicting or barring the farmers from the location.

However, the South-Central Farmers Feeding Families eventually failed to succeed in their efforts to save their farm. In June of 2006, L.A. county sheriff's deputies entered the site with orders to forcibly evict anyone who refused to evacuate. In all, forty people were arrested and bull-dozers were set loose upon the site to level the farm to the ground (see Figure 15.3). Following the destruction of the farm, the land remains contested ground, changing ownership at least one more time since the 2006 evacuation. The property was sold to a development company intent upon building warehouses for a retail garment distributor. Likewise, several more lawsuits were filed by the farmer's legal team, which stated that the continued plans to develop the site did not comply with existing environmental restrictions. In 2019, the farmers lost what is most likely their last attempt to regain the land that served to feed low-income members of the South L.A. community.

Defining informal settlement in the urban landscape of South Los Angeles

Up to this point, I have taken the liberty of referring to the formation of the former South Los Angeles Urban Farm a form of urban settlement. Before moving further, I would like to state that when I use the term settlement, I mean for it to be understood in the same manner as John C. Turner's description of urban settlement models (2007). Turner argues that," [u]rban settlement patterns can be seen as the product of the needs for location, tenure, and amenity combined with the means for their satisfaction – above all, land..." (2007, p. 358)

It is through the lens of that offering, and through the farmer's aggregated land use, that I make the argument that the individuals who farmed the land at 41st Street and Alameda Avenue satisfied the requisite need(s) for Turner's model of urban settlement, i.e., "location, tenure, and amenity" (Ibid). Therefore, the urban farm, the legal battle(s) over its contested ground, and the formation of a highly politicized, and highly organized, advocacy group, worked together to create what should be remembered as

Figure 15.3 Images of the South-Central Farm, South Los Angeles: it is the constant work of volunteers that transforms the area into a productive landscape.

Source: Jonathan McIntosh – Own work, CC BY 2.5, https://commons.wikimedia.org/w/index.php?curid=1461398. This image has altered in that it was converted to greyscale.

Figure 15.4 Images of the South-Central Farm, South Los Angeles: it is the constant work of volunteers that transforms the area into a productive landscape.

Source: Jonathan McIntosh – Own work, CC BY 2.5, https://commons.wikimedia.org/w/index.php?curid=775026. This image has altered in that it was converted to greyscale.

an urban settlement pattern that served as a self-constructed 'means for their satisfaction,' i.e., an answer to the negative effects of food scarcity.

I would like to add that the farm and the actions of the low-income, predominantly Hispanic, farmers qualify as 'informal' settlement in that they validate Dovey's contention that "[i]nformal urban design and planning is the means by which cities have absorbed most of the rural-to-urban migration over the past half century. We define such settlements as 'informal' because they emerge outside the formal codes of the state in terms of land tenure, urban planning, design and construction." (2016, p. 265) Since the planning and construction of the farm was performed within the means of those whom Turner describes as the "the lowest of three typical levels of income and social situation,[3] the "'bridge-header'...," or those who "...seek a toehold in the urban system" (2007, p. 358). I am further convinced that the operations of the, South Central Farmers Feeding Families provided a unique, and definitively necessary, type of informal urban settlement.

Defining sustainability in the urban landscape of South Los Angeles

While I am confident that the South-Central Urban Farm served/serves as a viable case study for informal urban settlement, I would also like to take some time to satisfy the challenge of this book in that we have been asked to speak to how the specific instances of informal settlement that we present here can be viewed through the lens of sustainability. I will do so by echoing the threefold domain of sustainable development as it was presented by the Netherlands in their 2003 summary report of their country's response to the 2002 UN's Johannesburg World Summit on Sustainable Development.

Coincidently, the year that the South-Central Urban Farm was initiated was the same year that the 1992 UN's Rio de Janeiro Conference on the Environment and Development crafted an international agenda to reconcile the global implementation of sustainable development. The commonly understood notion of sustainable development, or sustainability as it is more commonly referred to, reminds us that it is the responsibility of each current generation to meet their needs without jeopardizing each future generation's ability to do the same.

While a generalized notion of sustainability has become globally well-acknowledged and understood, it is my opinion that the follow-up work conducted during the U.N.'s 2002 Johannesburg World Summit on Environmental Sustainability lies more congruent to my argument that the South-Central Urban Farm is not only a viable case study of an informal urban settlement pattern, but one for sustainable development as well. It is my opinion that this greater sense of congruency is valid due to the 2002 summit's commitment to charging each nation in attendance to identify specific connection(s) between the reduction of global poverty and sustainable development.

More specifically, I will draw upon the threefold management domain offered in the 2003 Dutch summary report to the 2002 Johannesburg summit's charge. In that report. The Netherland's describes a threefold management domain needed to facilitate sustainable development. That threefold prescription promotes an equitable approach to maintaining the: "sociocultural (people), the ecological (planet), and the socioeconomic (profit)" realms of sustainability (Ministerie van Buitenlandse Zaken, 2003, p. 9).

The sociocultural domain (people)

It is important to understand that the sociocultural domain established by the South Central is one that is bound in Mexicana/o American politics, and culturally informed traditions. Likewise, these farmers adhered to customs that are deeply rooted in everyday, agrarian, practices. Many of the persons who took to growing food for their families at this site, were skilled farmers who gained practice and experience in rural Mexico and Central America, while others brought experiences gained working as migrant farm workers in California's Central Valley. According to anthropologist Devon G. Peña, the sociocultural makeup of those who farmed the South-Central Urban Farm included "native peoples of Mixtec, Tojolobal, Triqui, Tzeltal, Yaqui, and Zapotec descent." (2006, p. 2)

In order to define the unique sociocultural identity formed via the 'bridge-heading' activities of the farmers, and how they differ from the sociocultural settlement activities of those who inhabit the larger, more formalized urban landscape of Los Angeles, the work of the urban planner/theorist James Rojas lends a helpful viewpoint. In reference to the specific cultural identity that is formed via the activities performed by the city of Los Angeles' Mexicana/o American residents, Rojas contends that, "exterior space provides a background for people to manipulate as they please," and that these manipulated spaces become "enacted environments"(1999, p. 131) It is my argument that, when practiced at the scale, and with the specific intent of providing subsistence for themselves and their families, Rojas' conception of enacted environment transcends to the level of a sustainably sound urban settlement.

The ecological domain (planet)

To demonstrate how the South-Central Farm and its farmers contributed to the ecological domain of managing sustainability, I will again refer to Peña when he states:

> Like other anthropologists, I often marvel at the sustainable and equitable nature of the agricultural practices of indigenous farmers around the world. Mexico's native ethnic groups have created one of the world's great centres of agricultural innovation and botanical knowledge. Mexico is a 'Vavilov Centre,' an important world centre for the original domestication of wild plants, including mainstays of the global diet like maize, bean, squash, peanut, chocolate, tomato, sweet potato, avocado, guayaba, and chayote. The South-Central Farmers are a contemporary extension of this Vavilov Centre and thus stewards of a significant cultural and natural resource.
> (2006, p. 2)

In his personal experiences at the South-Central Farm, Peña has observed what he feels is representative of well over 130 different species of plants, including many different types of fruits, vegetables, and herbs. Given the Vavilovian quality of this site's agro-ecology (Peña, 2006), which was set about to sustain 360 individual families with food, in a way that was no longer possible or available in this community, it would be hard to argue that the actions of these farmers would not qualify as what was intended to serve as a long-running sustainable ecology.

The economic domain (profit)

In referring to a generalized understanding of the notion of profit, where profit is calculated by deducting opportunity costs and explicit costs from revenues earned, I will draw an analogy where the farmers' opportunity costs were equal to their labour, their explicit costs were those monetary costs directly associated with cultivating their crops, and their revenue was measured in terms of their harvest(s) plus the social and cultural capital built via the organized activities performed throughout their campaign. Considering that the farmers, who did not purchase or lease the land, but instead paid a nominal monthly fee for water, trash haul-off, and other services for almost fifteen years, it is without reservation when I suggest that their farming served as a viable example of providing a profit within the economic domain of sustainability.

In addition to my analogy listed above, I will return to Turner who also suggests that "...of the two archetypal low-income situations, it is clear that location, [of their settlement], will be determined by minimal subsistence costs in the case of the poorest..." (2007, p. 358) As such, the minimal subsistence costs endured by the South-Central Farmers Feeding Families also supports my argument that this case study answers to the third (economic) domain of sustainability as set forth in the Netherland's 2003 summary report to the UN.

Further offerings – Everyday life as a design influence in the urban landscape

Where I have used this work to delineate the South L.A. Urban Farm as a viable example of sustainable informal settlement(s), it is my contention that the farm's most significant contribution to the lexicon of urban design far transcends that context. I feel strongly that the South Los Angeles Urban Farm, and other similarly constructed 'enacted' landscapes, offer themselves to urban designers and urban planners as valid case studies in addressing the criticism of our built environment as it has been presented by Raymond Ledrut (1986). Ledrut's criticism suggests, that "[t]he problem today – which has nothing 'philosophical' about it – is that of the real life 'of' the city and 'in' the city. The true issue is not to make beautiful cities or well-managed cities. It is to make a work of life. The rest is by-product" (Ledrut, 1986, p. 133).

There is no more meaningful place to measure and/or 'make a work of life' than the arena of the everyday. Everyday life is situated in the commonplace, seemingly mundane, activities that constitute our daily experiences. The trip to and from work, going shopping, or grabbing a quick bite to eat are examples of daily activities that we often take for granted. While taking these actions for granted, we often tend to ignore the potential spatial and temporal qualities available in our built environment (Crawford, 1999). By ignoring these factors, much of our formally 'designed' urban landscape can easily become rendered anonymous, thus reinforcing Ledrut's criticism of the contemporary city.

With that in mind, I would like to return to Rojas' acknowledgment that, within L.A.'s Mexicana/o community, "exterior space provides a background for people to manipulate as they please," and that these manipulated spaces become "enacted environments" (1999, p. 131). If indeed 'enacted' environments, and therefore everyday manipulations/activities, can serve as possible programs for incorporating said activities into the design of our cities, be they cultural activities, ecological informed activities, economic activities, etc., into the more formally 'designed' fabric of our cities, then an examination into the possibilities of how everyday life can play such a role is necessary.

The French cultural theorist Henri Lefebvre has suggested that everyday life operates in a dualistic fashion. Lefebvre's pronouncement of a dualistic 'everyday life' construct recognizes what he refers to as the "quotidian" and the "modern" aspects of life. The "quotidian" reflects the unchanging or recurring measures of life, while the "modern" refers to those things that are at all times new and continuously changing (Lefebvre, 1971). The activities that surrounded the South Los Angeles Urban Farm begin to illustrate aspects of Lefebvre's notion of a dual everyday reality. Through the physically repetitive and modest acts of planting, mulching, harvesting, etc., the "quotidian" qualities of the garden can be recognized, whereas, community celebrations, chance social encounters, and even protests, that happen at the garden can be seen as examples of the "modern" (see Figure 15.4).

In addition to Lefebvre's dually structured theory of the quotidian and the modern, he and others, i.e., de Certeau (1980), have suggested that temporality is also a critically determinant factor in explaining everyday urban life. In order to illustrate the potential temporal influence of this farm on the urban landscape of L.A., one has only to consider Lefebvre's suggestion that time related circumstances are what allow for a necessary form of impulsiveness that results from conducting everyday activities (Lefebvre, 1991). It is precisely this combination of 'impulsiveness' and 'manipulation', in conjunction with the 'quotidian' activities of planting, cultivating, and harvesting, and the 'modern' opportunities to gather and socialize, found in this community farm that allowed for it to become a valuable case study in learning from everyday activities (see Figure 15.5). In turn, these actions should help us to become more informed when being charged with designing more relevant public landscapes.

Connectivity and human consequence

While the farm site was never zoned as public open space, the farmer's performance and exchange of Lefebvre's quotidian and modern activities created a sustainable form of *in situ* zoning reflective of cultural agency, personal need, and therefore human consequence. In as much, the farm site served as a "connective tissue that [bound] daily lives together" (Crawford, 1999, p. 9). As Crawford's work suggests, the bonds that are formed within these 'connective' landscapes are "[u]nrestricted by the dictates of the built form," and therefore "become venues for the expression of new meanings through the individuals and groups who appropriate the spaces for their own purposes." (ibid, p. 28)

This 'appropriation' is directly connected to the implications made by both Lefebvre and de Certeau in that the city is composed of both human and social discourses. As such, the city can become recognized as an entity that is created through the dialogue that occurs between the multitude of everyday activities and other more formalized efforts made by a city's inhabitants (Lefebvre, 1991). The implications made by Lefebvre and de Certeau have often been criticized as being too philosophical to make an applicable transition to the design practices typically involved in city making. However, both theorists have stated that connections must be made

Figure 15.5 Image of a South-Central Farm's community meeting.

Source: Jonathan McIntosh – Own work, CC BY 2.5, https://commons.wikimedia.org/w/index.php?curid=775005. This image has altered in that it was converted to greyscale.

between theory and practice as well as between consideration and conscious experience (Crawford, 1999).

As design professionals, we are well-aware of our charge to combine theory and practice while placing our ideas into specific context(s). However, in reality, urban designers often fall captive to design formulas and municipal restrictions that are abstractions of canonical postulates that leave little to no room for truly quotidian experiences. Acknowledging and ultimately practicing an urbanism that accounts for, and champions, the everyday activities that result in the formation of 'enacted' environments might help to fashion cities where the identity of place takes form as a "work of life" (Ledrut, 1986, p. 133). As such, recognizing those 'enacted' informal settlements, that arise from everyday activities as viable design typologies, can offer points of consideration that promote the necessary value of human consequence over more formal design considerations reflective of disassociated dogma.

Conclusions

Rojas suggests looking towards the vernacular landscapes of Los Angeles' Mexicana/o community to gain insight into the possibilities of creating more responsive urban spaces. "The beauty of the vernacular can be measured not by any architectural standard but by life experiences, which are ambiguous. The vernacular represents people's manipulation and adaptation of their environment" (1999, p. 137). The South L.A. Urban Farm and the actions of the South-Central Farmers Feeding Families illustrate a specific example of the power of connection between social action, environmental need, and cultural expression. This connection has served to create an identity of place that can act as a precedent when considering the strength of employing a more vernacular approach to creating responsive urban landscapes.

This work is not meant to imply that the South-Central Urban Farm serves only as a role model for a more responsive urban landscape typology. It is also meant to suggest that this particular landscapes' formation, through the quotidian and modern engagements of its users, serves as an influence to designers and city officials to look toward and allow for urban design typologies that are truly more responsive to human consequence. In suggesting as much, it should be understood that employing an urban design methodology that is truly more responsive to human consequence will challenge design professionals, and others whose decision-making authority affects the crafting of our cities, to become open-minded, diligent, witnesses of the informal settlement patterns of their constituents.

In this case, the South-Central Urban Farm, the everyday practices of agricultural cultivation, and the organized fight for land present a valid contribution to the discursive notion of a place-based, informal, settlement pattern within the urban landscape of Los Angeles. More specifically, the informal settlement activities that eventually amounted to the development of the South-Central Urban Farm offer a view of the potential for an informally aggregated, enacted, urban landscape to serve as a responsive design typology that respected human consequence above material, and perhaps legal, means.

Notes

1 On 3, March, 1991, an African American male, Mr. Rodney King, led policemen from the Los Angeles Police Department (L.A.P.D.) on a high-speed automobile chase. At the end of which, a private citizen video-taped several police officers repeatedly striking Mr. King with their batons, while nearly twenty other officers stood present in witness. The citizen submitted the video to the authorities and Mr. King was released without facing criminal charges. However, based on the video footage, four white male L.A.P.D. officers were indicted by a grand jury to face criminal charges related to the beating. Those who stood by and watched were never indicted. On 29 April, 1992, all four officers were acquitted of all charges related to the beating. Upon news of the verdict, public rioting ensued throughout South Central Los Angeles from April 29–May 4, 1992, during which nearly 9,000 soldiers from three branches of the U.S. military were deployed to patrol the streets of Los Angeles to quell the looting and rioting. In 1993, a federal grand jury indicted the four officers again on charges of violating Mr. King's civil rights. Two of the four were found guilty and sentenced to thirty months in prison.

2 The Alameda Corridor project is a twenty-mile-long rail line that connects the Port of Los Angeles to the city's downtown.

3 Turner's three typical levels of income and social situation are: "the "bridge-header" at the lowest level, the consolidator at the mid-level, and the third level is that of the "professionally secure," 'status seeker.' (2007, p. 358) Of these three typical levels of income and social situation, Turner considers these first two to be archetypal of low income.

References

Crawford, M. (1999). Introduction. In J. Chase, M. Crawford, & J. Kaliski (Eds.), *Everyday Urbanism* (pp. 8–15). New York: Monacelli Press.

Crawford, M. (1999). Blurring the Boundaries: Public Space and Private Life, In J, Chase, M, Crawford, & J, Kaliski (Eds.), *Everyday Urbanism (pp.)*. New York: Monacelli Press.

de Certeau, M. (1980). *The Practice of Everyday Life*. Berkeley and Los Angeles: U.C. Press.

Dovey, K. (2016). *Urban Design Thinking: A Conceptual Toolkit*. New York: Bloomsbury Academic.

LeFebvre, H. (1971). *Everyday Life in the Modern World*. New York: Harper.

LeFebvre, H. (1991). *Critique of Everyday Life*. London: Verso.

Ledrut, R. (1986). Speech and the Silence of the City. In M. Gottdiener, & A. Langopoulos (Eds.), *The City and the Sign: An Introduction to Urban Semiotics* (pp. 114–134). New York: Columbia University Press.

Ministerie van Buitenlandse Zaken. *Sustainable Action: Sustainable Development Program Summary* (2003). Retrieved from: https://www.un.org/esa/sustdev/natlinfo/nsds/summary.pdf

Peña, D.G. (2006, 4, March). Farmers Feeding Families: Agroecology in South Central Los Angeles. *Lecture Notes, Keynote Address presented to the National Association for Chicana and Chicano Studies*, Washington State University, Pullman, WA. https:www.ucdenver.instructure.com

Rojas, J. (1999). The Latino Use of Urban Space in East Los Angeles. In G. LeClerc, R. Villa, & M.J. Dear, (Eds.), *La Vida Latina in L.A.: Urban Latino Cultures* (pp.131–138). Thousand Oaks: Sage.

Turner, J. C. (2007). Housing Priorities, Settlement Patterns, and Urban Development. In *Modernizing Countries. Journal of the American Institute of Planners. 34 (6)*, 354–363. https://doi.org/10.1080/01944366808977562

Chapter 16

The hill and the asphalt

A 50-year perspective on informality in Rio de Janeiro

Janice E. Perlman

Introduction

In Brazil 13 million people live in informal communities called *favelas*. They are distinguished from formal communities in colloquial parlance as '*the hill and the asphalt*' *(o morro e o asfalto)*. As with the urban poor worldwide, favela residents are particularly vulnerable to natural and man-made disasters. Due to the extreme density of the communities, their precarious access to water and sanitation and the lack of adequate health care, Covid-19 has hit favelas hard and spread rapidly. When asked about this, Brazilian President Jair Bolsonaro is reported to have said, '*So what? What do you want me to do?*'[1]

Even before the new coronavirus the President had broadcasted his disregard for the lives of favela residents he considered dangerous through what has been called his 'extermination policy, stating publicly they should '*die on the streets like cockroaches [os caras vão morrer na rua igual barata]*'.[2] Rio State's Governor, Wilson Witzel, exhorted the police '*to aim at their little heads and fire' [vai mirar na cabecinha... e fogo]*.[3] This is only the most extreme expression of 'the war on the poor', which has been consistently hostile to informality in Rio's favelas since their first appearance in 1897.

To quote one favela resident before the new corona virus, '*our people make the city but do not have the right to enjoy it' ['o povo faz a cidade, mas não tem direito de usufruir]*.[4]

This chapter is based on 50 years of primary fieldwork in the favelas of Rio de Janeiro – and on involvement with informal settlements in megacities throughout the world. In Brazilian Portuguese, favelas are colloquially referred to as hills and the distinction between the informal and formal city is indicated as '*the Hill and the Asphalt*' [*O Morro e o Asfalto*]. Most cities have their own affectionate or disparaging terms – such as '*pueblos jovenes*' (young towns) in Lima or '*villas de miseria*' (towns of misery) in Buenos Aires. Reference to the *informal sector* applies to both informal settlements and to the informal economy. I have argued elsewhere that both types of informality are essential for the flourishing of urban centers. This chapter, in keeping with the entire volume, addresses primarily the physical territorial side of informality.

What is urban informality after all, and why does it matter?

Today informality is the term of choice to signify shanty towns, squatter settlements, degraded public housing projects, clandestine subdivisions, and multiple family use of abandoned office buildings, slums, tenements, and precarious neighbourhoods of various sorts. The term itself has become increasingly useful insofar as each of the terms I listed here is used differently and most have derogatory connotations in one context or another. The use of the term *squatter settlements* is most meaningful in the global south while in the global north the terms that fit better are slums and precarious neighbourhoods.

Specific characteristics used earlier to define squatter settlements have become irrelevant over time as they have improved the quality of their homes, installed urban infrastructure, participated in urban upgrading programs and/or received various forms of certification through payments to electric companies to government certificates of occupancy.

The one constant factor seems to be the absence of formal land title. Frequently, especially in older settlements, the parents or grandparents of the current residents squatted on unwanted land and built up their houses and community over several generations. It represents an ongoing investment of household resources. They are owners of their homes and many have occupancy permits (given by various local and state administrations) but they do not own the land on which their homes were built. The fight for formal title was a major struggle from the mid-60s through the mid-90s in Rio, but in the current configuration residents do not seem to want it. They see it as a financial burden (paying property tax) and a risk factor for gentrification (having legal title making it more appealing to buyers from outside).

Informal settlements are the fastest growing segment of the human population. Writing about *'the urban explosion,' a 'world of cities' or 'the urban age'* is really about the growth of informal settlements. The population of the formal sector is not growing and in some places is actually shrinking. It is now widely known that informal settlements are home to a billion people representing one sixth of our global population and are expected to double by 2030 and triple by 2050, reaching 3 billion – one of every three people on the planet.

Neither the state nor the market has the capacity to provide housing to meet this demand, so self-built homes in informal settlements are the only way to house newcomers. The fact that the informal sector has grown faster than the formal sector corroborates this view. For new arrivals, informal communities provide a toe-hold in the city; a stepping-stone to a better life and a source of mutual aid – all of which make the difference between life and death.

Over the past few years I have been reminded of a basic tenant of the Mega-Cities Project – that is, the similarities faced by people in squatter settlements in the global south and 'precarious neighbourhoods' in the global north. Precarious neighbourhoods is the term of choice to signify slums, tenements, shanty towns, squatter settlements, degraded public housing projects, clandestine subdivisions and informal neighbourhoods in highly industrialised countries. It is useful insofar as more specific terms, such as slums, invasions and social housing projects, have a derogatory connotation. They faced the same type of exclusion, stigma, and vulnerability as marginalised communities the world over.

There is a tendency in both cases to *conflate precarious neighbourhoods with precarious people.* Once an area is perceived as precarious, the people living there are seen as undeserving,[5] dirty and dangerous. Public policy and planning decisions flow from that perception. This is what I find so devastating – the mindset that a significant number of people in the city don't count, don't matter and don't deserve respect.

Vulnerability is a chronic condition of existence and constant stress associated with informality, marginality and precarious neighbourhoods in four ways:

1. Vulnerability due to *insecure occupancy of territory.* Uncertainty and fear are present in conditions running the gamut from homeless people living on the streets, in parks, or under bridges (as seen in New York City); to occupation of patches of grass in the middle of traffic circles (as seen in Paris); to living on construction sites (as seen in Bombay); to sharing abandoned office buildings (as seen in Johannesburg); to social housing projects and squatter settlements across Latin America Asia, and Africa.
2. Vulnerability due to the *instability or impermanence of the dwellings.* Construction materials are often taken from the garbage: scrap metal that becomes burning hot in the sun; plastic sheeting that becomes torn in wind and rain; packed mud, lean-tos and tents or even, as in the case of pavement dwellers in India, cloth saris strung on poles on the sidewalk (using the wall behind them as the back of the house). What these have in common is precariousness and danger for the inhabitants.
3. Vulnerability of *entire neighbourhoods,* which may be due to: *1) deterioration* due to neglected maintenance, lack of urban services, natural disaster, or population succession; *2) partially or totally demolished; or 3) abandoned* due to economic and social transformations.
4. Vulnerability *exacerbated by public policy.* The intention driving the programs may be rationalised as 'improving living conditions', 'regularizing land use', protecting the environmental' or 'opening space for the public good'. In any case, the end result is generally expelling the poor to the urban fringe.

Regardless of the circumstances, the cruel reality is that *precariousness erodes not only one's* ***sense of security*** but also one's **sense of self**. Families and individuals are put under constant stress. Their lives and the meaning they imbue to their home and community can be ripped apart at any time without justification. Decisions are made about them without including them. Health data shows that displacement increases high blood pressure, risk of stroke and heart attack and reduces life expectancy.

What was learned? Marginality disputed

My early research in the favelas of Rio de Janeiro was conducted in 1968 and 1969 at the height of the military dictatorship in Brazil. It was a time when everyone – from leftist students to taxi drivers – thought it was too dangerous to go near the entrance to a favela, much less enter one. I was interested in the impact of urban experience on newly arrived migrants from the countryside. I wanted to know how they managed in the city, given that most arrived with little or no money (having sold everything to afford the trip to the city); that few knew how to read or write; and that only a handful had gone beyond walking distance from their villages.

To do the study I selected one favela from each of the three areas of the city where migrants tended to go: 1) *Catacumba* from the upscale residential South Zone; 2) *Nova Brasília* from the industrial North Zone; and 3) *Vila Operária,* and two small favelas from the municipality *Duque de Caxias* in the *Baixada Fluminense.* I lived for six months in each favela and interviewed 200 people chosen at random (among residents from 16–65 years old) and 50 leaders from each community. I returned in 1973, after *Catacumba* was removed, to find out what had happened and learn about life in the housing projects.

The book resulting from that study in 1976, *The Myth of Marginality: Urban Politics and Poverty in Rio de Janeiro,*[6] was part of a paradigm shift from seeing squatter settlements as a problem to recognizing them as the solution to a problem; seeing the residents as parasites on the city to recognizing them as a valuable resource. This line of thinking had already been suggested in the work of John Turner, Lisa Peattie, and Anthony Leeds, with whom I studied – and Charles Abrams before them.[7]

A decade before Charles Abrams, Oscar Lewis had argued against the anti-urban bias in his article 'Urbanization without Breakdown' which took on Robert Redfield's premise of a 'folk-urban continuum' from an idyllic rural life to a depraved urban life.[8] Lewis later postulated a 'Culture of Poverty', a set of beliefs and behaviours passed from generation to generation thereby perpetuating poverty.[9] William Ryan called this, *Blaming the Victim*, claiming the poverty trap was structural and not a self-defeating subculture.[10]

In Brazil at roughly the same time, a body of work on marginality and dependency theory was emerging in the discourse on poverty, inequality, and development. At the height of the military dictatorship (1969), a group of university professors in São Paulo founded CEBRAP – The Brazilian Centre for Analysis and Planning. The group included Fernando Henrique Cardoso, Enzo Faletto, Paulo Singer, Francisco Weffort, Octavio Ianni and Jose Arthur Giannotti.[11] Shortly afterwards, this line of thinking was elaborated in the book, *Authoritarian Brazil,* edited by Al Stepan, which included chapters by Cardoso, Juan Linz, Samuel Morley, Philippe Schmitter, Thomas Skidmore and others.[12]

My research in Rio's favelas examined the stereotypes about favelas against the reality on the ground. I started with a set of questions about the 'Impact of Urban Experience' based on the disputes in the literature of the time. The research results contradicted assumptions that had never been empirically tested or contested. I found that the migrants were not the poorest or most desperate within their village, but the best and the brightest. They were the ones who had the courage and conditions to leave everything behind in search of a better life in the city. In other words, they were *not* the 'bottom of the barrel' but the 'cream of the crop'. And, in political terms, they were not resentful and radical and did not compare their conditions to that of those in the luxury apartment houses around them. Their reference group remained the people back in their villages who were much worse off and without future opportunities open to them. My main conclusions were:

1. Favela residents are not marginal to the city but inextricably integrated into it, albeit in an asymmetrical manner detrimental to their own interests
2. They contribute their hard work, their high hopes, and their loyalties, but do not benefit from the goods and services of the system
3. They are neither economically nor politically marginal, BUT exploited, manipulated, and repressed to maintain the status quo
4. They are neither socially or culturally marginal, BUT stigmatised and excluded from a closed class system

In short, favelas are not marginal but actively 'marginalised' by a system that benefits from maintaining inequality, exclusion, and repression.

What changed over 40 years and 4 generations?

In 1999, I returned to Rio to see whether it would be possible to find the 750 people who had been interviewed thirty years earlier. The prospects were especially dismal given that we had used only first names (to protect people's identity); that there were few street names and no housing numbers at the time; and the communities had grown and changed so much between 1969 and 1999. *Catacumba* had been removed in 1970 and its 10,000 residents had been relocated to distant housing projects. *Nova Brasília* had grown up and over the hillsides, merging with other favelas into what the government called the *Complexo do Alemão*, one of the most violent areas of Rio. Yet, due to the strong social networks it was easier than expected to track down original interviewees, even those who had left the area.

The idea of the study was to follow the evolution of these precarious neighbourhoods and the life trajectories of those who had been part of the original study.[13] However, there was no way to determine whether the people were better or worse off, because they were in a different stage of their life cycle. To deal with this we interviewed a sample of their children, whose age range was comparable to their mothers or fathers 30 years earlier (the study included males and females from 16–65). When the analysis of those data showed disappointing results as compared with the hopes of the migrants, we thought that perhaps it took another generation for integration. With that in mind we sampled the grandchildren. The research results are presented in the more recent book, *Favela: Four Decades of Living on the Edge in Rio de Janeiro.*[14]

Where were the original study participants?

After two years of detective work and travel to six states, we managed to find 41% of the 750 people interviewed despite not having their last names or addresses, and the fact that many had died since the oldest ones would have been 95. We found 50% of them in the same homes. But one in three had moved out of the favelas into the bottom rungs of the formal sector and by their grandchildren's generation half had done so.

Did things get better or worse?

The answer is 'both' – some things got much better and other things much worse. Among those that improved:

- **Living conditions improved.** During the years between the two studies, the residents had turned their ram-shackled homes into solid housing stock made of permanent materials, generally four stories high with a rooftop space. This allowed extended families to live together and often provided rental income as well. This settlement pattern prevented sprawl and allowed people to live close to multiple sources of work. The photographs below (see Figures 16.1 and 16.2) show what the favela of Catacumba looked like in 1968 and what it would probably look like now if it had not been removed in 1970.

Figure 16.1 Catacumba, 1968.

Source: Author.

The favelas did not have legal title to their land but they had 'de facto' tenure since it was unthinkable that they would ever be faced with removal. In fact, during the first decade of the 2000s, most residents were no longer interested in formal title as they saw it as unnecessary and adding the cost of property taxes.

- **Household consumption rose.** Ownership of electro-domestic appliances rose dramatically, especially in the grandchildren's generation whose score on the index of household consumer goods reached the median of the city as a whole. The younger generation owned plasma televisions, washing machines, and air conditioners unthinkable in earlier times. The only two indicators that were higher in the formal city were personal computers and cars. Even so, 34% of the grandchildren's generation owned cars or other vehicles and 27% of them had personal computers. This high degree of consumerism has been equated with the rise of a 'new middle class'. Yet *no degree of material acquisition can confer citizenship status, equal treatment under the law or the respect accorded to a middle-class person.*
- **Educational gains were impressive.** Illiteracy was 46% among participants in the 1968 study; was 82% among their parents; dropped to 6% for their children and no longer existed among the grandchildren. Over 11% of the grandchildren were studying or had completed university. In 2020 when this is being written, that percentage is estimated to be closer to 20%.

Among things that got worse are work, violence, schools, access to health care, bargaining power with political candidates and the degree of exclusion. For example:

- **Finding work was more difficult.** For the most part, gains in education did not translate into parallel gains in income. **85%** of kids had more years of schooling than their parents but only **56%** had better jobs and unemployment was much higher in the children's generation.

Figure 16.2 Rocinha, 2016.

Source: Bennett Cain.

Even more striking, the income gap between favela residents and the rest of the city increased with every additional year of schooling after the 3rd grade. The expected rise in incomes with additional years of schooling showed up for the city as a whole, but not so much for favela residents.

Among the explanations for this gap are the rising bar for entry into jobs which demands educational levels at higher rates than the gains made in the favela population; the changing labour market; the poor quality of schools in favelas; and **the stigma of living in a favela** – which is sufficient in itself to cut off job interviews when an address is required.

- **Lethal violence devastated community life.** In the intervening years between the first and follow-up studies, the single change, however, which most affected already precarious lives between my first study in the 1960s and my restudy in the 2000s, was ***the rise of the drug and arms traffic and the consequent high levels of lethal violence.*** Starting in the mid-1980s, the drug trade, especially in cocaine, grew rapidly and favelas provided a convenient locale for dealing. By the time I began the re-study in 1999, many favelas were controlled by drug traffic and by the end of the study almost all had expelled the elected Presidents of the Residents' Associations. People were living in constant fear of being caught in the crossfire between competing drug gangs or between the police and the traffickers. One in every five interviewees reported having lost a family member in a homicide.

The sharp increase in violence decreased the most precious survival mechanisms of the favelas: social capital, mutual trust, and sense of community unity. And the association of favela residents with danger and violence reinforced the old and ongoing stigma.

In response to the questions about sources of prejudice they had experienced personally, residents reported more discrimination based on favela living than on skin colour, 'appearance' (presentation of self), gender, being born outside the city or living in a 'bad' neighbourhood. While all other experiences of discrimination declined in each generation, the degree of discrimination of living in a favela remained high – reported by 80% or more in all three generations.

Fear of losing one's home was replaced by fear of losing one's life in the crossfire between police and gangs or among rival gangs at war over territorial control. Police tended to stay out of the favelas while the narco-traffic expanded their area of control by expelling or killing the elected Presidents of the Residents' Associations. By 2010, there were few independent favelas left; those not controlled by drug lords were controlled by self-appointed armed militias.

Contextual transformations

These changes in the lives of favela residents across time and generations were reflections of macro-level transformations in the political economy of Brazil and of Rio. Brazil went from dictatorship to democracy; from hyperinflation to stabilization to growth and then stagnation. Rio lost jobs as the pace of city growth declined, reducing construction work; as industrial costs became noncompetitive and manufacturing jobs moved out; and as port activities became obsolete with containerisation. The difficulties these contextual factors created for livelihoods among the favela population were compounded by public policies over the same period of time.

Evolution of favela policy: From hostile to hopeful and back again

The clear policy message from my earliest favela research was to stop favela removal and allow them to grow naturally into working class neighbourhoods, serving the needs of surrounding neighbourhoods. The government did the exact opposite, bulldozing down favelas, displacing over 100,000 residents from their homes, and moving them to remote public housing complexes. This proved disastrous for both the families, who never recovered from the trauma and loss of income and for the government, which was nearly bankrupted by the non-recoverable costs of the public housing.

By the first decade of the 2000s, it appeared that favela removal was a thing of the past. It seemed too politically risky for any candidate or office holder to antagonise the 20% of the electorate living in favelas. They had de facto if not de jure land tenure. No one expected the drastic policy pivot back to removal, once Rio won its bids to host the 2014 World Cup and the 2016 Olympics.

By 2016, 77,206 residents had been removed from favelas.[15] Most were sent to apartment units in the federal government programme, My House My Life (Minha Casa Minha Vida). They were generally separated from family and neighbours and moved far from their homes, reprising what had been done half a century before.

The rationale for removal was to make way for the Olympic venues (or parking lots), for the new Transcarioca or Transolímpica Bus Rapid Transit lines; or to protect them from 'environmental risks'. The real reason was the opportunity for low-cost acquisition of valuable lands for up-scale development. The numbers of people removed was almost twice that of the 1960s and 70s and the value of destroyed homes many times greater than 35 years before.

The images below show (see Figures 16.3 and 16.4) what removal looked like in 1969 in Praia do Pinto on the Lagoa Rodrigo Freitas and in 2015 in Vila Autódromo, in Jacarepaguá, the West Zone.

Figure 16.3 Praia do Pinto, 1969.

Source: Author.

Figure 16.4 Vila Autódromo, 2015.

Source: Catalytic Communities (CatComm).

Return to democracy

The end of the dictatorship in 1985 heralded the shift from hostile policies to helpful policies, specifically upgrading urban services and improving living conditions on site.

The first large scale upgrading project in Rio was **Favela-Bairro** (translated as Favela-Neighbourhood). It started in 1995 with funding from the Inter-American Development Bank, the Brazilian National government, and the city of Rio. Its mission was 'to improve the quality of life in favelas through urban infrastructure projects and soften the boundary between favelas and their surrounding neighbourhoods'. The initial two 5-year phases targeted small and medium-size favelas. It was the most ambitious squatter upgrading program of its time.[16]

The largest favelas in Rio were next to be upgraded in the third phase of Favela-Bairro. Due to changes in the local administration and the *not-invented-here* syndrome, the project was subsumed under the Federal Program for Accelerated Growth (PAC) and named **PAC-Favelas** (PAC-Slums). It was launched in 2008 with the advantages of a considerable budget, ten years of upgrading experience through Favela-Bairro and a semi-autonomous public management enterprise. But just when the actual upgrading was to begin – after years of painstaking work with the selected favela communities to build trust and goodwill – fund were abruptly frozen and the project dropped indefinitely.

There was one other extremely promising upgrading program in Rio, **Morar Carioca**. In 2008 when Rio won its bid to host the Olympics and the new Mayor, Eduardo Paes, took office, he saw an opportunity to take on-site upgrading to the next level. He announced his plan to *upgrade all of Rio's favelas by 2020,* as part of the Olympic Legacy and went so far as to promise land title for residents.[17] Like PAC, Morar Carioca met a painful death. By 2016, although it was never declared dead, it had been dismembered piece-by-piece and the name had become the new label for any public housing projects.

The Pacifying Police Program (UPP) was yet another example of a public policy that had the potential to improve safety and bring social services into the favelas but ended up doing more harm than good, ultimately increasing lethal violence. Most of the victims were young black males shot by the police without provocation and never held accountable. Lives lost in the crossfire were considered collateral damage whether children playing in their school yard during recess or mothers with their children sitting on the front steps of their homes. In the first eight months of 2019 police actions were responsible for the deaths of 1,249 favela residents.

With the election of a governor whose campaign slogan was ending violence and the 'taking back control of the territories' and Rio's selection as host of the World Cup and Olympics, the UPP – Pacifying Police Programme – was launched in 2008. Its aim was to end the use of ostensive arms and exert control of favelas through a permanent police occupation. The original concept was to pair the military side with strong social programmes and community services provided by the sister programme, the Social UPP. A political party deal destroyed the prospects for the much-needed Social Programme just before it was to go into effect. Without the human and social side, and in push for rapid expansion, the UPP police antagonised the communities with arbitrary brutality and disregard for the rights of residents. Rather than bringing peace, they increased the atmosphere of violence and opened the door for the return of the drug gangs even before the 2016 Olympics.

Favela Policy Overview. The figure below (see Figure 16.5) traces the major shifts in favela policy from the first favela in Rio, the Morro da Providência, in 1897, to the

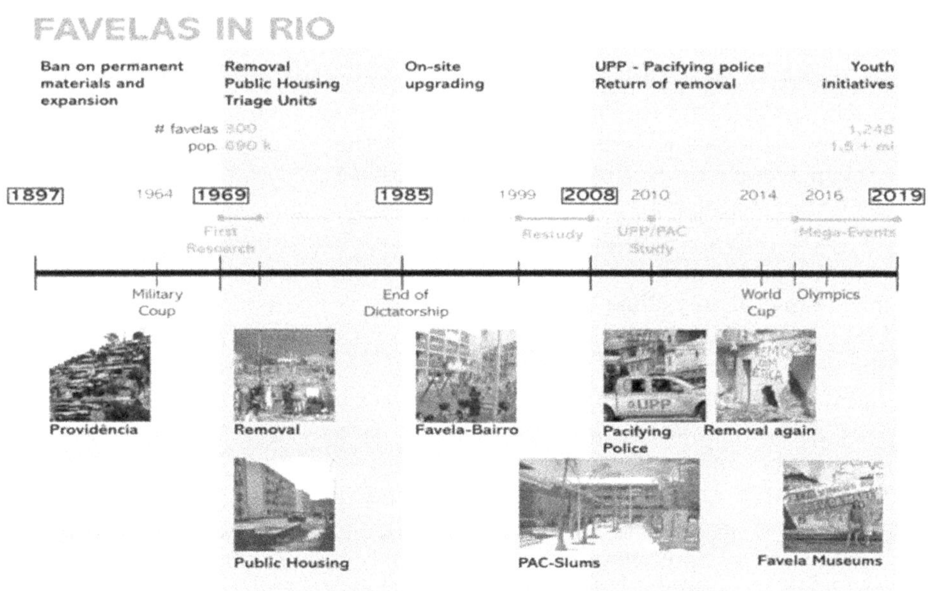

Figure 16.5 Trajectory of Favela Policy in Rio de Janeiro from 1897 to 2020.

current period. Along the bottom of the midline are milestones in Brazil's history – the military coup and the dictatorship, the return to democracy and then the mega-events in Rio de Janeiro. Above the line are the periods when the favela research was conducted. Below the line are photographs of the main policies: removal; public housing, Favela-Bairro upgrading program: PAC-Favelas upgrading in largest favelas; the UPP-Pacifying Police; return of Removal, and the favelas re-claiming their history and identity through museums they create.

By a year after the Olympics, the public policies put into place before and during the games had left Rio's favela population no better than, and in many cases, **worse off than before**. This makes any future work in the communities much more difficult. Any new initiative will be met with deep-felt distrust, cynicism, and anger.

In praise of informality

Although I have used the case of favelas in Rio de Janeiro, many of the points raised can be generalised to informal settlements elsewhere in Latin America, Asia, and Africa. One of the main observations is the importance of *mindset* concerning informal communities. Our perceptions, concepts, and even our words shape our mental map of informality, which in turn defines how we define problems/solutions or deficits/assets. Once we recognize the essential role of Informality for our cities to survive and to thrive we can rethink what matters, whose lives count and what might be done to move towards the city we want.

To illustrate this, I have specified five valuable contributions of informal settlements and what the city would lose without them:[18]

1. **Loss of labour** and **productivity:** informal communities have a thriving internal economy with commerce, services, real estate markets, restaurants, bars, and small-scale manufacturing. They also power most formal sector work by providing the cheap labour for local, national, and international production.
2. **Loss of consumer power:** the urban poor spend a disproportionate portion of their income on consumer goods and services, paying double or triple the shelf price because they buy on instalments. Favela residents in Rio account for 1.3–2 million consumers, with an annual income of 5–10 billion *reais* per year[19] (approximately 1.4 to 2.9 billion US dollars) keeping entire segments of the urban economy afloat
3. **Loss of cultural production and creativity:** new forms of music, art, dance, theatre, film, and fashion are born and nurtured in these 'alternative spaces' influencing trends in the rest of the city and indeed the world. Insofar as the future of cities depends upon innovation and adaptation to change, there needs to be space for deviance and non-conformism.
4. **Loss of social capital:** the strong kinship and friendship networks are coping mechanisms in day-to-day life and survival support in times of crisis. In the absence of any state safety net, the community becomes the safety net and the city depends on that, in fact, takes it for granted. That's how neighbourhoods in Mexico re-built after the earthquake, and how favelas are now dealing with the new coronavirus.

5. **Loss of intellectual capital:** the intelligence is not distributed along economic, racial or territorial lines, depriving the residents of informal communities of the opportunity to realize their full potential, limits the intellectual capital of the entire city. Some of the community leaders in Rio are as brilliant as any of my professors in graduate school at MIT. The intractability and complexity of the urban problem, requires the best minds, closest to the ground for solutions.

This is an abridged version of a much longer argument about the interdependence of the informal and formal sectors. Each needs the other to exist.[20]

There is a related truth here that is often overlooked. Many, if not most people I interviewed until the current moment of Covid-19, expressed a preference for living in informal communities even though they have sufficient income to move elsewhere.

Attachments to place run much deeper in the *morro than in the asfalto*. For them moving away means leaving behind the home that they watched their parents and grandparents build over a lifetime; leaving behind their extended families and friendship group – and the families of their friends; and giving up the freedom to be themselves.

For them, being forced out of their settlements and into apartments in public housing projects is *not a dream but a nightmare.*

Cities without slums are cities without soul[21]

Ridding cities of informal settlements altogether has been the dream of planners and policymakers for over a century, but was made explicit in 1999 through the '*Cities without Slums*' programme.[22] As these three little words embody the prevalent notion of slums as deleterious for urban order, they were readily picked up by the United Nations, folded into the 2000 Millennium Development Goals and then rolled over into the 2015 Sustainable Development Goals.

Ignoring for the moment the ongoing controversy over the derogatory nature of the word 'slum', the aim of formalising the informal sector is the polar opposite of what is needed. Why not use the same resources necessary to eliminate, clean up and control communities, to support the realization of their own priorities?

The very essence of urbanity is density and diversity. Conviviality, like innovation thrives on serendipitous encounters; on chaos and complexity and on the element of surprise when different knowledge comes together.

What needs to be eradicated is *not informality, but poverty, inequality, and exclusion.*

Going beyond the territorial perspective

Until this point in the chapter, the discussion has focused on one approach to addressing urban poverty, the ***place-based approach***. The focus is on the physical territory within the boundaries of informal settlements. The policies mentioned were targeted to informal settlements, whether for their benefit or detriment.

But the conditions that make informality so attractive to so many for so long – are not inside the communities. And as long as structural constraints produce and reproduce these conditions, informality will continue to grow faster than formality.

Other entry points and toolkits are needed to deal with the causes and consequences of poverty, inequality, exclusion, and lack of equal standing in the eyes of the law. Two other approaches might be based on conditions of scarcity and need or on the deprivation of rights.

The poverty-based approach focuses on those living below a set poverty line regardless of where they live. To be fair, this needs to be adjusted for purchasing power parity as living costs in a city are not comparable to those in a subsistence economy in the rural Northeast. This approach, generically known as Conditional Cash Transfers (CCTs) creates a monetary incentive for low income families to invest in the health and education of their children and the care of their elders. In Brazil the programme is called '*Bolsa Família*'.

The Rights Approach is based on individual and collective rights, applicable universally, to all people regardless of where or how they live. The argument for 'The Right to the City' was articulated by the French sociologist Henri Lefebvre in his 1968 book of that name.[23] He wrote: '*The freedom to make and remake our cities and ourselves is (…) one of the most precious and yet most neglected of our human rights*'.

This concept led to a global discussion on the 'right to housing' and the 'right to decent housing' at the Habitat II Summit in Istanbul in 1996, and on the 'right to the city' or the concept of '*The City for All*' at the UN Habitat congress in 2016 in Quito and every urban summit meeting since. Obviously these approaches are complementary, not mutually exclusive.

Place-based	*Poverty-based*	*Rights-based*
Favela-Bairro	Conditional Cash Transfers	Right to Housing
PAC	Bolsa Família	**Right to the City**
Morar Carioca		Right to Dignity
MCMV		

Three approaches to urban informality

My 50 years of research and practice in international urban development compel me to argue for the addition of '*The Right to Dignity*'. The concluding chapter of my 2010 book is called '*The Importance of Being Gente*'.[24] *Gente* is the Brazilian expression for *personhood*. Despite the many intelligent people and good intentions in the public sphere and in bilateral and international aid agencies – and despite efforts to incorporate new knowledge and to partner with community groups and NGOs – government interventions in precarious neighbourhoods often do more harm than good. I refer to this as '*the helping hand strikes again*'. The further removed from the on-the-ground reality, the more difficult it is to value the voice of the disenfranchised and to recognize the way society renders them invisible.

Ultimately, the lack of respect for the dignity and personhood of the urban poor means that right now, in 2016, the knowledge and talent of the billion people living in precarious circumstances are being wasted. By 2050, one of every three people on the planet will reside in these informal communities. Can we afford to ignore them?

Acknowledgments

Portions of this paper appeared earlier in *Trialog, in* Berlin, 2017, edited by *Kosta Mathéy* and the section on precarious neighbourhoods was informed by discussions at the International Conference on that topic, in Paris 2016, organised by Agnès Deboulet. The author would also like to thank Guilherme Rocha Formicki for his outstanding work and valuable contribution to this chapter.

Notes

1 Guimarães, 2020.
2 Istoé, 2019.
3 Pennafort, 2018.
4 Author's field notes from meeting of Pastoral da Favelas December 14, 2016.
5 See Bridges, 2017.
6 The book I am working on now shows how this 'non-personhood' plays out in Rio in the time of the mega-events. It is titled *The Importance of Being Gente.*
7 Turner & Fichtur, 1972; Peattie, 1986; Leeds, 1971; 1976; 1978; Abrams, 1964.
8 Lewis, 1952 and Redfield, 1953.
9 Lewis, 1969.
10 Ryan, 1971.
11 For a history of this period and the individual and collective publications of CEBRAP, see Goertzel, 1999 and Cardoso, 2001.
12 Stephan, 1976.
13 Perlman 2007.
14 Perlman 2010.
15 Vinicius, 2016.
16 See Osorio, Libertun de Duren & Perlman, (forthcoming).
17 See Paes, 2012.
18 Perlman, 2014.
19 O Globo, August 24, 2008, 'Sem direitos econômicos, favelas movimentam bilhões'.
20 Perlman (forthcoming). Informality: Choice or Consequence: Model for sustainable cities or child of scarcity.
21 Perlman, 2017.
22 The 'Cities Without Slums' action plan was developed by the Cities Alliance in July 1999 and launched at the inaugural meeting of the Cities Alliance in Berlin in December 1999. [www.citiesalliance.org/cws-action-plan]. For more on this theme, see Yusuf, 2014 and Perlman, 2014.
23 Lefebvre 1968.
24 See Perlman 2010.

References

Abrams, C. (1964). *Man's Struggle for Shelter in an Urbanizing World*. Cambridge, MA: MIT press.

Bridges, K.M. (2017). The Deserving Poor, the Undeserving Poor, and Class-Based Affirmative Action. *Emory Law Journal*, 66, 16–30. Retrieved from https://ssrn.com/abstract=2824433

Cardoso, F.H. (2001). *Charting a New Course: The Politics of Globalization and Social Transformation*. Washington DC: Rowman & Littlefield.

Deboulet, A. (ed.) (2016). Rethinking Precarious Neighbourhoods. Proceedings of the International Conference 'Rethinking Precarious Neighbourhoods: works, paths and interventions', Paris, 9 -10 June 2015. Paris: Agence Française de Développement.

Goertzel, T.G. (1999). *Fernando Henrique Cardoso: Reinventing Democracy in Brazil*. Boulder: Lynne Rienner.

Guimarães, L. (20 April 2020). Drauzio Varella prevê 'tragédia nacional' por coronavírus: 'Brasil vai pagar o preço da desigualdade'. *BBC Brasil*. Retrieved from: https://www.bbc.com/portuguese/brasil-52329579

Istoé. (6 August 2019). "Os caras vão morrer na rua igual barata, pô', diz Bolsonaro em entrevista. Retrieved from: https://istoe.com.br/os-caras-vao-morrer-na-rua-igual-barata-po-diz-bolsonaro-em-entrevista/

Leeds, A. (1971). The Culture of Poverty Concept – Conceptual, Logical, and Empirical Problems, with Perspectives from Brazil and Peru. In Leacock, E. (ed.) *The Culture of Poverty, A Critique* (pp. 226–284). New York: Simon and Schuster.

Leeds, A. & Leeds, E. (1976). Accounting for Behavioral Differences: Three Political Systems and the Responses of Squatters to them in Brazil, Peru, and Chile. In Walton, J. and L. H. Masotti (eds.) *The City in Comparative Perspective: Cross-National Research and New Directions in Theory* (pp. 193–248). Beverly Hills: Sage.

______. (1978). *A Sociologia do Brasil Urbano*. Rio de Janeiro: Zahar Editores.

Lefebvre, H. (1968). *Le droit à la ville*. Paris: Anthropos.

Lewis, O. (1952). Urbanization without Breakdown. *The Scientific Monthly*, Volume 75, No. *1*, AAAS.

______. (1969). Culture of Poverty. In Moynihan, D. P. *On Understanding Poverty: Perspectives from the Social Sciences* (pp. 187–220). New York: Basic Books.

Osorio, R., Libertun de Duren, N. &Perlman, J. (forthcoming). *The favela-bairro upgrading program: assessing results 10 years later*. Inter-American Development Bank.

Paes, E. (2012). Eduardo Paes: Os quatro mandamentos das cidades. *TED Talk*. Retrieved from: https://www.ted.com/talks/eduardo_paes_the_4_commandments_of_cities?language=pt-br

Peattie, L. (1986). *The View from the Barrio*. Ann Arbor: University of Michigan Press.

Pennafort, R. (November 18 2018). 'A polícia vai mirar na cabecinha e… fogo', diz novo governador do Rio. O Estado de S. Paulo. Retrieved from: https://politica.estadao.com.br/noticias/eleicoes,a-policia-vai-mirar-na-cabecinha-e-fogo-diz-novo-governador-do-rio,70002578109

Perlman, J. (1976). *The Myth of Marginality, Urban Poverty and Politics in Rio de Janeiro*. Berkeley, CA :University of California Press.

______. (1987). Misconceptions about the Urban Poor and the Dynamics of Housing Policy Evolution. *Journal of Planning Education and Research*, April 1987, 6 (pp. 187–196).

______. (2010). *Favela: Four decades of living on the edge in Rio de Janeiro*. Oxford: University Press.

______. (2014). What Happens When Marginal Becomes Mainstream? How to See the Challenge as an Opportunity. In Yusuf, S. (ed.) *The Buzz in Cities: New Economic Thinking*. Chapter IX: 117–141. Washington, DC: The Growth Dialogue.

______. (2017). Cities without Slums are Cities without Soul – Re-thinking Concepts and Consequences of Marginality in the Favelas of Rio de Janeiro. *In Trialog 123, A Journal for Planning and Building in a Global Context, Other Housing Strategies*, Vol. 4/2015 September 2017: 4–12.

______. (Forthcoming). Informality: Choice or Consequence: Model for sustainable cities or child of scarcity.
Ryan, W. (1971). *Blaming the Victim*. New York: Pantheon books.
Redfield, R. (1953). *The Primitive World and Its Transformations*. Ithaca, New York: Cornell University Press.
Stepan, A. (ed.) (1973). *Authoritarian Brazil*: Origins, *Policies, and Future*. New Haven, Connecticut: Yale University Press.
Turner, J.F.C. & Fichter, R. (eds.) (1972). *Freedom to Build: Dweller Control of the Housing Process*, Chapter 7 'Housing as a Verb'. New York: Macmillan.
Vinicius, G. (8 September 2016). Rio pós-olímpico: 77 mil removidos; Vila Autódromo vira rua. *Agência de Notícias das Favelas*. Retrieved from: http://www.anf.org.br/rio-pos-olimpico-77-mil-removidos-vila-autodromo-vira-rua/.

Part III

Informal behaviour as a form of community resilience

Alessandro Melis

Introduction

The determinism of modern architecture has shown its limits in overcoming a global crisis such as the environmental one.

The third part of this book discusses the informal hypothesis not as a result of the deterioration of the urban environment, but as an opportunity aimed at resilience to redefine the paradigms of human coexistence and the urban fabric in times of global crises.

This position is therefore the consequence of the failure of the order-oriented approach to planning and the awareness of the end of an alleged heroic phase of colonisation of the planet.

Following Freud's well-known perspective, each societal revolution occurs with the descent of a step by mankind from the Olympus in which he had narcissistically placed himself (Fletcher, 2007). As has happened during the revolutions of heliocentrism, Darwinian evolutionism, and the discovery of the unconscious in opposition to rationalism, today it is the environmental crisis that dethrones humanity and brings it back to the margins of nature and, hopefully, within the ecosystem.

If, on one hand, the organised city contributes to a negative environmental pressure, on the other hand, it is the informal settlement that suffers most of its negative effects, though sometimes it is there that you can find creative and unexpected solutions regarding solidarity and spatial practices, as the examples of the Mediterranean neighbourhoods, such as El Houma, the Algerian version of the Medina, suggest Khemri & Melis in 'Achieving community resilience through informal urban practices'. Nevertheless, we are usually faced with the paradoxical idea that the informal city is the problem.

This third part of the book aims at inverting the terms of the question and, without having the arrogance to provide a conclusive answer, discusses a series of hypotheses, which hopefully will be the subject of further studies in the near future. For instance, what can we learn from informal behavioural patterns in terms of low consumption of energy and resources, and about coexistence with non-human species?

In the following chapters, we will explore the apparent disorganisation and chaos, and, at the same time, the intertwining of relations, as forms of resilience, through variability, in opposition to the invariant presumed rationality of the conventional city.

The informal city is characterised by great complexity, as Cristina Dreifuss tells us in her chapter 'Learning place attachment from the informal city'.

The aforementioned complexity unfolds through the informal behaviour, as an antidote to determinism, which offers many opportunities.

The informal phenomenon is global as it takes place in all five continents and is present in several urban contexts, according to the authors of the chapters: Lara Hernandez, Khemri & Melis (Mexico City, Mexico), Khemri & Melis (Algiers, Algeria), Lai & Careri (Rome, Italy), Aliaj (Tirana, Albania), Ijatuyi, Ayoola & Melis (Akure, Nigeria), Chokhachian, Santucci and Auer (Amman, Jordan), and Pojani (Western Balkans).

Particularly Aseem Inam offers, in the chapter titled 'Designing the "Off-Grid" City', a transcontinental exploration of the phenomenon, from an infrastructural perspective, discussing case studies from America (Bogota, Colombia; Guadalajara, Mexico; Sao Paolo, Brazil), Africa (Cairo, Egypt), and Asia (Kuala Lumpur, Malaysia; Surat, India).

A further watermark denominator of the chapters, which joins a vast literature of international scholars, is the awareness that the status quo is not an option and that a societal shift is needed to build a new ecological alliance between humankind and nature.

Before going into the topic of the informal as an opportunity, it is worth remembering what the existing conditions which drive change are, and how these conditions have a negative impact, as stated, on the most vulnerable people who mostly belong to the informal parts of the city.

In this sense, we could consider the current pandemic as a symptom of the global crisis, previously described, leading to the need for change.

According to Ilaria Capua, director of One Health Centre of Excellence of the University of Florida, the COVID-19 pandemic confirms the critical relationship between environmental issues and human settlements (Cozzolino, 2020). Others, such as Andrea Tilche (2020), go further by assuming a more immediate relationship between the pandemic and climate change.

The environmental causes of the spread of viruses and diseases have long been established, beyond the COVID-19 pandemic. Morin et al. (2013), for instance, have highlighted the implication of climate change in the transmission of dengue, due to tropicalisation of climate. Wang et al. (2010) consider the reduction of precipitation in North America to be a potential risk for a West Nile virus outbreak.

The spillover of viruses, due to urban pressure towards reservoir-animals, will be only one of the negative impacts on health of the environmental crisis on our society.

The World Health Organization states that the impact of climate change on clean air, safe drinking water, and nutritious food supply will cause, between 2030 and 2050, "approximately 250,000 additional deaths per year, from malnutrition, malaria, diarrhoea and heat stress alone. The direct damage costs to health are estimated to be USD 2–4 billion per year by 2030". This will have major effects on informal settlements since "areas with weak health infrastructure – mostly in developing countries – will be the least able to cope without assistance to prepare and respond" (World Health Organization, 2018; IPCC, 2014). The United Nations, in fact, defines slums as settlements with inadequate access to safe water, sanitation, and other infrastructure, subject to structurally poor housing quality, overcrowding, and insecure residential status (Warah, 2003).

Snyder et al. (2014) stated that "these conditions are the perfect breeding ground for EVD (Ebola virus disease). Previously reported outbreaks of EVD occurred in rural and geographically isolated communities. The presumed introduction of the virus to the slums of Kenema and Freetown in Sierra Leone has undoubtedly augmented its spread. Sierra Leone is urbanising at a rate of 3% each year, and in 2005 more than 97% of its urban population lived in slums".

All this does not concern exclusively the southern hemisphere and the slums, but the weakest fringes of western society as well. Diane Yentel, president of the National Low Income Housing Coalition in the USA, reiterated the condition of particular vulnerability of homeless people (Yentel, 2020).

Both in the Global South and in Western countries, the effects of the environmental crisis can be mitigated through a radical rethinking of the human settlement, as ca. 40% of CO_2 emissions depend on buildings and their one-dimensional conception (Melis & Medas, 2020).

The above hypothesis became a fact in 1999, thanks to Mann-Raymond-Hughes's chart, indelibly renamed Hockey Stick by Jerry Mahlman (Rood et al., 2014), which demonstrates both the existence of global warming and its anthropogenic origin (Mann et al., 1999; Mann et al., 1998).

From that moment on, confirmations of the hockey stick multiplied until the zeroing of climate denial in the scientific field. A chart was formed based on the belief, then it became certain that trees, were a climate seismograph of absolute precision, capable of providing evidence of the presence of El Niño in 1791 (Mann et al., 2000), and the absence of summer in 1816.

The hockey stick, whose foundations date back to Michael Mann's postdoctoral research, is epochal for both the data collected, and for the use of an innovative and transdisciplinary methodology, which includes botany, microbiology and geology, crucial for an ecological understanding of the built environment.

Through this interpretation, therefore, the hockey stick is, at least symbolically, a first form of alliance between humankind and nature, aimed at overcoming the crisis, as stated in the premises.

Thanks to Mann's collaboration with Raymond S. Bradley, also a climatologist, and Malcolm K. Hughes, a professor of dendrochronology, it was possible to extend the results in different areas of the globe and for periods, through the intersection of quantitative data compiled from tree rings, ice cores, corals and lake sediments (Mann et al., 1998; Mann et al., 1999).

The worst predictions of the hockey stick became reality in May 2013 with the crossing, even psychological, of 400 parts per million CO_2 concentration (Bala, 2013).

That same year, Hurricane Sandy had a major impact on public opinion: $19 billion in damage and 43 deaths alone in New York. In Battery Park, the seawater reached 4 metres above the usual level then. Soon after, we became aware that the anomalous event, within a few tens of years, would become customary (Folger, 2013).

During the same period the Byrd Station, in western Antarctica, recorded an increase in the average annual temperature of 2.4 degrees Celsius from 1958 to today, a speed three times higher than the globally expected average of 0.8 degrees Celsius (Greene, 2013).

More than 136 large cities and over 40 million coastal inhabitants are at risk due to rising sea levels. The costs of protecting cities already seem very high but necessary today.

As anticipated, it is worth asking in this context, given that the conventional city has had a primary role as one of the causes of climate change, if the ecologic features of informal behaviour cannot play a role in mitigating its effects today.

The new terms of the covenant remain to be understood, as do whether or not the abandonment of the Oedipal perspective (Morton, 2016) leads humanity towards the renunciation of the Promethean position that the sapiens have maintained since they became aware of it.

Put more simply, does the awareness that human's perverse competition with nature, due to a distorted perception of progress (Gould, 1996), also lead to an abandonment of an active or creative role of humanity, in overcoming the current climate crisis?

The answer to this question has pushed many scholars to date to swing between some of the best known ecological theories, based on the coincidence of these two conditions, and other positions which might include the possibility of a new Renaissance.

Degrowth, as a reinterpretation of anti-capitalist ideas as an ecological key, including those disseminated by the *The Limits to Growth* report (Colombo, 2001) and expressed in the Malthusian theories (Neurath, 2017), has found its most influential thinker in Serge Latouche today. The key to the interpretation of the resulting movement is that the reduction of consumption does not require individual sacrifices or a decrease in well-being. Rather, it involves "decreasing" aim to maximise happiness and well-being through non-consumer means: sharing work, consuming less, and devoting more time to art, music, family, nature, culture, and community.

In the field of architecture, degrowth often overlaps the studies on the informal city, especially in the Global South, or in a regional approach towards sustainability and resilience. The contributions in this book, like the one signed by Olufunto Ijatuyi, Hezekiah Adadayo Ayoola, and Melis belong to this cultural territory.

These texts are an updated documentation of informal behaviour as a way to enforce sustainability and understand an emerging embodiment of the informal as a territorial phenomenon.

Several scholars have already analysed informal behavioural patterns that represent the collateral human component of the informal as a tangible phenomenon. Therefore, these chapters raise questions about significant circumstances which, in a way, have always characterised the history of the urban settlement transformations.

Particularly, the text written by Hernandez, Khemri and Melis discusses the issue of informality as a spontaneous act that informs the appropriation of a given urban context even when it is formally defined. This type of acts, underestimated by scholars up to now, will have a greater impact in the next decades than the informality of urban suburbs. As a matter of fact, informal behaviour seems to determine the intimate relations between human behaviours and public spaces.

Furthermore, this chapter highlights the need to include, within the discussion of informality, contemporary phenomena that are related to it and to motivate a new set of informal transformations which perhaps should be understood globally.

The complexity of the informal hypothesis, is emphasised, in the following chapters, by Dreifuss, on the sense of attachment to the place, Aliaj, about a programmatic dimension in the discussion of informality through the proposal of operational protocols, and Lai-Careri who also explore the political implications of the informal as an option of colonising the city.

As said at the beginning of this introduction, the study of the informal phenomena, in opposition to the determinism of the formal city, also leads to a more organic, and consequently less anthropocentric, approach to urban planning.

The ecologic reading of the informal phenomena is a pivotal in times of climate emergency, and implies a remarkable philosophical effort such as that shown, for example, by the theorists of the Heidegger-inspired metaphysics of object-oriented ontology.

Morton's dark ecology, which can be considered its ecological variant, also rejects the centrality of man with respect to the existence of non-human objects, in opposition to Kantian anthropocentrism, according to which phenomenal objects conform to the subject's mind, and, in turn, become products of human cognition (Morton, 2011; Harman, 2018).

The existence of objects independent of human perception and the fact that relationships, including those between non-humans, distort related objects as much as human consciousness and therefore exist on an equal footing with each other, leads Morton to state that "Anthropocentrism is a bug not a feature" (Matthews, 2017).

Dark ecology is based on the idea that ecology is "dark", as claimed by Morton, because it requires a rethinking of our most intimate relationship even with "inanimate" objects, which excludes a condition of human privilege. Unlike the conventional and obsolete idea of nature, ecology, therefore, is not necessarily beautiful and useful. In the process of rethinking the relationships between nature, ecology, and man, philosophy and the arts, according to Morton, are crucial (Morton, 2016).

The dissociation between the Oedipal and the Promethean stance towards ecology, in turn, includes very different theories, such as the "positive development" (Birkeland, 2012), the plethora of technology positivism to the extremes of post-humanism, and, in my specific research field, radical resilience, that is, in the ecological reading of the biology of evolution (and its application in the future projection of habitat).

The latter position is particularly characterised by the transdisciplinarity of the approach, around a core of research that includes, among others, authors such as Stephen J. Gould (1996), Heather Pringle (2013), Elizabeth Pennisi (2007) and Telmo Pievani (2006).

However, while Morton's philosophical interpretations, which converge with Gould's stances regarding the criticism of Huxley's chessboard (Gould, 1996), are shared by many of the advocates of a radically ecological approach in architecture, little of the work of Gould, Pringle, and Francois Jacob (Pievani & Serrelli, 2011) has been translated into architecture, despite offering incredibly practical ideas.

In fact, the use of expressions such as "spandrel" and "exaptation" (Gould, 1991; Pievani & Serrelli, 2011) is relatively new in architecture. Nevertheless, the application of exaptation in architecture confirms that determinism has been fatal to ecology, whilst exaptation's redundancy, variability, and randomness could be a solution embedded in informality.

By analogy with the biology of evolution, as an alternative model to the determinism of modern design, exaptation is intended as a process of radical and visionary elaboration, as well as privileged manifestations of associative thinking. The link between the terms of evolution biology and architectural design is corroborated by the evolutionary model based on the concept of crisis, described by both Gould and Pringle, as alternatives to evolution based on a gradual progression.

The sixth dictum of the panda (Gould, 1991) as well as the dinosaur feathers are the perfect representation of the concept of "spandrel" (Pievani & Serrelli, 2011), usable in the informal design.

The redundancy of forms and relationships (also called "spandrel") allows nature to adapt to unpredictable environmental conditions. Therefore, the survival and balance of ecosystems, according to Gould, is due to exaptation, i.e., the redundancy of forms and relationships allows adaptation.

In agreement with geneticist Ewan Birney, the structure of genome is also redundant, as well as all the "creative" structures. Another creative structure is the human brain thanks to the number of neuronal connections, and its most creative manifestation – associative thinking – is in turn also a creative structure, because it produces non-linear thoughts without a necessarily predefined utility.

According to Pringle (2013), art is the product of associative thinking. Throughout human history, art has often proved to be an essential tool of speculation to overcome emergency conditions. In *Full House*, Gould (1996) also mentions of the evolution model based on crisis rather than gradual progression, which would explain why the redundancy of forms, even without apparent utility, is fundamental to overcome the crisis.

In conclusion, informality can be considered a non-organised way to colonise the biosphere, which in biologic terms could also correspond to a non-anthropocentric way to do this. This condition, however, does not imply renunciation of creativity because variability – including the proliferation of forms without a predefined use and of interconnections – is an expression of creativity through which associative thinking is activated, when linear logic, which is the standard modality of survival, and its specialised and one-dimensional expressions, in the urban realm, are unable to respond to extensive global emergencies.

References

Bala, G. (2013). Digesting 400 ppm for global mean CO^2 concentration. *Current science*, *104*(11), 1471–1472.

Birkeland, J. (2012). *Positive development: From vicious circles to virtuous cycles through built environment design*. Routledge.

Colombo, U. (2001). The Club of Rome and sustainable development. *Futures*, *33*(1), 7–11.

Cozzolino, A. (2020, March 17). Il WWF: «Con i cambiamenti climatici, i virus diventano più pericolosi». *Corriere della Sera*. Retrieved from https://www.corriere.it/pianeta2020/20_marzo_17/wwf-coi-cambiamenti-climatici-virus-diventano-piu-pericolosi-1c1a8fd0-66fd-11ea-a26c-9a66211caeee.shtml

Fletcher, J. (2007). The scenography of trauma: A 'Copernican' reading of Sophocles' Oedipus the King. *Textual Practice*, *21*(1), 17–41.

Folger, T. (2013, September). Rising seas. *National Geographic*. Retrieved from https://www.nationalgeographic.com/magazine/2013/09/rising-seas-coastal-impact-climate-change/

Gould, S. J. (1991). Exaptation: A crucial tool for an evolutionary psychology. *Journal of Social Issues*, *47*(3), 43–65.

Gould, S. J. (1996). *Full house: The spread of excellence from Plato to Darwin*. Cambridge, MA: Harvard University Press.

Greene, C. H. (2013, Feb 13). Gli inverni del nostro sconttento. *Le Scienze*, n. 534, p. 46.
Harman, G. (2018). *Object-oriented ontology: A new theory of everything*. UK: Penguin.
IPCC (2014). Summary for policymakers. *Climate Change 2014: Mitigation of Climate Change*. Retrieved from https://www.ipcc.ch/site/assets/uploads/2018/02/ipcc_wg3_ar5_summary-for-policymakers.pdf
Latouche, S. (2009). *Farewell to growth*. Cambridge, England: Paperback Polity Press.
Mann, M. E., Bradley, R. S., & Hughes, M. K. (1998). Global-scale temperature patterns and climate forcing over the past six centuries. *Nature*, *392*(6678), 779–787.
Mann, M. E., Bradley, R. S., & Hughes, M. K. (1999). Northern hemisphere temperatures during the past millennium: Inferences, uncertainties, and limitations. *Geophysical research letters*, *26*(6), 759–762.
Mann, M. E., Bradley, R. S., & Hughes, M. K. (2000). Long-term variability in the El Nino southern oscillation and associated teleconnections. *El Nino and the Southern Oscillation: Multiscale Variability and its Impacts on Natural Ecosystems and Society*, 357–412.
Matthews, J. (2017). Book review: Humankind: Solidarity with nonhuman people by Timothy Morton. *LSE Review of Books*. Retrieved from https://blogs.lse.ac.uk/lsereviewofbooks/2017/11/03/book-review-humankind-solidarity-with-nonhuman-people-by-timothy-morton/
Melis, A., & Medas, B. (2020). Tecnologie avanzate per la resilienza dell'architettura e della comunità. *Bioarchitettura: Appunti per una città sostenibile*. Lucca, IT: Nardini Editore.
Morin, C. W., Comrie, A. C., & Ernst, K. (2013). Climate and dengue transmission: evidence and implications. *Environmental health perspectives*, *121*(11-12), 1264–1272.
Morton, T. (2011). Here comes everything: The promise of object-oriented ontology. *Qui Parle: Critical Humanities and Social Sciences*, *19*(2), 163–190.
Morton, T. (2016). *Dark ecology: For a logic of future coexistence*. New York, NY: Columbia University Press.
Neurath, P. (2017). *From Malthus to the Club of Rome and back: Problems of limits to growth, population control and migrations*. Abingdon, UK: Taylor & Francis.
Pennisi, E. (2007). DNA study forces rethink of what it means to be a gene. *Science*, *316*(5831), 1556–1557.
Pievani, T. (2006). *Homo sapiens e altre catastrofi: Per una archeologia della globalizzazione (Vol. 25)*. Roma, IT: Meltemi.
Pievani, T., & Serrelli, E. (2011). Exaptation in human evolution: how to test adaptive vs exaptive evolutionary hypotheses. *Journal of Anthropological Sciences*, *89*, 9–23.
Pringle, H. (2013). The origins of creativity. *Scientific American*, *308*(3), 36–43.
Rood, R. B., Ramaswamy, V., & Bierbaum, R. M. (2014). Jerry Mahlman: 1940–2012. *Bulletin of the American Meteorological Society*, *95*(1), 167–170.
Snyder, R. E., Marlow, M. A., & Riley, L. W. (2014). Ebola in urban slums: The elephant in the room. *The Lancet Global Health*, *2*(12), e685.
Tilche, A. (2020, April 3). *Coronavirus e clima: il nostro futuro tra due "epidemie"*. Retrieved from https://www.lavoce.info/archives/65095/coronavirus-e-clima-il-nostro-futuro-tra-due-epidemie/
Warah, R. (2003, Feb 1). *The challenge of slums: Global report on human settlements 2003*. Retrieved from https://www.globalpolicy.org/component/content/article/211/44579.html
Wang, G., Minnis, R. B., Belant, J. L., & Wax, C. L. (2010). Dry weather induces outbreaks of human West Nile virus infections. *BMC Infectious Diseases*, *10*(1), 38.
World Health Organization (2018, Feb 1). *Climate change and health*. Retrieved from https://www.who.int/news-room/fact-sheets/detail/climate-change-and-health
Yentel, D. (2020, March 30). *The End of the Beginning*. Retrieved from https://nlihc.org/resource/end-beginning-diane-yentel-nlihc-president-and-ceo

Chapter 17

Informal microclimates

Study on self-built settlements and human comfort in Amman

Ata Chokhachian, Daniele Santucci and Thomas Auer

Introduction

Over decades there have been efforts and challenges in different parts of the world in different scales to build a dialogue between formal and informal. Every so often, where the informal and formal meet, there is a predictable clash of top-down and bottom-up strategies. However the "New Urban Agenda", proposed by "Habitat III," challenges this approach, aiming for synchronization between these two black and white categories (Ababsa, 2010; Clos, 2017). This approach needs a better understanding of urban morphology and social factors. McCartney & Krishnamurthy (2018) highlights that even though the self-built settlements often present low-quality living standards, low accessibility to public facilities, or higher exposure of vulnerability, there are also existing capacities in informal settlements to be maintained and learnt from. In general terms, informal urbanization is a form of city construction defined as a production of urbanization independent from formal frameworks and assistance (Habitat, 2016). These forms of the cities are home for informal economic activities, small businesses and settlements which have a collective populations of 1.5 billion people (Das & Munoz Unceta, 2018).

In this chapter we are approaching the phenomena of self-regulated settlements with the question of how and to what extent they can create pleasant microclimates and what can we learn from those informal morphologies and densities for the development of future urban environments.

Duarte (2009) argues that even though the field of urban morphology has given more emphasis on the study of the broader city, little has been done to understand the characteristic of urban forms in self-regulated settlements causing the study of slums and informal areas to be almost completely absent from the morphological literature. For centuries, urban density has been referenced as an indicator for city development: reducing urban density was the agenda for urban planners to restore the congested industrial cities and escape from the unhealthy crowded urban spaces. In contrast, nowadays higher density has been linked to positive environmental impacts, more efficient infrastructure, economic benefits, social welfares and walkable public areas. Nevertheless according to Boyko & Cooper (2011), policymakers, practitioners, scholars and citizens are often unclear on how lower or higher density can be better utilized to create and support the design of urban environments. Density is one of the key concepts in urban planning since it is strongly coupled with historical, contextual, geographical and political aspects of the cities (Pont & Haupt, 2007; Rapoport, 2016;

Williams, 2020). It has been already proved that there is a strong link between density and use of public and outdoor spaces in cities. Newman & Kenworthy (1999) have found that as dwelling unit density increases above a certain threshold, automobile usage and total distance travelled by car per household decrease in favor of use of public transit, walking and cycling. Jacobs (2011) famously argued that increased intensity of human activity and 24-hour use of public spaces can promote safer urban environments through "eyes on the street" and more economically dynamic retail environments. Churchman (1999) proposes that higher residential population densities can, if appropriately configured, create a "critical mass" for pedestrian access to parks, community facilities such as libraries and schools, and shopping.

As in urban studies, there has been a wide range of literature body addressing the challenges of rapid growing rate of the informal housing sector where the formal sector needs time to be developed and implemented accordingly. Heisel (2016) in his chapter, "From density to intensity," approaches the case of Addis Ababa measuring the intensity of the interface with the urban environment that people encounter most directly on a daily basis. "Everyday Urbanism," known as appropriation of public spaces, is one of the informal approaches to characterize qualities of city life in urban studies, referring to everyday life without the necessity of creating ideal environment (Ahearne, 2010; Certeau, 1984; Speaks, Crawford, Mehrotra, & Kelbaugh, 2005).

In the context of increasing temperatures and urban structure complexity, urban climate is more likely to be encountered "as an agency rather than an index. Climate has more often been defined as what it *does* rather than what it *is*. Climate is generating also increasing social pressure with different local effects from place to place. Downscaling is proposed as one relevant way of approaching the issue" (Rodger Fleming & Jankovic, 2011). Moreover, urban environments, in fact, generate sequences of microclimates that elicit thermal experiences in the pedestrian that are vastly more complex than they would be under steady-state microclimatic exposures. Because of their material diversity and complex morphology and density, urban areas are characterized by varied microclimates across very small spatial and temporal scales. Accordingly, the crucial task of research in outdoor thermal comfort, generated by microclimatic conditions, consists of understanding and describing the correspondence between the artificial materiality of the "microclimate as human artifact, even though it appears to be a natural, nonmaterial and physical phenomenon" (Roesler & Kobi, 2018).

Rodger Fleming and Jankovic (2011) argue that:

> The layer of air within two meters of the ground, the noosphere, that is the most important of all in Earth's atmosphere. It is located in what meteorologists have come to call the anthroposphere, nestled in the "boundary layer," a turbulent, well-mixed zone at the very base of the sublunar realm. This is a space in which the "natural" atmosphere gets entangled with human energy. This is the anthropocentric layer is the interdisciplinary sphere of human affairs, the most influential layer of our planet's atmosphere. This layer has not been fully or even adequately explored, which is unusual, since it is so accessible to us—as intimately close as our next breath. Indeed, it has been consciously excluded from environmental analysis.

Within the methodological framework of microclimate sensing, the Amman case is part of the series of so-called "Climatewalks" experiments designed and developed to capture 3 domains of microclimate, human physiology and subjective responds in urban spaces. The experiment is based on georeferenced data acquisition techniques (Chokhachian, Ka-Lun Lau, Perini, & Auer, 2018) to find correlations between human outdoor thermal comfort, subjective responses and urban morphology.

Case study: Amman, Jordan

Context

The Climatewalk experiment in the metropolitan region of Amman (Jordan), is used as a downscaled method for identifying the formal and informal forces in the definition of territory. Working in collaboration with GIZ (Deutsche Gesellschaft für Internationale Zusammenenarbeit), the Ministry of the Environment and the Greater Amman Municipality (GAM), the project addresses the topic of redeveloping disadvantaged areas in East Amman's settlements that could be defined as informal as they were developed in absence of any master planning tool, which are home to more than two million people.

Involving participants from the local government and residents in Climatewalks opens up a new dimension as a method to generate participation in design processes: stakeholders such as citizens and administrations take part in an inclusive and common experience that creates consciousness about conditions in public space, not only from a bottom-up perspective but also with a deep physical experience. Suffering and feeling extreme heat conditions along with physical engagement are part of the format. The Climatewalks produced data that gives evidence to phenomena that can be used to redirect planning and design strategies to the Greater Amman Municipality and the Ministry of Environment, in order to use the methods on a larger scale.

Amman growth in the 20th century

Amman is the capital and the most populous city of Jordan, hosting half of the country's population with more than 4 million inhabitants. In 1921, the municipality of Amman was founded over an area of 31 km^2 with a population of around 10,000 inhabitants, replacing Salt as the Capital city of the then-Emirate of Transjordan, which would become the Hashemite kingdom of Jordan in 1950. By 1946, the population of the newly established capital had reached 46,000.

Since the declaration of Amman as a capital city in 1928, the city has expanded up to the slopes of the surrounding hills and spread over the mountain tops. However, the growth during the first two decades was slow. This is largely due to the slow pace of national economic development during that period. It was also partly due to the topographic characteristics of the valley with its narrow floor area and steep sides. By 1945, Amman was still viewed as a medium-sized town with a population of 56,000 (Findlay, 1986).

The war of 1948 resulted in an influx of 100,000 Palestinian refugees into Jordan, which entered Amman into a rapid growth phase. In the decades following the war, Amman witnessed rapid growth of informal settlements around the refugee camps. Another wave of refugees occurred after 1967 and resulted in an additional influx of 300,000 Palestinian refugees to Jordan with 150,000 of them settling in Amman

(Ababsa, 2010; Aljafari, 2014). From then on, the pace of Amman's urban growth intensified and was made up of three main phenomena: natural population growth, rural to urban migration and waves of refugees fleeing from war zones in the region. Therefore, the expansion of Amman and the sometimes unplanned nature of its development should also be read in light of the regional context. Most of the new Amman dwellers settle in the Eastern and Central parts of the city that are already the oldest and most densely populated sections of the capital, leading to the overburden of an already insufficient infrastructure.

Urban planning milestones in Amman

Amman has not had much of an urban planning history, and more or less has grown in an unorganized manner. In fairness, it should be stated that over the past half a century Amman has had to deal with a number of sudden population influxes. Under these circumstances, it may be argued that no amount of planning can fully accommodate such sudden population surges. Still, no clear planning strategies have been developed for Amman to address future scenarios affecting crucial issues such as land use or transportation (al-Asad, 2006).

For the longest time, the relatively small size of Amman allowed it to escape the consequences of not having any urban planning strategies. As a result, reactive, crisis-management actions usually provided acceptable short-term solutions to problems such as traffic congestion and urban sprawl. However, as Amman's population exceeded the two-million mark, such short-term fixes would no longer do. Decision-makers clearly became aware of the seriousness of the urban challenges facing Amman, and expressed a very serious will at tackling them. The Greater Amman Municipality consequently embarked on a process aimed at developing a master-plan for the city. Such a plan needed to work concurrently on two levels, a short-term one that addresses immediate concerns and problems, as well as a long-term one that addresses issues relating to long-term sustainability.

The most recent documents governing the development planning of Amman are the master plan for 2025 developed in 2006 which led to 2008's Transport and Mobility Master Plan (TMMP), designed in cooperation with the city of Paris, the Parisian Workshop for City-Planning (APUR), and the French Agency for Development, and the Amman Metropolitan Growth Plan, completed in 2006. Although these planning efforts were made before the latest influx of population in the city and therefore catered for a slower urban growth, they are still the reference documents for the development of the city.

Climatic challenges

According to the Köppen classification, Amman has a hot desert climate with summer temperatures of around 35°C. During extreme heat periods, the temperature even rises up to 40°C and is accompanied by sudden and heavy rainfalls, causing serious damage to buildings and infrastructures. The city climate intensifies the inequalities between the various social groups, as high-income groups tend more and more to leave the city center because of the urban climate, while lower-income groups prefer to live as close as possible to the job opportunities (Roesler, 2017).

There is an obvious need to mitigate these climatic conditions by increasing the quality of the built environment, in particular the one of public outdoor spaces. The vast majority of the neighborhoods in East Amman are not regulated by any kind of powered air-conditioning devices, added before or after the completion of the buildings. The builders and residents still trust in traditional mechanisms for controlling a building's temperature and enhancing the comfort of its inhabitants. Particularly the less wealthy part of the population spends time in public space and uses it as an extension of their living habitat. In the Mediterranean region, for centuries social life has taken place mainly in public space. Transformation of traditional building methods and the increasingly anthropogenic city climate affect the dynamics of the residential microclimates. The housing system of East Amman with its occupancy rates and the city climate of Amman with new climatic extremes (both in temperature and precipitation) are challenging the conditions for people in urban space.

The Climatewalk experiment

These new challenges and the need for livable urban space need to be addressed using both a participatory approach and the available technologies. The Climatewalk experiment is designed to collect microclimatic data and information about human response—its implementation with citizens and members of the local community allows to generate new insights on the analyzed areas.

The Climatewalk experiment in Amman (Jordan) was designed to understand interdependencies of microclimate conditions within a varied range of daily activities integrating the topic of adaptation in outdoor spaces. Furthermore, involving members of the local administration and citizens allows a participatory approach that gains knowledge about their point of views and generates consciousness about the environmental conditions and how they affect the way people use public space (see Figure 17.1).

Figure 17.1 Climatewalks in Al Quds area, Amman with participation of locals.

Source: Author.

Figure 17.1 (Continued)

The experiments were conducted in Amman, Jordan on October 8th 2019 and consisted of a path located in the Al Quds area (31°56′11.1 N 35°55′22 E), that was walked twice each day, in the morning and in the afternoon. The morning experiment started approximately at 10 a.m. and ended at 1 p.m., the afternoon experiment started at 2 and ended at 4 p.m. The weather conditions were fair, air temperatures up to 35°C, and with clear sky conditions. The participants were exposed to varying outdoor conditions in a dense urban context, simulating a common life experiences. The area was chosen according to the pilot sites in East Amman where GIZ is implementing practical networks of green urban design within the "Improving Living Conditions in disadvantaged Areas in Amman via the implementation of green infrastructure (ILCA)" project.

On October 8th, we met the participants in the Al Hussein Cultural Center where they had a brief introduction to the experiment and were equipped with wireless skin temperature sensors. Meanwhile, participants were exposed to a one hour 20°C preconditioning period (65% RH) at the beginning of each experiment. Following this, the walk started. Every 10 minutes the subjects were asked to do a survey about thermal perception. The walk had a moderate speed and ended around 1 and a half hour later. The experiment was repeated after lunch. This was done in consideration of circadian rhythms in core temperature, as well as the influence of prevailing weather on expectations and adaptation.

The walks were done in the Al-Quds neighborhood starting from the Al Hussein Center. The path was chosen to simulate an everyday life experience and started from a conditioned space (Center) to outdoor exposed conditions. The path included stairs, pedestrian streets and inclined slopes. The experiment was conducted with a group of four healthy male and eight healthy female subjects who were tested individually. All subjects were photographed to document their clothing factor.

Perceived temperatures

The collected microclimate data including air temperature, relative humidity, wind speed and solar radiation are translated to Universal Thermal Climate Index (UTCI) as an indicator about how the temperatures "feels like" on each measurement point. The collected data is georeferenced with GPS signals and mapped through the path (Figure 17.2).

Morning

In the morning walk (from 11:01 to 12:06), UTCI values range from 29 to 46°C equivalent temperature (ET), which corresponds to a range from moderate heat stress up to extreme heat stress. In the narrower street canyons (the staircases), shaded areas with lower radiation (0–200 W/m^2) contribute to lower UTCI values. Also the air temperature has lower values (between 26 and 28°C). The wider streets such as Al Quds street and Ali Ben Abi Taleb Street show a higher range, while the highest peaks were recorded on the highest point of the walk.

Afternoon

In the afternoon walk (from 13:47 to 14:42), UTCI values range from 30 to 45°C ET, which corresponds to a range from moderate heat stress up to extreme heat stress,

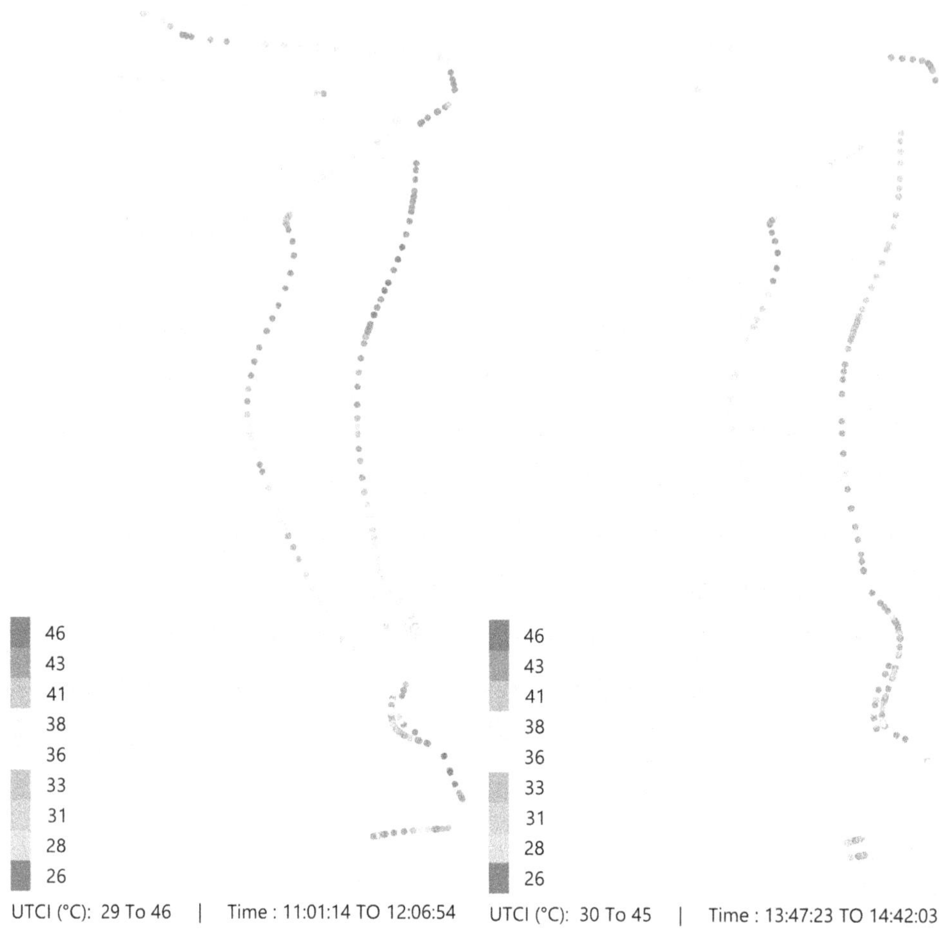

Figure 17.2 Measured UTCI values in Al-Quds neighborhood on October 8, 2019 (left: morning walk, right: afternoon walk).

similarly to the morning values. In the afternoon, also the wider canyons such as Al Quds street and Ali Ben Abi Taleb Street are shaded due to their orientation and provide similar comfort conditions as the narrow street canyons (the staircases), Also the air temperature has no significant changes than in the morning (between 26 and 28°C).

Comparing the data, we can recognize the significant contribution of the solar radiation which determines the most relevant differences between the morning and the afternoon: shaded areas provide 10 to 15°C lower UTCI values even with the same air temperature values.

Skin temperature

The second part of the Climatewalks experiment considers the human physiology and the way it reacts to compensate heat stress over a certain amount of walking activity.

For this reason, we used skin temperature sensors (iButtons) attached to hand and neck of the participants measuring continuously the variations.

Morning

The results (see Figure 17.3) show an already known phenomenon: the mean skin temperature (T_{skin}) of the female subject is higher than the male one. This is already known and has widely been demonstrated in literature, since the heat exchange in female subjects is higher. T_{skin} increases from 32.5°C steadily after the subjects enter the outdoor environment and follows the UTCI curve with a delay of around 1 min, which corresponds to the adaptation time. The highly variable microclimatic conditions given by the complex urban geometry generate a high fluctuation in UTCI.

Afternoon

In the afternoon, T_{skin} remains more stable even if UTCI shows strong variations. This phenomenon could be referred to the lower UTCI values, compared to the morning. The UTCI curve has the peak (45°C) at around 13:54 but decreases quickly to around 32°C within few minutes. The T_{skin} therefore remains more stable, still following the UTCI curve.

Subjective thermal sensation

The third pillar of the Climatewalks experiment evaluates the subjective responds of the people in terms of thermal acceptability and thermal preferences within the designed walking distances.

Morning

In terms of votes, subject express hot to very hot thermal sensation throughout the walk. Only in the beginning and at the end do the subjects express a sensation of neutrality, when reaching the conditioned indoor space. The strongest heat stress sensation is expressed at the top of the hill, after climbed two staircases within few minutes, reaching the fully sun exposed plaza. Also the thermal pleasure votes represent an uncomfortable condition. In general, the subject express a negative vote in terms of pleasure which can be related to the high thermal discomfort.

Afternoon

In the afternoon, the results show a different scenario: except point 6, which has the highest discomfort vote, the only other strong discomfort vote is given after the first staircase. Both votes, thermal pleasure and sensation, have correspondence in expressing the heat stress given by climbing the staircase under heat stress conditions. Here, besides the microclimatic conditions, the subjects are performing a fatiguing activity that adds heat transfer and therefore higher stress.

Results and discussions

The analyzed data of the Al Quds walk clearly shows that microclimatic conditions in the narrow staircases are better than in the wide exposed canyons. Narrow canyons

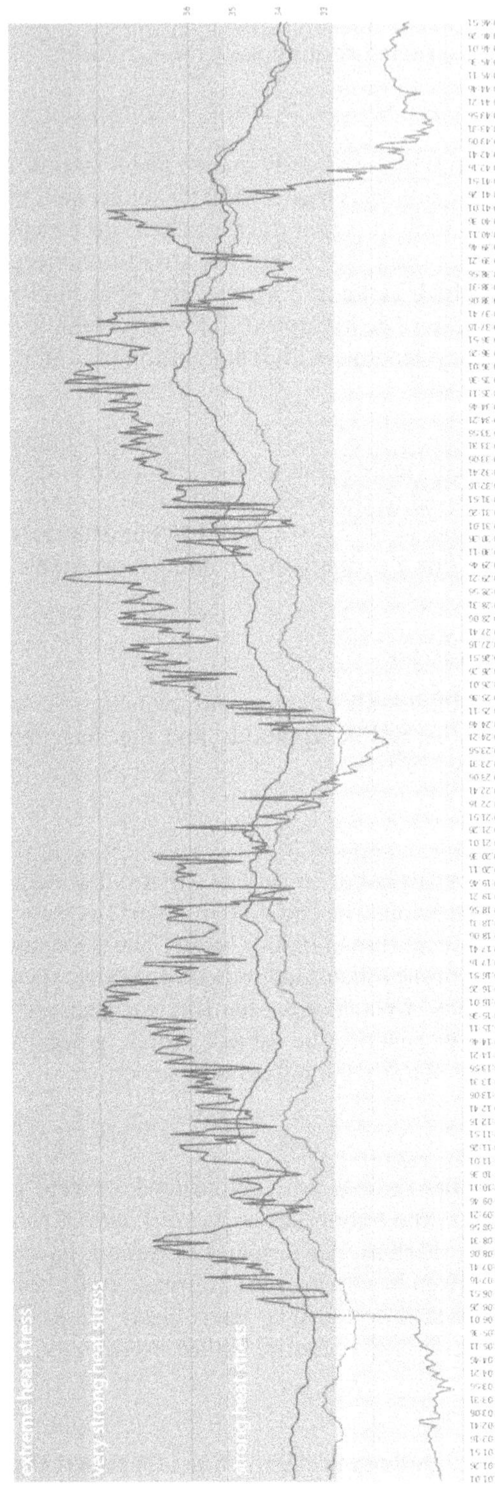

Figure 17.3 Correlation graph of UTCI and Mean Skin Temperatures of the morning walk.

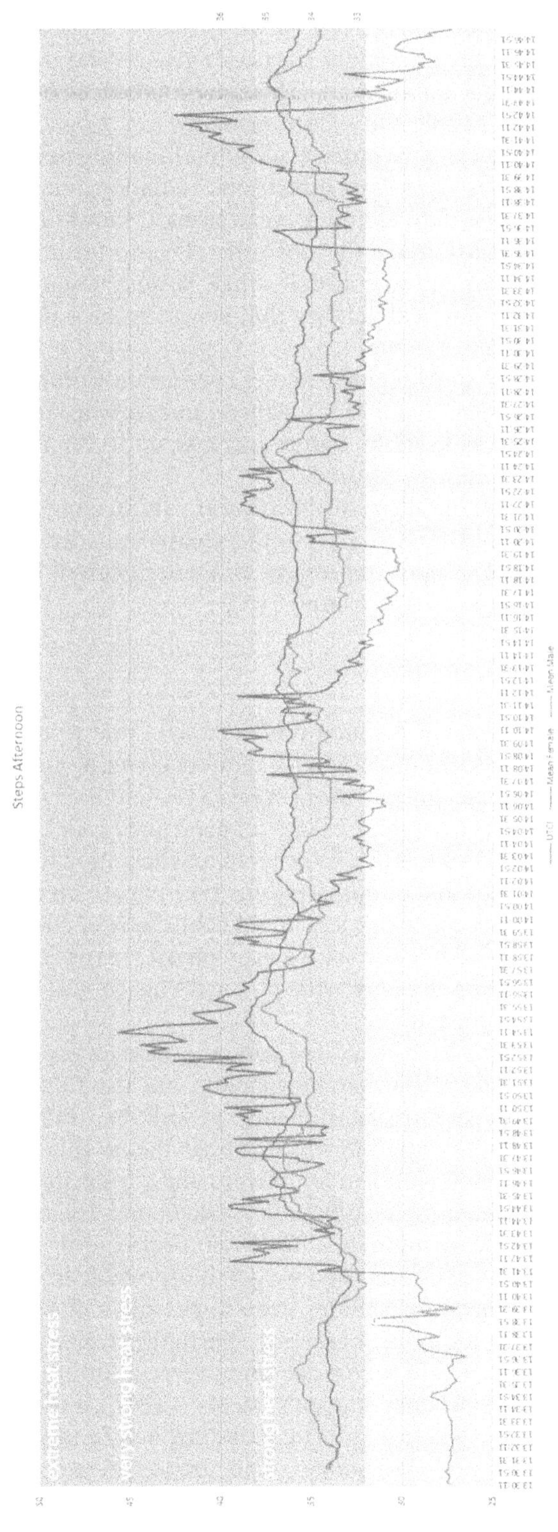

Figure 17.4 Correlation graph of UTCI and Mean Skin Temperatures of the afternoon walk.

have less direct solar radiation and provide shade by their morphological characteristics, however the results of the physiology measures give reverse indications in terms of comfort due to increased metabolic rate. This can be enhanced by providing proper sitting elements for elderly people and kids to recover.

On the other hand, wide canyons require additional shading devices, such as trees or canopies, to protect pedestrians from direct solar radiation, according to their orientation. We observed a lack of trees and in some cases, if they exist, they are located in places that don't constantly shade the sidewalks. Due to the articulated topography, narrow canyons correspond to staircases that, besides having lower UTCI values, require a more active physical activity that generates heat in the subjects, and therefore discomfort.

In the morning walk, the steps segment shows a variation within comfortable conditions (UTCI values between 28 and 36°C). Values increase when reaching the square on top of the hill. On the wide street, values increase up to the maximum value of 46°C, since the whole path is fully exposed.

In the afternoon walk, all the segments have lower values. Since the stairs are fully shaded, all values are around 33. Also part of the square is shaded and has lower values than in the morning. The most impressive difference is given by the wide street, that is shaded, and reaches values of around 33°C.

Conclusions

The Climatewalk experiments in Amman produced data that gives evidence to phenomena that can be used by administrations to redirect planning and design strategies on a larger scale with multiple impacts, working on a twofold level. During the experiment, involving participants from the local government and residents in Climatewalks opens up a new dimension as a method to generate participation in design processes: stakeholders such as citizens and administrations take part to an inclusive and common experience that creates consciousness about conditions in public space not only from a bottom up perspective but also with a deep physical experience. Suffering and feeling extreme heat conditions along with physical engagement (such as climbing steep steps) are part of the format.

In addition, Climatewalks have generated consciousness for the thermal and environmental qualities, related to the urban morphology but also to the contiguous conditions in urban space (waste burning, difficulty of walking, traffic safety, etc.) For locals, they also created additional knowledge about the neighborhood and set the basis for a common discussion platform for citizens and administrators.

After the experiment, mapping comfort allows detecting crucial points and heat and physical stress to intervene more specifically on the design strategies in a holistic design process. Scaling up the information we got, it is possible to summarize that:

The more compact urban tissue includes steep slopes and inclined street segments, or staircases, that generate additional heat stress due to the needed physical activity to walk through. Here microclimate becomes even more relevant because the topography and the absence of door-to-door transport means walking is required. Since these spaces are revealed to have better comfort conditions, it is fundamental to increase the dignity of the urban experience favouring walkability and increasing street safety, making them accessible for everyone without creating disenfranchisement.

Concluding, Climatewalks as micro-climatological surveys add to their human comfort experiment a new layer of cultural and social focal point. Microclimate ethnography centers precisely on these cultural and social implications by seeking insights into urban ethnography in order to enrich our knowledge of urban thermodynamics. By directing attention to cities, microclimate ethnography takes the growing significance of urbanization processes into account (Roesler, 2017). The task of these experiments is to build bridges between people and administrators facilitating an inclusive design approach to increase the quality of public space.

Acknowledgement

The authors would like to express their gratitude to the GIZ (Deutsche Gesellschaft für Internationale Zusammenarbeit) branch in Amman, Jordan, in particular to Katharina Manecke for coordinating the Climatewalks on site. Furthermore, they thank the representatives of the Ministry of the Environment and the Greater Amman Municipality (GAM), as well as all participants that took part in the Climatewalks, for their participation, their inputs and their strong empathy.

References

Ababsa, M. (2010). The evolution of upgrading policies in Amman.

Ahearne, J. (2010). Michel de Certeau, The practice of everyday life. *International Journal of Cultural Policy*, *16*(1), 2–3. doi:10.1080/10286630902971595.

al-Asad, M. (2006). The Urban Planning Moment. Retrieved from http://new.csbe.org/publications-and-resources/urban-crossroads/the-urban-planning-moment

Aljafari, M. (2014). *Emerging Public Spaces in the City of Amman, Jordan: An Analysis of Everyday Life Practices*. German Jordanian University.

Boyko, C. T., & Cooper, R. (2011). Clarifying and re-conceptualising density. *Progress in Planning*, *76*(1), 1–61. doi:https://doi.org/10.1016/j.progress.2011.07.001.

Certeau, M. d. (1984). *The practice of everyday life*. Berkeley. In: CA: University of California Press.

Chokhachian, A., Ka-Lun Lau, K., Perini, K., & Auer, T. (2018). Sensing transient outdoor comfort: A georeferenced method to monitor and map microclimate. *Journal of Building Engineering*, *20*, 94–104. doi:https://doi.org/10.1016/j.jobe.2018.07.003.

Churchman, A. (1999). Disentangling the concept of density. *Journal of planning literature*, *13*(4), 389–411.

Clos, J. (2017). Housing Policies: Affordable homes message by Dr. Joan Clos, UN-Habitat Executive Director. In.

Das, A., & Munoz Unceta, P. (2018). *Confronting Informality: Preserving communities and creating public goods in informal settlements*.

Duarte, P. B. (2009). Informal settlements: A neglected aspect of morphological analysis. *Urban Morphology*, *13*(2), 138.

Findlay, A. (1986). Amman: urbanization in a charity state. *Bulletin de la Société Languedocienne de Géographie*, *20*, 2–3.

Fleming, J. R., & Jankovic, V. (2011). Revisiting Klima. *Osiris*, *26*(1), 1–15.

Habitat, U. (2016). Urbanization and development: emerging futures. *World cities report*, *3*(4), 4–51.

Heisel, F. (2016). From density to intensity. In *Lessons of Informality: Architecture and Urban Planning for Emerging Territories-Concepts from Ethiopia* (pp. 157–165): Birkhäuser.

Jacobs, J. (2011). The uses of sidewalks: safety. *The City Reader*, 114–118.

McCartney, S., & Krishnamurthy, S. (2018). Neglected? Strengthening the Morphological Study of Informal Settlements. *SAGE Open*, *8*(1), 2158244018760375. doi:10.1177/2158244018760375.
Newman, P., & Kenworthy, J. (1999). *Sustainability and cities: overcoming automobile dependence*: Island press.
Pont, M. B., & Haupt, P. (2007). The relation between urban form and density. *Urban Morphology*, *11*(1), 62.
Rapoport, A. (2016). *Human aspects of urban form: towards a man—environment approach to urban form and design*: Elsevier.
Roesler, S. (2017). The Urban Microclimate as Artefact: Reassessing Climate and Culture Studies in Architecture and Anthropology. *Architectural Theory Review*, *21*(1), 73–88.
Roesler, S., & Kobi, M. (2018). Microclimates and the City, Towards an Architectural Theory of Thermal Diversity. In S. Roesler & M. Kobi (Eds.), *The Urban Microclimate as Artifact*. Basel: Birkhäuser.
Speaks, M., Crawford, M., Mehrotra, R., & Kelbaugh, D. (2005). *Everyday Urbanism*: University of Michigan, Taubman College of Architecture and Urban Planning.
Williams, K. (2000). Does intensifying cities make them more sustainable. *Achieving sustainable urban form*, 30–45.

Chapter 18

Urban form of informal settlements in the Western Balkans

Dorina Pojani

Introduction

This article discusses the urban form of informal settlements in the Western Balkans. Here this type of housing and built environment is widespread, sheltering hundreds of thousands of people (Tsenkova 2009). Despite the magnitude of the phenomenon, in-depth academic literature on the topic is limited for this region (see NALAS 2011; Tsenkova 2009; UN 2009; UN Habitat 2010). Elsewhere, the legal, political, anthropological, sociological, and economic frameworks of informality have been studied in depth (see Davis 2006 for a summary). However, informal settlements remain largely unstudied in terms of urban form, design, and image.

Recently, a theoretical framework has been set up for this purpose by Pojani (2019). It builds on early (and somewhat romantic) work on the vernacular architecture of informal settlements which focused primarily on visual appearances (Rapoport 1988; Rudofsky 1964), and later contributions, which added socio-economic layers to the discussion of the built artifact (Dovey and King 2012a; Kellet and Napier 1995). The framework is depicted in Table 18.1. It considers the *context* in which informality takes place; the *settlement* itself; the *houses* contained therein; the *dwellers* of those houses; and the *process* through which a settlement is originally formed and then transformed over time (see Pojani 2019 for a detailed discussion of the elements of the framework).

In this chapter, this framework is employed to analyze the urban form of informal settlements in the Western Balkans, with a focus on larger capital cities. Informal housing is now a permanent fixture of the urban landscape in this region. Given the widespread and increasing scale of informal settlements, it is important to record their spatial qualities and compare them to informal settlements elsewhere. Sustainable strategies to improve informal settlements depend on a better understanding of their urban space and residents. Finally, professional designers may be able to learn from this contemporary urban vernacular grammar (Kellet and Napier 1995; Pojani 2019).

This chapter is based on primary and secondary data, including (a) site and home visits in larger and more consolidated peri-urban informal settlements, which are representative of the Western Balkans context, (b) in-depth personal interviews with residents of informal settlements,[1] (c) photographs and plan sketches of residents' houses, and (d) official maps or aerial photos of informal settlements. The author's perspective is sympathetic to self-built form, and supportive of squatters, who seek to improve their lives in the face of adversity and with little assistance from the public largesse. However, this analysis is not an excursion into poverty tourism (see Roy and

Table 18.1 Theoretical framework.*

Context (social, economic, cultural, political, institutional – national and local)			
Settlement	*House*	*Dwellers*	*Process*
size and location layout and density land use public space image and identity	architecture and symbolism materials and technology	conditions of existence place attachment	origins consolidation gentrification redevelopment

* By Pojani (2019), based on Kellet and Napier (1995).

Alsayyad 2004). Glorifying informal settlements, despite good intentions, can harm local residents in various ways. Veering away from exoticism, nostalgia, or mere aesthetics, the author has sought to be realistic and nuanced in the following discussion.

Discussion

In accordance with the framework set forth earlier, the following discussion examines *context*; *settlements*; *houses*; *dwellers*; and *process*. Where information is available, the situation in Western Balkans settlements is compared to the broader international scene.

Context

In the Western Balkans, informal settlements have been a spatial manifestation of a painful transition from a socialist to a capitalist system, and an absence of respect for legal controls arising in response to decades of repressive socialist rule. Small informal settlements also existed during socialist rule, in what was Yugoslavia (Pojani 2018). But the fall of socialist dictatorships and their replacement by market economies set in place a combination of changes that spurred the growth of informal housing. Changes included: (a) the end of internal migration controls; (b) deindustrialization of areas outside capital cities and collapse of socialist production in rural areas, leading to mass migration, especially to capitals; (c) displacement caused by wars; (d) natural disasters and earthquakes that led to a movement of people to places of opportunity and/or safety; (e) poverty and a lack of low-cost housing and serviced land; (f) complex, lengthy, and costly bureaucratic procedures to build "legal" housing; (g) extra legitimacy conferred to illegal building because all social groups engaged in this activity; (h) egalitarian views in post-socialist societies which regarded housing as a right rather than a privilege (especially in the first decade of the transition); (i) hyper-inflation, which led people to invest in real estate in the absence of other viable investment alternatives (NALAS 2011; Tsenkova 2009; UN 2009; UN Habitat 2010; Pojani 2018).

In other parts of the world, informal settlements have been largely created by deprived and marginalized squatters from a poor underclass, in countries with longstanding and extreme class fissures (Davis 2006). In contrast, Western Balkans informal settlements were formed by households with more moderate means, in more egalitarian societies inherited from the socialist era. In all four case studies, the majority of squatters have built either on public land or on private land which they have purchased, sometimes informally (Pojani 2018). The informal nature of their houses is associated with the lack of formal masterplans and/or building permits rather than the character of their structures. Also, countless districts have expanded from permitted nuclei (Tsenkova 2009). Often "informal" homeowners hold building permits – though they have built much larger houses than the ones shown in the plans. As a consequence of this unique context, social and political responses to informal settlements have been far more favorable in the Balkans than elsewhere. Legalization processes are ongoing in all four settlements under study, although the process is slow, complex, costly for some (a few thousand dollars), and fraught with difficulties, inefficiencies, and uncertainties.

Settlement

Size and location

Generally in the Global South, informal settlers seek leftover, unsafe, unused, and unusable spaces (Dovey and King 2012a). Western Balkans settlements are often located in areas that are accessible from the inner cities either on foot or through a short bus ride. While the settlements may have originally formed in locations which were considered peripheral and marginal, they have come to occupy more strategic locations as a consequence of the rapid expansion of Western Balkans capitals from not very large nuclei at the outset.

A proximity to the inner city areas has been advantageous for squatters as they have been in a better position to access job, schooling, and other opportunities. Most settlements now constitute relatively large districts (by local standards), housing thousands of families. By the early 2000s, informal settlements had become a major public issue in the region. While alarmist, reports on the large scale of informality in reality helped squatters, in that they normalized and legitimized their actions.

In addition to *districts*, capital cities have seen the emergence of other types of informal settlements (as defined by Dovey and King 2012a) including: *waterfronts* (land prone due to flooding or exposure), e*asements* (railways, freeways, power lines, and sewer lines), *adherences* (informal additions or protrusions to formal public façades onto public space), *enclosures* (informal settlements contained within a formal building shell or institutional compound), and *backstages* (urban zones that become more informal the deeper one penetrates behind a relatively formal street frontage). While these types have smaller individual size, due to the fact that they crop up often in the urban fabric, in combination they give the impression that informality is pervasive.

Layout and density

Worldwide, many informal settlements are irregularly laid out – though still permeable at the local level. Their street layouts constitute a complex network of 'spatial decisions' informed by a set of social ideas and ideologies (Mills 1992). Other settlements have a clearly laid out internal structure, following a pure or modified gridiron pattern (Mukhija 2001). In the Western Balkans, layouts tend to be a cross between organic patterns and a modified grid (see Figure 18.1). This has been determined by

Figure 18.1 Morphology of selected settlements. Drawings courtesy Tigor Panjaitan.

topography (as many settlements are located on hilly terrain) but also by a particular culture and tradition of city building inherited from the Ottoman era (the region was part of the Ottoman Empire for nearly five centuries). Sidestepping formal planning controls, local residents have reverted back to traditional urban layout concepts – although building materials and architectural styles are contemporary.

Ottoman urban design traits included a close connection between city and nature and a loose articulation of the urban space. The building mass was organized into distinctive neighborhood units or small urban villages (*mahalla*). The density was relatively low and cities were lush with vegetation – a feature which blurred the urban-rural separation. The road systems were curvy, with many dead ends and no precise hierarchical transitions. No formal rules were in place to regulate urban form because Western-style government structures, such as charters and communes, did not exist in the Ottoman era. House construction rules were expected to respect accepted social behaviour, custom, ownership, and privacy (see Kostof 1993; Goodwin 1987; Mezini and Pojani 2014).

Many inherent Ottoman urban design traits, such as a lack of coordinated planning, low densities, open (unbuilt) spaces, organic street patterns, some clustering of houses, and respect for the privacy of others (by maintaining sufficient setbacks between buildings) are replicated in contemporary informal settlements. This has been advantageous in that it has made *a posteriori* service and infrastructure provision much easier than in very dense Brazilian favelas or Indian shanty towns (Mukhija 2001; Bernstein-Jacques 2002). Western Balkans layouts contrast to informal settlements elsewhere – especially poorer, centrally located, and more consolidated ones – which have much smaller lot sizes (Pugh 2000; Mukhija 2001).

Land use

As with layout and density, there are parallels between land-use distribution patterns in the Ottoman period and in contemporary informal settlements in the Western Balkans. In Ottoman cities, the residential fabric had primacy while public space was comparatively minimal. Representative public spaces in the Western sense were not present here; public life was on display in places associated with trade, such as bazaars, or with religious institutions. Virtually all houses were single-family (or housed families related by blood), reflecting a measure of individualism or tribalism (Kostof 1993; Goodwin 1987; Mezini and Pojani 2014).

These characteristics have reemerged in present day informal settlements. Like the rest of the Global South where the poor not only live in informal settlements but also earn their living therein through local activities (Muhkjiha 2001; Dovey and King 2012a), Western Balkans informal settlements tend to have mixed uses. Some buildings accommodate convenience stores, eateries, and microenterprises (such as repair shops and the like), and all settlements have access to a school (see Figure 18.2). Often, small religious buildings such as churches and mosques are present as well, whereas rental units are rare. However, many residents also commute to a job outside their settlement (they tend to work in manual labor or service sector jobs in the city). Modern zoning, with area-based uses sanctioned a priori, is, of course, absent. Similar to informal settlements worldwide (De la Hoz 2013), land uses are determined incrementally based on necessity. The ways in which unplanned storefronts appear in informal settlements have much to teach planners about the appropriate location of these commercial establishments – e.g., in places where there are strong flows of pedestrians (Tames 2004).

Public space

Typically, land is efficiently used for private development in all the informal settlements under study. While representative public spaces are not present anywhere, most

Figure 18.2 Convenience store in a tirana informal settlement (Kodra e Diellit), built as an extension of the owner's house.

Source: Dorina Pojani.

roads are wide enough for at least one car to pass, even in the hillier settlements. This is a measure of the squatters' status and contrasts to poorer informal settlements in many other parts of the world where homes are barely separated by narrow paths and sinuous alleys, with little to no room for cars (De la Hoz 2013).

As elsewhere, local landmarks consist of small stores or other functional elements rather than the squares, statues, and high-rises of the formal city. There are clear demarcations of defensible, private spaces. Although security is not a major concern in Western Balkans informal settlements (and cities more broadly) when compared to counterparts in Africa and Latin America (Kowaltowski 1998; Nguluma 2003), often burglar bars are provisioned around doors and windows on the ground floors, and fences or brick walls are also built around each lot. This situation – also a revival of the Ottoman tradition of privacy – differs to more convivial informal settlements in Latin America and South/Southeast Asia, in which the boundaries between public and private space (or even between homes) are more fluid (Hernandez-Garcia 2010; Tames 2004; Bernstein-Jacques 2002). However, in the Balkans too residents congregate and socialize outdoors, in streets and alleys, which tend to be pedestrian-friendly.

Image and identity

Often in the Global South, informal settlements are stigmatized as desolate improvisations by the undesirable (Peattie 1992). Meanwhile, some academic commentators have praised the image of informal settlements (including very poor ones) as picturesque, ingenious, porous, and full of vitality – qualities which the "formal" streamlined city does not possess (Hernandez and Lopez 2011; De la Hoz 2013). This positive imagery has helped foster place identity and legitimize squatting in some countries, especially in Latin America (Pearlman 1976; Turner 1968).

In the Western Balkans, most informal settlements have not been in poor-quality areas. Often they are perched above the respective cities on attractive hill sites that are almost within walking distance of the city center. Frequently, "informal" settlements are visually indistinguishable from "formal" settlements in the respective cities. As such, the discourse surrounding the construction of informal housing by low-income groups has been much more supportive and sympathetic. For example, in various ways and at various times, the press has questioned the state's legitimacy to govern and also de-legitimized controls on informal housing and the classes in power. Squatters have been characterized as citizens and while powerful elites (which have also engaged in informal construction) have been criticized and resented.

However, the public discourse towards squatters has also been exclusionary and criminalizing. As elsewhere, the "otherness" of squatters is informed by untested stereotypes and prejudices about their morals, abilities, and values (see Kellet and Napier 1995; De la Hoz 2013; Lombard 2014; Klaufus 2012; Pugh 2000). This explains why informality continues to carry a certain stigma in the Western Balkans, notwithstanding the fact that physical conditions and tenure have been upgraded most settlements.

House

Architecture and symbolism

As in vernacular settlements, squatters in a particular cultural and climatic context tend to rely on a shared architectural model which is varied from house to house based on an "ideal life" envisaged by users (Rapoport 1988; Kowaltowski 1998). Perhaps because informal settlement typologies mostly reflect "communal enterprise" rather than the work of individual architects, they have been resilient to the test of time (De la Hoz 2013; Rudofsky 1964).

The most distinguishing characteristic of informal settlements in the Western Balkans is their substantial dwelling size. Houses have at least two bedrooms in addition to a living room. Externally houses resemble single-family homes but in reality are often divided (horizontally or vertically) into apartments for extended family members – for example, a set of elderly parents and one or more married sons. Beyond meeting practical needs, squatters seek to assert themselves and achieve social recognition and self-esteem through the size and quality of their houses, as homeownership is central to the Balkan identity. (Avoiding rental tenure is crucial to residents.) Visually, squatter houses are hardly distinguishable from "formal" housing and are superior in quality and size when compared to the drab socialist multifamily housing stock occupied by a large portion of the population (Pojani 2018). In fact, some squatters have moved into their area to escape cramped inner-city apartments inherited from socialism.

"Informal" house layouts are rational and efficient (to minimize energy consumption and wasted space), have full functional separation, and include hygienic, indoor attendant services such as bathrooms and kitchens (although piped sewer systems are not always present and houses avail themselves of individual septic tanks). The main house layout typologies are shown in Figure 18.3. Often neighbors copy the house layout and décor from one another but also compete over house heights. This Western-style "keeping up with the neighbors" suggests that squatters have sufficient income or relatives abroad who send remittances. While large homes attenuate the stigma of poverty and informality, they also ignite resentment on part of the middle classes about squatters in urban peripheries.

In terms of style, some studies have found that squatter architecture often has a base in local heritage – either colonial or pre-colonial (Nguluma 2003; Kowaltowski 1998). In the Western Balkans, some dwellings bear testimony to the rural building traditions that squatters have imported from their villages of origin. And some traditional stylistic choices, such as red ceramic roof tiling and ornate railings, are present in Western Balkans informal settlements. This is mainly dictated by practicality, familiarity, and cost rather than a belief that the traditional is more beautiful or that heritage deserves preservation.

As elsewhere, the tastes of squatters cannot be separated from the tastes of the elite (Peattie 1992). Like the local elites, most Western Balkans squatters aspire to modernization in their architectural choices. This signifies their aspirations toward upward

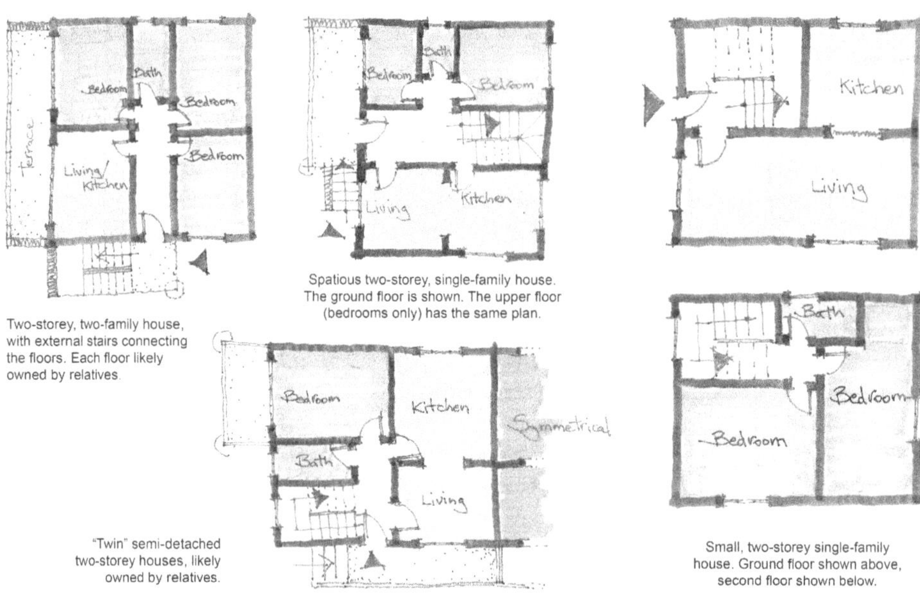

Figure 18.3 Main house types in Western Balkan informal settlements.

Source: Dorina Pojani.

Figure 18.4 Front yards decorated with golden statues in a Belgrade informal settlement.

Source: Dorina Pojani.

social mobility. For example, wooden window casings – once a defining element of Balkan traditional architecture – are replaced by the aluminum frames commonly employed in middle-class housing. Decorations, such as statues or appliqués which show others that one is achieving economic success, are often used (see Figure 18.4). While these may appear kitsch, they can also be interpreted as a showcase of strength and dignity. Furthermore, architectural modernity demonstrates long-term commitments and significant financial investments on part of squatters, and, as such it can be credited for the more supportive attitudes toward this social group which have prevailed in the Western Balkans.

However, where squatter families are truly poor, less effort than elsewhere (see Nguluma 2003; Klaufus 2012) is made to hide visible signs of poverty. Squatters prioritize the interiors of their homes over the public interface. It is common for lived-in houses to be fully functional and furnished inside but to have unfinished, bare façades which residents complete piecemeal as funding becomes available (see Figure 18.5). A lower concern for appearances is likely due to the more egalitarian context of the Balkans, where distances between social classes are not (yet) as large as in other developing contexts. Also, in the Balkan psyche, a clean and ordered interior of a home signifies "decency" and "civilization" (virtues which are typically associated with good moral standing, especially on part of women), whereas public space tends to be neglected (Pojani and Maci 2015). Public space neglect may be interpreted as another

Figure 18.5 Partly inhabited house in an informal settlement in Skopje (Pripor), with unfinished second floor and façade.

Source: Dorina Pojani.

measure of the Balkans' return to the individualism or tribalism of the Ottoman era, and of the region's rejection of the forced collectivism imposed by state socialism.

Materials and technology

As elsewhere (see Kellet and Napier 1995; Nguluma 2003; De la Hoz 2013; Lombard 2014), houses in Western Balkans informal settlements are usually built by a combination of self-help and paid labor. Many squatters are experienced builders themselves. Sometimes house plans are pre-determined on paper whereas in other cases construction proceeds based on a "typical" plan that the builder may have seen or implemented elsewhere. Collaboration in house construction requires financial and emotional investment and solidarity among nuclear and extended family members. Costs vary but can be as high as $50,000 for a completed, two-story house, and in many cases, householders obtain loans (from banks, friends, or relatives) to cover the expenses over time.

Construction materials are durable and industrially-produced. They range across steel, concrete, brick, and ceramic tile, which are purchased from commercial suppliers and transported to the building sites. Western Balkans squatters, just like the elites, admire pricey-looking and shiny materials, which signify progress, durability, health, financial means, and "good taste" (Peattie 1992; Dovey and King 2012b; Nguluma 2003; De la Hoz 2013; Elleh 2011). This is a major contrast with poorer informal settlements elsewhere, where lower cost, perishable, and natural materials are employed more often (e.g., bamboo sticks or scraps of recycled materials) (Dovey and King 2012a). In fact, amateur builders in the Balkans may be paying for more material than necessary by "overdoing" structural supports. On the other hand, in an earthquake prone region, a lack of professional engineering may place residents at risk.

A limited range of materials and heights bestows visual coherence and consistency to the settlements, at least in aerial views. At the ground level, however, every house and street is different. The monotony that prevailed in standardized socialist neighborhoods is avoided. Constrained by technology and limited means, most often builders adapt to topographical contours rather attempting to conquer those. But sometimes, the desire to appear modern trumps nature's imperatives. For example, in some cases, residents pave over their front yards rather than employing greenery for shading and cooling (as greenery is associated with the countryside and agricultural activities, which squatters have sought to escape). During the hot Balkan summers, these reflective surfaces need to be cooled with precious water.

Dwellers

Conditions of existence

This term (coined by Stea and Turan, cited in Kellet and Napier 1995) includes a squatter household's relations with various social groupings and the wider society, and that household's material conditions and access to resources. The conditions of existence of squatters in the Western Balkans may be "special" (see NALAS 2011; Tsenkova 2009; UN 2009; UN Habitat 2010; Pojani 2013). As noted, informal settlements in other parts of the world were largely created by deprived and marginalized squatters from an underclass, in countries with longstanding and extreme class fissures. Commonly the middle classes fear to enter informal settlements in Africa and Latin America. In contrast, Western Balkans squatters came from classes with significant resources, with a respected status during the socialist era. Unlike the extremely deprived and marginalized squatters of some countries in the Global South, many squatters here had access to financial resources either through remittances and savings or through the sales of housing inherited from the socialist era. While settlements do house some poor and marginalized populations, many residents belong to the working and even middle classes. Some rural occupations, such as micro-scale agriculture, continue to be practiced in some pockets, but most residents have urban occupations.

In most cases, squatting has been driven by younger, male family members who later have brought in their partners, siblings, and elderly parents. Traditional patriarchal family relationships persist in informal settlements, but a difference has been that younger couples are having fewer children (usually only two). Residents live modestly, on limited incomes, and limit their social activities in order to save money. Nonetheless, most claim that their living conditions have improved in the settlement compared to the past.

Place attachment

Place attachment processes are characterized by, and depend on, people's piecemeal, physical and emotional investment in their home and neighborhoods. As such, place attachment in informal settlements varies by the level of consolidation. In the Western Balkans, settlements have been taking shape over the course of nearly three decades. As such, a number of grassroots projects have taken place, such as road paving, purchase of electricity generators, or creation of rudimental sewer lines.

However, informal settlements are dynamic places, constantly growing and changing. Many residents are recent arrivals. While there is "neighborhood feeling," and some residents have family members living in the area, disputes with neighbors (e.g., over road access, building setbacks, or even blocked views) are commonplace. Some interviews hint that these aspects of life in informal settlements are a reflection of changing values towards individualism and materialism in Western Balkans societies more broadly. There is little political organization at the local level, except in moments of crisis – i.e., in a few instances when these communities have come under threat of demolition. Political allegiances reach outside the local settlement and, as it is generally the case in the Balkans, are based on personal and familial connections and patronage rather than ideology.

While many residents are quite attached to their settlement, many others are unhappy with a lack of planning and maintenance and aspire to move out if their finances permit it one day. Generally, informal settlement dwellers' expectations with regard to lifestyle match those of the middle classes. This situation contrasts to longer-standing informal settlements, such as Rio's favelas or Mexico City's barrios, which are characterized by collectivism. While this is part of the "authenticity" and placemaking of these spaces, it is necessitated by hardship, marginalization, and a need for security (Cummings 2013; De la Hoz 2013; Lombard 2014; Hernandez and Lopez 2011; Lastra and Pojani 2018). These issues are less present in Western Balkans informal settlements, due to less concern about security and a smaller social distance between squatters and the middle- and upper-classes than elsewhere.

Process

Origins

Informal settlements tend to emerge in conditions of instability, and remain subject to uncertainly and change for years afterwards (Kellet and Napier 1995). In the case of the Western Balkans, the post-socialist transition was a prolonged and painful period of political and economic instability, or deep crisis even, during which respect for legal planning controls evaporated. Undoubtedly, mutiny arose in response to decades of repressive socialist rule. However, informal settlement formation also owed to a traditional mentality – inherited from the Ottoman era, which preceded socialism – that a landowner ought to be able to use his/her land at will, as long as custom, ownership, and privacy were respected. Notions of any need for legal chain of title were beyond the squatters' purview (Pojani 2018). That this attitude perseveres is a testament to the importance of culture in enabling human behavior.

Generally, there are three primary modes through which informal settlements are established: (1) *settling* on unclaimed land; (2) *inserting* into uninhabited, abandoned, or leftover urban space; and (3) *attaching* to the structures of the formal city (Dovey and King 2012a). In the Western Balkans, the rapid changes in post-socialist period (noted earlier), triggered all forms of informal settlement formation, but especially the first. Due to tolerance but also inertia and fear of political frictions, demolition of informal housing rarely occurred in the Western Balkans. By the late 1990s, it became clear that mass demolition was no longer realistic. Once the fear of authorities evaporated, improvised shacks were converted into proper houses, some of which were built in a single weekend (see Pojani 2013). Now consolidated, most informal settlements constitute recognizable districts.

Consolidation

Globally, the dominant consolidation and growth process in informal settlements is incrementalism. This is conditioned by the slow accumulation of resources–scarce savings from salaries, remittances, or small businesses (Dovey and King 2012a), but also fear of government action. However, in the Global South accretion most often takes place on a room-by-room basis (Dovey and King 2012a; Nguluma 2003), whereas Western Balkans squatters tend build separate houses floor by floor – though room additions are sometimes built as well. (In capitals touched by war, many houses were renovated and expanded in the aftermath.)

Not infrequently, an upper floor may be completed before a ground floor. This occurs when the house will be inhabited by related families and the one which can finance construction first or has a more immediate housing need proceeds. Having secured the building shell, the other families wait until money becomes available or until they return from international migration. While in the Balkans such procedures are sometimes derided for their poor visual appearance, international academic commentators commend squatters' locally controlled, autonomous, and adaptive approaches. These can achieve a closer fit between dweller, dwelling, and settlement even as the needs and behavior patterns of the family change (Turner 1968; Bernstein-Jacques 2002; De la Hoz 2013; Dovey and King 2012b).

Gentrification

Based on the location logic of neo-classical economics, the poor are expected to live on poor land (Mukhija 2001). However, as a consequence of the rapid urban expansion of Western Balkans capitals, most informal settlements cannot be objectively considered as "peripheral" or "marginal." Now they have come to occupy more central locations. Better access, legalization reforms, and infrastructure upgrading programs are creating potential incentives for gentrification or redevelopment. Some settlements are already experiencing low- or mid-rise apartment construction. Thus the "formal" and "informal" cities are gradually merging.

This trend may eventually lead to loss of affordable housing, economic displacement, disintegration of communities, and cultural homogenization – as it has already happened elsewhere (see Cummings 2013). At the same time, Western Balkans squatters, being culturally attached to home and land, are very motivated to improve and expand their existing housing (for owner-occupancy or even rent) rather than move elsewhere. Also, sustained stereotyping of squatter areas by the middle classes, while negative in itself, can serve as a bulwark against gentrification and displacement. Moreover, many buyers consider the purchase of an informal house as undesirable given the legal complications associated with it (Pojani 2018).

Redevelopment

Proponents of the Modernist Movement promoted the forceful demolition of old, crowded, and dilapidated parts of the city and development of new, mass-produced housing (Mukhija 2001). Socialist governments in Eastern Europe and the Balkans adopted the same redevelopment paradigm. But rather than providing a solution to the housing problem, the ensuing urban renewal often aggravated the housing shortage. Since the '70s, urban renewal and slum clearance have become less prominent everywhere, as these processes have come to be considered contrary to the interests of low income groups (Mukhija 2001).

In the Balkans, as elsewhere, informal settlement policies are focused on in-situ infrastructural upgrading and legalization of land tenure. These approaches are sustained by the fact that the informal construction waves have decelerated, owing to an ongoing economic crisis (which reduces remittances), population aging trends, and a growing preference for international vs. internal migration (Pojani 2018).

Conclusions

The context of informal settlement formation in the Western Balkans may be unique given more egalitarian local societies inherited from the socialist era. Squatters do not constitute an underclass, and the visual, social, and cultural differences between the "formal" and the "informal" are not nearly as pronounced as elsewhere. By international standards, most informal settlements are easily accessible from the respective inner cities. They provide squatters with employment, in addition to housing opportunities. Conceptually, informal settlements replicate many traditional (Ottoman) urban design traits – although building materials and shapes are modern and seek to mimic middle class features. The most distinguishing characteristic of informal settlements is their substantial dwelling size, made of durable materials. Houses have been built in large increments, floor by floor, and often have expanded to accommodate extended families (in separate apartments).

As a consequence of the factors delineated above, social and political responses to informal settlements, and the image of the latter, have been far more favorable in the Western Balkans than elsewhere. While individual settlements are not very large, overall, the scale and permanent nature of informality has helped squatters legitimize their actions. Legalization and infrastructure upgrading processes are ongoing everywhere. While very positive, these reforms are also creating potential incentives for gentrification or redevelopment. As the "formal" cities infiltrate "informal" settlements, the two will fully merge and become virtually indistinguishable.

Note

1 In total, 200 interviews were conducted in Sarajevo (Buča Potok), Pristina (Kodra e Trimave), Skopje (Pripor), Belgrade (Kaluđerica), and Tirana (Kodra e Priftit) – 40 interviews in each. Snowball sampling was used, as it is practically difficult to collect a random sample in informal settlement settings. Interviews were structured and included 50 questions, as well as follow-ups as needed. All took place in person, in the native language of each country. Questions pertained to the house construction process, settlement formation and consolidation (legalization), and family history and lifestyle. The transcripts were later translated into English and analyzed deductively based on the template provided by the theoretical framework. They have been treated as qualitative rather than quantitative data; therefore, no tabulations are reported.

References

Bernstein-Jacques, P. 2002. *Esthétique des favelas*. Paris: L'Harmattan.

Cummings, J. 2013. Confronting the favela chic: Gentrification of informal settlements in Rio de Janeiro, Brazil. Master thesis, Harvard University, USA.

Davis, M. 2006. *Planet of slums*. New York: Verso.

De la Hoz, C. (2013) 'The favela typology: Architecture in the self-built city'. Bachelor thesis, Princeton University, USA.

Dovey, K., King, R. 2012a. Forms of informality: Morphology and visibility of informal settlements. *Built Environment* 37(1):11–29.

Dovey, K., King, R. 2012b. Informal urbanism and the taste for slums. *Tourism Geographies* 14(2):275–293.

Elleh, N. 2011. Perspectives on the architecture of Africa's underprivileged dwellers. *Social Dynamics* 37(1):43–77.

Goodwin, G. 1987. *A History of Ottoman Architecture*. London: Thames and Hudson.

Hernandez-Garcia, J. 2010. El parque de mi barrio: Production and consumption of open spaces in popular settlements in Bogota. Dissertation, University of Newcastle upon Tyne, UK.

Hernandez-Garcia, J., Lopez, C. (2011) 'Is there a role for informal settlements in branding cities?' Journal of Place Management and Development 4(1):93–109.

Kellet, P., Napier, M. 1995. Squatter architecture? A critical examination of vernacular theory and spontaneous settlement with reference to South America and South Africa. *Traditional Dwellings and Settlements Review* 6(2):7–24.

Klaufus, C. 2012. The symbolic dimension of mobility: Architecture and social status in Ecuadorian informal settlements. *International Journal of Urban and Regional Research* 36(4):689–705.

Kostof, S. 1993. *The city assembled*. Boston: Bulfinch Press.

Kowaltowski, D. 1998. Aesthetics of self-built houses: An analysis of a Brazilian setting. *Habitat International* 22(3):299–312.

Lastra, A., Pojani, D. 2018. 'Urban acupuncture' to alleviate stress in informal settlements in Mexico. *Journal of Urban Design* Doi: 10.1080/13574809.2018.1429902.

Lombard, M. 2014. Constructing ordinary places: Place-making in urban informal settlements in Mexico. *Progress in Planning* 94:1–53.

Mezini, L., Pojani, D. 2014. Defence, identity, and urban form: the extreme case of Gjirokastra. *Planning Perspectives* 30(3):397–428.

Mills, G. 1992. The spatial structure of ideology in informal settlements: A case study in Southern Africa. *Building and Environment* 27(1):13:21.

Mukhija, V. 2001. Upgrading housing settlements in developing countries: The impact of existing physical conditions. *Cities* 18(4):213–222.
Network of Associations of Local Authorities in South-East Europe (NALAS)). 2011. Challenges of regularization of informal settlements in Southeast Europe: Overview of the relevant urban planning and legalization laws and practice. Skopje: Report.
Nguluma, H. 2003. Housing themselves: Transformations, modernization and spatial qualities in informal settlements in Dar es Salaam, Tanzania. PhD thesis, Royal Institute of Technology, Sweden.
Peattie, L. 1992. Aesthetic politics: Shantytown or new vernacular? *Traditional Dwellings and Settlements Review* 111(11):22–32.
Perlman, J. (1976) The myth of marginality: Urban poverty and politics in Rio de Janeiro. Berkeley, CA: University of California Press.
Pojani, D. 2013. From squatter settlement to suburb: The transformation of Bathore, Albania. *Housing Studies* 28(6):805–821.
Pojani, D. 2018. Informal settlements in the Balkans: squatters' magic realism vs. planners' modernist fantasy vs. governments' tolerance and opportunism. In R. Rocco and J. van Ballegooijen, *The Routledge Handbook on Informal Urbanization*, Ch. 5. London: Routledge.
Pojani, D. 2019. "The self-built city: theorizing urban design of informal settlements." *Archnet-IJAR: International Journal of Architectural Research* doi.org/10.1108/ARCH-11-2018-0004.
Pojani, D., Maci, G. 2015. The detriments and benefits of the fall of planning: the evolution of public space in a Balkan post-socialist capital. *Journal of Urban Design* 20(2):251–272.
Pugh, C. 2000. Squatter settlements: Their sustainability, architectural contributions, and socio-economic roles. *Cities* 17(5):325–337.
Rapoport, A. 1988. Spontaneous settlements as vernacular design. In C.V. Patton (ed.), *Spontaneous Shelter: International Perspectives and Prospects*, pp. 51–77. Philadelphia, PA: Temple University Press.
Roy, A., Alsayyad, N. (eds.) 2004. *Urban informality*. New York: Lexington.
Rudofsky, B. 1964. *Architecture without architects*. London: Academy Editions.
Tames, E. 2004. Use, appropriation and personalization of space in Mexican housing projects and informal settlements. *Traditional Dwellings and Settlements Review* 15(2):33–48.
Tsenkova, S. 2009. The transition in housing and informal settlements. *Housing Policy Reforms in Post Socialist Europe, Lost in Transition*, pp. 187–208. Heidelberg: Physica-Verlag.
Turner, J. 1968. The squatter settlement: Architecture that works. *Architectural Design* 38:355–360.
UN Habitat. 2010. Informal urban development in Europe: Experiences from Albania and Greece. Tirana, Report.
United Nations. 2009. Self-made cities: In search of sustainable solutions for informal settlements in the United Nations Economic Commission for Europe region. Geneva, Report.

Chapter 19

Understanding temporary appropriation and the streetscape design

The case of Algiers, Auckland and Mexico City

J. Antonio Lara-Hernandez, M. Yazid Khemri and Alessandro Melis

Introduction

The present research seeks to explore the level of inclusiveness of the street by analysing the relationship between temporary appropriation (TA) understood as an indicator of social sustainability (Melis, Lara-Hernandez, & Thompson, 2020, chapter 2), and the design of the built-environment. TA is fast becoming a key indicator of the inclusiveness and liveliness of the urban landscape. Lara-Hernandez and Melis (2018) suggest that the way in which the built-environment is designed, and the manner in which people use it is culturally grounded and essential to the phenomenon of TA. Kent (1990) claims that culture (activities and uses) and the design of the built-environment are strongly related. Moudon (1991) supports this argument by claiming that the built-environment is a high-pitched display of cultural specificity in which each type of society generates a particular behaviour and it is reflected in the way people use the public spaces. Here the main challenge faced by many urban researchers is the diversity of places in terms of urban design and how environments are used by people. Not all cities have squares, green areas or high rises but they certainly share the street as a quintessential public arena. In this regard, it is now well established that "active facades" and mixed-use buildings play an important role in street's liveliness. However, the influence of streetscape design on TA is still unclear. The aim of the paper is to explore to what extent the design of the built-environment affects TA. This investigation takes the form of a cross-cultural case-study using an assemblage approach, analysing three different cities: Algiers, Auckland and Mexico City, resulting in the first study to explore the aforementioned relationship in three different cultural scenarios. In the following sections, it will be argued that the cultural dimension of the urban landscape plays a more decisive role on the emergence of TA rather than the design of the built-environment. This study sets out to assess the effect of the streetscape design on TA by using an assemblage thinking approach.

The first section of the chapter outlines the relationship between the built-environment and urban culture. The second section briefly explains the assemblage approach for analysing the urban landscape. The third section illustrates the case studies in terms of urban and cultural assemblages. The fourth section describes the methods, followed by the data analysis and results, followed by discussion and conclusion.

Built-environment and culture

The city is probably one of the most complex human products, a place where everything related to society occurs (Carmona, 2014; Madanipour, 1996; Mumford, 1938). It is the place where people interact, where society emerges, and evolves. (DeLanda, 2016) states that society is a sum or an aggregate of many rational agents or many phenomenological experiences shaped by daily routine, which implies, according to Rapoport (2005) that the city as an environment, consisting of two main components which are the fixed elements (built-environment) and non-fixed elements (people). Boaz (2017) implies that the built-environment is a social phenomenon deeply intertwined with communication and culture. These two components are in constant interaction producing and reproducing culture (Eliot, 1949). Bonfil Batalla (2004) supports this argument by arguing that culture from a wider perspective is formed by the group of values, symbols, skills, attitudes, meanings, social structure, communication methods and physical artefacts (including built-environment) that allow a determinate society a way of living.

The built-environment is a display of a high degree of cultural specificity strongly correlated to the uses and activities occurring in spaces (Moudon, 1991), thus a cultural product. Rapoport (2005) states that environments cannot generate behaviour, meaning that they are not deterministic. They either facilitate or inhibit behaviours, cognitive processes, moods, and so on. We agree with Rapoport (2005, 2008) when he claims that the environment could be seen as a form of non-verbal communication such as cues and meanings, because it has direct and indirect effect on people. For instance, the attributes and qualities of the built-environment could act on people's mood, activities and so on (see Toit *et al.*, 2007; Daigger *et al.*, 2015; Ellard, 2015). The cues and rules are part of culture because it dictates who does what, where, when, why, and including or excluding whom (Rapoport, 2005; Sibley, 1995). This is evident in the case that people prefer and select certain environments over others. Thus, if the cues are properly perceived and understood, and culturally appropriated, the social context can be judged correctly, and behaviour adjusted accordingly. This view is supported by several authors such as Graumann (1983; 1976), Pol Urrútia (2002), Vidal Moranta and Martinez (2005) who claim that people temporarily appropriate public spaces where they feel that they identify with the space or are somehow represented by it. The latter is one of the critical aspects of settings in which the cultural specificity is crucial for the organisation of environments by hosting a system of activities. A setting comprises a milieu, which defines a situation within which ongoing and predictable behaviour occurs (Rapoport, 2005). Its boundaries and regulations vary with culture, thus are culturally variable. It is a stage in which people play various roles, similarly to claims made by Choay (2001). Settings are not the same as spaces, for instance, a space could host many settings at one time, thus becoming a system (Rapoport, 2008). The emergence of a system of activities is strictly dependent on the conditions of a system of settings. In other words, activities that occur in some settings will not occur in another and vice versa (Rapoport, 2005).

As mentioned earlier, it is extremely difficult to make a comparison between built-environments of different cities because there are no equal urban scenarios, furthermore, they are not isolated elements of the urban realm. Rapoport (2005) suggests a useful conceptualisation to address this issue by suggesting that in order to do so, it is necessary to look at the systems of settings and systems of activities (such as TA) rather than the merely physical artifact (buildings, streets, boroughs, and so on). We agree with this conceptualization, but we suggest that the settings and the activities should be conceptualized as an assemblage rather than a system. An assemblage approach aims to connect categories or clusters of thoughts that are different. Unlike a "system" which implies hierarchy, assemblage thinking presumes an arrangement; it follows a pattern of entities interconnected without any apparent hierarchy. Marston et al. (2005) define it as a "flat ontology". In other words, it is the opposite to the reduction of the particular to the general, of smaller to larger scales (Dovey, Rao, & Pafka, 2018). Lara-Hernandez, Melis & Lehmann (2019) argue that the design of the urban environment could be understood as an assemblage product of other assemblages (such as visual complexity, building functions, and active façades) and could contribute to the emergence of TA (another assemblage). Their work suggests that we could compare different environments by analysing the design of the urban design and TA. The next section describes the assemblage thinking as a theoretical framework to analyse cross-culturally urban landscapes.

Assemblage thinking

DeLanda (2016) defines assemblage as a "multiplicity which is made up of many heterogeneous terms and which establishes liaisons, relations between them, across ages, sexes, and reigns – different natures" (2016, p. 1). Assemblage thinking is a practice of looking for relationships more than looking at things, seeking to understand how synergies and flows work. It has a "flat ontology" that opposes the reduction of the particular to the general, of smaller to larger scales (Dovey et al., 2018). Assemblage thinking provides an alternative for the logic of essence (Nail, 2017). An assemblage does not have essence because it does not have eternally necessary defining features, only contingent and singular features. The essence of a thing is what uniquely and necessarily defines it, which endures despite all its unessential aspects. On the other hand, assemblage thinking does not presume that the thing is the final product nor that this product is somehow independent of the network of social and historical process to which it is connected. Thus, there is no a final product, because we don't know what the wave will become or what relationships will be into. We solely know its collections of contingent features at a specific point in its incomplete process. However, it is not the aim of this paper to deeply discuss assemblage thinking, which has been widely studied elsewhere (DeLanda, 2016; Deleuze & Parnet, 1977; Dovey & Ristic, 2017; Marston et al., 2005; Nail, 2017). Rather, it is to use the assemblage approach to analyse urban phenomena in different contexts through a cross-cultural study. The benefit of this approach is that it focuses in the relations between the elements rather than the elements itself.

In terms of architecture and space, Gehmann (2009) supports previous arguments by suggesting that we cannot perceive space as a totality rather as the relations of the totality. The latter implies that, space is perceived as a constant or as a parameter as DeLanda (2006) describes. All assemblages populate the same ontological plane, and this is what differentiate assemblage theory from other realist philosophies in which they have strong ontological distinctions between levels of existence, such as genus, species, and organism. In this sense, TA emerges as an assemblage from the physical environment, the cultural context and the legal framework/regulations over the use of public space that allow it (Lara-Hernandez et al., 2019). TA could be defined in terms of Garcia Canclini (2005) as an assemblage process of hybridisation of other assemblages, first the architecture and urban design (built-environment) which is a formalise practice, and secondly the informal practices of people that use the public space. Garcia Canclini (2005) argues that hybridization is not a synonym of fusion. *Mestizaje*, syncretism and fusion are terms commonly used too but they differ from hybridization. Garcia Canclini defines hybridization as "the socio-cultural processes in which discrete structures or practices, previously existing in separate form, are combined to generate new structures, objects, and practices" that occupy space (2005, p. XXV). Thus, we can infer that an assemblage combined with another assemblage results in a completely new assemblage. This occupied space is certainly a constraint for some of their human components while at the same time they help to conform their cultural identity within the urban landscape.

An assemblage approach requires the use of jargon and neologism, in this regard it has been largely criticised. However, we agree with Dovey et al. (2018) when he states that learning new ways of thinking usually requires learning new languages. Such as a new language to describe the social realm spatialised in the urban landscape, this language is present in the city, but it is important to learn how to see it and read it.

Informal use of the public space

The way in which people use the public space varies across places and cultures. Humans have an intrinsic need to experience their social and physical environment kinesthetically through direct encounters with places that are associated with cues trough five senses (Hall, 1966). These encounters occur in what Choay (2001) calls "space of contact" in which the social actions either individual or collective activities unfold, thus shaping urbanity. Purcell (2002) argues that these activities allow citizens to contribute to the production of urban space rather than just to use the already produced urban space. These activities are what give citizens the right to fully use and manage their everyday life within the urban environment (Lefebvre, 1992). Moreover, the public space is where the power and resistance are spatialised in the city (Law, 2002), they support private activities and public relationships. The public space plays a key role towards the edifice of the social realm (Carmona, 2010; Efroymson, Than Ha, & Thu Ha, 2009; Gehl, 2011; Huffschmid, 2015; Jacobs, 1961; Mehta, 2018; Varna, 2014). Nonetheless, discussing the relevance of public spaces for the construction of the social urban landscape is beyond the scope of this study; neither debating around the categorisation of formal and informal activities which also has been discussed elsewhere (Bayat, 1997; Canclini, 2018; Dovey, 2012; Roy & AlSayyad, 2004; Sarmiento & Tilly, 2018). Rather, it is to briefly illustrate how the literature has portrayed the occurrence of informal activities as a feature of non-western countries.

It is commonly assumed that the informal use of the public space occurs predominantly in non-western countries. In an extensive review of the existing literature about informality, Marx & Kelling (2018) argue that essentially the use of the concept has been pushed forward as a way to understand non-western cities. For instance, bowling shoes in the street could be considered "formal" in Mexico City, while seen as informal in Oslo. Recently, Lara-Hernandez, Melis and Coulter (2020) argue that such informal uses of public spaces are an emergence of TA strongly influenced by the cultural landscape. This view is supported by (McAuslan, 2006), who claims that allowed and/or forbidden activities in public spaces are strongly dictated by state law, religious law, indigenous law, customary laws and local conventions. Moreover, such informal use seems not to be completely exclusive to non-western countries (see Lara-Hernandez, Melis & Coulter, 2020). Furthermore, (Lara-Hernandez & Melis, 2018) argue that TA could be used as an indicator of social sustainability of the urban landscape.

Let us now consider the design of public spaces and the activities hosted, such as TA. Urban designers have tried to compare urban landscapes in terms of design and how they are use between different countries. However, Rapoport (2005) argues that a mere comparison between built-environments is unable to grasp the complexity of the urban landscape. The urban landscape has other dimensions that influence how urban spaces are used such as social (Hillier, 1996), political (McQuire, 2006; Mouffe, 2000; Purcell, 2002), cultural (Heinemann, 2002; Low, 1999; Rishbeth, 2001) and environmental (Chan & Lee, 2009; Jackson & Kochtitzky, 2010; Plas & Lewis, 1996). Rapoport (2005) suggests that a comparison between urban landscapes must analyse the design of the built-environment and how it is associated with activities in a specific context. Thus, we could compare different urban landscapes by assessing the design of the built-environment and the activities hosted in the urban landscape.

A tale of three cities

Considering the cultural implications previously highlighted, the selection of the cities is pivotal to better understand how TA could be explained as an assemblage of assemblages within the built-environment. According to DeLanda (2016) some cities could be catalogued as a highly coded city, meaning that they have a unique regional culture and a well-defined identity. Global cities (e.g., London, New York or Tokyo) have a multiplicity of geographies (Fyfe & Kenny, 2005), which means that there is high dynamism between the cultural, social, and physical landscapes (Lima, 2001). The overlapping dynamism between social, cultural, and physical landscapes defines a specific place (Hubbard, Kitchin, Bartley, & Fuller, 2002). Brenner (2005) supports this argument by claiming that there is a "vertical" differentiation in which social relations are embedded within the hierarchical scaffolding of nested territorial units stretching from the global, the supra-national, and the national downwards to the region, the metropolitan, the urban, the local, and the body. Consequently, we have selected three cities with different histories and cultural backgrounds as examples of highly coded cities, which are convenient for illustrating one of the arguments presented in this paper.

The methodological approach used here is an instrumental multi-case study (Groat & Wang, 2013). This research is a theoretical replication of a case study by Lara-Hernandez, Melis & Lehmann (2018) previously carried out in Mexico City in which the streetscape design and TA of the urban landscape at the scale of the public space were analysed. The benefit of this approach is that it allows us to analyse the cross-cultural landscape looking at the physical and social environment (Rapoport, 2005). The study selected three cities Algiers, Auckland and Mexico City; the following table illustrates the criteria for selection in terms of similarities and differences:

Table 19.1 Selection criteria.

Characteristics	*Algiers*	*Auckland*	*Mexico City*
Economic capital	·	·	·
Former colony	·	·	·
Unique identity	·	·	·
Mixed use City Centre or CBD	·	·	·
Date of the city foundation	1200 BC	1840	1325
Population (City Centre, CBD)	68,364	22,804	61,229
Area in km^2 (City Centre, CBD)	1.21	4.33	9.10

In the following section a brief background of the three cities will be explained, in order to help understand the context of TA in each city.

Algiers City Centre

Algiers is the political and economic capital of Algeria; it hosts the Algerian central government, and important political, social, economic, and financial institutions (People's Democratic Republic of Algeria, 2015). Algeria is a country located in North Africa that has experienced numerous invasions and colonisations through history which had shaped its culture and built-environment (Saoudi & Belakehal, 2018). The city of Algiers was founded by the Phoenicians in 1200BC, and in the year 944, the Berber Muslim Bologhine ibn Ziri erected the modern city of el-Djezair, which then grew under the prominence of the Ottoman Empire from 1516 until the 17th century, in which the city centre of Algiers was the Casbah (the Ottoman Medina). When the French arrived in 1830, they introduced an urban renewal plan to modernise the city and change its status from an Arab/Muslim city into a European city through new buildings and urban planning approaches that consisted of large boulevards, regular streets, European apartment buildings, public spaces and plazas (Grabar, 2013). Following the independence in 1962, the Algerian population repossessed Algiers, but adapted the new built-environment to their socio-cultural life. Algiers City Centre (ACC), with an area of 1.21 km^2 (see People's Democratic Republic of Algeria, 2015) and a population of more than 68364 inhabitants, is a product of a mix of cultural heritages, which is evident in the building typologies. Today, the government of Algiers is keen to preserve the prestigious built heritage that charts the history and identity of Algeria by launching a strategic plan that aims towards the rehabilitation of the historic city centre, renewal of urban spaces, the improvement of the quality of the built-environment, and the quality of urban life (Amrouche, 2012).

Auckland's CBD

Auckland's CBD[1] (New Zealand) is one of the most extensive historical areas of the city, with a total area of 4.33 km^2 (Government of New Zealand, 2013) and a population of 22,804 inhabitants (Government of New Zealand, 2018). The CBD was the first land bought from Ngāti Whātua by the Crown in 1840. It covers 433 hectares in a triangular area bounded by the Waitematā Harbour and the inner suburbs of

Ponsonby, Newton and Parnell. The buildings with heritage value in Auckland's CBD were almost entirely created after the 1840s by European immigrants, and the street layout of Auckland's CBD would have been influenced by the regulations and models that were laid out by the Colonial Secretary's Office (1829) in Australia (Siksna, 2006, p. 90). However, the current plot pattern is the result of a combination of the amalgamation, subdivision and truncation of plots (Gu, 2010).

During the 1990s, education became the CBD's biggest export earner. The University of Auckland and Auckland University of Technology, as well as new English language schools, catered for large numbers of Asian students (Government of New Zealand, 2018). The inner city was revitalised by these incomers, and others drawn to apartment life in the city. Moreover, Auckland's CBD is one of the best examples of a multicultural area within the city (Dürr, 2011; Pearson & Kothari, 2007) and this defines its particular identity. Queen Street is one of the main streets within the CBD and it has remained the gathering point for festive parades and protest marches. Since 2006 public concern over shoddy commercial developments and the government's advocacy of a massive, port-side stadium has led to a review of the design of the CBD.

Mexico City Centre

Mexico City Centre (MCC) is the biggest colonial historic centre in America, with a total area of 9.1 km^2 and a population of 61,229 (INEGI, 2018). It was built on top of the ruins of Tenochtitlan, the capital city of the Aztec empire. It has five Aztec temples, the biggest cathedral in America and fine public buildings such the Palacio de Bellas Artes. In 1987 UNESCO declared it a world heritage site. Regarding the organization and logistics, Mexico is a centralised country; government, religious, and civil institution headquarters are located in the historic centre. The city centre is a symbol of national identity; it is the place for political, and cultural expressions of society in Mexico. Furthermore, the government has set an agenda of specific medium and long-term strategic guidelines for the preservation and sustainability of the site (Gobierno de la Ciudad de Mexico, 2016). Since 2008, various urban design interventions in public spaces have occurred, such as the transformation of the spatial configuration of streets and squares (Pantoja, 2010). The main purpose of those interventions was the improvement of the quality of the built-environment, and therefore the increase in the quality of urban life, such as the sense of community, inclusion, pluralistic function, and public space democracy (Autoridad del Centro Historico, 2011). Some areas of MCC have already been transformed, some are currently in process, and others will be developed in the near future. Thus, the city centre is still undergoing an urban design transformation process.

In terms of planning, MCC has the Spanish grid commonly used in Latin American colonies, starting from the main square, the church, and the council building. The centre was divided into boroughs to allocate the population according to their social status (Stanislawski, 1947). It could be described in terms of Fyfe & Kenny (2005) as an area of the city with a multiplicity of geographies (economic, social, and physical) overlapping and interacting with a strong correlation between them (Lima, 2001). Advocates of assemblages thinking such as Lara-Hernandez, Melis & Lehmann (2019) support this argument by claiming that Mexico City is a highly coded city, meaning that it has a unique regional culture and a well-defined identity.

Methodology

The present study analyses the streetscape as a design element of the built-environment (streetscape design) conceptualised as an assemblage of settings and TA as an emergence assemblage of activities (Lara-Hernandez et al., 2019). The streetscape design was evaluated through two main indicators; visual complexity and softness. These indicators help to isolate the individual components that as a whole either add to or subtract from street vitality (Porta & Renne, 2005). The benefit of this approach is that it allows us to quantitatively assess this connection. It draws upon the framework of the instrumental multi-case study approach (Groat & Wang, 2013).

The analysis of TA and the streetscape design were carried out on site, selecting Colonel Lotfi Av. in ACC (320 m long), Queen St. in Auckland's CBD (800 m) and Moneda St. in MCC (780 m), indicated in blue in Figure 19.1. In total, 77 photographs were taken across the three streets: 12 in Colonel Lotfi Av. (Algiers), 33 in Queen St. (Auckland) and 32 in Moneda St. (Mexico City). Streetscape design analysis in conjunction with a TA observation mapping is one of the more practical ways to assess both the assemblage setting and the assemblage activities. The following paragraphs describe in detail the methods used in the research.

Temporary appropriation analysis

The forms of TA that shape the urban realm in each local context were researched. In order to analyse TA this study uses a technique also known as "activity mapping" that has been developed to analyse the ground floor in relation to street uses and physical elements (Francis, 1984; Lara-Hernandez et al., 2019; Mahdzar, 2008). This technique is used to understand the "temporal city", stressing the process of interactions between people and the physical environment. The period of observation was

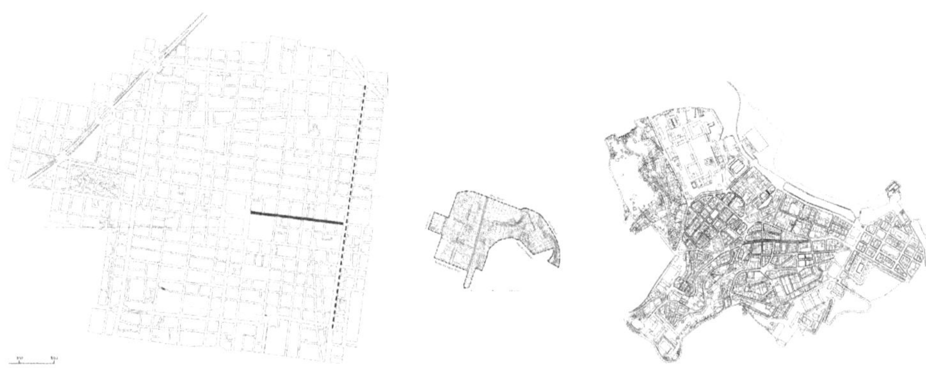

Figure 19.1 Moneda St. in MCC (left), Queen St. in Auckland CBD (Centre) and Colonel Lofti in Algiers City Centre (right).

Source: Author.

from 7th to 27th May 2018 in MCC, 4th to 30th June 2018 in Auckland's CBD, and 4th to 12th September 2018 for ACC. The observations took place on both weekdays and at the weekend, as well as at three different times during the day and for periods of one hour each. The activities were mapped as an expression of TA, illustrating the street section in which TA emerges. The observation was carried out as shown in Table 19.2, grouping activities into three main categories. First, TA activities related to work/trade such as selling products, selling/preparing food, advertising, promoting services, street vendors' guards, police officers, and prostitution. Second, TA related to leisure such as skate boarding, football, playing cards, playing music, dancing, singing, painting, acrobatics, playing with pets, watering plants, reciting, eating, resting, photo shooting and reading/studying. Lastly, TA related to sacralisation such as praying, processions, lighting candles and putting flowers. TA diversity is calculated

Table 19.2 Observation analysis.

Days of observation	*Time of observation*	*Observation technique*	*Diversity analysis*
Monday and Sunday, or Tuesday and Saturday.	1 7:00–9:00 h. The first period of observation is selected according to "rush hour" in MCC. Offices, shops and schools usually start their operation at this time of the day.	Three-round observations of two-hour periods were carried out each day. Each two-hour period consisted of 2 rounds of 15 minutes walking (to and from totalling 30 minutes in each hour); i.e., 4 rounds per 2-hour slot. These rounds of observations were conducted in 6 snapshots in two 20 minutes walking snap-shots, per hour, per area in a day of observation.	The diversity of TA is calculated using the Shannon-Weiner diversity index, which the formula comes as follows: H' = – ∑ piln in which pi = 1 /log S (S = total number of elements). Thus, the higher the value of diversity index, the higher level of TA. After calculating the diversity value of each street, the results can be compared and show which of the analysed streets have the higher diversity value of TA.
	2 From 13:00–15.00 h: The second period will be lunch time. Many people use this time to take a break, to go out, and have lunch, therefore the chances of observing a diversity of activities in public spaces are higher.		
	3 From 6.00–8.00 pm: The third period is when the majority of people finish their daily working routines. From 16:00–17:00 in the case of Algiers.		

Source: Lara-Hernandez, Melis & Lehmann, 2019.

using the Shannon-Weiner diversity index (SW), which the formula comes as follows: H' = – ∑ piln in which pi = 1/log S (S = total number of elements). Meaning that the higher the value of diversity index, the higher level of TA diversity. After calculating the diversity value of each street, the results can be compared and show which of the analysed streets have the higher TA diversity value.

Streetscape design analysis

The analysis used here is adapted from an Australian research-based team (Porta & Renne, 2005) and begins by analysing the Visual Complexity (VC) and softness as indicators of the streetscape design. The concept of 'visual complexity' is essentially multi-dimensional, thus is best evaluated by reference to four different sub-areas: colour, façade, street furniture, and pavement. The measurement of both indicators combined is what we call the Streetscape Design Value (SDV). A series of photographs were taken along the centre of the street, 25m apart. A total of 77 photos were taken along the three streets (see Figures 19.2–19.4) and categorised into five main groups according to the SDV. In order to ensure that each photo captured the same amount of visual field, a camera was attached to a tripod (eye level). Streetscape VC measures the amount of variety in the streetscape, seeking to describe the degree to which the street is a rich visual tapestry. One advantage of VC analysis is that it allows one to study the streetscape tri-dimensionally. Softness measures subjective elements such as transparency and transitional space that make the streetscape feel welcoming and safe (Anderson, 1986; Porta & Renne, 2005). Similarly to VC, the assessment of softness draws upon image analysis. The amount of window space/area that face onto the street allowing the view into and out of the building corresponds to transparency. While, transitional space is a measurement of the spaces visually accessible such as front yards, porticos, stoops, entry setbacks, *vestibule*, awnings, and so on, providing a soft transition from the public to the very private realm. Using AutoCAD software, poly-lines were drawn to define transparencies and transitional spaces, then each of them were calculated. The final measure was calculated separately for each of the two elements and then the average was taken. Due to the different nature of each sub-indicator, the data were normalized before calculating the average. The photos were compiled, and a computer program (Photoshop) was used to analyse the colour indicator precisely, while, for the others, we used a stratified sampling strategy (Groat & Wang, 2013) by inviting a group of five volunteer experts (ranging from Africa, Asia, Europe, America, and Oceania) who appraised and categorised the photos separately.

The streetscape was analysed by comparing the SDV of each photograph (or street section). Colour (the number of different colours, brightness, richness, and high contrast) by comparing the standard deviation index of the colour histogram of each photo. Colour histograms are frequently used to compare images (Arman, Hsu, & Chiu, 1993; Hampapur, Jain, & Weymouth, 1995; Ogle & Stonebraker, 1995; Pass, Zabih, & Miller, 1998). The photos were classified into five groups, the highest ranking five (above 80 Std Dev for Moneda St., 76 for Queen St. and 72 for Colonel Lotfi Av.) and the lower one (below 56 for Moneda St., 63 for Queen St. and 62 for Colonel Lotfi Av.).

Figure 19.2 Moneda St. photos, from M1 top-left to M32 bottom-right.

Figure 19.3 Queen St. photos, from Q1 top-left to Q32 bottom.

Figure 19.4 Colonel Lotfi Av. photos, from CL1 top-left to CL12 bottom.

Figure 19.5a illustrates the highest and lowest ranked photos respectively for each street.

- Façade (attractive doors and cornices, attractive height building articulation and details in roof lines, balconies, verandas, and material's variety). Each photograph was evaluated three times with reference to a 1–5 scale shown in Figure 19.5b.
- Street furniture (benches, street-art, alluring light posts, raised planters, etc.). Similar to the previous sub-indicator, it was also judged based on personal judgement from five different architects with reference to a 1–5 scale illustrated in Figure 19.5c.
- Street pavement (variety of texture, colour, different material, patterns, and attractive finishing). Similarly to the previous sub-indicator, it was also judged based on personal judgement from five different architects with reference to a 1–5 scale illustrated in Figure 19.5d.

Softness is a compound indicator with two elements; transparency and transitional space. Transparency is a measure of the amount of window space/area facing the street, allowing viewing into and out of the buildings. Transitional space is a measurement of spaces – visually accessible front yards, stoops, porticos, verandas, shelters, entry setbacks, balcony awnings, or the like – that provide a 'soft' transition from the private to the public realm. Transparency and transitional space were measured independently, then averaged to get an overall measure for softness. In AutoCAD, polylines were drawn to define the presence of transparencies and transitional spaces and each were calculated. The total measurement was separately calculated for each of the two elements and then the average was taken. Due to the different nature of each sub-indicator, the data were normalized before calculating the average. Figure 19.5e illustrates the highest and lowest for each of the assessed streets.

Figure 19.5 a) Colour sub-indicator from highest (left, rating 5) to lowest (right, rating 1). Colonel Lotfi Av. top, Queen St. middle and Moneda bottom row. b) Façade sub-indicator from highest (left, rating 5) to lowest (right, rating 1). Colonel Lotfi Av. top, Queen St. middle and Moneda bottom row. c) Street furniture sub-indicator from highest (left, rating 5) to lowest (right, rating 1). Colonel Lotfi Av. top, Queen St. middle and Moneda bottom row. d) Street pavement sub-indicator from highest (left, rating 5) to lowest (right, rating 1), Colonel Lotfi Av. top, Queen St. middle and Moneda bottom row. e) Softness indicator from highest (left, rating 5) to lowest (right, rating 1), Colonel Lotfi Av. top, Queen St. middle and Moneda bottom row.

Table 19.3 TA activities observed.

TA activity	*Colonel lofti Av.*	*Queen St.*	*Moneda St.*
Selling and preparing food	108	22	1144
Selling products	0	0	372
Advertising	134	2	21
Promoting services		66	38
Guards street vendors		0	23
Police officer		16	86
Prostitution		0	12
Refuse collectors	38	0	0
Begging	19	58	0
Taking care of children	0	0	2
Skateboarding	0	0	1
Football	0	1	1
Playing cards	0	0	1
Playing music	0	69	16
Dancing	0	2	1
Singing	0	6	8
Playing with pets	0	3	8
Watering plants	0	0	2
Reciting	0	1	12
Eating	51	101	429
Resting	82	281	279
Photo Session	0	5	0
Reading/studying	5	2	9
Ygasoro	166	0	0
Praying	0	0	48
Processions	0	0	0
Lighting Candles	0	0	7
Putting flowers	0	0	3
TOTAL	603	635	2523

Findings and discussion

Table 19.3 illustrates the activities observed in the three streets grouped into categories previously described.

The first set of questions aimed to describe the assemblage settings by analysing the SDV of the built-environment. Table 19.4, Table 19.6 and Table 19.8 summarise the results for each street. The tables indicate SW Div. value and the SDV value for

Table 19.4 Colonel Lotfi St. sections, TA diversity and VC values.

Street section	*SW Div*	*SDV*	*Street section*	*SW Div*	*SDV*
CL1	3.36	2.15	CL7	2.81	2.05
CL2	4.02	2.16	CL8	2.53	1.93
CL3	2.52	2.63	CL9	1.26	1.22
CL4	1.71	2.64	CL10	0.00	1.56
CL5	2.47	2.47	CL11	1.93	2.21
CL6	4.64	1.61	CL12	2.03	1.95

Table 19.5 Linear chart Colonel Lotfi St. sections and their corresponding TA and SDV.

TA (SW div) average	2.44
SDV average	2.05

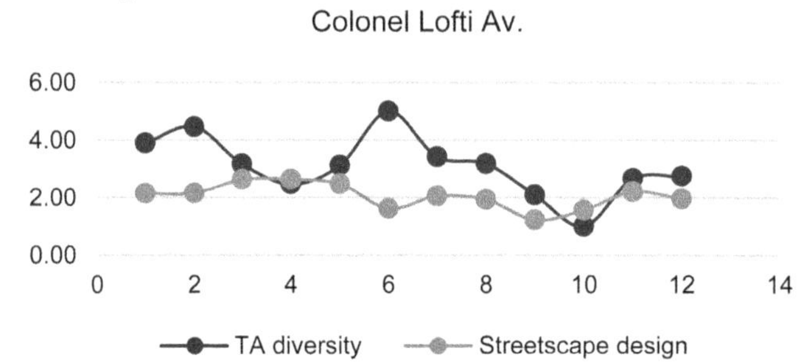

each of the street sections. On the one hand CL11 (Table 19.4), Q7 (Table 19.6) and M8 (Table 19.8) showed the highest values of SDV. On the other hand, CL9 (Table 19.4), Q28 (Table 19.5), and M32 (Table 19.6) were assessed with the lowest values of SDV respectively.

Figure 19.6a exemplifies street section CL4, Q7, and M18, which obtained the highest SDV value and TA value of 2.47, 3.45 and 3.04 SW div respectively. Figure 19.6b illustrates street section CL12, Q33 and M32 which obtained the lowest SDV value and TA value of 2.75, 3.80 and 0.74 SW div respectively. Figure 19.6c, and Figure 19.6d illustrate street sections CL6, Q9, and M17 with the highest TA of 4.64, 5.00, and 4.63 SW div values respectively. While CL10, Q22, and M31 with the lowest TA of zero, zero and 0.25 SW div values respectively.

Table 19.5 shows an overview of the values of TA and SDV along Colonel Lotfi Av. It is apparent from the linear chart that there is no apparent correlation between SDV of

Table 19.6 Queen St. sections, TA diversity and VC values.

Street section	*SW Div*	*SDV*	*Street section*	*SW Div*	*SDV*
Q01	3.37	1.82	Q18	1.01	2.63
Q02	2.86	2.36	Q19	1.60	2.53
Q03	4.80	2.37	Q20	1.41	2.09
Q04	3.73	2.70	Q21	2.05	2.58
Q05	1.25	2.61	Q22	0.91	2.20
Q06	1.04	3.01	Q23	2.65	2.57
Q07	3.45	3.15	Q24	1.33	2.36
Q08	1.24	2.90	Q25	2.60	2.83
Q09	5.00	1.48	Q26	1.00	2.65
Q10	1.10	2.15	Q27	1.88	1.64
Q11	1.07	2.64	Q28	1.82	1.20
Q12	1.91	2.52	Q29	2.49	1.04
Q13	1.16	2.84	Q30	0.85	1.29
Q14	3.37	2.42	Q31	3.44	1.63
Q15	2.89	2.56	Q32	2.16	1.15
Q16	1.38	2.83	Q33	3.80	0.71
Q17	1.49	2.85			

Table 19.7 Linear chart Queen St. sections and their corresponding TA and VC values.

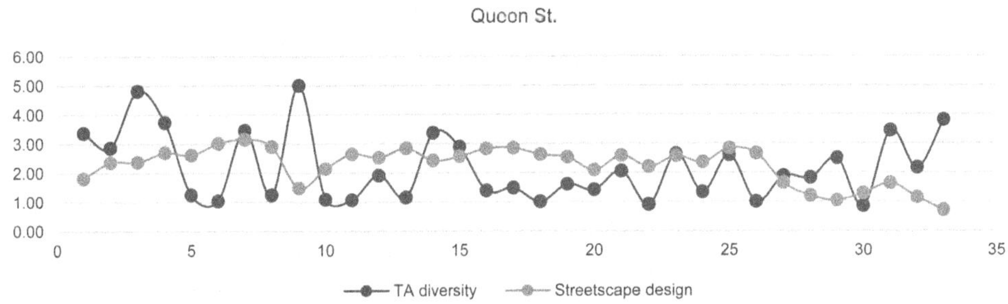

TA (SW div) average	2.42	Streetscape design average	2.25

the streetscape. Closer inspection of the table shows that the highest TA SW div value is in CL6 having a SDV value of 1.61, which is below the average of the whole street. If we now turn Auckland's CBD, Table 19.7 presents a completely different pattern. The most interesting aspect of this linear chart is that the two data values were not correlated. The SDV presents a constant and more or less steady decrease, although the TA value showed an erratic pattern. Interestingly, following previous case the highest TA value was observed in Q9 having SDV of 1.48, which is below the average of the whole street. Table 19.9 presents the summary of SDV and TA SW div analysis for Moneda St. in MCC. What is interesting about the data in this chart is that TA SW div values are lower at the extremes of the street while they rise along the centre. From the chart it can be seen that by far the highest value of TA SW div was observed in M17 having a SDV value of 3.06, which is above the average of the whole street. The more surprising correlation was found in Algiers and Auckland in which the maximum TA SW div value was located in a street section with SDV lower than the average of the whole street in both cases.

Table 19.10 illustrates the different types of TA activities observed in each of the streets. What is striking about the figures in this graph is the similarities between

Table 19.8 Moneda St. sections, TA diversity and SD values.

Street section	*SW Div*	*SDV*	*Street section*	*SW Div*	*SDV*
M1	1.78	2.83	M17	4.63	3.06
M2	1.02	3.18	M18	3.04	3.53
M3	0.62	2.84	M19	3.25	2.04
M4	0.36	3.42	M20	2.54	2.16
M5	2.41	3.11	M21	2.70	2.65
M6	2.45	3.04	M22	2.74	1.13
M7	2.28	3.34	M23	0.77	2.63
M8	1.77	3.09	M24	0.52	2.45
M9	1.68	2.88	M25	1.31	2.06
M10	3.01	3.02	M26	2.85	1.89
M11	2.25	3.08	M27	0.35	2.56
M12	1.69	2.67	M28	0.42	2.36
M13	2.47	2.76	M29	0.41	2.19
M14	3.97	1.63	M30	0.42	2.23
M15	3.96	2.72	M31	0.22	2.26
M16	2.90	2.22	M32	0.74	1.60

Figure 19.6 a) Street sections with the highest SDV, VC chart. Colonel Lotfi Av. (CL1) left, Queen St. (Q7) centre and Moneda (M8) right. b) Street sections with the lowest SDV, (left) VC chart. Colonel Lotfi Av. (CL9) left, Queen St. (Q29) centre and Moneda (M22) right. c) Street sections with the highest diversity level of TA SW Div, (left) VC chart. Colonel Lotfi Av. (CL2) left, Queen St. (Q9) centre and Moneda (M17) right. d) Street sections with the lowest diversity level of TA (left) VC chart. Colonel Lotfi Av. (CL10) left, Queen St. (Q30) centre and Moneda (M31) right.

Table 19.9 Linear chart Moneda St. sections and their corresponding TA and SD values.

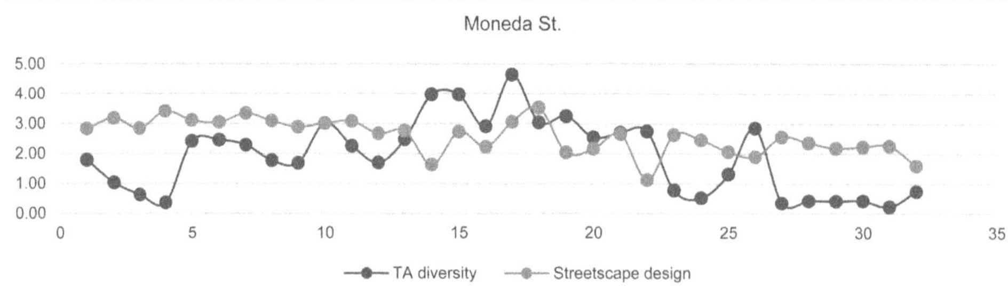

TA (SW div) average	1.92	SD average	2.58

Table 19.10 Schematic representation of the overall diversity of TA observed. Colonel Lotfi Av. top, Queen St. middle and Moneda St. bottom row with their respected TA activities observed.

	Work or Trade	*Sports, arts and leisure*	*Sacralisation*
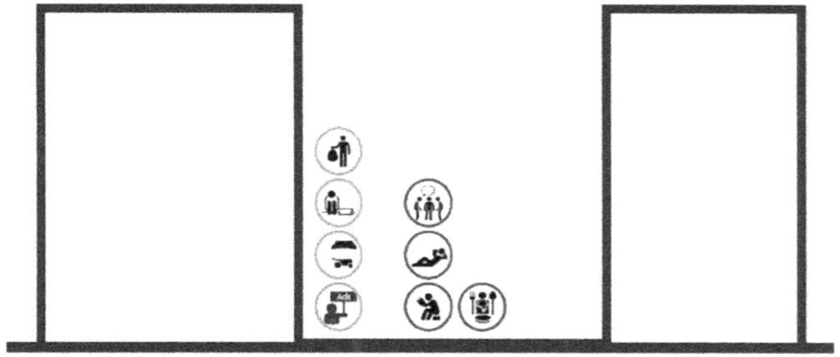	• Selling products • Advertising • Cleaning works • Begging	• Ygasoro • Resting • Eating • Reading	
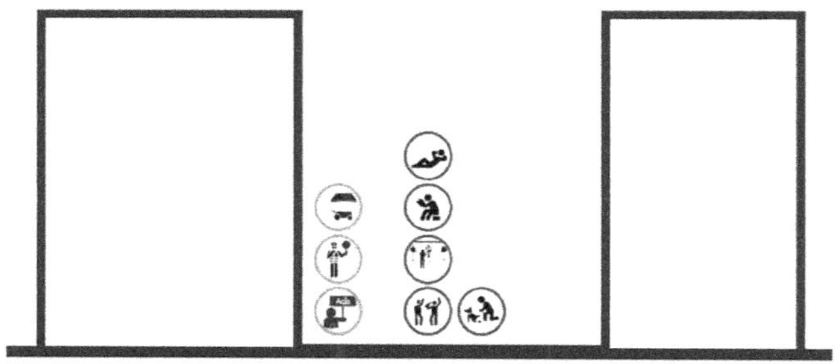	• Advertising • Cleaning works • Guards	• Dancing • Singing • Resting • Eating or drinking • Reading • Playing with pets • Photo session	
	• Selling products • Selling and preparing food • Advertising or promoting services • Guards • Guards street vendors • Prostitution	• Caring children • Skateboarding • Football • Playing cards • Dancing • Painting • Playing with pets • Watering plants • Eating or drinking • Resting • Photo Session • Reading/studying	• Processions • Lighting candles • Putting flowers

Colonel Lotfi Av. and Queen St. in terms of the different types of TA activities observed. Eight different types of TA were observed in the former, and nine in the latter. Considering the fact that Algiers and Auckland have completely different cultural origins and histories, thus built-environment, this result is meaningful. The most striking result to emerge from the data is that although Moneda St. is not the most appealing in terms of aesthetics compared to Queen St. the diversity of TA activities in the former is by far the highest among the analysed streets.

This finding broadly supports the work of other studies (Lara-Hernandez & Melis, 2018; Lara-Hernandez et al., 2019) in this area linking TA with the cultural dimension of the urban landscape. These results challenge previous and widely accepted arguments by authors such as Jacobs (1961), Gehl (2011) and Bentley et al. (1985), who claim that an "active façade" is an essential design strategy to achieve a lively street.

Conclusions

The first section of the paper described the strong relationship between culture and built-environment, theoretically highlighting the constant flux in how they influence one each other. It has shown that an assemblage thinking approach can be useful to compare urban landscapes culturally diverse. The study has identified that the built-environment and TA can be conceptualised as assemblage settings and an assemblage of activities respectively, which according to Rapoport (2005) allow us to make cross-cultural comparisons. The second major finding is that assemblage theory can be used as a theoretical framework for investigating cross-culturally urban phenomena. This research also contributes to the existing knowledge of TA by supporting assemblage thinking approach as an instrument for the study of urban phenomena at the scale of the public space.

In conclusion, this study is the first comprehensive cross-cultural investigation of TA in relation to the design of the built-environment. This approach will prove useful in expanding our understanding of how public spaces are used and culturally shaped. The research provides a useful method to assess and compare different urban-cultural landscapes. The study also enforces the idea that the study of assemblages' settings and assemblage's activities (TA) could provide useful insights about the relationship between people and their built-environment. We agree with DeLanda (2016) and Lara-Hernandez, Melis & Lehmann (2019) in supporting assemblage theory as a strongly resilient theoretical tool to analyse the urban landscape.

Research in the fields of the built-environment (architecture, landscape architecture, urban planning, and urban design) could provide further knowledge on the design settings (design features) of the built-environment (another assemblage) related to TA in any determinate context. In addition, the contribution to other fields of research (sociology, environmental psychology, urban ecology) could help us to shed light and increase certainty in this matter.

A limitation of this study is that the length of the streets among the selected case-studies vary, thus affecting the availability of TA and its distribution. Another limitation of the study was the dates in which the observation was carried out because it varied across cities, and thus weather conditions. Notwithstanding these limitations, the study suggests that cross-culturally studies utilising assemblage thinking approach are viable. A natural progression of this work is to analyse and study other streets among cities that share similar history and cultural context. Further research might explore and identify other assemblage's settings of the built-environment such as building land use, or even other assemblages such as legal and economic. Hence, there are some research questions that could be asked relating to the extent to which the design of the built-environment (another assemblage), which is also related to cultural meanings and symbols, may have an influence on TA. Further research needs to examine more closely the links between TA and weather conditions in relationship to the built-environment.

Note

1 Central Business District.

References

Amrouche, A. (2012). Projets prioritaires. *Vie des Villes*. (Vol. 3).

Anderson, S. (1986). On Streets. *In on Streets*. Cambridge, Massachusetts: Mit Press.

Arman, F., Hsu, A., & Chiu, M.-Y. (1993). Image processing on compressed data for large video databases. In *Proceedings of the first ACM international conference on Multimedia* (pp. 267–272). ACM.

Autoridad del Centro Historico. (2011). *Plan Integral de Manejo del Centro Historico de la Ciudad de Mexico (2011-2016)* (Vol. 9). Mexico: DF.

Bayat, A. (1997). Un-civil society: The politics of the "informal people." *Third World Quarterly*, *18*(1), 53–72. https://doi.org/10.1080/01436599715055

Bentley, I., Alcock, A., Murrain, P., McGlynn, S., & Smith, G. (1985). *Responsive Environments*. London, UK: The architectural Press Ltd.

Boaz, F. (2017). *Anthropology and modern life*. New York: W.W. Norton & Company Inc.

Bonfil Batalla, G. (2004). Pensar nuestra cultura. *Dialogos de Accion, Primera Etapa*, 117–134.

Brenner, N. (2005). *New state spaces: urban governance and the rescaling of statehood*, New York: Oxford University Press.

Canclini, N. G. (2018). A culture of informality. *Urban Studies*, (March 2017), 1–6. https://doi.org/10.1177/0042098018782635

Carmona, M. (2010). *Public Places Urban Spaces, The Dimensions of Urban Design (Second Edition)* (Second Edi). Burlington, USA: Architectural Press. https://doi.org/10.1111/febs.12167

Carmona, M. (2014). The Place-shaping Continuum: A Theory of Urban Design Process. *Journal of Urban Design*. Taylor & Francis. https://doi.org/10.1080/13574809.2013.854695

Chan, E. H. W., & Lee, G. K. L. (2009). Design considerations for environmental sustainability in high density development: A case study of Hong Kong. *Environment, Development and Sustainability*, *11*(2), 359–374. https://doi.org/10.1007/s10668-007-9117-0

Choay, F. (2001). Historic Heritage and the Contemporary Culture Industry. In *The Invention of the Historic Monument* (pp. 138–163). Cambridge University Press.

Daigger, G. T., Newell, J. P., Love, N. G., McClintock, N., Gardiner, M., Mohareb, E., … Ramaswami, A. (2015). Scaling Up Agriculture in City-Regions to mitigate FEW System Impacts, 69. Retrieved from https://works.bepress.com/megan-horst/7/

DeLanda, M. (2006). *A new philosophy of society*. London, UK: Continuum.

DeLanda, M. (2016). *Assemblage Theory*. Edinburgh, UK: Edinburgh University Press.

Deleuze, G., & Parnet, C. (1977). Deleuze and Claire Parnet. *Dialogues. Paris: Flammarion*.

Dovey, K. (2012). Informal urbanism and complex adaptive assemblage. *International Development Planning Review*, *34*(4), 349–368. https://doi.org/10.3828/idpr.2012.23

Dovey, K., Rao, F., & Pafka, E. (2018). Agglomeration and assemblage: Deterritorialising urban theory. *Urban Studies*, *55*(2), 263–273. https://doi.org/10.1177/0042098017711650

Dovey, K., & Ristic, M. (2017). Mapping urban assemblages: the production of spatial knowledge. *Journal of Urbanism*, *10*(1), 15–28. https://doi.org/10.1080/17549175.2015.1112298
Dürr, E. (2011). To belong in aotearoa new zealand: Latin American migrant experiences in multicultural Auckland. *Journal of Ethnic and Migration Studies*, *37*(3), 503–519. https://doi.org/10.1080/1369183X.2011.521359
Efroymson, D., Than Ha, T. T. K., & Thu Ha, P. (2009). Public Spaces: How They Humanize Cities. *October*, (October).
Eliot, T. S. (1949). *Notes Towards the Definition of Culture*. Retrieved from https://books.google.co.uk/books?id=QYR9FNyKMmwC
Ellard, C. (2015). *Places of the hearth: The psychogeography of everyday life*. New York, USA: Bellevenue Library Press.
Francis, M. (1984). Mapping Downtown Activity. *Journal of Architectural and Planning Research*, *1*(1), 21–35. Retrieved from http://www.jstor.org/stable/43028671
Fyfe, N. R., & Kenny, J. T. (2005). *The urban geography reader*. *The Routledge urban reader series*. Retrieved from http://www.loc.gov/catdir/toc/ecip0421/2004018547.html%5Cnhttp://www.loc.gov/catdir/enhancements/fy0650/2004018547-d.html
Garcia Canclini, N. (2005). *Hybrid cultures*. Minneapolis, USA: University of Minnesota Press.
Gehl, J. (2011). *Life Between Buildings*. Washington DC: Island Press.
Gehmann, U. (2009). Formatting and Loss of Space – Considerations (including Annex Typing & Loss). *Main*, *1*, 60–98.
Gobierno de la Ciudad de Mexico. (2016). Autoridad del Centro Historico. Retrieved April 1, 2016, from http://www.autoridadcentrohistorico.df.gob.mx
Government of New Zealand. (2013). Census map – QuickStats about a place. Retrieved November 11, 2018, from http://archive.stats.govt.nz/StatsMaps/Home/Maps/2013-census-quickstats-about-a-place-map.aspx
Government of New Zealand. (2018). Te Ara Encyclopedia of New Zealand. Retrieved November 11, 2018, from https://teara.govt.nz/en/auckland-places/page-10
Grabar, H. S. (2013). Reclaiming the city: Changing urban meaning in Algiers after 1962. *Cultural Geographies*, *21*(3), 389–409. https://doi.org/10.1177/1474474013506361
Graumann, C. (1983). On Multiple identities. *International Social Science Journal*. Retrieved from http://eds.b.ebscohost.com/eds/pdfviewer/pdfviewer?sid=4e7bdb42-733e-4fbb-98b0-3082b60477c5%40sessionmgr105&vid=7&hid=112
Graumann, C. F. (1976). The concept of appropriation (aneignung) and modes of appropriation of space. Universitat Heidelberg. Retrieved from http://iaps.scix.net/cgi-bin/works/Show?iaps_00_1976_009
Groat, L., & Wang, D. (2013). *Architectural research methods (Second)*. New York, US: John Wiley & Sons, Inc.
Gu, K. (2010). Urban morphological regions and urban landscape management: The case of central Auckland, New Zealand. *Urban Design International*, *15*(3), 148–164. https://doi.org/10.1057/udi.2010.4
Hall, E. T. (1966). *The Hidden Dimension*. New York, USA: Anchor Books and Colophon.
Hampapur, A., Jain, R., & Weymouth, T. E. (1995). Production model based digital video segmentation. *Multimedia Tools and Applications*, *1*(1), 9–46.
Heinemann, M. (2002). *A culture of appropriation: Strategies of temporary reuse in East Germany*. Technical University of Berlin, Germany.
Hillier, B. (1996). *Space is the machine*. *Design Studies* (Vol. 18). London, UK: Press Syndicate of the University of Cambridge.
Hubbard, P., Kitchin, R., Bartley, B., & Fuller, D. (2002). *Thinking Geographically*. London, UK: Continuum.
Huffschmid, A. (2015). From the City to "Lo Urbano": Exploring Cultural Production of the Space in Latin America, *45*(45), 119–136. Retrieved from http://www.jstor.org/stable/41677562

INEGI. (2018). Clima. Distrito Federal. Retrieved July 30, 2018, from http://cuentame.inegi.org.mx/monografias/informacion/df/territorio/clima.aspx?tema=me&e=09

Jackson, R. J., & Kochtitzky, C. (2010). Creating A Healthy Environment: The Impact of the Built Environment on Public Health. *Director*, (October), 20. https://doi.org/10.4037/ccn2009716

Jacobs, J. (1961). *The Death and Life of Great American Cities. New York* (Vol. 71). https://doi.org/10.2307/794509

Kent, S. (1990). *Domestic Architecture and the Use of Space. New Directions in Archaeology*. Cambridge, UK: Cambridge University Press.

Lara-Hernandez, J. A., & Melis, A. (2018). Understanding the temporary appropriation in relationship to social sustainability. *Sustainable Cities and Society*, 39C, 1–14. https://doi.org/10.1016/j.scs.2018.03.004

Lara-Hernandez, J. A., Melis, A., & Coulter, C. M. (2020). Temporary appropriation and informality: a nuanced relationship. In J. A. Lara-Hernandez, A. Melis, & J. Thompson (Eds.), *Temporary Appropriation in Cities: Human Spatialisation in Public Spaces and Community Resilience*. London, UK: Springer Nature Limited.

Lara-Hernandez, J. A., Melis, A., & Lehmann, S. (2018). Temporary appropriation and social sustainability: the case of the historic centre of Mexico City. In *APRU Sustainable Cities and Landscapes 2018*. Hong Kong. Retrieved from https://apru.org/

Lara-Hernandez, J. A., Melis, A., & Lehmann, S. (2019). Temporary appropriation of public space as an emergence assemblage for the future urban landscape: The case of Mexico City. *Future Cities and Environment*, *5*(1), 1–22. https://doi.org/10.5334/fce.53

Law, L. (2002). Defying Disappearance: Cosmopolitan Public Spaces in Hong Kong. *Urban Studies*, *39*(9), 1625–1645. https://doi.org/10.1080/00420980220151691

Lima, J. J. (2001). Socio-spatial segregation and urban form: Belem at the end of the 1990's. *Geoforum*, *32*(4), 493–507. https://doi.org/10.1016/S0016-7185(01)00019-7

Low, S. M. (1999). Spatializing Culture. *Theorizing the City*, (August), 111–137.

Madanipour, A. (1996). Urban design and dilemmas of space. *Environment and Planning D: Society and Space*, *14*(3), 331–355. https://doi.org/10.1068/d140331

Mahdzar, S. S. B. S. (2008). *Sociability vs Accessibility Urban Street Life*. University College London, United Kingdom.

Marston, S. A., Jones, J. P., Woodward, K., Paul, J., Iii, J., Woodward, K., … Woodward, K. (2005). Human Geography without Scale. *The Royal Geographical Society*, *30*(4), 416–432. Retrieved from www.jstor.org/stable/3804505

Marx, C., & Kelling, E. (2018). Knowing urban informalities. *Urban Studies*, *1*(16). https://doi.org/10.1177/0042098018770848

McAuslan, P. (2006). Legal Pluralism as a Policy Option: Is it Desirable, Is it Doable? *Land Rights for African Development From Knowledge to Action*, *2005*, 9–10. Retrieved from http://www.capri.cgiar.org/wp/.%5Cpdf%5Cbrief_land-04.pdf

McQuire, S. (2006). The politics of public space in the media city. *First Monday*, *11*(SPEC. ISS. 4), 17–34. https://doi.org/http://dx.doi.org/10.5210%2Ffm.v0i0.1544

Mehta, V. (2018). Streets and social life in cities: a taxonomy of sociability. *URBAN DESIGN International*. https://doi.org/10.1057/s41289-018-0069-9

Melis, A., Lara-Hernandez, J. A., & Thompson, J. (2020). *Temporary Appropriation in Cities: Human Spatialisation in Public Spaces and Community Resilience* (1st ed.). London, UK: Springer Nature Limited. https://doi.org/10.1007/978-3-030-32120-8

Moudon, A. V. (1991). *Public Streets for Public Use*. New York, US: Columbia University Press.

Mouffe, C. (2000). Deliberative Democracy or Agonistic Pluralism. *Social Research*, *66*(3), 745–758. https://doi.org/10.2307/40971349

Mumford, L. (1938). The Culture of Cities. In *The Culture of Cities* (pp. 405–481). London, UK: Anthony Rowe.

Nail, T. (2017). What is an Assemblage? *SubStance*, *46*(1), 21–37.

Ogle, V. E., & Stonebraker, M. (1995). Chabot: Retrieval from a relational database of images. *Computer*, *28*(9), 40–48.
Pantoja, S. (2010, June 11). Obras de peatonalización de Madero inician el lunes. *El Universal*.
Pass, G., Zabih, R., & Miller, J. (1998). Comparing images using color coherence vectors. *Proceedings of the Fourth ACM International Conference on Multimedia (MULTIMEDIA '96)*, 1–14. https://doi.org/10.1145/244130.244148
Pearson, S., & Kothari, S. (2007). Menus for a Multicultural New Zealand. *Continuum: Journal of Media & Cultural Studies*, *21*(1), 45–58. https://doi.org/10.1080/10304310601103950
People's Democratic Republic of Algeria. (2015). Wilaya of Algiers. Retrieved December 12, 2018, from http://www.wilaya-alger.dz/en/wilaya/
Plas, J. M., & Lewis, S. E. (1996). Environmental factors and sense of community in a planned town. *American Journal of Community Psychology*, *24*(1), 109–143. https://doi.org/10.1007/BF02511884
Pol Urrútia, E. (2002). El modelo dual de la apropiación del espacio en Mira, R., Sabucedo, JM y Romay, J. *Psicología y Medio Ambiente. Aspectos Psicosociales, Educativos y Metodológicos*, 123–132.
Porta, S., & Renne, J. L. (2005). Linking urban design to sustainability: formal indicators of social urban sustainability field research in Perth, Western Australia. *Urban Design International*, *10*(1), 51–64. https://doi.org/10.1057/palgrave.udi.9000136
Purcell, M. (2002). Excavating Lefebvre: The right to the city and its urban politics of the inhabitant. *GeoJournal*, *58*, 99–108. https://doi.org/10.1023/B:GEJO.0000010829.62237.8f
Rapoport, A. (2005). *Culture, Architecture, and Design*. Chicago: Locke Science Publisher.
Rapoport, A. (2008). Some Further Thoughts on Culture and Environment. *Archnet-IJAR*, *2*(1), 16–39.
Rishbeth, C. (2001). Ethnic Minority Groups and the Design of Public Open Space: An inclusive landscape? *Landscape Research*, *26*(4), 351–366. https://doi.org/10.1080/01426390120090148
Roy, A., & AlSayyad, N. (2004). *Urban Informality*. (A. Roy & N. AlSayyad, Eds.). Maryland: Lexington Books.
Saoudi, H., & Belakehal, A. (2018). World's urban sustainable policies and sustainability in Algeria. *Courrier Du Savoir*, (26), 593–604.
Sarmiento, H., & Tilly, C. (2018). Governance Lessons from Urban Informality. *Politics and Governance*, *6*(1), 199. https://doi.org/10.17645/pag.v6i1.1169
Sibley, D. (1995). *Geographies of Exclusion*. London, UK: Routledge. Retrieved from http://books.google.com/books?id=ZyNT3uZQnqgC&pgis=1
Siksna, A. (2006). The study of urban form in Australia. *International Seminar on Urban Form*, *10*(April), 89–100.
Stanislawski, D. (1947). Early Spanish Town Planning in the New World. *American Geographical Society*, *37*(1), 94–105.
Toit, L. Du, Cerin, E., Leslie, E., & Owen, N. (2007). Does Walking in the Neighbourhood Enhance Local Sociability? *Urban Studies*, *44*(9), 1677–1695. https://doi.org/10.1080/00420980701426665
Varna, G. (2014). *Measuring the public space: The star model*. Surrey, UK: Ashgate Publishing Group.
Vidal Moranta, T., & Pol Urrútia, E. (2005). La apropiación del espacio: Una propuesta teórica para comprender la vinculación entre las personas y los lugares. *Anuario de Psicologia*, *36*(3), 281–297. https://doi.org/10.1006/jevp.2000.0185

Chapter 20

Reinventing city planning in a context that "hates" planning!

A new role for architects, city planners and institutions

Besnik Aliaj

Albania experienced the most orthodox system of centralised planning in the former "East-European" block. For 45 years, it suffered denial of the freedom of speech, religion, and movement. It acted almost as a "North Korea" of Europe. Citizens were not invited to influence decision making, which was highly centralised and usually a fake process. The early '90s inherited no tradition on community participation, as the past system abused the concept of "collective" work to the point that almost everybody hated planning. The early '90s influenced Albania with radical political, social, and economic changes that totally transformed East-Europe. A difficult and volatile transition with chaotic and dramatic events started. Severe setbacks followed, including 1997 social unrest caused by the collapse of fraudulent financial schemes and the war of 1999 in Kosovo with a wave of one million refugees that flooded Albania.

The second decade of transformations brought certain progress and prosperity for the country with growth rates at 6% per annum (World Bank Technical Assistance Project, 2013, p. 11). Come 2010, problems reappeared again, as global recession and the stabilocracy logic slowed down both the economy and democratization processes. However, Albania is a member of NATO and committed to opening negotiations with EU. It is such complex and fast changing social, economic, and political background, which gave birth to *Co-PLAN Institute for Habitat Development* (About Co-Plan, 2010), as one of the first and most reputable civic initiatives in the country specialised on community and city planning. Co-PLAN emerged in 1993 with a start-up logic and almost "business" attitude of participatory planning. Ground activities emerged during the difficult years of 1995–1999. Initially a modest Dutch-financed social program in the informally developed peripheries of the capital Tirana, Co-PLAN would soon distinguish itself as a pioneering organization committed to contributing to the difficult transformation of Albania. Planning and participation were instruments for societal change to Co-PLAN (Aliaj, Shutina, & Dhamo, 2010). The most distinguished radiation of its energy remains the establishment of the academic and research platform: POLIS University in Tirana (About Polis University, 2006).

Almost a heroic phase: Establishing the Co-PLAN NGO at a grassroots base

By the early 90s, the urbanization level in Albania was the lowest in Europe at a rate of approximately 35% (Misja & Vejsiu, 1996). Tirana was the biggest city with around 250,000 residents. Despite an estimated exodus of the population abroad at 20%, many cities grew in population over 5%. Tirana grew at an alarming rate of 7% per annum, doubling its surface and tripling population over one decade. The city expanded by 200 hectares each year. Analysis of aerial photography (1994 by LMTF (see Figure 20.1) and 2001 by Co-PLAN(see Figure 20.2)) proved a growth of at last 1,100 new housing units per annum, built mostly without permission (LMTF, 1995). The high housing demand of overcrowded urban dwellers and pressures from rural-urban migration lead to the construction boom, but also the rise of informality and the concentration of poor in urban areas too. The new arrivals in Tirana often belonged to the lowest income groups, which included 25–30% of the city population. Another 30% that belonged to the low and middle-income group could easily be attached to the first group if any social or economic shock hit them (Aliaj, 2002). Without basic facilities, uprooted and surrounded by others equally as poor and struggling as themselves, they found themselves isolated from Tirana's dwellers and highly vulnerable. In this context, Co-PLAN was born.

Co-PLAN is a good example of synergy generated among key local actors and international development assistance. The founders were young enthusiastic professionals graduated at local universities just at the collapse of communism. At that time, one in four Albanians emigrated. What made a difference for CoPLAN-ers

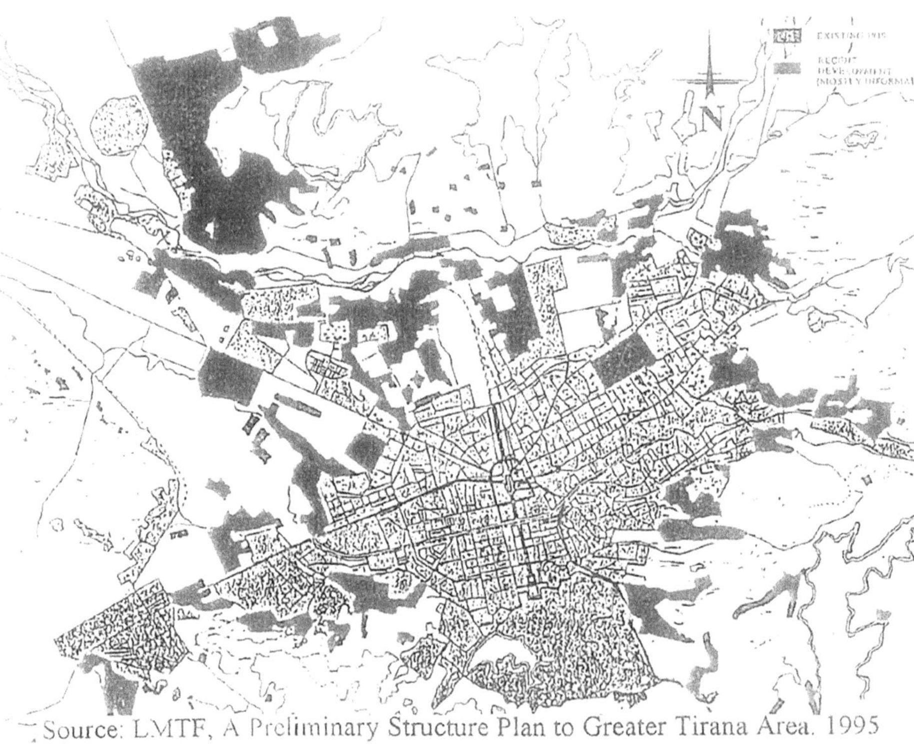

Figure 20.1 The growth of Tirana and informality developed areas in 1990–1995.

Source: LMTF, 1995.

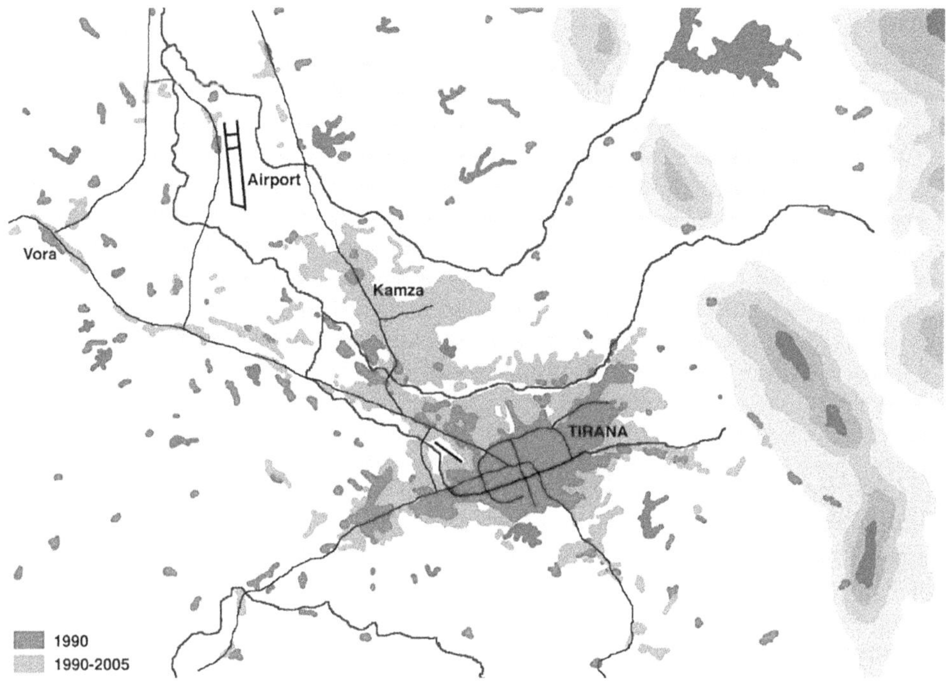

Figure 20.2 The growth of Tirana and informality developed areas in and 1995–2005.

Source: LMTF, 1995.

was that after specializing internationally they returned home with the mission to help rebuild the country. Their own interests met the interests of local and international development stakeholders. The objective was to ensure a long-term development perspective, beyond the mere logic of project financings. The article describes such an experience, focused on the aspects of organizational development and institutional strengthening (Niented, 2016), which in return promotes the sustainability of developments, instead of short-term actions and superficial transformation of physical nature.

The first actions of Co-PLAN were taken in the muddy poor peripheries of the capital Tirana (Co-PLAN, Annual Report, 2007), aiming to organise communities to address problems of public space, social disarray, health, and education. It was unusual for the Albanian context to address community, especially informal settlements (Aliaj, 1998). It always existed an opposition of small groups of former landowners, conservative citizens, and public administrators, or "old-school" professionals, etc., as at initial stages Co-PLAN was misunderstood as a "protector" of the informality (Accioly, Aliaj, & Kuçi, 2004). However, Co-PLAN remained firm in its views of advocacy towards groups in need and vulnerable communities that could never get access or a chance to influence decision making, even when said decisions directly affected them. Co-PLAN did not act as a charitable organization either. The persistent crisis of the country and a high presence of international aid of emergency nature often spoiled local development objectives and slowed down Co-PLAN's work.

A clash of ideas and institutional philosophies happened between *long-term development programs* and *short-term emergency actions* (Co-PLAN, Annual Report, 2004). However, over time communities proved the value of the long-term partners. Therefore, time was of the essence! To Co-PLAN, it was nearly impossible to initially negotiate newcomers' mentality giving up part of their "own" (occupied) land in favour of planning broader public interest (say like a new road network), because people's attitude shifted orientation from "*collective*" into "*highly-individual*". Changes in mentality has always proven to be difficult and usually take time (Aliaj, 2002); but probably due to this fact, it became a challenge that CoPLAN-ers embraced. Surprisingly, the real battle was not to be faced with the communities, but rather at the "sophisticated" level of professionals and authorities, with whom advocating for the "informal" was considered almost a heresy.

Moving to another scale: Municipality of Kamza and greater Tirana area

Co-PLAN's main objective of bringing together communities with policy makers called for another level of professionalism in Albania. It undertook several initiatives to establish networks, build partnerships, and organise citywide forums where different stakeholders could pose, defend, and debate views and interests. All these initiatives helped establishing a new culture of communication, while Co-PLAN shifted slowly towards the role of intermediary between the communities and local-central authorities. This included the introduction of: i) comprehensive tools to cope with the challenges of new urban dynamics during transition, ii) comprehensive level of human capacities, and iii) strong willingness to lead the entire process (Co-PLAN, 2003). The new challenges had to be faced cyclically because of the systematic shifts towards higher level of professionalism and decision-making. This imposed on Co-PLAN the need for a broader view of *the neighbourhood to the city scale*. Kamza became Co-PLAN's first municipal test for scaling up the challenge from the subject of informality towards municipal autonomy.

Co-PLAN tried to emphasise the potential in these areas. Thanks to the implementation of periodical socio-economic surveys, Co-PLAN estimated at the time an incredibly large amount of 110 million USD investments in housing made by residents, while the municipal budget spent on public investments, in the best year, never surpasses 100,000 USD (Hope, 2013). Unfortunately, such potential was ignored. Dealing with it often resulted in conflicts between authorities and the local population. In 1995, 1998 and 2003, the government tried to relocate settlers forcedly, but they united in harsh confrontations with police (Aliaj, Shutina, & Dhamo, 2010). It all resulted in dramatic events that made everyone aware that making war with broad segments of the society was not a feasible option, especially when dealing with poverty and accumulated problems of the past. It also became clear that the authorities lacked vision in coping with growing informality. In contrary, the issue has been misused politically, offering unrealistic promises during electoral campaigns in favour of the legalization. The governments indeed never elaborated such an option professionally.

Box 1: Municipality of Kamza, Greater Tirana Area (Co-PLAN, Strategic Urban Development Plan of the Municipality of Kamza, 2002)

Kamza Municipality was established in 1996 because of the need to cope with the unprecedented development growth. It inherited a strong agricultural background, but within the first decade of post-communist transition population saw 20-fold increase from 7,000 to 140,000 inhabitants, because of radical processes of informal land conversion from agricultural-rural to urban. It is not difficult to imagine the challenge and scale of the problems for a newly established municipality, confronting an alarming rate of 90% informal building, with practically no institutional memory and capacity (Aliaj, 2008). All this happened in a moment of legal and institutional vacuum, while national politics had other priorities, and support/financing from the central government was nonexistent. One should also consider country's context of decentralization with transference of problems rather than empowerment of the local administration. Local elections often created blackouts for local administration because of arbitrary staff firing due to political changes.

Neighbourhood development agenda: Building bridges of mutual trust by motivating actors!

Co-PLAN undertook several initiatives aimed at i) building the bridges of mutual trust and ii) disclosing actors and their own motivations. This approach intelligently combined local resources with initial institutional-financial support given by donor organizations, such as the Dutch NGOs Cordaid and Novib. The encouraging results of the first actions were used pragmatically later on to establish communication with local governments. This would eventually serve to address issues of common interest with community, and serve as a strategy to identify potentials for joining forces to overcome other existing problems.

Co-PLAN worked initially at a neighbourhood scale, in two very specific informal areas: i) *Breglumasi-Lapraka, Tirana Municipality*, around 13 hectares and 600 families; ii) *Bathore, Kamza Municipality, Greater Tirana Area,* which expanded in a few years from 30 to 200 ha involving 4,000 households. Residents came originally from harsh remote mountainous areas of the country, where, after the 80s, chances for a normal life were practically zero. Indicators of health and education in the origin regions were two times less than the national average, and ten times lower than the capital Tirana (Co-PLAN, 2002). Many people were unemployed after the collapse of local industries and failure of state farms. To be able to work successfully with planning as a transformation tool in such social, economic, and cultural tissue, it was essential to initially look carefully into i) the stages and reasoning for migration and ii) understanding the processes behind the informal urban development which people went through in order to gain access to land and neighbourhoods. For such tasks, city planners must cooperate closely with social scientists, anthropologists, economists,

Figure 20.3 Steps of informal housing development, Bathore neighbourhood, Kamza municipality. (Aliaj, NGOs/CBOs and housing for low-income people in Albania, governing cities – new institutional forms in developing countries and transitional economies, 2002).

Box 2: Demystifying the process of informal development in the Greater Tirana Area (Accioly, Aliaj, & Kuçi, 2004)

Stage 1: Decision to migrate – Originally life was organised around "clan" logic, which meant an extended family with a common economy. Therefore, decisions were jointly taken. Take an average family of 4–5 brothers: after they realise that life in their village is no longer feasible, they make the decision to move towards the capital city, with more chances of a better life. There are a few implications to this decision. In order to afford such an important and financially costly decision, the clan decides on a "sharing of responsibilities" among brothers. One of them (usually the youngest and possibly the single one) gets the mandate to search for the appropriate and affordable location for the whole family, while others are responsible for securing financial means to afford the move and new shelter. Often someone has to emigrate abroad. The oldest brother or grandfather always remains to look after the family.

Stage 2: Identifying the location for a new house – This step is taken in a very discreet way. The criteria are: i) vicinity to the urban area, ii) affordability, iii) land and property titles. This is a delicate process, as newcomers must be well informed about the location's tenure. If government owns the land plot, the risks are considered minimal for settling. Such attitude originates from the post-communist belief that "collective property is nobody's land". However, there always exists a "fee" to enter an area. Often the first comers in the neighbourhood act also as "middlemen", subdividing the big chunks of land they controlled, and thus making profits by selling it out to other newcomers. The transactions are informal, although "written declarations" are signed. In reality, everybody knows that they do not actually buy land, but rather the "right" to settle in the neighbourhood. The deal would be invalid if the government or the real owner or third parties were to step in.

Stage 3: Testing the authorities – The "purchase" of land-plot is not followed by immediate house construction. Initially, residents build a "shack" or they put foundation stones on the site as a sign of plot "control" and announcement for later construction activity. This step is taken for two reasons: i) newcomers test the reaction of authorities toward their actions; ii) they state a signal to the neighbours to prevent any risk of plot "occupation" from others. Sometimes problems happen, but this is the reason why initially only one family member deals with the new plot.

Stage 4: Starting the investment – Having gained a little security, the investment in housing starts. An interesting point about this step is the fact that investments follow the cycles of financial flow. This means the progress of the investment relies a lot on incremental income generated mostly from emigration, or selling out old properties, or by income thanks to the work in city. Residents appear to be very creative in decreasing their own construction costs. The tools range from cheap materials to decreasing labour costs by involving relatives and neighbours in the building process. If the household economy grows, one can easily realise how this effects the investment: better materials are used and roofs replace terraces.

Stage 5: Moving into the new house – The big family moves into the new house when the investment is complete. An interesting point about this step is that the big family still lives within a common economy. They keep such a protection system alive until housing for each individual family is secured. This solidarity system stimulates the assistance among family or "clan" members. (see Figure 20.3).

Stage 6: Improve services and surroundings – Until this stage, services and infrastructure provision are not a priority. Once the plot is bought, the buyer is supposed to have the right of access. As this is not always the case, it can become a source for conflicts, because there is no planning layout in the area to guide land occupation process, despite the inherited reference of agricultural patterns. At this point, the process meets with the needs and the difficult task of generating common understanding to mobilise joint efforts, contributions and financing for infrastructure and services. Exactly here is the need for organizations like Co-PLAN!

and demographers, in order to undertake detailed field surveys. That was already a big change for the mentality of physical planners of Albania.

Enemies or partners? Discovering the need to reinvent a "new" planning!

The focus of Co-PLAN in the informal settlements of Tirana was to create examples of community mobilization in order to identify, plan and secure public space that is vital for normal urban development. In practice, it takes enormous efforts to convince people who work hard to "buy" a land parcel so crucial for their own families and future life. They struggle every day with poverty; they resist police pressure, and all this is just to ensure a minimal living! At the end, the right for housing and basic employment is an issue of human rights (Constitution, Republic of Albania, 1998). So considering the clearance option for their life investments, or even more asking them to move back depots, walls or fences to make space for the benefit of public interest, requires a big change of mentality and attitude towards the community. No matter how enthusiastic this small group of professionals was, nothing much could be done without first establishing human relationship and trust among local residents. Building trust in itself is a lengthy process that takes time and effort, and cannot be achieved without understanding the real human side behind the entire process (Aliaj, 2002).

Therefore, trust was established based on tangible actions and results, and only when people could quickly see the benefits. Such a "snowballing" process (Accioly, Aliaj, & Kuçi, 2004) was meant to break the ice and have more people follow the example in favour of a longer-term development mechanism. It takes more people to accept

Box 3: Steps of realistic community-based planning at Bathore neighbourhood, from (Aliaj, Misteri i Gjashtë. Cili është kurthi që mban peng zhvillimin dhe integrimin e ekonomisë shqipetare në botën moderne., 2008)

1. **Entering the area** – Establish the first contacts within the neighbourhood via recommended trustable sources. Informally visit the neighbourhood with them as social guarantees.
2. **Entering within households** – Have spontaneous meetings to inform the purpose of your presence in the area. Ask for time. Introduce yourself humbly door to door. Implement first socio-economic surveys to understand the profile of community and average residents. Explain and reassure people that you are there simply for professional interest and no other agenda.
3. **Identify local community leaders** – Find reputable persons and potential community leaders whom have the sympathy of the broad public, as a baseline for promoting later on social structures like the representative local community-based organization (CBO).

4. **The start-up workshop** – Work with community leaders and CBO representatives to identify main neighbourhood development issues. Explain to them how to strategically plan a process of transformation and guarantee the implementation within own limited resources. Subdivide neighbourhood in smaller units of 15–25 households in order to work more closely with people.
5. **Drafting the first charrettes** – Design with community leaders the first sketches of a bottom-up neighbourhood concept-plan, and expose it publicly to initiate a process of feedback, interaction, and broad consensus. Discuss the concept plan door-to-door and explain the physical impact of the plan for each plot/property. Identify and mark future road network and public spaces.
6. **Implement the plan of public spaces** – Encourage residents to remove voluntarily and timely fences, walls, depots, in order to make way for the re-establishment of public space and roads.
7. **Identify, gravel and protect the newly open public space** – Improve the quality of access in the neighbourhood from (narrow) muddy paths into (wide) gravelled roads and public spaces. It visually marks and protects newly opened public spaces. Coordinate with the community and donors the building of playgrounds and sport facilities, basic educational, healthcare or community meeting infrastructure, etc., in order to ensure space for bringing people together.
8. **Work with vulnerable groups** – Invest in strengthening women, youth, and children, who have not had the best position in such communities, but play a significant role in the process of improving and prioritization. Promote social life to integrate them. Stimulate productive economic activities in order to generate income for them, and have in return a stronger role within the local CBO. Undertake training to stimulate concrete actions of public improvements and gain sympathy.
9. **Invite authorities to visit the neighbourhood** – When the first results of community interaction become tangible via low-cost, community-based, and self-help actions, invite authorities to visit the area, to understand the positivity of local development processes, reduce prejudice, misunderstanding, as well as reflect on potential future cooperation.
10. **Help authorities to have representation in the neighbourhood** – Encourage them to have a basic local office within the neighbourhood, in order to follow up daily with the situation and provide advice or services. Further on, facilitate the access of people in headquarter municipal offices, as a step towards full servicing, formalization, and integration.
11. **Promote democratic elections and registration of the local CBO by the Court** – This is an intensive participatory process and a mature step towards the legal recognition of the community, which makes them legal partners for negotiations and agreements with authorities.

12. **Coordinate actions among authorities and stakeholders** – As the community shows positive attitude and progress, more stakeholders intend to enter in the neighbourhood and play a role. To avoid a clash of development strategies and synergise the impact, organise a coordinated round-table for development purposes, usually chaired by the most trusted stakeholder.
13. **Hand over the development process to local authorities and CBOs** – A smooth "exit" strategy on how to get out of the neighbourhood with no harm must be well thought and gradually implemented by the development organizations, NGOs or start-up professional structures. When local CBOs and authorities show good capacities for jointly managing the development process, a "Memorandum of Cooperation" must be signed between them to institutionalise i) future responsibilities and duties, and ii) clear timeline and resources, in favour of a transparent plan implementation, including improvement of basic services, infrastructure, and full legalization.
14. **Intermediate implementation of the cooperation agreement** – Make sure the implementation of the plan and other priority services push the development process towards full legalization and community integration, by making them normal citizens and taxpayers. Then fully hand over development process to authorities and local CBOs, by making sure to train local authorities.
15. **Periodically organise citywide actions of information and awareness** – Undertake training and community visits for students and scholars, workshops and tours for municipal and ministry staff, citywide public debates for professionals and broad public, open lectures, forums, publications, exhibitions, conferences, and TV-debates, focused on city development issues by confronting different opinions and promoting contemporary ideas. It is essential these actions be taken on a city scale, and not just in the area.
16. **Draft professional, legal, and political platforms of city transformations** – Ask political candidates during electoral campaigns (both at municipal and national level) to publicly express their opinion on how they will solve community problems of broad public interest. Prepare technical platforms and submit them at the municipal council and national parliament, proposing legal changes in favour of the communities and local development. Put positive pressure via (social) media, polls, and surveys, disseminating the public opinion, etc., always from a neutral basis. Help reformation of the decision-making by providing professional arguments.
17. **Periodical long-term monitoring of the development process** – This can be done by the NGOs, academia or even municipalities by hiring independent experts or involving diploma students and researchers to study and analyse the long-term effects of transformations in the development process. Always share such surveys and research findings among all stakeholders involved.

it through a soft and timely based "*social community pressure*" (Aliaj, Shutina, & Dhamo, 2010). After that, community residents convince their neighbours to embrace the "rules" of the process and speed up. Most importantly, all is done with no need for the presence of authorities or police. The first positive impact materialised soon! *World Bank* in Albania joined the process. They asked Co-PLAN and local CBOs to help adapting such experience as a main philosophy within their own national "*ULMP Urban Land Management Project*" jointly financed with the Albanian Government (Jarwood, 2010). Breglumasi and Bathore neighbourhoods were the first among a few others to benefit from the investments.

Bringing community puzzles together – The making of the strategic urban development plan

An important milestone in the process of reinventing planning at city scale in Albania has been the tactic of ***organizing several scientific events of national and international impact***, as strategic instruments to further advance urban knowledge/agenda in Albania. The first one was jointly organised with *Municipality of Tirana* and *Ministry of Public Works*: the international conference of ENHR *European Network of Housing Research*, namely "*Making Cities Work*" in May 2003 (Aliaj, 2005). The conference was followed then every year by similar events of the same importance. The international debate was a tactical move of Co-PLAN to use the situation of Tirana as a case study and a working laboratory among local and international experts, researchers, decision makers, and institutions. It aimed the confronting ideas and changing attitudes as a real educational atmosphere. Such presence in the city was seen as an instrument of raising awareness among the broad public. Participants were "provoked" to shift out from the auditors of the conference towards communities in need, and ongoing peripheral development programs. For Co-PLAN this was also a moment of shift beyond the work in the informal areas. It meant moving strategically towards planning for the formal context and city centres! Such events were carefully designed as open platforms for frank debates between highest local and national authorities, and international keynote speakers. Tangible recipes and concrete recommendations were asked on how to go further on! From that moment, Co-PLAN was practically in the lead of reforming the planning agenda of Albania.

Another tactical instrument became the preparation of qualitative contextual ***publications***. Books could be crucial reference and support tools to bring together professionals and students in common understanding of the needs for a "new" planning system. The initial series of "*City Made by People*" (Co-PLAN, 1998) transformed later on into a scientific journal known as "*Forum A+P*", (POLISPress, 2006). Such publications summarised the positive local experiences of urban development in Tirana, thus creating institutional bridges for debate amongst professionals and authorities. As result of that, Co-PLAN became the main advocate for formulating ***bottom-up strategic neighbourhood/city development plans*** for the *Greater Tirana Area*, as a model that would cater Albanian reality and integrate informally developed areas. World Bank and the Albanian authorities joined again the exercise that was completed by 2003 (Kacani, 2019), despite problems with the existing *status quo*. Neighbourhood and municipal plans of Kamza were also integrated with the city.

The activities of Co-PLAN on ***capacity building*** were backed in the long term by *IHS Rotterdam, Institute for Housing and Urban Development Studies, Erasmus University Rotterdam,* the Netherlands. Such an alliance has been crucial. More than 50 staff of Co-PLAN were systematically trained over time there, together with key staff from the local and national institutions. This was an internal and city capacity building strategy of Co-PLAN in order to cater better for the needs of the authorities. Several ***on-the-job trainings***, priority needs assessment, operational plans, etc., were undertaken as well. The approach used was based on the PACA and OOPP methodologies(Peace_Corps, 2007; UN, 2002). Thanks to that, Co-PLAN could identify three issues: i) urban development; ii) infrastructure; iii) economic development, which meant employment as the main priorities of the municipal administration on a city-wide scale. In order to respond to those needs, the following objectives were formulated: a) drafting a vision for urban development; b) establishing a capacity-building program; c) having concrete investments.

Previous planning initiatives in Albania failed to meet the real needs of people. Until then, plans were produced that ended up not approved in shelves. It is a fact nowadays that the only approved plan in almost 2.5 decades of transformation was the participatory plan designed by Co-PLAN, and the communities and authorities of Kamza Municipality (Co-PLAN, 2002). Recognizing that, Co-PLAN was invited to plan other municipalities too. To date, 40% of the municipalities in the country are planned thanks to the experience of Co-PLAN, and its spin-off POLIS University (AKPT, 2016). It has been clear for those institutions that only ***the process makes the difference*** from others. For Co-PLAN the plan in itself is seen not as an end but as a long-term instrument in the hands of the authorities to foster the development of the neighbourhoods and cities.

The ***tangible investments*** were the last but not least component. Given the financial constraints, they were not meant to meet the huge needs for municipal infrastructure. This necessitated that the choices should be addressing specific issues and models (Co-PLAN, 2002). Co-PLAN wanted to use investments to assist municipality, rather than taking over its duties to meet the needs of public infrastructure and services. Co-PLAN's bottom up philosophy of work was always based on sharing contributions to improve through the steps and stages of betterment of the area. Initially all these were perfectly understood by the residents but not immediately by the authorities and professional communities. Thus the move to a "***higher/city scale***" – along with the shift from an "*action oriented experience*" towards "*policy formulation*" – implied that the terms of discussion with the residents needed to reform further. Co-PLAN learned that the municipal planning document must always be easily translatable into actions and phases expressed in operational terms. The same problem was also encountered by the municipal staff.

Moving to the national scale: Education, education, and education! – Drafting Albania 2030

After the first decade of grass-root experiences of Co-PLAN, the organization moved qualitatively and gradually from community to city and national scale. The methodological approach remained bottom up. Co-PLAN was always the voice of the people and society. Between 2003–2005, Co-PLAN drafted a policy document addressed to all political parties in the Parliament of Albania (Aliaj, 2008). Between local and national elections, the document opened a good technical debate at highest decision-making levels. The platform has been mostly adopted, although further interpreted by the last two governments in power. It is still a running project at national scale that includes a qualitative role of Co-PLAN and POLIS University as watchdogs, but also in advising new legislations on: territorial planning and development (Law 107/2014); formalization of buildings, properties and economy (Ligji 9482, 3 April 2006); decentralization, administrative division and regionalization (Co-PLAN, 2014); education and science; etc. The impact has been maximal but not easy going. Maintaining independence and neutrality has been always a struggle, but de facto successfully achieved. The key staff of Co-PLAN assisted Government of Albania for drafting and implementing a specially designed program on "the rule of law", supported by UNDP and ILD Peru, (UNDP, 2007), and preparing the methodology for the national spatial development plan as well.

The establishment of POLIS University: Creating a critical mass of reformed expertise

Moving ahead with city planning and territorial development agendas via reforms and by working at macro policy-making level made Co-PLAN understand once more the need for a new soft "exit" strategy, handling the job gradually to the national authorities, and maintaining its own neutral position. Co-PLAN's philosophy has been always self-adapting and "one-step ahead" of others. By understanding the magnitude of national problems, Co-PLAN founders and staff concluded that in order to guarantee resilient city's approach, there was an urgent need to establish a critical mass of expertise within the city/country, able enough to work in line with the comprehensive and bottom-up philosophy of Co-PLAN. Among many spinoffs of Co-PLAN, (Aliaj, Shutina, & Dhamo, 2010), therefore ***education*** has been seen as the next strategic step.

Between 2000 and 2005, Co-PLAN established initially a ***training centre*** for local authorities and communities (NET – Network of Exchange and Training). In 2006, this was transformed into a private with non-for-profit logic, namely *POLIS University* of Tirana, or otherwise known as the *International School of Architecture and Urban Development Policies* (POLISPress, 2006). POLIS University nowadays is established as a "space for thinking" in the fields of sustainable design, engineering and territorial development policies, including technology, civic leadership and private entrepreneurship. The mission of POLIS today is to provide knowledge, technology, and leadership for people and communities, encouraging local and national development, and innovation. Through its unique applied and alternative scientific research, POLIS today develops and promotes scientific excellence and innovation (POLISPress, 2006). Through its non-conventional academic and practical teaching, it enhances creative and comprehensive competences (POLISPress, 2006). The impact radiates also in Western Balkans and Adriatic-Ionian region. All it started up with a grassroots project in the outskirts of Tirana.

Conclusions

Both Co-PLAN and POLIS University are well established "civic movement" institutions with a strong social responsibility and resilient local resources. It has been shown in this article that the development of both institutions can be understood in terms of their deep grassroots and professional approach, as well as in the entrepreneurial start-up logic. Such logic is naturally and intelligently applied in the case of Co-PLAN and POLIS University for the benefit of communities, cities, and their needs of contemporary planning and development. Without such pioneering organizations, it is very hard to think nowadays tackling complex realities such as Albania.

The innovative and socially responsible founders of Co-PLAN acted as successful professional entrepreneurs in a given dynamic urban context. One could say that creative startups could be everywhere – and not just in a "*LA garage in USA*" – but also in any size and type of institutions, and even in countries like Albania. The founders of Co-PLAN and POLIS University started in a very modest office in the peripheries of Tirana, bound to the local Albanian context and trained internationally (Niented, 2016). Apart from studying architecture, engineering, planning, etc., they all also studied on creative management and entrepreneurship, which was highly beneficial for them, for their institution, and its mission in the society. They made plans, rented a building for a pragmatic NGO organization, which later on developed into a qualitative University premises. The design processes always went via rigorous and creative participatory processes. The location of offices was purposely selected near the targeted communities, and later on near business clusters. The entrepreneurial spirit from the "start" has been and is still part of the growing creative culture of Co-PLAN and POLIS University, and their own projects. It responds flexibly to the daily work, providing comprehensive expertise of high social responsibility, beneficial to people and communities, thus making them highly useful for the society and institutions.

However, the entrepreneurial spirit in city planning imposes the need for a balanced resilient city management culture. This implies that Co-PLAN and POLIS became not simply standard professional organizations, but remain first of all human institutions designed to create new thinking, new products, and services for architecture, city planning, and broader territorial policies. Growing into a critical pool of expertise with around 100–150 local and international staff, and significant imposed rules and bureaucracy, they demand fine and innovative management, while keeping focus on what they are about: their mission and independence; their advice, research and academic activities; and their civic activism. They did so under highly uncertainty conditions, unfair competition, and pressure from political factors.

Co-PLAN's start-up experience in applied architecture and city planning teaches others lessons that in order to build resilient communities and cities, one must first build sustainable and resilient institutions, in order to achieve social missions and public objectives. This is why Co-PLAN and POLIS are still successful respectively since 1993. Over time, they demonstrated a successful internal capacity building strategy, which in return rewarded them with a dynamically stable and creative institution, despite turbulent Albania. It is because of the "high uncertainty" of Albania's environment and the limited financial means, that made Co-PLAN fit regularly: try initially something as small as possible; than learn and improve towards bigger and higher scale (Bonazzi & Perruchoud, 2014). Therefore, this lesson is simple:

build-measure-learn. In the case of Co-PLAN and POLIS University, the feedback cycle (Thompson & MacMillan, 2010) has been always based on the response of people/partners, but the organizational cycle is longer than that; as feedback often comes from many different sources (not only citizens, researchers, students, but also from parents who pay, from government officials, donors, professional circles, and so on). More is to be researched in the future on the case of Co-PLAN, POLIS University, and their start-up logic.

References

About Co-Plan. (2010). Retrieved 5 2020, from Co-Plan – Institute for Habitat Development: http://www.co-plan.org/en/rreth-co-plan/

About Polis University. (2006). Retrieved 2020, from Polis Univeristy: http://www.universitetipolis.edu.al/?q=en/node/80

Accioly, C., Aliaj, B., & Kuçi, F. (2004). A path to citizen participation in urban management. *Adequate and Affordable Housing for All* (p. 25). Toronto: Univerisity of Toronto.

AKPT. (2016). *Plani i Pergjithshem Kombetar*. Tirana: Agjensia Kombetare e Planifikimit te Territorit.

Aliaj, B. (2005). Comparing between Transitional and Developed urban housing models. *ENHR04: Making Cities Work* (p. 12). Tirana: Co-PLAN.

Aliaj, B. (2008). *Misteri i Gjashtë. Cili është kurthi që mban peng zhvillimin dhe integrimin e ekonomisë shqipetare në botën moderne*. Tiranë: CoPlan.

Aliaj, B. (2002). NGOs/CBOs and housing for low-income people in Albania, Governing Cities – New institutional forms in developing countries and transitional economies. *Urban Managment Series*, 109–128.

Aliaj, B. (1998). Pilot Actions for Community Based Planning of Irregular Settlements in Tirana – Albania. *City and Culture, Urban Sustainability and Cultural Processes* (p. 12). Stockholm – Cultural capital of Europe '98: International Conference.

Aliaj, B., Shutina, D., & Dhamo, S. (2010). *Between energy and the vacuum*. Tiranë: CoPlan.

Bonazzi, R., & Perruchoud, A. (2014). Combining the notions of "lean startup" and "effectuation" to train future entrepreneurs. *Interdisciplinary European Conference on Entrepreneurship Research* (p. 7). Chur: IECER.

Co-PLAN. (2004). *Annual Report*. Tirana: Co-PLAN.

Co-PLAN. (2007). *Annual Report*. Tirana: Co-PLAN.

Co-PLAN. (1998). *City Made by People. Vol 1*. Tirana: Co-PLAN.

Co-PLAN. (2003). *Neighbourhood Development Agenda.*. Tirana: Co-PLAN.

Co-PLAN. (2002). *Strategic Urban Development Plan of the Municipality of Kamza*. Retrieved from: https://www.researchgate.net/publication/280578412_Strategic_Urban_Development_Plan_of_the_Municipality_of_Kamza

Co-PLAN. (2014). *The Regionalisation of Albania, The Governance, Administrative, and Territorial Reform that Albania needs on a Regional Level*. Tiranë: Co-Plan.

Hope, K. (2013). Albania playing catch-up. *Financial Times*, 1.

Jarwood, J. (2010). *Strategic Planning: Greater Tirana Strategic Plan (Urban Planning After War, Disaster and Disintegration*. Cambridge: Cambridge Scholars Publishing.

Kacani, A. (2019). F.I.S.I.A assessment and the territorial impact. Measuring and comparing the policy efficiency and effectiveness of the Urban Agenda on informal areas in Tirana and Durrës region. Doctoral dissertation, POLIS University. Tirana: Polis Press.

Law 107/2014. Për Planifikimin dhe Zhvillimin e Territorit.

Ligji 9482. (03.04.2006). Per legalizimin, urbanizimin dhe integrimin e ndertimeve pa leje. Tiranë.

LMTF. (1995). *Land development Pilot Project in Western Tirana: A Public/Private Partnership, Land Management Task Force*. Tirana: USAID.

Misja, V., & Vejsiu, Y. (1996). *Aspects of Demographic Development in Albania*. Tirana.

Niented, P. (2016). *U polis as Lean Startup Innovation*. Tirana: Polis Press.

Peace Corps. (2007). *Participatory Analysis for Community Action Training Manual*. Washington: Peace Corps Information Collection and Exchange.

POLISPress. (2006). Retrieved 2020, from Polis Univeristy: http://www.universitetipolis.edu.al/?q=en/node/175

Republic_of_Albania. (1998). *Constitution, article 59*. Tirana: Kuvendi i Shqiperise.

Thompson, J., & MacMillan, I. (2010). Business Models: Creating New Markets and Societal Wealth. *Long Range Planning. Volume 43, Issues* 2–3, 291–307.

UN. (2002). *Participatory Project Design to combat trafficking in children and women. Objective Oriented Project Planning (OOPP) as design tool*. Bankok: Mekong Sub-Regional Project to Combat Trafficking in Children and Women.

UNDP. (2007). *Albania: transition to the rule of law and inclusive market economy*. Lima: ILD Peru.

World Bank Technical Assistance Project. (2013). Retrieved from: https://data.worldbank.org/indicator/NY.GDP.MKTP.CD?locations=AL

World Bank Technical Assistance Project. (2013). Retrieved 2020 from: https://projects.worldbank.org/en/projects-operations/project-detail/P004339?lang=en

Chapter 21

Roman lessons

What if informality was not a bug to be corrected but a bacterium capable of reactivating a dormant urban metabolism?

Alessandra Lai and Francesco Careri

Introduction

As is well known, the world population tends to move to cities, which, together with their metropolitan areas, represent today the centre of economic production. Living in or around cities means increasing opportunities to escape extreme poverty. However cities do not seem equipped to accommodate and manage this very rapid urbanization process, so more people than ever before are now responsible for creating their living spaces, and they do so within different economic contexts, and different climatic and cultural conditions, which generate a wide range of solutions to the problem of living (Pojani, 2019). These are spaces, places and communities where residents adapt to the circumstances at hand using locally based rules, processes and governance. These actions are generally 'outside' the structures and processes that guide order and control in the formally planned city (Jones, 2017). Therefore, it has become common practice to define them as "informal".

As Lefebvre reminds us, illustrating the concept of "right to the city", "[people in informal settlements] are excluded, so they take; they are not seizing an abstract right, they are taking an actual place. And this act to challenge society's denial of place by taking one of your own, is an assertion of being in a world that routinely denies people the dignity and the validity inherent in a home" (Neuwirth, 2005).

This chapter illustrates, through a passionate interview with Francesco Careri, the events, tools, problems and perspectives that have characterized some emblematic attempts to accompany the creation of alternative living models to those formally defined by the system of rules that would like to design the contemporary city, but which prove to be unable to provide the conditions for dignified living and enjoying the opportunities of the city for the weaker segments of the population.

In particular, Careri, with Stalker and other associations, worked on the themes of the intercultural city and nomadism in Rome, recognizing the importance of informal settlements as an alternative expression of contemporary, otherwise prosaic, artificial and sanitized urbanity (Cummings 2013; De la Hoz 2013).

Careri's building activity focuses on the intangible. Rather than modifying the informal spaces of the city, he is interested in "building situations" to make them visible, to transform the perspective from which we observe the communities that inhabit them, to recognize their identity and values. To affirm the "right to difference" (Careri, 2018).

The purpose of this contribution is not to enrich the case studies on informal settlements, neither from the point of view of the economic, social, legal and political aspects, already widely debated by other scholars, nor from the point of view of the formal analysis of the design solutions that have been adopted. Instead, the interest of the authors is to offer, through the story of Roman cases, new opportunities for reflection on the plurality and equal dignity of forms for contemporary living. If the right to housing and the city were recognized as one of the expressions of the "right to difference", a more fertile rethinking of the fate of the spaces of the contemporary and future city could be launched. And in fact the image of informality is already not uniformly negative: dystopic, poor settlements simultaneously attracts and repel visitors (whether researchers or "slum tourists") (Pojani, 2019).

LAI: The climate emergency represents, at a global level, the strongest push for the search for new forms and new languages to design the cities of the future, but also to outline more responsible behaviour. However, the 17 objectives contained in the 2030 Agenda for Sustainable Development remind us that climate change is not the only threat: common urban challenges include the lack of funds to provide basic services and the lack of adequate housing.

In the big cities, which welcome a fluctuating population with increasingly heterogeneous characteristics in terms of culture, education, language or religion, the ordinary challenges are joined by those related to the search for new forms to encourage a fruitful coexistence between new or temporary citizens and old citizens.

The consolidated urban space planning models reject any element that lies outside their own schemes and the traditional assistance tools complain of insufficient endowments to manage the dimension of the social transformations taking place. Is it possible to introduce informal appendices to the consolidated model to make it more porous and flexible or has the time come for a radical rethinking of the system of rules on which the growth of the city is based?

CARERI: To the word Rome our brain immediately associates that of ruins and immediately the stereotyped image of people who inhabit them in a picturesque, "informal" way we would say today, appears to the mind. For external and internal tourists – even for those who live in the city but superficially – Rome appears as an opaque marsh from which few islands of ancient ruins emerge, freed, for some time now, from their inhabitants and enhanced for the tourism show.

All around, on the surface of the pond, nothing moves, everything floats inert. No brave burst of urban audacity moves the surface of the water. But if you dive deeper into the contemporary city we still find the Eternal Rome, that of ruins and poor people, old and new poor, old and new Romans, all always foreigners.

The city is again the one portrayed by Piranesi and the Grand Tour landscape painters. Discarded lives who live among the waste: poor, homeless, migrants, Roma and unwanted people of all kinds, who rebuild their lives no longer among the ancient ruins but in the ruins of the contemporaneity. It seems that they have always been there, that they are part of the local fauna. Here, in fact, the city must be invented because otherwise no form of life would be possible.

In recent years with Stalker we have started to re-read the eternal theme of ruins and foreigners. I must say that it was in particular Lorenzo Romito,[1] in the early months of 2015, who proposed to all of us at Stalker the myth of the foundation of Rome, of the pagan gods, of the imperial myths ... the fact of getting to re-read the Aeneid of Virgil seemed crazy to me: I thought he was joking! Then I understood the depth of the operation: undressing the fascist and imperial rhetoric that has always appropriated all this and affirming that the Genius Loci of Rome is founded on the hospitality of the foreigner, that Rome has always been a great multicultural capital, that in eternal history they were the foreigners who cyclically re-inhabited the ruins and re-founded Rome.

With Stalker we have done two actions to re-read and reactivate the ancient myths: a first walk *On the Ruins of the Contemporary*[2] to witness the new costly architectures of the archistars left unfinished, and a second, *Xeneide*[3] to go over the traces of Aeneas: progenitor of Romulus and Remus. Aeneas, the Trojan, arrives in Rome as a refugee, runs away from the war, has lost many companions in the dangerous journey in the Mediterranean, lands on the Italian beaches, among the ruins of the Palatine (there were already ruins before there was Rome) meets another foreigner, Evandro the Greek, to whom he is bound by a previous bond of hospitality, the *xenia*.[4] Aeneas will bring his foreign blood to mix it with that of the Latins and the Etruscans to give life to Eternal Rome, a city cyclically in ruins and reactivated by foreigners who live there.

Despite the myth, and I come to answer the last part of your question, today in Rome neither ruins nor foreigners are recognized as a resource to reactivate the wheel of the Eternal city and bring down the waters that have flooded the marsh. We want those waters to keep still and to hide what cannot yet emerge. Here it is not possible to make the consolidated model more porous and flexible although it would be necessary and although the virtuous informal experiences from which to learn exist and are also many. And it also seems to me that the turning point for a radical rethinking of the system of rules you are talking about is actually taking place, but that it is taking place in the opposite direction. It is an authoritarian turn that is changing the rules of civil and democratic coexistence, increasingly intolerant toward any form of resistance to the dominant model. For a different change today there are no political conditions, even if there are physical, economic and human resources. Although what is happening at the bottom of the marsh is well known to the administration, it is not intended to proceed towards the legalization of informal experiences, nor to offer spaces and opportunities in which to experiment with alternative formal models.

LAI: Your answer seems to suggest enormous potentiality and then burn them permanently. Yet I have read that you had started to conduct a census of the places of degradation in Rome (perhaps referring to the ruins of the contemporary). Here came to mind the self-management experiment of Torre David, the abandoned skyscraper of Caracas following the death of its builder and the collapse of the Venezuelan economy, which later became an improvised home for over 750 families. Where some saw only a failed project (a ruin of the contemporary?), others saw an opportunity and a laboratory for studying informal vertical communities, which drove to the conclusion that the future of urban development lies in the collaboration between architects, private companies and the global population

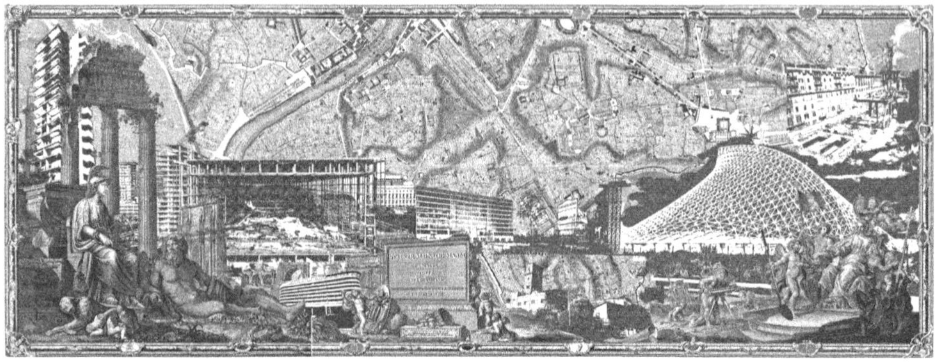

Figure 21.1 Map of the seven ruins. Digital collage. 2014.

Source: Carlo Prati.

of slum dwellers. No mention of administrations or political forces. Is this collaborative scenario with private companies a utopia, a provocation, or there are elements that give hope?

CARERI: I'm sorry that it seemed that I wanted to burn all hope, but it would actually be easier to operate on these issues with other political scenarios than the current ones, and if politics does not follow us we would go on as you say, as architects-artists, private companies and population. Unfortunately, in fact, it does not seem to me a historical moment in which the public could be the only solution. And I do not exclude the possibility of collaborating with private actors at all: it is not a problem of ideological barriers. I think private capital can and should be stimulated, educated and convinced of the fact that in some cases decreasing profit to support welfare is important for everyone, even for private individuals if they do not want society to collapse violently, bringing them into the abyss as well.

Today there are some solutions for the lower-middle class, the so-called Social Housing Policies for those who can afford to pay at least 500 euros per month. I believe that this type of operation should be also extended to those in emergency circumstances and paupers, perhaps leveraging on their constructive, organisational and evolutionary abilities, and this is possible by understanding and favouring the microeconomies and mutual aid systems that are created, for example, in housing occupations. Given that, however, I believe that also with regards to the public, the time has come to reverse the course: we have to stop with selling off and "securitizing" public housing, we need to start expanding the public real estate assets again, starting to experiment on an ever-growing range of increasingly differentiated public solutions. This cannot be invented from scratch as a table, and can only be done by observing and understanding the reality and urban life that surrounds us, which in order to survive finds infinite solutions.

LAI: In 1971, Victor Papanek wrote a book, *Design for the Real World*, which revolves around the question: how is it possible to "design for the real world"? You did it, facing the exceptions that our rule system rejects. How do you deal with informality without pretending to bring it back, by distorting it, within rigid and formal schemes? What can be transferred from your experiences in traditional planning or assistance tools and what is holding back this "transfusion" process?

CARERI: Yes, you are right, for twenty years now we have been dealing with informality with Stalker, and we have ripened a certain awareness and attitude towards the problems of relational approach and cultural appropriation that they propose. But after so many experiences we have not succeeded either in having a real mandate to work in a formal way, or in transferring what we learnt in our experiences to the traditional instruments.

With Stalker we have worked not only to *design for the real world*, but also to "*build*" with the real world, and always addressing the theme of ruins, foreigners and informal living. The first realization was the Ararat center, an abandoned building of the former slaughterhouse in Testaccio, which we occupied and reactivated together with Kurdish activists and refugees in 1999. It is still the only place created for the hospitality of refugees in the city center, inside the Roman walls and not in the unattainable metropolitan suburbs. It is entirely self-managed and more than twenty-five thousand refugees have passed through it, without ever burdening public funds.[5]

For years we have also dealt with the issue of the Roma, and with them we have worked in the slums, we have built a model house, *Savorengo Ker*, which means 'the house for everyone', we have made proposals to the administrations to overcome the system of camps. But the house was burned, the Roma were evicted and locked up in mono-ethnic camps, and no reasonable policy came from the successive administrations to overcome a situation that has always been absolutely unacceptable for a European capital.[6]

After the experience with the Roma community, we worked with the Civic Arts Laboratory on the theme of housing occupations, in particular with those of Metropoliz[7] and the Porto Fluviale,[8] witnessing yet another world that inhabits the ruins and makes them the garrisons of the fight for the right to housing. They are people with a lucid political awareness that comes from the struggles of the Seventies, but whose discourse has changed profoundly. They have made many important steps,

Figure 21.2 Stalker e casilino 900, savorengo ker – house for everyone, 2008.

Source: Giorgio de Finis.

such as that from the *struggle for home* towards a wider *struggle for living*, that is not only to have a roof but a set of services, spaces, relationships and policies that coincide with the city itself.

The movement in the last twenty years has greatly grown in number, from the few hundred people of the Eighties to the many thousands today. It has diversified in its composition: first they were almost entirely Italian and today there is a large foreign majority; and the way of presenting itself to the city has changed: no longer only antagonist but also proactive and with a great ability to create alliances with previously unthinkable actors, for example the Vatican, and to solve the problems that administrations do not even want to face. The movements of fight for the right to housing are managing to bring out from the marsh what in the perception of the city was previously invisible. But they still lose a lot of energy in defending themselves from threats of eviction and live a daily precariousness that does not allow them to evolve into formal models.

LAI: Cases of occupations and self-managements are ways of appropriating urban space perceived with diffidence as parasitic, at least in today's sense of the word, which indicates as a parasite someone "who lives behind others." In the experiences you mentioned like Ararat, the Roma community of Casilino 900 and the mixed-race communities of Metropoliz, Porto Fluviale, and now Spin Time, it seems that it is possible to recover the original sense of the term, where the nickname "parasite" was referred to "those who participate in a banquet without having a defined role (without having organized it and without having particular merits to be invited)," positioning themselves "around the food or the source of sustenance," but, gladdening the hosts with games and jokes. In short, it testifies to the willingness to exchange.

What kind of exchanges can we expect to observe between new communities settled in residual or abandoned spaces and the neighbourhood or the city? What kind of resources can the new inhabitants bring into play, to start establishing fruitful relationships of reciprocity with the context in which they settle?

CARERI: Today, apart from the hostile gaze of a few, even ordinary people begin to understand that the many buildings occupied in Rome are a barrier to degradation and a solution which, although precarious, is not only capable of offering spaces for a dignified and human living, but also services and innovation for the rest of the city. They are places where intercultural living is experimented in different forms, where people are not numbers and bodies to manage, but women and men free to express their culture and desires. Even institutional politics sometimes look at them with interest, as in the case of R-Home, a day in which administrators, occupants, activists, artists and intellectuals made a long bus tour to understand the phenomenon more closely.[9]

The academy also did its part to make the phenomenon read from a different point of view. There are increasingly studied experiences on which many degree and doctoral theses are made. In short, I would say that the exchange exists and it is getting stronger.

I like your definition of "parasite" and it is very suitable for the C.I.R.C.O. project, an acronym that stands for Casa Irrinunciabile per la Ricreazione Civica e l'Ospitalità.[10] It is a project that proposes to put together, as eternally happened in Rome, the ruins with foreigners, learning from the occupations how the institutional reception machine could be replaced with a network of places based on hospitality. The acronym explicitly refers to the imagination of the circus: that colourful, magical, nomadic place and alien to the city, proud of its diversity, which is installed in waste land and where the circus performers have skills to put together in a project common.

First of all, we elaborated the theme of the ruins with a mapping that is divided into different layers: military barracks, Atac[11] remittances, cinemas, theaters, schools, sports facilities, health facilities, ecclesiastical goods, factories. All abandoned. The proposal is to inhabit and recover wastes as hybrid, porous, inclusive, original places, in which to relaunch culture by giving space to the Other: to the Roma, to the migrant, to the off-site student, to the seasonal worker, to the artist, to the craftsman, to the traveler, to the homeless and also to tourists.

Later we proposed several projects that pivot on the O of the acronym Circus, hospitality (in Italian "Ospitalità"). As I said before about the Xeneide project, this takes up the Greek word *xenía*, the gift that the host gives to the guest, but more generally concerns the complex of reciprocal rules that underlie the hospitality, which was sacred to all the ancient world and which today has lost its meaning and has been replaced by the word "Reception." While "Reception" is a one-way word, which refers to needs, to blankets, hot meals, legal and health assistance, to looking after bodies and not people with their desires, "Hospitality" is based instead on a mutual exchange, looks at the guest as a bearer of the gift, of culture, of resources. Rome continues to be a city where you are not hosted, but also where hosting is prevented by all means, as it was evident in the Baobab Experience, a city network of solidarity and hospitality for so-called migrants in transit that organized a space informal reception next to the Tiburtina station which has been periodically cleared for years.

The migrant issue is complex and varied: some are economic migrants who prefer not to be registered in Italy and try to reach Northern Europe, others have refugee status but when the reception period is over they have nowhere to go, others are Dubliners, those that Europe sends back because of the Dublin Treaty which obliges to apply for asylum in the country where they landed. Until the city realizes that migrants are a resource and not a problem, they will not make great progress.

Conclusions

Careri's Roman lessons on informality are upstream. There is no interest in regulating informality by reporting it within formal canons. On the contrary, his research focuses on building opportunities to reveal its characteristics and values. Careri is a scholar and an explorer – with his students and different associations, he travels and crosses Rome, not the eternal city of the imperial ruins, but the ephemeral city of the voiceless people who today, as in its glorious past, reach the capital through different life paths.

The first lesson we learn from these case studies is that on "building together." It can assume different meanings, like building spaces, architecture, homes, relationships, or social, cultural and economic opportunities. The focus lies in the word "together," where active listening represents a very powerful tool to know other worlds and to make other worlds known, because it invites the Other to express himself and tell about his differences. Listening evolves into sharing knowledge when the exchange is not one-way, when nobody excels, when all voices have equal dignity. As Senneth (Watchel, 2013) reminds us "Cooperation is a lesson that needs to be learnt, by listening. Not by showing hyper-empathy (the reception), but by becoming curious, and accepting that we cannot all be inside it in the same way, but we collaborate the same despite the fact that people do not really understand each other at all."

The construction of Savorengo Ker, the house for everyone at the Casilino 900, had many values, but above all, it gave space to the comparison on the ways of thinking about the meaning of house and the ways of building it.

This is also linked to the concept of hospitality as a guiding attitude in approaching the theme of informal living and more generally in establishing fertile exchanges between the guest and the host. The Italian word "guest" derives, in fact, from the Latin *hospes-pitis* and alludes to the reciprocal duties of hospitality; therefore, in the Italian language a guest is a person who receives in his own home and a guest is a person who enjoys hospitality and presents himself in the house. This is so clear in the case of Metropoliz, the abandoned factory that houses families belonging to different ethnic groups and in the free and collective spaces welcomes the works and installations of various artists. On Saturday the doors of this world open to tourists and citizens allowing them to understand who the Other is and what the Elsewhere is.

Roman experiences also tell of the ability of these new citizens to resurrect otherwise forgotten spaces and buildings simply by inhabiting them. Hence the other project, C.I.R.C.O., dedicated to the mapping of the ruins of the contemporary, of those spaces that the formal city, with all its political, administrative, professional and common citizen components, ignores. To ask oneself about the fate of these places means to ask oneself about the fate of Rome. Perhaps it is in the resources of the ephemeral city that eternal Rome could find the strength for its re-foundation, especially now that news tells us of a city out of control, unmanageable and decadent. Rome is a city that, like many other capitals, sees its national and international influence very weakened, and needs to find new perspectives and new motivations to recover. Perhaps through works such as Careri's it becomes possible to imagine the rebirth of Rome as a real re-foundation by recovering "his Genius Loci founded on the hospitality of the foreigner. Rome has always been a great multicultural capital, which in eternal history were the foreigners who cyclically re-inhabited the ruins and re-founded Rome."

In the end, the project C.I.R.C.O. invites us to re-think the global approach we've always had towards informality management: instead of trying to legalize informal settlements and occupations, why don't we imagine a complete radical change of the paradigm? Why don't we explore the opportunity to open the city's elements to welcome new models of living, new ways of housing? This type of operation would be able to activate new social housing policies to include people in emergency and often paupers, leveraging on their constructive, organizational and evolutionary abilities, understanding and favouring the microeconomies and mutual aid systems that emerge, for example, in housing occupations.

Instead of a stereotyped capital that chooses to compete with the others through high tech skyscrapers, we can think of Rome as a New Babylon fragment of Constant's utopia, which in 1956 imagined a "city for homo ludens," a "nomad camp on planetary scale."[12] Some fixed, immanent elements, such as the ruins of ancient Rome, the monuments of the Fascist era, the headquarters of the institutions that govern the country and a series of spaces in the making, built, inhabited and modified by a crowd in transit. A crowd made by the migrants, the students who come from the South of Italy, the regional delegates, the tourists, the artists, those who must request permits, the workers who have been sent to Rome but can't wait to return to their villages, the nomads and all the fragile segments of our society. What if we start to consider them a resource? Instead of looking at them as common "parasites," we should start to imagine this crowd like those bacteria capable of preserving a healthy state of balance in the urban environment, by re-activating the metabolism of the inert spaces of the city.

Notes

1 Romito L. (2014), *Walking out of Contemporary*, in Mitrasinovic M. (Ed.) Concurrent Urbanities: Designing infrastructures of Inclusion, Routledge, 2015. (https://www.academia.edu/12089692/Walking_out_of_Contemporary)
2 *Among the ruins of the contemporary* is a Stalker project, developed on the occasion of the artistic residence Studio Roma, at the Swiss Institute in Rome, and it is the title of the walk between 18 and 20 March 2016 which led us from the Colosseum to the skeleton of the "white shark" designed by Santiago Calatrava via the "beached whale" of Fuksas in EUR and the "city of moles" of Koolhaas in Ostiense.
3 *Xeneide – the gift of the Other. Myths, Practices, Poetics of Hospitality* is a project curated by Stalker and NoWorking in 2017. The project produced a first experimentation of the Gift Space at the AuditoriumArte and then, with the Civic Arts Studio, retraced on foot the journey of Aeneas from Torvaianica beach to the top of Monte Cavo on the Alban hills, the legendary Albalonga from which Romulus and Remus came to found Rome (https://xeneideblog.wordpress.com/).
4 From the Greek word ξενία «hospitality»
5 On Ararat, today known as the Kurdish Cultural Center of the Ex Slaughterhouse of Testaccio, and on all of Stalker's experience at Campo Boario, there is an unpublished book by Stalker Nomad Observatory, *Circles. Campo Boario 1999–2009*, available online (https://www.dropbox.com/s/uoe777ovcg9fmdg/librostalker%20campo%20boario.pdf?dl=0)
6 On the actions and projects made by Stalker with the Roma, cf. Francesco Careri, Lorenzo Romito, *StalkerOn / Campus Rom*, Altrimedia edizioni, Matera 2017. The film *Once upon a time Savorengo Ker*, by Fabrizio Boni and Giorgio de Finis on the house built together with the Roma of Casilino 900 in July 2008 is on Vimeo (https://vimeo.com/showcase/1540238)
7 Metropoliz is a residential occupation of the Metropolitan Precarious BPM-Blocks located on Via Prenestina and is now also home to the MAAM, Museum of the Other and the Elsewhere, designed by Giorgio de Finis. See Francesco Careri *Autodialogo su Metropoliz*, in Fabrizio Boni and Giorgio de Finis, "*Space Metropoliz. L'era delle migrazioni esoplanetarie*," Bordeaux Editions, 2015.
8 Porto Fluviale is a housing occupation of the City Fight for Home Coordination. On Porto Fluviale see the 2011 *Good Buy Roma* film by Gaetano Crivaro and Margherita Pisano (https://goodbuyroma.wordpress.com/) and Francesco Careri, *Tano, Blu e il Porto Fluviale*, in Giorgio de Finis, Fabio Benincasa, Andrea Facchi, "*EXPLOIT. Come rovesciare il mondo dell'arte. D-Istruzioni per l'uso*," Bordeaux Edizioni, Rome, 2015.
9 The experience told by all the participants is in the book by Giorgio de Finis and Irene Di Noto, *R/home. Diritto all'abitare dovere capitale*, Bordeaux Edizioni, Rome 2018.

10 CIRCO is a research developed since the autumn of 2017 within the Laboratory of Urban and Architectural Design of the Master's Degree in Urban Design of the Department of Architecture of Rome TRE, with the participation of Francesco Careri, Fabrizio Finucci, Chiara Luchetti, Alberto Marzo, Sara Monaco, Enrico Perini, Serena Olcuire e Maria Rocco (https://laboratoriocirco.wordpress.com/).

11 Atac is the acronym for Agenzia del Trasporto Autoferrotranviario del Comune di Roma (Road transport agency of the Municipality of Rome)

12 For more information please look at Careri F., 2001, *Constant. New Babylon, una città nomade,* Testo & Immagine, Torino; Wigley M., 1998, *Constant's New Babylon: The Hyper-architecture of Desire,* 010 Publishers, Rotterdam.

References

Cummings, J. 2013. *Confronting the favela chic: Gentrification of informal settlement in Rio de Janeiro, Brazil.* Master thesis, Harvard University, USA.

De la Hoz, C. 2013. *The favela typology: Architecture in the self-built city. Bachelor thesis, Princeton University, USA.*

Careri, F. 2018. *Poesia, architettura, ospitalità. Dialogo sui territori dell'informale.* Intervista di Gissara, M., Percoco, M., Rossini, E., in Gissara, M., Percoco, M., Rossini, E. (edited by) *Città immaginate. Riuso e nuove forme dell'abitare.* Manifestolibri, Castel San Pietro Romano (RM).

Jones, P. 2017, Housing Resilience and the Informal City, *Journal of Regional and City Planning* vol. 28, no. 2, pp. 129–139, August 2017.

Neuwirth, R. 2005. *Shadow Cities: A Billion Squatters, A New Urban World,* Routledge, New York.

Pojani, D., 2019, *The Self-Built City: Theorizing Urban Design of Informal Settlements,* in Archnet-IJAR: International Journal of Architecture Research, available online at https://www.emeraldinsight.com/doi/full/10.1108/ARCH-11-2018-0004.

Watchel, E., 2013, *An interview with Richard Senneth,* in "Brick. A Literary Journal", n. 92.

Chapter 22

Informality in formality

The case of a neighbourhood in a Nigerian city

Olufunto Ijatuyi, Hezekiah Adedayo Ayoola and Alessandro Melis

Introduction

Urban informality, often considered synonymous with poor urban neighbourhoods, develops through the procedures of self-organisation and incremental alterations (Kamalipour, 2016), occasionally on unutilised lands (Van Gelder, 2010) that are sometimes illegally occupied. Poorly-serviced, unregistered, sub-standard, and overcrowded houses in low-income urban settings are essential parts of the make-up of informality.. Urban informality defies the regulating power of the state, perhaps not blatantly, but on account of the circumstances imposed on it by the dominance of urban socio-economic disparity. This is accentuated by Varley (2013) that some groups are deprived by the offering of formality through repression and informal taxations. Relegating low-income groups to measures disfavouring informality only engenders law-contravening responses against the elitist nature of planning and building codes (Watson, 2009). This highlights that the breach of planning and building regulations seems to be the only available option for the urban poor to secure housing.

Reactions posed by informal activities against urban regulations are perceived as anti-state or direct resistance to formality (Banks, Lombard, & Mitlin, 2019); however, the generalisation of anti-state actions is cautioned against by Varley (2013) who, when considering the erstwhile work of Gilbert and Ward (1985), warned that some of the activities of informality were part and parcel of the urban economy and the political system of Columbia, Mexico and Venezuela. Informality is thus a strategy that is employed by different actors—the indigent for survival and the affluent for accumulation (Banks, Lombard, & Mitlin, 2019, p. 6).

Attention to informality usually comes with the emphasis on the dystopian conditions of those who are unable to be formal; it also indirectly suggests the capacity of some others who are selectively informal (Banks, Lombard, & Mitlin, 2019). To be selectively informal is to have the capacity to be formal but to elect to be informal for circumstantial and subjective reasons. This disposition is typically buoyed by the tenuousness of urban governance and rules. In other words, informal housing activities are not the exclusive preserve of the urban poor, but they embrace the actions of diverse sectors that involve business interests, the state, and urban populace that include middle and high income earners (McFarlane, 2012). Therefore, defining informality within the context of cities in the Global South is challenging; while Ranganathan (2014) sees it as the absence or suspension of regulations, Varley (2013) differs to see it as the absence of the law or direct resistance to rules in an anti-state manner, but supports Bayat's (2004) argument that views it as a quiet, prolonged, unassuming yet illegal encroachment of the ordinary.

Past literature established that informality could be found all over the place across the social spectrum in Global South Cities (Yiftachel, 2009; Roy, 2011). In the words of De la Cueva (1987), informality exists in the formal spaces belonging to the elites, just as the law exists in informal spaces. Put simply, 'illegal settlement processes are conditioned by the law' (De la Cueva, 1987, p. 524). Hence, if informality is witnessed in the domain of the elite, then it is necessary to study this version of informality, which erstwhile literature has not comprehensively examined.

One of the ways middle and high income earners (just like low-income earners) indulge in informality in the Global South is through the design and construction processes of houses, which could be incremental in approach. Incremental housing, a slow step-by-step procedure that allows building components to be added, altered or improved by owner-occupiers as money, time, or materials become available (Wakely & Riley, 2011) is not alien to the construction practices in the informal sector. Incremental housing is evidently occasioned by socio-economic differences across the urban social spectrum in consequence of the fact that the capacity to meet housing need by majority of urban dwellers is low, and housing programmes have always been priced out of the monetary reach of the poor (Olotuah, 2009; Kolawole, 2011). As a result, many manage to house themselves, albeit poorly, through incremental construction process (Olotuah, 2009; Housing Microfinance Report, 2012).

With reference to a study conducted by Wakely & Riley (2011) in third world cities, housing is commonly procured as incremental process that spreads over several years. Low-income earners without access to indemnity or collateral securities build small, rudimentary dwellings for a start. Thereafter, contingent on available resources, they expand and improve on this initial construction as the need for bigger or better structures becomes a primary concern. Wakely & Riley (2011) also averred that only the affluent—who are typically a small section of the people—have the luxury of either purchasing their homes without instalments or constructing their buildings as a one-off process as opposed to an incremental/gradual process. These have steady incomes and collateral that can easily be used to procure access to mortgage, which could take between 15 and 30 years to pay off. Incremental development can take several decades or may never end (Wakely & Riley, 2011); this is an expression of poverty. As stated by a study by Erubami and Young (as cited by Okpoechi, 2006), though the urban area is the centre of attraction with various sophisticated urban infrastructures that serve as urban magnets for the many immigrants, about 50% of urban dwellers in Nigeria are poor. The result of this, coupled with inadequate and unmanaged planning is substandard housing of slums and squalors. This is the status of a typical city in Nigeria. However, if high-income earners engage in informality in the form of incremental construction, then this may not be the case of economic constraints, but more of an idiosyncratic choice of engaging in practices that are inadvertently supported by the society in context.

From the foregoing, a desertion of multidimensional connections and events outside the urban poor that form and define them in their milieu, could be the consequence of a blinkered attention to such a cohort (Banks, Lombard & Mitlin, 2019). Therefore, this paper presents an understanding of urban informality, capturing its intricacy in regard to the close connections and intersections between formal and informal urban construction practices within the context of residential buildings. It sheds light on informal measures adopted by actors within the context of formal urban neighbourhoods in a typical African city—Akure Nigeria. The paper draws on empirical evidence from this study area, and aims to provide a better understanding of the context of informality within supposedly formal areas inhabited by the elites.

An overview of incremental housing

Unmanaged incremental construction activities are acknowledged to be prevalent at the fringes of most Nigerian cities where they experience centrifugal urban extension. Indeed, this has made many people self-actualised owners of houses (Olotuah, 2009), most of which are utterly substandard. Interestingly, the group of people who are involved in incremental construction activities may not entirely be limited to low-income earners. In other words, incremental housing is not limited to the precincts of informal settlements. This assumption is substantiated by the relative values or costs of land on which some incrementally-procured building constructions are found. Though the feeling of self-actualization is derived from home ownership, such houses are barely completed before they are occupied, and their completion may take close to ten years (Kolawole, 2011) or even more. The prevalence of uncontrolled incremental housing was initially seen as an unconventional housing project, but it is no more alien to the construction industry in the Global South; although its unrestrained prevalence threatens occupants' health as well as the liveability of the environment.

In more advanced countries, consideration is giving to the triad of sustainability, resilience and liveability of the environment at large (Maddox, 2013); however, developing countries like Nigeria have these concepts only on paper! And where these are claimed to be adopted, it is with an abysmally self-centred approach, having a very bleak hope of realisation. Although there are planning laws governing building construction, such laws are not properly enforced. Construction processes—incremental or not—are not monitored in most places to ensure adherence to planning regulations. The result of this finds expression in an uncontrolled housing not only at the peripheries of Nigerian cities, but also in core areas. This engenders the off-shoot of incremental slums that could hamper the safety conditions of the built environment.

There may be concerns and questions against informality in developing economies, but there are also arguments that this approach meets the needs of those who adopt it. Ibem, Aduwo & Uwankoye (2012) discovered that 50% of respondents felt that housing environment in Ogun State, Nigeria was adequate in meeting their needs, and that incremental housing construction strategy could offer adequate housing for both low and middle-income civil servants in the Global South. In Zimbabwe, a study by Nevhunjere & Mutsindikwa (2012) discovered that policy and legislation are key factors in human settlement development. These factors create either an enabling or disabling environment for actors to participate effectively in incremental development approach. The study also showed that an incremental development approach was adopted to condone the situation that was created by Operation Restore Order where people were left homeless after the clean-up operation in urban areas of Zimbabwe. Furthermore, the study revealed that housing finance was the key question that hindered housing provision in urban Zimbabwe, making it necessary for public-private partnerships to play an essential role in resolving this issue.

In Chile, Greene (2010) observed incremental housing as a way of meeting housing challenges. She identified three aspects of this informal concept, these areas entail reaching a minimum space, developing construction as an improvement process, and having a family and house time line. Similar to the formal housing process, the informal sector in Chile makes use of public housing programmes and legal structure to create housing. This sector develops minimum solutions provided by different housing programmes, and also complements state's social housing. However, the incidence of informality in formal neighbourhoods has not been well explored for the purpose of providing a better understanding of the pervasiveness of this phenomenon in the urban environment.

Method

The periphery of a popular formal neighbourhood—Alagbaka phase 1—has been purposively selected in Akure, Nigeria (see Figure 22.1). The criterion for selection is the middle-high income status commonly ascribed to this area on account of the relatively high land value, the luxurious outlook of existing buildings, and the fact that it is close to the location of State Government House, Secretariat, office buildings and big commercial buildings. All these lend credence to the formality of this location. The general vista of this area suggests that except through inheritance, lower-income earners cannot afford a plot of land or to rent a building in this location. Based on physical observation, purposive selection was used for buildings that were identified to have been incrementally constructed in the study area. Consideration was also given to the buildings' outlook in terms of their materials and the procedures applied

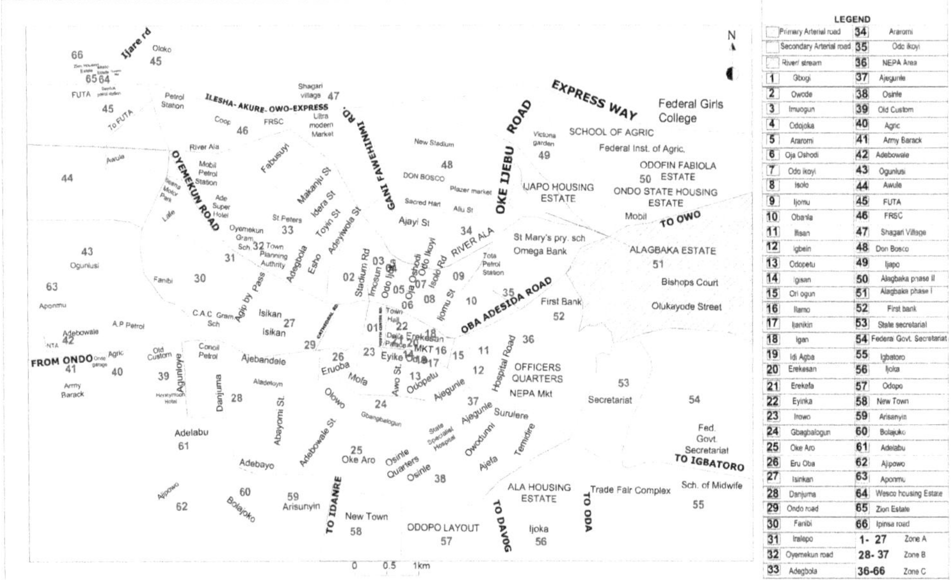

Figure 22.1 Map of Akure showing Alagbaka phase 1 (hatched area).

Source: Fakere, Folorunso, Fadairo & Arayela (2018).

Table 22.1 Sequence of procurement processes for formal and informal housing.

Informal settlements			**Formal** settlements
1.	*Move onto land*	4.	
2.	*Build house*	3.	
3.	*Install infrastructure*	2.	
4.	*Obtain title to land*	1.	

Source: McLeod & Mullard (2006) as adapted by Wakely & Riley (2011).

in their construction. It is worthy of note that the observed processes of informal construction activities in this area are not entirely akin to the processes described by Wakely & Riley (2011) in Table 22.1 although they share several similarities.

For informal settlers depicted in Table 22.1, the typical sequence of procurement processes involves moving unto the land, building the house, installing infrastructure and obtaining land title. The reverse order of this informal procurement sequence is what obtains in formal situations (see Table 22.1). Using this table as a guide, this paper expounds some observed informal practices at the fringe of Alagabaka area of Akure. This is an area that would normally be considered formal, although the criteria for what is known as formality are not covered in this paper. The methods of data collection are direct observation, visual recording (Kamalipour, 2016) and casual interactions with residents in the area. Observation involved noting the buildings' general outlook [sub-structure (if possible) and super-structure] in relation to the occupancy of these buildings.

Discussion

Moving onto land and obtaining land title

Physical observation of the study area that includes transect walk reveals that 'moving onto land' was not the first step in the established sequence presented in Table 22.1. The reason for this was not investigated, but this could largely be influenced by the socio-economic status of most households, who do not settle on just any vacant land (public or privately-owned). Thus, land ownership is not usually contested because land acquisition is mostly formal with appropriate reference to some form of land titles. This is not to make a sweeping statement that land procurement is also formal in all other ostensibly formal neighbourhoods. In fact, the purchase of plots could be formal but there are alleged cases of sales of unregistered land subdivisions in some parts of this middle-high income area. This aligns with a study by Holston and Caldeira (2008) that most occupants of informal settlements in Brazil purchase plots that could be from illegal sub-divisions, hence they are not unlawful tenants/squatters, and they do not reside in favelas. Also, there is no serious issue of insecurity of title to land and property. Intending buyers are sometimes given conditions to develop their lands within a stipulated period, after which they could forfeit such lands. With respect to illegal subdivisions, there could also be some eviction threats by appropriate government authorities, but these are not pronounced, because sub-divided lands can still be registered by land speculators even after being sold to people, this usually comes with penalties. Consequently, ownership of land is somewhat secured and eviction threats are minimised. However, on account of widespread construction practices that contravene planning rules, there could be infrequent demolition threats from planning authorities.

Survey plan is the land title that many households hang on to and retain as a major reference to ownership, although this document does not really ascribe a decisive ownership right to anyone who has it. Ownership that is merely based on reference to a survey plan alone could be contested. A statutory right of occupancy or a Certificate of Occupancy is considered as strong indication of absolute land title but is not commonly held by most households. A property without a Certificate of Occupancy can still be disputed, particularly in places where land speculators hoodwink many prospective buyers. A rampant situation is where a plot of land is sold to more than one person at different times.

Depending on the choice or priority of homeowners, any of the other three stages—building the house, installing infrastructure, and obtaining title to land—as identified by Wakely & Riley (2011) could come first. What comes first does not depend on finances, but on what homeowners consider more important on their scale of preference and not what planning regulations stipulate. This substantiates the tenuousness of planning rules as well as the muted ratification of informality, which finds expression in the sheer reticence of the state to this situation. Going by the process of land acquisition that appears to have some tenor of formality, the scenario here reveals an impression of a blend of formal and informal construction practices in a supposedly formal environment. Formal-informal connection has been observed in different scenarios (Bunnell & Harris, 2012; Pasquetti & Picker, 2017; McFarlane, 2019). In particular, (McFarlane's, 2012) re-conceptualisation of informality as a review unravels a comprehension of the relationship between formality and informality (Banks, Lombard, & Mitlin, 2019). This relationship find is the reticent approval of informal activities by the state. This is because informality is not alien to the state for indulge in informality.

Building the house

With respect to the construction of residential buildings in Nigeria, informality is symptomatically marked in little or no adherence to any specific monitoring system that guarantees a liveable environment; this is also evident in the study area. However, some attempts to control the construction of unregistered residential structures are observed in cities such as Abeokuta, Abuja and Lagos; there may be others. Therefore, because construction activities do not really follow any formal design and construction process, the challenge of denoting a neighbourhood as formal is obvious.

Informality also manifests in the fashion in which professional services are procured or not procured by actors. Typically, intending landlords do not always employ the services of building professionals because they are not prepared to pay for professional services, which they perceive as unnecessary. This perception is not based on a question of the socio-economic status or level of education of such people. It is simply a way of life that subsists in a developing economy like Nigeria. However, what is definite is that the services of local tradespeople such as bricklayers, carpenters, welders, plumbers, and electricians, whose technical know-hows could be difficult to investigate, are employed. The competence of these tradespeople can only be ascertained by recommendations from friends and family members. When tradespeople make suggestions to provide building plans or help you to illegally alter existing plans in their possession and sell them out, informality is clear. It is a setting whereby some professionals also pose themselves to be what they are not in order to obtain construction jobs.

Another key question here relates to the over flogged issue of poor materials and workmanship. In most construction works, the commonly used material for walls (both exterior and interior walls) is what is generally called 'sand-crete blocks.' These blocks are routinely made of a poor mixture of cement, sand and water; consequently, many of these sand-crete blocks break into pieces on the road to the construction site. Some of the blocks that survived road potholes during transportation would not withstand the test of the torrential downpour of rain and the scorching heat of the sun. Visible structural cracks on walls during pre-occupancy and in post-occupancy state of such buildings attest to this situation as well. These practices translate to the well-documented collapse of buildings (Akinyemi, Dare, Anthony & Dabara, 2016; Ayedun, Durodola, & Akinjare, 2011; Fagbenle & Oluwunmi, 2010; Oke, 2011; Windapo & Rotimi, 2012), which is common to buildings with several floors in Nigeria.

With poor workmanship goes the rather unprofessional practice by which building constructions are performed (see Figures 22.2 and 22.3). Some methods of construction that literally depart from standard construction practices are common with all buildings, whether or not they have been incrementally constructed. A common scenario is that proper site analysis and soil tests are not usually carried out to determine suitable foundations for many buildings. Because professional help is rarely sought, people use a one-size-fits-all approach for constructing foundations. The usual foundation type used in almost all cases in the study area is the wide strip foundation. The condition is exacerbated by the fact that the sand-crete blocks used for the foundation are ironically structurally weak in compression. In some cases, concrete slabs and damp proof membranes are not used at all (see Figure 22.4). Structural cracks and water capillarity in walls are the leading consequences of these poorly constructed foundations in most buildings.

In view of these, some buildings that are proximate to the middle course of Ala River in the study area have become awful targets of flooding and capillarity. The appearance of these buildings vividly betrays either a lack of professional service or insufficient resources to execute a standard job during construction. Apart from these, one thing is certain in the study area: regulating authorities display no interest in how well building constructions are performed, what they seem to care about is whether such constructions are registered or not. In other words, there is no interest or formal procedure that ensures that building constructions are not sub-standard or whether health and safety procedures are observed during the construction process. Landlords can decide to move into their buildings at any stage of the building construction whether or not such buildings have windows, floor finish, internal doors, and the required basic infrastructure and services.

Figure 22.2 An incrementally constructed building in the study area [the latest addition to the roof and wall (bottom image) was made during the field work. Initial construction was more than 10 years ago.]

Source: Authors' fieldwork, 2019/2020.

Setting up infrastructure and services

In the study area, the state's responsibility regarding the provision of basic infrastructure has indubitably been left in the hands of property-owners. Although the government paved some sections of the major roads, most inner street roads have been left out. In some cases, house-owners contribute money for road grading. Generally, no neighbourhood can vaunt the state's provision of pipe-borne water, sewers or uninterrupted supply of electricity. In particular, power supply is abysmally epileptic. Many neighbourhoods do not even have access to it at all. Small private generators are consistently procured by most households for subsistence. It is a nation-wide fact that

Figure 22.3 An incrementally constructed (gated) building in the study area.

Source: Authors' fieldwork, 2019.

reliance on the government for power supply is unrealistic. This is a national problem that has been a running battle since the nation became independent in 1960. Billions of Naira and dollars have been allocated to electricity supply projects across the country (Da Costa, 2009; Fakoyejo, 2019; Okwumbu, 2020; Olukoju, 2004; Osae-Brown & Olurounbi, 2019) but there is no substantial positive outcome, and there seems to be no optimism in sight. Solid waste disposal is horrible in some parts of the study area; most places in Nigeria also experience this. Although this is not common in the study area, but wastes (of different types) are dumped on roads and on vacant plots.

Because the government does not supply pipe-borne water to households anymore, people have resorted to digging bore-holes or well water. What the government occasionally provide are bore-holes in locations where people travel to (through motorbikes, bicycles, cars, or by walking) in order to fetch water. Septic tanks and soakaways are dug—by home-owners—in every compound (sometimes, close to well water); and this raises the question of well water purity. In summary, the involvement of the government in the provision basic infrastructure is deplorable. In formal scenarios, installing infrastructure should follow the erection of the building, which is usually the case in the study area. However, households in the study area are not bound by any sequential construction procedure. They simply organise their construction process as they desire. The foregoing implies that formal settlements regularly undergo changes as basic infrastructure become obsolete due to lack of maintenance

Figure 22.4 A building without a concrete slab.

Source: Authors' fieldwork, 2019.

or because basic infrastructure are non-existent in the first place. Consequently, what is considered formal in Nigeria could be marked as informal in advanced nations. In addition, reasons, motives or persuasions for subjective informal activities by people in the Global South remain largely unknown. Consistent with the views of Gilbert and Ward (1985) along with that of Varley (2013), the activities of Local Authorities in Nigeria evasively corroborate informality at all levels. This makes it challenging to delineate some practices as formal or informal, and shows that Local Authorities are part of informal practices (McFarlane, 2012). All these prompt a couple of questions that could be relevant to future research: can scenarios which constitute formality or informality be generalized? What knowledge of settlement informality is pertinent to city authorities?

Conclusions

Informal construction practices within the context of a formal urban neighbourhood have been discussed drawing on evidence from Alagbaka in Akure Nigeria. Physical observation and visual recording have been utilized as one of the key methods of exploring informality in the study area.

The sequence of procurement processes for formal and informal housing (Table 22.1) has been referenced to illustrate the peculiarity of the study area. One key point noted in this paper is that informal construction practices are observed within the ostensible formality of this area. This indicates that formal neighborhoods are also inhabited by a few poor households. It is highlighted that incremental construction is observed in this neighbourhood, substantiating De la Cueva's (1987) position that informality is present anywhere and everywhere and it subsists in elites' formal spaces. In the words of Banks, Lombard, & Mitlin (2019, p.4), various actors that include "city-based or national elites" often negotiate and impose a set of rules different from the ones defined by the state. These rules are what Kamalipour (2016, p.71) implicitly referred to as 'underlying logic' even in the random and chaotic outlook of informal morphologies. This is in contrast to what Ranganathan (2014, p. 90) advanced, stating that informality is "the flexible and uneven suspension of regulation and law in the production of urban space and materiality." In other words, informality, which appears as an absence of the state's presence in a place, is in fact the expression of a different set of rules that, at times, radically or quietly contest the failure of formality.

Note

1 The Ala River is a tributary of River Ogbese in South-west Akure, Nigeria. It has a total length of about 58km; about 14.8km of this length is within Akure city (Ayeni, Balogun & Soneye, 2011).

References

Akinyemi, A., Dare, G., Anthony, A., & Dabara, D. I. (2016). Building collapse in Nigeria: Issues and challenges. *Conference of the International Journal of Arts & Sciences*, CD-ROM, 9(1) 99–108. Ayedun, C. A., Durodola, O. D., & Akinjare, O. A. (2011). An empirical ascertainment of the causes of building failure and collapse in Nigeria. *Mediterranean Journal of Social Sciences*, *3*(1), 313–322.

Ayeni, A.O., Balogun, I.I., &. Soneye, A.S.O. (2011). Seasonal Assessment of Physico-chemical Concentration of Polluted Urban River: A Case of Ala River in Southwestern-Nigeria. *Research Journal of Environmental Sciences, 5(1),* 22–35. DOI: 10.3923/rjes.2011.22.35

Banks, N., Lombard, M., & Mitlin, D. (2019). Urban informality as a site of critical analysis. *The Journal of Development Studies*, *56*(2), 223–238.

Bayat, A. (2004). Globalization and the politics of the informals in the global south. In A. Roy & N. Alsayyad (Eds.), *Urban informality: Transnational perspectives from the Middle East, Latin America and South Asia* (pp. 79–102). Lanham, USA: Lexington Books.

Bunnell, T., & Harris, A. (2012). Re-viewing informality: perspectives from urban Asia. *International Development Planning Review*, *34*(4), 339–348.

Da Costa, G. (2009, November 1). Nigerian Lawmakers Probe $16 Billion Spending on Power. *VOA News.* Retrieved https://www.voanews.com/archive/

De la Cueva, A.A. (1987). Low income settlements and the law in Mexico City. *International Journal of Urban and Regional Research*, *11*(4), 522–542.

Fagbenle, O.I., & Oluwunmi, A. O. (2010). Building failure and collapse in Nigeria: The influence of the informal sector. *Journal of sustainable development*, *3*(4), 268–276.

Fakere, A.A., Folorunso, C. O., Fadairo, G., & Arayela, O. (2018). Effects of Socioeconomic Characteristics on Residents' Satisfaction with Housing Infrastructural Facilities in Akure, Nigeria. In S.N. Zubairu & O.F. Adedayo (Eds.), *Inclusive city growth and the poor: Policies, Challenges and Prospects* (pp. 88–101). Community Participation Research Group (COPAREG).

Fakoyejo, O. (2019, December 27). FG allocates N61 billion to Nigeria-Siemens power deal. *Nairametrics business news*. Retrieved https://nairametrics.com/

Gilbert, A.G., & Ward, P. M. (1985). *Housing, the State and the Poor: Poverty and Practice in Three Latin American Cities*. Cambridge, UK: Cambridge Univ. Press.

Greene, M.Z. (2010). *Incremental Housing: The Chilean Experience*. Retrieved from http://web.mit.edu/incrementalhousing/WUF-Rio/pdfs/CHILE-Greene.pdf

Holston. J., & Caldeira, T. (2008). Urban peripheries and the invention of citizenship. *Harvard Design Magazine* 28(spring/summer) 18–23.

Housing Microfinance Report (2012). *Sustainable housing finance in Nigeria*. www.housingfinanceafrica.org/...3/HMF-Nigeria...1.pdf

Ibem, E.O. Aduwo, E.B. & Uwankoye, O. (2012). Adequacy of incremental construction strategy for housing low-income urban residents in Ogun State. *Built Environment Project and Asset Management*, *2*(2), pp. 182–194. https://doi.org/10.1108/20441241211280918

Kamalipour, H. (2016). Forms of informality and adaptations in informal settlements. *ArchNet-IJAR*, *10*(3).

Kolawole, Y. (2011). 85% of Nigeria's urban populace lives in rented houses. *Vangaurd News*. http://www.vanguardngr.com/2011/10/85-of-nigeria%E2%80%99s-urban-populace-lives-in-rented-houses/

Maddox, D. (2013). The Cities We Want: Resilient, Sustainable, and Livable. *In Sustainable cities collective*. Retrieved from http://sustainablecitiescollective.com/nature-cities/149306/cities-we-want-resilient-sustainable-and-livable?utm_source=scc_newsletter&utm_medium=email&utm_campaign=newsletter&inf_contact_key=7be3bad89ee52080826fd34361d038cd-3dd6bb11e27b806390726f1f2017d4f0

McFarlane, C. (2019). Thinking with and beyond the informal–formal relation in urban thought. *Urban Studies*, *56*(3), 620–623.

McFarlane, C. (2012). Rethinking informality: Politics, crisis, and the city. *Planning Theory & Practice*, *13*(1), 89–108.

McLeod, R., & Mullard, K. (2006). *Bridging the Finance Gap in Housing and Infrastructure*. London: ITDG Publishing.

Nevhunjere, H., Mutsindikwa, N.T. (2012). *Incremental housing development in Zimbabwe: Case for Hatcliffe Extension*. http://www.amazon.com/Incremental-housing-development-Zimbabwe-Hatcliffe/dp/3848402440

Oke, A.E. (2011). An examination of the causes and effects of building collapse in Nigeria. *Journal of Design and Built environment*, *9*(1).

Okpoechi, C. (2006). Urban Design Issues in the Provision of Public Infrastructure and Improvement of the Quality of Nigerian Cities. *Journal of Urban and Environmental Sustainability: Interventions and Responses*, (1)1, 19–28.

Okwumbu, R. (2020, March 11). Nigeria's Power sector loses N117.8 billion in 66 days. *Nairametrics business news*. Retrieved https://nairametrics.com/

Olotuah, A.O. (2009). *Demystifying the Nigerian Urban Housing Question*. Inaugural Lecture Series 53 Delivered at The Federal University of Technology, Akure.

Olukoju, A. (2004). 'Never Expect Power Always': Electricity consumers' response to monopoly, corruption and inefficient services in Nigeria. *African Affairs*, *103*(410), 51–71. DOI: 10.1093/afraf/adh004

Osae-Brown, A., Olurounbi, R. (2019, September 23). Nigeria Runs on Generators and Nine Hours of Power a Day. *Bloomberg Business*. Retrieved https://www.bloomberg.com/africa

Pasquetti, S., & Picker, G. (2017). Urban informality and confinement: Toward a relational framework. *International Sociology*, *32*(4), 532–544.

Ranganathan, M. (2014). 'Mafias' in the waterscape: Urban informality and everyday public authority in Bangalore. *Water Alternatives*, *7*(1) 89–105.

Roy, A. (2011). Slumdog cities: Rethinking subaltern urbanism. *International journal of urban and regional research*, *35*(2), 223–238.

Varley, A. (2013). Postcolonialising informality?. *Environment and Planning D: Society and Space*, *31*(1), 4–22.

Van Gelder, J. L. (2010). Tales of deviance and control: on space, rules, and law in squatter settlements. *Law & society review*, *44*(2), 239–268. https://doi.org/10.1111/j.1540-5893.2010.00406.x

Wakely, P. & Riley, E. (2011). Cities without slums – The case for incremental housing. *Research and* Working Papers Series No.1. Retrieved from http://web.mit.edu/incrementalhousing/articlesPhotographs/pdfs/Case-for-Incremental-Housing.pdf

Watson, V. (2009). Seeing from the South: Refocusing urban planning on the globe's central urban issues. *Urban Studies*, 46, 2259–2275.

Windapo, A.O., & Rotimi, J. O. (2012). Contemporary issues in building collapse and its implications for sustainable development. *Buildings*, *2*(3), 283–299.

Yiftachel, O. (2009). Theoretical Notes On Gray Cities': the coming of urban apartheid?. *Planning theory*, *8*(1), 88–100.

Chapter 23

Achieving community resilience through informal urban practices

The case of El Houma in Algiers

Mohamed Yazid Khemri and Alessandro Melis

Introduction

Cities around the world are exposed to a growing range of challenges in the 21st century, from climate change-related issues to rapid urbanisation and population growth to inadequate infrastructures to disasters. In the meantime, more urban areas are expected to be built since it is estimated that over 70% of the world population will be living in urban areas by 2030 (Komeily & Srinivasan, 2015).

Recently, the concept of resilience has been a focal point as a subject of study and debate among many disciplines, whereas resilience is fundamental to the sustainability and durability of cities, as it helps urban systems to resist to disruptions, adapt and prepare for (un)expected challenges, and bounce back (100 Resilient Cities, 20179). The concept of resilience is defined as the capability of urban systems to withstand, resist and bounce back from disruptions. In order to achieve that, a holistic approach that integrates tangible and intangible aspects of urban systems needs to be implemented and promoted.

There is a growing belief that ensuring social sustainability at the neighbourhood level is a significant step towards planning for resilience. The concepts of sustainability and resilience have been at the centre of debate over the last few decades, whereas, looking closely at the two concepts, many scholars have rejected the idea of replacing one with the other, but instead, of combining them both into achieving a more holistic planning approach.

The concept of sustainability has been vaguely defined and used, portrayed as a development that balances three important pillars, which are environmental, social and economic. However, it has been claimed that the social aspect is the least researched element among the three, whilst its importance in achieving sustainability and resilience is as important as the other two. For instance, many scholars have argued that social sustainability aspects, such as solidarity, trust and sense of belonging, are crucial to get community members to collaborate and respond to disasters (Leap & Thompson, 2018).

Moreover, the lack of intensive research and consideration of the social aspect has caused several failures to urban planning and architectural projects around the world, especially in the global south (Khemri et al., 2020); these failures are a result of ignoring local contexts and the local socio-cultural way of life while designing projects. Many of the so-claimed sustainable projects in the global south are criticised for their social failures, as a result of ignoring local lifestyle and incorporating a planning approach designed for the global north or by being inspired by the modernism movement, which has equally caused social and spatial segregation in European cities.

Many scholars consider the urban practices of local residents as powerful tools in achieving sustainable and resilient communities, whereby these urban practices serve as a showcase of the lifestyle of people, which can be used to tailor urban spaces that are responsive to the social needs of residents (Gehl, 2010). Jacobs (1961) argued that the everyday life of people produced lively and well-functioning neighbourhoods, through improvised and innumerable activities.

Residents' social activities and urban practices not only contribute to urban life, but also serve to achieve urban resilience. Some of these urban practices are considered as an expression of "informality", because they are performed outside the framework of architects, urban planners and policy makers. Devlin (2018) considers them as "off the books" or "under the radar" employment activities, public transportation and informal housing... These informal practices, among others, performed in some urban spaces, are informed by several factors, such as quality of the built environment, living in proximity, social ties among residents and sense of belonging ... all of which contribute to social cohesion and solidarity within the community.

Some of these urban practices contribute highly to resilience, for instance, informal commerce helps people to be resilient against unemployment and to make ends meet, or hosting various activities in public spaces ensures social inclusion and justice in the face of social exclusion and discrimination.

Despite the large expansion of research on social resilience, this body of knowledge has not paid enough attention to resilience strategies employed locally by residents in urban neighbourhoods in the face of their local challenges (Pu & Qiu, 2016).

While most of the literature on resilience discusses how cities and neighbourhoods fight against natural disasters, this chapter takes Algiers as a case study and draws on the local informal urban practices employed by residents of urban neighbourhoods in the Algerian capital, as a way of resilience to local disruptions. These urban practices emerge from being part of "El Houma", which is a concept of neighbourhood peculiar to North Africa that is characterised by strong social relations and social cohesion. This concept is explained further in Section 4 of the chapter.

The aim of this chapter is to shed light on different approaches of social resilience, undertaken by residents as signs of solidarity, trust, social cohesion and sense of belonging that emerge from social interaction and sharing a place of residence. The chapter also attempts to bridge the gap between theory and practice of social resilience in urban areas by answering the following questions: what is the relationship between urban informality and resilience? How do residents of El Houma adapt and respond to social disasters? How can local informal urban practices be considered as social resilience strategies? How do these urban practices emerge?

The urban practices studied in this research as a form of resilience, were found in neighbourhoods that are considered as true embodiment of El Houma, as many urban sociologists have highlighted the presence of strong social relations, social urban practices and positive lifestyles (Bouaouina, 2007; Dris, 2005; Grangaud, 2009; Icheboudene, 2002).

The chapter is formed of two important parts; the first part provides a general understanding of the concepts of resilience and urban informality and identifies the relationship between the two concepts. As for the second part, the chapter critically uncovers how informal urban practices serve as social resilience strategies in urban neighbourhoods, while presenting examples from case study analysis of El Houma in Algiers. In this respect, the chapter is formed of five sections. Section 1 includes the introduction to the research and outlines the aims and methods used in the investigation. In Section 2, the chapter conceptualises the concept of resilience, providing definitions and explications of urban and social resilience. Next, in Section 3 which is divided into two subsections, the chapter sheds light on the literature regarding urban informality and its contribution to resilience and explains how informal urban practices contribute to social resilience. In the following Section 4, the concept of El Houma is introduced and explained, and examples of informal urban practices and their contribution to resilience are presented. Finally, Section 5 offers a conclusion recapitulating the findings of the chapter while highlighting the correlation between informal urban practices and resilience.

Aims and objectives

The main aim of the chapter is to bridge the gap between theory and practice in urban resilience, and to demonstrate the correlation between urban informality and social resilience in urban areas.

The chapter will present results of mapping informal urban practices in urban neighbourhoods to highlight how residents react to local disruptions by means of solidarity, trust and sense of belonging.

As part of the overall objectives of the chapter, the research will identify the main drivers (social dynamics) that promote resilience strategies, and how social use of urban spaces can create these social dynamics.

The outcomes of this research enable, on the one hand, to systemize the literature on the concepts of urban informality and community resilience and, on the other, to present examples of how people in urban neighbourhoods seek the right to the city by performing informal urban practices to achieve resilience and resistance to local disruptions.

Methodology

The methodology used in the chapter is qualitative and is formed of two important methods, a critical analysis of the literature and activity mapping. The literature review focused on exploring the concepts of resilience in urban planning and social science, as well as urban informality. A critical analysis of the two concepts allowed an identification of the main drivers to inform informal urban practices and their correlation to community resilience.

The main aim of the literature review is to provide an overview of the concept of community resilience and urban informality, and to identify and explain how informal urban practices can contribute to resilience.

The second method is activity mapping also known as snapshot observation. It has been used by many pioneers of urban planning researchers to study public life in urban areas, such as Jane Jacobs, William Whyte and Jan Gehl. The method used in this research is based on their methods and techniques to identify informal urban practices that lead to community resilience.

This method of observation is a combination of urban planning and sociology research strategies, which allows for a study of human activities within urban spaces. It has been developed to study social life in urban areas (Francis, 1984) and people's activities in urban spaces (Gehl, 1987; Mahdzar, 2008; Shirazi, 2018).

This strategy is considered as an ethnographic approach by Groat & Wang (2002), because it inserts the researcher in the actual world with the object of inquiry, in order to identify urban practices in their natural setting.

The observations of the different urban practices in El Houma were conducted in two different neighbourhoods in the city of Algiers; the two neighbourhoods are explained in Section 4 and 5.

The observations and mapping focused on urban practices, formal and/or informal, that have the potential to inform resilience strategies, such as informal commerce, street art, informal use of urban spaces, informal gatherings, etc. The list of activities was identified from the literature review; however, an open mode of data collection was followed to capture spontaneous and unexpected activities.

The observations of urban practices were conducted during weekdays and weekends of the last two weeks of August 2019 (Friday and Saturday constitute the weekend in Algeria). The observations were conducted during different times of the day, in order to capture different and unexpected urban activities on different days of the week, and different times of the day. The observations and mapping were carried out in different spaces of the two neighbourhoods, from public (public spaces, squares and main streets), to semi-public (secondary streets) to private spaces (residential areas) of El Houma.

The following section attempts to conceptualize resilience and the different facets of the concept, which will pave the way towards an understanding of potential strategies.

Underlying principles of resilience

Conceptualising resilience

The concept of resilience has gained significant importance in the last few decades among many academic disciplines and research fields, ranging from biology, ecology, socio-ecological studies, social science, psychology and engineering to urban planning and sustainability (Folke, 2006; Brand & Jax, 2007; Keck & Sakdapolrak, 2013).

Although there is no single agreed upon definition of the concept, most definitions share an intentional repetition of the fact that resilient systems should be resistant and able to bounce back from disasters.

Initially, when it first emerged, resilience as a concept only concerned natural disasters and climate change-related issues. Subsequently, however, attention has been devoted to broadening resilience application in order to respond to other urban and social disruptions.

The concept of resilience was researched and applied in the discipline of urban planning. UN Habitat (2018b) defines urban resilience as the ability of an urban system with its residents to ensure continuity and survival when exposed to various kinds of disruptions, while positively adapting, adjusting and transforming towards sustainability. A resilient city has the ability to plan, prepare and act to respond to hazards – be they natural and/or human made, expected or unexpected, chronic or acute – with the aim to protect and improve people's lives, ensure development and positive change (UN Habitat, 2018b).

Urban resilience is defined as the capability of individuals, communities and other various formal institutions, businesses and systems within a city to survive, resist, recover and bounce back from disruptions, be they chronic stresses and/or acute shocks (100 Resilient Cities, 2019).

In order to achieve urban resilience, a holistic approach needs to be researched and implemented. This holistic approach combines both tangible and intangible components of the city, starting with an understanding of the different constituents of the city and their interdependencies, and the potential risks they may face (100 Resilient Cities, 2019).

Several studies have acknowledged the informal strategies developed by urban residents to recover from disruptions, for instance, in the Philippines, residents of villages rely on cooperation and collective problem solving that emerge from the trust, social cohesion, shared culture and values among neighbours in order to survive and recover from landslides and floods caused by typhoons (Usamah *et al.*, 2014).

Social resilience

In social sciences, resilience is defined as a cooperative action in the face of disruptions that caused damage to infrastructures and disturbed normal operating conditions (Comfort et al., 2010). Most social resilience definitions are based on the collaborative work between social entities; whether individuals, organisations or communities, and their capabilities to tolerate, survive, resist, cope with and adapt to various kinds of environmental and/or social threats (Keck & Sakdapolrak, 2013).

Maguire & Hagen (2007) argue that social resilience refers to the ability of a social entity, be it a group or a community, to "bounce back" and to react positively to stresses and disasters, and state that the society's capacity is related to three approaches of how people respond to disruption: "resistance, recovery and creativity".

Social resilience acknowledges the various roles played by social entities, the independent responses taken by members of the community, or, with the help of formal organisations, to be prepared for uncertainty and surprise and recover from shocks and stresses (UN Habitat, 2018a).

Social resilience in cities refers to the capability of urban systems, with all their socio-ecological components and socio-technical networks, to perform across temporal and spatial scales. The main aim is deal with disruptions, both in the present and in the future, through an urban ecosystem that is able to protect, resist and return to function, while adapting and preparing for future (un)expected disasters (Meerow, Newell & Stults, 2015)

While there is a growing body of research on social resilience, there is still ambiguity and lack of consistency on how the concept is applied by communities (Saja et al., 2019). Social resilience of urban areas can be achieved through a series of factors that are embedded within communities, namely, trust, solidarity, social cohesion and sense of community, social interaction, shared community activities, communication and information (Gibberd, 2017; Wang, Guo, & Kuo, 2020).

In this respect, this research attempts to demonstrate how urban practices within neighbourhoods of Algiers, even when considered informal, serve as resilience strategies to local challenges. The urban practices mentioned in this study as resilience strategies were informed by an individual's feeling of solidarity, trust, sense of belonging, social cohesion and support.

The following section sheds light on urban informality and its implication with everyday urban life and resilience.

Urban informality

De Soto (1989) argues that, when talking about informality in urban design, it doesn't refer to the individual as informal, but, rather, their actions and activities. Supporting this claim, Roy's (2009) definition of informality refers to a state of deregulation, a state where the possession, use and purpose of land are not defined by any prescribed rules or laws. For Roy (2009), informality lies in the blurry relationship between legal and illegal, legitimate and illegitimate, authorised and unauthorised.

The complexity of the notion of informality involves many spheres, it is a term that describes and theorises not only the spatial aspects of a city, but also its economic, social, cultural and political organisation (Hernåndez et al. 2010).

Informality is not predefined by policy makers, planners, architects or any decision-makers at the city or neighbourhood level, who plan and design spaces for the use of people. In fact, informality is defined by people's needs and aspirations to support their way of life. Informal practices react and respond to local culture and community, and can evolve and adapt according to people's developing needs and lifestyles (Revell, 2010).

Various situations can be considered informal, like the spontaneous processes of occupying a land or territory, illegal inhabiting, constructing and self-building of dwellings, temporary occupation of spaces, self-organising and developing urban area at the edge of cities, etc. (Revell, 2010). Informal urban practices can also refer to unauthorised and place-based modifications and occupations of urban spaces, examples of these phenomena being graffiti, street dance, street art, guerrilla knitting, guerrilla gardening, guerrilla theatre, happenings, street games, art interventions and art exhibitions, space hijacking and place hacking, craftivism and artivism ... the list goes on to include occupation of public spaces and 'do it yourself' urban design activities and many others. These activities are informed by different motivations and have impacts of different scales, yet they can be considered as urban practices performed by individuals or informal groups who challenge and go against normal and expected uses of urban spaces through unauthorised and unexpected actions (Douglas, 2014). Other informal urban practices mentioned by the literature are street vending, community gardens, informal housing, squatting, vernacular practices of 'everyday' urbanism, public art activism and informal physical planning (Devlin, 2018).

Qualifying some activities as informal, unauthorised or unwanted indicates a strong denial of urban residents' right to the city. According to Lefebvre (1968), the right to the city gives people the right to occupy urban spaces, which does not only include certain economic elite or specific class of the society, but every resident. Allowing residents to express themselves through social use of urban spaces, without excluding any member of the society, promotes inclusiveness and urban life and allows the city to express itself as an oeuvre. In this respect, the right to the city allows every citizen to access, appropriate and use urban spaces to perform various activities.

Harvey (2003) claimed that the right to the city should enable residents to contribute to the development of the city through a rich urban life that is formed of collective urban practices. The right to the city does not include accessing city space and merely accepting what professionals have designed in terms of urban spaces but is a right to show diversity of the city's inhabitants through expressions of their lifestyles (Harvey, 2003; Huchzermeyer, 2011; Simone, 2005).

Roy (2009) suggests that activities that happen in urban areas that lead to gain the right to the city or sense of belonging are considered informal when they are out of the ordinary or against the intended objective of the designed space.

However, Landry (2006) argued that informal practices should not be considered as processes of marginality but should be framed as concepts that could mix with other formal activities to develop simultaneous ways of "making the city". Yiftachel (2009) added that urban population who work and live within informal sectors are part of the overall urban community, economy and space.

Roy (2005) argues that urbanity is very complex and requires a new planning theory that attempts to acknowledge and accommodate the diversity and richness of urban life. In this respect, contemporary urban life is complex and diverse, and composed of different urban practices that are considered both formal and informal; most of these activities serve not only to promote urban life, but also to illustrate resilience strategies undertaken by urban neighbourhood residents.

It is important to reframe how resilience is understood and applied, since the essence of resilience is to fight against disruptions. A greater understanding of residents' lifestyles and how they collaborate to improve their local conditions could highly inform holistic and more effective resilience strategies.

Social dynamics as drivers for resilience

In this study, social resilience strategies are linked to solidarity, trust, social cohesion and sense of belonging, among other aspects of social sustainability and urbanity. The next section explains how these social aspects can be sustained through (informal) urban practices.

As mentioned previously, a combination of both tangible and intangible aspects is fundamental in order to form a holistic resilience approach.

The physical (tangible) elements of a city need to be flexible to support residents' activities, while, at the same time, enable frequent and continuous use of these spaces by community members to promote social sustainability and social resilience of the area.

There is a growing belief among researchers in social sciences that social dynamics are drivers for social resilience (Berkes & Ross, 2013; Clarke & Mayer, 2017; Davidson, 2010). These social dynamics are defined as an individual's feeling of cohesion, belonging and solidarity with other members of the community (Hunt & Benford, 2004). All of these, in addition to trust, collective identity and place attachment, encourage people to work together to respond to disruptions (Adger, 2003; Pretty & Ward, 2001).

The notion of collective identity emerges whenever there is a positive and shared sense of belonging, and social solidarity, because a collective identity indicates who does and does not belong to the community (Gamson, 1997; Taylor & Whittier, 1992).

Collective identity and sense of belonging help in uniting individuals and aligning their perceptions of what, to whom and how they ought to apply resilience strategies (Polletta & Jasper, 2001). On the other hand, the lack of social solidarity causes difficulties to individuals to cooperate and gather their forces to respond to disruptions (Leap & Thompson, 2018).

These social dynamics emerge from social relations and social interaction between people and their built environment. This research argues that social use of urban space, while performing informal urban activities, promotes and enhances resilience, as it creates the fundamental basis for social resilience, which comprises trust, solidarity, social cohesion sense of belonging and right to the city.

The next paragraph shows how social use of urban space contributes to strengthen the different social dynamics that are required for social resilience.

Social dynamics: A construct that results from social use of urban space

Some activities of social use of urban spaces which contribute to resilience are considered informal; however, the right to the city strongly advocates that these activities should be accepted. Mehta (2014) called the variety of activities in urban spaces as meaningful activities, given their importance in making public spaces inclusive.

Mitchell (2003) argues that the space becomes public when it is socially used by people to fulfil their needs. Debates on the use of public spaces often focus on the types of activities and behaviours that are acceptable and permitted, whereas inclusiveness consists of a flexible design that accommodates and supports various activities and behaviours of people (Mehta, 2014). Additionally, diverse activities in public spaces promote social sustainability between people and enrich urban life (Gehl, 2010).

Meaningful spaces are also considered useful spaces, because they are the arena for a variety of activities and diverse people (Mehta, 2014). Phenomenology studies argue that such spaces encourage repeated and frequent visits, which generate a familiarity with the space and the people that attend them, creating a sense of place and building trust and collective identity between users (Jacobs, 1961; Seamon, 1980). The consistent social use of urban spaces reflects the level of democracy within the area, whereas the more diverse people and activities take place, the more social cohesion and inclusion increase, and encourage people to acknowledge the presence and diversity of each other (Arendt, 1958; Mehta, 2014).

An inclusive public space is open and accessible to different members of the society and provides opportunities for various activities to happen in a safe and secure environment (Mehta, 2014). Inclusiveness of urban spaces refers to the notion of the 'Right to the City', a concept initiated by Henri Lefebvre (1991) and recalled by many authors, such as David Harvey (2003). The right to the city refers to the right for the users to re-invent and recreate the physical aspect of the city and, in turn, recreate themselves and the urban society.

By attending public spaces regularly, the user builds a relationship with the place and the people they see there, which is fundamental for building relationships and trust (Gibberd, 2017). Public spaces are arenas for social interaction, they provide a space for planned and unplanned meetings, and for residents to interact and perform various activities enriching urban life, which, in turn, promotes a sense of belonging, and increases residents' attachment to their locality (Dines et al., 2006; Low, 2000; Worpole & Knox, 2007).

Place attachment and sense of belonging are centrally important to community resilience, while feeling identified with the spaces encourages people to care about the area and generates a feeling of responsibility to react to disruptions.

Collective identity groups people around a common identity and gives them a common cause to fight for. Collective identity can be achieved through social interaction in urban spaces within a neighbourhood, whereas social interaction between people unites communities and grants residents a common identity with the place and with each other (Ralph, 1976).

A flexible design of urban areas allows community members to display and promote their culture, through art shows, food festivals, music and dance performances, all of which strengthens the collective identity of the area and its residents and increases awareness of diversity (Thomas, 1991).

Public spaces also provide a place for socialising and interacting, a place where people can play cards, dominos or other games, chat, read, eat and drink or just relax, a place where informal commerce could take place through people selling street food for visitors. They are a resource for children to play away from the hustle and traffic while their parents can meet to watch over them and create a local network of acquaintances and mutual support (Khemri, Melis & Caputo, 2020; Mehta, 2014).

Placemaking through regeneration of spaces contributes to solidarity and sense of belonging. Placemaking is a result of a collaborative action by community members to re-shape and revitalize the area socially and physically and the process is informed and accomplished by solidarity and common identity between people and the space they share (Project for Public Spaces, 2010).

Placemaking also fosters a sense of community and collective identity, by enabling different people to participate in community activities to transform and improve their shared area of living (Aravot, 2002; Dixon & Woodcraft, 2013; Kohon, 2018).

The case of El Houma

This research presents results of an investigation into how informal practices within a neighbourhood can be considered as social resilience strategies. These informal practices are consequences of being part of El Houma, which is a term specific for North African neighbourhoods that are characterised by strong social cohesion.

As mentioned previously, social resilience in urban areas is based on individuals' feeling of solidarity, trust, social cohesion, sense of belonging and sense of community. These aspects, when grouped together, create a socially sustainable neighbourhood. In Algiers, which is the area of this investigation, the term for socially sustainable neighbourhoods is "El Houma", a term peculiar to North African neighbourhoods with strong social relations.

The concept of 'El Houma' was a main driver to carry out this research, wherein various activities are performed within the area that contribute to the social resilience of the area. The different activities performed by residents could be considered informal because they are out of the ordinary; however, because people feel identified with the space, they deem all activities appropriate and normal.

Origin and evolution of El Houma

El Houma (or EL Hawma) is an expression for a neighbourhood in the Maghreb, one that is defined by social relations rather than territorial boundaries (Dris, 2005; Grangaud, 2013).

In Algeria, El Houma holds an important part in the city's organisation and people's lifestyles. It is pronounced slightly different around the country, because of the variety of accents across regions. In Algiers, the capital, it is pronounced and written 'Houma' or 'Huma', and both words can be found in several written documents, on the other hand, in the western and eastern parts of Algeria, it is pronounced 'Hawma' (Grangaud, 2009).

El Houma is a North African concept and it is equivalent to 'Mahalla' and 'Hara' in the Middle East (Hourani et al., 1993). El Houma comes from Maghribi Arabic, and is only used in North Africa (Dickie, 1994). While 'El' is the Arabic definite article for 'the' in English. The origin of the word 'Houma' comes from the Arabic word HA-WA-MA, a word that means the environment, a circular perimeter within the eye's purview, it also means a density of an area, a quarter, a section of a city (Wehr, 1976).

The concept of El Houma is believed to have emerged in Algiers since the first settlement and developed during the medieval ages. The first settlement was made of a series of enclosed quarters that were inhabited by homogenous communities, which were people from the same tribe, clan, family, religion, ethnicity or profession (Abu-Lughod, 1987). Every quarter housed residents that share mutual rights and duties, and occupied the same area for living, playing and working, which strengthened their sense of common identity, solidarity, trust and sense of community.

El Houma in contemporary times

A neighbourhood can be considered El Houma only when some aspects of urban social sustainability are ubiquitous, such as intricate social ties among neighbours, social cohesion, trust, solidarity and sense of belonging, etc. These features emerge from sharing life and experiences between people in a common area of residence. For residents, El Houma is as much as a social reality as it is a spatial one; it is a place that accommodates everyday life, and a place that people attend daily to chat, play and socially interact with their classmates, playmates and neighbours who have been part of their life for a while (Grangaud, 2009).

As a result of intricate social ties that members of El Houma share, they support each other during different events of their life, for instance, when one gets married, members of the community get together and occupy the space to host the wedding ceremony and share a meal in the public space of El Houma. This is also similar in the case of funerals; as a sign of support, members of El Houma gather around the deceased's house to show support during the crisis. These informal occupations of the space are informed by sense of belonging and the right to the city, whereby people feel identified with the space and reclaim the right to appropriate it informally to satisfy their needs.

El Houma is a socio-spatial reality formed by strong social ties between residents and the space that accommodates their shared activities (Grangaud, 2013). The boundaries of El Houma fluctuate with the intensity of social interactions (Gentz & Kramer, 2006), and its physical unit is a space that hosts local socio-cultural practices; as for its social construct, it concerns a community of neighbours sharing a common identity, sense of solidarity and belonging to El Houma (Bouaouina, 2007; Grangaud, 2009).

El Houma can be considered as a representation of local social life through use of urban space, it shows how people express their sense of belonging through occupying and using the space, both formally and informally. Belonging to El Houma gives its members the right to appropriate the space to perform various socio-cultural practices, such as: appropriating the space to chat, relax, play cards or dominos, play football or any other games, informal commerce activities, social meetings, gathering around houses to show support in weddings and funerals, etc, (Dris, 2005; Gentz & Kramer, 2006; Grangaud, 2009).

It could be concluded that the definition and attributes of El Houma are aligned with claims that these social dynamics not only contribute to create socially sustainable neighbourhoods, but also to inform collaborative actions by community members to tackle local disruptions, as a result of solidarity, social cohesion and trust.

The next section will illustrate the different resilience strategies performed by residents of el Houma as a result of the strong social relations between them.

Case study: Design overview of El Houma

Algeria was exposed to many invasions and colonisations through history which contributed to create its rich and diverse culture and built environment (Saoudi and Belakehal, 2018).

Algiers is the capital city, and is located north, opening up on the Mediterranean Sea. The city's built environment has been influenced by the several civilisations the country has hosted, from Phoenicians, to Berbers, to Arabs, to Ottomans and French, and, in 1962, the country regained its independence.

Nowadays, the influence and remains of some of these civilisations is still apparent and inhabited by people and, therefore, eligible for a contemporary study on the way of life of residents. The most apparent and influential styles are the Ottoman and French, due to their planning principles that proved to be adequate for Algerian way of life; in other words, residents were able to adapt their lifestyles to the existing planning. Two neighbourhoods that embody the concept of El Houma are investigated in this research, one from the Ottoman era, and one based on 19th century European urban planning designed by the French.

The Casbah, which is the Ottoman Medina, is a compact and dense urban town, built on a hilly site and is divided into two main parts, based on a hierarchy of spaces dictated by socio-cultural factors (Raymond, 1998). The town is characterised by a clear separation between public and private spaces, the public realm, is in the bottom part of the town and includes economic and religious activities and public services, such as Hammams (public bath), mosque, bazaars, markets and many other shops, whereas the upper part of the town is the private space that contains the residential area, and is formed of clusters that contain houses and a few necessary shops. The two parts are linked by a network of narrow irregular and winding streets and dead-end alleyways. The shape of the town is believed to be informed by the topography of the site, but also to benefit from the fresh breezes coming from the sea by introducing them into the town through streets oriented towards the sea. The narrow streets are to ensure privacy and provide shade for passers-by and reduce the area of the house exposed to the hot sun, thereby reducing cooling demand (Michell, 1978).

With the arrival of the French in 1830, they sought to modernize and civilize the city through changing its status of an Arab/Muslim city into a modern and European city. They applied an urban renewal plan based on 19th century European principles of urban planning, starting by demolishing a portion of the lower part of the Casbah and introducing large plazas and a boulevard. They also extended the city by building neighbourhoods with apartment buildings of regular façades and arcades at the ground floor, public spaces with vegetation and streets characterised by regularity, proportion and symmetry (Icheboudene, 2002; Grabar, 2014; Kobis, 2017).

In 1962, Algeria regained its independence and the Algerian population repossessed the city of Algiers, and some moved to live in the inherited French colonial city and adapted the built environment to their socio-cultural life, by means of frequent socialisation of urban spaces and occupying the spaces, both formally and informally, which led to create the concept of El, which was also informed by strong social relations (Bouaouina, 2007; Dris, 2005).

Informal practices and social resilience in El Houma

The informal practices were observed in two different neighbourhoods, and each neighbourhood is characterised by a peculiar urban planning and architecture related to a time in history and design principles, as mentioned in the previous section.

El Houma is a place where social cohesion between residents is strong and leads to create solidarity between neighbours. Residents of El Houma, like any other neighbourhood, face many challenges from environmental, to economic and social, and they have responded to the different challenges through social activities that could be classified as informal.

As mentioned in the previous sections, social resilience in urban neighbourhoods can be achieved through social cohesion, solidarity, trust and collective identity, among others. These aspects are a result of residents' social interaction among themselves and with their built environment.

Resilience strategy linked to place attachment and sense of belonging

Informal spatial practices

During the observations, the author encountered several informal activities performed by residents in order to face different disruptions. The derelict state of some parts of the town – due to its long existence, previous earthquakes and lack of maintenance – has made the area unsafe and unpopular among tourist; therefore, residents of the neighbourhood got together to collaborate in beautification/revitalisation projects financed and run by themselves. Being part of the neighbourhood or El Houma gives them the right to occupy urban spaces and modify them according to their needs. This sense of belonging to the area and to the community naturally encourages people to care about their neighbourhood and work together to respond to disasters and bounce back.

Street art was performed in different parts of the neighbourhood as a form of placemaking and resilience to bounce back from lack of safety and poor quality of the area (see Figure 23.1).

Street art as a social resilience strategy is a double-edged sword. In fact, another disruption in the area tackled by this resilience strategy was unemployment. Many people in Algiers suffer from unemployment and they tend to rely on informal commerce activities to survive. Street art performance in the neighbourhood helps to attract more tourists to the area, thereby improving the local economy by setting up restaurants and souvenir shops. Some houses have even opened their doors to visitors

Figure 23.1 Street art in the Casbah, designed in order to revitalize the space and enhance the image of the neighbourhood.

Source: Author.

to raise awareness about the architectural heritage and history of the town and grow a sense of community.

Even though these spatial performances through street art galleries are informally conducted, they contribute, however, highly to the resilience of the neighbourhood, through improving the deplorable state of the area, attracting tourists and improving local economy.

Resilience strategy linked to solidarity and support

Informal use of urban space

Disruptions are not just shocks and stresses related to natural disasters, death is also considered as a disruption that causes people discomfort, sadness and stress. As a sign of sense of community, members of El Houma show support and solidarity to the deceased's family, by attending the funerals and gathering around their house to show solidarity. People will occupy streets and/or public spaces using urban furniture, movable chairs or just standing (see Figure 23.2).

Algiers, as any other Mediterranean city, is known for its hot summer days, which cause people to be thirsty and need water to refresh. Another sign of solidarity is providing water for passers-by and members of the community. In large streets and boulevards, and next to informal markets, residents of El Houma set up drinking water dispensers for people (see Figure 23.3).

Despite this activity being an aspect of informal use of urban space, it contributes highly to resilience and represents a local resilience strategy performed by members of El Houma to fight against discomfort and heat.

Resilience strategy linked to right to the city

Informal commerce activities

Informal commerce activities have been considered by many scholars as a strategy to achieve community resilience, whereby people who practice this activity tend to seek right to the city and use it as a way not just to survive, but to integrate into urban life.

Unemployment, as a disruption, leads people to opt for informal commerce to make ends meet which is an activity that was considered as an urban informal practice by many scholars (Roy, 2009; Devlin, 2018), but which is necessary, however, for urban poor residents to resist stresses such as poorness and unemployment. It is considered informal because it takes place in a space that was not designed for such activity, and, in some contexts, this activity is against regulations.

Informal commerce activities are ubiquitous in Algiers, people use streets, building entrances, public squares and plazas … to sell different products and/or food. These activities are informed by both tangible and intangible aspects of the neighbourhood.

The intangible aspects are right to the city and sense of belonging. As mentioned previously, being an active member of El Houma, people feel the right to occupy the space, formally or informally, to fulfil their needs and consider all their activities appropriate. They may use the space to socially interact and/or as a place of work by occupying a space that was not dedicated to such activity.

Figure 23.2 Groups of people gathering around a deceased's house to show support and solidarity using movable chairs. Top: The Casbah. Bottom: Bab el Oued.

Source: Author.

Street vending, which may cause places to be overcrowded or untidy, seems as a solution against unemployment and contributes to urban life by increasing people's presence and, thus, safety. On the other hand, the right to the city indicates that people of different social classes can access public spaces, and are able to recreate and modify the physical space to suit their needs, and, in turn, reinvent the social aspect of the space by changing its uses and meanings.

The design implications for street vending or informal commerce activities could be understood from the investigation carried out in two neighbourhoods of different urban planning. Informal commerce activities can take place in various urban planning scenarios. As mentioned before, the Casbah is divided between public space in the bottom part and private space in the upper part. The lower part of the Casbah

Figure 23.3 Providing drinking water dispensers for passers-by in summertime, as a sign of solidarity and support. Top: Lower part of the Casbah. Bottom: Bab el Oued.

Source: Author.

contains public buildings and various shops, and that encourages people to occupy the space for informal activities and to contribute to urban life.

In the French designed neighbourhood, named Bab El Oued, it was noticed during the observations that street vending took place mostly in the arcades on the ground floor of buildings, or in main and secondary streets that are equipped with trees. The arcades play an important role in fostering urban life and informal commerce, whereby not only do they provide protection from the hot sun, they are also wide enough to allow circulation and stalls to take place.

These activities can also take place when the dimension and design of the space allow; large avenues and boulevard encourage these activities to take place, due to large number of passers-by and enough space to accommodate different activities,

Figure 23.4 Informal commerce activities in El Houma, enabled by the size and design of the street and right to the city. Selling food and various products. Top: Lower part of the Casbah. Bottom: Bab El Oued.

Source: Mohamed Yazid Khemri.

and, in some areas, these activities take place in secondary streets, due to the shade made by trees and/or the two buildings that limit the street (see Figure 23.4).

Conclusions

This research demonstrated the strong correlation between urban informality and community resilience, highlighting the different disruptions that a community may face and the various resilience strategies of urban neighbourhood residents.

It is fundamental to reframe how resilience is understood and applied, since resilience aims to enable communities to resist and bounce back from disruptions. As such, a deeper understanding and acknowledgment of residents' way of life and their local socio-cultural practices are important to understand how they collaborate to improve their living conditions.

A holistic resilience approach requires a balance and integration of tangible and intangible aspects of urban systems. This research proved how the social dynamics of a community and the place in which they take place could achieve community resilience.

Informal activities should not be considered as illegal or a sign of marginality, they are called informal because they can be unexpected, unplanned and unusual and, as such, the opposite of what designers planned or anticipated; however, they constitute an important contribution to urban life and community resilience.

The research emphasised on the fact that solidarity, trust, social cohesion and sense of belonging should be incorporated into future considerations of resilience strategies. The chapter also showed how different facets of social use of urban space contribute to create and promote the social dynamics that are responsible for achieving social resilience.

The analysis of El Houma as case study allowed an understanding of how social dynamics within neighbourhoods of Algiers encouraged residents to seek right to the city, express themselves in urban areas and apply resilience strategies against local disruptions.

Street art was used as a strategy to enhance the image of the deplorable state of some urban areas, and, thanks to a strong degree of sense of belonging and sense of community, members of El Houma worked together to improve their neighbourhood and, at the same time, to encourage visitors and promote the local economy. While some people consider this activity as informal, in fact it serves as an initiative to both strengthen social relations between neighbours and to bounce back from a disruption.

Showing solidarity and support in funerals by gathering in streets and public spaces is also an important element of keeping a sense of community alive. This kind of activity happens when people need support; therefore, making informal occupation of urban space acceptable.

Lastly, informal commerce activities have been discussed by many scholars and considered as a way to seek right to the city. In this research, these activities were also considered as a resilience strategy to fight against employment. In the meantime, the right to reserve a spot on the street emerges from a sense of belonging to the area to obtain that right.

The study of local contexts prior to designing urban projects is fundamental, whereby studying people's lifestyle and their behaviour not only helps understanding how to design responsive projects for local population, but also to gain insights on the peculiar resilience strategies each community is taking in order to survive disruptions.

References

100 Resilient Cities. (2019). What is urban resilience? Available through: https://www.100resilientcities.org/resources/#crf-infrastructureenvironment. Accessed on 20/04/2020.

Abu-Lughod, J. L. (1987). The Islamic City – Historic Myth, Islamic Essence and Contemporary Relevance. *International Journal of Middle East Studies*, pp. 155–176.

Adger, W. Neil. (2003). Social Capital, Collective Action, and Adaptation to Climate Change. *Economic Geography*.

Aravot, I. (2002). Back to Phenomenological Placemaking. *Journal of Urban Design*, 7(2), pp. 201–212. doi: 10.1080/1357480022000001223.

Arendt, H. (1958). *The Human Condition*. Chicago, IL: University of Chicago Press.

Berkes, F. and Ross, H. (2013). Community Resilience: Toward an Integrated Approach. *Society and Natural Resources*, 26(1), pp. 5–20. doi: 10.1080/08941920.2012.736605.

Bouaouina, N. (2007). Alger à travers sa « houma »: Formation et déformation des espaces identitaires communautaires de quartier. *Esprit Critique*, 10(1), 1–16. Retrieved from http://www.espritcritique.fr/Dossiers/dossier.asp?idcode=66.

Brand, F. S. and Jax, K. (2007). Resilience as a Descriptive Concept and a Boundary Object. *Ecology and Society*, 12(1), p. art23. doi: 10.5751/ES-02029-120123.

Clarke, H. E. and Mayer, B. (2017). Community Recovery Following the Deepwater Horizon Oil Spill: Toward A Theory of Cultural Resilience. *Physiology & behavior*, 176(1), pp. 139–148. doi: 10.1016/j.physbeh.2017.03.040.

Comfort, L. K., Oh, N., Ertan, G., Scheinert, S., 2010. Designing adaptive systems for disaster mitigation and response. In Comfort, L. K., Boin, A. and Demchak, C. C. (Eds.), *Designing Resilience: Preparing for Extreme Events*. Pittsburgh: university of Pittsburg Press 33–62.

Davidson, D. J. (2010). The applicability of the concept of resilience to social systems: Some sources of optimism and nagging doubts. *Society and Natural Resources*, 23(12), pp. 1135–1149. doi: 10.1080/08941921003652940.

De Soto, H. (1989). *The other path*. London, Harper and Row.

Devlin, R. T. (2018). Asking "Third World questions" of First World informality: Using Southern theory to parse needs from desires in an analysis of informal urbanism of the global North. *Planning Theory*, 17(4), pp. 568–587. doi: 10.1177/1473095217737347.

Dickie, J. (1994). Granada: a case study of arab urbanism in Muslim Spain. In Jayyusi, S. K. & Marin, M. (2nd ed.), *The Legacy of Muslim*. Spain: E. J. BRILL.

Dines, N. Cattell, V. Gesler, Wil, & Curtis, S. (2006). Public spaces, social relations and wellbeing in East London. *The Policy Press for the Joseph Rowntree Foundation*. Available through www.jrf.org.uk

Dixon, T. and Woodcraft, S. (2013). Creating strong communities: measuring social sustainability in new housing development. *Town and Country Planning Journal*, (November), pp. 473–480.

Douglas, G. C. C. (2014). Do-it-yourself urban design: The social practice of informal "improvement" through unauthorized alteration'. *City and Community*, 13(1), pp. 5–25. doi: 10.1111/cico.12029.

Dris, N. (2005). Formes urbaines, sens et représentations: l'interférence des modèles. *Espaces et Societes*, (122).

Folke, C. (2006). Resilience: The emergence of a perspective for social-ecological systems analyses. *Global Environmental Change*, 16(3), pp. 253–267. doi: 10.1016/j.gloenvcha.2006.04.002.

Francis, M. (1984). Mapping Downtown Activity. *Journal of Architectural and Planning Research*, 1(1), pp. 21–35. doi: 10.2307/43028671.

Gamson, Joshua. (1997). Messages of Exclusion: Gender, Movements, and Symbolic Boundaries. *Gender and Society*.

Gehl, J. (1987). *Life between Buildings: Using Public Space*. New York: Van Nostrand Reinhold.

Gehl, J. (2010). *Cities for People*. Washington D.C: Island Press.

Gentz, N. and Kramer, S. (2006). *Globalization, Cultural Identities, and Media Representations*. State university of New York press.

Gibberd, J. (2017). *Social Resilience in Urban Areas*. in *11th Built Environment Conference*.

Grabar, H. S. (2014). Reclaiming the city: Changing urban meaning in Algiers after 1962. *Cultural Geographies*, 21(3), pp. 389–409. doi: 10.1177/1474474013506361.

Grangaud, I. (2009). Masking and unmasking the historic quarters of Algiers: the reassessment of an archive. In Celik, Z. Clancy-Smith, J, A. & Terpak, F. (Eds). *Walls of Algiers: Narratives of the City Through Text and Image*. University of Washington Press.

Grangaud, I. (2013). *The Hawma: the processes of disqualification of an Ottoman institution (Algiers 1830)*. Insaniyat/1, تإنسانيا –18.

Groat, L. and Wang, D. (2002). *Architectural research methods*. New York, US: John Wiley & Sons, Inc.

Harvey, D. (2003). Debates and Development, The right to the city. *International Journal of Urban and Regional Research*, 27(4), 9–44.

Hernández, F., Kellett, P., and Allen, L. K. (eds) (2010) *Rethinking the informal city: critical perspectives from Latin America*. New York: Berghahn books.

Hourani, A., Khoury, P. S, & Wilson, C. (1993). *The Modern Middle East: A Reader*. University of California press.

Huchzermeyer, M. (2011). *Cities with slums: From informal settlement eradication to a right to the city in Africa*. Cape Town: UCT Press.

Hunt, Scott A., and Robert D. Benford. (2004). Collective Identity, Solidarity, and Commitment. In David A. Snow, Sarah A. Soule and Hanspeter Kriesi (Eds.). *The Blackwell Companion to Social Movements*. Malden: Blackwell Publishing Ltd., pp. 433–57.

Icheboudene, L. (2002) 'de la houma à la cité I Larbi.pdf'. *Revue algerienne des sciences juridiques, economiques et politiques*, (40).

Keck, M. and Sakdapolrak, P. (2013) 'What is social resilience? lessons learned and ways forward'. *Erdkunde*, 67(1), pp. 5–19. doi: 10.3112/erdkunde.2013.01.02.

Jacobs, J. (1961). *The death and life of great American cities*. New York: Random House.

Khemri, M. Y, Caputo, S. & Melis, A. (2020). The drawbacks of a global concept of sustainable neighbourhood in developing countries. In Maruthaveeran, S., Mahgoub, S., Alberti, F., Versaci, A., Mohareb, N. (ed). *Cities' Vocabularies: The Influences and Formations..*, Springer.

Khemri, M. Y., Melis, A. and Caputo, S. (2020). Sustaining the Liveliness of Public Spaces in El Houma through Placemaking. *The Journal of Public Space*, 5(1), pp. 129–152.

Kobis, R. (2017). al-Madīnah or la ville? An architectural & urban "clash of civilizations" – the example of the city of Algiers. *Urban Development Issues*, 54, pp. 27–34. doi: 10.1515/udi-2017-0009.

Kohon, J. (2018). Social inclusion in the sustainable neighborhood? Idealism of urban social sustainability theory complicated by realities of community planning practice. *City, Culture and Society*. Elsevier, 15(August), pp. 14–22. doi: 10.1016/j.ccs.2018.08.005.

Komeily, A. and Srinivasan, R. S. (2015). A need for balanced approach to neighborhood sustainability assessments: A critical review and analysis. *Sustainable Cities and Society*, 18, pp. 32–43. doi: 10.1016/j.scs.2015.05.004.

Landry C. (2006). *The art of city making*. London: Earthscan.

Leap, B. and Thompson, D. (2018). Social Solidarity, Collective Identity, Resilient Communities: Two Case Studies from the Rural U.S. and Uruguay. *Social Sciences*, 7(12), p. 250. doi: 10.3390/socsci7120250.

Lefebvre, H. (1968). *Le Droit a la Ville (The right to the city)*. Paris: Antropos.

Lefebvre, H. (1991). *The Production of Space*. Oxford: Blackwell.

Low, S. (2000). *On the Plaza: The Politics of Public Space and Culture*. Austin: University of Texas Press.

Maguire, B. and Hagen, P. (2007). Disasters and communities: understanding social Resilience. *The Australian Journal of Emergency Management*, 22(2). doi: 10.4324/9781315678726.

Mahdzar, S. S. B. S. (2008). *Sociability vs Accessibility Urban Street Life*. PhD thesis. University of London.

Meerow, S., Newell, J. P. and Stults, M. (2015). Defining urban resilience: A review. *Landscape and Urban Planning*. Elsevier B.V., 147, pp. 38–49. doi: 10.1016/j.landurbplan.2015.11.011.

Mehta, V. (2014). Evaluating Public Space. *Journal of Urban Design*. Taylor & Francis, pp. 53–88. doi: 10.1080/13574809.2013.854698.

Michell, G. (1978). *Architecture of the Islamic World «its history and social meaning»*. Thames and Hudson.

Mitchell, D. (2003). *Right to the City: Social Justice and the Fight for Public Space*. New York: Guilford Press.

Polletta, F, and Jasper M. J. (2001). Collective Identity and Social Movements. *Annual Review of Sociology*. 27, 283–305.

Project for Public Spaces (2007). What is placemaking? Available through https://www.pps.org/article/what-is-placemaking

Pretty, J. and Ward, H. (2001). Social Capital and the Environment. *World Development 29*, 209–27.

Pu, B. and Qiu, Y. (2016). Emerging Trends and New Developments on Urban Resilience: A Bibliometric Perspective. *Current Urban Studies*, 04(01), pp. 36–52. doi: 10.4236/cus.2016.41004.
Ralph, E. (1976). *Place and Placeness*. London: SAGE.
Raymond, A. (1994). Islamic City, Arab City: Orientalist Myths and Recent Views. *British Journal of Middle Eastern Studies, 21*(1), 3–18. Retrieved from http://www.jstor.org/stable/195564
Revell, K. (2010). Working with informality: increasing resilience in cities of the Global South. *Isocarp*, pp. 1–13.
Roy, A. (2005). Toward an Epistemology of Planning. *Journal of the American Planning Associarion*, 71(02). doi: 10.1080/01944360508976689.
Roy, A. (2009). Why India cannot plan its cities: Informality, insurgence and the idiom of urbanization. *Planning Theory*, 8(1), pp. 76–87. doi: 10.1177/1473095208099299.
Saja, A. M. A. *et al.* (2019). A critical review of social resilience assessment frameworks in disaster management. *International Journal of Disaster Risk Reduction*. Elsevier Ltd, 35(December 2018), p. 101096. doi: 10.1016/j.ijdrr.2019.101096.
Saoudi, H. and Belakehal, A. (2018). World 's urban sustainable policies and sustainability in Algeria. *Courrier du Savoir*, (26), pp. 593–604.
Seamon, D. (1980). Body-subject, Time-space Routines, and Place-ballets." In Buttimer, A. and Seamon, D. (Eds.). *The Human Experience of Space and Place*. New York: St. Martin's Press.
Shirazi, M. R. (2018). Mapping neighbourhood outdoor activities: space, time, gender and age. *Journal of Urban Design*. Routledge, 4809(May), pp. 1–23. doi: 10.1080/13574809.2018.1458607.
Simone, A. (2005). The right to the city. *interventions. International Journal of Postcolonial Studies*, 7(2005), pp. 321–325. doi: 10.1080/13698010500268189.
Taylor, Verta, and Nancy E. Whittier. (1992). Collective Identity in Social Movement Communities: Lesbian Feminist Mobilization". In Aldon D. Morris and Carol McClurg Mueller (Eds.). *Frontiers in Social Movement Theory*. New Haven: Yale UP, pp. 104–29.
Thomas, M. (1991). The Demise of Public Space. In V. Nadin, and J. Doak (Eds.). *Town Planning Responses to City Change*. Avebury: Aldershot.
UN Habitat (2018a). Social Resilience Guide. *City resilience profiling programme*.
UN Habitat (2018b). Urban Resilience. *City resilience profiling programme*.
Usamah, M., Handmer, J., Mitchell, D and Ahmed, I. (2014). Can the vulnerable be resilient? Co-existence of vulnerability and disaster resilience: Informal settlements in the Philippines. *International Journal of Disaster Risk Reduction*. Elsevier, 10(PA), pp. 178–189. doi: 10.1016/j.ijdrr.2014.08.007.
Wang, C. yuan, Guo, J. and Kuo, M. feng (2020). The building of social resilience in Sichuan after the Wenchuan earthquake: A perspective of the socio-government interactions. *Safety Science*. Elsevier. doi: 10.1016/j.ssci.2020.104662.
Wehr, H. (1976). *A Dictionary of Modern Written Arabic*. Edited by J. Milton Cowan. Spoken languages services, Inc.
Worpole, K. and Knox, K. (2007). The Social Value of Public Spaces. *Joseph Rowntree foundation*, p. 15. Available at: https://www.jrf.org.uk/sites/default/files/jrf/migrated/files/2050-public-space-community.pdf.
Yiftachel, O. (2009). Theoretical notes on "gray cities": The coming of urban apartheid?. *Planning Theory*, 8(1), pp. 88–100. doi: 10.1177/1473095208099300.

Chapter 24

Learning place attachment from the informal city

Cristina Dreifuss-Serrano

Introduction

> 'The building is a moment of becoming and not a solidified end.' (Schneider & Till, 2016, p. 18)

Turner (1976), one of the first scholars on the informal city, observed that dwellers involved in the design and construction of their house show strong subjective, affective relations with the environment. Further research on the subject seems to have proven this first impression right (Porteous, 1976; Pierce, Kostova, & Dirks, 2003). Participation and self-help are key to strengthening place attachment and identity, both important to guarantee sustainable care in any given urban environment (Varley, 2015; Soyinka & Siu, 2018). When there is a lack of place attachment, disinterest ensues, frequently followed by neglect and even vandalism.

By systematic observation of informal settlements in the periphery of Lima, Peru, we were able to analyse ways in which self-built neighbourhoods incorporate the appropriation of both home and public space, leading to a possible increase in place attachment and identity. Whereas informality presents many negative aspects to the contemporary consolidation of urban settlements, we argue that DIY architecture and collective use of resources might lead to interesting, original ways of relating to city life, born as responses to everyday needs. Informal settlements offer a possibility for learning lessons that could be applied not only in peripheral neighbourhoods, but also in formal, consolidated areas of our cities.

Place attachment: Definition and considerations

One of the main concepts to understand subjective emotions and relationships with space and place is place attachment. With almost fifty years of ongoing research, both theoretical and on the field, place attachment refers to 'emotional bonds which people develop with various places' (Lewicka, 2011, p. 219). It is an approach to people's affects when dwelling or simply occupying their environment, and considers 'a broad range of physical settings and emotions', which are in constant change, 'both unconscious and conscious, (...) and exist within a larger socio-political milieu' (Manzo, 2003, p. 48).

Most of the literature on place attachment regards it as a positive attitude, since it enhances the feeling of belonging, and thus allows the consolidation of both individual and group identities. Conversely, a lack of an affective positive relationship to places could provoke alienation, disinterest and even vandalism.

Despite some negative connotations to the term (Lewicka, 2011), there is a consensus on the benefits of adequate place attachment. Porteous (1976) identifies three territorial satisfactions, linked to it: identity, security, and stimulation. Scannell & Gifford (2017) list thirteen categories of reported psychological benefits, as shown by previous studies: memories, belonging, relaxation, positive emotions, activity support, comfort-security, personal growth, freedom, entertainment, connection to nature, practical benefits, privacy, and aesthetics. It has been proven that factors related to neighbourhood improvement, such as investments of time and money, social cohesion, and social control are directly linked to place attachment (Manzo & Perkins, 2006), since it's because of affective bonds that people start to invest in their communities and watch over them.

Methodologically, place attachment can be described and studied through three dimensions: Person, Place and Process (Scannell & Gifford, 2010). *Person* refers to the individual's characteristics affecting the presence and intensity of the attachment, and can vary according to age, occupation, time of permanence in a particular place, etc. *Place* seeks to explore the physical characteristics that could strengthen or weaken place attachment, in terms of objective architectural characteristics (Hummon, 1992), such as form, functions, and connections to other parts of the city.

Process refers mainly to the psychological internal path that generates place attachment, through time and action in and on the space. Manzo and Perkins (2006) distinguish three areas of research on this particular dimension: affect, cognition, and behaviour. It is in this last area that DIY and self-help are to be taken into consideration, as the activities of construction/occupation/adaptation in and of spaces contribute to the forging of affects and emotions (Kaltenborn, 1997). This aspect of place attachment has been frequently overlooked since most of the research on the area comes from the social sciences and is centred on the person. However, it is important to notice that place attachment linked to self-construction is a relevant aspect to be taken into consideration both for the study of the existing city and for the planning on new dwellings, and it is necessary to address it from the point of view of the built environment as a process.

Method

Even though there are many instruments and approaches to study place attachment, most of them focus on the inhabitants' histories and perceptions, while there is scarce methodological information that assess architecture as a process, and even less information on place attachment in the informal city.

We documented several peripheral, informal neighbourhoods in Lima, Perú, through photography, video, and interviews. Aiming to focus on the physical aspects and processes, we focused on describing and analysing ways in which people appropriate their environment while showing affective bonds. We consider the following indicators: (a) additional value over the basic housing unit, (b) personalisation through design and ornament; (c) social organisation and self-regulation mechanisms; (d) statement of identity through visible signs. For this study, factors related to person (family and individual stories, demographics) were not considered.

The four indicators are characteristic of the processes of dwelling in the informal city, while focusing on affective aspects linked to place attachment. Since not all informal settlements are equal, it is possible that different social and spatial circumstances call for new instruments.

The role of the (informal) process

Informal settlements are parts of the city that did not originate from state policies. Depending on particular local circumstances, they can take different forms, such as the occupation of empty structures, the sub-renting of spaces inside 'formal' housing, or the occupation of empty land to build structures from scratch. 'For a long time the housing problem in Third World cities did not receive the attention it deserved. As a result, a majority of the urban poor have had no choice but to try and solve their problems themselves, which most of them did by squatting or by buying plots in illegal subdivisions. Thus, large illegal, or "autonomous" or "spontaneous" settlements, were formed' (Kool, Verboom, & Van der Linden, 1989, p. 87). For this study, we will only consider informality by self-construction.

Most informal settlements have a common origin in the lack of state response to the problem of massive migration. As an effect of industrialisation in the 1940s (Rodriguez, Riofrío, & Welsh, 1971), large groups of people from the country moved to the city in search of better living conditions and the promise of modern commodities. Confronted by the need to find a place to live, groups first occupied existing empty structures. However, soon afterwards, because of a lack of free space, migrants organised in groups to occupy empty land on the outskirts of the consolidated city (Matos Mar, 2012), in neighbourhoods known as *barriadas*. Time has proven that, eventually, most of these informal neighbourhoods are absorbed by the formal city; the occupation in more recent settlements considers this by leaving empty spaces for roads and plazas, and planning the size of the plots according to the dimensions of those in the nearby areas.

The occupation of the land was possible by a combination of three factors: the lack of solutions that the state could offer; the lack of proper law enforcement, through evictions or surveillance of empty land; and more importantly, official policies that allowed this occupation as the only feasible solution at the time. In exchange for votes or popular support, local authorities even offered land deeds after short periods of occupation, thus legitimising the entire procedure.

Regarding houses, what starts as a small unit made of wood or cane changes over the years, with the incorporation of permanent materials and the addition of new rooms and floors (see Figure 24.1). Following the family's history, spaces change to host new members and rooms are assigned to productive activities. As Turner describes it, unlike the buildings in the formal city, regarded as *objects*, the self-constructed informal house is a *system*, which 'can respond to the changing demands and is left in the hands of the user' (Turner, 2018, p.98) who directs it as needed.

The process shows people's strategies and solutions born out of precarious conditions and poverty. 'That is, their ability to absorb, recycle, provide services, establish networks, celebrate, play and essentially extend the margins of the urban system to new levels of robustness' (Mehrotra, 2010, p.xiii). The stories of the houses are about invention, the combination of vernacular and modern resources, and the construction

Figure 24.1 San Juan de Lurigancho, self-help houses.

Source: Dreifuss-Serrano, 2019.

not only of a living space, but of an urban identity. Some of the processes that were essential for the initial occupations, such as solidarity, group cohesion and, of course, self-construction, are still in place as new *barriadas* continue to expand the borders of the city.

The informal city presents us with a situation in which inhabitants search to compensate 'for the unequal distribution of resources in an urban condition' (Mehrotra, 2010, p.xiii), through activities that solve their everyday problems despite the scarcity of means, which translates to a rational use of available resources (Dreifuss-Serrano, 2015).

The process of decorating and furnishing a house accompanies the story of families, and intrinsic meanings are always in process (Putnam, 1995). In the particular case of informal settlements, the precarious first units develop according to their inhabitants' needs and preferences and, despite the already mentioned economic problems, they are interesting examples for understanding the process of place attachment, linked to the process of appropriation through self-construction.

Additional value

One of the first reasons why inhabitants of *barriadas* prefer their situation to moving to a low-cost apartment in the formal city is that the self-built house allows the incorporation of productive activities. The ground floor becomes a workshop, a small store or a nursery for the neighbours, and there is always the certainty that, in case of necessity, other parts of the house could be used as well, or the main productive activity could change. The house is even understood as an asset to be inherited (Ward, 2015).

That added value also works in terms of urban life and neighbourhood cohesion. Small stores frequently appropriate part of the pavement, for customers to wait or consume their purchases, creating a semi-public space that improves the exterior conditions. It has also been observed that the presence of small-scale commerce increases casual encounters and conversations between neighbours, and thus the use and occupation of public space (Seinfeld Lemlig, 2019). Figure 24.2 shows a small convenience store in the district of San Juan de Lurigancho, installed and run by the owners of the upstairs dwelling (Image 2:). The owners installed a small roof over the entrance, and a bench outside, so that people can stop and rest on their way up the hill, and that gives the opportunity for transactions and dialogues. The simple design features become a point of reference for the neighbourhood as part of the public space.

Figure 24.2 Convenience store at San Juan de Lurigancho.

Source: Dreifuss-Serrano, 2019.

When there is not enough space inside the house, or where it is being used for other activities, inhabitants do not hesitate to use the pavement as an extension of their space. Such is the case of occasional informal commerce, like selling beverages during hot days or food during lunchtime.

The house also encompasses the evolution of the family and the changes in its composition. When children grow, the upper floors are used as independent units, with exterior stairs that allow a second or even a third entrance. If grown-up children decide to move away from the family home, the owners offer those units for rent or for hosting other members of the extended family. We have even observed cases in which the house, now four floors high, works as a hostel.

Ultimately, added value is also shown in the upgrading of the neighbourhood (Ward, 2015), which in turn increases property values. What once started as a precarious structure becomes part of a consolidated, integrated neighbourhood, and families have been able to sell their self-constructed properties at a profit.

Personalisation though design and ornament

Despite the efforts towards standardisation and uniformity put in place by modern architecture, people seek ways to personalize their dwellings. The case of Le Corbusier's housing units in Pessac, and the adaptations made by their inhabitants almost from the moment they moved in is a good example (Schneider & Till, 2016).

In the informal city the roles of user, designer, and builder are sometimes taken by the same individual. The process of decision-making is easier and faster, and there is no risk of it getting lost in the interpretation of a professional who might not understand the user's motivations or objectives. It is also cheaper, since it employs fewer people and leans heavily on the participation of the family and the collaboration of neighbours in exchange for similar favours. This simplified chain of command is shown in the design of the façade, the incorporation of ornament and the internal distribution of the house.

The resulting design might not be very functional. We have observed houses with low natural light due to the over-occupation of the plot; interiors with too many columns, constructed by the owner 'just in case'; badly designed stairs added years after the consolidation of the first floor; poor ventilation. However, there are also cases in which traditional organisation schemes are ignored in favour of solutions closer to the family's needs, such as a shop right next to the living room, allowing the mother to attend while supervising what the children are doing.

In terms of aesthetic solutions, ornament shows figures related to traditional Andean cultures, copies of elements seen in other parts of the city, fancy materials that give the impression of belonging to richer neighbourhoods, and decorative green areas (see Figure 24.3). The result can be read as a combination of traditional and aspirational identities (Dreifuss-Serrano, 2011). Since it's not mediated by a professional

Figure 24.3 Decorative garden area at Manchay.

Source: Dreifuss-Serrano, 2015.

(Atkinson, 2006) who might be more concerned about stylistic unity or aesthetic harmony, it works for the family as an instrument to navigate their assimilation into a new place and a new way of living. The possibility of showing one's identity 'is paramount in any building, but most of all in housing, where there is an ethical imperative to allow the dwellers to live out their own lives and not that of the architect' (Schneider & Till, 2016, p. 8).

Social organisation and self-regulation mechanisms

The establishment of the house and the building of the first structures are essentially group activities. Confronted by a precarious, unstable situation, the first dwellers of a *barriada* are aware that their strength is in the cohesion of the group (Hordijk, 2015). As it achieves a certain stability, the group becomes a mechanism for political decisions, participation in the life of the formal city, and the establishment of self-regulation mechanisms and 'rules of conduct and obligations' (Portes, Castells, & Benton, 1989, p. 305), that allow the proper functioning of the neighbourhoods.

The established social relations and their relative success in solving some of the everyday problems, in a short span of time, produces a common identity between participants. At the same time, a sense of empowerment emerges in the community (Manzo & Perkins, 2006), which is essential for participation in urban life in connection to the formal city. '(…) becoming an amateur builder and taking on the role of producer rather than consumer gives individuals a valuable sense of agency' (Beegan & Atkinson, 2008, p. 310).

One relevant indicator for assessing place attachment, from the point of view of the person, is the establishment of social ties with neighbours. Even though we cannot evaluate friendship or companionship just from studying the built environment, we can see this in the organisation of public space, its occupation and eventual signs of territoriality. For example, neighbours in San Pablo Mirador in Manchay worked together to install vegetation on one of the public stairs, in order to make a resting place for everybody using that particular path. Another example, the opposite of this, is the use of small fences to protect green areas from being stepped on or used in any other way (see Figure 24.4).

Statement of identity through visible signs

The migration process implies a shift in the identity traits of the dwellers. Some of the changes are deliberate attempts to adapt customs to the requirements of the city; others are part of a much slower, unconscious process of appropriation in the new dwelling. It is important to acknowledge how an individual can host many identities at once (Castells, 2010 [1997]), and some of them are constructed by belonging to a group and participating in its proposed activities, which establish interdependencies (Sassen, 2006). The personal and the collective identities construct themselves in a continuous process.

The act of building a house becomes a statement of identity, 'the production of "presence" of those without power' (Sassen, 2006, p. 315). According to Vasudevan (2014), this occupation becomes a place of collective world-making, even encouraging new modes of living. Conversely, the collaboration in the construction of other's houses helps to consolidate the collective identity and strengthens the bonds between members.

Figure 24.4 Fences protecting a small garden in the public pavement, put in place by the nearby house's inhabitants.

Source: Dreifuss-Serrano, 2015.

Some early occupations, still aiming for recognition and legitimisation, paint the early structures in the same colour (see Figure 24.5), regardless of the poor quality of the materials being used, or of the extra cost of the paint. There is not only the need to have the community's support, but also to show this to other communities and to the authorities. The act of painting alone won't build a common identity, but it is a powerful message and a first step towards a group's cohesion.

DIY and self-construction, the legitimisation of informality

Most authors identify that the main asset of self-construction processes is the appropriation that occurs from a psychological point of view, which adds to the individual's and group's identity.

Figure 24.5 Early structures, painted, at San Juan de Lurigancho.

Source: Dreifuss-Serrano, 2018.

The intervention of users in their own dwelling, also known as do-it-yourself (DIY) architecture, is a human practice that can be observed in formal and informal situations. From the rearranging of furniture to the complete self-construction of a house, people plan for modifications, extensions or change of uses in their own dwelling, conceptualising, designing, and building (Brown, 2008).

The house, or rather the home, is regarded as a process 'in which past and future trajectories (inseparable from external abstractions such as 'class') are negotiated through fantasy and action, projection and interiorization' (Clarke, 2001, p. 25). Even when resources are limited, there is creativity in the implementation, and the act of building is a consequence of people's and families' dreams, a materialisation of an ideal home (Klaufus, 2000). 'The house objectifies the vision the occupants have of themselves in the eyes of others and as such it becomes an entity and process to live up to, give time to, show off to' (Clarke, 2001, p. 42).

Whereas some authors have studied the implication of DIY interventions in consolidated dwellings (Beegan & Atkinson, 2008; Brown, 2007; Brown, 2008; Clarke, 2001; Dreifuss-Serrano, 2012), or in new ones that follow the logics and rules of the formal city (Brown, 2007; Brown, 2008), little has been said about the affective characteristics of the process in the informal city, where the lack of regulations contributes to more possibilities for the exercise of creativity and self-expression. 'Self-building allows for a flexible design methodology that is far from the norm in architecture and design. (...) The self-builders were able to creatively shape homes that evolved over relatively long periods' (Beegan & Atkinson, 2008, p. 310)

If every DIY project is a practice 'integral to the process of identity formation' (Brown, 2007, p. 263), the slow process and the precarious characteristics of the informal city regarding home construction have a very important social function.

The construction of identity starts even before the actual construction of the house, and with this the attachment to the new place of residence, because of the affordances identified in the land to occupy. Understood as 'a resource that the environment offers to any animal that has the capabilities to perceive and use it' (Chemero, 2003), affordances are the dreams and hopes informal habitants constantly have regarding their houses and neighbourhoods, even preceding subjectivity, interpretation, use, and meaning (Gibson, 2015 [1979]; Almquist & Lupton, 2010). Rather than understanding the house as an incomplete project, its inhabitants see it as a work in progress, which encompass their own wishes to improve and grow.

From an aesthetic point of view, the choices in style and decoration work as distinction signs (Bourdieu, 1984) between the neighbours of a *barriada* but especially towards the external formal city, 'enabling individuals to negotiate their position in a group or groups to acquire a position in a society' (Klaufus, 2000, p. 344).

Conclusions

Place attachment presents itself differently in the informal city, in comparison with the formal, consolidated city. The self-construction of houses and neighbourhoods is an important factor. However, we observe other distinctive characteristics in the social dynamics of displacement and occupation.

There are two opposing forces regarding place attachment in the informal city. Since it originates from the displacement of communities, sometimes as the result of violent episodes or extreme poverty, the decision to move implies the loss of social contacts and familiar views, the change of routines and the adaptation of new habits (Lewicka, 2011). The forced dislocation 'represents a disruption in the sense of continuity; it brings about a fragmentation of two cognitive components of identity, that is spatial and group identity, both of which have associated, strong affective qualities' (Giuliani & Feldman, 1993, p. 267). Poor living conditions, especially when first arriving in the city, increase the feeling of uprooting. The expected result is a lack of place attachment, shown in dissatisfaction and disinterest regarding the dwellings.

And yet, the study of the informal city shows that, not long after the establishment of the *barriada*, people start showing signs of care and affection towards the new dwelling, consistent with place attachment. Small actions like establishing outside gardens, painting, and decorating the façade, or even just leaving space for future constructions, show emotional attachment and psychological bonds to the location, even when occupation was recent (Giuliani & Feldman, 1993).

This second tendency seems to be stronger than the first, which raises the following questions: what processes or mechanisms in the informal city help to overcome the negative connotations of displacement and precarious living conditions? What is the role of architecture in this process?

We argue that it is in the characteristics of DIY architecture that the strength of the informal city lies. Allowing the occupation and the continuous improvement of living conditions, the manifestation of place attachment also facilitates the consolidation of new identities.

However, it is important to notice that due to economic reasons, inhabitants of the informal city have little to no choice regarding housing mobility. Once established in the settlement they become less capable of changing their place of residence since they rarely have access to formal financing (Ward, 2015). 'Emotional attachment to place may then be a result of the absence of life alternatives, as opposed to some form of conscious choice' (Lewicka, 2005, p. 382).

Still, the processes of place-making and attachment take place, and we argue that the formal city could learn from a situation where the lack of regulations could become an asset. Spontaneous design in the formal sphere is usually scrutinized by local planning authorities, thus limiting the freedom of the builder (Beegan & Atkinson, 2008); even in formal contexts, DIY architecture sometimes choses an informal path in order to regain said freedom. Whereas some rules are necessary regarding safety and respect for others' spaces, the simplification of regulations allows for more freedom in design, and eventually the increased satisfaction produced by DIY processes. Even though a lack of proper training and the strong influence of mass media prevent a truly creative use of this freedom, the case studies observed in the informal city have shown imaginative responses to everyday situations that could also be used in more formal environments.

We are not implying the end of the functions of architects or professional builders, but the beginning of a much closer collaboration, in which co-creation (Brown, 2008) supports and expands the ideas and possibilities dreamt by informal designers.

Informal building mechanisms seem to be the natural, spontaneous way of dwelling when there is a lack of guidelines or regulations. It also becomes an asset in the construction of place attachment. Learning about said processes aims to improve formal design processes, as well as regulations and mechanisms in the formal or consolidated city, aiming for a better understanding of housing in order to truly host people's life.

References

Almquist, J., & Lupton, J. (2010). Affording Meaning: Design-Oriented Research from the Humanities and Social Sciences. *Design Issues, Vol. 26, No. 1*, 3–14.

Atkinson, P. (2006). Introduction: Do It Yourself: Democracy and Design. *Journal of Design History, Vol. 19, No. 1*, 1–10.

Beegan, G., & Atkinson, P. (2008). Professionalism, Amateurism and the Boundaries of Design. *Journal of Design History, Vol. 21, No. 4, Ghosts of the Profession: Amateur, Vernacular and Dilettante Practices and Modern Design*, 305–313.

Bourdieu, P. (1984). *Distinction. A Social Critique of the Judgement of Taste*. Cambridge, MA: Harvard University Press.

Brown, R. (2007). Identity and Narrativity in Homes Made by Amateurs. *Home Cultures, Vol. 4, No. 3*, 261–285.

Brown, R. (2008). Designing Differently: the Self-Build Home. *Journal of Design History, Vol. 21, No. 4*, 359–370.

Castells, M. (2010 [1997]). *The Power of Identity*. Oxford: Wiley-Blackwell.

Chemero, A. (2003). An Outline of a Theory of Affordance. *Ecological Psychology, Vol. 15, No. 2*, 181–195.

Clarke, A. J. (2001). The Aesthetics of Social Aspiration. En D. Miller, *Home Possessions. Material Culture Behind Closed Doors* (págs. 23–46). Oxford: Berg.

Dreifuss-Serrano, C. (2011). *L'estetica (del huachafo) nell'architettura contemporanea a Lima.* Roma: Tesi di Dottorato, Università degli Studi di Roma, La Sapienza.

Dreifuss-Serrano, C. (2012). Adaptation processes in Middle-Class housing units. Interaction with built space through everydayness. *Middle-Class Housing in Perspective. From Post-war Construction to Post-Millennial Urban Space* (págs. 1–18). Milano: Politecnico di Milano. School of Architecture and Society.

Dreifuss-Serrano, C. (2015). Sustainability through Informality. *European Journal of Sustainable Development, Vol. 4, no. 2*, 1–8.
Gibson, J. J. (2015 [1979]). *The Ecological Approach to Visual Perception*. New York: Psychology Press.
Giuliani, V., & Feldman, R. (1993). Place Attachment in a Developmental and Cultural Context. *Journal of Environmental Psychology, 13*, 267–274.
Hordijk, M. (2015). Debe Ser Esfuerzo Propio: Aspirations and Belongings of the Young Generation in the Old Barriadas of Southern Lima, Peru. En C. Klaufus, & A. Ouweneel, *Housing and Belonging in Latin America* (págs. 81–103). New York: Berghahn.
Hummon, D. M. (1992). Community Attachment. Local sentiment and sense of place. En I. Altman, & S. M. Low, *Place Attachment* (págs. 253–278). New York: Plenum Press.
Kaltenborn, B. P. (1997). Nature of place attachment: A study among recreation homeowners in Southern Norway. *Leisure Sciences: An Interdisciplinary Journal, Vol. 19, no. 3*, 175–189.
Klaufus, C. (2000). Dwelling as representation: Values of architecture in an Ecuadorian squatter settlement. *Journal of Housing and the Built Environment, Vol. 15, No. 4*, 341–365.
Kool, M., Verboom, D., & Van der Linden, J. (1989). Squatter Settlement Improvement and Displacement. *Habitat International, Vol. 13, No. 3*, 187–199.
Lewicka, M. (2005). Ways to make people active: The role of place attachment, cultural capital, and neighborhood ties. *Journal of Environmental Psychology, Vol. 25*, 381–395.
Lewicka, M. (2011). Place attachment: How far have we come in the last 40 years? *Journal of Environmental Psychology, 31*, 207–230.
Manzo, L. C. (2003). Beyond house and haven: toward a revisioning of emotional relationships with places. *Journal of Environmental Psychology, 23*, 47–61.
Manzo, L. C., & Perkins, D. D. (2006). Finding Common Ground: The Importance of Place Attachment to Community Participation and Planning. *Journal of Planning Literature, Vol. 20, No. 4*, 335–350.
Matos Mar, J. (2012). *Perú: Estado desbordado y sociedad nacional emergente*. Lima: Fondo Editorial Universidad Ricardo Palma.
Mehrotra, R. (2010). Foreword. En F. Hernández, P. Kellett, & L. K. Allen, *Rethinking the Informal City. Critical Perspectives from Latin America* (págs. xi–xiv). New York: Berghahn Books.
Pierce, J. L., Kostova, T., & Dirks, K. T. (2003). The State of Psychological Ownership: Integrating and Extending a Century of Research. *Review of General Psychology, Vol. 7, No. 1*, 84–107.
Porteous, J. D. (1976). Home: The Territorial Core. *Geographical Review*, 383–390.
Portes, A., Castells, M., & Benton, L. A. (1989). The Informal Economy. *Studies in Advanced and Less Developed Countries*. Baltimore: The Johns Hopkins University Press.
Putnam, T. (1995). Between Taste and Tradition: Decorative Order in the Modern Home. *Bulletin John Rylands Library*, 91–108.
Rodriguez, A., Riofrío, G., & Welsh, E. (1971). *De invasores a invadidos*. Lima: Desco.
Sassen, S. (2006). *Territory, authority, rights: from medieval to global assemblages*. New Jersey: Princeton University Press.
Scannell, L., & Gifford, R. (2010). Defining place attachment: A tripartite organizing framework. *Journal of Environmental Psychology, 30*, 1–10.
Scannell, L., & Gifford, R. (2017). The experienced psychological benefits of place attachment. *Journal of Environmental Psychology, 51*, 256–269.
Schneider, T., & Till, J. (2016). *Flexible Housing*. New York: Routledge.
Seinfeld Lemlig, C. (2019). *La conformación física y el uso como posibilitadores de relaciones sociales entre los residentes de los megaproyectos Mivivienda. Lima: Tesis para optar por el grado de Magister en Ciencias con mención en Arquitectura*. Universidad Nacional de Ingeniería.

Soyinka, O., & Siu, K. (2018). Urban informality, housing insecurity, and social exclusion; concept and case study assessment for sustainable urban development. *City, Culture and Society*, 1–14.

Turner, J. (2018). *Autoconstrucción. Por una autonomía del habitar*. Logroño: Pepitas de calabaza.

Turner, J. F. (1976). *Housing by People: Towards Autonomy in Building Environments*. New York: Pantheon Books.

Varley, A. (2015). Home and Belonging: Reflections From Urban Mexico. En C. Klaufus, & A. Ouweneel, *Housing and Belonging in Latin America* (págs. 275–293). New York: Berghahn Books.

Vasudevan, A. (2014). The autonomous city: Towards a critical geography of occupation. *Progress in Human Geography*, 1–22.

Ward, P. M. (2015). Housing rehab for consolidated informal settlements: A new policy agenda for 2016 UN-Habitat III. *Habitat International*, 1–12.

Chapter 25

Designing the "Off-Grid" city

Empowering the transactions of infrastructure

Aseem Inam

Introduction

This chapter fundamentally rethinks what constitutes urban infrastructure and its future design by proposing a theoretical framework and attendant research agenda. The chapter investigates how residents transact i.e. have interactive exchanges, with urban infrastructure (e.g. water, sanitation, transportation, communication, energy), in the global south via "off-grid" approaches (i.e. highly creative ways, such as informal strategies and social innovations). The theoretical framework is based on two innovative premises. The first is that the conjunctions of people and their transactions with each other and with urban infrastructure in the global south in fact constitute a type of unique infrastructure itself i.e. people as infrastructure, following Simone (2004). The second is that these types of people/people and people/infrastructure transactions can be further designed to empower residents and create transformative urban practices i.e. designing urban transformation, following Inam (2014). Integrating these two premises, the paper further develops this theoretical framework via a research agenda focusing on the global south, where the most ground-breaking innovations in informality have been integral to cities for centuries e.g. in Africa, Asia, Latin America. By pursuing this research agenda, the chapter proposes new ideas about the power of design, such as the everyday creativity of citizens, and the transdisciplinary collaborations necessary to redesign urban infrastructure. This is also an approach for learning and theorising from the global south that is highly relevant to the global north (e.g., in terms of radically democratic design, innovation in the face of resource constraints, horizontal networks rather than top-down expertise).

Theoretical framework

What follows is not a conventional academic paper. Rather, it is a proposal for a research project – in terms of being a larger intellectual and operational endeavour – that consists of a theoretical framework driven by sets of research questions and objectives, and an operational strategy articulated by research methods, ethical challenges and approaches, and finally, impacts and benefits. Thus, it is nakedly much more of a proposed collective brainstorming and work in progress, than a supposedly finished and clearly defined scholarly paper. I adopt this stance because in order to confront the myriad of challenges and crises that cities face in the 21st century, we need more

Figure 25.1 The Ocupação São João in São Paulo addresses the critical shortage of housing by through a residential squatting strategy that also contributes to the cultural infrastructure of the city through a self-managed cultural center, the Centro Cultural São João. The mural in the cultural center symbolizes how citizens can empower the transactions of such infrastructure through radically democratic strategies and informal urbanisms.

Source: Aseem Inam.

open-ended, collaborative and experimental approaches that will lead to fundamental change; that is, towards urban transformation (Inam 2014).

The research project examines how residents interact with urban infrastructure in highly creative and productive ways in the global south, including via informal strategies and social innovations. Further, the project fundamentally rethinks what constitutes urban infrastructure and its design by proposing approaches based on two innovative premises. The first is that the conjunctions of people and their transactions with each other and with infrastructure in fact constitute a type of unique infrastructure itself (i.e. people as infrastructure). The second is that these types of people/people and people/infrastructure transactions can be further designed to empower residents and create transformative urban practices (i.e., designing urban transformation). The ultimate goal of this project is to create a global platform that will reshape the disciplinary landscape of urbanism and create empowered urban practices through south-south learning and south-north knowledge exchange.

The first innovative premise for this research project, people as infrastructure, is derived from the work of AbdouMaliq (Simone 2004, 2009, 2018). Infrastructure is commonly understood in physical terms as systems of highways, pipes, wires, or cables. I extend the notion of infrastructure to people's activities in the city. Cities in the global south are characterised by flexible, mobile and provisional intersections of residents that operate depending on the ability of residents to engage in complex combinations of objects, spaces, people and urban practices. These networks and conjunctions themselves become a platform and an infrastructure providing for and reproducing life in the city. This is how we can fundamentally rethink urban infrastructure, its transactions with people, and its future design.

In this manner, a significant source of innovation in cities are informal urbanisms. I define informal urbanisms as the transactional conditions of ambiguity that exist between that which is acceptable and that which is unacceptable in cities. Thus, informal urbanisms constitute the transactive realm between coded formalities (e.g., engineered infrastructures, legal and financial rules and regulations), and fluid informalities (e.g., social networks, political negotiations over resources and spaces). In fact, informal urbanisms are not marginalised forms of urban practices and places; they are central to understanding the logic of urbanism because they constitute debates about what is legal and illegal in the city, what is legitimate and illegitimate, and with what effects. As an illustrative example, informal urbanisms are partly constituted by the everyday informal strategies that the most marginalised (i.e., least resourced) residents deploy to navigate the everyday city in order to survive and even thrive (e.g., service delivery innovations such potable water delivery to informal settlements, political negotiations to obtain services such as sanitation systems, extralegal housing and infrastructure construction of things like roads). This research project would develop a systematic and in-depth understanding of these types of informal urbanisms, in order to develop their potential for transforming cities through "off-grid" strategies. The purpose is to harness the everyday knowledge and informal strategies of marginalised residents in order to flip the narrative from them being marginalised to them being empowered, especially in face of urban change and crises.

The second innovative premise for this research project, designing urban transformation, draws from and further builds upon my previous work (Inam 2014, 2016, 2018, 2021). The argument of this work is a theoretical one (i.e., we need radical shifts in how we think about how cities are actually shaped or "designed"), and an empirical one (i.e., there are existing yet overlooked design strategies and transformative urban practices we can learn from). We can understand informal strategies as potentially transformative design practices that yield systemic, long-term and large-scale impacts. Ultimately, this transformative approach can yield far more empowered ways of redesigning urban infrastructure.

The research project examines the potential of this "off-grid" city via the powerful lens of design, which has witnessed increasing interest from, and collaboration with, the fields of social sciences and policy. Design can be empowering in terms of the larger spatial political-economic structure of the city because:

- It emerges out of human creativity, an inventiveness that every citizen and every organisation have the potential to imagine and realise bright new futures, provided there are mechanisms and networks that enable such potential.
- It is inherently transdisciplinary, because it rests on the premise that design projects require cutting across conventional disciplinary boundaries whilst focusing

in-depth on the issue at hand, such as the design future of urban infrastructure seen from different perspectives.

- It engages with the everyday material realities of the city, including infrastructure, because it engages directly with matters of space and place.
- It embodies learning by doing, in which we test ideas in iterative and reflective ways with partners and collaborators.
- It is propositive (i.e., focused on putting forth intentional propositions) such that whilst it understands the need to conduct serious research in order to systematically understand existing problems, in the end it is action-oriented.

Through this lens of design, we can acknowledge that whilst cities face enormous challenges and crises, they also constitute places and networks of innovation and transformation.

There is a growing and rich body of work on urban infrastructure to draw from. For example, Karvonen and van Heur (2014) discuss urban laboratories and experimentation, Coutard and Rutherford (2016) explicate the post-network city hypothesis, and Björkman and Harris (2018) analyse the relationships between power, politics, materiality and urban engineering. Whilst there is some overlap with this literature, my focus is much more on investigating and designing, in highly creative and spatial ways, the "off-grid" city by collaboratively empowering the people/people and people/infrastructure transactive nature of urban infrastructure. Essentially I am treading substantially new ground at the intersection of the two seminal bodies of work referenced at the beginning of this section, and by also drawing from related literature on urban informality (Bunnell and Harris 2012; McFarlane 2012) and on design innovation (Bhan 2019; Hou 2010). My project proposes that there are "off-grid" approaches that are more accessible, affordable, and adaptable to current and future realities. These approaches are investigated and further developed by first examining a series of research questions and objectives, described in the following sections.

Research questions

The proposed multi-year multi-partner multi-country multi-city collaborative research project would be driven by a number of critical research questions that have implications for new theories of contemporary urbanism as well as alternative forms of urban practice, especially transformative approaches that can bring about fundamental changes to the local spatial political-economy of urban infrastructure (e.g., how power is exercised over spatially expressed outcomes in cities, including how policy decisions are made and how resources are allocated, such as for distribution of infrastructure investments to meet urban challenges and crises). The questions that inform the theoretical framework include:

- What are the contemporary findings and the implications of theoretical work in urbanism and empirical research in terms of "off-grid" creative and innovative approaches to people/infrastructure and people/people transactions (i.e. interactive exchanges) in cities of the global south, especially the most marginalised residents?

- What are specific ways in which creative transactions among people constitute people as infrastructure (e.g., in social, economic and political interactive exchanges such as around provision of water and sanitation through self-build, self-financed or cooperative models)?
- For each in-depth case study analysis (see brief descriptions of potential and illuminating case studies below), how are the concepts of people as infrastructure and designing urban transformation embodied and operationalised?
- Viewed through the lens of transformative design practices, what do more creative and effective (i.e. more open, democratic and transformative), approaches to designing the "off-grid" city look like, such that they not only challenge conventional disciplinary boundaries but also develop new theoretical and policy frameworks for effective action in people/infrastructure transactions?

Objectives

The proposed research project would significantly advance our knowledge of cities as complex systems, particularly how the most marginalised urban residents not only transact with existing infrastructure, but also how they create their own vital infrastructure (e.g., supply chains, exchange systems, social networks, governance structures), through symbiotic transactions with each other. This will contribute to a greater understanding of how such transactions are often based on informal and innovative strategies throughout cities in the global south (e.g., Chen 2012; Jaglin 2014; Caldeira 2017), and how they possess the potential of being further designed as empowered and indeed, transformative urban practices (e.g., Mieg and Topfe 2013; Vasudevan 2015). Within this overall goal, these are the principal objectives:

- Through critical analysis of existing research and literature, to fundamentally rethink the concept of urban infrastructure in terms of human transactions with each other and with material grids and service flows in the cities of the global south.
- Through systematic documentation and analysis of grounded case studies in different contexts of the global south, to gain an in-depth understanding of the vast creative potential of informal strategies that marginalised residents already deploy individually and collectively to address current urban challenges and crises.
- Through collaborations, partnerships and networks with researchers, practitioners and activists across the global south (e.g., Brazil, Colombia, Egypt, India, Malaysia, Mexico) and the global north (e.g., UK, USA, Sweden, Canada), to develop common understandings and examine the propositive implications of this fundamental rethinking of urban infrastructure as systems of informal transactions.
- Through the urban practice implications from the literature review, case study analyses, and south/south and north/south knowledge exchange, to propose new ideas about the power of design in terms of the everyday creativity of citizens and the transdisciplinary collaboration necessary to address pressing urban challenges and crises.
- Through the in-depth research, on-the-ground fieldwork and international collaboration enabled by this research project, to ultimately shift the disciplinary

landscape of urbanism and the thinking behind urban practice, towards a more open, democratic and transformative approach that challenges conventional disciplinary boundaries by developing new theoretical and policy frameworks for effective action.

Research methods

One of the biggest strengths of this research project is that it would operate across multiple cases and multiple geographies in particular ways. Firstly, it pays close attention to the specifics of particular social, political and economic contexts while simultaneously seeking generalisable commonalities across the cases from different parts of the world; and secondly, it refines comparative research methods collaboratively, especially by highlighting perspectives from the global south as well as south-south and south-north learning through the global platform that it creates. The detailed and in-depth case study analyses offer the kind of fine-grained empirical analysis that yield the thick descriptions necessary to tease out the truly creative and innovative urban practices found within the contextually social and political nuances that sometimes get lost in broad-brush universal generalisations. I will now briefly describe a number of potentially illuminating case studies to document, analyse and further develop the basic theoretical framework outlined so far in this project.

Bogota, Colombia: Resident-operated artisanal water systems in San Germán

San Germán is an informal settlement located in Usme on the eastern side of Entrenubes Park in Bogota. The location is part of an urban edge territory that was declared as protected and its growth monitored for the past fifteen years by local authorities. However, this institutional action has not been sufficient in managing its growth or improving living conditions for inhabitants. Moreover, even without adequate public investment in such informal settlements, self-managed developments such as this continue to increase on the urban peripheries of Colombia. Recent research conducted at the Universidad de Los Andes in Bogota has highlighted the collective action that fostered the growth and development of artisanal water systems in San Germán. San Germán is a fascinating case study for analysis for four reasons. First, there is a conjunction of tensions between the formal and informal logics that shape the city. Second, it represents an alternative response to the unfulfilled basic needs of residents. Third, this settlement highlights the importance of understanding links established between the community and infrastructure in terms of self-management of the "off-grid" city. Fourth, it exposes the ineffectiveness of formal institutional action resulting from a misunderstanding of the territorial dynamics that then yield informal urbanisms.

Guadalajara, Mexico: Independent moto-taxi operators in Tlajomulco de Zúñiga

Low-cost housing in Mexico, as in many countries in the global south, is located in urban peripheries, resulting in a large percentage of the population having to live far from work, education and health facilities, with few public transportation options. Guadalajara's metropolitan area grew rapidly in the 2000s towards a municipality called Tlajomulco de Zuñiga. Such spread-out urbanisation created long walking journeys from bus stops to houses, and thus triggered spontaneous "off-grid" solutions to long trips, especially for disabled people, those carrying groceries, those with young children, and so forth. This movement started with a few neighbours who decided to offer a *bicitaxi*, a cart powered by a bicycle, to provide low cost rides through the subdivisions. The idea then evolved into a motorcycle-based *moto-taxi*, allowing drivers and passengers to travel greater distances and make more trips per day, whilst still being cheaper than regular car-based taxis. The moto-taxi thus fulfils the need for local mobility in an informal way, which has now become an integral part of urban infrastructure.

Cairo, Egypt: Zabaleen informal garbage collectors in El Mokattam

Cairo is home to more than 15 million inhabitants and like other mega-cities, solid waste management is a huge challenge for the municipality and local stakeholders. The city produces more than 15,000 tons of solid waste every day, which puts tremendous strain on its infrastructure. Waste collection services in Cairo are provided by the formal sector (e.g. local agencies such as the Cairo Cleanliness and Beautification Authority), as well as by the informal sector (e.g. traditional garbage-collectors such as the *zabaleen*). The *zabaleen* (or '*zabbaleen*' in some sources) have been Cairo's informal garbage collectors since around the 1940s and are spread around seven different settlements in Cairo, with the largest settlement at El Mokattam (or Mokattam Mountain) with a population of approximately 30,000. There, they sort the garbage and then either sell it to a middleman or create new products from the recycled garbage. The zabaleen recycle up to 80 percent of the waste that they collect, in the process soliciting the help of goats and pigs to consume much of the organic waste. This hardworking and self-sustaining group offers informal and yet well-organised services throughout the city and represent a thriving example of the "off-grid" city.

Kuala Lumpur, Malaysia: Street traders and light rail lines in the central business district

The case study consists of five light rail transit (LRT) stations that cut across the heritage zone, the recently regenerated River of Life, and the central business district of Kuala Lumpur, starting from the Central Market LRT Station to the Ampang Park LRT Station. Within a walkable distance from each of these stations are informal street traders that temporarily use the sidewalks and roadsides, either from tables or trucks, in the morning, afternoon and evening, offering quick breakfast, lunch and evening take-aways for urban commuters and corporate office workers. Although the LRT Stations are provided with built-in convenience shops and kiosks, the informal traders provide greater selections of food and goods to commuters as they walk in and out of the stations. Street food culture is a daily essential for Malaysians in urban areas due to the affordable prices, speed of purchase and a plethora of choices, while being a critical source of income for the poor. However, the integration of this "off-grid" yet essential phenomenon of the transport planning network was missed due to overly-formal oversight, leaving potential street entrepreneurs potentially seen as illegal or out of place traders who are supposedly hazards to pedestrian and vehicular movement as well as contributors to sanitation problems.

Surat, India: Stakeholder coalitions around water and power provision

This potential case study looks at the design of governance networks that shape access to two specific types of infrastructure: water and power. The emphasis on designing governance networks is deliberate because governance networks include state, and non-state actors, institutions, civil society, and grassroots communities. Rather than focusing only on state-led analyses of access to infrastructure, this perspective allows us to examine how coalitions formed of a wide range of stakeholders may be brought together to improve the manner in which access to water and power is governed. In the coastal city of Surat in the state of Gujarat in western India, the case study would examine how marginalised and vulnerable communities become more resilient to environmental and economic shocks as a result of variable and unreliable access to water and power. Surat has a long history of widespread engagement across different communities and socio-economic groups, as well as state and regional institutions, to deal with pressing environmental, economic, and public health challenges that includes "off-grid" city approaches.

São Paulo, Brazil: Squatters who create cultural infrastructure in abandoned buildings

The social movements for housing and related infrastructure in Brazil organised to demand more effective policies from the government, beginning with the re-democratisation process in the 1980s. The primary demands of these movements were focused on the outskirts of the city, where land is cheaper. In the 1990s, demands by part of the movements shifted from land and housing to the right to the city. In 1997 they started to promote organised squatting in buildings in the central areas, where the city is replete with jobs, infrastructure and facilities. Since then dozens of buildings have been squatted in, and some of them have been converted into social housing projects.

The first buildings that were squatted were heavily guarded and enclosed spaces, reflecting the need to protect the squatters from the police and forced evictions. In the last few years a different kind of squatting started to appear, which is more connected to surrounding areas by performing as neighbourhood infrastructure. In the city of São Paulo, two squats in the city that adopted a proactive, rather than defensive strategy, are Hotel Cambridge and Ocupação Nove de Julho. They offer meals at reasonable prices, spaces for workshops and exhibitions, and have reserved rooms for residents. By embracing the "off-grid" city approach and turning the squats into part of the city's cultural infrastructure, these social movements for housing thereby strengthen their political position and avoid evictions by organising for longer-term stability.

In order to analyze case studies such as the potential ones sketched above, the research project would employ innovative methods in order to be far more interactive, collaborative and interdisciplinary (in addition to well-established and rigorous social science research methods), including:

- A collaborative brainstorming workshop early in the life of the project would bring together all partners and stakeholders to further discuss in person an overall analytical framework for the various case studies, initial ideas about differences and similarities between the case studies, and different approaches to the case study analysis, including the potential of participatory action research, smartphone-based online surveys, ethnography as non-linear dynamic system, journal-keeping as reporting and as research, crafting and telling of narratives of analytical research, visual story-telling by participants, diagramming power networks of power structures and dynamics, identifying infrastructure as agent in actor-network theory, etc.
- A series of collaborative workshops with stakeholders from each case study to take place in each city to create collaborative documentation of the work on the ground, as a form of self-reflective urban practice, and to investigate future creative potential in terms of the concepts of "people as infrastructure" and "designing urban transformation," each of which would be broadly defined such that they are adaptable to each context. Rather than traditional top-down versus bottom-up research methods, such local workshops form a type of sideways collaboration for mutual learning and benefit between research project team members and community stakeholders to investigate these ideas together.
- An overarching research design that cuts across not only traditional academic boundaries (e.g., design, geography, political-economy), but also challenges traditional academic hierarchies (e.g., senior versus junior scholars) by developing a more horizontal and collaborative research process. Each member of the team and each of the case study stakeholders would bring their own knowledge, experience and perspective to the research project in a process of mutual learning and benefit, through the workshops as well as the final public conference, which would be as much about presenting research project findings as about learning from others, including invited keynote speakers, selected speakers from an open call for papers, as well as activists and practitioners.

Ethical challenges and approaches

The innovative nature of this research project would take into account ethical challenges and approaches, such as:

- Inclusion of people belonging to vulnerable groups: People living in "off-grid" cities are likely to belong to one or multiple vulnerable groups (e.g., internally displaced, living under the poverty line, by gender or age group, etc.). We would carefully tailor our methods of engagement to ensure we handle such vulnerabilities properly so that they are not reinforced by their participation in the project.
- Inclusion of participants involved in extralegal activities: Because of the diversity of the contexts we would be working in, it is likely that some of the participants in this research project (i.e., people from the communities in the cases we would be

studying) are involved in activities that are marked as "illegal" in such contexts (e.g., informally supplying water or energy to the neighborhood without planning consent). We would carefully consider the context of each case study before starting our fieldwork and in the case we need to include participants involved in illegal activities, we would keep their personal information strictly confidential and make sure any sensitive information doesn't leave the research team.

- International fieldwork: There are significant cultural differences between the variety of contexts we would be working in. To ensure our work is sensitive to those differences, local partners in each city would take leadership when conducting fieldwork and their research organisations would review our research methods to ensure they are appropriate.
- Consent to participate: All participants in our research project would be asked to give written consent to be interviewed, observed, surveyed, etc. We would give them information about the project and their involvement before they sign. We would also make it clear that they have the right to withdraw from the project at any time they wish.
- Data protection: All data collected should be compliant with the European Union's General Data Protection Regulation guidelines. We would ensure data is handled confidentially and anonymity is guaranteed, in particular whenever we are handling input from vulnerable groups or people involved in extra-legal activities. Personal data should only be stored for key informant interviews as long as the participants agree to this.

In general, while conducting such type of research around the world, we must learn to work in such truly international, multicultural and multilingual teams so that we are extremely sensitive to cultural and ethical issues in each context. From the very beginning of such a research project, one has to discuss, agree upon, and follow principles of mutual respect, reciprocal consultation, and a genuinely collaborative spirit – as suggested in the points above.

Types of impact and beneficiaries

While there is ongoing and even increasing research on informal urbanisms in the global south, the fact of the matter is that we actually do not know enough about the often subtle and invisible innovative urban practices in many parts of the world. In addition, even with this emerging research, we have not yet generated enough shared concepts and new directions that can shape urban theory and policy in different parts of the world, whether it is the global south, the global north, or formerly socialist countries of Eastern Europe. The other value of examining the cities of the global south as one point of focus is that it is where that the majority of the population lives in a constant state of economic, political and ecological precarity, a condition that is increasingly prevalent in the rest of the world as we face the urgency of the climate crisis and growing urban poverty.

From the outset, this research project would be designed to deliver impacts at the local, city and international levels. The case study analyses would deliver impacts to local organisations and municipal governments by reflecting on "off-grid" strategies and lessons learned therein, for example within each type of illuminating case study described previously and equally importantly, across case studies to ascertain common patterns and lessons:

- Bogota, Colombia: Resident-operated artisanal water systems in San Germán
- Guadalajara, Mexico: Independent moto-taxi operators in Tlajomulco de Zúñiga
- Cairo, Egypt: Zabaleen informal garbage collectors in El Mokattam
- Kuala Lumpur, Malaysia: Street traders along light rail lines in central business district
- Surat, India: Stakeholder coalitions around water and power provisions
- São Paulo, Brazil: Squatters who create cultural infrastructure in abandoned buildings

The potential inclusion of other organisations in the field in such case study analyses, such as the URBZ collective in Colombia or the UN Habitat office in Egypt, would be instrumental in fostering partnerships and alliances with the third sector and civil society organisations needed to put new approaches into practice. On a practical level, funds would be needed to carry out international and local workshops to promote knowledge exchange, collaboration and potential partnerships between key stakeholders in each country. Fieldwork and workshop costs reflect the possibility of maximizing the impact of these spaces to engage in conversations and learning such that they can enable fundamental change to take place.

Community members and activists in the selected case studies will have meaningful participation throughout the project. In addition to bringing their voices into the discussions about what it means to actually design the "off-grid" city, we would invite them to take leadership in helping guide these conversations, especially in the workshops with other local stakeholders (e.g., from local government). This would foster spaces of knowledge exchange and learning in multiple directions: the research team and local stakeholders would learn from the strategies employed by community members in their specific contexts; community members and other local stakeholders would learn from broader theoretical and methodological contributions from the research team; and community members and the research team would learn from the experience accumulated by local stakeholders such as civil society organizations or local governments. Knowledge exchange between partner countries would also allow for south-south collaborations so that researchers and practitioners in every country can learn from experiences in other countries.

At the international level, the project would have multiple beneficiaries as well. International organisations such as United Nations Habitat (UN Habitat) and their Sustainable Development Goals (SDGs), as well as the World Urban Forum (WUF) global gatherings would benefit from such practice-oriented research that directly addresses urban challenges and crises. Findings would also benefit international coalitions and organisations, such as Slum/Shack Dwellers International (SDI) and Women in Informal Employment and Organizing (WIEGO). Since these organisations work with the most marginalised populations, research that highlights highly accessible, low cost and participatory practices towards different aspects of infrastructure provision is of great value (e.g., self-build and cooperative models of water or transportation provision).

The process by which these different groups would contribute to and help shape the research project will be facilitated through a series of collaborative, participatory and dissemination activities. For example, as mentioned previously, at the onset, we would convene a collaborative workshop with all project team members from countries in the global south and the global north to exchange experiences and ideas, to seek common ground in terms of theoretical approaches and research methods, and to further fine-tune our collective approach towards the project. In each of the selected cities, the team would also participate in locally-organised workshops to critically reflect upon case studies and ongoing projects in partnership with the lead stakeholders and residents. Finally, we would have a number of dissemination and feedback activities, such as thematic panels at international conferences, a major international conference organized by us at a suitable location to present and discuss our findings, and publications such as an edited book and an online platform to foster further research.

The impact of these outputs would be multiple:

- Building a global platform for an international network for collaboration, including south-south learning and south-north exchange of ideas and knowledge.
- Fostering new models of mutual learning and mutual benefit between senior and junior scholars, between scholars and practitioners, between practitioners and activists, and between different geographical contexts.
- Bringing the most marginalised urban residents from the fringe to the centre by making them not only the primary focus of practice-oriented research, but also bringing a comparative and collaborative aspect to their creative efforts and accomplishments in people/infrastructure transactions.
- Providing both context-based and more generalisable urban practices and common patterns for local stakeholders, municipal governments, and international networks of organisations and scholars to test out, learn from, and develop further to address people/infrastructure transactions in the face of pressing urban challenges and crises

In the longer term, I envision building a global network for intellectual exchange around the topic of designing "off-grid" cities via informal human-infrastructure transactions. In this sense, we would foster relationships of mutual benefit with our fellow academics in the global south; we would learn from them as much as they would learn from us. The in-depth case study analyses from different countries would allow us to highlight locally-grounded practices and cross-border lessons, as well as emergent commonalities and more generalised patterns of practice, with theoretical implications. Such network-based globally-oriented research projects are being increasingly deployed. However, we should think carefully about beneficiaries to remedy the current power and resource imbalances of global north countries vis-à-vis the global south.

The first tier of academic beneficiaries of this research project, therefore, would be the investigators and their research teams, as well as colleagues and students at their respective institutions, both educational and third-sector ones. In this manner, the project will have a direct impact on academic research in the countries of the global north and global south and would showcase social innovations based in the global south taking place in "off-grid" cities. Furthermore, such design-based proposals would bring new theoretical and methodological approaches to current research on informal urbanisms in the global south and create a dialogue with work being done on this topic in the social sciences (e.g. integrating design approaches with geography, anthropology, sociology) so as to create mutually-enriching bodies of knowledge.

A second tier of academic beneficiaries would be researchers on informal urbanisms mainly in global south countries that are not part of our project, but would be exposed to its outcomes through an active public discourse and dissemination strategy. We would have to seek funds for an ambitious dissemination strategy in which our team of investigators would travel to multiple international conferences to present our work, publish in a series of peer-reviewed journal articles, and prepare an edited book to be published after the project. We would also organise a cumulative public and international conference at a suitable location, where we would invite distinguished keynote speakers as well as emerging scholars on designing "off-grid" cities via informal human-infrastructure transactions from across the world, including several who would be funded through bursaries. These would be selected after a call for papers to elicit and support research that is innovative, and has both practical and theoretical contributions from global south countries that are not explicitly covered by our project.

A third tier of academic beneficiaries would be those actively joining efforts to theorize from social innovations occurring in the cities of the global south. Renowned scholars such as Faranak Miraftab, Vanessa Watson, Jennifer Robinson, Ananya Roy, and AbdouMaliq Simone are developing an increasing body of literature that produces theory from experiences in the global south (e.g., Simone 2009, Roy 2011, Miraftab & Kudva 2014, Watson 2014). Our project is aligned with such views, and therefore our outcomes would contribute to this growing literature, which that treading exciting new ground in urban theory and on-the-ground practice.

Finally, I return to the question of design, its role in these processes, and its future. We would further pursue the benefits to academics and educational institutions by looking into the impact of our research project into design-related curricula in the global north (e.g., UK, USA, Sweden, Canada) and global south (e.g., Brazil, Colombia, India, Mexico). The suggestion resonates because it is something of great interest to many of us around the world, it is very much part of the discussions that come up in conferences, and most of all, it is what some of us are already pursuing (e.g., at Cardiff University, University College London, Indian Institute of Human Settlements, Universidade de São Paulo, University of Nevada Las Vegas). In fact, one of the explicit impacts of the outputs of this project is to foster new models of mutual learning and mutual benefits between different realms of engagement, such as between academic scholarship and grassroots practice. The same principle can be applied systematically to radically revise design curricula at our partner universities, for example, especially since many of us are in leadership positions that can help initiate such discussions at our respective departments.

Conclusions

In conclusion, let me highlight a few key aspects of the research project I have just sketched out. First, a significant source of innovation in terms of sustainability are informal urbanisms, which I define as the transactional conditions of ambiguity that exist between what is acceptable and what is unacceptable in cities. Furthermore, informal urbanisms are not marginalised forms of places and practices; rather, they are central to understanding the logics of urbanism. Second, using informal urbanisms as a starting point, this chapter fundamentally rethinks what constitutes urban infrastructure and its future design by proposing a theoretical framework and attendant research agenda, with a focus on investigating how residents transact (i.e., have interactive exchanges) with urban infrastructure in the global south via "off-grid" approaches (i.e., highly creative ways, such as informal strategies and social innovations).

Third, the research proposes new ideas about the power of design, such as the everyday creativity of citizens and the transdisciplinary collaborations necessary to redesign urban infrastructure in a sustainable manner. This is also an approach for learning and theorising from the global south that is highly relevant to the global north (e.g., in terms of radically democratic design processes, innovation in the face of resource constraints, horizontal networks rather than top-down expertise, etc.). Fourth and finally, rather being a conventional academic paper, it is a proposal for a research project – in terms of being a larger intellectual and operational endeavour – that is nakedly much more of a proposed collective brainstorming and work in progress, than a clearly defined and supposedly complete scholarly paper. The most vital aspect of this approach is that in order to confront the myriad of challenges, crises and uncertainties facing cities in the 21st century, we need much more open-ended, collaborative and experimental approaches that will lead to fundamental change; that is, towards urban transformation.

Acknowledgements

I would like to acknowledge the valuable contributions of colleagues from around the world towards this chapter: Renato Cymbalista, Clemencia Escallon, Ghada Farouk Hassan, Elahe Karimnia, Nastaran Peimani, Neha Sami, and Juan Usubillaga. The final responsibility for the chapter rests with the author.

References

Bhan, G. (2019) "Notes on a Southern Urban Practice," *Environment and Urbanization*, *31*(2), 639–654. https://doi.org/10.1177/0956247818815792

Björkman, L, and Harris, A. (2018) "Engineering Cities: Mediating Materialities, Infrastructural Imaginaries and Shifting Regimes of Urban Expertise," *International Journal of Urban and Regional Research*, 42(2) pp. 244–262. 10.1111/1468-2427.12528

Bunnell, T. &Harris, A. (2012) "Re-Viewing Informality: Perspectives from Urban Asia," *International Development Planning Review*, 34(4), 43–51.

Caldeira, T. P. (2017) "Peripheral Urbanization: Autoconstruction, Transversal Logics, and Politics in Cities of the Global South," *Environment and Planning D: Society and Space* 35, 1, 3–20.

Chen, M. (2012) *The Informal Economy: Definitions, Theories and Policies*. Cambridge MA: Women in Informal Employment: Globalizing and Organizing.

Coutard, O. and Rutherford, J. (2016) *Beyond the Networked City: Infrastructure reconfigurations and urban change in the North and South*. London and New York: Routledge.

Hou, J. (ed) (2010) *Insurgent Public Space: Guerilla Urbanism and The Remaking of Contemporary Cities*. London and New York: Routledge.

Jaglin, S. (2014) "Regulating Service Delivery in Southern Cities: Rethinking Urban Heterogeneity," in S. Parnell and S. Oldfield (editors), *The Routledge Handbook on Cities of the Global South*, London: Routledge.
Inam, A. (2021) "Reclaiming Urban Practice for India: What Can Design Teach Us?," in A. Kumar (ed.) *Future of Cities: Opportunities and Challenges*. London and New York: Routledge, forthcoming.
Inam, A. (2018) "Designing New Practices of Transformative Urbanism: An Experiment from Toronto" in *Urban Design International*. (Online) Available at: <https://doi.org/10.1057/s41289-018-0058-z> (Accessed 17 August 2018).
Inam, A. (2016) "Extending Place: The Global South and Informal Urbanisms," in R. Freestone and E. Liu (eds.) *Place and Placelessness Revisited*, London and New York: Routledge, 242–256.
Inam, A. (2014) *Designing Urban Transformation*. London and New York: Routledge.
Karvonen, A. and van Heur, B. (2014) "Urban Laboratories: Experiments in Reworking Cities," *International Journal of Urban and Regional Research* 38(2), 379–392.
McFarlane, C. (2012) "Rethinking Informality: Politics, Crisis, and the City," *Planning Theory and Practice* 13(1), 89–108.
Mieg, H. and Topfe, K. (eds) (2013) *Institutional and Social Innovation for Sustainable Urban Development*. London: Routledge.
Miraftab, F. and N. Kudva (eds.) (2014) *Cities of the Global South Reader*. New York, London: Routledge.
Roy, A. (2011) "Slumdog Cities: Rethinking Subaltern Urbanism," *International Journal of Urban and Regional Research* 35(2), 223–238.
Simone, A. (2004) "People as Infrastructure: Intersecting Fragments in Johannesburg," in *Johannesburg: The Elusive Metropolis*. Durham: Duke University Press.
Simone, A. (2009) *City Life from Jakarta to Dakar: Movements at the Crossroads*. New York and London: Routledge.
Simone, A. (2018) *Improvised Lives: Rhythms of Endurance in an Urban South*. New York: Wiley.
Vasudevan, A. (2015), "The Makeshift City: Towards a Global Geography of Squatting," *Progress in Human Geography* 39, 3, 338–359.
Watson, V. (2014): "The Case for a Southern Perspective in Planning Theory," *International Journal of E-Planning Research*, 3(1), 23–37.

Index

Note: Page numbers in *italics* indicate figures, **bold** indicate tables and numbers with "n" indicates endnotes in the text.

For Product Safety Concerns and Information please contact our EU
representative GPSR@taylorandfrancis.com
Taylor & Francis Verlag GmbH, Kaufingerstraße 24, 80331 München, Germany

www.ingramcontent.com/pod-product-compliance
Ingram Content Group UK Ltd.
Pitfield, Milton Keynes, MK11 3LW, UK
UKHW052054230926
475702UK00026B/1213

* 9 7 8 0 3 6 7 3 5 4 7 7 0 *